Illustrated Dictionary
of Practical Pottery

DEDICATION

To the memory of
DORA BILLINGTON
for the sound basic knowledge
and appreciation that her training gave me
and many others.

Illustrated Dictionary
of Practical Pottery

THIRD EDITION

Robert Fournier

CHILTON BOOK COMPANY
Radnor, Pennsylvania

Published in U.S.A.
in Radnor, Pennsylvania 19089,
by Chilton Book Company

Third edition first published in 1992 by
A & C Black (Publishers) Limited
35 Bedford Row, London WC1R 4JH

ISBN 0-8019-8248-0

© 1992, 1973, 1977 Robert Fournier

First edition 1973
Second edition (paperback) 1977
Publishing by Van Nostrand Reinhold Inc.

Library of Congress Cataloging-in-Publication Data
Fournier, Robert L., 1915–
   Illustrated dictionary of practical pottery/Robert Fournier.
3rd ed.
     p. cm.
   Includes bibliographical references and index.
   ISBN 0-8019-8248-0
   1. Pottery craft—Dictionaries.
TT919.5.F68   1992
738.1'03—dc20

Photographs by John Anderson, Robert Fournier and others.
Diagrams by Sheila Fournier

Typeset by Florencetype Ltd, Kewstoke, Avon
Printed in Great Britain by Butler & Tanner Ltd,
Frome, Somerset

Acknowledgments

Without John Anderson's fine series of action photographs
together with other essential illustrations, and my wife
Sheila's diagrams, this book would be a shadow of its
present self; my sincerest thanks are offered to them. Also
to F Stop Photography (Bath) and Derek Parker for their
work on my negatives.

Other contributors to the illustrations include: Ron
Sloman, of the St. James Gallery, Bath (including the
dramatic 'porcelain' and charming 'flute'); Reg Singh, Beaux
Arts, Bath; and the potters Jack Doherty, Jim Robinson,
Monica Young, Joan Hepworth, Mike Dodd, Eric Mellon,
Dave Roberts, Maggie Berkowitz, Joanna Constantinidis,
Barbara Lock, John Leach, Rosemary Cochrane, Owen Rye,
Greg Daly, John Maltby, Kevin White, Michael Casson, and
many more. William Hunt, Editor of Ceramics Monthly
(U.S.), and Janet Mansfield, Editor of Ceramic Art &
Perception (Australia) gathered welcome examples of their
country's work.

Many others have also helped; Peter Smith gave
generously from his recipes and research; Frank Hamer's
'Dictionary' has been a valuable authority; John May put me
right on computers; Leslie Savage on electrical matters; and
the Editors of Ceramic Review, Eileen Lewenstein and
Emmanuel Cooper, have contributed not only material from
the magazine but also pictures from their archives. Steve
Mills, of Bath Pottery Supplies, has given useful advice.

The various suppliers listed sent catalogs and other
useful material. The Southwest Gas Board, the Electrical
Development Association and the British Ceramic Research
Association have allowed adaptations of their diagrams to
be used.

Mike Casson, Alan Caiger-Smith and other potters have
given time and expertise, while valuable information has
been derived from writings by Ken Clark, Ivan England, Ben
Cooper, Jane Lord, A Lewis-Evans, Richard Behrens, and
many others. Maurice Ball meticulously corrected the
revised edition of 1977 (he is not responsible for any errors
which may have crept in since!).

My gratitude to them all.

INTRODUCTION

This dictionary collects into an easily available form much of the practical information now open to craft potters. It stays strictly within the scope of its title: aesthetics are considered only where inseparable from discussion of the entry, while historical references are kept to a minimum. Similarly industrial or archaic terms have generally been omitted, entertaining though these often are (I have been unable to resist one favorite old term; a small prize for the first reader to spot it!). All the material will, it is hoped, be of practical use to potters: student, amateur and professional alike.

Materials and equipment which you may encounter in merchants' catalogues have been covered together with terms used in books on ceramics. Some duplication of information has been inevitable in order to avoid constant cross-reference by readers. Charts have been compiled where necessary to make facts as accessible as possible. Sources are mentioned where appropriate and a bibliography will be found at the end of the book.

The factual nature of the book is balanced by the illustrations of completed work which help to keep the craftsman's ultimate goal in sight—the production of good and individual pots. The author's other two Dictionaries of FORM and DECORATION deal with the historical and aesthetic aspects of ceramics and include more extensive discussions of specialised techniques than is possible in this book.

REVISED EDITION, 1990

Many entries have been updated and expanded and new ones added. Over one hundred of the illustrations have now been replaced. While the basic information is timeless there has obviously been technological progress since the last edition which needs to be incorporated in the entries. Certain health aspects have also been stressed.

The name and initials mentioned in the text (e.g. Cardew PP, or Rhodes CGP) are authors and abbreviated bibliographic references. The full titles will be found in the Bibliography at the end of the book.

FOUR NOTES

Analyses The analyses by weight included in this dictionary have been arranged with the various oxides in their $RO: R_2O_3: RO_2$ columns, i.e. in a similar way to glaze formulas. It is hoped that this will give potters a more immediate picture of the material than the normal listing which places the higher percentage first. It has been carefully stated in each case that the analysis is by weight, not molecular parts as would be represented in a formula.

Italicization The words printed in *italics* indicate a reference to another entry which may help to clarify the definition or the discussion. Minerals and oxides have not, in general, been treated in this way, it being understood that each has its own entry to which reference can be made if required.

Atomic and Molecular Weight The number immediately following any element, oxide or mineral mentioned in the dictionary indicates the atomic or molecular weight of that material to the nearest whole number or one decimal point.

Spelling The earlier issues of the dictionary used a mixture of British and American spellings. In this edition U.S.A. versions of such terms as lustre, colour, metre have been used: i.e. luster, color, and meter. We hope that this will not offend the British readers: after all, 'metre', for instance, is hardly Anglo-Saxon in origin, and is certainly not pronounced logically!

ABRASIVE

A hard, sharp material used for cutting, grinding or polishing. The usual abrasives for potter are *silicon carbide* and *fused alumina*, the latter avoiding carbide contamination of the surface of biscuit which can cause scum in the subsequent glaze firing. The Cintride range of abrasive blocks are useful although the base metal to which the tungsten fragments are attached is too soft; the file with fine and coarse faces is preferable. A small, high-speed electric grinding wheel can be used on minor glaze faults. There is a wide range of wheel qualities and bonding materials which are listed in Dodd DC. See *grinding wheel* for some details.

Dry clay or soft biscuit will respond to medium glass paper, the several grades of emery paper (or, better still, emery cloth which can be washed), or an abrasive pad as made for sanding machines. To level unstable pots, clip the abrasive sheet to a whirler or wheel-head and rotate it while holding the piece firmly in the centre.

A pot which needs a lot of grinding is usually a 'second', anyhow, and prevention is better than cure. An exception must be made for *crystalline glazes* which often necessarily involve extensive grinding. Abrasive blocks of calcined alumina are available for cleaning shelves, sharpening tools, etc.

ABSOLUTE TEMPERATURE

A scale on which 'absolute zero' (−273°C.) become 0° Kelvin, symbol K. The boiling point of water—100°C. —thus equates with 373° K. It is used to determine *gas expansion*, essential data in kiln design, and approximate *sintering* temperatures. (See also *temperature conversion table*.)

ABSORPTION

The taking up of liquid into the pores of a pot. The water absorption of a ceramic material is an indication of its degree of *vitrification*. It is expressed as a percentage of the weight of the dry material.

If a pot weighing one kg. absorbs 150 gm. of water it has an absorption of

$$\frac{150}{1000} \times \frac{100}{1} = 15\%$$

A rough test is to weigh a pot after thoroughly drying it in an oven, then to immerse it in water for twelve hours and reweigh it. Absorption can also refer to the taking up of gases, light, or heat. (See also *porosity*.)

ACID, acidic oxides

Among potters, the term 'acid' is used rather loosely. Strictly speaking an acid is a compound containing hydrogen which will combine with a base to form a salt, releasing the hydrogen in the form of water (H_2O) and rendering each material chemically neutral.

Example: HCl + NaOH = NaCl + H_2O.

Where an acid contains oxygen, the abstraction of water H_2O will leave the acidic oxide, and it is this acid oxide which is referred to when 'acid' is mentioned in this book. For instance, silica SiO_2, and not the true silicic acid H_2SiO_3, is listed under the heading *acid* in *glaze formulas*.

It is useful to know to which main chemical group an oxide belongs, for this will give some indication of its behaviour in the kiln. The principal acid oxides used in pottery are silica and the oxides of boron, antimony, tin, chromium, titanium and zircon. Two others of less importance are phosphorus and germanium which, together with the first three listed above, act as *glass formers*. In general, acids are refractory: *boric oxide* is an exception. (See also *chemistry of pottery*.)

An acid such as vinegar or calcium chloride will retard glaze settling. Acidic fumes from kilns, especially unventilated electric kilns, can attack window glass (and lungs!).

Rocks which are high in silica, such as granite and rhyolite are known as acidic even though they may also have higher proportions of R_2O than the 'basic' basalt which is higher in calcia. Sutherland GNS lists the mean composition of the main types of igneous rocks which well repay study.

ACID RADICAL

An acidic substance without acidic hydrogen. Most pottery 'acids' are acid radicals.

The main acidic oxides (acid radicals) used in pottery.

Oxide	Chemical formula	Main use
Silicon oxide (silica)	SiO_2	Glass former
Boric oxide	B_2O_3	Glass former/flux. See *boron*.
Antimony oxide	Sb_2O_3	Yellow pigment with lead. Glass former.
Phosphorous pentoxide	P_2O_6	Glass former.
Tin oxide	SnO_2	Opacifier
Titanium oxide	TiO_2	Opacifier
Zirconium oxide	ZrO_2	Opacifier
Chromic oxide	Cr_2O_3	Pigment

ACID RESISTANCE

It is essential that glazes used on wares which will come into contact with chemically active substances should be stable and well-balanced. Vinegar, wines (especially if fermented in the vessel) and some fruits are the main sources of danger, which arise from the tendency of some glaze ingredients, especially lead, to separate and dissolve into the liquid forming a poison.

Adherence to the *Seger formula* principles in formulating earthenware glazes will minimise the risk (e.g. a lead glaze formula 1.0: 0.3: 3.0) but the use of totally leadless glazes for cooking ware may be made compulsory. All glazes containing lead (or selenium) made for table or kitchenware must be tested to the British Standard (in Great Britain), see *lead solubility*, *metal release*, *Thorpe's Ratio* and the various glaze entries. Needless to say, the glazes should not be crazed.

Industrial sanitary wares, acid holders, and the like are vitrified, and sometimes salt-glazed, one of the most acid-resistant of all glazes.

ADHESIVE

Adhesives in general have little place in pottery; water is the 'adhesive' for clay! Glazes or colours may be treated with gum (see *gum arabic*) to make them less friable, for use on low-absorbency biscuit, or for glaze-over-glaze techniques. Potclays sell an adhesive called Propit for fastening props into place before firing.

ADOBE

A sun-dried clay-mud, with additions of straw or chaff, used in hot, dry climates for building. Very substantial buildings—a majority of the older, traditional houses of Cyprus for instance—demonstrate the high dry strength of some clays and clay-sand mixtures.

The adobe bricks of blocks, usually 12–18 in. (30–45 mm.) square and 4 in. (100 mm.) thick, are not, of course, subjected to sufficient heat to turn them into ceramic material, and they would disintegrate in persistent rain. Adobe is an excellent heat *insulator*. G. Woodman describes an adobe kiln for firings up to 1100°C. (PQ 23). See also *brick* for a useful press for adobe slabs.

ADSORPTION

The taking up of a liquid, vapor or gas on a solid surface. Adsorption may cause expansion of a body (even a fired one) and is one of the causes of delayed *crazing* after a period of exposure to the atmosphere. It is, of course, more likely on low-fired porous ware.

Water adsorbed on clay particles is resistant to evaporation and requires a temperature of at least 120°C.

(figures as high even as 200°C. have been mentioned) to remove it. The volume of liquid is small but nevertheless expands very quickly and can break a pot. Clay cannot therefore be considered to be completely dry at room temperature. Ware which has been heated at 120°C. and allowed to cool again will readsorb moisture and be more susceptible to damage than before.

AGATE

Cryptocrystalline (chaldonic) silica. Also known as 'agata'. A banded, variegated hard stone. Polished, it is used to burnish gold (and, in South America, for burnishing pots), or for making small mortars and pestles.

AGATE WARE

A pottery body resembling agate stone in its marbled appearance. Produced by layering different color clays, pressing them together and using the resultant multi-sandwich for throwing or hand-building. Care must be taken that the relative shrinkage of the layers is as nearly uniform as possible. For this reason stains or oxides are used to derive different colors from a single body.

The technique is used by a number of modern potters and can give results which are sharp and bright or merged and subtle. A thrown agate vessel will generally

A subtle use of the agate technique by Marianne de Trey. (See also a variety of other styles in Fournier DPD.)

need to be turned over its whole visible surface to reveal the pattern. A more controlled effect is achieved by Jack Doherty who places a thin slab of colored clay onto the surface of a half-finished pot or bowl, then continues with the throwing; a technique closer to *rolled inlay* (where it is illustrated). In yet another variation Jennifer Lee uses different colored clays (based on T-material) as flat, shaped strips in constructing a coil pot, (CR 95). See also *marbling* and *neriage*. Agate ware is discussed and illustrated fully in Fournier DPD.

AGGREGATE

The non-cement materials in a cement or concrete mixture. These comprise stones and sand in ordinary concrete; sand and crushed firebrick, grog or other refractories in a kiln mortar or brick mixture. Normally about five times the volume of the cementing material.

AGING OF CLAY

Also known as 'souring'. Authorities differ on the period necessary for the attainment of full plasticity and workability in a clay: a generation in China; two years according to Leach and Billington; a week (Rhodes). Isaac Button's procedure of two months in a damp atmosphere followed by re-plugging yielded excellent results. Hamer gives a useful article on aging. (See also *algae*, *weathering*.)

AIR

The gaseous envelope or atmosphere which surrounds the earth. Composed (on average) of 78% nitrogen, 21% oxygen, with very small amounts of other gases, water vapour and dust. The oxygen is 'free', that is, available to maintain life, or to form *oxides* of elements. *Oxidation* produces heat; when the reaction is very rapid (e.g. the oxidation of carbon) the heat can be used as a source of energy.

AIRBRUSH, aeography

A method of applying color and, occasionally, glaze by means of a spray-gun powered by compressed air, see also *spraying*. Airbrushing equipment sold for art-work is widely available using a canned propellant though, because it is intended for easel paints, the nozzle may clog with the sometimes coarser pottery pigments. A model supplied by a potter's merchant should be selected to deal with this problem—you can then complain if it doesn't work. Spraying from cans could prove expensive where much work is done but they are useful for experimental pieces. For regular use a motorised compressor is essential. (See *spraying*.)

AIR-SETTING MORTAR

Normal clay/grog mortar hardens on firing but fire resistant mortars or cements are available which harden at air temperature. Useful for setting arches and unsupported parts of a kiln structure, but not essential. The makers of 'Sairset', a commercial air-setting cement, suggests its use as a protective coating on furnace linings, or mixed with crushed firebrick for patching kilns. (See also *kiln wash*.)

ALBANY SLIP

A clay found near Albany, New York. Quoted analysis CaO 5.7, MgO 2.7, alkalis 3.1, Al_2O_3 14.5, Fe_2O_3 5.2, SiO_2 57.6.

The high proportion of fluxes, combined with a very fine grain, causes it to melt at around 1240°C., and it is used as a *slip glaze*. Recipes for its use may be found in Rhodes CGP. Color brown to black. Behrens in CM 20/4 gives two recipes using 90% Albany clay with 10% wollastonite or cryolite, the latter producing a 'patterned' glaze. (See also *temmoku*.)

ALBITE

Soda *feldspar*. Ideal formula Na_2O, Al_2O_3, $6SiO_2$, 524. Most commercial feldspars are mixtures of soda and potash spar (orthoclase). Can cause unwanted bubbles in a glaze above 1200°C.

ALGAE

In the *souring* and *aging* of clay, it was formerly believed that the activity of microscopic single-cell plants broke down the particles and increased plasticity. It now appears that the algae are a secondary but linking factor in the process of *ionic exchange*. The CO_2 released will slowly alter the pH factor of the clay which, in turn, affects its plasticity.

ALKALI

A subdivision of the chemical *bases*. Strictly speaking the term refers to soda, potash, and lithia but it is also used to cover the *alkaline earths*. Alkalis are *glass-modifiers* and strong *fluxes*. Soda, especially, produces intense colors, e.g. *Egyptian paste*. Unfortunately the alkalis have high *coefficients of expansion* with consequent glaze *crazing* and, in many forms, are soluble, (see *alkaline frits*).

Feldspar, china stone, lepidolite, nepheline, petalite, and spodumene are insoluble sources of the alkalis (see under individual minerals).

ALKALINE EARTHS

The oxides of calcium, magnesium, barium, and strontium (see under these headings). All operate as *bases (glass modifiers)* in glaze function. Normally more active at higher temperatures although they also appear as secondary fluxes in many earthenware glazes.

ALKALINE FRITS

It is difficult to include the alkalis in significant proportions in a glaze, particularly a *soft glaze*, due to their solubility. For this reason they are normally added as *frits* and as such are widely available.

Useful for lowering the maturing temperature of glazes, including stonewares; for affecting the color response in earthenware; and for use in larger proportions at the low end of the scale in *raku*, etc. The suppliers will usually tell you the make-up of any particular frit.

ALLUVIAL CLAY

Deposits of this clay left by rivers and by flood. In England, for instance, the valley clays of the Humber and Thames are alluvial. Composition varies, but the clays are fine-grained, plastic, often iron-stained and sticky.

ALPHA FORM

A term given to the crystalline form of quartz at temperatures below the *inversion* point.

ALTERED FORM

Today many potters use a thrown form simply as a starting point for more complicated shapes; cutting, pressing, or otherwise distorting the original shape. In extreme instances it is cut up and reassembled.

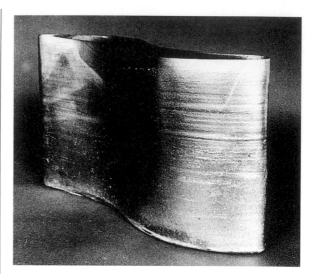

A thrown cylinder reformed into an 'envelope' shape by Joanna Constantinidis.

A pedestal bowl, wheel-thrown and altered with fine-line brushwork in underglaze cobalt blue. By Kevin White (Australia).

ALTERNATING CURRENT (or AC)

Mains electricity supply which alternates or changes direction of flow at a very rapid rate. The number of changes or cycles per second is called the frequency. In England the normal frequency is 50. Certain pieces of equipment, especially motors, are designed either for AC or for direct current (DC), and these must only be used on the supply specified. It is possible to pass AC through a rectifier to convert it into DC.

The very direct handling of a (probably thrown) cylinder, bought in a Northern Italian market.

4

ALUMINIUM

A metallic element, Al. 27. It occurs in a crystalline form as corundum, and as the gems, sapphire, ruby, and topaz. Manufactured as a metal by calcining alumina hydrate from bauxite. (See *alumina*.)

ALUMINA

Oxide of aluminium. Al_2O_3, 102. m.p. 2050°C.

Supplied as aluminium hydrate, $Al_2(OH)_6$, which decomposes at around 300°C to alumina: or as calcined alumina. The latter is preferable for *setting* etc.

One of the essential ingredients of all clays and most glazes. Chemically *amphoteric*, it has a balancing and unifying effect between bases and acids and between glaze and body. It is rarely used as a separate mineral in glazes; instead it is introduced by adding clay or 'natural frits', e.g. china stone, feldspar, and nepheline syenite, which are the main sources; there are others. See list of minerals. The normal molecular equivalent in a glaze is from 10–12% of the silica content. It acts as a *network modifier* and helps to lessen recrystallization during cooling (for this reason it is kept to an absolute minimum in *crystalline glazes*). Alumina will also increase the hardness and stability of a glaze; its tensile strength; and its resistance to *crazing*. In excess it will produce a matt surface, pinholes, and other faults associated with too 'stiff' a glaze.

As a separate oxide it is used mainly for *placing* pottery and as a wash to prevent lids sticking in the firing. Calcined alumina is preferable to the hydrate for this purpose. It is also used in special forms (bubbles, etc) as a heat insulator.

High alumina clays (silliminite, some fireclays, etc) are used for making kiln furniture and other refractories.

ALUMINOUS REFRACTORY

Materials high in alumina will be less subject to damage from *thermal shock* than high-silica refractories. The best grades of fireclay are aluminous. (See also *bat, brick, firebrick, kiln shelf*, etc.)

AMBIENT TEMPERATURE

The temperature of the surrounding atmosphere.

AMBLYGONITE

A lithium mineral of variable composition, high in alumina. *Ideal formula* Li.AlF, PO_4, but can contain sodium and fluorine, e.g. (Li, Na) Al PO_4 (F,OH), L.o.i. 17.4. Typical analyses: Li_2O, 7.8; Al_2O_3. 34.2; SiO_2, 2.8; P_2O_5, 47.5. Used in small amounts in glazes.

AMMETER

An instrument for measuring the current flow in *amperes*. Useful for checking the correct working, and the effects of aging, of kiln *elements*. A low reading will suggest that the elements are wearing thinner; a reading of no current on the ammeter indicates a broken circuit.

AMMONIUM META-VANADATE

A less dangerous form of vanadium, NH_4VO_3. 117. 10% gives a rather weak yellow, improved by the use of an *opacifier*. Not greatly affected by stoneware temperatures (up to 1280°C.) or, according to the Fulham Pottery catalog, by reduction. (See also *vanadium*.)

AMORPHOUS

Without a structured shape. An amorphous mineral is one that does not build up regular crystals. Diatomite is an amorphous silica. Flint was once considered to be amorphous but is now classed as micro-crystalline. Glass is an amorphous 'frozen' liquid, and is without a definite melting point.

AMPERE

An electrical unit of current (symbol I) that one *volt* sends through one *ohm* of resistance.

Useful equations to calculate amperage:
$I = P \div E$, or, $E \div R$, or, the square root of $P \div R$.
(P in watts; E in volts; R in ohms). (See also *electrical symbols*.)

AMPHORA

A general name for pointed or very narrow-based pots, generally with handles, typified by the Greek amphora.

They are still thrown in a few places in the Mediterranean countries. The top half is thrown first, half dried, reversed onto a chuck, and the pointed base thrown onto it from a thick coil. This method is useful for any narrow-based form. (See also *two-piece throwing*.)

AMPHOTERIC

'Amphi'—two ways, or half. Applied to an oxide which does not exhibit strong acidic or basic characteristics. The middle column of the *Seger formula*. Alumina is amphoteric; iron oxides vary in effect; ferric being amphoteric, while ferrous iron will act as a flux.

ANALYSIS

The theoretical breakdown of a material into its constituent *elements, oxides* or *minerals*. A laboratory can produce an elemental or ultimate analysis listing the oxides as comparative or percentage weights. It is possible to re-group these into probable minerals—sometimes known as the rational analysis.

Example: Tony Benham's hop ash.

Soda Na_2O	0.3
Potash K_2O	10.8
Lime CaO	12.9
Magnesia MgO	1.5
Alumina Al_2O_3	0.9
Iron Fe_2O_3	9.6
Silica SiO_2	35.3
Phosphate P_2O_5	2.8
Sulfate SO_3	9.0
Chloride Cl	1.6
Moisture H_2O	2.5
Carbon C	2.8
Undetermined	2.1
Carbonates CO_2	7.9

These oxides can be re-grouped as probable minerals:

Fine sand	26	*The greater part of the silica*
Chalk	15	*Most of the lime and some carbonate*
Calcium silicate mineral	9	*The rest of the lime and some silica*
Potassium sulfate	20	*Potash and sulfate*
Hematite	10	*The ferric iron*
Magnesium carbonate	3	*Magnesium and the remaining carbonate*
Granite minerals	4	*Bases, alumina, the remaining silica*
Minor compounds carbon and moisture	13	

Some reasonable inferences as to the behavior of this ash in a glaze are:

With 10% iron it will give a stained glaze.

Some of the 'fine sand' will fail to pass a 120 sieve.

Lack of alumina suggests instability and poor interface development if used alone.

The bases are adequate, over half consisting of lime. The alkalis may be soluble and will be lost if the ash is washed.

With some feldspar and a little clay it should give an interesting iron glaze.

While analyses are useful in forming a general impression of a material, their value is limited especially in assessing clays. Other factors, such as grain size, are important. Practical experiment is essential. An analysis can be reformulated in terms of the *Seger formula* (see *analysis into formula*). Cardew PP. Appendix 10, gives details of a method for deriving the probable minerals from a list of oxides (calculated formula).

Potters' merchants will sometimes provide analyses, or there are firms of analytical chemists who will quote.

What is known as the ultimate analysis in ceramics will take into account the changes which take place in the kiln, i.e. some molecules will split up and dispel one or more of their constituents as gases, marked in these analyses as 'Loss' or 'Loss on ignition'—l.i.o. Materials can also be analysed according to physical qualities such as *grain size* in clay, etc.

ANALYSIS INTO FORMULA

Where an analysis of a mineral or other material is given as parts-by-weight it is useful to be able to convert it into *molecular* parts for a truer appraisal of its behavior, especially in a glaze. It is usual to group the constituents in the general order of the *Seger formula*.

Method: Divide each of the figures by the molecular weight of that oxide. Group the RO and the R_2O oxides and total the parts. Divide each figure in the formula by this total.

Example. A mineral with the analysis by weight:

$$12.40 \ K_2O \div \text{mol. wt.} \ 94 = 0.132$$
$$3.15 \ Na_2O \div \text{mol. wt.} \ 62 = 0.05$$
$$18.60 \ Al_2O_3 \div \text{mol. wt.} \ 102 = 0.182$$
$$65.85 \ SiO_2 \div \text{mol. wt.} \ 60 = 1.096$$

Thus in the total RO group $0.132 + 0.05 = 0.182$.

If we divide each of the results of the example above by this total we arrive at the formula:

Na_2O and K_2O	1
Al_2O_3	1
SiO_2	6

which is near the ideal formula for orthoclase feldspar.

A natural mineral will be more involved than the simple example above, but the method can still be applied.

CO_2, H_2O, and other *loss on ignition* oxides, if listed separately, can be ignored. If quoted as *carbonates*, the molecular weight of the carbonate will allow for the CO_2. See also charts at *formula into recipe*.

ANATASE

One of the ores of titanium. A crystalline form of TiO_2.

ANDALUSITE

A mineral, $Al_2O_3SiO_2$, 162. One of the *silliminite* group. Converts by firing into mullite $3Al_2O_3.2SiO_2$ plus silica (as cristobalite).

ANHYDROUS, anhydrite

Without water of *crystallization*. A natural anhydrite is $CaSO_4$, often found in close conjunction with gypsum.

ANION

A negatively charged particle, i.e. with surplus electron(s). (See also *canion*.)

ANISE, aniseed oil

Used as an *enamel* medium. Potclays issue a substitute called 'Aniseed Turpens'.

ANISOTROPIC, anisometric

Different values in different directions, applied to *crystals*. The *lamellar* structure of clay can lead to uneven shrinkage if some plates are aligned and others random.

ANNULAR

A disc with a hole in it—like a doughnut! Some potters consider it an easier shape to center on the wheel, especially with large masses of clay. A *bottle kiln* would have an annular *bag wall*. (See also *centering*.)

Annular centering is especially useful for larger pieces of clay. (See also Isaac Button at throwing.*)*

ANORTHITE

A calcium *feldspar*, $CaO.Al_2O_3.2SiO_2$, 278. There is a series of solid solutions known as the *plagioclase* feldspars between anorthite and albite, also called the Ab-An series.

ANORTHOCLASE

A soda spar, some way between *albite* and *orthoclase*. Written as $NaKO. Al_2O_3, SiO_2$. Term often used for any mixed-based feldspar.

ANTI-FLUX

A term used by Hamer to describe the temperature range below which certain RO oxides fail to act as effective glaze fluxes though this is complicated by the interaction of one on another and by the amount used. All are active at stoneware temperatures, though their effect varies. See under individual materials and at *fluxes*. The effect of red iron oxide as an 'anti-flux' is reversed under reduction.

ANTIMONIATE OF LEAD

Approximately $3PbO, Sb_2O_3$, sometimes written $Pb_3(SbO_4)_2$. A yellow pigment for earthenware, also known as Naples yellow. Toxic. Although unstable above 1150°C. it has a *refractory* nature and needs the addition of a soft lead frit in the proportions of 1:1 when used as a pigment. It is not very satisfactory in or on a leadless glaze. Apply evenly and fairly thinly on *majolica*.

ANTIMONY, oxides

A metallic element Sb (Stibium), 122.
Oxide Sb_2O_3, 291.5 m.p. 630°C., s.g. 5.5.
A low-temperature *opacifier*. With lead oxide yields a yellow pigment (see *antimoniate of lead*). Also listed as a *glass-former* in the Seger formula. Toxic.

APPLIED DECORATION

Three-dimensional decoration with a wide variety of character and method. It can be as simple and direct as the pressed or stroked-on pellets of clays found on English medieval jugs, or as mechanical and intricate as Wedgwood sprigs. The thumb pot illustrated shows how applied decoration can become part of the form.

The clay can be applied direct if the decorative element is small, but larger pieces must be slipped and carefully pressed on from the center outwards. (See further illustrated examples under *sprig*, *lug* and *knob*.) More extensive discussions and illustrations may be found in Fournier DPD.

Pads of clay applied to a slab-built plant trough by Margaret Shotton.

1

2

There is no clear borderline between applied decoration and modeled form as is illustrated in
(1) The multi-rim additions to a handbuilt bowl by Sheila Fournier and
(2) The strips and bosses incorporated into a pinch pot by Alex Watson.

ARCH

See *bricklaying*.

A

B

An arch can be built over a former made (A) from hardboard or (B) slats nailed over arch-shaped wooden ends. These are removed when the mortar between the bricks has set. (See also bricklaying.)

ARENACEOUS

Sandy. Some arenaceous rocks however, may be quite hard, e.g. greywacke and millstone, the sands cemented by silica or limestone.

ARGILLACEOUS

Clayey. Materials with layered crystals, as clay, also including mica. Hamer, however, gives it as 'mudstone' which 'often contains a proportion of clay'. 'Illite is the commonest clay mineral in argillaceous rocks' Cardew PP.

ARGILLITE

A sedimentary rock containing clay minerals.

ARK

A quaint name for large slip and glaze containers with mechanical stirrers.

ARMATURE

A supporting core of wood or metal wire used in *modelling*. It must, of course, be removed if the piece is to be fired. Sculptors' techniques often trap air in the clay and also develop very uneven wall thicknesses, both of which can be disastrous in the kiln. Coiling or similar building methods are advised if the piece is intended for firing.

A sort of armature can be built of crushed and bound paper to give some support to hollow shapes; either pulled out piecemeal when the model is completed and dry, or burned out in the firing (with much smoke in an electric kiln!). Theoretically any combustible material could be used but may give rise to other problems.

ARMENIAN BOLE

An earthy compound of iron, used as a pigment. Now seldom listed by merchants. (See *bole*.)

ARSENIC oxides

As_2O_3. Very toxic. A glass-forming oxide which has been used in ceramics in the past. Very small quantities act as a decoloriser.

ASBESTOLUX

A trade name for a steam-pressed insulating and fire-proof material originally made from asbestos but now known as 'Non-asbestos Asbestolux'! Standard size 8 × 4 ft. (approx. 2.4 × 1.2 m.), thicknesses up to $\frac{1}{2}$ in. (approx. 12.5 mm.). Reasonably strong, but liable to crush at the corners. Can be cut with an ordinary saw. It does not easily warp and 'will not crack or shatter at furnace heat' say the makers. It is useful for the outer cases of kilns, where it will prove good thermal *insulation*, and also for working *bats* and for stiffening pots after throwing. If used for *throwing bats*, however, its high absorbency needs quenching with a coat of polyurethane varnish. It is still essential to use a mask when cutting this or any similar material.

ASBESTOS

A fibrous natural mineral consisting of silicates of magnesia and calcium with iron. It loses water at 400°C. and rapidly weakens about 500°C. Because of its carcinogenic effects this very useful material has been phased out from most of its applications, to be replaced by mineral wool and other materials in heatproof sheeting, electric wire insulation, etc., the latter now using butyl- and silicone-rubbers which have lower operating temperatures. White asbestos is reputedly less dangerous than the blue type but great care should be taken (always use a mask) when cutting or handling the material in any way which may send dust or fibres into the air, especially sweeping up afterwards. (See *asbestolux*.)

ASBESTOS CEMENT

Cement and asbestos cast into thin sheets, one side smooth and the other textured. Strong but brittle, slightly absorbent, and liable to warp unless braced with timber. Will crack or shatter under heat and is not recommended for kiln casing. Now generally made with mineral wool or other asbestos substitute, but check with your supplier. *All* dust promoting activities are dangerous to health.

ASBOLITE

An impure *cobalt* ore, used by Chinese potters. Yields a pleasant quenched blue which we can approach by adding red clay, ferric, manganese etc to the pure oxide. Has been quoted as containing 2–20% CoO with Mn O_2, Fe_2O_3, etc.

ASH

A powdery residue left after the combustion of any material. The ashes useful in ceramics are those from trees and plants (*bone ash* is dealt with separately) where the incombustible residue is composed of the *inorganic* substances, mainly metal oxides and silica, which they have taken up from the soil during their lifetime. The different parts of a plant will use or store certain groups of minerals: grass stems obtain much of their brittle strength from silica, and straw ash is therefore refractory. The trunk of a tree is likely to store lime in greater quantities than the bark, and the bark may become richer in silica as it ages. Box and apple wood, for instance, yield 5–10% of silica and 40% or more of lime; in reed ash the proportions are reversed. Cardew suggests that the first be considered an interesting alternative to limestone, the latter an impure silica. In general the harder and more woody the plant, the softer (more *fluxing*) the ash is likely to be. I have used a cedar ash which, alone, melts to a shiny liquid at 1260°C. This is a guide only, there are exceptions such as the Australian mahogany mentioned in Cardew PP. The younger, sappy wood from a large tree will be higher in CaO and alkalis. Apple ash can have as much as 50% CaO.

Other factors influence the behavior of an ash, the type of soil and, possibly, the time of year the plant is cut. Few ashes are high in alumina, although those from fruits may contain more than others. The *alkalis* are often soluble and can be lost in washing. Magnesia and phosphorus can impart a milky lustre sometimes known as the '*Chun*' effect.

The very considerable variation, even in the narrowest field of study, makes the direct testing of every ash sample indispensable. A typical ash analysis is given at *analysis*. Several others are given in Leach PB, Cardew PP, and other books.

Ash needs to be burnt well to a pale gray or white power; black ash contains carbon. It can be reburnt or calcined to about 700°C. in the kiln after washing. Reburning will also have the advantage of curing its tendency to *flocculate*. A great deal of vegetable material is required to produce a small amount of washed, sieved ash; the final count might be as little as 3% of the plant weight! (See *ash preparation*.)

Coal ash is fundamentally an aluminium silicate with iron and other impurities. It has low fluxing power and acts in a similar way to clay.

ASH GLAZE

Glazes which contain large proportions of plant ash are not necessarily superior to more consciously formulated ones, though the subtlety of the natural ash compounds can give unique results. There is little value in using ash in glazes to be fired below stoneware temperatures. The particular qualities of ash glaze are better exploited in reduction rather than in oxidation, although interesting results can be achieved in electric kilns. Owing to *soluble* constituents, ash glazes are liable to give variable results even during the use of a single glaze batch. In partially burnt ash the carbon provides local *reducing* conditions during the firing of the glaze.

Few ashes will provide a satisfactory glaze used alone, and they tend to give a poor and powdery dip. Small test bowls will, however, give some idea of the *fusibility* or *refractoriness* of a sample. Normally an ash is used as an ingredient in a recipe. The 'classic' starting-point is 2 ash: 2 feldspar: 1 clay. Dolomite and nepheline are also useful additions, although the former may overload the lime content. One of the most interesting constituents of many ashes is the phosphorus (pentoxide P_2O_5) which can give a pearly or opalescent quality. (See also under *ash* for more discussion of ash behavior.)

An unusual coal-ash glaze suggested by Peter Smith is:

Coal ash	20.5
S. Devon ball clay	8.3
Whiting	21.5
Feldspar	31.8
Red clay	3.1
Ochre	1.6
Quartz	13.2

ASH-PREPARATION

To prepare plant ash for use, one must first ensure that it is well-burnt. Some potters go to great trouble to obtain a clean and perfect example, burning on a swept stone slab. Ash burned in a Baxi or other domestic fire with an efficient draft will give a good white ash. Cardew recommends calcining the washed ash in a kiln to about 900°C., packing it in a *saggar*. For practical work the ash must also be available in sufficient quantity—at least half a dustbinful, and preferably more. Ashes from various sources can be mixed though this would be frowned upon by the dedicated ash-experimenter. Ash dust is *caustic* and care must be taken not to inhale it.

A careful initial sieving through a garden sieve will remove the rough stuff. It is then soaked in plenty of water and passed through a 30 mesh. As the ash settles, the surface water will contain a considerable concentration of soluble alkalis and will be *caustic*. This liquid can be poured or scooped away and replaced with clean water. The ash is well-stirred and again left to settle. It is advisable to carry out these operations wearing rubber gloves. The 'washing' process can be repeated two or three times, during which *fluxes* will be removed and the ash will become progressively more *refractory*. Reasonable washing is essential for ash which is to be added to tableware glazes, but for purely decorative purposes a totally unwashed ash can give entertaining results.

After the final settling and decanting, the sludge is spread out to dry (beware of ash on plaster slabs—the alkalis will attack the surface). When dry it is stored and weighed like any other glaze ingredient, care being taken not to raise a dust.

ATOM

The unit particle of a chemical *element*. Often cited as the smallest particle of matter which can partake in chemical action, though certainly not the smallest particle which exists. The make-up and behavior of atoms is continually under revision but simple, basic *molecular*

'Ash glaze' with a vengeance! The fascinating surface of this 'bag form' by Owen Rye (Australia) was achieved by laying it on its side under the stokehole (thus protecting it from the direct flame) of a wood-fired kiln which was fired with periods of heavy reduction over five days. One side of the pot has the accumulation of ash from the fuel (and a fireclay wad used for setting another vessel on top of it is still attached). Owen describes the glaze as 'golden Shino' (kaolin, soda, feldspar, and nepheline syenite) over a sandy body with 'pinholing – and crawling characteristic of this glaze type'.

theory is normally sufficient for the pottery. Hamer (PDM) deals extensively with the atomic make-up of pottery materials.

A representation of the oxygen atom. The nucleus is composed of 8 protons and 8 neutrons and is surrounded by two 'orbits' of electrons, the first of 2 electrons and an outer one of 6, a total of 8 to balance the positive charge of the protons. Oxygen occurs only as molecules of 2 atoms which share two electrons to make up the magic stable number of 8 in the outer shell.

ATOMIC NUMBERS

The atomic number is derived from the number of protons (or electrons) in an atom. Thus hydrogen has a single proton and is number 1, helium has two protons and is number 2, and so on. (See *periodic table*.)

ATOMIC RADIUS

The 'size' or radius of an atom will determine how it will act and which combinations it can form. Potassium and sodium have large atoms which are close enough in size to be interchangeable in feldspar etc. Sodium and calcium are also very close and form the plagioclase series. Silicon is a small atom and can fit within a pyramid of four (large) oxygen atoms, forming the SiO_4 group on which all ceramics are founded. The radii are measured in ångström units, 10^{-8} cm., and vary between 0.20 (boron) to 1.43 (barium) in common pottery *elements*. (See Cardew PP for list.)

ATOMIC THEORY

The 'classical' theory of the structure of matter is still broadly valid for potters. To quote H.IPC:

1   All elements are made up of small particles called atoms. Atoms are defined as the smallest particle of an element which can take part in chemical action.
2   Atoms cannot be created or destroyed.
3   Atoms are indivisible.
4   Atoms of the same *element* are alike in every way.
5   Atoms combine in whole numbers.

All these have been modified in the light of later research (we know to our cost that atoms can be 'split') but insofar as we are dealing with chemical change and

inorganic materials, Dalton's postulates above are still useful in practice. The fourth is complicated by the discovery of 'isotopes', but constant isotopic mixtures occur so that, again, for practical purposes, the application of this principle will be valid. The main effect of isotopes is to complicate *atomic weights*, which are no longer convenient whole numbers but are worked out as averages of the isotopes, and can therefore run into many places of decimals. In this book atomic weights are confined to one or two decimal places.

The application of simple atomic science to pottery is dealt with under *elements, molecules, valency*. Here we can discuss briefly the way in which the modern chemist views the structure of matter. For deeper insight into the theories see Holderness IPC and CR 2–14.

The atom, once thought to be the ultimate particle, is now considered as having some parallel with a solar system and to be made up of a number of still smaller fundamental units. These are distinguished by their electrical characteristics: the neutrons, electrically neutral; the positive protons; and the much smaller negatively charged electrons, are the principal units. The first two make up the nucleus or core of the atom and account for most of its 'weight'. The electrons have 'orbits' round the nucleus and form from one to seven layers or 'shells' at various distances from it. The number of protons in the nucleus and, when the atom is electrically neutral, the number of electrons surrounding it, is called the *atomic number*. The chart of atomic numbers is called the *periodic table*.

The total weight of an atom consists of its total number of protons and neutrons as compared with hydrogen. Hydrogen is unity with one proton (no neutrons); oxygen has eight of each. Thus the atomic number of oxygen is 8 and its atomic weight 16. In the heavier atoms there are more neutrons than protons in the nucleus.

Isotopes are those atoms in which the proton number is constant but the number of neutrons varies. Since the atomic weight (a.w.) equals the sum of these particles, an element can have more than one atomic weight. Within the mass of an element, however, these variations occur in regular proportions, so that the atomic weight can be given as a mean weight. Thus chlorine has an a.w. of 35.5—most of the atoms weighting 35, but some 37.

The electrons directly affect chemical behaviour. The shells lie at various distances from the nucleus, and each contains a fixed number of electrons. The outer shell is crucial to chemical action and to the formation of molecules or linked groups of atoms (lattices). It may hold from one to eight electrons. An outer shell of two or eight electrons is the stable state to which all atoms aspire, and the atom will borrow or share one another's electrons to make up eight or to lose all so that the next innermost shell becomes the 'complete' one. Atoms behaving in this way are joined one to another in groups or chains or networks which make up the involved, infinitely various, and apparently distinct compounds which constitute the world as we experience it.

When an atom 'loses' an electron it ceases to be electrically balanced and has a spare positive 'charge' from a proton. The element symbol is altered from R to R^+. If, on the other hand, two electrons are 'gained' it is written R^{--}, and so on. Unbalanced atoms are known as ions. In many cases a number of elements enter into combination, and the sharing becomes complicated and on several planes, leading to the build-up of crystal structures. The bonds formed between ions are 'electrovalent'; where sharing which does not disturb the balance takes place 'covalent' bonds are formed and molecules result. (See also *valency, electron, electrovalent, covalent.*)

ATOMIC WEIGHTS

The 'weight' of an atom is derived from the total of the *protons* and *neutrons* in the nucleus. It is a comparative number based on hydrogen at one or oxygen at sixteen. Used by potters as a means of translating *molecular* parts into tangible *recipes*. The 1961 International Atomic Weights Table is taken to seven decimal places, but we can be content with approximation to a single decimal place (it would not greatly affect the result to use the nearest whole number considering the empirical nature of most calculations and the comparatively small amounts). Atoms, in fact, obviously occur only in whole numbers but the presence of *isotopes* complicates the 'weight' of elements.

Element	Symbol	Weight
Aluminium	Al	27.0
Antimony	Sb	121.8
Barium	Ba	137.3
Bismuth	Bi	209.0
Boron	B	11.8
Cadmium	Cd	112.4
Calcium	Ca	40.0
Carbon	C	12.0
Chlorine	Cl	35.5
Chromium	Cr	52.0
Cobalt	Co	59.0
Copper	Cu	63.5
Fluorine	F	19.0
Germanium	Ge	72.6
Hydrogen	H	1.0
Iron	Fe	55.8
Lead	Pb	207.0
Lithium	Li	7.0
Magnesium	Mg	24.3
Manganese	Mn	55.0
Nickel	Ni	58.7
Oxygen	O	16.0
Phosphorus	P	31.0
Potassium	K	39.0
Praseodymium	Pr	59.0
Selenium	Se	79.0
Silicon	Si	28.1
Silver	Ag	107.9
Sodium	Na	23.0
Strontium	Sr	87.6
Sulfur	S	32.0
Tin	Sn	118.7
Titanium	Ti	48.0
Vanadium	V	51.0
Zinc	Zn	65.3
Zirconium	Zr	91.2

AUTOCLAVE

An airtight chamber which can be used to test the liability of a glaze to *crazing* by heating it under steam pressure. The method is not entirely satisfactory as it confuses the effects of moisture expansion (*adsorption*) with *thermal shock*.

AUTOMATIC KILN CONTROL

Sophisticated electronic apparatus is widely available for terminating or soaking a firing automatically according to the programme set by the potter. The rate of rise and fall of temperature is also controllable. Cromartie issue a good range. Many potters would prefer to have direct control but such equipment is useful for repeating a programme of firing once it is established.

A simpler mechanical device usually makes use of *mini-bars*. A rod, set within the kiln, introduced through the spyhole, rests on the bar and when the bar sags, indicating that the required temperature has been reached, the rod drops and switches off the kiln. Also known as a 'kiln sitter'. (See also *kiln-sitter, controlling pyrometer.*)

AVENTURINE GLAZE

Aventurine is a mineral, a feldspar with small shiny crystals of hematite. In glazes it is therefore a decorative surface effect produced by the formation of small, sometimes bright crystals (*devitrification*). Larger, sometimes very large and impressive crystals can also be generated, see *crystalline glazes*. The aventurine crystals are generally of hematite and the method is similar to that described at crystalline glazes. High iron oxide content in lead glaze, combined with low alumina will help to develop the effect. Zinc (around 0.3 equivalents in the glaze formula), rutile, and titania have been mentioned. Slow cooling especially in the 900–700°C. range is essential. Quoted recipe:

Lead/borax frit	75
Cornwall stone	15
Oxide of iron	6
Oxide of copper	1
Chromate of iron	3

from Billington TP with the usual advice for the type 'apply thickly, fire and cool slowly'. The glazes are suitable only for decorative pieces.

BACKSTAMP

A printed or impressed stamp beneath a pot giving information about the maker or the making of the piece. Not often used by the studio potter who generally prefers to stamp the footring or outer base of the piece.

A backstamp could be useful to collectors and historians, not to mention the interested public; the average potter today is very anonymous.

BACTERIA IN CLAY

It is thought that the growth of bacteria in damp clay promotes acid gels which have a beneficial effect on *plasticity*. Rhodes recommends mixing a little well-matured clay with new batches. The bacterial action will assist vegetable decomposition which is a link in the chain leading to ionic exchange, a factor in plasticity. (See *algae*.)

BAG WALL

A wall of brickwork built between the firebox and setting-space of a kiln. It deflects the heat upwards and also serves to prevent the flame from impinging directly onto the ware or the *saggars* (although it is possible to build a bag wall of saggars). Cardew recommends the use of a thin brick, 9 × 4½ × 1–1½ in. (approx. 220 × 110 × 30 mm.), with 3 in. (70 mm.) between the bag wall and the kiln wall, and terminating 5 in. (about 120 mm.) or so below the springers of the dome. These measurements, especially that of the distance between the bag wall and the kiln wall, will vary with the design of the kiln but too great a gap will waste heat. Bag walls are sometimes built with apertures to spread the flames

through the ware nearest them. Lightweight or *insulating* brick have obviously no advantage for bag walls which, anyhow, are subject to fierce fire.

A section through the bag wall of a down-draft (or cross-draft) kiln.

BAIL HANDLE

An overarching handle, sometimes used on teapots and more commonly on pottery 'baskets'. Pottery bail handles give a firmer grip than cane ones but are more vulnerable.

A ceramic bail handle on a teapot by Sheila Fournier; attractive and easy to use but somewhat vulnerable.

BALANCE

Finely suspended scales used in chemistry. Essential for weighing quantities under 10 g. Normally only cobalt is likely to be used in such small amounts in working glaze batches.

BALL CLAY

Secondary, transported (*sedimentary*) clays which are very plastic and fire to a pale color. The name derives from the 30–35 lb. balls into which form they were originally made up for horse transport. As dug they often contain carbons which stain them blue or dark grey; these will be dispersed during firing. They have a high shrinkage rate and are difficult to handle on their own due to very fine particle size, e.g. their failure to settle as a slip or to dry easily from slurry to plastic. Other, coarser-grained clays are therefore added and the ball clay content of a body is normally restricted to about 30%. It has high dry strength which is valuable.

In England the main beds are at Wareham, Dorset, and in Devon; in the U.S.A. in Kentucky and Tennessee. Ball clays vary considerably in their mineral content: Sutherland GNS quotes: kaolinite from 20–90%; micaceous material 5–45% (illite or hydrous mica); quartz 1–70%. Remarkably wide limits.

'Free' silica is often a feature of ball clays, which are then known as siliceous ball clays. They are all too sticky and fine-grained to use alone but are an essential ingredient of most pottery bodies, increasing *plasticity* and *dry strength*, and assisting *vitrification* upon firing.

A typical analysis by weight:

K_2O	1.8	Al_2O_3	33.0
Na_2O	0.2	Fe_2O_3	1.0
CaO	0.3	SiO_2	49.0
MgO	0.3	TiO_2	0.9

A *body* recipe for a 1290°C. firing might read:

Fireclay or stoneware clay	50
Ball clay	25
Flint	10
China stone or feldspar	5
Fine grog	10

(See also *clays, throwing, body*.)

BALL MILL

A machine for grinding rocks and minerals, consisting of a horizontal cylinder made from, or lined with, an abrasion-resistant material (e.g. stoneware or porcelain), and of some mechanical means of making it revolve.

The materials to be ground are put into the cylinder together with flint pebbles, porcelain or hard steel balls, and water. As it rotates, the balls, rolling continuously to the bottom of the curve, grind very efficiently. In the industry dry milling may be practised, with a current of air taking away the finer material (elutriation). There is also a wet system where the mill is vertical and vibrates rather than rotates. The craftsman who buys commercial materials will rarely require a mill—the materials will be sufficiently ground (often too finely)—but a mill is useful for experimental and special purposes. For the pioneer potter it is indispensable. The smaller ball mills are called *jar mills* and are discussed under that entry.

Various critical factors must be taken into account when constructing a ball or jar mill.

Speed varies with the size. Slightly differing equations have been put forward; the simplest is

Revs. per minute = $58.18 \div \sqrt{r}$

where r is the radius of the interior of the mill in feet. Thus for a 6 in. (approx 150 mm.) diameter mill the rev./min. would be $58.18 \div \sqrt{0.25}$, i.e. $58.18 \div 0.5 = 116.36$. This is the maximum working speed, and one would grind at about 75% of this, i.e. 80 rev./min. Other mill sizes work out at 100 rev./min. for a 4 in. (approx. 100 mm.) mill; 70 rev./min. for 8 in. (approx. 200 mm.); 50 rev./min. for 12 in. (approx. 300 mm.).

Balls. Flint pebbles or porcelain, called the 'grinding medium' in merchants' catalogs. Size $\frac{1}{2}$–2 in. (10–50 mm.) in diameter, and filling about 50% of the mill's capacity. ('Capacity' meaning two-thirds of the total space in the mill.) Some authorities recommend no more than half full.

Water and charge are each 15–25% of capacity. The charge must already have been ground to 'sand' size.

Time varies with hardness and grain size required, from two to eight hours. The mill will become warm if the charge is grinding correctly.

Cardew PP has an appendix on ball mills and also an ingenious system of finding the square roots of numbers below unity, useful in the speed equation above.

If a ball mill is working at its optimum efficiency, Brian Sutherland GNS romantically but evocatively suggests that it should sound 'like a breaking wave'! See *jar mill* for principle of operation. The ball mill has been

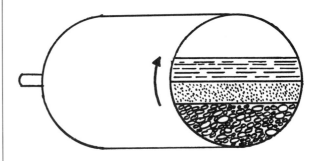

A diagrammatic section of a ball mill showing pebbles, charge, and water in their approximate proportions. These will, of course, be intimately mingled when the mill is turning.

largely superseded in the industry by the *vibratory mill* which is also coming onto the market for studio potters and has a much more rapid grinding action.

BALLOON

The use of a rubber balloon as a former or support has been mentioned in CM 20/6 and elsewhere. A rounded shoulder on a slab pot for instance, can be formed from a soft slab worked over a balloon, which has been sufficiently inflated just to fill the top of the pot.

BANDING

The spinning of pigment lines onto a pot. The brush should hold sufficient liquid to complete the band without a refill, and the hand must be held perfectly still once the brush is in contact with the pot surface. Some support which will incline the hand towards the pot, such as an elbow set on a firm surface, is useful. Needless to say, the pot must be centered on the wheel or whirler, and

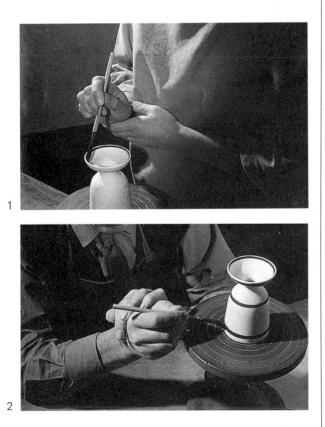

1

2

Two methods of supporting and steadying the hand for banding.
(1) The left hand holds the right wrist, the potter standing to the work.
(2) When seated the elbow can be used as a pivot, resting it on the bench.

sufficient smooth turning momentum obtained. A heavy *whirler* is essential for technically efficient banding. Banding is somewhat mechanical in appearance but is useful as a frame and foil for more *calligraphic* work— and to do it well is very satisfying!

The freer spinning of lines is dealt with under *spun colour*.

BANDING WHEEL

Although the term is used for any free-spinning circular turntable it is, strictly, a floor-standing wheel often with a cork inset surface. Also called a lining wheel. The term 'whirler' or 'bench whirler' is now more general for the table wheel normally used by potters. (See *whirler*.)

BANK KILN

A kiln constructed against a hill or bank, the slope, usually about 30°, providing the draft. Though crude in conception, bank kilns were probably responsible for some fine pottery. Small bank kilns are sometimes constructed by potters today and they can be excellent teaching aids. The body of the kiln can be actually cut into the slope which will then supply efficient insulation. See Rhodes K 18–20. The oriental many-chambered *climbing kilns* are based on a similar principle.

Section diagram of a simple kiln built into a sloping bank of earth and suitable for raku and other low-fired ware where a certain amount of smoky atmosphere is not a problem. The black dots represent firebars on which the fuel, usually wood, is burnt. The pots are set on a shelf which is built up on brick columns.

BAR, pyrometric

See *Holdcroft bar, mini-bar*.

BARBOTINE

A French word for *slip* occasionally used in older books on pottery, often applied to the high-relief slip patterns of the type so brilliantly achieved by the Roman Rhenish and some Romano-British potters whose precise technique has never been rediscovered or equalled.

BARITE

See *barytes*.

BARIUM, compounds

A metallic element Ba. 137.3
Oxide BaO, 153.3. Baria.
Carbonate $BaCO_3$. 197.3.
Sulfate $BaSO_4$. 233. *Barytes*.

An alkaline earth. Most compounds toxic. The carbonate is relatively insoluble and is normally used in glaze mixes (though it may react with any flocculant present). Decomposes to the oxide at 900°C.

Baria acts as a *base* in glazes at high temperatures, its action similar in some respects to lime (calcia). A high proportion, 20% plus, may dull the surface of the glaze and cause pinholes unless the recipe also contains boron. Vivienne Foley (CR 78) and Behrens suggest as much as 50% in a 1250°C. glaze but the average is 10–20%. Baria can give a hardness and brilliance to a glaze at 1150°C and over. Behrens gives recipes:

Baria	30.4	21.5
Feldspar	46.4	—
Nepheline	—	24.7
Zinc	7.5	—
Flint	15.7	31.5
Strontium	—	12.4
Whiting	—	2.8
China clay	—	7.1
	1190°C.	1225°C.

Barium also occurs in a surprising number of Japanese recipes (see Sanders WJC). It will modify pigments sometimes in a startling way, as with copper. Proportions are critical and considerable experiment is necessary. Behrens mentions a red with nickel in CM 19/8.

It is used industrially to prevent scum on bricks: the addition of 2–3% of the carbonate will do the same for red-clay biscuit ware (terracotta) which is liable to white discoloration. Wedge the carbonate into the body. The scum is caused by soluble salts, especially calcium chloride when the surface crystals are destroyed in handling. To quote Billington 'the barium effects a substitution $CaCl_2 + BaCO_3 = BaCl_2 + CaCO_3$'. The sulphate will have a similar effect.

BARYTES

The natural rock of barium sulfate. Associated with lead and consequently sometimes known as heavy-spar. Used to introduce baria into a glaze so long as the sulphur can be efficiently dispersed. Usually fritted with carbon into barium carbonate. (See also *witherite*.)

BASALT

The characteristic volcanic basic rock, smooth and black. High in iron. Ground and fired it can form a glassy material with a melting temperature variable between ca. 1150–1250°C. but must be used with additional silica and feldspar to form a dark-colored glaze. Ivan England's analyses and discussion of basalts and basalt glazes appeared in PQ. 31, together with his glaze recipes using an 'average' basalt.

1 For a dark glaze:
basalt 66; whiting 6; flint 28.
This is the maximum possible proportion of basalt.

2 For a lighter colour:
basalt 17; feldspar 49; whiting 10; silica 16.
Add bentonite 2% for suspension.
A basalt is listed by Ceramatech, and others.

BASALT WARE

Originated by Wedgwood as a name for a black vitreous body resembling *basalt*. A recipe quoted is:

Ball clay	47.0
China clay	3.0
Ironstone	40.0
Manganese	10.0

In effect basalt ware is a black slip body fired to vitrification. The recipes for *black slip* using iron, manganese and cobalt in various proportions can be adapted. A 'basalt' body is now supplied commercially. Among modern potters, Colin Pearson has used it effectively in winged cylinders.

A basalt body recipe given in CM 17/3 is:

Red clay	40
China clay	18
Ball clay	15
Ferric oxide	16
Manganese	6
Nepheline	2
Bentonite	3

BASE, basic

One of the main chemical groupings. Inorganic materials may be classed as bases or acids. In general the bases cause ceramic mixtures to become *fusible*: they are *glass modifiers*. Bases and acids combine to form 'salts'. The bases are listed under the general term RO in the *Seger formula*; they also include the R_2O oxides, usually of metals.

The principal bases in pottery are the oxides of lead, sodium, potassium, magnesium, zinc, lithium, calcium, strontium and barium. Also the pigment oxides of manganese, copper and cobalt.

The bases include the alkalis and the alkaline earths. (See also *flux*.)

BASE CRACKS

During throwing the base of a pot undergoes less pressure, and is worked on less, than the walls. It is thus less aligned in particle structure and liable to greater shrinkage. The compression of the base from the outside at any time in the throwing process can help to prevent base cracks. During drying bases must always be free to contract. See *cracking*. Hamer PDM has an exhaustive study of base cracks.

BASIC ROCK

Igneous rocks comparatively high in basic minerals. They may contain 45–55% of silica but most of it is locked into silicate minerals so that there is little of the 'free' oxide. Basalt is the main type; generally volcanic in origin. It can decompose into clay material but, to quote Cardew, 'tends to produce montmorillonite rather than kaolinite'. The high iron content of these rocks limits their use as a glaze material.

BASIC SLAG

A byproduct of the steel industry, rich in phosphorus and iron, with some silica and calcium. Obtainable as fertilizer. Occasionally occurs in glaze recipes. Mentioned in Green EP, and Cardew PP. The slag can be used in stoneware glazes where it will introduce an interesting, if not always predictable, well-combined batch of ingredients. *Opalescence* can result from the phosphorus. It can be used with red clay for *temmoku* type glazes.

BAT, batt

Applied to various types of sheet material:

1 Kiln shelves or cranks of refractory clays.
2 A slab of plaster or low fired biscuit for drying clay.
3 Sheet material used for supporting, transporting or drying pottery. Should be slightly porous so that it releases the clay as it dries. It is easy to slide a wet pot onto a glazed surface but almost impossible to remove it when leather-hard.
4 A removable disc of wood, plaster, or other material which is fastened to the wheel-head but can be easily removed. For repetition throwing or for large pieces. See *ejector head, wheel bat*.
5 A bat-shaped piece of wood (e.g. a butter pat) for beating pots or stirring glaze.

6 A short brick. In U.S.A. a broken brick—hence brick-bat.

(See also under *kiln shelves*.)

The use of a fairly stiff ring of clay to adhere a throwing bat to the wheelhead.

BATCH, batch weight

A proportioned mixture of materials. Batch weights are in fixed proportions to one another but have random totals. For easier comparison and calculation bring batch weights to percentages.

Method: Multiply each number in the recipe by 100 and then divide by the total, i.e. $\frac{BW}{T} \times 100$.

An example of the same recipe as batch weight and percentages:

Batch weight	Percentage weight
143	44
65	20
13	4
103	32
325	100

The answer in line 1 is worked out thus: $143 \times 100 \div 325 = 44$.

BAT WASH

A *refractory* material applied to *bats, saggars* etc, to prevent ware sticking to them during firing. Flint or calcined alumina and a little clay mixed with water may be brushed on. The disadvantage of coated shelves is that they cannot be reversed. A thin dust of dry alumina is usually sufficient—this can be brushed off. *Kyanite* has been mentioned as a bat wash, as has the similar mineral *sillimanite*, also bauxite, and zircon. Glaze rarely sticks to *silicon carbide* shelves. Layers of glossy paper have been suggested, relying on the clay content of the coated surface. Avoid any mixture of alumina and silica for setting or bat wash when salt-glazing.

BAUXITE

The ore of aluminium, Al_2O_3, $2H_2O$ with iron, titania and other impurities. The name derives from an early source at Beaux in France. A sedimentary rock with clay and iron. For a detailed discussion of 'bauxitization' see Cardew PP, 58–9. (See also *diaspore*.)

BEAD

Jewelry beads are often made in ceramic. The work is somewhat tedious, especially the glazing. Biscuit beads in coloured or variegated bodies can be fired in bowls or on tiles. Beads need not be spherical, but may be square, cylindrical, conical, or of a flattened shape, with carved, rolled, painted, or molten glass decoration. Rolling a bead across a textured surface will transfer the pattern to the bead. The true bead will have a hole through it. This needs to be clear and without excessively sharp edges which may cut the string.

Glazed beads must either have a hole large enough to allow them to be threaded over a heat resisting (*nichrome*) wire, or be designed with one flat, unglazed surface on which they can rest. The wire can be supported at each end on a 'cradle' which you can make yourself. Partial or spot glazing is easier than full glaze covering, although even majolica painting is possible if you are prepared for the rather tiresome work of ensuring that the hole in the bead and a small circle around it are free from glaze. One can apply a spot of wax to one end, impale the other on a toothpick and then dip the bead into the glaze. Threading the beads onto a fine drinking straw has been suggested, the nichrome wire being inserted through the straw. The straw burns away during firing. The use of *Egyptian paste* will obviate much of this work.

A bead can be glazed by impaling it on a cocktail stick or toothpick. The other end of the hole is sealed with a blob of wax.

The conception of a necklace has widened beyond the traditional string of beads, and the elements may be joined together in different ways—perhaps in combination with metals.

Special ceramic beads are used as electrical insulators threaded onto wires which are subject to heat. Can be used for sheathing connections on electric kilns.

A bead firing 'cradle', formed from a strip of clay and a length of nichrome (or Kanthal for higher temperatures) wire, if the wire is too long (over about 8 in. (150mm.)), or over-loaded, it may sag during firing.

BEADING

Lines of dots in relief, often slip-trailed, used decoratively. Hamer uses the word to describe excessive crawling of glaze into blobs. See Fournier DPF for illustration and discussion.

BEAKER

A drinking vessel with or without a handle and usually without a saucer. A very wide range of shapes is possible —the stumpy barrel being the least attractive. See Fournier DPF for a variety of forms.

BEAM SCALE

Perhaps the most accurate and sensitive of scales, but rather expensive although, with the influx of electronic instruments, it may be possible to pick one up second hand. Can weigh from 5–10,000 grams and be zero adjusted to take account of containers.

BEATEN DECORATION

Similar to impressed decoration, but more spontaneous and direct. The edge of a stick, or a textured surface such as a butter pat or string wound round a bat, can be used with wide-ranging effects from subtle indented marks to deep three-dimensional impressions. The beater can be ragged or irregular although too obvious a repeat in the pattern can become rather mechanical. The edges can be left sharp, or softened with a sponge.

Beaten patterns retain more of their characteristic quality under thin, spare glazes—dry ash glazes are very suitable—than with full thick coatings.

The actual surface of a pot can be decorated, or an applied slab of softer (perhaps differently colored) clay can be luted on. Large decorative 'sun' forms can be beaten from circular slabs of clay. These are attractive in themselves, and the exercise can be useful in releasing pent-up tensions in the potter!

1

2

1

3

5

(1) The surface of a pot may be simply ridged with a sharp-edged bat.
(2 and 3) Here a circular 'sun' is beaten into a slab of clay which is then applied to the slipped surface of a pot.
(4 and 5) An irregular slab of plastic clay is luted on and the pattern then beaten in. Further subtlety can be obtained by later planing of the half-dry surface.

BEATEN FORMS

Thrown or hand-built pottery can be gently beaten to alter form, profile or emphasis, or to provide panels for decoration. It is a favorite technique among modern potters, offering a subtle contrast between curved and plane surfaces. The beating can be done as soon as the surface loses its stickiness or at any subsequent stage up to stiff leather-hard; the different clay states yield different styles and qualities of form. The bat should be wide enough to avoid edge marks; slightly chamfered or rounded corners will help. The clay undergoes considerable strain and the blows should be just hard enough to ease it into a change of shape without forcing it. Alternatively the pot can be flattened or rocked on the bench surface.

Thrown or built pots are often distorted, more or less violently, by beating with a flat bat, a shaped piece of wood or other object, or with a sharper edged tool, at the extreme giving the almost 'destroyed' forms favored in the U.S.A. especially during the 1970's and 1980's when iconoclasm was all.

A variety of bats and beaters: two butter pats, a paddle, a flat-backed wooden spoon, and a cooking spatula. Beaters wrapped with string or cord, or cut with grooves have been used for many centuries to develop patterns and textures on clay. The Japanese 'Jomon', the oldest known pottery, means 'cord impressed'.

These pots were formed as rounded 'envelope' shapes and then beaten to form ridges or spines down the front and sides (more distinct in the right-hand piece), the form resembling a brazil nut. By Robert Fournier.

BEATER

For light work, butter pats make excellent beaters for knocking pots into, or out of, shape. Old pats can be found in junk shops and new ones are now available. For work requiring a heavier tool a cricket bat shape can easily be cut from a piece of $3 \times \frac{3}{4}$ in. (approx. 75×20 mm.) timber. Wood is the best material for beaters, non-porous surfaces such as plastic tend to stick to the clay. Edges should be rounded and faces sanded smooth.

Beaters or 'paddles' can be carved to give a simple overall pattern and many Japanese potters keep a stock of decorated paddles. Plain beaters can double up as glaze stirrers. (See illus. under *paddle*.)

BEDDING

See *placing*.

BEIDELLITE

A clay mineral of the montmorillonite group from Beidell, Colorado. Rich in alumina.

BELLY

The widest part (where this is not the *shoulder*) of a full-bodied pot form.

BENTONITE

A very fine-grained (*colloidal*) clay of the *montmorillonite* type containing bases and iron, derived from volcanic ash. The name originated from a source at Fort Benton, U.S.A. The particle size is probably under 0.03% of the average kaolinite grain. It is a very sticky clay with a high shrinkage (the bonding between the unit layers allows the ingress of more water than does *kaolinite*) and a tendency to crack during firing and cooling. It is therefore unworkable alone or in any large quantity in a body, but its super-plasticity (at least as far as *thixotropy* is concerned) can help short bodies such as porcelains. It also assists the *suspension* of a glaze.

Calcium bentonite is the most useful type. Sodium bentonite will swell as it takes up water. The iron content always colors bentonite but there is a so-called white bentonite with an analysis by weight:

20

K_2O	5	
Na_2O	2.0	Al_2O_3 64.2 12.0, SiO_2
CaO	2.0	
MgO	2.3	Fe_2O_3 2.0

This will give a better color in reduction than in oxidation, if used in a porcelain body. Bentonites vary widely in plasticity and purity. A few, such as fuller's earth, may be relatively unplastic.

Bentonite is difficult to mix into a glaze batch. Work it into a thick slurry with a little water first and add further water only very gradually. If it is tipped dry into a glaze it will merely float in small globules. Pass the bentonite slip several times through a 120 mesh or small 200 color lawn. 3% is the normal maximum for addition to a body or glaze but up to 12% has been suggested. (See *once-fired ware*).

BERKELY CLAY

A plastic refractory clay from South Carolina.

BERYLLIA

An expensive (and toxic) glaze flux for high temperatures. Emerald and aquamarine are natural forms.

BETA FORM

Generally applied to the crystal form of quartz at temperatures above the *inversion* point.

BI−, or DI−

Indicating double; in chemistry the terms are used to describe a combination with two atoms or molecules, e.g. carbon-di-oxide (two oxygen atoms); bisilicate of lead (two molecules of silica).

BIN TROLLEY

A variation on the old 'sack truck'. A two-wheeled trolley with a flat base ledge, on which bins or sacks of material can be supported or moved. Also listed are 'stair climbing' bin trolleys. A bin 'dolly' is a wheeled flat platform for moving bins around which can save many a back-ache or slipped disc though, to be really efficient you would need one for each bin.

BIOTITE MICA

See *mica*.

BISCUIT, bisque

Unglazed ware, usually porous. In the USA and in the pottery industry the French form 'bisque' is preferred.

The biscuit firing is for convenience, to render the pots less fragile and to make glazing easier. It is also reputed to produce a tougher glazed fabric. This is certainly the case in the industry, where the biscuit fire may be 150°C. higher than the glaze fire. *Earthenware glazes* are less likely to craze on a high-fired biscuit (see *cristobalite*) but it is difficult to apply the raw glaze onto a body which has *vitrified* to any great degree.

Clay turns into ceramic at 500–600°C. so that is the minimum for a biscuit fire (primitive *sawdust* and similar firing do not always reach this temperature). At least one authority believes that the change is instantaneous at a certain temperature rather than progressive. Above 600°C. clays behave in different ways, i.e. approach sintering and vitrification at different temperatures. The more 'impurities' present, the lower the temperature. Biscuit firing should be oxidised except for special unglazed effects. For stoneware the biscuit need not exceed 850–900°C. but for earthenware glazes a firing approaching 1100°C. will produce some *cristobalite* which will help to prevent *crazing*.

Ground-up biscuit is known as *grog*. The term terracotta is often applied to biscuit modeling, especially in red clay.

BISCUIT FIRE

A number of alterations and stresses occur during the firing of the clay into ceramic. The principal ones are:

Up to 100°C.	'Mixed' or water of plasticity is driven off as vapor.
100–200°C.	The adsorbed water is lost and organic materials begin to burn out (carbonise).
573°C.	*Quartz inversion*.
500–600°C.	*Chemically combined water* is lost and a new (ceramic) material is formed.
600°C. upwards	Carbons, sulfur, etc. continue to burn out. There is a certain expansion in volume up to 800–850°C. *Vitrification* begins (different temperatures for different clays), the particles pack more closely, and shrinkage occurs.

The greatest risk of breakage or explosion is in the 90–150°C. range. Thick pieces are obviously more at risk than thin-walled ware. From 200°C. fairly quick firing is possible, indeed the clay-ceramic conversion may be virtually instantaneous (Peter Smith). One can quote the twenty-minute African brushwood firings, while the industry has experimented with even shorter periods. My own biscuit, fired (after thorough drying) in four hours, has a good ring at 980°C. However clays and kilns are so variable that no one can be dogmatic about their behaviour. An average and conservative biscuit graph is shown.

With some clays it is considered useful to slow down the rate of rise or even *soak* at around 900°C. in order to fully dispel impurities and to oxidise any carbon to CO_2, or *black core* and *bloating* can result in the subsequent glaze fire, caused by trapped carbon.

A biscuit firing graph showing three to four hours drying, including 'water smoke', a slight slowing down between 400–600°C (a by no means essential refinement), then a faster rise to 1020°C. A stoneware biscuit can be terminated earlier (900–960°C) but for earthenware a higher temperature (to ca, 1090°C. if this can be reached without vitrification) will help to avoid future glaze crazing. Some clays benefit from a slowdown between 900 and 1000°C to burn out any carbon content. An indication of this is shown on the graph.

BISCUIT STOPPING

See *stopping.*

BISMUTH, oxide

A metallic element Bi, 209.0.
Oxide Bi_2O_3, 466, m.p. 825°C.

Can be used to produce a mother-of-pearl luster. Listed as a base in glazes, although its oxide suggests that it is *amphoteric*. Parmelee describes the preparation of bismuth luster using the resinate of bismuth, and suggests its addition to yellow and gray-brown lusters. Bismuth can also be used as a carrier for other luster colours (Hamer). See also *luster.*

BISQUE

See *biscuit.*

BIT

See *crank.*

BIVALENT

A valency of two (will combine with two hydrogen atoms), e.g. the valency of oxygen in water (H_2O) is two. Thus it follows that the valency of calcium in calcium oxide (CaO) is also two—it is bivalent. See diagram at *valency.*

BLACK BODY

Similar considerations arise as to *black slips*. Only a vitrified body will approach a true black. (See also *basalt ware*.)

A construction in partly glazed black clay, "Firmer Ground II", by Henry Pim.

BLACK CORE

Bricks, shards of primitive pottery, and even seventeenth-century slipware often show a section which is red for a few millimeters from each face, but black in the centre. Caused by an inadequately oxidized or too rapid firing of a carbonaceous and generally high-iron clay.

In sawdust firing the black core is inevitable, but it can be a great decorative asset where it breaks through to the surface.

A shard of Hertfordshire (England) slipware showing the black stripe in the thickest part of the section.

BLACK GLAZE

The standard black earthenware glaze has been quoted as 4% each of iron, cobalt and manganese. Many black glaze and pigment recipes approximate to this combination. Rhodes recommends 2% of each; Billington 6% manganese, 4% iron in a lead and soda glaze, or 7% manganese, 1% cobalt and 2% iron in a lead glaze.

The high pigment content necessary to produce a near-black will affect glaze fusibility. The manganese is also liable to cause bubbling. Copper blacks are possible but rather tricky: 3–5% will produce a *matt* surface at earthenware temperatures (see also 'gun-metal' black mentioned under *black pigments*). Copper can be combined with iron to produce a 'mirror black' (Rhodes). Manganese/copper combinations have a very low *eutectic* and can cause running in glazes or pigments. Also beware of manganese with zinc.

In stoneware, especially in reduction which turns red iron oxide to the black oxide, between 5% and 12% or iron oxide in a *siliceous* glaze, and preferably on a siliceous body, should give black, although in some glazes the higher proportions may oxidize on the surface to produce *kaki* reds. A different quality of color can be developed with 6–8% iron and 1–2% cobalt. A high concentration of manganese in a oxidized fire can give a metallic pewter-like surface up to about 1270°C. The finest quality black wares were produced in Song China. Leach quotes the addition of 10% of medium wood ash to Hamada's 'building stone' glaze for temmoku. Potclays' 'black feldspar' could be the basis for a similar experiment. The so-called 'oil spot' or 'hare's fur' glaze markings may have derived from settled-down bubble craters. Some authorities, however, consider that they are more likely to be glass-in-glass melts. Rhodes is convinced that these are natural slip glazes, similar to Albany clay glazes. Manganese earthenware glazes, which also bubble, occasionally exhibit similar patterns.

As well as Albany clay, ochre, burnt sienna, and spodumene have been suggested. See Rhodes CGP 187.

BLACK PIGMENT

A true black pigment is difficult to mix from raw materials. The standard cobalt/manganese/iron mixture will tend to separate out, though often in a pleasant way. It will also run. In ready-made industrial colors the oxides are *sintered* together, with opacifiers and *refractories*, and are blended to maintain the hue and to minimize running and blurring. Black prepared pigments (underglaze or stains) will almost certainly contain chrome (so beware of chrome-tin reactions), and nickel will often be present.

'Standard black' quoted by Dodd consists of 30 cobaltic oxide, 56 ferric oxide, 48 chromic oxide, 8 nickel oxide, 31 alumina. Other black mixtures quoted in Webb CNS are for underglaze: ferric oxide 36, chrome 7, manganese 12, cobalt 32, nickel 13; and for stains—iron chromate 51, nickel 9, cobalt 21, chrome 4, ferric 15. A simple mixture of 9:1 MnO_2:CoO with perhaps a little iron oxide will give an approximation to black at earthenware temperatures.

There are also iridium blacks. A gun-metal black results from equal parts of copper, manganese and cobalt. Copper and manganese can give black with a gold sheen. (See *copper/manganese gold*.)

BLACK SLIP

The traditional black slip for lead glazed slipware is red clay with up to 10% dry weight of manganese dioxide. The biscuit fire must be kept low (ca. 1000°C.) to avoid vitrification which inhibits the glaze take-up.

Some of the manganese can be replaced with either iron and cobalt or both, but the distinctive quality of the simple slip will be lost. Manganese slip under a tin glaze will produce warm grays and even, on occasion, a gentle salmon blush. The *fusible* nature of manganese is ideally suited to staining through a normally opaque glaze. Any trace of cobalt will cool the color. Black slip applied thinly (flooded over or brushed on) on a buff body will fade unevenly under a lead glaze to browns and yellowish colors. Difficult to control but very attractive at its best.

The high shrinkage of red clay based black slip necessitates its use on clay which is slightly softer than leather-hard. Black slip, with perhaps a more sophisticated body base (see *engobes*) will be self-glazing (vitrified) at stoneware temperatures.

BLACKSMITH'S SCALE

Iron spangles. Originally the blue flakes resulting from

hammered iron, now produced by roasting scrap iron. (See also at *magnetite*.)

BLEB, blebbing

An American term for small blisters on pottery caused by air pockets just below the surface. A minor form of *bloating*. Avoided by careful *wedging* and clean clay.

BLEED-THROUGH

A colloquial term for the breaking through of impurities in the body to speckle or color a glaze. The commonest source is pyrites (iron sulfide) in the clay, especially fireclay. Largely an aspect of reduction at high temperatures. Attempts have been made to simulate and control the effect artificially in oxidation using iron spangles and other coarse-grained pigments.

BLISTERING

Bubbles of escaping gas are an inevitable feature of glazes at some point in their firing. Raw material glazes are more liable to blister than *frits*. Most of the bubbles settle down as the glaze melts, but if the firing is terminated too early, or is carried on to a point where further reactions begin (often thought of as 'boiling') then unhealed craters will be left in the cooled glaze. The bubbles may be of oxygen from manganese dioxide, fluorine from some china stones, or any other gaseous material released by the firing.

Blistering may be aggravated by too thick a coating of glaze; by the slight reduction of a lead glaze; by too rapid an end-fire (1240–1280°C. in stoneware); by sulfur compounds, perhaps in the body; by the use of *fluorine* minerals in the glaze; and, probably the commonest cause of all in earthenware, by the setting of newly glazed and inadequately dried pots in the kiln. Even a preliminary warming-up does not always help in an electric kiln and it is advisable to dry the pots thoroughly before packing.

BLOATING

The development of gas pockets in a body after it has started to vitrify and is *pyroplastic*, causing it to develop local swelling. Bad mixing or wedging, or sulfides in the clay can be causes. Gas may also be generated by carbon obtaining oxygen from the body and forming carbon dioxide, or by minute pockets of water in closed pores deep in the fabric.

Care must be taken, when firing the biscuit, to avoid *vitrification* by sudden or local temperature rise (see also *flashing*), especially in bodies high in carbonates. In the stoneware fire Cardew recommends that oxidizing conditions be maintained to 1150°C. My own firing sched-

ule is a rapid one and I find that, using comparatively high iron bodies in an oxidizing fire, there is a critical temperature—about 1275°C.—where bloating may occur.

As bloating normally occurs only when the clay is sufficiently 'molten' to swell without breaking, it is thus a feature of high-fired pottery. Most bodies will bloat if they are overfired or if they have a premature glass phase e.g. an excess of feldspathic material. Needless to say, any tiny pellets of body ingredients or 'foreign' materials will increase the risk. David Leach suggests an oxidized *soaking* at 1000°C. to burn out carbon. Hamer mentions too 'stiff' a glaze layer or a vitrifying slip as contributory causes. For *once-fired ware* there must be plenty of ventilation for the first 1000°C. especially when using high sulfur clays. In this connection Alan Graham (CR 75) suggests half an hour of light reduction at 800°C. to produce sulfites which will decompose and disperse.

Good preparation, clean clay, avoidance of overfiring, the addition of some opening material such as grog or calcined china clay will all help to avoid bloating. Potters have been known to bloat pots deliberately as a decorative feature.

BLOWN SLIP

A layered effect produced by blowing across a newly slipped surface which can then we used as a ground for further embellishment.

BLUE PIGMENT, glaze stain

There is a bewildering variety of blue colors listed in suppliers' catalogs. Most of them derive from cobalt, which can be mixed and fritted with other materials to give various shades of blue. Some of the shades quoted are:

Willow blue: recipe by Dodd DC—cobalt oxide 40, feldspar 40, flint 20. A diluted blue.

Manzarine or royal blue from cobalt with various fluxes.

Matt blue: Cobalt 20, alumina 60, zinc 20. A cobalt aluminate which would need to be fritted.

Peacock blue, with china stone, *standard black* (see *black pigments*) and flint.

Early blue frits were zaffre and smalt. Most fritted blues are for use on earthenware. At high temperatures it is difficult to prevent the formation of rather strident cobalt silicates. Even with the use of cobalt aluminates, a eutectic is formed with the silica of the glaze at around 1200°C.

Many potters find modern cobalt oxides used as

pigments too pure and stark and make additions of other materials to modify their stridency. Various combinations (up to 80% of the total pigment batch) of manganese, iron, red clay, nickel, or rutile have been suggested in an attempt to approximate to the impure *asbolite*. A simple dilution for use on earthenware is one part of cobalt to four parts of china stone. Unless specking is required, cobalt colors need careful sieving through a 200 mesh lawn, or levigating in the way described by Cardew PP 29, who considers it a mistake to sieve pigments.

Some prepared blues will contain chrome, particularly the dark blues and slate colors. Blue is also prepared from vanadium and zircon for temperatures up to 1280°C. e.g. 3–5% vanadium oxide; 60–70% zircon; with some silica, for a very dependable pigment. An involved formula for producing steel blue crystals from nickel at 1280°C. is described in Webb CNS. Reduced rutile is reputed to produce blue glaze, as is reduced vanadium. For a discussion of *turquoise* blue from copper see under that heading. (See also *cobalt*.)

BLUE SLIP

The addition of 0.5–2.5% of cobalt oxide to a pale-firing clay body will produce light to dark blue slip. The higher concentrations are useful under a *tin glaze*. The color can be rather hard and characterless, but may be softened by using a little red clay or any of the modifiers mentioned under *blue pigments*. Grind and sieve the colors through a 200 lawn.

BLUNGER

A machine for stirring and mixing ceramic materials, usually the ingredients of a clay body, with water. The slip is then used as such, or dried to a plastic body. The machine consists of paddles revolving horizontally in a vat, usually hexagonal or octagonal in plan, the angles exerting some resistance to the circulation of the mix. A 15 gallon industrial blunger may be fairly costly but the mechanism is simple and a potter who wished to prepare his own clays could build one. The paddles are driven from above the vat at between 100–200 r.p.m. There are also impeller blungers which force the slurry through radial channels. 'Blunging' by hand can be done with a simple paddle or the old-fashioned washing 'dolly' or 'peggy stick'.

Smaller electric high-speed mixers are available for up to four gallons, and are suitable for clay which has already been broken into small pieces. Rhodes suggests an old washing machine. For small quantities clay need merely be steeped in water. The major problem in 'temperate' climes is not the mixing but the drying of the slip. The use of *dough mixers* bypasses the liquid stage. (See also *clay preparation*.)

BLUSH

A pink area on a glaze caused by a reaction with a *volatilized* coloring oxide, usually either chrome or copper. Chrome can react with lead, lime and tin in an earthenware fire (see *chrome-tin pink*), or even in stoneware if a high-dolomite glaze with zinc is used. In reduction, copper can also stain adjacent pots. Prepared colors, especially dark hues, often contain chrome and may give rise to *blushing* on tin glazes. Occasionally iron from the body can break through as a rosy area where it has been licked by the flames during firing.

BODY

Any clay, mixture of clays, or admixture with other ceramic materials. Few natural clays are used alone but are blended together to produce a mixture with specific qualities. For instance, a plastic and *fusible* ball clay may be combined with a *refractory* fireclay, a little red clay and some grog to produce an easily workable, buff-colored, open textured stoneware body. Non-clay minerals—flint, china stone, sand, etc. may also be included. These will lessen plasticity.

Non-clay minerals: flint, sand, etc. can be added to increase silica content or to 'open' to give texture to the body. Fluxes such as china stone, nepheline syenite, feldspar or even boric oxide or calcia are sometimes added, especially to *porcelain* to increase vitrification. Those bodies with a considerable mixture of non-clays are often known as pastes. All will reduce plasticity and may be balanced to some degree by the further addition of *montmorillonites* such as *bentonite*.

There are as many body recipes as there are potters. Industrial earthenware bodies are still based on Wedgwood's eighteenth century experiments. The simplest recipe is equal parts of ball clay, china clay, stone, and flint. This is fired to about 1200°C., when it becomes a tough but still porous biscuit. At 1300°C. it vitrifies into a near-porcelain, but still opaque material. For 1220°C., firings in an electric kiln, Richard Zakin (USA) uses a fairly complicated body: stoneware clay 45%; kaolin (china clay) 35%; nepheline syenite 5%; wollastonite 5%; flint 5%; ball clay 5%. He also adds dolomite in some recipes.

A potter can modify a prepared plastic body to suit his particular purposes. I use five parts of a buff stoneware body with one of a Staffordshire red clay, wedged together, for a 1260°C. oxidized firing. It rings well, is reasonably vitrified, and of a warm color (and is almost chip-proof!). Simple additions include sand or grog to give 'bite' and to open texture; ball clay to improve fusibility and plasticity (in very short bodies, e.g. porcelain, up to 3% bentonite); quartz or flint or a siliceous *fireclay* to increase refractoriness and to decrease *shrinkage*; red clay for fusibility and to warm the color; china clay for whiteness and to vary particle size; feldspar or stone to increased fusibility. Silica, in some form, added to earthenware bodies will assist *craze* resistance. The effectiveness or otherwise of body mixtures or additions must always be tried and proved in the kiln. The correction of vices in clays—*warping, shattering, cracking* etc.—can be a complicated process. *Porcelain* poses special problems which are discussed under that heading. Ready-blended plastic clays are often too smooth and refined and need further adjustments.

The preparation of bodies can be by simple layering and *wedging*. This is hard work but quite effective if done thoroughly. Cardew, however, gives a surprising warning concerning the wedging of unplastic materials (e.g. china clay) into plastic clay. The mixture, he states, will approximate to the *least* plastic of the ingredients! He recommends that china clay be added as a *slip*.

If a high proportion of powder or dry materials is used it is necessary to mix them together on a clean floor, work them into a slurry with water, dry to a plastic state, and wedge thoroughly. Alternatively one becomes mechanized and uses a *blunger* (or a large ball mill), followed by sieving, drying (see *de-watering*), and *pugging*. In all cases at least a week's rest is necessary for the clay to mature before use. Other body-mixing equipment includes batch mixers with rotating runners, and *dough mixers*, which have had quite a vogue among studio potters.

A special addition to a red body is barium carbonate to prevent scumming. (See also *ovenware, glaze-body fit, shrinkage* etc.) Many body recipes can be found in pottery primers and magazines. See especially Ceramic Review CG.

BODY-GLAZE LAYER

See *interface*.

BODY STAIN

Most of the pigment oxides and prepared stains can be used to produce colored bodies (see also *slips*, and under individual colors—*blue, green,* etc.) It is advisable, however, to limit body color to a few simple mixtures of iron, copper, manganese, or cobalt. Stoneware and porcelain glazes over stained bodies can be interesting. The swirling bands of subtle color in some of Lucie Rie's bowls and bottles are derived from 'marbled' stained bodies, generally manganese bodies, in an oxidized fire.

Unless speckling is required it is advisable to sieve all body stains through a 200 mesh lawn. (See also *distinguishing stain*.)

BOILING POINT

Strictly speaking, the point at which the vapor pressure of a liquid is equal to the atmospheric pressure. The most familiar boiling point is that of water—100°C.—but many glaze constituents, and their mixtures, will 'boil' at some point during the maturation of a glaze, giving off a gaseous vapor and causing bubbles. These must be given time to settle although too high a temperature or excessive *soaking* can lead to further reactions. Fritted materials are obviously less liable to cause trouble. (See also at *blistering*.)

BOLE

A friable, earthy clay, stained with iron oxide. It was the type used in Turkey for their famous underglaze red (so also called Armenian bole), and today a similar mixture of iron and clay is used for the much higher-fired red dots on David Leach's work. (See *red colors and glazes*.)

BOND, atomic

Molecules and *networks* owe their structure to bonds or linkages between *atoms*. These can be of several kinds: *electrovalent* where electrons are transferred from one atom to another, producing *ions*; *covalent*, where electrons are shared; and weaker bonds involving electrically neutral particles known as Van der Waals forces. Also various combinations of these types. (See also *atomic theory, valency*.)

BONE ASH

Calcium phosphate, $3CaO.P_2O_5$ [sometimes written $Ca_3(PO_4)_2$]. 310 (equivalent weight 103).

A typical analysis by weight (Wengers):

MgO 1.27	Al_2O_3 0.36	P_2O_5 40.9
CaO 53.9	Fe_2O_3 0.11	TiO_2 0.01

Made by calcining bone, mainly cattle bone. Its principal use is in *bone china* bodies which may contain up to 50% of the ash. Occasionally used in a glaze (phosphorus is one of the glass-forming oxides although Hamer asserts that it does not enter the silica lattice), giving a milky quality and a more matt surface, but can also lead to bubble trouble.

BONE CHINA

An English hybrid between soft-paste and true porcelain. The refractory and unplastic nature of English china clay inhibited the successful manufacture of porcelain. Bone china was developed during the eighteenth century and its ingredients fixed by Spode in 1800. It is a very translucent ware with great toughness, resembling *porcelain* though not in 'coldness' or structure at a fracture. The calcined bone forms about half the body. Billington gives a recipe: bone ash 40; china clay 32; china stone 28. This is obviously unplastic and must be thrown very thickly and *turned* to a thin wall, or, as it is more usual, *slip cast*. Additions of ball clay, bentonite etc are liable to spoil color and *translucency*. Shrinkage is around 10% up to 1250°C. Industrially it is *biscuit* fired at 1250°C. and lead glazed at ca. 1080°C. but it is possible to reverse this schedule. It is increasingly used by studio potters, notably Glenys Barton (designing for Wedgwood), Jacqueline Poncelet, and others. The work is slip cast and the walls are sometimes paper-thin. Slip cast bone china is given a first firing to 1050°C. by Sasha Wardell in order to be able to complete the *fettling* without endangering the frail ware (CR 111). Color and glaze are applied with a spray gun. She also recommends a one and a half hour soaking at the final 1260°C. firing.

Graphic permutations on cubes of precision-ground bone china, by Glenys Barton.

BONFIRE FIRING

The primitive method of bedding posts in brushwood, heaping wood and grass on top of them, and setting the heap alight. The method can still be a valuable educational exercise and may yield pots of a highly decorative character.

In other than tropical climes, the main danger is the *dunting* of the pots through sudden and uneven cooling. Pots must be resistant to *thermal shock*. This can be achieved by the addition of grog (preferable to sand), though the grog makes burnishing more difficult. Well rounded forms, thin-walled but with sturdy rims, are most likely to survive. Make all joins secure and keep the pots, during building, as evenly damp as possible. *Pinching, coiling* and *throwing* are suitable techniques; slab pots are not recommended. Pots can be prefired to a low biscuit and the bonfire used as decorative treatment.

For raw clay firing the pots should be pre-heated to expel *adsorbed* water. The African potter inverts her large pots over a small heap of glowing embers. The pots in the bonfire are protected by shards which also probably conserve some heat.

Method. Build your bonfire on dry ground or on a brick bed. Pre-heat the pots in a kiln or over a small fire, perhaps on a grill or grate, and immediately bed them in dry grass and brushwood. Lay radiating rings of sticks or brushwood against the pots, topping with grass or straw. Light at several points simultaneously. The firing can be maintained for a time with fresh fuel. Protect against wind if possible. Cover with leaves and soil as the fire dies down, to minimize *dunting*. The use of a pit and a grill or grate (of metal, or fired pottery cylinders) will increase heat and can also be used for the initial warming.

Experiments carried out by Southampton University confirm that good results are possible only on a fairly still, warm day. Their best pots were fired in a pit dug into a pile of used stable straw, layering the pots with dry leaves and burning from the top as in *sawdust firing*. 780°C. was reached. (See also *kiln* for a paper version.)

BORATE

A combination with boric oxide. In glazes, boric oxide is combined with other elements. The minerals colemanite and borax are borates. Their molecular structures are diverse and involved.

BORAX

Sodium diborate, $Na_2O. 2B_2O_3. 10H_2O$, 381.5.
Calcined (anhydrous) borax, $Na_2O, 2B_2O_3$. 202 m.p. 600°C.

All forms of borax are soluble to a greater or lesser degree and are normally used in a fritted form. Borax provides the *base*, soda, and a very fusible *acid*, boric oxide. It is therefore very efficient at lowering the maturing temperature of any glaze. Soft glazes must contain either lead oxide or borax—often both.

A typical borax frit, melting at 1000–1020°C.:
Molecular parts—

CaO	0.632	Al_2O_3	1.15	Na_2O	0.336
SiO	2.6	K_2O	0.032	B_2O_3	0.644

A similar frit formula is given by Hamer as $Na_2O. 2B_2O_3. 3SiO_2$.

Very soft borax frits (850°C.) can be used, with the addition of 3% of bentonite, for *raku*. Borax can also be added to salt to assist *salt glazing*, although it may destroy the characteristic aesthetic values of salt glaze. (See also *boron, Gerstley borate*.)

BORIC ACID, boracic acid

Given variously as $B(OH)_3$, H_3BO_3, or B_2O_3, $3H_2O$. (See *boron*.)

BORO-CALCITE

CaO. $2B_2O_3$. $6H_2O$. 304, also given as $2CaO$. $3B_2O_3$ $5H_2O$, 412.

The natural mineral, with a slightly different molecular formula, is *colemanite*. Can be used in small amounts (up to 3%) to lower the maturing point of a stoneware glaze without materially affecting its character.

BORON, boric oxide

An element B. 10.9.
Boric oxide B_2O_3 69.6.
Boracic acid B_2O_3. $3H_2O$. 123.7.
Also occurs as borax, and, in an insoluble form, as colemanite.

Boric oxide occupies an ambiguous position in the *Seger formula*. It is an acidic oxide and a *glass former*, and as such is normally listed with the silica. Its apparent effect, however, is to soften (flux) a glaze and it replaces lead oxide in earthenware. Its formula suggests a third place, with alumina, as an *amphoteric*. As boric oxide in a glaze it has no melting point but a long melting range.

It has the great advantage over lead in that it is non-toxic—boracic acid is, of course, a mild disinfectant. However, little of the rich quality of a lead glaze is apparent in a borax glaze. With the increasingly stringent controls over lead compounds boron is becoming more generally used by craft potters, although it is still possible for lead glazes to pass all the tests. Earthenware leadless glazes are all boron glazes. They are confusingly marked L in catalogs, as distinct from LS, or low-solubility lead glazes. A typical soft L *frit* is given under *borax*.

Soft borax frits (boric oxide is usually added in the form of borax) can be used as a fusible foundation for subsequent additions by the potter. The frit *formulas* now more frequently supplied by merchants are invaluable when modifying them with raw materials. Some clay in the batch will help the physical behavior of a boron frit, improving its suspension in water. Boric oxide tends to brighten colors in a rather unsubtle way. Copper may tend towards turquoise, and manganese towards purple.

The usual molecular proportion of boric oxide to silica in a glaze formula is around 1 boric oxide, 4 silica. In larger amounts it develops milkiness and surface peculiarities such as glitter and shiny patches in a duller glaze.

For the use of boron in the form of colemanite, see under *colemanite*. A curious property of boric oxide, which makes it very useful in earthenware glazes, is that, in amounts less than 10%, it has a 'negative' *coefficient of expansion* which helps craze resistance.

BORON PHOSPHATE

Compound BPO_4. Has been used as a constituent of a ceramic body which fires to a translucent porcelain at 1000°C. (Dodd DC); a soft-paste.

BOROSILICATE OF LEAD

See *lead*.

BOSS

An age-old decorative feature; a spherical hump traditionally formed by pressing from the inside of a pot but today more frequently applied to the outside.

A salt-glazed pot with a nicely placed 'boss' with amusing overtones of a Roman face-pot, "created by throwing wads of clay at the internal surface while still on the potter's wheel, creating very fluid changes in form" (William Hunt U.S.)

28

BOTTLE FORM

Any pot form with a narrow neck tends to be called a bottle. It allows the maximum exploitation of contour and is favored by potters who wish to show glaze quality or other decoration to the full, the upper curve or *shoulder* being the most positive and eye-catching area of any pot.The neck is often too small to allow of any 'useful' function.

Genuine bottles such as cider jars, bellarmines and the like include some of the most noble shapes in ceramics. It is not, however, easy to attain the generous sweep of shoulder when throwing a large bottle; it poses considerable problems of clay control. When throwing the initial cylinder, concentrate on the lower half and do not overwork the top; it will need all the strength and freshness it can be given. After opening out the belly throw the shoulder inwards rather than simply compressing it, and increase the wheel speed as the circumference decreases. Avoid soaking in water. Hold a finger inside when *collaring* to avoid buckling. Isaac Button, the Yorkshire potter, threw large bottles with very little collaring, but eased the shoulder over with the same movement as the rest of the throwing, using a steel rib outside. He may be seen working 28 lb. of clay in the film *Isaac Button, country potter*.

Another method is to throw an open ovoid onto which, when it has stiffened a little, a thrown ring is luted and the neck is then thrown from this. (See also *two-piece throwing*.)

Bottles can be made by coiling, with multiple *pinch-pots*, or with slabs. Bernard Leach has made some very handsome large rectangular *press-molded* bottles with thrown necks. Bottles with more than one neck, or with tube necks as in pre-Columbian American pottery, are entertaining variations.

BOTTLED GAS

A conventional term for liquified petroleum gas which is either supplied in cylinders or delivered to special storage tanks. It is an efficient but fairly expensive alternative to town or natural gas, and needs slightly different types of burners.

Bottled gas involves very little in the way of a chimney and can be useful for the occasional reduction-firing. It is clean enough for earthenware glazes.

Nearly a whole cylinder will be used in a single stoneware firing of a 6 cu. ft. (0.2 cu. m.) kiln. Pressure drops as the gas is used, due to a lowering of temperature. At a constant temperature it will stay at a constant pressure until empty, but a standby cylinder to boost the end of the firing is essential. Supply can revert to the partly empty cylinder at the beginning of the next firing.

A changeover valve can be fitted, or two or three cylinders can be connected to a manifold and a pressure regulator and gauge. Other hazards are pressure fall in cold weather through freezing caused by the rapid evaporation of the gas liquid, and the collection of any escaping gas at ground level (the gas is heavier than air).

With tank installations pressure is more easily maintained, but a guarantee of a large yearly consumption must be given to the installing company.

Bottled gas may be supplied as Butane, Propane, Calorgas, etc. Butane has been quoted at 3200 Btu per cu. ft. propane at 93,000 Btu per gallon (20,700 kjoules per liter). These figures compare very favorably with natural gas. (See also *gas fuel*.)

BOTTLE OVEN

As late as the nineteen-fifties every street in Stoke-on-Trent, England, seemed to have its cluster of kilns. The kiln or oven itself was surrounded by a bottle-shaped casing or 'hovel'. They were coal-fired. The splendid skyline disappeared in a few years (together, it must be admitted, with a lot of smoke and grime) with the rapid introduction of *continuous* kilns.

Stoke-on-Trent in the 1950's with bottle ovens of many shapes and sizes plus what, today, would be an unacceptable pall of smoke and fumes.

BOULDER CLAY

Clay which together with an assortment of stones and rocks has been transported by glacial action and then dumped as the glacier has melted. Common to large areas of North America and Europe. Used for brickmaking in the north of England. The clay itself is fusible and of an even particle size which makes the removal of impurities difficult. It has been suggested as the basis for a fusible slip.

BOW

A single clay-cutting wire held taut by a curved strip of bamboo or metal. In a looser way the term is applied to the more elaborate *harp*.

A bow made from a strip of metal or bamboo. The cutting wire may be of metal or nylon.

BOWL FORM

At once the easiest shape to throw and the most difficult to succeed with. The subtleties of a really lively bowl are not easy to analyse. To some potters a bowl should have a sense of enclosure, of cupped hands, but this excludes

A section through a partly thrown bowl showing the outer finger tucked well into the junction of the clay and the wheel-head and supporting the base of the wall as the inner hand begins to leave the base and starts to thin and shape the wall, thus preventing a dip in the curve at this point which is a common fault in thrown bowls.

a great family of flaring forms. If the bowl has a well-defined practical purpose its shape must, of course, be suited to its use, as seen in the Peter Dick mixing bowl illustrated. A sense of growth and spring from the base is essential and this involves a careful proportioning of the foot ring. The rim needs consideration, as its style will fundamentally affect the character of the bowl. A sturdy rim is more likely to maintain a circular plan but this is not always aesthetically desirable.

When throwing a bowl perhaps the commonest fault is caused by the sudden lessening of support as the inner hand leaves the base clay and begins to exert pressure on the walls. Unless a finger or a knuckle of the outer hand is tucked right against the base to take the pressure, the all too common ridge and valley is formed. This becomes weaker as throwing proceeds and may finally collapse. In the earlier stages of throwing keep the wall more upright and with less curve than will be finally required, even to the extent of reversing the form—i.e. slightly convex instead of concave. The full curve is the last operation of all. The rim will benefit from being kept slightly thicker than the walls both throughout the throwing and in the finished piece. A generous rim can be an important feature and will help to maintain the bowl's circular plan.

For all sizes of bowl the wheel speed should be progressively lessened as work proceeds, in order to balance the centrifugal force exerted on the ever-widening wall. Do not over-wet the clay, and complete the throwing with as few movements as possible. Large bowls are more easily controlled on a kickwheel. The centering and initial throwing can be done on a power wheel, and then the wheel head transferred.

One can complete the bowl on the wheel, trimming the base with a bamboo or metal tool. The flat base must be reflected inside the bowl if a thick wedge is not to be left at the outer edge of the foot. Most bowls, however, will need turning, and sufficient clay must be left to form the *foot ring*. Cardew, some Japanese potters, and others throw a foot ring onto a reversed leather-hard bowl.

A number of bowls can be thrown from a large block of clay. This method is useful for test bowls. The mass of clay is roughly centered, the top part fully centered and the bowl thrown from this. Cutting off can be done Japanese-fashion with a loose thread which is allowed to wind itself into the clay and is then whipped sharply out, or a fine needle awl can be held sloping slightly upwards and cut in towards the center of the base.

Bowls may be *beaten* or cut (see *facet*). Other illustrations may be found under *foot ring*. Handbuilt bowls are less common, but for details see under *handbuilding*.

The Peter Dick mixing bowl referred to in the text. A basic container form with a powerful rim.

BOX

Pottery boxes rarely have a definite functional purpose, but are often very attractive objects and present the potter with interesting technical and aesthetic problems. The lids, especially of flattened forms, beg for decoration, even if this is simply the turning spiral of some of Richard Batterham's best boxes, or the speckled salt glaze of Gwyn Hanssen. A smooth curve will burnish well for *sawdust firing*. There are also unexploited possibilities for modeled knobs on lids. Many of Bernard Leach's earlier boxes had attractive, lively modeled knobs.

The method of holding the lid in place (the style and placing of the flange or slope) is open to many interpret-

A three-tier box by Sheila Fournier; the wave-like junctions (shown here slightly separated) ensuring that the sections will stay in place when closed.

ations. The proportions between base and lid can be a recurring challenge and delight.

Boxes can be made by any technique. Rosemary Wren has shown how lively little boxes with excellently fitting lids can be made from *pinch pots*. Boxes may be thrown as two shallow bowls or short cylinders. Slab boxes pose their own problems; the flange can look heavy, and the sides are liable to warp inwards. They should be fairly flat in profile and put together from quite stiff clay, the joints pressed home with a wooden tool.

A good fit between lid and base will be best maintained during firing if they are fired in place. This necessitates care and thought when glazing. Sticking is less likely if the rims are waxed where they are to be left unglazed. A very thin wash of china clay and flint or alumina can be spun onto the rim before waxing.

A charming modeled bird lid on a box by Barbara Colls, the head or tail providing a convenient handle.

Two lively modeled boxes by Peter Phillips. Note his method of holding the lid in place.

BOXING

The packing of pottery, especially bowls and cups, rim to rim, and foot to foot. They must be of similar size with level rims. The method is most often used for biscuit firing but can also be used in the glaze fire where the rim and foot are free of glaze. The method is more wasteful of space than sitting bowls one in another but helps to lessen warpage. Boxing bowls and plates during drying can also help in retaining shape.

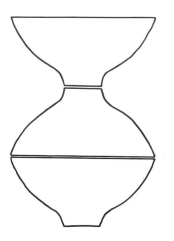

Boxed bowls in a biscuit fire. The pile or 'bung' can be extended to six or eight bowls depending on their sturdiness. It is also possible to fire glazed pieces in this way if they have biscuit rims and there is no danger of the glaze running. (See also warping.*)*

BRASS

A zinc-copper alloy occasionally used as filings to speckle bodies and glazes. It will dissociate in an oxidizing fire to a flux and copper oxide giving speckles, sometimes with a green halo.

BRAZIER KILN

A very simple type of coke kiln used for *raku*. First developed in England by David Ballantyne. It can be built in half an hour from common bricks—Flettons or any open-textured house brick. Fifty to eighty are needed. Also a saggar of approximately 12 in. (300 mm.) diameter, which can be purchased, or coiled from a well grogged body. Diagram A shows the plan, including the three half bricks on which the *saggar* stands; diagram B is a section through a completed kiln. A dry site is needed, or a foundation of bricks laid down. The interior diameter will depend on the size of the saggar which should preferably be about 9 in. (230 mm.) high. Allow 3 in. (75 mm.) between saggar and walls all round. The space between the three supporting half

bricks is filled with coke or a smokeless fuel before the saggar is positioned, and paper or firelighters placed near the bottom gaps between the bricks so that they can be lit from the outside. A layer of sticks is laid on top.

Walls are built up dry to a height of 6 in. (150 mm.) or so above the saggar, leaving $1-1\frac{1}{2}$ in. (30 mm.) gaps between the bricks. The top row may be placed close together. A saggar lid must be provided, together with some means of removing it when hot. If your *tongs* will open wide, then the lid can be a simple kiln bat, otherwise a handle should be built onto it. The space between saggar and bricks is now filled with coke, or smokeless fuel if coke is unobtainable. The fire is lit at the base holes.

See *raku* for details of firing. The film 'Raku, English style' shows the building and firing of a brazier kiln; also the book Riegger RAT contains useful information.

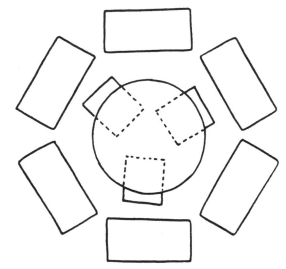

(A) Palm of a brazier kiln. (See text.)

(B) Section through a brazier kiln.

BRICK

A clay or ceramic unit of building construction, the commonest shape being a rectangle of around $9 \times 4\frac{1}{2} \times 2\frac{3}{4}$ in. ($228 \times 115 \times 70$ mm.). Bricks have changed little over the centuries, though they are now made in an ever-widening range of materials from red surface clays to bauxite and chrome ore.

The three main types of brick used by potters are easily distinguishable. They are:

1. Open-textured red clay building bricks, the cheapest being called Flettons in England.
2. Hard, heavy, close-grained refractory bricks.
3. Lightweight *insulating* bricks.

Group 1   Apart from their obvious building purposes, they can be used for the outer skins of kilns where they will provide better insulation than heavy bricks. Also for low temperature and 'primitive' kilns such as the brazier type.

Group 2   Includes all grades of *firebricks* from Super-duty, PCE.33, for working temperatures up to 1550°C., to Low Heat Duty, PCE 15, which soften at 1400°C. and must be used at well below that. Grading in England is by alumina content—45% downwards.

Group 3   These are easily abraded, very porous, light in weight, and superb *insulators*. They are made in many qualities and degrees of heat resistance. Those made from *diatomaceous earth* are either quarried and cut to shape or fired into blocks with a little clay. These are weak in structure and are comparatively fusible. The more *refractory* types are made from very pure and iron-free ceramic materials and have an open, sponge-like appearance achieved by physical means (mixing the raw material with sawdust, for instance) or chemical processes. These are graded by a K factor, the number denoting the degrees Fahrenheit which they will endure without failing, e.g. K26 = 2600°F. or 1430°C. The higher numbers are stronger but marginally less effective as insulators. They are all more expensive than firebricks.

The choice of bricks will depend on a balance being struck between the extra initial cost of high insulation qualities and the extra fuel costs due to the *heat storage* and *heat loss* of hard firebrick. (See *insulation, heat storage, conduction of heat.*) The care needed to avoid abrading or breaking the softer bricks may also weigh in your decision. For electric kilns, group 3 is the obvious choice.

The standard insulating brick size is $9 \times 4\frac{1}{2} \times 3$ in. ($228 \times 115 \times 76$ mm.) but there is a wide range of special shapes and sizes designed for arches, bevels, domes, etc. Insulating-brick is also available in blocks up to $18 \times 9 \times 4\frac{1}{2}$ in. ($460 \times 230 \times 115$ mm.). Kiln bricks can be molded by the potter either as fireclay and grog mixtures (see details in Cardew PP, Appendix 3), or cast from special bodies made from heat-proof calcia/alumina cement (not ordinary Portland cement) with an aggregate of crushed firebrick, insulating brick, grog, or expanded *perlite*. Use one part cement to four or five aggregate. See *insulation of heat* for a home-made insulating brick recipe. A useful piece of equipment for making large unfired slab-bricks, (*adobe*), even from any 'handy local dirt' (Parks, PGRG)! mixed with some clay and perhaps 5–10% cement, is the Cinva-Ram press which both exerts great compressive power (by hand through a long lever) and also eases the completed 'brick' out of the mould. The blocks need a considerable time to dry out thoroughly (after a few days in the damp state if they contain cement). Illustrations can be seen in Parks' excellent book, and the address is given at the end of this dictionary. It was found that a kiln cased in this type of blocks needed a coating of stucco to prevent damage in bad weather.

The use of bricks both for hot face situations and especially for backing insulation has been superseded in many instances by *ceramic fiber* but clay bricks of one sort or another still have a role to play in kiln construction. High insulation hot-faced bricks and slabs have become very expensive (an increase of 1800% since the first edition of this book was published) but are still essential for wire element electric kilns and some other applications.

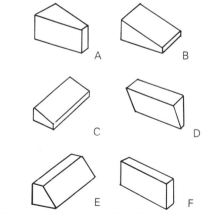

Some of the special shapes of bricks available. A. End Arch brick; B. a Feather End; C. a Feather Side; D. a Side Arch; E. a Side Skew; F. a Split. All are useful in arch building and a Split is almost impossible to cut from a whole brick.

BRICK CLAY

A general name for a variety of clays, mostly red-firing and *fusible* and containing lime and other impurities. Fired at 900–1100°C. Bricks can be made from many surface or near-surface clays so long as their shrinkage is not too great and they are not contaminated with lime nodules. Some 'brick earths' such as those of the Thames valley in England, are of recent origin, geologically speaking (Pleistocene, two to six million years ago), but others are from much older carboniferous times. Their quality depends partly on the underlying rock.

The addition of sawdust, chopped grass, or brick-dust can be added to brick clays to lessen the wet-dry shrinkage. Refractory bricks are made from the purer *fireclays*. (See also *marls*.)

BRICKLAYING

Most of the potter's work in this field will be in the building of kilns. Here bricks are laid almost in contact with one another—merely a 'buttering' of mortar between them. The mortar must be a high-temperature clay slurry or a special heat-proof cement such as Ciment Fondu or other commercial aluminous cement, and is used as a fairly sloppy mix. The bricks themselves are either soaked or, at least, well wetted on the surface. Some constructions, electric kilns in particular, can be dry built. Andrew Holden (CR 87) suggests the use of ceramic paper (made from *ceramic fiber*) between Sayvit bricks (U.S.A.) in a dry-built gas kiln.

Long horizontal joints in brickwork are inevitable, but vertical joints are avoided by overlapping. There are

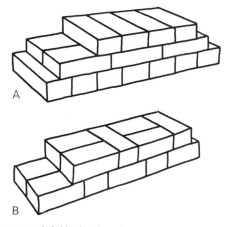

Two common bricklaying bonds.
(A) The English bond, which may consist of alternate header and stretcher courses (short and long face of the brick), or one header to two or three stretchers.
(B) The Flemish bond; bricks laid in alternate directions within each course.

several systems, but the principle is similar in each case: that each brick should, as often as possible, span the join between the two below it. In 9 in. (230 mm.) walls, courses can be laid across the width (called 'header' courses because the head or end of the brick shows on the face), as well as along its length ('stretcher' courses). Bricks will often be needed in half-lengths and can be cut with a brick hammer which has a chisel end, or with a 'cold' chisel or bolster. The brick may be chipped or scored along the line of the break and then tapped sharply across a hard edge.

Accurate bricklaying depends on a level and firm foundation and the frequent use of a good spirit level at least 18 in. (500 mm.) long. Stretched lines or board can guide straight walls, wooden templates are often constructed over which to build arches and domes. Rhodes gives advice on bricklaying in Chapter 4 of 'Kilns', also Cardew PP.

A brick structure will expand on heating; open (unmortared) joints about $\frac{1}{4}$ in. (6 mm.) wide should be left every four bricks. (See *expansion*.)

Three ways of 'springing' an arch of bricks.

BRIGHT GOLD
See *gold*.

BRISTOL GLAZE

A medium temperature glaze containing zinc oxide, originally developed in an attempt to avoid the use of lead. It is a difficult glaze to control and is subject to *crawling* and pinholes. The zinc-alumina-silica eutectic is fairly high—1360°C.—but can be brought down to below 1200°C. by the addition of feldspar and whiting. The use of clay in the recipe makes it suitable for use on green (unbiscuited) ware. Zinc glazes are not suitable for reduction.

Typical recipes:

Feldspar	56.6	
Whiting	9.5	
Nepheline		40.0
Lithia		5.0

Zinc oxide	6.5	12.0
Clay	13.0	8.0
Flint	14.5	35.0

And from PQ 13 (Merritt):

Calcined zinc oxide	24.3	
Feldspar	113.2	
Colemanite	51.5	
Barium carbonate	19.7	Firing
Talc	18.9	1140°C.
Flint	66.0	
Calcium nitrate	2.9	

The zinc is sometimes used in a calcined form to lessen drying shrinkage. (See *zinc*.) The zinc will affect colors (not often to their advantage), though copper is reputed to produce turquoise (Rhodes) and uranium a bright yellow in zinc glazes. The average firing temperature for Bristol glaze is around 1180°C.

BRITISH THERMAL UNIT, Btu

A measure of heat quantity. The heat required to raise 1 lb. of water through 1° Fahrenheit. Equal to 252 calories. 100,000 Btu = 1 *therm*. The heat value of various fuels can be stated in Btu for comparison.

The unit *joule* is now superseding the Btu. One Btu is equivalent to 1055J or 1.055kJ (kilojoules).

BROKES

Term used for a type of English ball clay which will not 'cut into balls' (Dodd). Generally of low plasticity. Fires grayish.

BRONGNIART'S FORMULA

A method of determining the weight, on a pint basis, of suspended solids in a slip or glaze, devised by 'the father of ceramic chemistry' who was Director at Sevres in the first half of the nineteenth century.

Method: First weigh the container empty, then with one pint of the slip to be tested. The liquid weight is arrived at by subtraction. We then use the formula

$$P - 20 \times \frac{\text{s.g.}}{\text{s.g.} - 1}$$

in which s.g. stands for *specific gravity* of the solid material and P for the pint weight arrived at as above. The 1 stands for the s.g. of the water.

Example: The average s.g. of plastic clay is 2.6. If the pint weight was 27 oz. then:

$$(27 \text{ [oz.]} - 20) \times \frac{2.6}{2.6 - 1} = 7 \times 1.62 \text{ oz.}$$

i.e. 11.34 oz of dry clay.

The calculation is complicated for glazes by the fact that materials with different specific gravities are mixed together. However, most common glaze minerals are in the range 2.5–3.0. Where the s.g. is much above this figure it has generally been noted in this book (e.g. lead oxide). A good approximation to the pint weight can therefore be arrived at.

BRONZE LUSTER

Obtained by firing chromium and lead compounds in reduction, but the system is too complicated for the studio potter who can buy prepared bronze lusters. A bronze-like finish can also result from copper/manganese mixtures at most temperatures from low earthenware to porcelain. The color is brushed onto the biscuit. (See *copper-manganese*.)

BROOKITE

One of the oxide ores of titanium.

BROWN PIGMENT, Glaze

Iron oxide is the commonest brown pigment: 4–8% in most glazes, but will tend to bleached if calcium is present. Rutile gives broken cream-browns and ilmenite darker colors. *Albany slip* and some other fusible red clays including Fremington give a dark brown glaze.

Small amounts of zinc (0.5–1.5%) can develop browns from chrome. Manganese as a pigment tends towards the purple-browns. Nickel can be brownish in a barium glaze. Rutile gives broken browns. A recipe for a brown pigment given by Miss Pleydell-Bouverie is: 1 measure of cobalt oxide, 10 iron, 5 manganese, 10 china clay. Grind together in a mortar. Unglazed iron and copper will give blacks and browns.

BRUSH

The painting brush traditionally used in the industry is the 'liner', very long-haired and square-ended. The high absorption of pigment by biscuit or glaze makes it essential that any brush should hold a great deal of it. It is a wonder that no-one has come up with a 'fountain-brush' for pottery.

For the more calligraphic style of painting, liners have limited value. The *cut liners* are more lively. Goat-hair *mops* are useful for background washes, e.g. in preparation for *sgraffito* or *wax resist*. Japanese brushes are more responsive but, being designed for inks, are, in general, rather soft, a quality which can, however, give great sensitivity to a stroke. There is an attractive hand-made flat brush on the market which is called a 'hake' brush (from hakeme?) available in both 44 mm. and 76 mm. (approx. $1\frac{3}{4}$ and 3 in.) widths. Cardew mentions a resilient type called Sen Pen Banka, from Muruzen Co., P.O. Box 605, Tokyo Central.

'Majolica pencils' are of sable, are slightly wider than paintbrushes and give a good point. Three basic brushes will fulfil most requirements: a large sable watercolor brush, a square shader (about $\frac{3}{4}$ in. (15 mm.) wide), and a liner, or medium Japanese brush. Experimental potters can try any sort of brush-like object with which to apply their slip or color: shaving brushes, cheap paste brushes (which give a useful dry, striated line), dabbing and working the surface to provide fresh textures. The 'throw-away' plastic sponge brushes may also have possibilities for backgrounds. Brushes for *wax* need to be resilient and have a good body. The modern potter uses a great variety of materials apart from the traditional brush to transfer slip or pigment to ceramic surfaces, as have peasant potters through the ages using frayed plant stems, cloth, feathers, etc. Nylon is replacing hair in some traditional brushes.

Brushes must be cared for. Wash and stroke to a point after use, store preferably hanging hair-downwards. If kept heads-up in a jar, dry well or the hairs may rot at the base. Do *not* use brushes to mix colors. One cannot easily clean wax brushes unless water-soluble emulsions are used. Smooth the hairs to a point and leave them to set. A brush will be destroyed if dipped into hot wax when wet.

There are, as ever, quirky exceptions to all these 'rules' such as potters who prefer their brushes curved to a quarter circle through being left in the wax pot!

Lawn brushes should be easily cleanable or they will contaminate the next batch of glaze. It is advisable to keep a brush, clearly labelled, for each group of glazes and slips that you use, e.g. one for clear glaze, one for

dark colors, and so on. The large bristle brushes often listed in merchants' catalogs are not easy to clean and they retain a lot of sludge during sieving. I consider the common nylon washing-up brush to be one of the most suitable. Unfortunately they do not have very strong handles.

BRUSH-APPLIED GLAZE

There is little evidence that glaze was applied to pottery with a brush in past times, and today the method is normally used only where glaze is in too short supply for dipping or pouring. However the method has possibilities for particular effects and is used by Otto Natzler among others. Without experience the result can be thin and sketchy and if one glaze is brushed onto another the first is liable to be lifted off (the addition of a *siccative* might help here) but with practice individual results can be obtained. A thin initial poured or dipped coat can ensure that bare patches are avoided.

Pottery suppliers now list special brush-on glazes. The brush can also be used to flick the glazes on with somewhat haphazard results.

BRUSHED SLIP

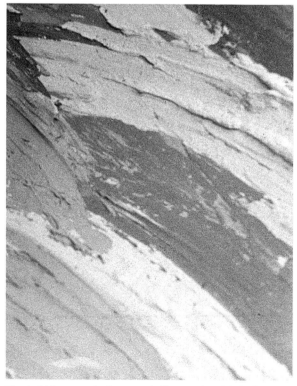

The bold impasto laying on of slip on a hand-built form by Irene Vonck.

A Chinese multi-brush, the elements of which can be slipped, from the cross-bars which hold them together, through holes in the bamboo handle, allowing for groups of two to six.

If slip is used like a pigment it must be applied very liberally if it is not to vanish in the glaze fire. This is especially true with earthenware lead glazes which use a layer of the surface clay to fulfil their glass-forming functions. As well as clay slips used in the manner of *hakeme*, slips heavily loaded with pigment oxides are used for painting on or under stonewares; either a natural iron-rich red clay, ball clay alone or stained e.g. 98 parts of clay to one of cobalt oxide and one of iron chromate. Also cobalt with ochre. The slip is laid on generously. See also *engobe*. Henry Hammond used a series of slips for painting his famous fish and other designs using 50% each of iron oxide and a local red clay, plus those mixtures mentioned above.

Pate-sur-pate was a typically painstaking Victorian method of building up a variable slip layer but the technique could be adapted to modern use.

BRUSHWORK

A serious gap in the potter's library is an expert and wide ranging discussion of brushwork. Once the most widely practised technique for decorating ceramics, it has been overshadowed by textural and glaze surfaces and by the less consciously designed applications of slips and colors. The reputation of Eastern calligraphy which is, at its best, as taut as a spring and as individual as hand-writing, has suffered through the careless and flabby copying of historical work. A few potters continue with majolica and luster in skilful Moresque-type patterns. Kenneth Clark and others made an impact with brush decorations in the nineteen fifties in England but he has little to say in his books except to try using brushes other than the traditional ones to achieve fresh and exciting marks. With the inevitable reaction against the more muted and mannered work on stoneware, splashes and dabs of bright color have become fashionable in the late eighties, the brush used simply to transfer pigment rather than to make its own mark.

For the more traditional application of brushwork a few do's and dont's quickly become obvious. The body of the brush is used as a reservoir and kept full of pigment; the temptation to drain it on the side of the color container should be resisted—shape the point of the brush only. Use as large a brush as the design will allow. Keep the hand floating and free, and let the brush itself do as much of the work as possible by varying the pressure upon the hairs.

It is important to practise with any one particular brush to find out what it will do, and to adapt your design to the particular marks it makes most naturally and easily. There is no quick route to good brushwork but the best advice is to paint freely and rapidly; although you may spoil a lot of pieces, control will come and liveliness is essential. Do not retouch. Many potters limit themselves to a narrow range of designs. If you adopt the path of copying natural objects, put your notebooks aside as soon as possible and make the adaptation of the design to the pot form your first consideration. The term 'brushwork' is usually associated with Oriental styles or with Hispano-Moresque and other Western wares deriving from calligraphy, but it can also include the more individual work exemplified by modern American and other innovative less, reflective and stylized pottery decoration, sometimes wild and chaotic but striving for new approaches.

Still the benchmark for the economical and expressive use of the brush is the best work of Bernard Leach. Here, basically, a mere couple of strokes delineate a leaping fish, combined with equally fresh sgraffito.

Lively brushwork by a Spanish country potter (1989) showing a familiar farmyard occurrence!

The great advantage of the older style of brushwork is that it accommodates the semi-transparent nature of pottery oxides. Unless special techniques are used (see *ground-lay*) strokes of color will almost always show up after glazing. Engobes help in this respect.

Wax resist has attracted as much significant work as has brushed pigment. It lends itself to strong blocks of color and to *glaze-over-glaze* techniques. It cannot be fussed over but must be completed quickly and firmly and has those elements of 'accidents and incidents', to quote Leach, which still find great favor. (See also *calligraphy, decoration, latex, resist, etc.*)

Delicate brushwork by Vic Greenaway (Australia).

A combination of brushed wax and spun colour on a stoneware glaze, suitable for repetition work on tableware. By Sheila Fournier.

BRUSSELS NOMENCLATURE

An attempt made in 1955 to agree on an International Tariff Nomenclature of terms and meanings. Chapter 69 includes ceramics, listing china, earthenware etc. The definitions are occasionally mentioned in this dictionary, but are more applicable to industrial work.

Btu

See *British thermal units*.

BUBBLES IN GLAZE

Most glazes go through a bubbling (gas releasing) stage. It is very marked in lead glazes. The bubbles must be given time to break and to settle down. If a glaze is fired beyond its optimum melting temperature, decomposition is likely to take place with the emission of further gases. The firing should therefore be terminated between these two phases.

Craters, pinholes, blisters, and milkiness in a clear glaze are evidence of bubbles. (See under *pinholes* and *blistering* for discussion of cause and cure.) Precautions that can be taken are the full *oxidation* of earthenware glazes and the careful drying of glazed pots *before* they are packed in the kiln. An even and adequate but not too thick glaze coating followed by accurate firing and possibly some *soaking*, especially of earthenwares, will minimise bubbling.

Some celadons owe their quality to myriads of minute bubbles possibly due to the breakdown of whiting and the release of CO_2. Its replacement by *wollastonite* gives a more transparent color.

High manganese glazes are liable to gas release: $3MnO_2 = Mn_3O_4 + O_2$. Bubbles trapped in a stoneware glaze but not evident on the surface are often an attractive characteristic; they are less welcome in a too thickly applied earthenware glaze. Deliberate 'cratering' of the surface is used as a decorative finish—barium sulfate has been mentioned.

BUFF CLAY

Few plastic clays fire white. Those containing 2–4% of iron fire cream in earthenware (the color depending on the degree of *calcia* content), buff or grayish at high temperatures. The term 'buff body' is often applied. The clay may be much darker in the raw state, due to carbon stained ball clay or fireclay in the recipe. Many buff bodies have a long firing-range: that from Potclays (England) is adequate from 1000–1280°C.

Some local river clays will fire to a deep buff, but local surface clays which may be yellow-buff in the raw state are most likely to fire to a red-brown. Buff clays are very suitable for slips, taking some of the brashness from cobalt and giving a slight grayness to green slips.

BULLDOG

An impure iron silicate, giving browns and blacks. Used in reduction to produce blue bricks. It has now disappeared, at least under this name, from the catalogs.

BULLER'S RING

Annular rings, like large washers $2\frac{1}{2}$ in. (65 mm.) in diameter and made from ceramic materials. They are placed in a kiln near a spyhole or at a point where they can be hooked out during firing. Their contraction in diameter is measured in a special triangular gauge, a reading indicating the heat it has reached. Introduced about 1900.

They are normally used only in fairly large kilns but could be a post-firing guide to the temperature in various parts of any kiln. Their advantage over cones is that they do not melt and stick. They are made in four temperature ranges covering 960–1400°C.

BULL'S HEAD WEDGING

See *wedging*

BUNG

Bungs of pots, a mixture of boxing *and bowls sitting one in another. The lower bowls have decorative bosses which rest on the rim of the bowl below. Garden containers by Mike Bailey.*

1 The spyhole stopper of a kiln. Generally of a truncated cone shape and either cut from a refractory brick or thrown from grogged clay.

2 A vertical setting in a kiln, either of saggers, usually separated by a broken coil of clay round the rim; ware supported by special kiln furniture; or pots simply sitting one upon another. For the last category see *boxing*.

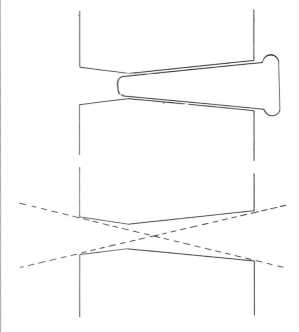

Kiln spyhole bung and sightlines.

BURNISH GOLD

See *gold*.

BURNISHING

The compacting and polishing of the surface of the clay by rubbing with smooth tools. A burnished pot can give considerable visual and tactile pleasure. It is developed from the clay itself, with a consequent sense of unity between body and surface. A burnished pot will rarely be watertight, although Siddig El 'Nigoumi burnishes coffee-pots and similar household vessels which he declares to be quite impervious.

Most bodies, even grogged ones, will burnish; the finer grained smooth secondary clays are the easiest to work on. Some micaceous material probably helps (see *mica*). The technique involves some restriction on form. Concavities, as well as lugs or other applied decoration, make work difficult. An unbroken rounded profile is the most satisfactory. Thrown boxes burnish well and show off the color variations of *sawdust firings*. The main

39

polishing is done at the firm leather-hard stage of drying. The clay's response to burnishing can be tested at intervals during drying until the best results are obtained. Thrown pieces can be polished on the wheel immediately after turning, although this gives a somewhat more mechanical appearance. A final rub with the hands (so long as these are not calloused or rough) is given at the near-dry stage. Cardew mentions beating the surface in order to consolidate it: this may be useful with coarser bodies.

Although hematite is the classic surface coating, I have found that pigments, such as ferric oxide, or high iron slips, can be disappointing both as to surface and color. A fine-grain red clay is perhaps preferable. John Ablitt (now, sadly, no longer working in this field), and others, have developed a stronger and more varied palette than the more subdued colors previously used.

A fine levigated slip was reputed to have been used for Roman Samian ware and a similar material helps the development of burnish. Ben Cooper mixes clay with a water softener and a small amount of organic acid (ox-gall, wine lees), a couple of tablespoons to 35 lbs of clay.

A thin slip is made and only the top finest particles used, after a fortnight's resting, and passed through a 200 sieve. With much less hassle, as mentioned above, Siddig El 'Nigoumi simply burnishes the leather-hard body with a spoon to a virtually watertight finish, using a similar slip of Fremington Clay (from the West of England) with 10% or more of precipitated iron oxide. Magdalene Odundo's splendid large pots are burnished to a black mirror finish. Burnishing is combined by Martin Smith with sophisticated arrangements of metal and epoxy resin.

Variations on an all-over sheen may be to leave certain areas matt for decorative purposes, or to comb or scratch through the shiny surface and through the slip, if used, to give contrasts of color and texture. The 'unka' or cloud-flower effect is achieved by Gen Asao (Japan) by touching the hot surface with vegetable oil. Siddig El 'Nigoumi obtains variations by smoke-staining the fired pot over a twist of burning newspaper. Clamp-firing, of course, will also vary the surface color, sometimes subtly, sometimes strikingly.

The burnishing tool can be any conveniently shaped

(1) Burnishing with a wooden tool, and

(2) Finishing with the flat of the palm.

An elegant, if fragile, handbuilt burnished pot by Tina Vlassopulos.

smooth object: a water-worn pebble, bone, plastic, metal, or hard wood are all possible materials. The only essential is a firm, perfectly smooth surface, preferably slightly convex and without sharp corners or edges. Work with a steady, even pressure in small circular movements. Glass burnishers are supplied for gold burnishing, and these may be used too.

The shine will diminish as the pot dries and should be further treated: often it suffices to work it in the hands or on a piece of cloth. The leg of one's trousers can often be used! Burnish may be lost if the firing is too high—850°C. is sufficient. Loss of shine can be remedied by re-rubbing with the hands or a soft cloth. The carbon saturation associated with sawdust firing assists the polish. A high burnish can be achieved even with a porcelain body. (See also *polishing clay, sawdust firing*.)

BURNT SIENNA

Calcined *ochre* or ochrous earth. A reddish-brown pigment. (See also *sienna*.)

BUTANE

$CH_3 (CH_2)_2 CH_3$ or C_4H_{10}.
See *bottled gas, gas fuel*.

BUTTER PATS

See *beater*.

BUTTON TEST

A test of the behavior of ceramic materials in the kiln. Many materials and minerals can be formed in a damp state into small balls or buttons. If these are fired on a biscuit tile one can obtain some idea of their fusibility and other qualities from the state of collapse or flow at a

A tile with six depressions in each of which a ball of pottery material – a mineral, frit, or a mixture of several constituents – has been placed. The 'buttons' can be made by moistening and rolling the material. These are fired (the hollows retaining any fusible melt) and the results studied.

given temperature. An excellent educational exercise. The results of this test, however, can be slightly misleading. It is the reaction of one material with another which is of prime interest when compounding bodies or glazes. (See *chemistry of glazes*.)

The simple, individual materials could, of course, be replaced with mixtures, which would be even more illuminating but need more careful recording. Possibilities are 50% each of feldspar and clay; clay and an alkaline frit; or whiting and flint.

CADMIUM, compounds

A metallic element Cd. 112.4. Used as cadmium sulfide CdS in low temperature pigments (enamels). Produces yellow and orange. Often combined with selenium which will withstand higher temperatures. *Volatile*. Obtainable only as a prepared pigment. May blacken in the presence of lead. Hamer recommends fast firing in reduction. Cadmium released into food acids is a health hazard and it should not be used on jugs or storage vessels. (See *metal release*.)

CALCEROUS CLAY

Clays containing lime and thus liable to 'blowing', if the lime is in the form of even very small nodules. (See *marls, lime blowing*.)

CALCINE, calcination

To disintegrate by heat: the strong heating of a material resulting in physical or chemical alteration, generally to a friable state without fusing.

Flints, very hard in the raw state, become a friable

A flint pebble and the calcined flint powder. The chemical make-up is not altered but the physical state is very different.

41

white powder at around 900°C. but retain the same chemical composition. Bone, when calcined, loses its carbon and only the *inorganic* residue of calcium and phosphorus remain. Some metal oxides can be calcined: manganese will give a more powerful pigment; cobalt oxides are prepared by calcining, the gray oxide CoO to 1050°C., the black oxide to 750°C. The gray oxide is thus slightly more concentrated in use, and will not change its form or lose oxygen in firing. Some wood ashes can be usefully calcined at about 750°C. Calcining is also practised to eliminate water of hydration, e.g. calcined borax. China clay is fired into *molochite*.

The combination of two or more materials to form a new compound by heating is known as *fritting*.

CALCITE, calcspar

A natural crystalline calcium carbonate, $CaCO_3$. It is the mineral constituent of limestone, chalk and marble. Many natural rocks are almost pure calcite, as also are oyster and some other shells. A method of determining the purity of a calcite rock sample is described in Cardew PP 51–2. Also, confusingly, known as Iceland spar.

CALCIUM, oxide, compounds

A metallic element Ca, 40.8.
Oxide CaO.57 (quicklime), m.p. 2570°C. Calcia.
Carbonate $CaCO_3$. 100, (lime). L.o.i. 44%.

The carbonate decomposes into the oxide at about 850°C. Although the melting point is very high its reaction with other ceramic compounds induces a much lower melting point. A eutectic is: CaO 1.0.Al_2O_3 0.35.SiO_2 2.48, as represented by 33.6% calcite, 30.39% china clay, 35.95% quartz.

$CaCO_3$ is almost pure in limestone and chalk, which are prepared as *whiting*. Because it is a pure material its proportions in a glaze must be carefully calculated. Its effect in glazes can be to shorten the solid to liquid phase. Either too much or too little can reduce the brightness of a glaze.

Lime is usually placed low in the table listing the *fusible* properties of bases. This is true for soft glazes, but somewhat misleading when considering stonewares, where it can be a major flux rendering the glazes more 'watery' or less *viscous*. In a series of experiments carried out some years ago it was found that 40% could be added to a stoneware glaze (at 1285°C.) before a scum began to form. In most glazes, however, the maximum fluidity may be developed with the additions of around 15%. Hamer lists it among his 'anti-fluxes' up to 1100°C. but it appears to have beneficial effects in

combination with lead and soda in earthenware glazes at a little below this temperature.

The *coefficient of expansion* of calcium is only half that of the alkalis. It is reputed to assist iron reduction for celadons, and has no bleaching effect on black (reduced) iron oxide. It gives hardness and durability and is responsible for the great strength of *bone china*. It tends to bleach color from red clays at lower temperatures. Lime in red clays will therefore yield yellowish colors as in some bricks which are fired at 1000°C. or less. In the Netherlands, up to 25% of a limey clay (marl) or lime was added to the body of majolica (Delft) tiles. According to Berendsen TGH, this helped to stick the glaze to the clay and to prevent crazing, although it also lowered its resistance to chipping.

Other calcium minerals are:

Wollastonite	$CaSiO_3$
Fluorspar	CaF_2
Dolomite	$CaCO_3$. $MgCO_3$ (approx.)
Calcium chloride	$CaCl_2$
Bone Ash	$3CaO$. P_2O_5
Colemanite	$2CaO$. $3B_2O_3$
Wood ashes	Variable
Plaster of Paris	$CaSO_4$. $\frac{1}{2}H_2O$
(Gypsum)	$CaSO_4$. $2H_2O$
Anorthite	CaO. Al_2O_3. $2SiO_2$.

(See also *efflorescence on clay, lime, lime blowing*.)

CALCIUM BORATE

A frit of similar composition to *colemanite* obtainable from W.G. Ball and other suppliers. Jane Lord (CR 107) suggests a 'base' glaze of 1 clay: 2 calcium borate for around 1080°C. earthenware glazes.

CALCIUM CHLORIDE

$CaCl_2$. 111. Occasionally used for the *flocculation* of glazes — 0.05%, and can be used in combination with bentonite. Also accelerates the setting of Portland cement.

CALCIUM PHOSPHATE

$3CaO$. P_2O_5. See *bone ash, bone china*.

Also present in small quantities in some vegetable ashes.

CALCIUM SILICATE

Can be bought in sheet form for the insulation of kilns. (See *mineral wool block*.)

CALCIUM SULFATE

An anhydrous gypsum. Can be used as a flocculant.

CALCSPAR

An old name for calcite and has been listed as such in suppliers' catalogs.

CALCULATOR

The standard sliderule is useful in glaze computation, but the most ingenious specialist calculator is the 'Rapid Glaze Calculator' which speeds up the arithmetic involved in converting recipes to formulas, shrinkage percentages, and the like. It would be better if a little larger and correspondingly more accurate, but even so it is very useful. Available from Ceramic Calculations, Marston Magna, Yeovil, Somerset, England. The 'Dial a glaze' calculator, available in the U.S.A. (CM 18/9) was reviewed in PQ 38.

Modern electronic calculators and computers have rendered most of the manual types virtually redundant. They are not in general, of course, particularised to ceramic problems although this is probably only a matter of time and a number of specialised programs have been worked out. Conversion of *batch weights* or *analysis into formula* are, however, greatly eased by the use of even the cheapest calculator. (See also *computer*.)

CALIPER

A compass of wood, metal, or plastic, usually with curved arms or arms curved at the ends. Used for measuring the inner or outer diameters of bowls, pots, lids, lid seatings, etc. Metal calipers are the most accurate but can corrode in pottery conditions. An arm length of 8–9 in. is the most useful; one does not often need to repeat pots or bowls above 14 in. (350 mm.) wide, but 10 in. and 12 in. are available. Cromartie (Kemper Tools) offer a handsome hardwood caliper.

Using calipers to fit a lid.
(1) The inside measurement of the flange is taken with the points curving outwards.

(2) Calipers used to check the lid diameter either by recording the width on a rule and reversing the caliper arms or as

(3) Using two calipers to tranfer the measurement.

Their most frequent use is for the fitting of lids. It is useful to have two calipers in order to transfer an inner to outer measurement, or vice-versa, see diagram in Flight CM. In Fournier PT is shown in ingenious if rather cumbersome double caliper for determining the thickness of the wall of a pot. Almost any strips of metal, wood, etc can be made into simple straight calipers but a long curve as shown has great advantages.

CALLIGRAPHIC

In pottery the term is used rather loosely to indicate a free style of brushwork which uses the movement and shape of the brush itself from which to derive the design. It comes more from Oriental brush-script than from Western broad-nib writing, though there are some parallels here too. (See also at *brushwork*.)

CALORIE

A unit of heat: that required to raise 1 g. of water through 1°C. The 'large' or food calorie substitutes a kilogram for a gram. and is sometimes written Kc. The *British thermal unit*, equal to 252 calories, is a more useful scale for potters. (See also *joule*.)

CALORITE

A cylindrical pyrometric cone.

CANDLE

Household candles vary in composition—wax, tallow, spermaceti etc—but most are suitable for wax resist work if melted with an equal volume of thin machine oil. Sharpened into a 'pencil', a candle can be used directly on biscuit or fired glaze as a *resist*.

CANE CLAY, ware

Cane marl is a low-quality fireclay from Staffordshire though Hamer described cane clay as 'a refined fireclay'. Cane ware was a light brown to straw color, fine in texture, and fired to stoneware temperatures.

CANE HANDLE

The diagram shows how the attaching tag of a cane handle is cut and bent. Cane is difficult to cut and needs sharp tools and a good vice. The bending will involve steaming or soaking.

A semi-circular hoop of cane or bamboo used for teapot handles, or occasionally for storage jars. Each end is split, one section cut away, and the remaining strip looped back round a lug on the pot.

The cane must be soaked or steamed, the ends slowly drawn together until they form rather more than a semi-circle (the curve will always spring out a little). (See *lugs* for fitting to teapot.) Cane handles are available from the Craftsmen Potters' Shop and several suppliers.

Vine roots have been used in a similar way, giving a more variable form with sharp angles.

CANION

A positively charged particle (ion), i.e. lacking balancing electron(s). (See also *anion*.)

CANTILEVER

An area projecting beyond its support. Can be dangerous in kiln packs, leading to warped or even broken shelves. The diagram illustrates such a situation.

A cantilevered kiln pack where the whole weight of shelves (B) and (C) are unsupported on the left hand side and shelf (A) is liable to warp or even break if the pack is a heavy one. Sometimes, over large dishes etc., some cantilevering is necessary and this is best done higher in the pack to minimize shelf stress.

CARBON, oxides, compounds

A non-metallic element C. 12.
Monoxide CO. 28.
Dioxide CO_2, 44.

Carbon occurs in all organic compounds and also in a pure state as graphite, charcoal and diamond. In pottery materials it is represented by the carbonates, where a *basic element* is in combination with carbon and oxygen as CO_2, an 'acidic' gas. In the carbonate form the bases are chemically stable, though often toxic, and often in a convenient physical form for use in bodies and glazes e.g. lime (calcium carbonate). The CO_2 is released as a gas during firing, leaving the oxide, RO. Carbonates are therefore always RO + CO_2 or RCO_3, where R is the basic element.

Carbon has a melting point of 3500°C. and is therefore one of the most refractory materials known and is also a good insulator (see caption at *saggar firing*), but this is only true in the absence of oxygen. With a plentiful supply of oxygen, i.e. in air, the gas CO_2 is produced in great quantities when burning carbonaceous fuels in kilns. Insufficient air (oxygen) will cause this to be 'reduced' to CO, carbon monoxide, an unstable and very poisonous gas. This, in turn, will extract oxygen from the glaze pigments in order to regain its stable CO_2 form. Carbon itself, as smoke, will also act as a reducing agent, see *reduction*. The carbon in incompletely burnt ash used in a glaze can act as a reducing agent in an electric kiln. Carbon can be dissolved to a small extent in a melting glaze. A speck of carbon falling onto a melting glaze will reduce it locally.

In clay carbon can lead to bloating and other troubles and must be burnt out by slowing down the biscuit firing at 850–1000°C. if present in any quantity.

The commonest carbon compound, apart from the carbonates, used in pottery is *silicon carbide*, SiC, a highly conductive material both of heat and electricity.

Some coloring metals can be used as carbonates: copper carbonate is green which helps to distinguish it from other oxides when painting, similarly cobalt carbonate is a purplish blue in the raw state. Unfortunately these advantages are balanced by the toxicity of many carbonates. This does not preclude their use but suggests care.

CARBON DIOXIDE

CO_2. The stable oxide of carbon. The product of *combustion* now in disrepute as causing harm to the environment via the ozone layer. The gas is, however, taken up by vegetation and it is the balance between its production and assimilation that is under threat. Potters, therefore, plant trees!

CARBONIZATION

In raku and sawdust firing the body may be partly reduced but is more likely to be saturated with unburnt carbon which will turn it grey or black, often with dramatic and pleasurable results. Partial carbonization can be achieved by simply holding low-fired biscuit over burning newspaper or other material. Cut paper shapes have been laid on raku for special effects.

Smoke carbon, introduced too early in the kiln can cause grey stains in glazes which may not subsequently burn out.

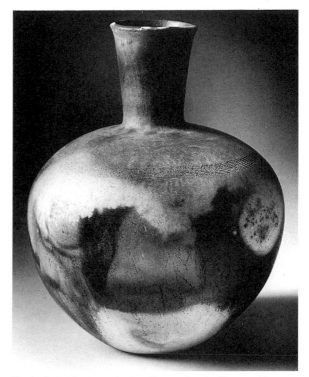

Typically intricate and attractive carbonization markings on a bottle by Naomi Ogilvie-Browne.

CARBON MONOXIDE

CO. A poisonous oxide of carbon; a heavier-than-air gas which can collect at ground level. Can be fatal if inhaled in concentration. Unstable in atmosphere. The major *reducing* agent.

CARBORUNDUM

A trade name, now become a household word, for *silicon carbide*. Used for grinding-stones. Biscuit which has been rubbed with carborundum must be well cleaned or it may cause scum on the glaze. (See also *abrasive*.)

CARD MEASURE

A piece of card cut in such a way that it can indicate 'vital statistics' of a pot for repetition throwing and for future reference. Other details such as clay weight and a diagram of the shape with handle position etc. can be recorded on it.

The card can be sprayed with varnish to prevent water saturation and to retain the information written on it. Linoleum or thin plywood are also excellent materials. The illustration overleaf shows one type but there are other styles, see Fournier PT, 41, and other books.

A card measure for a saucer, giving the shape, code number, weight of clay, width, height at the rim, and the width of well.

CAROLINA STONE

An American *china stone*.

CARVED MOLD

Since early times biscuit and plaster molds have had designs cut into them for repeat relief designs. For clay molds one obviously inscribes the leather-hard body before firing. This will give a relief design and if the more usual intaglio style is required a second reverse mold must be cast from the first. Thus, if the original was cut into a bowl shape, the final mold will be in the form of a bowl via a hump mold: if a *hump mold* (drape mold) is wanted the original design must be cut into a 'hump' of clay.

Using the mold presents certain technical problems. One is faced with the problem of damage to the design through the shrinkage of the clay before the cast can be removed and it is no accident that all the Roman molds, used to give decoration in fairly high relief, restricted it to the upright top half of a bowl, the curve being plain. Press molds are more flexible as the cast can be removed almost immediately after pressing and this must have been the method for the often delicate Song plates and dishes.

Carved molds may not, of course, be made only for a whole piece but may be used like a large stamp or for *sprigging*.

CARVING

As distinct from incising and *fluting*, carving suggests a more radical cutting away of the surface. It is popular today in porcelain, often penetrating the pot wall, producing decorative pieces of rare fragility. Fine-bladed penknives or renewable-blade surgical scalpels are favorite tools, though there is also the school of hacking away at the surface with any sharp instrument. In gen-eral, the more gradual removal of material is likely to be more successful than fierce cuts, liberating to the spirit though the latter may be! Cut edges and corners left sharp can break through dryish glazes in a pleasant manner though they may be somewhat damaging to the hands.

CASSEROLE

A deep lidded bowl for cooking in the oven, it should be of generous form with a well-fitting lid and an adequate knob, or a strap handle (see *handle*). The casserole usually has two *lug* handles or a short thrown one. The height of the average oven should be considered when designing pot and lid. (See also *ovenware* for discussion of body, glaze, etc.) The usual precautions association with *thermal shock* and *heat resistance* must be considered.

CAST

Three associated general usages:
1   Made in a mold.
2   The method of molding, e.g. slip cast.
3   The molded object itself.

CASTING

If a hollow plaster shape is filled with slip, water will be absorbed and a coating of clay will be deposited on the inner surface of the plaster. The level of the slip is kept topped-up as it is absorbed, and when the coating has become thick enough the remaining slip is poured out. The clay shape will slowly shrink away from the plaster mold and can be removed.

Casting is an industrial technique intended to produce a large number of identical objects, the initial shape often having been carved in plaster. It has less relevance to the work of the individual potter, though it is often used for bone china and sometimes for porcelain. Casting calls for its own skills, and professional results demand practice and experience. See also *mold*.

There are many points at which slip casting can go awry. The mold will, of course, become saturated after several casts have been taken and need careful drying. (See *plaster of paris*, *casting-slip*.)

CASTING-SLIP

A normal potter's slip has too high a proportion of water to solid material to be effective as a casting-slip. A slip which is too thick to pour can be made fluid by the addition of a deflocculant (electrolyte) which weakens the bonds between particles. Sodium silicate and soda ash are *deflocculants*. Hamer recommends the use of

FAULTS IN CASTING

FAULT	DESCRIPTION	CAUSE	REMEDY
Pinholing	Small holes just beneath the surface on the mold side of the article	Fluidity too low	Increase water addition
Wreathing	Small uneven ridges on the slip side of the article		
Brittleness	Difficult to fettle or cut	*Thixotropy* too low	Decrease alkali content
Casting spot	Discolored patch appearing on the mold side after firing		
Cracking	Small cracks where handles join the body of the article		
Flabbiness	Soft casts difficult to handle without distortion	Thixotropy too high	Increase *alkali* addition
Slow casting	Casting time too long	Fluidity too high or thixotropy too low	Decrease water or decrease alkali addition
Bad draining	Slip failing to drain from narrow sections	Fluidity too low or thixotropy too high	Increase water or increase alkali addition

By kind permission of the British Ceramic Research Association

two deflocculants to avoid thixotropic setting of slip in the mold. The slip itself can be made less *viscous* by using only small amounts of plastic clay. The normal industrial slip is composed of ball clay, china clay, feldspar or stone and flint. (See *body*.) The high proportion of non-clay materials ensures that the wall of the pot will dry and stiffen rapidly and evenly.

The percentage of deflocculant will vary with the type of slip from 0.5–1.5% of the dry weight. Most merchants list casting-slips and recipes. Some clays will not deflocculate. As a batch of casting-slip is used and re-used, plaster from the molds will reverse the action so that more alkali will be needed to maintain fluidity. Eventually the slip must be discarded. Non-electrolyte deflocculants are being developed.

CATALYSIS

The effect of some chemical substances to influence change in others without itself being fundamentally altered by the change. The presence of alkalis and alumina for instance assist the quartz/cristobalite conversion.

CATENARY ARCH

If a length of chain or rope is allowed to hang free between two level points it assumes a catenary curve. This curve, reversed can be used as the basis for a very stable arched kiln. Rhodes recommends that the height and width be nearly equal—'it is a beautiful structure'.

CAUSTIC

The burning or eroding effect of certain substances, notably, in potting, the *alkalis*. Water in which plant ash has been steeped for cleaning and sieving will feel soft and slippery (which means that it is dissolving a layer of your epidermis!). It will be caustic and obviously may damage sensitive skin. It may be necessary to use gloves. Caustic soda is sodium hydroxide, NaOH.

CELADON, celedon

The general name given to a *solution color* range of subtle green to blue-gray stoneware and porcelain glazes, deriving from iron in reduction. The name is said to originate, somewhat inconsequentially, from a character in French classic drama who wore green clothes.

The Yueh wares of China, dating back to early Han, were the forebears of the later and very fine Song celadons (A.D. 960–1260) where its quality was likened to jade. The color is shown to greatest advantage on porcelain or pale bodied stonewares, although it can also produce a rich olive on darker bodies.

From 0.5 to 2.0% of ferric oxide is added to a transparent glaze, which should be applied fairly generously to obtain the depth and richness of color and to maintain the iron in the ferrous state during cooling. (See *reduction*.) A particular quality of slight opacity in a celadon is due to minute bubbles in the glaze. Cardew suggests a viscous glaze with an RO of 0.25–0.45 KNaO, and 0.55–0.75 CaO, with very little magnesia. This may eliminate some wood ashes from which the early celadons are thought to derive. Rhodes mentions a little bone ash to provide *opalescence*. A series of recipes is given in Leach PB which include ochre (up to 9%) as all or part of the iron content, also Fe_3O_4 (black iron) instead of ferric.

In PQ 17 A. Lewis-Evans quotes the (now obsolete) Seger cone 3 formula:

$$\begin{array}{llll} K_2O & 0.3 & Al_2O_3 & 0.45 \\ CaO & 0.7 & Fe_2O_3 & 0.05 \end{array} \quad SiO_2 \; 4.0$$

which he translates into:

China clay	7.5
Potash feldspar	45.0
Whiting	17.5
Quartz	27.5
Ferric oxide	2.5

CELSIUS

The internationally approved name for the Centigrade scale. Luckily the sign °C can stand for either.

CEMENT

Any adhesive material which hardens as it dries, and particularly the large family of heat-treated mixtures of limestone, clay, bauxite, etc. These provide various grades of hydrated cements which set and gain strength when mixed with water. True refractory cements harden only as a result of ceramic alteration at high temperatures.

The ubiquitous Portland cement will explode or melt if strongly heated, but high-alumina cements such as Ciment Fondu, Lumnite etc, can be cast with suitable *aggregates* into kiln blocks, element wire holders, etc for firing up to 1320°C. Morgans and Gibbons (England) make refractory jointing cements. Keene's Cement is a hard setting *gypsum* plaster. (See also *air-setting cement*, and *mortar*.)

CENTIGRADE SCALE

A temperature recording scale in which the interval between the freezing and boiling points of water is divided into 100 degrees. The symbol 'C' also refers to the Celsius scale which is now the approved international scale and increasingly used outside the laboratory, and is for most practical purposes parallel to Centigrade. To convert degrees Centigrade to the other commonly used scale, *Fahrenheit*, divide by five, multiply by nine, and add thirty-two. (See also *temperature conversion, temperature degrees*.)

CENTERING

Pressure applied to a ball of clay on the wheel as it spins, to persuade the whole mass to run true. Potters develop their own methods, but a steady pressure in one horizontal direction, either thrusting or pulling, is the basis of the action, with a secondary downwards thrust to maintain a roughly semi-circular mass. See also the third

(1) Centering by a sideways pressure with the left hand, the right palm holding the mass down.

(2) The block may also be centered by a pull with the right hand towards the potter's body. (See also coning.*)*

(3) and (4) Show Isaac Button at work where centering and the commencement of throwing so merge that it is difficult to decide where one finishes and the other starts. See the film 'Isaac Button'; also annular.

and fourth illustrations and *annular* for another possible approach. *Coning* is an associated but separate action. Pots are also centered on a throwing wheel or on a *whirler* for turning, banding and other work. Wheel heads are usually marked with concentric rings to simplify centering, but it can also be accomplished by a series of rapid taps on one side of the pot as it spins, a knack requiring practice.

CERAMIC

Derived from the Greek *keramos*, 'burnt stuff', or 'an earthen vessel'. This suggests pronunciation with a hard 'c', but the soft 's' is popularly sound especially in the U.S.A.

The term has now so wide an application as to have lost much of its meaning. Not only is it applied to the silicate industries but also to 'articles or coatings from essentially inorganic and non-metallic materials made permanent by heat—at temperatures sufficient to cause sintering—or conversion wholly or partly to the glassy state' (from the U.S.A. definition, 1963). The net is now cast even wider to include cements and enameling on metal.

CERAMIC FIBER

A mass of thread-like crystals, known as 'filaments' or 'whiskers', produced by very hot air being driven across the surface of a melt of *fused silica*, alumina, potassium titanate and other ceramic compounds. Used as a lightweight insulating material resembling felt. More expensive than traditional heat insulators though the gap in price is narrowing. More refractory than glass-wool (fiberglass) and can be used as a hot-face as well as a backing material, the best quality graded up to 1800°C.

One method of fixing ceramic fiber sheeting (or blanket) in a kiln. The (black) metal pin holds a ceramic 'cup' with a flanged rim which is pressed into the fiber and tightened by means of a nut on the outside of the kiln wall. The end of the pin is protected from the full heat of the hot-face by a stuffing of ceramic wool. (See also a simpler method described in the text.)

Colson KBSM discusses its use in fuel-burning kilns; Fournier EKP in electric kilns. There are a number of trade names: Fiberfrax, Ceafibre, etc.

Because of its light weight, its efficiency as in insulator, and its ease of handling, ceramic fiber in the form of blocks, 'modules', 'blanket', 'wool', or paper, is now more widely used in fast-firing kilns for raku, etc (see *top hat kiln*) and is replacing brick in many others where there is little mechanical stress, e.g. gas kilns. Fordham Thermal systems make useful 18″ × 12″ × 6″ 'modules'. The 'blanket' or board can be fastened to the casing with the special 'cups' as in diagram but a similar system is that used by Steve Mills of Bath Pottery Supplies (U.K.) for both low and high temperatures. He makes stoneware clay buttons, about 2 inches across, with a lug or loop on the back. Nichrome or other heat-resistant wire is taken from this loop and through the casing, held in place either by a twist in the wire on the outside of the kiln or another button. The fiber may also be 'glued' into place with a special cement. Off-cuts have been recommended for clamming-up; and even introduced into bodies for dry strength and to prevent *dunting*, being ground wet in a mortar and wedged into

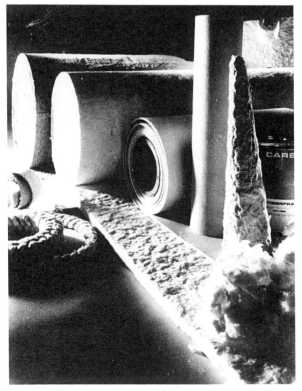

Ceramic fiber in the form of felt, blanket, string, paper, etc.
Photograph reproduced by kind permission of Carborundum Company Ltd.

the clay. Simple, light-weight *top hat* lift-off raku kilns can be constructed from a forty-gallon oil drum and ceramic fiber blanket cemented to the inner surface. See *top hat kiln*. The paper form can be used in dry-built kilns, see *bricklaying*. There is also a sprayed-on ceramic fiber available but this appears to be used on too large and technically involved a scale to be of practical use to studio potters at present (1991).

Like all inorganic fibrous materials care must be taken not to inhale fragments into the lungs.

There are shrinkage problems associated with the continued use of ceramic fiber but Rath's Denka mullite fiber (see List of Suppliers) has, in trials, shown little evidence of this trouble.

Although its comparatively low mechanical strength limits its use in some situations, and earlier electric kiln element holders, for instance, were not very successful, especially hardened and machined shapes are now available.

The simple attachment for the ceramic fiber blanket in the kiln illustrated at top-hat kiln. *See information in the text and also in the caption at* reduction.
Note the use of square shelves in a round kiln which Steve Mills finds useful in maintaining an even temperature through the pack.

CERAMIST

Applied generally to potters making non-functional pieces, most commonly in the U.S.

CERAMIC PENCIL

See *pencil*.

CERAMIC SCULPTURE

A term generally applied to those ceramics which are not used as pots, or where form, invention, and decoration are the sole consideration. It occupies the attention of an increasing number of potters today but detailed discussion is outside the scope of this dictionary.

CERIUM

Oxide, ceria, CeO_2.
A rare earth derived from monazite. Has a high melting point (specialized crucibles have been made from it). Used as a stabiliser for yellow vanadium and antimony stains. Dissolves in a glaze above about 1000°C.

CERMET

Material containing both ceramic and metals. Can replace silica for *thermocouple* sheaths.

CHALK

A white earthy limestone, $CaCO_3$. Ground and levigated into *whiting*. Formed from the shells of minute marine organisms. Deposits in England up to 2000 feet (about 600 m.) thick. French chalk is a soapstone or *steatite* used for marking on cloth.

Blackboard chalk is made from calcium sulfate, $CaSO_4$. Sticks of chalk (or cylinders or other shapes cut from larger pieces) can be used like stamps, or as *roulettes* to roll repeat relief patterns into clay. (See also at *plaster of paris*.)

CHAMBERED KILN

Generally applied to the climbing kilns of the Orient, e.g. Hamada's at Mashiko (see Rhodes K). In the West, semi-continuous brick kilns have twelve or more chambers (see *reverbatory*). Two-chambered kilns are quite common in studio potters' workshops, the second sometimes used for biscuit, or for oxidation. (See also *climbing kilns*.)

CHAMOIS

A very soft and pliable leather, unrivalled for smoothing the rims of pots on the wheel. Unfortunately it soon becomes clay colored and not infrequently it is lost in the slurry to turn up later in a pot! An attached tab will help to avoid this.

CHAMOTTE

A term found in Scandinavian and European books on pottery to denote a heavily grogged stoneware, often unglazed. It can also refer to the refractory grog itself. Also used in the U.S. Listed in some suppliers' catalogs.

CHANGE-OVER SWITCH

See *electric wiring to kiln*.

CHARCOAL

Vegetable or animal substance heated with the exclusion of air. Impure carbons. (See also *reduction*.) Useful for preliminary drawing on raw clay or biscuit. Could be adapted for raku firing (and for cooking the sausages at raku parties!).

CHATTER

Corrugation of the surface of clay which can develop quite suddenly during turning. The turning-tool will begin to vibrate. A slack hold, clay which is too hard (or, occasionally, too soft), too sharp a tool, and uneven texture or hardness of clay, can all contribute to chatter.

To cure, continue turning with the long edge of the tool or a *steel palette*, held at acute angle to the corrugations so that it rides across the tops and cannot fall into

A two-chambered kiln of the type often used by craft potters. Sometimes a bag wall is built of packed saggars at each setting. The second chamber may be used for biscuit or for oxidized firing. Occasionally a large chimney is utilized for biscuit.

Showing the position of the turning tool to cure chatter (the corrugated surface).

the dips. As soon as the surface is smooth again, revert to the normal position.

Chatter has been used as a decorative texture since Roman times and is codified as 'kasurmon' in Japan where it cuts segments from a slip coating in the manner of *sgraffito*—though deliberately to develop chatter in a controlled way sounds even more difficult than avoiding it when it is not wanted.

CHEESE-HARD

Term sometimes used as a synonym for *leather-hard*.

CHEMICAL ANALYSIS

One can analyse a pottery material in more than one way. The commonest is a list of parts by weight of all the separate elements, oxides, carbonates, sulphides, etc which can be isolated from it by various physical or chemical means.

A good supplier will give analyses of the materials he sells and is useful in warning us against variations from the *ideal formula* which is used in glaze calculations. (See also *analysis*.)

CHEMICALLY-COMBINED WATER

The water of hydration. Specifically, in clay, the H_2O which is expelled at 500–600°C., altering the molecular pattern and forming a new material. The process cannot be reversed. Distinct from *absorbed* and *adsorbed* water. Leach PB refers to it as 'hygroscopic water'.

CHEMICAL CONSTANTS

Theoretically unvarying qualities of minerals, etc as predicted by their *ideal formulas*: melting points, conversion factors, specific gravities, hardness, etc. In practice only a chemical analysis can tell us how near is any sample to the pure form though, from a good supplier, it will be near enough for practical purposes.

CHEMICAL SYMBOL

The letters (or pairs of letters) which denote the chemical *elements* either singly or as combined *molecules* are international. The symbol is either a single upper-case letter: e.g. C for carbon, or O for oxygen; or a capital and lower-case such as Si for silicon but, because the symbols are often based on Latin names, they are not always as straightforward and recognisable. Tin, for instance, uses the Latin 'stannum' and its symbol is Sn; sodium is 'natrum', Na. But we need only be able to recognise about a third of the hundred odd total. When two or more elements are combined in a molecule the symbol also indicates the relative number of atoms of each of them; e.g. SiO_2, one silicon to two oxygen. (See

also at *atomic theory, compound, element, periodic table*.)

CHEMISTRY OF POTTERY

The early potters worked miracles of clay and glaze compounding and firing without true chemical knowledge, but their time scale was in generations while ours is in years. An ability to think in terms other than those of pure day-to-day experience has become essential. Simple chemistry and an outline of the current explanation of the behavior of atomic particles can short-cut many a tedious trial series and will help to explain and control results. On the other hand it is always what happens to your glaze in your kiln that matters.

One problem in presenting the subject of chemistry is that extreme simplicity can be misleading, the actual changes and reactions being complex. However, since the whole story is not known even to the specialist scientist, a general framework will be valid for most practical purposes. 'A complete chart of information . . . would probably be out of date before we had learned to read it' (Cardew). Chemistry should be seen as one of the many valuable sources of information.

The raw materials of our world are legion. Their names tell us little about their make-up or properties. This endless diversity can be greatly simplified in chemical terms. All physical materials are combinations of a mere one hundred or so unique and separate parts called the *elements*. Potters use some twenty of these regularly, and another twenty occasionally. The field is thus dramatically reduced. The elements sometimes exist alone, e.g. as the metal 'iron' or the element carbon as 'charcoal', but more often in combinations of two or more. These compounds are more than mere mixtures; they will rarely resemble in appearance or in general behavior any of the constituent elements. To take an extreme instance the dangerously unstable metal sodium, in combination with chlorine, a poisonous gas, forms the harmless and useful sodium chloride—table salt.

It is possible, therefore, to describe materials by listing the elements which make them up. These can be written out in full but are generally noted as abbreviations or symbols. A list of the elements relevant to ceramics will be found under *elements* and *atomic weights*. The element symbols are international.

The commonest simple compound in *inorganic* chemistry is between an element and oxygen (another element). The result is called the *oxide* of the element e.g. iron oxide, silica (oxide of silicon). Elements form oxides under the influence of heat, the science of ceramics is, therefore, the study of reactions between oxides at high temperatures. Once compounds have been formed they can be separated only by other chemical reactions or by the application of energy such as heat. Firing is essentially the rearranging of existing compounds e.g. clay, and the formation of new compounds from mixed materials e.g. glaze.

Oxides can be listed in three groups: the *bases*, the *acids*, and the *amphoterics*. In ceramics, the first group has a fluxing action i.e. it lowers melting points; the second comprises the *glass formers* and is usually considered as refractory—it raises melting points; the third group has an intermediate balancing and uniting role. This rather crude view of the three groups is open to criticism, but will be found generally valid in practice. To decide the proportional amounts which enter into combination to produce a desired result e.g. an earthenware glaze or a porcelain body, we must enter at least the fringe of atomic and molecular science. (See also *atomic theory*.)

Atoms combine into compounds in certain fixed proportions. This proportion is indicated in the symbol by a number written after and below the element. For example, in silica the silicon, symbol Si, and the oxygen, symbol O, combine in the proportion of one to two. This is written SiO_2. The reverse is true when sodium, Na, combines with oxygen, given Na_2O. Ferric oxide combines 2.3 i.e. Fe_2O_3. These proportions can be taken to apply to the atoms (the smallest particle of an element), the actual material being a repeat pattern in infinite extension of connected atoms known as molecules. (See also *crystal, network, valency*.)

A mineral will often contain several oxides. Its chemical symbol will always be made up of the constituent elements and their atomic parts, but these can be arranged in several ways. The most obvious is to note each element and its proportion, for instance, potash feldspar, $K_2Al_2Si_6O_{16}$. This is, however, of little practical use for obtaining a general picture of the mineral or guessing its probable behavior in the kiln. A more practical grouping, and that normally used by potters, would be $K_2O. Al_2O_3. 6SiO_2$. It will be seen that, instead of writing SiO_2 six times, the number 6 has been placed before it. This grouping corresponds to the *Seger formula* and the base, amphoteric, acid divisions mentioned above. The mineral has six times as many molecules of acid oxide as it has of basic: we can therefore guess that it would make a glaze but only at stoneware temperatures—1250°C. and above, and this in fact is the case. (See *Seger formula, base, acid* etc for further discussion.)

The letter R does not occur in the list of element symbols and so it can be used to indicate any element in combination with oxygen. Thus R_2O_3 includes any

compound which unites in a 2:3 ratio. The whole of the bases in a glaze formula may be denoted by RO in order to compare them with the amount of acid. All these symbols denote molecular parts and must be multiplied by their molecular weight to translate them into weighable materials. (See *formula-into-recipe*.)

For convenience, *minerals* are symbolized by their 'ideal' formula, i.e. as if they were quite pure, unadulterated materials. This seldom occurs in nature but rocks are selected which have the nearest approximation. The perfect mineral may be given a separate name. For instance, pure clay material—$Al_2O_3. 2SiO_2. 2H_2O$—is 'kaolinite'. For practical computation, china clay may be considered as kaolinite although it has some 2% or more of impurities. Similarly potash feldspar has the ideal formula as listed above, but the base is nearly always a mixture of potash and soda with very small amounts of other materials, and is sometimes denoted as NaKO. Luckily the two alkalis act in a fairly similar way. A *chemical analysis* will show how far the sample strays from the pure mineral. Secondary clays, on the other hand, may stray a long way from kaolin and be composed of associated minerals such as illite and other micaceous substances. These variations, while necessitating practical trials, do not invalidate an understanding of the fundamental make-up of the materials a potter uses.

CHIMNEY

A vertical shaft of brick, metal or asbestos. A warm, rising column of air exerts a 'pull', drawing air and gases in from the base of the shaft. Different types of kiln require widely differing sizes of chimney. An electric kiln needs none at all; gas kilns often require only minimal chimneys, or may be quite efficient with the near horizontal 'balanced flue' taken straight through a wall. Oil, wood and coal, respectively, need increasing size and height. An up-draft kiln forms its own chimney, and little if any extension is required at the top. The down-draft type obviously needs sufficient pull to force the hot gases to travel downwards through the chamber against their natural inclinations. As a rough guide, for solid fuel kilns, every 30 cm. (1 ft.) of downward draft and every 120 cm. (4 ft.) of horizontal movement needs one metre (say 3 ft.) of chimney height.

A tall narrow chimney is generally considered to exert more 'pull' than a short wide one but Harry Davis disputes this and states that they are equally effective. The expansion of gases is very considerable (in the range of 1–5) and must be taken into account in any design, see *gas expansion*. However the movement of gases through the kiln can be maintained by forced draft at the firemouth or a fan in the chimney, thereby cutting the chimney height to a minimum though increasing the setting-up and running costs.

CHINA

In England the term officially refers to *bone china*. Its wider use in the U.S.A., and common usage elsewhere, covers any domestic vitreous whiteware. The Brussels Nomenclature equates it with *porcelain*.

CHINA CLAY, kaolin

A general name for an almost pure clay material containing, on average, 98% kaolinite, Al_2O_3. $2SiO_2$. $2H_2O$. 258. A *primary clay*. Found in comparatively few areas though in great quantities in Cornwall, England, in the U.S.A. (Florida, Carolina) and elsewhere. Usually very white, though iron-stained kaolins are found. Of the millions of tons used annually only one fifth or less is absorbed by ceramics. It is usually 'won' by washing from the rock face with high-pressure hoses, the resultant slurry carried along channels to settling troughs. The *micaceous* matter is separated out—this eventually forms the 'white mountains' of the St. Austell district of England.

Because of its large particle size its plasticity is poor. Some samples are more workable than others; Chinese kaolin being probably the most plastic and the Cornish clay one of the least. China clay is used in many bodies to increase the whiteness and *refractoriness* and to vary the particle size of secondary clays. Industrial bodies may contain 30% or more; porcelains, 50%. In glazes it represents pure *kaolinite*. The term kaolin is often used as a synonym for china clay, but this is deprecated by some authorities. Calcined china clay is used as an 'opener' in bodies and to minimize wet-dry shrinkage. (See also *kaolinite, clay, molochite*.)

CHINA STONE

A feldspathic mineral with the general formula of NaK_2O. Al_2O_3. $8SiO_2$, 644, but variable with an RO which may also include 0.30 equivalents of lime. Also known as pegmatite, Cornwall stone, Cornish stone, or, simply, stone. Godfrey spar from the U.S.A. is a similar material, as is *Manx* stone.

An analysis (Wengers) by weight:

Na_2O	4.0				
K_2O	3.81	Al_2O_3	14.93	SiO_2	72.9
CaO	2.06	Fe_2O_3	0.13	TiO_2	0.02
MgO	0.09				

This is an analysis of a 'de-florinated' china stone. Raw stone often contains fluorine and is purple colored. There are 'hard' and 'soft' white grades (referring to *fusibility*) in which the alteration to kaolin or secondary mica is more or less advanced (Dodd).

Stone will form a glaze between 1300–1400°C. It is used in bodies and glazes to provide some soda. Also used as a dilutant for cobalt.

CHITTERING

Glaze flaking, especially on rims. (See *shivering*.)

CHROMATE OF IRON

See *iron chromate*.

CHROME

Often used to denote pigments or glazes containing chromatic oxide (see *chromium*) e.g. 'chrome green', and sometimes, loosely, for the oxide itself.

CHROME-TIN PINK

A pottery pigment, normally used on earthenware, for underglaze painting, in enamels and as a *stain*. Used in the eighteenth century and originally called English Pink. It is derived from a reaction between chrome, tin oxide, and lime (calcia). 'The precipitation of fine particles of chromic oxide on the surface of tin oxide in an opaque glaze' (Dodd). It has a long firing range but becomes volatile at high temperatures. The color does not often blend happily with craft pottery. For use in glaze, Stephanie Kalan (CR 47) states that fluxes should be 'mostly lime and lead with a minimum of alkalis'. Lime stabilises the color. Accidental blushes can occur in a firing where the necessary ingredients are present, usually in lead glazes but has also been known in stoneware if commercially prepared color is used. There is also a chrome-zircon pink.

CHROMIUM, oxide, compounds

A metallic element Cr. 52.
Chromic oxide Cr_2O_3, 152, m.p. 2270°C.
Chromate of potash $K_2Cr_2O_7$, 294

Can be toxic and carcinogenic, so take care not to inhale as dust. The green oxide of chrome is the form most used by potters. Although refractory it is also *volatile* over 1000°C. and can cause pink reaction. 'The potassium form is used in glazes and frits' Billington TP.

The oxide is a very versatile coloring agent, especially at low temperatures. In a high-lead, low-alumina glaze red, orange and yellow can be obtained. 1–2% can give red or orange at 900°C. or below, using the dichromate of potash (toxic). Lead/silica frits are good starting points for recipes. As the firing temperature is increased the color turns through orange to yellow (ca. 1050°C.) Hamer suggests the addition of red iron and zinc oxides at higher temperatures but the results hardly sound worth the trouble. Yellow is also reputed to be possible with lead and soda. At more practical temperatures chrome yields dullish greens in a lead glaze and browns with zinc oxide. Colors are apt to be rather heavy and flat and are always opaque. Cardew suggests the addition of *fluorspar* for a clearer color in reduction up to 1320°C. The green may be spoiled by the presence of tin oxide. A brighter, lighter green can result from a high lime glaze. Lithium carbonate (6–8%), in a soft lead glaze with chromium has also been mentioned. A small quantity (0.25–1.0%) with cobalt is reputed to give good colors in reduction. Chromium, with tin and calcium, and especially in *lead glazes*, can develop pinks and browns which are not always attractive. This reaction is the basis for many prepared pinks—known as chrome-tin pinks. Chromium is a favorite addition to many prepared stains and colors, especially dark ones; its opacity, refractoriness and low solubility make it valuable as a stabilizer. Chrome-magnesium ores are made into specialist refractories.

CHUCK

As applied to throwing, a chuck is a ring or block of clay for supporting a pot or bowl on the wheel head while turning, or for secondary throwing (see *amphora*).

A chuck of stiff clay inside an inverted bowl or pot is preferable to dabs of clay round the outside. The piece can be removed to check thickness etc, and is held true during the work. A chuck can be cut for the largest piece to be turned and pared down progressively smaller for the rest, or a stock of leather-hard chucks can be made and kept in condition in polythene.

Method: Stiff clay is beaten out to a flat block on a dampened wheel head and the piece to be turned pressed gently on to it, making a mark which will indicate its width. The block is then cut to fit with a pointed turning tool. Billington TP, illus. 71 shows bowls supported above the wheel head, but it is easier to maintain the same plane between rim and foot ring if the former is hard down, though this necessitates a precisely fitting chuck. (See also *turning*.)

A hollow chuck for supporting tall pots is usually in the form of a diabolo. It may be thrown and wrapped in polythene when leather-hard, or else biscuited prior to use. Biscuit chucks should be soaked in water before use. *Cup heads* can also be utilised. In CR 58 David Lloyd Jones illustrates a chuck for large plates: a wide *annular* ring thrown on a wheel head, cut to a bevel and scored. The plate rim sits on the bevelled surface and the scoring prevents movement in relation to the chuck. (See also *turning*.)

A beaten-out slab of stiffish clay has been cut on the revolving wheelhead to receive the bowl for turning.

A circular plastic box used as a turning chuck by Jack Doherty.

CHUN GLAZE

See new spelling at *jun effect*.

CIRCUIT, electrical

The complete path travelled by an electric current. An unbroken length of conductor between two terminals.

The wiring in a kiln will usually be split into several circuits, each one carrying a certain current (in amperes) and exerting a certain resistance (in *ohms*).

If a circuit does not embody apparatus which exerts resistance, unlimited current will flow—it will be short-circuited or 'shorted'. A weak link of easily melted wire—a 'fuse'—is put into all circuits to guard against this eventuality. See also *E.L.C.B.*

CIRCUIT BREAKER

See *fuse, ELCB*.

(A)

L

(B)

N

A single electrical circuit, the current flowing between L (line or, in common parlance, 'live') and N (neutral) through a length of resistance wire which limits the current. The resistance may be a light bulb, or may represent a series of elements in an electric kiln but each circuit must stem separately from the mains input at points (A) and (B). (See parallel wiring and diagram at series.)

CLAMMING

The sealing of a kiln door and, after firing, the hearths, with coarse *slurry*.

CLAMP

A heap of bricks or, in primitive firings, pots, either covered with brushwood or other fuel, or built to allow fires within the clamp. In a simple brick clamp only about 50% of the bricks are adequately fired. (See Cardew PP Appendix 3.)

CLAMP KILN

A firing method similar to *bonfire*. A shallow pit is dug and lined with wood or brushwood which is set alight. On to the glowing embers bone dry pots are set and more fuel is laid over them. Turves are finally laid over the whole area and the kiln left for several hours before being unpacked. Pre-heating of the pots to the *water-smoking* stage is advisable.

CLAY

The 'ideal' clay material is *kaolinite*, Al_2O_3. $2SiO_2$. $2H_2O$. 258. This never occurs pure in nature. China clay averages 95% or more kaolinite, but this is not the case in *secondary* clays. It has been stated that in most fine, very plastic clays kaolinite is frequently absent and the main constituents may be illite ('London clay is thought to he 90% illite' Cardew), montmorillonite, and muscovite. We must therefore be wary of equating many clays, apart from primary 'china clays', with the usual formula for *kaolinite*. In practice, of course, it is

the physical behavior of clays which is important but a theoretical background is useful in assessing their behavior, especially when things go wrong. For more exhaustive studies of the science of clay materials see Worrall C. and Hamer PDM and C.

Clay is the result of the decomposition of granite and igneous rocks. The alkalis are leached out; quartz, mica and clay remain. 'Primary' clay is found on the site of its formation and is therefore purer, whiter, but less weathered and plastic than are 'secondary' clays. The latter have been moved by glacial and rock-folding action (boulder clays), by water (alluvial, *estuarine*, fluvine, *lacustrine*), or by wind. The weathering and general battering they have received, together with natural *levigation*, have reduced the particle size with a corresponding increase in plasticity. Secondary clays have also picked up 'impurities' which lower their melting point, increase drying and firing shrinkage, and darken color. They occur very widely and are infinitely variable, but can be grouped, broadly, in order of refractoriness:

1 *Fireclays*: up to 1500°C.
   Associated with coal seams. Often black and compressed (see *shale*). Some free silica. Often high in alumina and low in alkalis. Fire cream to gray. Often excellent plasticity.
2 *'Stoneware' clays*: to 1350°C.
   Any plastic and reasonably refractory pale firing clay.
3 *Siliceous ball clay*: to 1300°C. *Ball clay*: to 1250°C. *Sedimentary clays*: of very fine grain which is an important factor in their *fusibility*, high plasticity, and comparatively high shrinkage. They fire ivory. Use in association with other clays.
4 *Red clays*: to 1100°C. (1250°C.)
   Plastic, very fusible, fire brown. Earthenware, slipware, *terracotta*, bricks, etc. A few stand the lower stoneware temperatures. Very variable. High in iron. Some so fusible that they will form a glaze at 1280°C. e.g. *Albany clay*.
5 *Other*: Various minor deposits such as *pipeclay*. Also the widely distributed *marls* and 'loams'. Very contaminated surface clays have too high a shrinkage to be useful, though they can sometimes serve as an iron pigment.

Between the types listed there are many graduations. There are untypical examples within the categories, such as the Yorkshire potter Isaac Button's red clay, the melting point of which was reputed to be above 1400°C.

While most clays are derived from granite, similar minerals have formed from diorite, *volcanic ash*, *basalt* and other rocks. These include the *montmorillonite* additions to less plastic bodies. As mentioned above,

Two representations of clay 'scales'.
(A) Shows the presumed molecular formation, the top and bottom rows representing repeats of the center group. The forces of attraction between each layer are weak. (Diagram based on Worrall, C. Pl6.)

(B) Is perhaps a more comprehensible but still diagrammatic suggestion of plates of clay (each consisting of a grouping of the above 'scales') with water between. The plates can slide over one another but there is enough attraction between the plates to maintain their formation once pressure on them is removed. The amount of water is obviously important; too little and the plates would break apart rather than slide, too much and they cease to have sufficient cohesion and would result in slip rather than a workable body. (See thixotropy.)

The landscape of Cornwall (England) with the 'white mountains' of china clay waste, mostly micaceous material, on the horizon.

some clays are considered to be largely composed of illitic minerals.

The structure of clay is lamellar (flat scales). In simplified terms, the electrical cohesion between the 'sheets' is sufficient to maintain the mass of a clay in any given shape, but can be momentarily disturbed by pressure. The scales, in effect, can slide over one another, lubricated by the molecular-thin layer of water between them. On the release of the pressure the form-holding qualities are restored. The lamellar hypothesis assumes that other rock minerals, no matter how finely ground do not exhibit plasticity and this proves true in practice. This unique quality is known as thixotropy. Other virtues we look for in a good potters' clay are a low water absorption, and standing strength. In *monimorillonites* the link or bond between plates is weaker and up to four 'thicknesses' of water molecules can penetrate. Substitution can also take place, iron and alkalis for alumina, for instance (base exchange), lowering refractoriness, darkening the color, and resulting in very variable compositions. Some bentonites swell when wetted.

For workable clay bodies, not only are different clays blended together for their individual properties (plasticity, color, refractoriness, etc) but non-clay minerals are frequently added, the commonest being sand, grog, or quartz, but also including china stone, nepheline syenite, feldspar, mica, iron compounds, molochite (in porcelain), and talc. See CG for examples.

CLAY MEMORY

A slightly fanciful term coined by Cardew for the fact that a pot, for instance, which has been 'out of shape' and subsequently corrected, will return in some degree to the original distortion, possibly in the firing.

CLAY TESTING

Any new clay, whether purchased or 'found' (see *clay winning*) will have its own distinctive qualities and vices. 'You cannot know too much about your subtle and elusive raw material . . . any clay must be deemed guilty until it is proved innocent' (Cardew).

Some simple tests can be made which will build up an overall picture of the clay you are dealing with:

1 *Free lime.* A pellet of clay dropped into dilute hydrochloric acid will effervesce if lime is present.

2 *Soluble alkalis, or lime,* will cause staining or a whitish scumming on the surface of a dried or fired example.

3 *Plasticity.* A $\frac{1}{2}$ in. (12 mm.) coil rolled out and bent round a 1 in. (25 mm.) rod (a broomstick) should not crack unduly. A pinchpot is a fairly stern test. Try throwing. Newly prepared clay should be given at

least a week's rest in a damp atmosphere (wrapped in polythene) before plasticity tests are made.

4 *Shrinkage*. Roll out and cut a strip of plastic clay, to 10 in. (or 250 mm.) long. An engraved ruler can be pressed into the clay to leave an accurate mark of length. Measure again when dry (keep the strip flat), if it has shrunk to less than 9 in. (or 225 mm.) the clay is not likely to be very useful. Test also for dry strength at this stage.

5 Inspect dried samples for cracks or other faults.

6 *Fire samples of pots and measured strips*, preferably, at first, to about 900°C. If this biscuit is free from faults, try again at higher temperatures until it shows signs of *vitrification* and/or collapse. If a strip is supported at the ends only, the sag during firing will be an indication of pyroplastic *deformation* and *refractoriness*. Check the measured strip for firing shrinkage and compare with a known clay at the same temperature.

7 If you now have a biscuit sample of 'won' clay which is neither too dark nor faulted (cracks, bloats etc) at 1000°C. then you are lucky and can go on to try the clay on the wheel for standing-strength and water-absorption.

8 Finally, try the clay with slip and glaze.

More elaborate trials establishing particles size etc are described in Cardew PP. 255–8. (See also *shrinkage, porosity, water of plasticity*.)

A clay may fail on its own but still be a useful addition to other bodies, or its vices may be minimized by additions of flint, china clay, sand or grog. (See also *body*.) 2% of barium carbonate will cure lime scumming.

CLAY WINNING

Or clay getting. The practical work of finding and extracting clays. Books on geology are generally disappointing in their references to clay. Details of the younger sedimentary rocks, where useful materials may be found, are sparse. Layers and deposits of clay may be revealed by deep cut river-beds or roads, records of old potteries are valuable, as is local soil knowledge and 'folk memory'. In some regions geological surveys have been made which are available on application to the appropriate authority. White clays found outside the recognized areas are usually in small pockets, are often unplastic and sandy, and may be contaminated with lime ('pipeclays' etc.). Surface clay topped by soil will be stained with organic matter to a depth of one to two feet. Hill clays which may once have been buried much deeper may be more rewarding. Soil Hill Pottery, on the

Yorkshire moors, had a fine red clay topped by a buff slip clay further up the hill, and a refractory clay at the top—all on a single slope of about 400 yards. What you are least likely to find is a workable pale stoneware clay, and that is what most of us want.

Commercially, clay is dug from a pit, mined or washed from the surface with high-pressure hoses. Seams and deposits are under continuous scrutiny and analysis.

Clay getting is exciting, if not always rewarding. Sticky garden clay is usually too contaminated for practical use other than as a pigment where it can be considered as an impure iron oxide. Local brickworks may guide you to clay. Few 'local' clays will take a glaze and many will *slag* above 1000°C., but for educational purposes (your own education as well as the children's) the work is of value and the material can be used in sawdust or other simple firings.

Method: Dig a pound or two of clay from various parts of your 'seam'. Immerse it in buckets of water and leave to soak. The way that it breaks in the water will give some ideas as to whether it is sandy and *short*, or sticky and cohesive. Stir and skim off any floating matter. Heavy, coarse materials will sink and the clay slip can then be poured off. Pass through a cooking sieve and then a 60 lawn. One can see how much is left in the sieves and whether enough slip has gone through to make worthwhile the work of extracting it. Dry the slip to a plastic state. The sample can then be subjected to the tests listed under *clay tests*. A very pure-looking sample could be tried in the dug state. Try the slip also for slipware and as a pigment especially on stoneware.

A useful book on finding and dealing with clays and other pottery minerals is Sutherland GNS.

CLEANLINESS

Cleanliness in working practice is anathema to some potters but the continuous dust raised by disturbing deposits of clay, glaze, and colors can seriously injure your health and potters so exposed have suffered. Tidiness is more subjective but can save the one commodity which is finite—time—which may otherwise be spent searching for tools and materials. Lack of labelling can also cause waste and spoiled work. (See also *health hazard, poisonous materials, spraying, sweeping compounds*.)

CLIMBING KILNS

Many-chambered Oriental semi-downdraft kilns built on a hillside or on an artificial slope. The heat is drawn from one chamber to the next which is, in turn, side-stoked with wood until the required temperature is reached. Rhodes calls it a 'near perfect design'. Kilns may be 200 ft. long (60 m.) and 10 ft. (3 m.) high. (See also *chambered kilns* and *bank kilns*.) Rhodes K contains many illustrations.

CLOTH PATTERN

Soft clay will readily take an impression of the weave of cloth pressed onto it. The fabric can be beaten into the surface all over or in strips and other shapes. If the cloth texture itself is irregular—knotted, very open, coarse, seamed, torn—a great variety of decorative effects are possible as has been shown by the work of Otto Heino, Stig Lindberg, Ruth Duckworth and others. There are many other variations of the technique: an open weave pressed firmly onto the surface, covered with slip (or glaze) and then peeled or burnt away; setting one string texture against another; rubbing color or glaze into the texture; using a fine pattern as a basis for further embellishment. Other ideas will arise out of the work in this field.

A cloth pattern with a slip overlay on a stoneware pot by Jim Robison. The pattern was created by rolling over a strip of strongly textured cloth laid on a slab of soft clay.

COAL

Ancient underground carbon deposits formed by the decomposition of vegetable matter over many millions of years. Peat, lignite, household bituminous coal and anthracite are the main types. Most of the *bottle kilns* in Stoke-on-Trent, England, were fired with coal up to the late nineteen-fifties. High quality coal was required and was available nearby. A 9×9 ft. (3×3 m.) setting space would take about 4 tons (4000 kg.).

Coal is not very suitable for small kilns. It needs a generous grate and a high chimney. Nevertheless Geoffrey Whiting (England) fired a coal kiln until 1970. It had two chambers. The final temperature of around 1300°C., however, was achieved with wood, (see the film *Geoffrey Whiting, craftsman potter*). Coal lies between oil and wood for optimum efficiency per lb. of fuel at around 12,000 Btu or 12.6 kJ.

COAL ASH

Has been used in glazes, see *ash*.

COAL GAS

Now almost extinct in England—but see *gas*.

COBALT, oxides

A metallic element Co, 59.
Black oxide Co_3O_4, 241. Equivalent weight 80.3.
Gray prepared oxide CoO, 75.
Carbonate $CoCO_3$, 119.

All oxide forms give stable blues at all pottery temperatures. The hue can be modified by the alumina/silica balance of the glaze and by other additions. (See also *blue pigments* and *stains*.) A cobalt aluminate is also quoted by Dodd as a stable color. Cobalt reactions are very complicated.

The blue from cobalt is strong and insistent. 'A few of the blues were overdone and the cobalt, in its horrible purple intensity, had triumphed over the iron' (Leach PB). This intensity can be subdued by using red clay, iron oxides and manganese as dilutants. This dilution is especially important for painting on stoneware. Leach used 98 raw ochre to 2 cobalt. Boiled green tea is used as a vehicle for cobalt in Japan; the tannin is reputed to prevent spread under the glaze. Sheila Fournier has used a mixture of cobalt, manganese and red clay in electric stoneware firings at around 1250°C. to produce a subdued blue with gold-brown streaks which is very pleasant and individual, based on suggestions in Cardew PP.

Its stability has made cobalt a favorite pigment on majolica where it was often used to outline more fugitive colors, and on porcelain—the ubiquitous 'blue and white'. It can be diluted with china stone when used thinly as a wash. Talc will also diminish its stridency. Excess cobalt will separate out during firing, causing 'ironing', a rusty surface which is, however, not always unpleasant on stoneware. In soft glazes cobalt can be *fritted* with alumina etc to produce various tones (see *blue*), but in stoneware it tends to revert to the purplish-blue silicate.

Owing to its high melting point cobalt is difficult to 'fix' on biscuit. China stone, a frit, or a little clay can be mixed with the pigment. In zinc glazes cobalt can produce a purple-blue or a green; with magnesia pink. In a glaze it acts as a weak base. (See also *asbolite* (the ore of cobalt), and *smalt*.)

COEFFICIENTS OF EXPANSION

Materials expand upon heating at a steady and progressive rate. There is a similar contraction on cooling. The rate varies between materials, and the various degrees of expansion have been worked out as a coefficient based upon expansion per unit length per degree Centigrade and conversely, its contraction during cooling. It is the latter which is of primary interest to potters because it affects glaze-fit. Knowledge of the coefficients is also essential in preparing bodies of ovenware and fireproof ware.

There is some disagreement in the figures usually quoted for reversible linear thermal expansions of the various oxides and compounds. Also, since the expansion is a continuing process, it is usually given as a figure for a certain range e.g. 100–1000°C. This is a useful range for glazes which all harden on cooling between 800–500°C. As mentioned above, there is need for more expert research on the coefficients. The tables generally available are those of English and Turner, and Winkelmann and Scott. The marked disagreements are for the values of alumina, silica, and boric oxide. We can strike a balance, but the figures should be considered as qualitative rather than literal. The progression from high to low values is borne out in practice and can be considered reliable.

It will be seen that *body* constituents have lower coefficients than have the glaze *bases*. Hence one of the causes of crazing, as the glaze contracts more than the clay. In CR 113 Potclays Ltd list the c.o.e. of all their clays and they show, in general, lower figures for raku and stoneware bodies; the highest for red clays and bone china. The negative expansion (i.e. expansion on cooling) of boric oxide is one reason for its wide use on earthenware. The physical meaning of the figures is that they indicate the expansion multiplied by 10^{-6}, i.e. to six places of decimals. Potash thus expands 0.000033 of its length for each degree Centigrade of temperature rise.

The final computation is always complicated by *quartz 'inversion'* which, in effect, puts silica higher in the list and so eases matters for the potter. Also the reversible expansion we have been considering should not be confused with the changes in size which occur in ceramic materials, clay especially, due to *sintering* and *vitrification*, and which are non-reversible. (See *shrinkage*.) These do not greatly effect glaze-fit.

COEFFICIENTS OF EXPANSION FOR SOME POTTERY MATERIALS

(All figures to power of 10^{-6})	*Oxide*	*English and Turner*	*Winkelmann and Scott*	*Whole number average*
Highest expansion and contraction	Soda	41.6	33.3	37
	potash	39.0	28.3	33
Medium	Calcia (lime)	16.3	16.6	16
	Baria	14.0	10.0	12
	Titania			
	Lead oxide	10.6	10.0	10
	Antimony oxide			
	Alumina	1.4	17.0	9
Lowest	Lithia			
	Magnesia	4.5	0.4	2
	Zirconia	2.3		2
	Tin oxide			
	Silica	0.5	2.7	1
(Negative expansion up to 10% of glaze material only)	Boric oxide	−6.5	0.33	−3

Coefficents are additive and one can get an overall value of a glaze by the following computation:

1 Multiply the analysis figure of each oxide by the coefficient.
2 Total the answers.
3 Divide the total by 100.

(For expansion of gases see *absolute temperature scale, gas expansion*.)

While there are obvious discrepancies in the readings the *order* of expansion from the high figure of soda to the low or negative figure for boron is still valid and useful. The temperature range is also significant (Hamer quotes soda at only 5.8 to 600°C.) He also gives alumina and calcia at a similar reading of 2.9.

COGGLE

A wooden or metal *roulette* wheel which was reputedly used to compact the rims of cooking dishes and some pots, decorating them with notches or other patterns at the same time, and which might be a useful tip for today. In a looser sense the word is used to describe any roulette.

COG WHEEL

Increasingly difficult to obtain since the Electronic Revolution but have been used to impress a variety of patterns into clay.

COIL CUTTER

Hollow, circular, spring steel tools (available from most potters' merchants) which can be drawn through a block of clay to cut coils for pot building, handles, or decoration. Quite a large block of clay would be necessary if used for coil pots.

COIL-FORM DECORATION

As well as being used to build ceramic forms, coils or ropes of clay are increasingly used as decorative elements: on the edges of dishes or rims of pots, or over the surface, building up sculptural details on casseroles, etc of great effectiveness; sometimes even rolled in. It is also possible to make patterns of coils on a flat surface— lines, spirals, etc— and then to flatten them with a rolling pin to join them into a solid sheet. The design will be sharpest if the coils are applied, lightly adhered, and the slab turned over before the final rolling-in. This can be used for making dishes, wrap-round pots, etc. (See also *rolled inlay*.)

COILING

An age-old technique of building pots by laying coils or ropes of clay one upon another and working them together. Until recently pots in which three or four people could stand were coiled in Cyprus. Built to hold wine they were affectionately known as 'honeymoon pots'.

Pots can be coiled, after a little practice, to a size which it would take many years to learn how to throw. Coiled pots have their own character and should not be looked upon as a stage on the way to throwing. Large models and asymmetric forms intended for firing can best be made by coiling.

Rosemary Wren uses a special coil for her large models. It resembles a stubby inverted T in section and speeds up the building, while the wide base gives plenty of clay to work downwards, maintaining a wall of even thickness. The coil is first rolled and then worked into shape with the finger and thumb.

Rolling the coil is perhaps the most difficult part of the operation. I have found the following advice useful in teaching:

1 Use reasonably soft clay.
2 Give yourself plenty of room to work in.
3 Cut your clay from a block with wire and work it into a rough thick coil before starting to roll.
4 Use long, even movements from the shoulders.
5 Use the whole length of your hand.
6 Start with the hands close together and move them apart as the coil lengthens. Inspect the ends of the coil occasionally to see that you are not forming macaroni!
7 Needless to say, the working surface must be clean, smooth, dry, and slightly absorbent.

The lazier potter will extrude coils from a *wad mill*. Some use flattened coils or even strips cut from rolled-out slabs which I cannot imagine being very easy. Some comb and slip each surface (especially for the flat strip type), but, as I recommend below, I have never found this essential and it results in slippery surfaces which are difficult to join by the stroking down method. However, it is not wise to be dogmatic as all systems can obviously be made to work. In most countries where coiling is a traditional craft, coils are rolled vertically between the two palms (and they don't use slip to join them!). See film Ladi Kwali (Films for Potters).

Method: There is no point in coiling the base of a pot. This can be a flat, beaten-out, circular slab of clay. Cut a piece of paper to stick underneath so that the base will not adhere to the working surface. When building the coils, make a complete ring for each layer, it is much more difficult to control the form if the coils are spiralled. Cut or nip the ends to a wedge shape so that they can be overlapped. Do not wet or slip the surfaces. Coiling, with a relatively soft clay, is one exception to the rule that joins must necessarily be moistened. The first few coils will take all the weight, so make them fairly sturdy and work the base coil well into the base slab. Always join downwards from the latest coil to the wall already built, using the ball of the thumb to drag a little of the coil clay downwards, inside and out. If the form is widened too soon or too suddenly the whole thing is likely to heel over or collapse.

(1) Monica Young rolling a fine, long coil

Starting a coil pot.
(1) The cut out base with the first coil in process of being rubbed in.

(2) The pot is built up by stroking each coil into the wall beneath.

(2) An example of the elegant result of her work; showing a smooth and sophisticated form which betrays no sign of its method of construction.

Coiling can be treated as a preliminary to pinching, stroking, or even throwing, and can be added to molded dishes. One must always take care, however, not to produce a characterless hybrid. Various illustrations in this book show coiling as an auxiliary technique. *Saggars* can be coiled. (See *formers, hand building.*)

Dave Roberts moistening the rim of a large pot preparatory to adding the next coil.

A Cypriot village potter rolling coils vertically. Note the large cone of clay beside her from which she scoops the material for each coil.

Rosemary Wren coiling one of her large animal figures using inverted T-shaped coils. (From film/video 'Creatures in Clay', see list at end of book.)

(1) Unloading fine coiled pottery from a wood-fired kiln in the same village in Cyprus, and

(2) A corner of their storeroom.

A coiled Cypriot kebab pot (meat cooked in tomato juices) fired in a simple up-draft wood-fired kiln.

COKE

Now almost extinct, in England at any rate, since it is a by-product of burning coal for gas. Some processed coal blocks are useable in its place. As a fuel it gives a glowing radiant heat rather than a long flame, and is therefore more efficient as a contact fuel. (See *brazier kiln*.) Less air is needed for combustion than with coal or wood. Producer-gas kilns have been designed which drip water onto hot coke.

COLD COLOR

Unfired pigment in the form of enamel paint, etc. In America especially, non-ceramic finishes have been widely used including poster colors and oil paints. Perhaps, with the easing of the threat of nuclear doom, these short-term finishes will diminish! Unfired pigments, however, have been applied to pottery throughout its history.

Some pottery suppliers list 'cold colors' for use in schools.

COLEMANITE

A naturally occurring calcium borate, $2CaO. 3B_2O_3. 5H_2O$. 412. Convenient formula weight 206, giving $1CaO:1.5B_2O_3$ in the melt. Found in Nevada and California. *Gerstley borate* is a colemanite. Only slightly soluble. The actual composition of colemanite is variable, that from the U.S.A. being nearest to a pure *borocalcite*, while Turkish colemanite contains a number of other materials in small proportions: alumina, soda, potash, and magnesia. See CR 28.

A powerful flux for most glazes. In earthenware it can be used to introduce boric oxide in a relatively insoluble form (though it can cause a glaze to thicken or flocculate). More than 10% is likely to cause crawling due to an unfortunate effect known as 'dusting' which can even detach the glaze from the pot just before red heat. The boron content can give opalescence in a glaze and, according to Rhodes, a broken mottled colour, especially with rutile.

COLLARING

Isaac Button collaring the neck of a large cider jar. From the film/video 'Isaac Button, Country Potter' (Films for Potters).

64

Reducing the size of the neck of a pot on the wheel by encircling it with the thumb, index finger, and crooked second finger of each hand spread out, and exerting an inward and upward pressure. Another position, which helps to prevent buckling, is to hold the index finger of one hand inside the rim. Increase the wheel speed as the circumference gets shorter.

COLLOID

Particles of matter which are ultra-fine to a degree where some are smaller than the wavelengths of visible light. The colloidal content of secondary clays is often as high as 25–30% and is thought to be associated with their plasticity. The word derives from 'Kolla'—glue. Colloidal particles dispersed in a liquid will remain in suspension for a long time but, once settled, are difficult to remix. Red copper glaze gets its color from colloidal particles, as does the bluish opalescence of *Jun*. In slips they assist burnishing and are probably responsible for the non-glaze shine on Roman and other ware, which has been successfully imitated today, using very finely levigated colloidal clays. (See *gloss*.)

COLOR

The physicists' explanation of color—the absorption, reflection, and refraction of different light wavelengths —may seem largely irrelevant when we are mixing oxides or reducing iron glaze, but it is useful to know the various ways in which color can develop.

The simplest and commonest is the solution color. All wavelengths other than those we see are absorbed. The hue is similar by transmitted (seen through) or by reflected light. Many of our pottery colors are in this category. 'The color is influenced by the abundance or scarcity of oxygen in the atomic environment' (John Dunn PQ 17), which is a way of saying that the type and condition (i.e. reduced or not) of the glaze will affect the color derived from any one *pigment oxide*.

More difficult to comprehend is the effect of particles or fine films of matter so tenuous as to approximate to the light wavelengths. Examples are the iridescence of oil on water or the devitrifying surfaces of ancient lead glazes. Here there are no coloring pigments, but what might be called an optical effect, the cause of the color being in itself colorless. The blues of Chun glazes and the very subtle Imperial wares, Kuan and Ju from Sung China, are said to derive from ultra-fine particles in suspension. There is also an elusive opalescence on the surface of some white raku glazes. Cardew refers to optical colors as glass suspended in glass. In practice, a thick coating of glaze is necessary and probably a fairly dark slip or body. Billington mentions

oxide of bismuth to produce mother-of-pearl luster. Slightly larger particles—the colloids—are responsible for many red-purple colors, e.g. reduced copper in which comparatively few particles of sub-wavelength copper will produce red.

Lastly, there are the very thin films of metal, usually copper or silver, sometimes so fine as to show iridescence which we call 'lusters'.

Color terminology is imprecise and somewhat chaotic. Various attempts, such as in the British Standard Colors, and the *Dictionary of Color* by Maertz and Rea Paul, have been made to standardize names.

COLOR-AFFECTING MINERAL

Some glaze ingredients can alter the tone or the hue of pigment oxides. Magnesia and baria tend to influence copper towards blue, and cobalt to purple. Baria can turn even iron to a bluish hue. Zinc will deaden some colors. The lists of colors derived from metal oxides often given in textbooks, though accurate in general, may not always work out in practice and variations can be assessed only by testing. Copper is particularly susceptible to the foundation glaze and is an exciting and valuable pigment for this reason, especially in non-reduction stoneware firings. Different wood ashes will affect iron, as will the efficiency with which they were originally burnt. (See *carbon*.)

COLORED BODY

A colored slip can be dried to the plastic state and used as a body. A cruder alternative is to damp a finely ground oxide to a thick sludge, spread it onto thin layers of plastic clay, and then to wedge them all together. This is something of a hit or miss method as regards final hue, but one can consider the plastic clay as two-thirds (0.66) solid material and weigh the oxide accordingly. Coarser pigment oxides—ilmenite etc—or colored grog can be added to a body to give mottled and textural effects. *Red clay* is, in effect, a colored body.

Colored bodies are used industrially for colored tableware, sometimes with a skin of white clay inside cups. For the craft potter they can be useful in modelling, giving a decorative result without resorting to colored glazes. (See also *agate, basalt, inlay, marbling, neriage*.)

COLORED GLAZE

Color can be added to an otherwise clear glaze in the form of pigment oxides (the metal oxides) or prepared stains (*fritted* mixtures of oxides). If iron is required it is available in various subtle forms as red clay, ochre, etc. Many of the coloring oxides are dissolved and therefore transparent in a clear glaze, forming 'stained glass'. The hue will be stronger where the glaze is thicker, an effect which can be exploited by engraving the clay. *Celadon* glazes are often used in this way. The body color will have a direct influence as it is visible through the glaze. Optical color and iridescent glazes are not stained. (See *color*.)

A completely different effect is obtained by the use of *opacifiers*, most of the light then being reflected back at or near the surface. The body still has some influence, but it is not so marked. Majolica painting is the local staining of an *opaque* glaze. Color will also diffuse upwards through an opaque glaze, but the effect will be more subdued and outlines less sharp. (See *underglaze, tin over slip*.)

The ingredients of a glaze will control the particular hue derived from any pigment. A glaze will have its own saturation point which varies with each oxide; an excess will render it opaque or be precipitated onto the surface. Remarkable effects will arise from the saturation of glazes, especially in stoneware, but beware *metal release* in kitchen or cooking ware. *Temmoku* and tessha are iron saturated. (See also *glaze trials* and under *black glaze, red glaze* and so on. Also *line blends, color trials*, etc.)

COLOR TRIALS

The color of a glaze does not necessarily proceed by simple stages from light to dark as *pigment oxides* are added to it. Nor can one very accurately guess the effect of a certain proportion of *oxide* in a glaze. The variables —type of *bases*, base-*acid* relationship, *opacity* etc—all contribute to an infinite variety. Statements such as 'copper gives green colors', while broadly true, must always be tested in your particular glaze in your kiln.

Random tests can be made and are sometimes successful, but the most attractive combination is likely to be missed or a whole range condemned on insufficient evidence. More methodical trials, though by no means infallible, are more likely to be useful. The obvious method is to weigh and add progressively larger amounts of an oxide to a glaze, testing at each addition. This has its disadvantages: it involves a great deal of work weighing and sieving each time; cumulative error is likely; and one cannot easily return to a promising range.

An alternative is known as *line blending*. First determine the limits between which you wish to explore. A simple example would be a clear glaze as one limit and the accepted maximum proportion of the oxide in a similar glaze as the other. Make up these two samples in equal quantities and, as far as you can judge, of equal consistencies. They are then combined in certain pro-

portions, a test-piece being glazed at each stage. The series can consist of as many steps as you consider useful or practicable. Ten combinations will tell you quite a lot. The measures are by volume, using any spoon or small container as a standard unit.

A line blend is usually given as:

Glaze	Percentage mixtures										
A	100	90	80	70	60	50	40	30	20	10	0
B	0	10	20	30	40	50	60	70	80	90	100

This does not represent ideally equal steps, however, and is not immediately obvious how to use it in practice. I suggest the following method which fulfils the same function. We will call the glazes to be blended C and D—clear and dark, if you like.

Test				Total additions
1	To 10 measures of C add 1 measure		D	1
2	To above mixture	add 1 measure	D	2
3	To above mixture	add 2 measures	D	4
4	To above mixture	add 2 measures	D	6
5	To above mixture	add 4 measures	D	10

In test 5 you have equal parts. It is extravagant in glaze to go on from here: we would need to add 50 measures of C to achieve a radio of 1D-5C. We therefore start again from D, adding C in similar proportions.

Test			
6	To 10 measures of D add 1 measure		C 1
7	To above mixture	add 1 measure	C 2
8	To above mixture	add 2 measures	C 4
9	To above mixture	add 2 measures	C 6
10	To above mixture	add 4 measures	C10

This brings us again to equal parts. You will in fact find that Test 5 is not identical to test 10, due to slight differences in the consistencies of the glazes.

The series can be translated into percentages of oxide; if glaze C has no pigment oxide and glaze D has 4%, then in Test 1 the proportion of D in the batch is 1 part in 11 and the percentage of oxide is $\frac{1}{11} \times \frac{4}{1} = 0.36\%$. Test 2 is 2 parts in 12 and the percentage of oxide $\frac{2}{12} \times \frac{4}{1} = 0.66\%$ and so on through the series. When we reach the changeover point the proportion of D becomes 10 in 11 in Test 6; 10 in 12 in Test 7 and so on.

The whole range works out as follows:
Test 1: 0.36%; 2: 0.66%; 3: 1.14%; 4: 1.5%; 5: 2.0%. Test 6: 3.64%; 7: 3.33%; 8: 2.86%; 9: 2.5%; 10: 2.0%.

Dual blending can be practised with any two glazes, with two pigments, or with glaze ingredients. One can make a diagram for three variables (see *triaxial dia-*

grams). But for more than three the calculations become very involved.

All this work is useless if the actual firing tests are not fully valid. Brushing a large number of test glazes onto a single tile or shard may be just adequate for pigment trials, but it gives little or no indication of a glaze potential. Make *test-pieces* of each of the bodies you are likely to use; dip the glaze carefully and try different thicknesses of glaze coating. Keep an accurate record. (See also *glaze trials, records.*)

COMB, combing

Decoration by scoring with a multi-toothed or pronged instrument. The technique has a long history. In its wider sense, the term also applies to sgraffito-like decoration through slips or glazes. The simplest 'combs' are always with us—our fingers. Finger combing must be done very rapidly with the slip or glaze in an almost liquid condition. Old English Devonshire slipware was sometimes finger-combed; Leach, Cardew and Whiting have used it extensively. Mixed color wet slips may also be gently combed to give marbled effects.

The more traditional combs may be of wood, metal, stiff leather, rubber, felt, etc, each of which will give its own character to the line. Broken saw blades, hacksaw blades and Surform tools are useful. Simple pieces of broken wood or twigs can be utilized for irregular textural patterns.

The teeth of pottery combs are usually quite broad and well spaced. Hair combs often have too sharp a point and plow up a rather unpleasant furrow. The illustration shows a few types of comb and the marks

Marks made by various tools used for combing through pigment to leather-hard clay. From left to right: a broken piece of Surform blade, a hacksaw blade fragment, and two metal sculptors' tools.

they cut through pigment. Flexible or convex combs are needed for the inside of bowls etc.

Rough edges to the cuts can be removed with a stiff brush when quite dry. This work must be carried out with discretion, or the sharp quality of the decoration will be smudged.

Some delicate combing combined with colored slips on a porcelain dish by John Glick (U.S.A.).

COMBINED WATER

See *chemically combined water.*

COMBUSTION

The *oxidation* of *organic* materials, producing CO_2 (with H_2O, SO_2, etc) and heat.

Combustion is the source of heat in all kilns except those fired with electricity. It needs a free air supply in a continuous draft, and hence a chimney. Fuels vary in their readiness to oxidize (burn). Gas is instantaneous, wood has a low ignition point, but oil must be vaporized by a jet of air, or evaporated by dripping onto a red-hot metal plate. Coal and coke need 'starters'—wood, firelighters, etc—to bring them to a temperature at which they will ignite. All fuels burn more readily the hotter the kiln becomes: heated secondary air therefore increases efficiency. Kilns are designed to provide a steady supply of oxygen (air) to carbonaceous fuels, to convert them into carbon dioxide, and then to trap and utilize as much as possible of the heat-energy which is released in the process.

When combustion takes place a good deal of water is produced, a pint of paraffin (kerosine), for instance, will liberate 1.5 pints of water. The formation of water vapor helps *reduction*.

COMPOUND

A material of uniform composition containing two or more *elements* in a state of chemical combination. A compound possesses characteristics different from either of the elements which compose it. Iron (a blue-gray metal) plus oxygen (an invisible gas) produce the compound ferric oxide (a red powder). All pottery materials are *oxides* and, therefore, compounds.

Elements combine in fixed whole-number proportions. These are indicated by numbers following and slightly below the symbols for the elements. The compound mentioned above combines as two parts of iron to three of oxygen and it is written Fe_2O_3. Fe being the symbol for iron. Chemical combinations are now interpreted in electrical terms (see *atomic theory*, but for practical purposes a simplified view is generally sufficient. A glaze itself is not a compound, but is made up of a number of compounds.

Two elements may combine in a variety of proportions, although one is generally the more stable (inert). More than two elements can enter into a compound. Carbonates are made up of the oxide plus carbon dioxide, e.g. $CaO + Co_2$ gives $CaCO_3$ — calcium carbonate. The formula for complex minerals may include the compound symbol with a prefix figure. This is a convenient way of indicating the comparative number of whole molecules of an oxide in the make-up of the mineral. Clay, for instance, contains the oxides of aluminium (alumina), silicon (silica), and hydrogen (water) in the proportions 1.2.2 and is written Al_2O_3. $2SiO_3$. $2H_2O$. (See also *chemical background, valency*.)

COMPRESSION

Squeezing. Fired glazes should be in a state of slight compression, that is the body should shrink a little less than its overlaying glaze. A glaze can stand more compression than tension but, in excess, it will *shiver*. *Cristobalite* formation in the body is useful. (See also at *crazing, shattering, shivering*.)

COMPUTER

Although many potters are uninterested in ceramic science or are perhaps wary of computers, these machines will undoubtedly play an increasing role in ceramics. In addition to its well-known use as a word processor (this book was written on the cheapest Amstrad), the computer can help with many of the business tasks of the potter: stock control, accounts, forecasts, etc in a compact, space-saving and easily accessible way. It can

store, sort, and retrieve data (formulas, analyses, information, etc), repeat procedures to manipulate figures and, of course, calculate quickly and accurately, and it can store and print out results.

A spreadsheet program will store and sort any data, but there are also specialised programs which can be purchased which avoid having to learn complicated procedures or having to find out and enter every item of basic information and calculation oneself. They are designed to do tasks specific to ceramic chemistry such as calculating from recipe to a Seger formula, thermal expansion, displaying limits, and so on. Such programs are not yet commonly on the market but names and addresses of some people who may be able to help are given under Suppliers at the end of the book. As an instance of their possible use, in CR 116 Tony Hansen (of IMC who issue 'Insight', a chemistry computer program) suggests a system for altering glazes to fire at higher or lower temperatures while retaining similar basic qualities.

While programs are not necessarily limited to any given make and model of computer, their portability between makes can be restricted by any number of differences in specification of hardware or operating systems. Thus the choice of program is likely to influence or be influenced by the choice of computer. IBM (International Business Machines) with MS-DOS (the operating system) dominates the computer market, but for the average potter a good program on a comparatively cheap machine will cope with any task he or she is likely to require.

Any specific advice on computers and their use is likely to be out of date almost as soon as it is given, so rapidly is computer science developing, but for the potter's practical purposes he does not need to be in the 'front line' and can consider his modest machine as a rapid and flexible aid to the storage and manipulation of the information he most needs in his day to day business. Attendance at a school or short course on basic computing will dispel much of the mystique which many consider still surrounds computers, especially in the explanation of the strange language which has developed round them and is sometimes a bar to an appreciation of their usefulness.

CONDUCTION OF ELECTRICITY

Electricity will 'travel' through some materials more readily than others. Metals are usually good conductors. Most dry-clay materials are non-conductors; although they contain a metal, aluminium, this does not conduct in its oxide form. Silicon carbide is a conductor but in the form it is used in kiln shelves it is not dangerous in an electric kiln. Wet materials are better conductors than dry ones. A person standing on a wet concrete floor will conduct current (to earth) if he is in contact with 'live' or faulty equipment and the result could be fatal.

Copper metal is an almost perfect conductor and is used to carry current in wires. Other materials may conduct in some degree but at the same time put up some resistance to the flow of current, developing heat in the process. Electric kiln elements are especially designed to control conduction/resistance ratios.

Conductors	Poor or non-conductors
Metals, especially copper, iron, aluminium, tin.	Dry or fired clay, hence bricks etc, and most clay materials.
Impure water and wet materials in general.	Rubber, Plastic.
Silicon carbide (in the form of kiln elements)	Distilled water.

CONDUCTION OF HEAT

The rate at which heat is transferred through a material. An important consideration in kilns (and the walls of your pottery on a cold day). In general, the denser the material the more quickly it will conduct heat. In metal this is very rapid; *silicon carbide* is also a good conductor. A porous brick has more resistance to the passage of heat than a non-porous one. The inner parts of a kiln—the shelves, saggars, kiln furniture, etc—should be reasonably good conductors, the walls poor conductors. (See also *insulation, heat loss, heat storage.*)

CONE

More accurately 'pyrometric cone'. Made from mixtures of ceramic materials formed into triangular elongated pyramids, and designed to melt and bend over or 'squat' at a given temperature. The standard size is $2\frac{5}{8}$ in. (65 mm.) high, miniatures 1 in. (25 mm.) high. They are numbered to indicate the temperature at which the point will have dropped level with the base if placed in the kiln at a slight angle (8° for Orton). Because cones are composed of similar materials to the ware in the kiln, they are considered by many potters to be better indicators of *heat-work* than *pyrometers*, which measure temperature only. The speed of firing will affect the behavior of a cone, a fast firing needing a slightly higher temperature to bend the cone. Quoted firing rates of optimum cone performance vary widely. Rhodes' 10°C. an hour is impracticably slow: *Orton* cones are quoted for 60° and 150°C. per hour. In practice one can accept the nominal temperature equivalent and work from there according to practical experience of one's own kiln and glazes. It is often recommended that three

cones of successive numbers be used, the first as a warning, the second being of the temperature required. The third should remain standing at the end of the firing. A personal system of one-cone firing may be of interest. I placed the cone and socket on a piece of flat shelf so that the moment can be ascertained when the point of the cone just touches down onto the shelf as it melts. This is the point of reference, and the firing is continued for a certain number of minutes after this according to the pack and contents of the kiln. A potter need stock only one cone number for a 20–30° range of firing. A kitchen timer is invaluable.

At high temperature, cones may be difficult to see in a kiln. They can be brought momentarily into relief by blowing gently into the spyhole. Beware singed hair!

There are several makes of cones. Numbers begin at about 022, diminish to 01, and then increase again to 42. Staffordshire and German Seger cones have a close similarity in temperature equivalents, but the American Orton cones do not often correspond with them. This leads to confusion when glaze maturing points are quoted as cone numbers, e.g. a cone 6 glaze which would indicate 1200°C. for a Staffordshire cone but nearer 1225°C. at the same firing speed for Orton. There is some disparity between official lists of end points for cones, probably due to different rates of firing.

The squatting temperature is something called the 'end point'. Always leave enough room in the kiln setting to place the cone accurately and visibly. An error in reading the cone can ruin all the rest. (See also *P.C.E., Holdcroft bars, Orton cones,* and *cone socket* for self-supporting cones.)

No.	Seger	Staffs	Orton
022	600	600	600
020	670	670	635
018	710	710	717
017	730	730	747
016	750	750	792
015		790	804
015a	790		
014		815	838
014a	815		
012		855	884
012a	855		
		900	894
010a	900		
09		920	923
09a	920		
08		940	955
08a	940	950	
07		960	984

Cone			
07a	960	970	
06		980	999
06a	980	990	
05		1000	1046
05a	1000	1010	
04		1020	1060
04a	1020	1030	
03		1040	1101
03a	1040	1050	
02		1060	1120
02a	1060	1070	
01		1080	1137
01a	1080	1090	
1		1100	1154
1a	1100	1100	
2		1120	1162
2a	1120	1130	
3		1140	1168
3a	1140	1150	
		1160	1186
4a	1160	1170	
5		1180	1196
5a	1180	1190	
6		1200	1222
6a	1200	1215	
7	1230	1230	1240
7a		1240	
8	1250	1250	1263
8a		1260	
8b		1270	
9	1280	1280	1280
9a		1290	
10	1300	1300	1305
10a		1310	
11	1320	1320	1315
12	1350	1350	1326
13	1380	1380	1346
14	1410	1410	1366
15	1435	1435	1431

CONE SOCKETS, plaques

These can be purchased as singles or in groups of three or four. Considering the fact that they can often be used only once, they are expensive and it is easy enough to press a cone into a small block of grogged clay.

Self-supporting Orton cones are made which stand at the correct angle and do not need a socket. They are, as may be expected, half again the price of a normal cone and might stick to the shelf if melted too far, e.g. if used as a warning cone. If you make your own socket each time from clay, a small bowl shape can be pinched into it to receive the melting cone.

CONE WHEEL

See *power wheel*.

CONGRUENT MELTING

See *melting point*.

CONING

A movement preliminary to throwing and associated with centering. The clay is allowed to rise into a column on the rotating wheel under horizontal pressure between the palms of the hands. The hands rise with the column, which is then forced down again with the right hand while the left controls the spread of clay. At the end of the movement the hands will regain the centering position.

(1) Coning by evenly-maintained side pressure from both palms.

(2) The position of the hands for depressing the cone to a centering position.

CONSISTENCY OF GLAZE AND SLIP

The assessment and control of the relative consistencies, or thicknesses, of glazes and slips is a continuing problem for the potter. Industrial potters, even with their great experience, still use a number of scientific checks while most craft potters rely on guesswork.

Dipping a finger into glaze and assessing the coverage is a crude check. The relative amounts of water and solid matter are an important guide, and this can be established, approximately, by a *hydrometer*. Other factors to be taken into account are:

1 *Flocculation* and *thixotropy*. Ash glazes and those containing colemanite are liable to thicken as they stand.

2 Frit glazes should be used thinner than raw ones. They are more concentrated and their glassy nature renders them more transparent when wet.

3 A clear soft glaze needs to be applied more thinly than an opaque one.

4 When trying a new glaze, check its hydrometer reading. After inspection of the fired result you will then know which way to alter the reading.

5 Glazes and slips will not maintain their consistency unless closely covered. Evaporation at room temperature is considerable.

6 Consistency is only one factor: biscuit porosity and speed of glazing are others. The more porous the biscuit or, for slips, the drier the clay, the thinner the mixture needs to be.

One cannot over-stress the necessity of repeated stirring before testing or during the use of the glaze or slip, especially lead or frit glazes. (See also *glazing, slip, casting slip, porosity, Brongniart's formula*.)

CONTINUOUS KILN, firing

Most industrial ware is now fired in long tunnels, the center of the tunnel being maintained at the peak temperature. Pottery travels through on special trucks, heating and cooling in a slow continuous motion.

There is also a type of multichamber brick-kiln where the heat is transferred from one chamber to the next, using it efficiently to pre-heat, fire, and control the cooling of the loads. The craft potter normally fires in an *intermittent* kiln but the many chambered Oriental climbing kilns were, in effect, similar to the brick kiln.

CONTRACTION

See *shrinkage*.

CONTROLLING PYROMETER

A *pyrometer* equipped with mechanism which can partially or completely control the firing according to a prearranged schedule worked out by the potter. The simplest type merely switches off the current at a given temperature, others will supply intermittent current to maintain top temperature (soaking).

There are many models between the fully automated type which can set you back £500 to £1000, and the simple pyrometer. (See also *kiln sitter*.)

In schools especially, these controllers can be of great benefit—if they work. But we have all heard of burnt-out kilns which have been left on 'control' over a weekend. If they are to be used in this way a 'fail-safe' device such as a *heat-fuse* must be fitted. (See at *fail-safe*.)

Today, the microprocessor has largely taken over from mechanical control, fully programmable for firing and cooling: time, rate, soak, etc. However the warning above still holds: the instrument may be reliable; the setter is human and can make mistakes. Check and double-check, the cost may be a ruined kiln if it is left entirely to its own devices.

CONVECTION OF HEAT

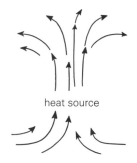

heat source

Heated air becomes expanded and therefore lighter than the surrounding air, rising and drawing cooler air in from below. As the warm air rises it cools again and movement ceases or a circular motion may be set up as in a room with a radiator. (See also heat*).*

hot zone

The standard type of kiln used in the industry with the ware moving very slowly on trucks through a tunnel the central area of which is kept continually at optimum temperature.

All fuel burning kilns are built on convection principles. Hot air or gas, being lighter (more expanded), will rise (e.g. in a chimney) so long as there is a supply of cooler air to take its place. Effective convection is negligible in an electric kiln, where the top is often the coolest spot. If top and bottom bungs are removed at the same time, however, then convection will take place into the outside atmosphere, so beware of this when peering at the cone if you value your eyebrows. Heat is transmitted by convection, *conduction* and *radiation*.

CONVERSION FACTOR

A figure used to convert one scale or type of measurement into its equivalent in another scale with which it has a regular co-relationship. For instance the factor turning inches into centimeters (both regular scales of linear measurement) is 2.54. Any number of inches multiplied by 2.54 will equal the same length in centimeters.

To convert any list of figures to percentages, divide each figure by the total of all of them and multiply by 100. In this case the total is the conversion factor. Useful lists of conversion factors are given in Hamer PDM, the better suppliers' catalogs and other manuals. Full conversion tables are, of course, even more valuable, although modern electronic calculators make the work comparatively simple. The table for temperatures is given at *temperature conversion*. See also at *centigrade* and *fahrenheit*. Another aspect of conversion concerns the amount, compared with the recipe weight, of any raw oxide which will be present in a fired glaze (will enter fusion) after carbon dioxide, fluorine, and other molecules have been driven off as gases. Other oxides might take up more oxygen and have a higher figure for the fired state.

As most glaze recipes have been tested empirically this becomes of less importance but the knowledge is useful when trying new formulations based on molecular parts and weights. Some conversion factors are mentioned under the relevant headings and there is an exhaustive table in Hamer.

Some physical factors a potter might need are:

To change	into	multiply by	to obtain converse multiply by
inches	cm	2.54	0.394
feet	meters	0.305	3.281
gallons	liters	4.546	0.22
Imperial gallons	US gallons	1.201	0.833

To change	into	multiply by	to obtain converse multiply by
pints	liters	0.568	1.760
ounces	grams	28.35	0.035
pounds	kilograms	0.454	2.205
cwt.	kilograms	50.8	0.02
oz./pt.	g/cm^3.	0.05	20.0
Btu	watt/hours	0.29	3.41
Btu	joules	1050	

COOLING OF GLAZE AND BISCUIT

The effort and expense of firing go into the heating up of pots, but changes important to the finished article occur also on cooling.

For the majority of glazes, cooling to 1000°C. can be quite rapid. This inhibits the growth of crystals and keeps the glaze surface 'bright'. David Leach cools rapidly to 750°C. in a two-chamber kiln: the second chamber is brought up to temperature while the first is cooled by the incoming draft. Slow cooling while the glaze is still fluid will develop *matt* qualities in certain glazes and is essential for *aventurine* glazes. Below 900°C. the glaze become increasingly rigid, but subsequent changes occur which put either the glaze or the body into a state of stress. If this is excessive *crazing*, *shivering*, or *shattering* can occur.

The main factors at work are:

1 The comparative *coefficients of expansion*.
2 *Inversions* of quartz and cristobalite, at 573 and 220°C. respectively.

The ideal is, therefore, reasonably slow cooling from red-heat almost to touch-heat. For most potters the cooling rate is built into the kiln design. Hearths and all vents in a fuel burning kiln must be *clammed*. An electric kiln could be covered with a ceramic fiber blanket. The particular qualities and vices of a glaze or body will be affected by the heating and cooling behavior of the kiln—no two of which are identical. This fact lessens the value of *test kilns*. (See also *dunting*.)

COPPER, oxides, compounds

A metallic element Cu. 63.5.
Black cupric oxide CuO, 79.5. m.p. 1149°C.
Red cuprous oxide Cu$_2$O. 143.0.
Carbonate CuCO$_3$. 123.5 [strictly CuCO$_3$. Cu(OH)$_2$].

The cuprous oxide is in the 'reduced' or lower oxide state and will revert to CuO in a glaze unless the reduction is maintained. (See *copper red*.) The green carbonate will decompose in hot water and is more toxic than the oxide.

A *basic*, versatile pigment, slightly *fluxing* in a glaze. Liable to *volatilize*. A great variety of transparent green colors derive from 1.3% of copper oxide: apple green in lead glazes; turquoise in low alumina alkaline glazes; and various shades in leadless glazes. Produces a rather watery color in slip and is usually combined with chrome.

In oxidized stoneware copper will usually give a rather characterless green-brown, but will sometimes surprise with buff to black in a high base matt, or rich blues with barium.

Copper increases lead solubility to a significant extent and must not be used in this combination on tablewares or kitchenware. An excess of copper—3% and upwards—in any glaze will generally produce a rather cindery black. With careful experiment and control this can be made quite attractive in an earthenware glaze.

As a pigment, copper is used for green colors on glazes, or for browns and blacks on unglazed biscuit. It will tend to separate out if mixed with other pigments. Copper/manganese mixtures can give a definite gold color on biscuit at any temperature, but the low eutectic can cause running if thickly applied. Copper chloride is used in lusters. (See also *copper/manganese gold*.)

An interesting if rather tedious method of preparing your own copper oxide for painting is given in Sanders WJC. Copper filings are soaked in salt water for a week, stirred and washed with water and finally with strong tea. Dry and remove the top layer which will contain the tannin. Carefully separate the middle from the bottom layer (which will be metallic) and use this as a pigment. (See also *copper red*.)

A rosebowl by Robert Fournier thrown in a coarsely grogged clay. The wide rim has been turned to bring up the texture and then spun with copper oxide. Only the center well is glazed. A thicker application of a copper/manganese mixture on the edge of the rim has given a gloss; coppery gold in places. (See copper-manganese.)

COPPERAS

A ferrous sulfate $FeSO_4$. Calcined for enamels, giving nasturtium reds at 600°C. and violet at 1000°C. Shaw SCP.

COPPER LUSTER

A metallic, ruby-red luster can be achieved by painting onto a soft (1000–1050°C.), fired glaze which has been opacified with tin or titianium, with copper/clay (usually ochre) mixture, refiring to about 780°C. and reducing at the top temperature and during cooling. The clay is cleaned away when the piece is cold. In-glaze luster is fired to glaze maturity and reduced during cooling, intermittently but fairly heavily. All luster firing is very tricky. Prepared lusters are available. (See also *luster*.)

COPPER/MANGANESE GOLD

The lustrous sheen on two handbuilt 'pebble' forms sprayed with a copper-manganese pigment (see text) and fired to 1225°C. By Robert Fournier.

Mixtures of black copper oxide and manganese dioxide with a greater proportion of the latter, can produce bronze-gold on biscuit over a wide range of temperatures. The biscuit can be first brushed over with manganese and the copper (or a copper/manganese mixture) then applied with a brush, sponge, or spray where the gold color is required, all over if necessary. Too heavy an application of copper will, as ever with this oxide, burn an ashy black. Temperatures may be from high earthenware to porcelain. Around 1220°C. is optimum to avoid running which is always a problem. If crinkled or immature in appearance it can be refired. Lucie Rie is reputed to use copper carbonate in place of the oxide, or even manganese alone although I have not had success with these—which only goes to show—!

COPPER RED

Copper oxide, in reduction, will yield colloidal particles of cuprous oxide to produce red glazes. This can be achieved at any temperature from 800–1400°C. but is fugitive and difficult to retain in the cooling glaze. The color can range from blood red through purple to a rather muddy khaki. Billington recommends a little borax, and even lead, at slightly sub-stoneware temperatures (1150–1200°C.). At any temperature the glaze needs to be fairly fluid. Small amounts of tin oxide or zinc in glazes low in alumina and magnesia have been recommended. Finely ground silicon carbide in the same proportions as the copper carbonate can give a streaked red.

One can buy red cuprous oxide which some potters believe should be used for reduced copper glazes. It will quickly revert to cupric green in *oxidation*.

Use 0.5–1.0% of the oxide or carbonate. Maintain at least a non-oxidizing atmosphere during cooling i.e. keep the kiln as airtight as possible. The typical *sang de boeuf* Chinese reds occur on a blue Chun glaze. (See *color*.) A small amount of iron is reputed to help the red hue. It is difficult to duplicate copper red effects in detail. The colors, even at their best, are rather strident and need handling with discretion if they are to be anything more than technical achievements.

A copper glaze which local reduction has turned blood-red on one side while the right-hand area has remained a pale apple green on a thrown pot by Greg Daly (Australia).

CORDIERITE

Magnesium-aluminium-silicate. $2MgO. 2Al_2O_3. 5SiO_2$.

It exists as a mineral—there are deposits in Wyoming, USA—but is usually synthesized at a very high temperature from clay, talc and alumina. It has a low and uniform thermal expansion (*coefficient* 1–2.5) and attempts have been made to incorporate it in fire-proof bodies. Serious difficulties, however, arise when it is combined with plastic clays.

CORD IMPRESSION

The impressing or rolling of cords (string or rope) into the surface of wet clay has been practised world-wide for millennia and is still a valid method of decoration. The cord can be used as it is, or wound round a length of wood or dowel and rolled or beaten onto the slab or pot. Japanese 'nawame' cords of this type are widely used. The resultant pattern can be inlaid, wiped over with pigment or glaze before or after biscuit firing, or treated in other ways.

CORDON

A strap or raised continuous band round a pot, formed during throwing or turning, or applied. It can give vigor and interest to the profile and, on beakers and the like, can form a springing-off point for a handle. A cordon which has been impressed with the fingers up and down into a wavy shape is called a 'frilled cordon'.

CORNWALL STONE

See *china stone*.

CORUNDUM

A natural crystalline alumina, nearly as hard as diamond. Used as an *abrasive*. Also derived from high-fired bauxite.

COSTING AND PRICING

It is said that an object is worth whatever someone will pay for it. Up to a point, this is true of pottery. Pots, even of the highest order, do not in the West often command the prices paid for even second-rate paintings though the gap is narrowing.

The pricing of an individual piece is not, however, the main problem, which is how to arrive at a fair price for the run of tableware and 'useful' pieces which may constitute many a professional potter's bread and butter. A balance must be struck between the estimated production costs and the average price range for similar wares. A comparative beginner will use more time and materials than an experienced potter, but cost cannot be expected to cover lack of skill!

One system is to keep a kiln log of the number and description of pieces produced. Over several months an average figure will emerge. If an approximate wholesale price, based on those prevailing in the shops, is given to each piece, an estimate of one's likely gross income per week or per month can be arrived at. The wholesale price is normally the shop price minus 40–60%. The retail price should be approached even if you sell a number of pots from your own showroom; remember that it may take ten minutes or more to sell a few pounds or dollarsworth of pots (longer if the customer is an interesting one!). Halve the gross figure of the total sales and if the final sum is not sufficient as a private income you must work harder, or more efficiently, or persuade customers that your pots are worth more. The method is rough and ready but better than none. A more logical system, though often as arbitrary, is to try to estimate the actual cost of production. To arrive at the precise cost of each article is impossible, but again, averages can be struck. Some recording and 'office work' will be involved however you arrange your accounts and the various tax people have to be satisfied.

Cost is made up of materials, time and 'overheads', plus a sum to cover future development, taxes, travel and 'profit'.

1 *Materials.* Assess all materials used over a given period (not less than six months). Clay, glaze, minor materials such as cones, sponges, wax, fuel for kiln, etc which are 'consumed' or used up.

2 *Time.* Your wages and those of any assistants. Make an assessment of hours worked and an hourly rate which would be acceptable.

3 *Overheads.* The proportion of rent, mortgage, telephone, building repairs, lighting, heating, which are attributable to the pottery. Exhibition and professional society charges.

4 *Equipment.* Capital costs, wear and tear, and depreciation. See note below.

5 *Development.* You should build up some capital for the future. The equipment figure is a guide to possible requirements.

6 *Taxes.* Value Added Tax if applicable, or its equivalent outside the European Economic Community. National Insurance, other insurances, other taxes, bank loan or overdraft charges.

7 *Other.* Traveling: allow mileage costs as estimated by motoring organizations. Costs of post and carriage. Boxes and other packing, office materials, and sundries (laundry etc).

Items 1, 2, & 3 must be calculated on the basis of six months or a year's total cost. No. 4 is more difficult. The

following example may help. The figures are arbitrary: If your kiln and kiln furniture cost $1000 with an estimated $300 a year for replacement and repairs, then the charge to be added to a year's costs will be: $100 + (3300 \times 5) \div 5 = 2500 \div 5 = \$500$.
Add at least the same amount and preferably double the figure arrived at in No. 4, to cover No. 5. The higher figure will help to take inflation into account.

The calculations for 6 and 7 are based on one year's expenses.

The figure for each category can be reduced to a monthly rate by simple division. Add 10% for 'profit'. This final figure is the sum you should be getting for a month's gross output, as arrived at by the first system mentioned above.

This need not be a continuing process. One calculation can serve as a basis for several years, balancing prices against inflation.

COST of setting up

The individual potter is obviously restricted by limits of time and skill as to the number of pieces of work that can be turned out. His or her returns can only be enhanced by keeping the cost of production as low as possible. It is easy to spend many thousands of pounds or dollars on elaborate equipment; pug-mills, slab-rollers, blungers, extruders, vibratory sieves, electronic kiln controllers, etc which would be unlikely to be recouped by the average potter for many years when, fundamentally, all that is needed is some clay, a few minerals, a kiln, and skilful fingers! Resist the temptation to order by leafing through suppliers' catalogs, and buy equipment only when it becomes essential for a line or type of work which you have experimented with and decided upon. Look through Harry Davis' 'The potter's alternative' and other manuals before embarking on purchases. The total money spent on setting up, including any interest on borrowed money, should be set against returns for a true appraisal of the financial success of a pottery venture.

On the other hand it is economical in the long run to buy materials in as large quantities as you can afford and house. This will not only be cheaper pro rata and save the aggravation of waiting for supplies, but has the great advantage that you can become familiar with a particular batch of clay or mineral. We are lucky that the materials of pottery do not deteriorate with age, may even improve—like the potter!

COUNTER CHANGE

A design in which one half of a pattern is a mirror image of the other but in reverse colors; e.g. one part black on white, the other white on black. The diagrams illustrate the principle of the method. The style is useful as an exercise for students since it makes clear that the spaces between elements of a pattern have as much 'shape' as the elements themselves. It is particularly suited to sgraffito and paper resist, and slip trailing. Sometimes the reversals can be in panels on each side of a wavy line as often practised by Leach (see illustrations in Fournier DPD).

A cut paper counterchange design, in this case one element has been cut from the other.

Three examples of the principle of counterchange. These diagrams are, necessarily, in the extremes of black and white but the use of slips and engobes can add variety, while Leach and others have used brushwork in more subtly contrasting colors.
1. A stylized leaf, one side of the center stem reflecting a 'negative' image of the other.

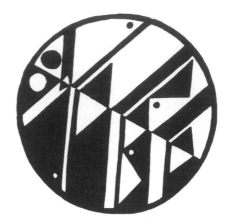

2. A more involved pattern but using the same system and presenting a striking design.

3. The counterchange principle applied to a bowl, the light and dark elements reflecting one another.

COVALENT BOND

The sharing by two atoms of a pair of *electrons*, one provided by each atom. (See *atomic theory*, *valency*.)

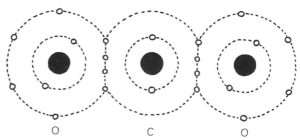

Covalent bonds between atoms of oxygen (O) which has 6 electrons and carbon (C) with 4. Two electrons from each atom are shared, making up 8 in each orbit and forming the carbon dioxide molecule.

CRACKING

Cracks often result from the mishandling of clay at the leather-hard stage e.g. careless correcting of deformed pot or bowl rims. The strain may not show until the pot is bone dry or biscuit. Cooling too quickly through the *inversions* of quartz and cristobalite may cause cracks or *dunting*. This would be aggravated by an excess of silica in the body. A cooling crack is usually curved and sharp. Other causes of cracking:

1 Over-wetting parts of a pot, e.g. water left in the base during throwing.
2 Stretching the clay when making.
3 Uneven or forced drying—the last part to dry may crack.
4 Applying slip to a dish which is either too dry, or, conversely, has only just been pressed into a mold.
5 Very uneven wall thicknesses, especially the bases of pots.
6 Wet clay joined to drier clay.
7 High shrinkage-rate of clay.
8 Pieces of lime or stone.
9 Excessive weight on a pot or 'bung' of pots in the kiln, including piles of six or more tiles in plastic clay.
10 Slabs bent when too stiff, e.g. pots made around cylinders.
11 Over-*wedging*, giving a very short body.
12 Thick glaze on one side of a dish only.
13 The working of clay after it has dried beyond the plastic stage.

This is a formidable list, but in fact clean, well-prepared clay made into reasonably even-walled pots which are allowed to dry naturally will not suffer. (See *base cracks*.)

The filling (stopping) of biscuit cracks is not recommended, although preparations are sold for this purpose. Hamer gives a remarkably detailed analysis of many types of cracks and their possible causes.

CRACKLE

A term applied to the intentional *crazing* of stoneware or porcelain glazes. *Vitrification* of the body prevents excessive absorption of moisture.

On porcelain, crackle is used decoratively and can be stained with manganese or other color while still hot from the kiln. Nitrates of the pigment oxides are suggested by Behrens. If pottery color is used it can be fixed in a second fire. Non-ceramic materials such as tea and water-based paint have been used to stain crackle. Brian Beaven (CR No 73) warns against handling the ware

before staining—finger marks will show up—and to hold the warm pot with a clean rag. Rapid cooling of raku, etc will induce crackle and Martin Smith wipes wet strips of cloth over the areas he wants affected. In this case, of course, the result if more accurately '*crazing*'. A second and wider crackle may form long after firing. Crackle is best avoided on tableware.

Thick glaze with a high *coefficient of expansion* is needed for the development of crackle. Behrens (CM 17/8) suggests a body of 58 ball clay, 39 talc, 3 bentonite, with a glaze of volcanic ash, china clay, and frit, fired to 1220°C. The formula for a talc crackle glaze by Victor Margrie, given in CR 2, reads:

K_2O 0.20
CaO 0.29 Al_2O_3 0.20 SiO_2 2.0
MgO 0.51

firing to 1260°C. on David Leach porcelain body. (See also *crazing*.)

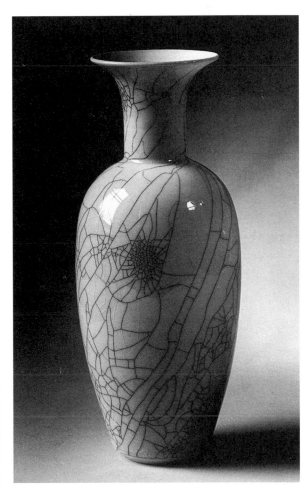

An interesting spider-web crackle on a porcelain bottle by Christine-Ann Richards. (St. James Gallery).

CRANK, bit

A thin refractory kiln shelf up to about 12 in. (300 mm.) long. May be rectangular or triangular, and have bent-over tabs for spacing. Used mainly for tiles. Small blocks to hold the cranks apart are called 'bits' or 'dots'.

A crank can also be a vertical structure with a series of 'pins' to hold plates or tiles of identical size. Maximum kiln temperature 1200°C. More supportive cranks have three turned-down feet which span the tile or plate but these are not often used by the studio potter.

Thirdly, the term may be used to cover all *kiln shelves*.

CRANK MIXTURE

A coarse, *grogged* body of refractory clays used for making 'cranks' or kiln shelves. Used as a trade name for a somewhat variable mixture by Potclays, Stoke-on-Trent.

Useful for mixing with other clays to impart a more open texture, allowing thicker walls in models, coiled pots, etc. Very little shrinkage if used alone. Can be made into *saggars* for *raku*.

CRAQUELE

An alternative term for *crackle*.

CRATER GLAZE

A rather tricky decorative finish derived from burst *bubbles* in a glaze. The use of sulfates such as barium sulfate has been suggested. The 'craters' should be suf-ficiently melted to lose their dangerous sharpness. A recipe in CM 17/3 (Behrens) is given as:

Talc	43.5
Lepidolite	54.4
Bentonite	2.0

Coarse-grained silicon carbide in the body has been suggested. A light colored 'stiff' (refractory) glaze over a darker more fusible one can trap escaping bubbles which will finally break through to form a 'crater'. Any material which will liberate gases—the fluorides, etc—will help to form the required effect. Hamer gives the optimum temperature range as 1000–1200°C. The result is only occasionally worth the trouble!

"A crater glaze – using outgasing from a decomposing clay body as a source of the cratered surface, rather than anything special about the glaze itself" (William Hunt, U.S.A.)

CRAWLING

A glaze fault, the glaze bunching up in places leaving other parts bare. Some likely causes are:

1 In general, glazes with a high surface tension.
2 Too thick a coat of glaze, or repeated coatings. If the

Tea bowl with 'cratered' glazes by Ewen Hendersoh.

78

glaze shows signs of cracking as it dries then it will almost certainly crawl.

3 Glaze which has *flocculated* in the batch, due to soluble alkalis (e.g. ash) or colemanite.

4 Greasy or dusty biscuit.

5 Overloading with opacifying materials, or with feldspar, making the glaze too *viscous*.

6 Underfiring.

7 Glaze materials too finely ground.

8 An exceptionally smooth body can aggravate crawling.

9 Thick underglaze pigments, especially barely *sintered* oxides which have the same effect as dust.

10 Double glazing with the first glaze too dry.

11 Very 'hard' water used in throwing or sponging has been given as a cause.

12 The commencement of firing before the glaze water has fully dried from the body. This is one of the commonest causes. Do not dry off the glaze water in the kiln.

Crawling on the rim of a pot is difficult to cure. I have had to abandon otherwise excellent glazes because of this fault. Cardew suggests a higher biscuit fire, or altering the body by the addition of quartz or a hard, fine grog.

Crawling has been exploited as a decorative finish—for instance Hamada's white crawled glaze on the necks of pots. Sheila Fournier's handbuilt bowls where the crawling is made to 'heal over' in a second fire; Lucie Rie's very controlled all-over crawling, etc.

Deliberate decorative crawling achieved by pouring a thick glaze over a rough, sand-beaten surface. Hand-built stoneware by Robert Fournier.

CRAYON

Underglaze colors in the form of pencils or crayons are available from several suppliers. Use like an ordinary crayon, blow away loose dust, and fire. The effect is generally paler than when using a brush and more allied to drawing. A home-made crayon may be made by mixing a pigment with clay and a little glue or binder into a stiff paste and then rolling it into a cylinder, perhaps covering it in a strip of thin paper to make it more rigid.

Joan Hepworth's detailed and crisp decoration using ceramic crayons. She warns that their use is not quite as simple as it may appear to be; they need continual sharpening and tend to be soft, brittle, and easily broken. They are, nevertheless, an interesting and valuable addition to the potter's palette.

CRAZING

A network of fractures in a glaze caused by differences in contraction between body and glaze during cooling, or by subsequent expansion of the body. Term generally applied to earthenware; a similar effect on high-fired ware is often called *crackle*. It should be avoided on all pottery made for table or kitchen use. If a glaze regularly crazes despite efforts to cure it, dispense with it. One may also have to abandon a body on which crazing regularly occurs.

Crazing is most apparent in clear glazes; it can be difficult to detect in *tin* or opaque glazes—until you wash up after that delicious bowl of raspberries. *Slip* can craze.

In general, the whiter, prepared bodies may be most liable to crazing under craft conditions since they are designed for a much higher biscuit fire. Industrial frits are often applied too thickly by the student potter. Too thick a coating of any glaze will increase its susceptibility to crazing.

The perfect glaze is in slight compression after firing: it has contracted a little less than the body during the final 600°C. of cooling. The main factor working against this ideal state is the high *coefficient of expansion* of many of the *bases* used to *flux* a glaze. Soda and potash are the worst offenders, while silica and alumina have comparatively low coefficients. This means, in practice, using less feldspar or stone and a little more flint or clay, or a little boric oxide (as borax frit). (See *negative expansion*.) Lead is reputed to have more elasticity than the other bases; some bi-silicate or a low-solubility frit may therefore be advantageous.

A more fundamental approach is to tackle the body, increasing its contraction to put the glaze into *compression*. Silica, in a glaze, does not *crystallize* on cooling, and so contracts evenly throughout the temperature range. Crystals of silica in the body, however, undergo a very sudden change in molecular shape at 573°C. (*inversion*) accompanied by a contraction of around 1%. This helps to balance the glaze contraction and we get the apparently anomalous situation where the addition of silica to either glaze or body will help to minimize crazing. If the silica in the body is fired high enough to form *cristobalite* then another and proportionally greater contraction occurs at 250°–220°C., further aiding glaze compression, and at a critical temperature when the glaze is quite rigid. Cristobalite forms only very slowly at 1060°C. and above. A 1080–1100°C. firing, with soaking, is therefore necessary to achieve significant results. Very finely ground flint or quartz will form cristobalite more rapidly. Prepared cristobalite can be purchased and added to a body. Remedies for crazing must be used with discretion.

Free silica in the body must be kept below 20%. To go too far in the alteration of glaze and body can build up too great a compression with subsequent *shattering*. Also a fired body with expansions in the cooking temperature range will suffer thermal shock, which may cause the crazing, during normal household use, of a glaze which came whole from the kiln.

Ordinary precautions include careful temperature control, neither under- nor *over-firing*; the *soaking* of soft glazes for 20 minutes or so; refraining from opening the kiln too early (above 100°C.); avoidance of sudden drafts of cold air at dull red heat and cooler.

An indication of glaze-body fit can be obtained from the degree of deformation of a thin bar of clay coated fairly thickly with glaze on one face only, and fired on its side on a bed of alumina. Ideally it should curve slightly with the glaze side convex. (See also *Seger's rules, Harkort test*.)

Slips can craze due to excess shrinkage. It becomes apparent during glazing when the cracks show up as thicker deposits. To cure, apply slip on slightly damper clay or stiffen the slip with a refractory material such as china clay or fireclay. Slip-cracking is more often due to wet/dry shrinkage than to firing reactions.

A quite distinct cause of crazing is water *adsorption* which slightly increases the volume of the body. This may show weeks or months after firing. A pot which is fully covered with a good glaze will not be at great risk.

CRISTOBALITE

A crystalline form of silica with an *inversion* which is greater than that of quartz (3% linear expansion as compared with around 1%), and taking place at a lower temperature, 220°C. Beta quartz will slowly convert to cristobalite from 1050°C. Conversion continues to 1550°C. and is therefore never complete in a pottery body. Lime is said to accelerate its formation. Even small amounts, however, can be valuable in the prevention of crazing, known by some potters as the 'cristobalite squeeze'. *Soaking* during the biscuit fire at around 1070°C. will help earthenware. It can be obtained in a synthesised form, often in conjunction with *tridymite*.

CROCUS MARTIS

A natural ferric oxide, Fe_2O_3, 'with some nitrate' (Billington); 'an anhydrous ferrous sulphate' (Hamer). Soluble, but partially decomposes at around 900°C., rendering it insoluble. May turn greenish in boric glazes. Can give darker browns than red ferric, and black with cobalt.

CROSS-DRAFT KILN

A semi-downdraft kiln usually with a single firemouth. (See figs. under *bag wall* and *chambered kiln*.)

CRUSHING ROCK

Small experimental quantities of rock can be crushed with a 2 lb. (1 kilo) hammer on a steel slab and then ground in a mortar and pestle, a teaspoonful at a time, or in a *jar mill* or *ball mill*. Larger quantities require a jaw crusher and a plate mill, normally beyond the resources of the craft potter. A rare exception was Harry Davis who crushed and compounded local Cornish rocks into glazes. Rocks vary very greatly in hardness, see *Moh's scale*.

Calcining to around 900°C. will loosen the bonds between molecules and render the rock easier to crush. A hammer (with the rock well covered under thick cloth, e.g. a strong sack) may then be sufficient to break it up. The easier way is to collect rock dust from granite and other workings. Read Sutherland GNS, Cardew PP, and Davis PA, for practical details.

Harry Davis describes a rock crusher made by West Shore Machine Works (Box 512, Trona, California 93562) which is hand operated and will crush one kilo of rock to mesh size in a few minutes. (See also *vibratory mill*.)

CRYOLITE

A sodium-aluminium fluoride Na_3AlF_6, 210 (convenient formula weight 420). Fires to $3Na_3O. Al_2O_3$. m.p. 1020°C.

Can be used as a source of insoluble soda, but the accompanying fluorine will bubble through the glaze on escaping during the firing, and will leave pinholes unless the glaze is very fluid. The alumina is likely to give a matt surface. Used in the vitreous enamels.

CRYSTAL, crystallization

Molecules or *lattices* which have built up into a three-dimensional repeat pattern. The solid substance assumes an individual and geometric form with plane faces. Most pure materials can be found in crystalline form, the large crystals often used as gemstones, e.g. crystal-lized carbon as diamond or aluminium silicate as topaz. Crystals can be very large or micro-crystalline and invisible to the naked eye, as in clay or flint. They form either in the melted, fluid state, or in solution. Their study is a wide-ranging and fundamental science. Perfect crystals

The regular shapes built up by crystal formation in a tin/lead alloy.

may be transparent, hence the use of terms crystal-clear, or crystal-glass (the latter very much a misnomer). Non-crystalline materials are *amorphous*.

Crystals need time in which to form from a fluid compound. Glaze is normally cooled too quickly and remains largely *amorphous*, though some crystals can form to show as a matt surface if very small, or to sparkling or *aventurine* glazes if larger. A bright, clear glaze is wholly non-crystalline: it is a supercooled or frozen liquid.

High alumina or calcium glazes are apt to form crystalline matt glazes 'thought to be anorthite' (Cardew PP). Zinc and titanium promote crystallization. (See also *devitrification*.) Soluble material and very soft frits will recrystallize from a solution, e.g. a frit raku glaze. See further discussion in next entry.

CRYSTALLINE GLAZE

Glazes which have been subject to partial devitrification are dealt with to some degree under *aventurine glaze*. The crystals can vary from a slight all-over sparkle to large, striking, crystalline patterns. They are formed principally in the 900–700°C. range during cooling which should take place very slowly. Suitable glazes can be refired. Many of the glazes become very fluid and can run badly. Some potters accept this; use drip bowls beneath the pieces; and spend a long time grinding off. Alumina in the glaze is kept at a minimum. Stephen Booth in CR 80 goes as far as leaving out alumina altogether and using only zinc oxide, soda, and silica—a very fluid glaze. He gives a four hour soak at 1080°C. after cooling rapidly from 1290°C. Titanium, zinc, cal-cium, magnesium, and ilmenite (some form of iron ox-ide is mentioned in most recipes) are quoted as useful in initiating or 'seeding' (Hamer) the process. Parmalee recommends using elements with low atomic weights: calcium, magnesium, iron, lithium, and, to a lesser degree, titanium, uranium, phosphorus, and bismuth. Kenneth Clark (Clark PM) gives some percentage limits: alkaline or borax frit 45–62, flint 5–21, zinc oxide 22–27, titanium dioxide 5–9, fired to 1260°C., cooled rapidly to around 1140°C. then very slowly for the next 60–100 degrees. Rada mentions up to 25% of rutile with 5% each of copper and manganese. The main difference between crystalline and aventurine glazes is that, in the latter, the crystals are embedded in the glaze and are usually smaller.

CUENCA

A Spanish decorating method used on countless thou-sands of tiles and other pottery in which the areas within raised outlines of a design are filled with glaze or color, similar in technique to cloisonne enamel. The depressed areas can be formed by stamping, casting, slip-trailing, or can be cut away from a flat surface. Glazes or colors are poured, trailed, or brushed on. (See also *tube lining*.)

A striking copper luster tile pattern from Granada, the pools of color held apart by lines in relief.

CULL

US equivalent of a 'waster', a kiln-spoiled pot.

CULLET

Pieces of colored glass used in pottery decoration. Also supplied, finely ground, as a cheap but variable glaze flux.

CUP

The design of a cup should always be considered in relation to the saucer on which it is set. There must be enough room under the handle to accommodate a spoon and to allow the cup to be lifted without tipping it. The handle itself should be easily gripped without the fingers contacting the hot cup surface. The lip should not turn inwards nor flare excessively. A heavy handle will deform a thin rim in the firing, if not before.

In common with the teapot and the jug the cup form has been taken over as an art object or what is fashionably known as an 'icon' by various potters, notably Ron Nagle; 'not cups but about cups', Garth Clark.

CUP HEAD

A hollow *wheel head*. Can be used for supporting circu-

lar molds, e.g. for *jigger and jolley*, or for turning narrow-necked pots. (See also *molds, turning*.)

CUP LAWN

A small conical or cup-shaped sieve, usually of metal, and 2–3 in. (50–75 mm.) wide.

CUPRUM, cupric, cuprous

Copper Cu. The cupric is the higher oxide CuO, cuprous the lower or reduced oxide Cu_2O. (See *copper*.)

CURRENT, electric

The flow of electricity as measured in *amperes*. (See *electricity*.)

CUT BRICK

Soft insulating bricks can be cut into relief or intaglio patterns for stamping onto soft clay to produce three-dimensional textures or more controlled designs. Can also be used as a stamp for printing.

CUT-CORNER DISH

A slab technique for making dishes. Allows variations in size and shape which the mold denies. It has its limitations, and some practice is necessary. The dishes look their best in a fairly chunky style. They can be stoneware fired.

The photographs show the principal stages. The template, cut in stiff paper, is laid on a slab or fairly soft plastic clay, and the clay cut to shape. The corners must be cut at a slant so that they can be overlapped to give a strong joint. The surfaces are slipped, the sides raised up until the corner can be luted together. Overlap the faces by about $\frac{1}{8}$ in. (2 mm.) to avoid any thinness when the joint is worked together. Supports must be prepared.

Stages in making a cut-corner dish.
(1) A template is cut from a sheet of paper folded in four.

The inside face can be smoothed with a *kidney rubber* and, later on, with a *steel palette*. The top edge will need trimming flat and the back must be scraped or planed when stiff. Any style of decoration can be used on these dishes. A fairly fine grog in the clay helps, especially for stoneware.

(5) Clay supports in position to hold the dish in shape while it stiffens up.

(2) The clay slab is cut to the template shape.

(3) The corner segment is cut at a 45° slope.

(6) The joins must be gently smoothed over and the inside of the dish shaped by stroking with a rubber kidney. When leather-hard the inside can be further smoothed and the outside finished with a steel palette or plane.

CUT LINER

Also called a 'sword liner'. A soft squirrel brush cut at an angle and pointed at the end.

CUT PAPER RESIST

See *paper resist*.

CUT SPONGE

Originally patterns were cut from the dense root of a sponge for printing pigment onto pottery. More open and free-formed designs can be 'printed' with foam sponges which can be cut, or burnt away with a hot metal rod into a broad pattern.

(4) With the segment removed the faces are slipped and brought up together.

CUTTING CLAY

The choice of tools for cutting clay will depend on its state of dryness. For plastic clay a wire can be used for trimming the rims of molded dishes and the like, a wooden spatula tool or a very fine metal tool such as a needle awl. If wide metal tools are used on soft clay they will tend to stick and tear. For leather-hard clay, use a slender *knife* with a good handle. When cutting clay for slab pots take care to hold the knife vertical and always draw it towards you. For a new cut turn the clay; do not turn the knife to an awkward angle.

Cutting through a block of clay with shaped wires or tools can also provide interesting and dramatic surface patterns, textures, or bold, three-dimensional results as shown in the illustrations as *texture*.

CUTTING OFF

After throwing, pots are normally cut from the wheel with a twisted wire or thread. This may be drawn through the base, holding the stretched wire hard down on the wheel head with the index fingers and cutting away from the body. The Japanese method is to hold a thread at one end only, allowing the free end to wind round the base of the pot, then to give it a sharp horizontal pull. This involves throwing the pot on a mound of clay an inch or two above the wheel head.

The two-handed technique will give various patterns beneath your pot according to whether you pull the wire through straight, allow it to curve as you cut, or cut as the wheel is coming to a halt.

(2) The typical shell pattern from a twisted wire used just before the wheelhead comes to a halt.

CUTTING WIRE

A wire for cutting pots from the wheel should be strong, fine and flexible. It is difficult to find one material which combines these qualities and which will also twist into the stranded form which acts like the 'set' of a saw, thus making the cutting both easier, more efficient, and decorative in the bargain. Steel wire is too springy for comfort; copper is too weak. A brass wire with a steel strand, as sold for picture hanging, is a compromise. Nylon is strong but will not remain twisted. A fine nylon can be plaited.

The degree of twist is important. It should not be too tight; the normal twisted steel wire is too finely wound. The gauge of wire used should be heavier for wedging and cutting blocks of clay. Coarse nylon can be useful here. Treat cutting wires with care and avoid pulling a loop which may result in an eradicable kink. Bends can be smoothed out by pulling the wire tightly back and forth across a piece of wood or table-edge. Wires for *harps* and multiple cutters can be of steel, sometimes known as 'piano wire'.

Handles are essential (it is painful to use a wire loop). They can be of wood dowelling, or made from clay and fired. Wires of varying lengths are required: a long wire shortened by twisting it round the fingers will not last long—neither will the fingers.

Fastening the wire to the handles or toggles is a perennial problem. If the ends are simply twisted round to fasten them they can present danger to the fingers. Soldering is one answer: the use of a sheath such as the rubber covering of electric cable, is another. Some potters bypass the difficulty by using fishing line and other types of thread. For more ideas see Fournier PT.

(1) Cutting through the base of a thrown pot, holding the wire hard down onto the wheelhead with the forefingers while drawing it under the base.

D

DAMP-CUPBOARD, damp-room, damp box

A cool, airtight cupboard with non-absorbent walls. A saturated atmosphere is built up which ceases to absorb further moisture from the pots. There has often been some confusion, especially on the part of school architects, on the subject of damp-cupboards. Various measures, such as trays of wet plaster—even felt walls in one new building—have been tried. But every time the door is opened (in a school read 'left open') the built-up humidity is dispersed. The damp-cupboard is now virtually obsolete, having been replaced by the widespread use of polythene. A cool cupboard with well-fitting doors by all means, but polythene as well!

A clay cellar or damp-room as described by Cardew PP is a major construction and suitable only for the large-scale professional potter. For the amateur, the polythene box or well-sealed plastic bag has happily replaced the rusting biscuit tins of a few years ago.

DAMPER

A sliding plate which can close or decrease the chimney opening and thus the draft through the kiln. Must be of stout iron or of refractory ceramic. The removal of a chimney brick will have a similar effect, by-passing the pull through the kiln chamber.

DARNING HEAD

A wooden mushroom shape used normally for darning, but useful to potters for pressing clay into molds and formers. Very useful if you can find one (but does anyone darn these days!) or you can make one.

DE-AIRING CLAY

The removal of air from clay by passing it through a partial vacuum, usually in a special *pug mill*. The clay must be shredded prior to de-airing. De-aired clay is denser and, reputedly, more plastic. For the enthusiast Harry Davis invented a splendid de-airing pug. Though he is, alas, with us no more he has left plans for this and a multitude of other machinery and tools in his book, Davis *The Potter's Alternative*.

DECAL, Decalomania

Lithographic *transfers* (U.S.A.). The term 'decalomania' has been traced to the craze among amateur potters and pottery decorators for paper transfers at the end of the nineteenth century in America.

DECOMPOSITION

The breaking up of chemical compounds. During firing carbonates decompose into the oxide and CO_2 which is given off as a gas, red lead breaks down, $(2Pb_3O_4) = 6PbO + O_2$, and so on. Vegetable and other organic matter present in clay will decompose at about 200°C, but the residual carbon will not burn away until the temperature has reached 800–1000°C.

In a slightly different sense glazes can decompose with age. (See also at *devitrification*.)

DECORATION

Two voices from the past, discussing the decoration of pottery, still have valid points to make for today: Dora Billington (Billington TP) 'Design freely, do what and only what pleases you, and only apply principles as an aid to criticism if something goes wrong', and Leach 'Subordinate to form but intimately connected with it is the problem of decoration and whether the increased orchestration adds to the total effect or not'.

Dora Billington goes on 'diffidently' to give advice on the fundamental basis of design and discusses scale, balance, variety, contrast and tension; the last conspicuously absent from much modern work. Her remarks are based on a lifetime of experience and are well worth assimilating. The potter Kenneth Clark also gives advice from a painter's point of view. His 'range of visual contrasts' is useful (Clark PC).

It is difficult to disassociate decoration from some of the discredited nineteenth century ideas of 'applied art'. For a time, especially during the 1960's, many potters followed the rule: 'if in doubt, don't!'. 'Texture' and 'glaze quality' were paramount.

Recent times, however have seen a much more uninhibited approach, with bright colors both in underglaze and enamels. A glance at the pottery of the past from Suza slip to Spanish luster will indicate a perennial preoccupation with over-all decorated ceramics with as much brilliance of color as the craft will allow. Much of the work has been in earthenware but the white ground of porcelain, too, invites and aids brilliance of tone. Our palette has also been enlarged with chrome colors, selenium, and the like.

The techniques of pottery decoration are discussed under *sgraffito*, *slip trailing*, *brushwork*, *wax resist*, *applied decoration*, *beaten decoration* and *paper resist*.

DEFLOCCULATION

The dispersion of particles especially in a clay slip leading to increased *fluidity*. Its prime use is in *casting slip*. It assists particle *suspension* and reduces comparative shrinkage (less water is needed) in a body mixture. It is achieved by the use of an *electrolyte* (usually sodium) in silicate or carbonate (soda ash) form. The electrolyte alters charges on the molecules, causing them to hold away from one another (disperse). Potassium carbonate will have the same effect. Sodium tannate, pyrophosphate, and other compounds are used in special cases. If a clay already contains *free alkali* it will not defloculate. Excess deflocculant will reverse the effect, the slip thickening again, while coarse grained materials such as flint will not defloculate at all.

Recipes and instructions for using electrolytes appear in most suppliers' catalogs (see also Rhodes CGP 29–32). For maximum effect the balance is a delicate one and will vary from body to body. Add electrolyte drop by drop if you are working with liquid slip, or weigh dry against dry powdered body according to the advice of the suppliers of the body. 'One half per cent dry weight will turn soft plastic clay into slip' (Billington). Potclays market 'Sodium Dispex' for which they claim 'improved stability amd mold life'. Sodium silicate is sold in *Twaddle* degrees.

DEFLUORINATED STONE

China stone from which fluorine has been extracted, now often listed by merchants. May help to prevent *pinholes* in glaze.

DEFORMATION

Pyroplastic deformation occurs at the temperature at which a ceramic body can no longer hold its shape due to the formation of molten compounds within the fabric. It is normally a slow and continuing process, but can be quite sudden in high-calcium bodies and artificial low-temperature porcelains. Deformation usually leads to slumping. *Warping* may have other causes (see *plastic memory*).

Kiln shelves are tested for 'deformation under load'. The softening effect occurs at each firing so that a curved or sagged shelf can be reversed in the next firing. (See *kiln shelves*.)

DEHYDRATION

The removal of water. In pottery generally confined to the loss of the *chemically combined water* in clay at 600–700°C.

DELIQUESCENT

A material which will absorb moisture from the air to such a degree that it will itself become liquid. The commonest deliquescent pottery material is potassium carbonate. (See also *hygroscopic*.)

DELTA WIRING

See *star and delta*, *three phase*.

DEVITRIFICATION

The change from a glassy to *crystalline* state. Glaze may partially devitrify during a slow cooling (see *aventurine*, *crystalline*, *matt*) giving a frosty look 'common in high clay or silica glazes' (Rhodes), or, in the case of glazes designed to crystallize readily, larger, often striking colored crystal formations.

Soft glazes, especially the early high-soda glazes from the Near East, will devitrify with great age, often developing a silvery or iridescent sheen which may obliterate the decoration. The effect is similar to that on very old glass and is most marked on early Islamic alkaline glazes. If melted glass, especially colored or stained-glass, is used in the embellishment of pots it can sometimes devitrify on cooling. (See *melted glass decoration*.)

A much magnified view of the remarkable crystalline pattern, resembling frost, developed by glass which has started to devitrify during cooling. To the naked eye it appears as a whitish rough patch about $\frac{1}{2}$ in. (8mm.) across.

DEWATERING CLAY

The drying of *slip* to plastic clay. It is the practice in the pottery industry to render all bodies to slips, which are then *filter-pressed* to a plastic state. A craft potter can easily rig up a blunger but, in temperate climes at any rate, the dewatering of the slip is a major problem. The slip will settle and the surplus water can be poured, scooped, or siphoned off but we are still left with a runny slurry. If space is available this can be poured into cloth bags (a fine one inside a stronger coarser one) which can be hung up to drip and stiffen, like cheeses for three or four days. Dave White recommends old corduroy trousers with the leg bottoms sewn up! and Mrs. S. Hardwick an old leaky wheelbarrow lined with denim (see Fournier PT). Plaster or biscuit molds, raised on blocks are useful for small quantities but soon saturate. Shallow troughs such as those used at St. Ives need roofing over if they are not to flood in winter, and they entail space and time. In hot weather the simplest method is that practised by Harry Davis: the slip is poured into a large sheet spread in a depression in the ground, the corners of the sheet being brought together and knotted. The knot acts as a wick, the water is drawn up and evaporates in the sun. Davis has also designed a piece of home-made dewatering equipment which is an ingenious reversal of the industrial filter-press. In it the water is extracted by suction in a semi-vacuum. See Davis PA. At Soil Hill Pottery the hot gases from the kiln were drawn under a long brick trough before they reached the chimney. Cardew shows plans for brick dewatering-troughs in PP 85.

Most potters bypass the problem by buying plastic clay or by mixing clay powder and water in a dough mixer.

DIASPORE, diaspore clay

Diaspore is a hydrated alumina, found in massive form. The term diaspore clay is used for one rich in alumina, valuable for making *refractories*.

DIATOMITE

Sometimes called 'infusorial earth' or 'Kieselguhr'. Formed from the accumulation of the siliceous remains of minute aquatic vegetable organisms (diatoms). It has very high porosity and heat resistance up to about 800°C. making it a useful, if limited, kiln insulation material. It can be used as granules, or as bricks cut from reefs, the granules are also used as a concrete aggregate for insulation. *Ceramic fiber* and other synthetic insulators with greater refractoriness have all but replaced diatomite.

DIE

A *pug* or *wad box* attachment which fastens over the mouth of the machine. The clay is forced through holes to form coils and other shapes. Some very large forms can be made in this way, see *extrusion*.

A 'die-press' is a damp-clay tile press.

DIELECTRIC

Capable of withstanding electrical stresses, e.g. porcelain insulators. An iron-free *vitrified* body is essential.

DIGITAL

The indication of temperature, time, etc in actual numbers instead of by a marker on a dial as on the older style of pyrometer. For firing, digital readings are obviously more precise—so long as the instrument is accurate. See *controlling pyrometer*, *pyrometer* for comments.

DILATANCY

The opposite of *thixotropy*, i.e. becoming less fluid when stirred or under pressure. Wet sand 'dilates'. Dodd mentions ceramic bodies which are deficient in fine particles, the coarser ones dilating, which is the opposite effect to that required by the potter.

DIOPSIDE

A calcium mineral, free of alumina, $CaO.MgO.2SiO_2$. Occurs as a crystal and in basalt, and can be precipitated from glazes high in dolomite, giving a matt surface.

DIRECT CURRENT

Or DC. Electric current flowing in one direction only. Batteries and most home generators will develop direct current. The normal mains supply is *alternating current*.

DIRECT FIRING

Given by Dodd as synonymous with open firing i.e. firing without saggars.

DISAPPEARING FILAMENT PYROMETER

See *optical pyrometer*.

DISH

A shallow container which may be thrown, molded or built. *The Concise Oxford Dictionary* defines it as a 'flat-bottomed, usually oval or oblong vessel'. Both of these shapes can be developed from thrown dishes by cutting the base (see *oval shapes*) or by *beating*. Molded dishes benefit from good craftsmanship and a tidy finish. It is because the technique seems simple that those made by students and in schools are often scamped and poor.

The method for non-circular molded dishes is shown in the figures under *pressed dishes*. For dishes made over, rather than in, a plaster or biscuit mold, see *hump mold*. For cutting circular molded dishes a wheel is needed. The mold is dropped into a *cup-head* or centred and fixed to the wheelhead. The clay slab is eased into or over it (*hollow* or *hump* mold) and roughly trimmed. The final cutting of the rim is done on the spinning wheel with a wooden spatula tool. Hold the tool with both hands, approach the surface of the clay slowly, and hold the tool firmly as it cuts into it.

Andrew and Joanna Young make large dishes by throwing the rim or wall and luting it to a separately made base with a coil pressed into the join. By this method any plan (shape of dish) can be accommodated and the rim given crispness and character on square, oblong, or oval forms. For circular flat-bottomed dishes and plates, a coil can be attached to a thrown base and the rim formed from it on the wheel. A variation on the simple method of making a shallow rectangular dish shown at *former* is demonstrated in CR 72; a flat wooden block is placed on a slab of clay and the whole reversed, the block underneath. Wooden edge pieces are then used to press the clay over the edge of the block. The whole is reversed again, the top surfaces of the edge pieces (2–3 in. wide) forming a wide rim. The clay is trimmed and the blocks removed as soon as it is stiff enough to stand its own weight (David Morris).

Molded dishes do not develop that parallel-plated structure in the clay fabric which gives thrown ware its strength and stability (see *clay, lamellar, plasticity*) and they are thus more liable to warp if not well supported during drying and firing. With the exception, perhaps, of flat-based pie dishes they are rarely suitable for stoneware firings. The method of making *cut corner* dishes is described under its heading. See also *oval dishes*. Slab and coil dishes are possible though perhaps less suitable for kitchen use.

DISINTEGRATION OF GLAZE
See *devitrification*.

DISSOCIATION
The reversible decomposition or alteration of the *molecules* of a compound. In pottery dissociation is usually brought about by heat, the products recombining on cooling, e.g. the reoxidation of ferrous iron to ferric where it can come into contact with the oxygen in the air.

DISTINGUISHING STAIN
An organic dye which will burn away on firing and is used to identify otherwise similarly colored bodies, glazes, etc. At Bullers Electrical Porcelain factory the

bright pink and blue large-scale electrical porcelains are quite striking!

DISTORTION
See *deformation, clay memory, pyroplastic, warping*.

DOD BOX
See *wad mill*.

DOG'S TEETH, dragon's teeth
Irregular tears in an extruded length of clay from the *pug*. Caused by friction against the mouth of the pug or the edge of a die. Clay which is too dry, *short*, or unevenly mixed is liable to this fault, but a badly cleaned pug mill is most often to blame.

DOLOMITE
A mineral $CaCO_3.MgCO_3$, 184. The double carbonate of calcium and magnesium. Typical analysis: CaO 31%. MgO 20%. Loss (CO_2) 43%, minor impurities: silica 1.5, with other bases and alumina 4.5%. The calcia content is sometimes greater than these figures suggest. The high 'loss' (L.o.i.) figure is, of course, due to the dispersal of the CO_2.

Dolomite is used mainly in stoneware glazes (temperatures above about 1175°C.). Although of worldwide occurrence it only became generally available to the craft potter in the 1960's but has enjoyed a considerable vogue since. There are other suitable sources of calcia but insoluble magnesia is less common. (See *talc*.)

Dolomite acts as a *flux* but, if used to replace whiting, it will raise the maturing temperature of a glaze. (See *magnesium*.) Average proportion in a glaze is 3–6% but up to 20% can be used for special effects. 2% or so may be added to a porcelain body. The typical magnesia effect derived from the use of dolomite is a smooth, buttery surface. With higher concentrations and slower cooling, however, it tends to form crystals of calcium and magnesium silicates with a consequent, *matt* surface.

DOUBLE GLAZING
See *glaze-over-glaze*.

DOUBLE EUTECTIC
See *eutectic*.

DOUGH MIXERS
These machines, until recently used by small bakers, have found a new lease of life in craft potteries for mixing powdered clay and bodies with water into a plastic state, thus bypassing the blunger, drier etc.

Large mixers can deal with 150 kg. (330 lb.) of dry powder and water in 30 minutes; smaller ones 100 kg. (220 lb.) an hour. There are two types: the one illustrated in which the arm moves forward, down and up, turning and mashing the mixture; and the revolving arm type. The former needs some attention but the latter can be quite automatic in its action.

A large dough mixer from an old bakery used to ease the labor of mixing clays and water into a condition suitable for pugging or wedging. The revolving pronged arm alternately turns and mashes the mixture. About 30 cwt. (170 kilograms) can be prepared in thirty minutes from dry clay (here being emptied into it by Mick Casson) and water.

DOWNDRAFT KILN

A kiln in which the hot gases from the fireboxes rise first to the roof and are then drawn down through the setting and out into the chimney through flues in the kiln floor. The heat is better distributed and more efficiently used than in an *up-draft* kiln. The hot gases can be subsequently channelled under a brick floor for drying clay or pots. Rhodes K 48–53, shows several types of downdraft kilns, while Cardew PP 184 discusses the general principles. A good chimney is needed to exert the necessary 'pull' which forces the heat downwards against its

inclination. A starting-fan or small chimney fire may be used to create the initial draft.

Climbing kilns and the Western two or three *chambered kilns* utilize a diagonal downdraft.

A down-draft kiln with more than one fire mouth.

DRAFT

The upward movement of hot gases as a result of their expansion, and their replacement by further air from the atmosphere. This process is controlled in a fuel-burning kiln by the concentrated rising column in the chimney, the replacement air being drawn through the firebox or through secondary air vents. A slide or check put across the chimney, or a vent in the chimney (withdrawal of a brick) will both decrease draft.

Forced-draft may be introduced either by the use of a fan to speed the exit of gas in the chimney, or by pumping compressed air or gas into the kiln at the firemouth.

Draft is dependent on the diameter and height of the chimney and on the sizes of inlet and outlet apertures relative to the *expansion of gas*. (See also Cardew PP 180–6.)

DRAINOIL

Dennis Parks PGRG deals extensively with the use of waste oil for firing. The main disadvantage (apart from the smell and mess of dealing with it and removing any unwanted solids) is the high flashpoint which is around 245°C. as against 40°C. kerosene. An efficient starter fuel such as propane or wood is therefore essential. On the other hand the fuel is obtainable without charge and has a high heat value per gallon. See *Btu*, and *fuels*. Good kiln design and efficient burning can minimise the smoke produced.

Parks gives a number of suggestions for burners: both *drip-feed*, and pressure types. He reverts to diesel during reduction. Oil/water mixtures have also been used.

DRAPE MOLD

An American term for a mold or former over which a slab of clay is pressed or 'draped'. (See *hump molds*, *formers*.)

DRAWING A KILN

Unpacking a kiln.

DRAW TRIAL

A test piece withdrawn from the kiln during firing. Only practical with a large spyhole or when a brick can easily be withdrawn. *Buller's rings*, glazed rings or small pots can be quickly cooled and inspected. They will show shrinkage and the degree to which the glaze has melted, but color and other characteristics will be falsified to some extent by the rapid cooling. (See also *glaze melt indicator*.)

DRIP-FEED, oil

A simple type of burner in which the oil is dripped onto a heated metal plate or plates. The heat *volatilizes* the oil, which will then ignite. An ingenious horizontal box burner is illustrated in Rhodes K 69–70.

There must be some method of supplying initial heat to the pan to start the process. This could be by the use of a more volatile material such as paraffin (kerosene), or with a gas jet (perhaps *bottled gas*). Cotton waste to soak up oil and act as a wick has also been suggested. An oil and water mixture, dripped simultaneously from separate jets, has been found to be more efficient than oil alone. The plate must be protected from too direct an inrush of cold air. It has a relatively short life, but the whole burner is so simple that this is no great drawback. An attractive looking design using a small coke fire to

An oil-drip pan based on a design in Rhodes K. Oil and water are dipped onto it from above. A removable gas jet is shown which can heat the plates in order to start the process without too much smoke. Oil, of course, will burn only as a vapor.

heat the drip pan, and utilizing a reverbatory design, was published in PQ 7 by John Dan.

It has been found that drip-feed systems are very smoky, especially early in the firing, and an open site is required. They have other limitations and are not suitable for large kilns. On the other hand crude or sump oil can be used for cheapness. The firing is liable to be smoky, and, with today's sensitivity to the emission of smoke and gases, it is advisable to be as efficient as possible in the burning of all fuels.

DRYING OF CLAY AND GLAZE

Drying from slip to plastic state is dealt with under *dewatering*.

When plastic clay dries, water evaporates from the surface which becomes porous, further moisture being drawn by capillary attraction from the body of the clay. This action is sufficient to bring a thin-walled piece of pottery into balance with the humidity of the surrounding air. Further evaporation requires artificial heat or a drier atmosphere, and is assisted by the movement of air. The dryness of the air explains why clay may dry more rapidly on a cold night when most of the water in the air has been precipitated than on a humid day in summer.

Drying is accompanied by shrinkage. A thick wall of close-texture clay will tend to enclose a core of moisture which will have difficulty in getting away.

This slows down the capillary effect and is the reason why a pot seems to stay *leather-hard* for quite a time and then change color quite quickly. The inclusion of grog or other coarse-grained material is necessary to maintain open pores in thick pots or models. Shrinkage is caused by the particles of clay packing closer together as the layers of water between them disappear; the greatest shrinkage is therefore from plastic to leather-hard. At leather-hard the lubrication between particles is poor and they can be moved relative to one another only by careful beating. When dry this lubrication is nil. Rapid drying is not dangerous in itself, but any unevenness in the drying will cause one part of a pot to shrink, putting the fabric into tension which can be relieved only by warping or cracking.

The precise state of dryness is not easy to establish. As mentioned above, *ambient* air humidity will control natural drying. A pot, even though thoroughly dried over heat, will reabsorb moisture if left long before firing. There are various ways of testing for dryness: David Leach places the rim or other surface of a warm pot against a pane of glass; any steam will soon be precipitated onto the glass. A thick-walled piece may be too hot to touch and yet still show steam if a piece of glass or plastic is held over the mouth of the pot.

Apart from the water mixed with the clay, which is driven off at 100°C., there remains the more stubborn adsorbed water which may need 200°C. to disperse fully. (See *absorbed water, water-smoke*.)

The technique of *wet-firing* (described in CR 1) seems to contradict these statements, but other factors are at work here (e.g. the cooling effect of very rapid evaporation) and the system is hedged about with special provisions.

Not only the clay but also glazes, especially *soft glazes* although it is equally recommended for stonewares, should be fully dried *before* packing in the kiln for firing, in order to avoid blistering and other faults.

DRYING SHRINKAGE

The shrinkage of a clay or body from plastic to dry is usually expressed as a linear percentage. Dodd quotes 6–10% for china clay; 9–12% for ball clay. Most of this occurs up to the leather-hard stage. Drying shrinkage is one indication of the value of a clay sample (see *clay tests*). It is useful to work out the factor for your particular clay body; it will allow you to calculate the size of a lid, for instance, which is needed for a dried pot. The equation is $\frac{X}{Y} \times \frac{100}{1}$, where X is the percentage shrinkage of your test-piece and Y is the dry length of the test-piece. Example:

$$\frac{15 \text{ (\% shrinkage)}}{85 \text{ (dry length)}} \times 100 = 17\%.$$

The lid, therefore, needs to be 17% larger than the dried pot. For replacement lids of fired pots the calculations are more difficult but could still be based on a wet clay to fired ceramic test strip, (though there are other factors involved here so don't be too hopeful!). Hamer has an extensive analysis of the science and mechanics of drying. (See also *shrinkage*.)

DRY STRENGTH

Clays vary greatly in their dry strength. A porcelain body will be very weak, a *secondary clay* may be nearly as hard as *biscuit*. Dry strength is probably increased by a well-graded particle size from medium to very fine, allowing a close 'pack'. It is associated with plasticity. Ball clays have a high dry strength, partly due to their fine grain, but also to the lignin humus (organic wood tissue) content of 'black' ball clays. Coarse-grained bodies such as porcelain will be easily shattered.

The form of a pot and the technique used in making it will have some effect on its dry strength. A bottle or other well-rounded thrown shape has greater resistance to knocks and stresses than, for instance, a slab trough or a molded dish.

Resinous and fibrous bodies have been developed to obviate the firing of clay models in schools, e.g. *Newclay*. They can be useful in the wider field of modelling or handbuilding for dry strength, and can be thrown, though there is little advantage in the latter case.

DUNTING

The cracking of pottery in the kiln due to drafts of cold air striking it when firing or cooling, causing one area to contract more than the rest. *Free quartz* will increase the risk of dunting at dull red heat, and *cristobalite* at lower temperatures. A more rapid rate of cooling from top temperature to about 1100°C. will lessen the chances of this happening by keeping the silica in flux. A more vitrified body: one containing more fluxes or fired to greater maturity will lessen the chances of dunting from silica inversions.

Thermal shock can cause cracking during the use of a piece after firing. A poor glaze fit, especially one in excessive compression, can crack a piece during firing or afterwards; and at the other extreme high shrinkage of thick glaze can also tear a pot apart as sometimes happens when *melted glass* is used decoratively. Tensions can be set up during uneven drying of the clay, or even before that through excessive moisture or insufficient working on the base of a pot; too great a discrepancy between the thicknesses of various parts of the piece; or, of course, by a blow or pressure. Variations in cooling between pot and kiln shelf can cause dunting of the base wall; large flat dishes or tall pots especially should be raised on rings, clay wads, or setters. Rapid all-over cooling will not necessarily cause dunting—if it did, there would be no raku. *Sawdust firing* is very prone to severe dunting if not protected from draft. Ray Finch once-fires his large plates to minimize dunting, while others set large flat plates on clay wads so that they will not be affected by the different cooling rate of the kiln shelf. (See also *cracking, shattering*.)

DUST

All excessive dust from pottery activities is a danger; there is no way out once inorganic materials settle in your lungs. The cheapest way to lay dust is to sprinkle water on it. There are also *sweeping compounds*. In particular danger are potters who habitually abrade dry clay or biscuit, as are those who regularly use sprays for glazing. A light *mask*, costing very little, will help. See *poisonous materials* for specific dangerous minerals.

DUSTER, flat duster

An unlikely name, used in the industry for a soft flat brush, $\frac{1}{4}$ in.–1 in. (6–25 mm.) wide, for laying on background colour.

EARTHENWARE

The dictionary definition is 'vessels of baked clay'; in general usage it indicates pottery ware with a porous body which may or may not be covered with glaze. The Brussels Nomenclature agrees with this definition but excludes 'pottery made from common clay'—we are not told what this is to be called. The bulk of all ceramics has been earthenware, ranging from the 1200°C. fine-grained 'Queen's ware' of Wedgwood, to a soft, red 'earthen platter' from Portugal, and including majolica, delft, faience, and most slipwares. Many of the Near Eastern pots are in an anomalous position, as is *soft paste*.

The same clay body can sometimes be used to produce earthenware or stoneware, according to whether it is been taken to vitrification temperature or not, but, in general, mixtures of various clays, and sometimes other minerals, are blended specifically for a given range of firing temperatures. The dividing line between earthenware and stoneware is normally in the region of 1200°C. but the craft potter's earthenware is rarely taken above 1150°C. and more often fifty degrees or so below this figure. Because of its innate porosity the body of earthenware is usually entirely covered with glaze unless the porosity is utilised for keeping water cool or other particular purposes.

EARTHENWARE GLAZE

Also known as 'soft' glazes. Broadly speaking, they are those glazes which mature below 1150°C. and are used to cover a porous body. The typical earthenware glaze is shiny and smooth; it can be brilliant and transparent, or white and fully opaque, the latter providing a background for bright clear colors. Its qualities have been exploited through the ages giving us splendid slipwares, painted tin glazes, lusters, intense turquoise colors, raku, underglaze decoration, and enamels, from all parts of the world.

The formulas for earthenware glazes differ from those of stoneware and porcelain mainly in their choice of *bases*, and in the ratio of base to silica. A soft glaze can be prepared with soda as the only *flux* (the basis of Egyptian turquoise), but these are unstable, difficult to handle, and they always craze. More commonly, lead oxide has been used as the sole or major base. This type is now called into question (see *soluble lead*), but a well-balanced and adequately fired lead glaze will be safe for the majority of tableware purposes. Lead gives a richness of quality which other fluxes cannot imitate. If a soft glaze does not contain lead oxide in significant amounts (at least 0.5 equivalents in the *RO group*) then it will need to contain boric oxide. This is generally added in the form of borax which is a soluble material and requires *fritting*. (See also *colemanite*.)

Soda, potash and lime are the usual secondary fluxes, with zinc oxide, lithia, strontia and magnesia sometimes playing a minor role. Boric oxide, though technically an acid and a *glassformer*, nevertheless lowers the melting point of a glaze and to this extent can be thought of as a fluxing agent. Lead and boron are used in the form of silica frits, the first because of its toxic nature; the second because it is soluble in water. Recipes are legion and we cannot explore them in detail, several are quoted in Rhodes, Billington, and a host of other manuals. It is more important to have some understanding of the principles, and to be able to use the *Seger formula*.

The RO/RO_2 ratio of the majority of soft glazes is between 1:2 and 1:3. The R_2O_3/RO_2 ratio is between 1:8 and 1:12. (R stands for any appropriate element.) A typical formula might therefore read:

1 RO : 0.25 Al_2O_3:2.5 SiO_2 where the RO group includes at least 0.5 PbO. If lead is absent, then boric oxide must comprise about 0.2 of the total RO_2 group (a little confusing as boric oxide is both a strong flux and chemically an acid). (See *base*, *formula into recipe*, *glaze*, and under all the glaze *oxides*.) A variety of bases will help to give a more transparent and fully matured glaze.

The choice of bases will also influence the color reaction of any *pigment oxides*. An increase in the alumina content will take the shine from the surface, opacifying agents will tend to harden and so raise the firing temperature; manganese will act as a flux. *Oxides, minerals* and *frits* can be combined in one batch—a mixture is, in fact, advisable. It makes the physical process of glazing easier. Earthenware glaze is generally applied as a somewhat thinner coating than are the stonewares; this is especially true if *frits* are used. A soaking fire of about twenty minutes will improve the quality of soft glazes and also the *glaze/body fit*. (See *crazing*, *glazing*, and other entries.)

EARTH LEAKAGE CIRCUIT BREAKER
See *E.L.C.B.*

EASY-FIRE
Firing terminated below the maturing temperature of a body. Soft biscuit.

EFFLORESCENCE ON CLAY
A white surface scum which forms during firing, or occurs later, usually on red clays. It cannot be easily removed, even with abrasives. It is caused by soluble salts, mainly calcium, but occasionally other bases, sulfur, or chlorine, migrating to the surface during drying as crystals, and being crushed in handling (the efflorescence is often recognisable as finger prints). Modelling or any pottery subject to a lot of handling is especially prone. The addition of 1–2% of barium carbonate to the body will help; Billington mentions a teaspoonful to a pint of red clay slip. In CR 123 Bo Ratcliffe finds (in connection with Egyptian paste) that the efflorescence may continue after firing (as happens in some bricks) which she prevents by steeping the raw clay in vinegar for 24 hours (a smelly remedy!). See also *Egyptian paste* for deliberate efflorescence and *lime blowing*.

EGOTE
Japanese name for a *throwing stick*.

Three Japanese egote or throwing sticks. They are of wood with one rounded or beveled edge.

EGYPTIAN PASTE
The body of the original Egyptian turquoise ceramics is reputed to be about 90% quartz with some soda. The glaze has been given as 75% silica, 20% alkalis and calcium, 1.8% copper oxide, by analysis. A. Lucas suggests common salt added to the body to give some dry strength and to add the soda flux. The body is very open and therefore *short*.

An approximation in modern materials may be made as a paste or body from which soluble glaze materials will 'migrate' or effloresce onto the surface during drying. It follows that the drying should be slow

and that the piece should be handled as little as possible. Place it on stilts ready for the kiln as soon as it is completed. Firing temperature 950–990°C.

No glaze is applied to the modern style of Egyptian paste, (although, as mentioned above, the ware was often glaze dipped in early times).

The usual colouring material is copper carbonate which gives the characteristic turquoise, but other *carbonates* can be used, e.g. manganese. The material has little plasticity when moist, and is friable when dry. It is generally restricted to jewelry and other small pieces, although the Ancient Egyptians achieved some very large objects.

Typical recipes:

A measure recipe (Behrens CM):
- Flint or quartz 16 spoons
- Bentonite 4 spoons
- Sodium bicarbonate 2 spoons
- Copper carbonate $\frac{1}{2}$ spoon

By percentage weights

Feldspar	35
Flint	35
China clay	12
Bentonite	2
Sodium bicarbonate	6
Sodium carbonate	6
Copper carbonate	2–3

A more plastic version given in CM 16/2:

Ball clay	25
Nepheline syenite	25
Frit ferro 3134	15
Flint	20
Fine sand	5
Anhydrous (calcined) borax	3
Soda ash	4
Bentonite	3
Copper carbonate	2–3

Dextrin or other *siccative* can be added for dry strength. Also note that copper carbonate is toxic. Variations may be made in the feldspar/flint ratio between 20 and 40%; some ball clay can replace china clay. Up to 5% of whiting is sometimes recommended, while borax can be used to supply soda. Soluble varieties of the color oxide, e.g. copper chloride, may help.

More recipes are given in Fournier PT.

EJECTOR HEAD
A wheel head in the form of a shallow dish, the base of which can be raised to eject a plaster or wooden throwing-bat. Useful for large pots or for *repetition throwing*. (See also *wheel bats*.) When casting plaster bats in ejector heads the inner surface must be lightly wiped over with Vaseline or similar grease.

A pot on a plaster bat being lifted from an ejector head by upward pressure on the metal ring underneath.

ELASTICITY

Strictly the word implies the resumption by a material to its original shape and size when forces acting on it are removed. In pottery it is used more loosely to suggest the ability of materials to withstand stress and in this sense is a valuable quality. It is said that lead glazes are more 'elastic' than others.

E.L.C.B.

An acronym for Earth Leakage Circuit Breaker; a type of electric trip switch which automatically isolates the demand from the supply if a fault occurs. It is usually fitted between the meter and the fused switch box, and is activated by any slight leak between line and earth. It can be manually reset by pushing the switch button upwards but if it fails to hold then the fault must be traced and corrected. It may sometimes 'trip' off during a thunderstorm and can even be affected by a neighbour's electrical fault if exterior leads to earth at not far enough apart.

A type of trip-switch is now often attached to individual pieces of equipment which, like the ELCB, both protects the user from electric shock and lessens the chance of having to perform the tedious business of repairing fuses.

ELECTRICAL INSULATION

See *insulation, electric.*

ELECTRICAL PORCELAIN

A very hard 'proto'-porcelain with high *dielectric* strength but little or no *translucency*, from which electrical insulators, switches etc are made. A recipe quoted is similar to that for industrial earthenware, but fired to *vitrification*: ball clay 28: china clay 22: quartz 25: feldspar 25. (See also *porcelain.*)

ELECTRICAL SYMBOL

The principle shorthand symbols used in electrical computations are:

1. Electromotive force, E, measured in volts, V.
2. Current, I, measured in amperes, A.
3. Power P, measured in watts, W.
4. Reistance R, measured on ohms, Ω.

See at *electricity* for further information.

ELECTRICITY

Electricity is a form of energy generated by the movements of electrons. The concept of electrical charge is the basis of *atomic science*, and enters into all chemical changes.

The term is commonly applied to the energy supplied as electric current either through metal cables from a generating-station or across the terminals of a battery. If a conducting material is placed across the terminals of an electric supply between that marked L, (which popularly is thought to stand for 'live' but actually stands for 'line'), and neutral (N), current will flow. It will flow to an excessive and dangerous degree if there is nothing to stop it, a state known as a short circuit. However all materials exhibit a greater or lesser *resistance* to this flow, and it is in overcoming resistance that electrical energy is converted into heat.

The heat produced is proportional to the square of the current flowing. Where resistance is total no current flows, and the material is known as an insulator; where current flows with negligible resistance the material is a conductor. Many materials, especially in the presence of water, fall between these extremes. Even the best conductors will get hot and eventually melt if too much current is passed through them. A conducting wire must therefore be stout enough to withstand the current it is expected to pass. As explained below, the thicker the wire the less resistance it will exert. *Kiln element* wire has a controlled resistance in-built to produce heat according to certain equations.

Electricity is supplied at a given 'pressure' (to use an

understandable but not quite accurate term) called the *voltage*; the amount of current is measured in *amperes*; the total power in *watts*. The resistance mentioned above is calculated in units called *ohms*. These four factors—voltage, symbol E (electromotive force), measured in Volts (V); current, symbol I, measured in Amperes (A); power, P, in Watts (W); and resistance R, in Ohms (Ω), are all interdependent. It is not necessary to understand the exact nature of these units to use them in simple electrical calculations.

Basic arithmetic:

If you have figures for any two unit values it is easy to arrive at a third by means of simple equations:

$$E = I \times R \quad \text{or} \quad \frac{P}{I} \quad \text{or} \quad \sqrt{P \times R}$$

$$I = \frac{P}{E} \quad \text{or} \quad \frac{E}{R} \quad \text{or} \quad \sqrt{\frac{P}{R}}$$

$$R = \frac{E}{I} \quad \text{or} \quad \frac{E^2}{P} \quad \text{or} \quad \frac{P}{I^2}$$

$$P = E \times I \quad \text{or} \quad \frac{E^2}{R} \quad \text{or} \quad I^2 \times R$$

To turn the equations into a specific example: If our supply is at 240 volts and we want to design a 10,000 watt (10 kilowatts or kW) kiln then we need to pass $\frac{10,000}{240} = 41.6$ amperes of current.

If the kiln is wired in a single *circuit*, the resistance of the total wire (all the elements in *series*) must be $\frac{240}{41.6} = 5.76$ ohms.

If it is to be wired in two circuits then *each* must pass $\frac{41.6}{2} = 20.8$ amperes, and the resistance in **each** circuit would need to be $\frac{240}{20.8} = 11.53$ ohms.

There are two laws concerning resistance in a wire which have, in fact, some parallel with the way water flows through a pipe. The first is that the thicker the wire (the greater the cross-sectional area) the less resistance it will offer and the greater amount of current will flow; and the second law states that the longer the wire the more resistance it will offer, and this will reduce the current which will flow. Thus a long thin wire will pass less current than a short thick one of the same type. These considerations must be borne in mind when conducting current to a kiln as well as in the kiln itself. (See under *electric kiln elements, electric wiring to kiln*.)

The third connection which you will find on all appliances is the E (earth) terminal. This is a safety measure. Normally the flow of current will be through the apparatus connected between Line and Neutral and will be under control. If, however, a 'live' conductor accidentally comes into contact with another conductor not in the circuit, current will start to flow through it and it will become 'live'. A direct line to the ground, especially under damp conditions, will conduct a very high current, heating up rapidly in the process. This sudden surge can cause electric shock (burning) in human beings, or fire in a building. The earth terminal is literally what it says it is—a connection direct to the ground which will help to siphon off current which has strayed out of the circuit, and out of control. A long continuation of the flow is prevented by the insertion of a weak link in every circuit (the fuse) which will melt and break the line before much damage is done. An *ELCB* will fulfill a similar function. (See also *heat fuse*.)

ELECTRIC KILN

A pottery kiln heated by *resistance wire* or rods. It is, fundamentally, a simple piece of equipment. No provision need be made for the disposal of gases (chimney), for ash waste, or for vast supplies of air. All that has been done at the power-station, and energy is derived at 'second hand'. Like other 'canned' products it lacks 'incidentals', and variety must be attained through the ingenuity of the potter.

The kiln can be of any type: front loader; top loader, 'top-hat', etc. The hexagonal or circular top loader (not the easiest shape to pack pots shapes into) is popular in America and increasingly in Great Britain. Its advantages are ease of construction and compactness (narrow walls, small stress). The elements are mounted as circles or spirals. The development of ceramic fiber has revolutionised the building of small kilns of all types.

Whatever its shape the electric kiln is fundamentally a box, constructed of insulating material, and housing a length of resistance wire. The heat is 'radiant', and this limits its size to about 24 cu. ft. (slightly less than 1 cu. m.). The proportions of the box will affect its efficiency (see *heat loss*). *Insulation* is of prime importance. A comparatively high initial outlay will soon be repaid in lower fuel bills. (See *insulation of heat*.) The inner brickwork must be very refractory and the element slots must be of an iron-free ceramic. The slots can be cut from H.T. insulating bricks such as those supplied by Gibbons or Molers in England, or they can be cast as larger units from alumina *cements*. The outer insulation may be of lower heat resistance bricks or slabs (around 850°C. for stoneware firing), or of ceramic fiber, *micropore*, Moler's 'Kipsulate' etc. The casing should be of *Asbestolux* or similar (not a cement bonded material),

Power/chamber-volume relationships in commercial kilns. (A) in the United Kingdom, and (B) in the United States. (Permission of Russell Davies). Much of the difference in the rating is due to the heavier build of many British made kilns and consequent heat storage (leading to slower cooling). This graph was drawn up some years ago and the advent of ceramic fiber will have lowered the ratio of wattage to volume, i.e. has made them faster (both heating and cooling) and more power efficient.

A system of cutting element slots with a grinding wheel developed by Mike Harris. The drill (A) is clamped into position. The brick (B) is guided by a length of angle iron which is tilted and fastened to a block (D) so that the wheel grinds the groove to the required depth. The method produces considerable dust, so wear a mask.

The ideal shape for an element slot.

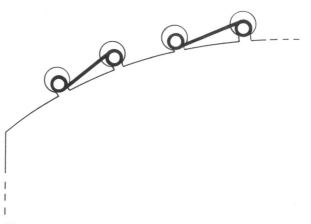

Elements in a kiln roof, the openings necessarily restricted to prevent them falling out. A method must be found for inserting them into the slots from the front of the kiln and efficiently shielding them.

1

Cutting slots in insulating brick to house wire elements. (1) The slots are marked and sawn. A sideways pressure on the saw at the completion of the cut will usually snap the section out but a third, central cut may be needed.

2

(2 to 4) The grooves are routed out by the use of a turning tool as shown or with a short length of wound element.

or sheet metal (though beware electrical connections when using metal). The skeleton structure is of angle iron or a similar material (Dexion etc.).

The fact that an electric kiln has no chimney means that sulfurous and other gases liberated by some clays pollute the atmosphere of the kiln room or pottery. Ventilation is essential but experiments in venting the actual kiln atmosphere through an outside wall have seriously retarded the temperature rise rate. The weight of a kiln should also be considered when planning an installation; at one time the weight could be up to one cwt. for every kilowatt in smaller kilns but modern materials have drastically reduced this figure. For detailed instructions on building a kiln see Fournier EKP.

A rather elaborate idea is illustrated in Potclays' catalog for levelling out the temperature and ventilating in an electric kiln in which air is drawn in from top vents through to minute ports in the base. In my experience, however, the top is rarely the hottest area. This is especially true of top loaders.

(See also *electric wiring to kiln, element, element winding, fail/safe, kanthal, silicon carbide, top-loading kiln, etc.*)

ELECTRIC WIRING TO KILN

Apart from the computations involved in the *resistance* wiring of a kiln, the current must be conducted to it. The wire used for this purpose must be able to take the full load for long periods without getting hot. The same rules hold as for resistance wire: less resistance in thicker, shorter wires; more in longer or thinner ones. Short runs between supply and kiln are therefore preferable where possible.

A composite cable holding the live, neutral and earth can be used to conduct *single-phase* current, but *three phases* and neutral are carried on wires which are then housed separately in protective metal or plastic tubes or 'conduits'.

Switchgear etc must all be rated at or above the load your kiln will need. *Three-phase* switches are rated at *amperes* per phase, e.g. a 30 amp fused switch will carry a total of $30 \times 3 = 90$ amps.

The following is a guide to the wire gauges for conducting various loads. The heavier wires are stranded. The first figure denotes the number of strands, the second the diameter of each strand in millimeters. The table is for p.v.c. insulated cables.

Size	Nominal cross-section area in mm²	Current rating (amps)	
		In conduit	On surface
1/1.13	1.0	11	13
1/1.38	1.5	13	16
1/1.78	2.5	18	23
7/0.85	4.0	24	30
7/1.04	6.0	31	38
7/1.35	10.0	42	51
7/1.70	16.0	56	68

A diagrammatic layout of the maximum electrical installation required in Great Britain. (1) switch (2) fuse (3) meter (3a) earth leakage circuit breaker, or ELCB (4) time switch clock (4a) contactor isolating switch (5) contactor (6) fused switch (6a) change-over switch (7) kiln isolating switch (8) kiln. Nos. 1, 3a, 4 and 5 are at the discretion of the supply company and depend on the conditions of supply, e.g. cheap rate arrangements. Change-over switches allow two or more kilns to be connected to one system of supply, firing alternately.

A two-way three-phase change-over switch with cover removed. This piece of equipment allows two kilns to be powered alternately from one system. In the photograph the blades are standing out horizontally and all power is off. When the handle is pressed downwards the blades connect three circuits; when pressed upwards, three different circuits.

An isolator (a fused switch box) and usually an *ELCB trip switch* as well, with possibly a contactor if you are using off-peak current (England), will all be required by the Electricity Authority.

ELECTROLYTE

'A compound which, when dissolved in water, partially *dissociates* into *ions* (electrically charged atoms and molecules). Added to clay slips ... to control flow properties' Dodd DC. Electrolytes in common use in ceramics are sodium silicate, soda ash and sodium tannate. (See *deflocculation*.)

ELECTRON

An elementary particle or basic unit constituent of an *atom*. Electrons make up the outer 'shells' and determine *valency*. An electron bears a 'negative' electrical charge. They can be freed from their atomic orbits and taken up by other atoms which then become electrically unbalanced—a negative *ion*. The atom which 'loses' an electron becomes positively charged.

Atoms are most stable when their outer shells contain two or eight electrons. To achieve this state, sharing and transfers occur between atoms of elements forming 'bonds' and building up molecules and networks—i.e. *crystals* and all the materials of the physical world. (See also *atomic theory*, *valency*, *ion*, *latice* etc.)

An aluminium atom, showing 'orbits' of 2, 8, and 3 electrons round a nucleus which consists of a similar number, i.e. 13 protons and 13 neutrons.

The number of *electrons* in the successive orbits of 'shells' of atoms in the commonly used pottery elements:

Element		1st	2nd	3rd	4th	5th	6th	7th
Hydrogen	H	1						
Lithium	Li	2	1					
Boron	B	2	3					
Carbon	C	2	4					
Oxygen	O	2	6					
Fluorine	F	2	7					
Sodium	Na	2	8	1				
Magnesium	Mg	2	8	2				

Element		1st	2nd	3rd	4th	5th	6th	7th
Aluminium	Al	2	8	3				
Silicon	Si	2	8	4				
Phosphorus	P	2	8	5				
Potassium	K	2	8	8	1			
Calcium	Ca	2	8	8	2			
Titanium	Ti	2	8	10	2			
Chromium	Cr	2	8	13	1			
Manganese	Mn	2	8	13	2			
Iron	Fe	2	8	14	2			
Cobalt	Co	2	8	15	2			
Nickel	Ni	2	8	16	2			
Copper	Cu	2	8	18	1			
Zinc	Zn	2	8	18	2			
Selenium	Se	2	8	18	6			
Zirconium	Zr	2	8	18	10	2		
Cadmium	Cd	2	8	18	18	2		
Tin	Sn	2	8	18	18	4		
Barium	Ba	2	8	18	18	8	2	
Praseodymium	Pr	2	8	18	21	8	2	
Lead	Pb	2	8	18	32	18	4	
Uranium	U	2	8	18	32	21	9	2

ELECTROVALENT

Bonds formed between atoms through the transfer of *electrons*, forming positive and negative *ions*. (See also *atomic theory*, *bond*, *valency*.)

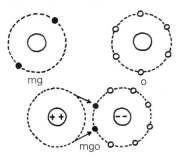

Electrovalent bonding of magnesium with 2 electrons in its outer shell and oxygen with 6. The oxygen makes up an orbit of 8 by annexing 2 from magnesium thus becoming a negatively charged ion, known as an O^{--}ion. The magnesium loses the whole of its outer (third) shell leaving a complete second shell of 8 electrons. The loss leaves two unbalanced positive protons and it becomes a Mg^{++}ion.

ELEMENT, chemical

'A substance which, so far as we know, contains only one kind of matter' (Mellor). There are about one hundred elements and all creation is built up from these simple materials.

Elements are denoted by internationally agreed symbols. These may correspond to the English name or may be derived from the Latin e.g. tin from *stannum*. Elements seldom exist alone in nature, but are found as compounds of two or more. Those elements of specific interest to potters are listed with their symbol and atomic weight under their English name in the entry for *atomic weight*. Here they are listed alphabetically according to their symbol. This will be a convenient reference when deciphering formulas.

Al	Alumina	Li	Lithium
Ag	Silver (argentum)	Mg	Magnesium
B	Boron	Mn	Manganese
Ba	Barium	Na	Sodium (natrum)
Bi	Bismuth	Ni	Nickel
C	Carbon	O	Oxygen
Ca	Calcium	P	Phosphorus
Cd	Cadmium	Pr	Praseodymium
Cl	Chlorine	S	Sulfur
Co	Cobalt	Se	Selenium
Cr	Chromium	Sn	Tin (stannum)
Cu	Copper (cuprum)	Sr	Strontium
F	Fluorine	Ti	Titanium
Fe	Iron (ferrum)	U	Uranium
Ge	Germanium	V	Vanadium
H	Hydrogen	Zn	Zinc
K	Potassium (kalium)	Zr	Zirconium

ELEMENT, electric kiln

A convenient section of a *circuit* which can be housed in an electric kiln, sometimes in a single slot, but often in two slots when it is known as a 'hairpin'. Fitting into more than two slots presents physical problems but is possible. The elements which go to make up one circuit are connected one to the other on the outside of the kiln wall (properly and fully shielded, of course) by *line taps* and heat-resistant covered wire, or by other means (solid brass connectors are sometimes used). An element is, therefore, a suitable length of wire wound into a spiral, with a 'tail' or connecting length at each end long enough to go right through the kiln wall. Occasionally an entire circuit is wound as a single element (as in circular kilns) but very long or multi-length elements are difficult to manipulate with wire thicker than 15 s.w.g. (1.8 mm.).

The following sample calculations for circuit lengths should be read in conjunction with the information given at *electricity*.

The wiring for a kiln is first broken down into suitable circuits. A convenient maximum load is around 5 kW per circuit. Each circuit is then considered separately in calculating the length of wire needed. There are factors limiting the rating (wattage) of a circuit. If too much current is passed through too short or too thin a

1

A simple system of winding electric kiln elements.
(1) After measuring the length of wire needed (see text, and Fournier EKP) allow a further 18 in. (45cm) and bend half of this extra length back at each end. With the last inch or so secured between the wooden jaws of a vice twist the double wire into a spiral as shown. This is the 'tail' which pierces the wall of the kiln. Doubling the thickness reduces the resistance of this section by three-quarters with the result that it will produce less heat.

2

3

(2) and (3) A general view of a primitive but practical element winder which is within the competence of any potter, and a closeup of a double (hairpin) element in the process of being wound.

4

(4) Showing how the bar can be removed from the bearing (a simple hole in the wood!) and the wound element slid over the handle.

5

(5) The final stage: pulling out the close-wound element to the length required for fitting into the wall slot. Always use wooden clamp jaws in order not to damage the wire. (See also electric kiln.)

wire, the wire will be unable to disperse the heat produced and will burn out.

Nichrome wire is suitable only for low temperature kilns. *Kanthal* or a similar wire is needed for regular firings above 1000°C. Each gauge or thickness of wire is given a rating of so many ohms of resistance per foot or meter length. It is a simple matter to divide the total ohms required by this figure to arrive at the length of a circuit. The gauge recommended for stoneware is 13 s.w.g. or thicker. (See *Kanthal*.) The ohm rating (for *Kanthal* A1) is roughly 0.1 per foot or 0.33 per meter. The wire needed for a 5 kW circuit on a 240 volt supply is therefore:

$$\frac{5000}{240} = 20.8 \text{ amperes}$$

$$\frac{240}{20.8} = 11.5 \text{ ohms}$$

$$\frac{11.5}{0.1} = 115 \text{ feet of 13 s.w.g A1 Kanthal}$$

$$or \quad \frac{11.5}{0.332} = 34.6 \text{ meters}$$

Replacing the above with symbols so that the equations become general:

$$\frac{W}{E} = A$$

$$\frac{E}{A} = R$$

$$\frac{R}{R \text{ per foot}} = \text{circuit length of wire}$$

The individual element length can be varied so long as the total wire length over the whole circuit is not altered. Elements can also be in the form of resistance tapes or rods. (See *silicon carbide elements.*)

It is possible, for stoneware firing, to use one gauge thinner than that quoted above i.e. 14 s.w.g. 2.03 mm; and down to 18 s.w.g. (1.219 mm.) for earthenware. It is difficult for a potter to wind wire thicker than 13 s.w.g. (See *element winding.*)

Note. s.w.g. stands for 'standard wire gauge'.

As mentioned above there is a minimum practical length for a circuit. As a very rough guide, reject any computation arrived at by means of the above equations which results in less than 100 ft. (30 m.) of wire to produce $4\frac{1}{2}$ kW.

The diameter and spacing of the coils will affect the efficiency and useful life of an element. There are two rules to be observed:

1. The diameter of the coil should measure 6–8 diameters of the wire. In practice this means winding 13 and 14 s.w.g. wire on a $\frac{3}{8}$ in./9 mm. mandrel. This gives a coil of approximately 15 mm. diameter. Applying the above criterion; the diameter of 13 s.w.g. is 2.33 mm.; multiplied by 7 gives 16.3 mm. for the average coil diameter—near enough. For thinner wires—15 to 17 s.w.g.—a $\frac{1}{4}$ in./6 mm. winding rod gives 12 and 11 mm. coils respectively,

2. The space between one coil and the next must equal at least one wire diameter, and preferably 1.5*d*. A

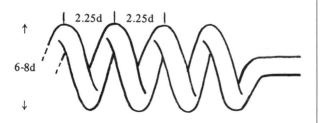

The spacing of coils must be at least 1.25 diameters between the faces of the coils; or 2.25 from the topmost point of one coil to the topmost point of the next to avoid each overheating its neighbor.

close-wound coil must therefore be stretched to two to three times its original length. It must be possible to insert a piece of the same wire between every coil and its neighbor. On the other hand, there is a limit to the degree to which one can stretch coiled wire. For 13 s.w.g. this is about a foot of wire to 5 in./125 mm. of slot—about 7 diameters between coils.

Never attempt to lay a straight length of wire in a slot. Although this may seem a simple method of taking all connections to one end, it will expand during heating and the arc of wire will fall from its slot and may easily short circuit to the element above or below. Attempts have been made to fit elements into the roof of front-loaders; these pose obvious difficulties which are, however, not insurmountable. The main disadvantage is the narrowness of the gap left open for radiation.

There are conflicting reports as to the damage caused to wire elements by *reduction*. The generally accepted theory is that reduction destroys the protective oxidised layer which the element builds up in normal firings and the advice is to arrange at least two oxidised firings to each reducing one. Stephen Coulston, however, (CR 88), does not experience any detriment to his Kilns & Furnaces AB40HT even though he fires at 1311°C. though he does not reduce (with gas) at much above 1220°C. Element life may be reduced by allowing glaze to splash onto the coils, preventing oxidation at that point. (See also *element winding, Kanthal, silicon carbide elements.* Fuller information in Fournier EKP.)

Where a continuous element is used in an oblong kiln some system must be devised to stop it pulling out at the corners as it expands and contracts during firing. Even in a circular or hexagonal muffle this is a danger. If an element does ease out of its slot it can only be pushed back in when it is hot; it will be too brittle when cold. It can be heated with a gas torch or the kiln can be switched on for a period (switching off, of course, before attempting a repair!).

An obvious limitation on possible wiring schedules is the length of wire which can be physically accommodated in a kiln. As a guide, 17 ft. (5 m.) of 13 s.w.g. wound on a $\frac{3}{8}$ in. (10 mm.) mandrel will give 30 in. (760 mm.) of stretched element. The arrangement of elements is important. They should be housed in the floor, rear wall and two side walls of a front-opening kiln; in the floor and all four walls of a top-opener. There is always loss of heat through the roof especially in *top loaders*, which can be minimized by placing the upper elements closer together. The floor needs about one-fifth of the total circuitry.

Connections: the length of the element 'tails' must be the width of your kiln wall plus an extra inch (25 mm.).

It is a good idea to allow twice this length so that the tail can be doubled back on itself and twisted together. This effectively doubles its cross-sectional area, lowering its resistance and preventing heat being generated where it will do no good. The connectors known as *line taps* are the best type for securing the element to the connecting wires. At one time the wires would have been asbestos covered but now substitute and somewhat less heat-resistant materials are used. These wires join the elements which make up a single circuit into a continuous run, the ends of which are connected to a live and neutral of the electrical supply. (See also *circuit*). All connections must, of course, be shielded from any possibility of being accidentally touched, or of touching one another apart from the required junctions. See also *silicon carbide elements* for their particular requirements.

Resistance wire tends to be more brittle in cold weather even before being fired. After a few firings it becomes almost as brittle as glass and it is difficult to extract a fired element whole.

The power input to a kiln averages 3–3.5kW per cubic foot for stoneware. With the increasing efficiency of modern insulators (ceramic fiber, etc) it may be possible to reduce these figures but a reserve of power is always useful. (See also *heat loss*.)

ELEMENT-WINDING

Electric kiln resistance-wire up to 13 s.w.g. (2.34 mm.) can easily be wound into elements by hand. The winder is simply a length of iron rod bent into a handle at one end and set in two bearings [holes in a piece of $\frac{3}{4}$ in. (20 mm.) timber are sufficient]. The length of the frame depends upon your element length when tightly wound (i.e. not the stretched length). The bearings will need to be about 6 in. (150 mm.) further apart than this. As a guide: 17 feet (5 m.) of 13 s.w.g. will wind into about 14 in. (350 mm.) of close coils. An element must always be pulled out to twice its wound length, so this example will span a 30 in. (750 mm.) kiln slot. 18–22 in. (460–560 mm.) is therefore a reasonable distance between bearings. Some means of gripping one end of the wire must be provided, and it must be possible to slide the completed coil from the rod. The illustrations show one system, but others will occur to you. An old wallpaper trimmer has been utilised but these are probably extinct.

During the winding, the wire must be kept taut by feeding it through a V-slot in a wooden block which runs along a second shaft. Single and hairpin elements can be wound on this machine at the rate of a dozen or so an hour. (See illustrations at *element*.)

Method. Cut the wire to the appropriate length, leaving enough for twisted tails at each end. The tails can be twisted in a vice before you start winding. Always use wooden jaws in the vice, and take extreme care never to nip, score, or damage the wire with metal tools during any process—it will only be as strong as its weakest part. Wind at a regular speed and keep the coils touching one another. Perfect elements will come with a little practice. Remove the coil from the rod, grip one end in a vice and the other with pliers or both hands, and pull it steadily apart until it has reached the length of the slot in which it is to be housed. You should be able to slot a piece of the same wire between the stretched coils which is the minimum distance apart to avoid overheating. For further details see Fournier EKP.

ELUTRIATION

The separation of particles according to their *specific gravity* by a controlled jet of air or water. Can also be used as a method for determining particle size.

EMBOSSING

Three-dimensional decoration applied to clay. Strictly speaking it should be in the form of a 'boss' or circular motif as has been used to embellish pots through the centuries, but the term is also used in a more general way. Lively single or repeat patterns can be achieved with deft strokes of the finger on pellets of clay applied to the dampened surface, as on some splendid Medieval jugs. A potter's seal can form a significant embossed break on a smooth surface. One can model or incise added clay to emphasise or isolate it or build up three-dimensional patterns. (See also *applied decoration*, *boss*, *seal*, *sprigging*.)

EMPIRICAL FORMULA

The simplest type of formula, merely listing the proportions of the elements which make up the material. Example: for potash feldspar: $K_2Al_2Si_6O_{16}$, which can more informatively be written as the *rational formula*: $K_2O, Al_2O_3, 6SiO_2$.

ENAMEL

Enamels, or enamel colors, are on-glaze pigments with a firing range of 690–850°C. They are applied to already fired glazed ware, which is then given a third firing to melt and fix the enamels. They are, in effect, very soft colored *frits*. They may contain slightly toxic materials.

The term 'enamel' (like 'majolica' when applied to a glaze) is sometimes used, in a confusing way, to indicate opaque, stained earthenware glazes, but we will confine discussion here to the low firing pigments.

The color range is wide, with many strong reds which do not feature in the higher-fired pigments. The general tone is bright and clean. In the past enamels have traditionally been handled in a rather genteel fashion but some Japanese and, in the later twentieth century increasing numbers of Western potters, have developed a bolder approach with vivid and spontaneous sweeps of the brush, especially on raku.

Enamels are mixed rather like oil paints, working and grinding the pigment with a *palette knife* on a glazed tile or a glass *muller*. The traditional medium is *fat oil* of turpentine (not substitute turpentine). It can be prepared by leaving turpentine in a cup to evaporate for a few days until a gummy residue remains. Prepared medium can be bought with the colors. The industry has a method of applying an even coating called *ground lay*. *Silk screen* printing can give interesting and bold effects.

The kiln must be well-ventilated during the early burning-off stage of the firing, and accurate temperature control established. Frequently more than one firing is required, the higher temperature range of colors being painted and fixed first, with subsequent firings for the more fugitive reds and golds. Enamels can be combined with underglaze pigments and even used on stoneware, though they may be difficult to 'fix' and will require a fairly smooth glaze.

Enamels will eventually wear away in use. A special type is commonly used on metal.

A combination of resist glaze techniques with a charming ship in crimson enamel. Stoneware by John Maltby.

ENCAUSTIC

A somewhat misleading term for pottery *inlay*, especially tiles.

ENDOTHERMIC

Heat absorbent. Clay has an endothermic peak during firing at 580°C., when it releases its combined water, slowing down the rate of temperature rise. The corollary of *exothermic*.

END POINT

The squatting temperature of a cone.

ENGINEERING BRICK

A highly vitrified brick which may be red, gray, or black according to kiln atmosphere. Of low *porosity* and great strength. A poor heat *insulator* and not suitable for kiln building. Used where high mechanical strength is the prime consideration. Made of etruria *marl* or clay with a fairly high flux content.

ENGOBE

An American term for *slip*, but which also covers a wider field than traditional *slipware*.

Engobes may contain very little plastic clay, being largely composed of materials more usually associated with glazes—feldspars, flint, opacifiers and fluxes. As distinct from the earthy qualities of European slipware, engobes are sophisticated and often white or near-white, providing a base for coloring oxides. Engobe recipes may appear involved and artificial but they are more adaptable to stonewares and can even be used on biscuit.

Colored engobe painting by Barbara Lock. The engobe (slip) is unglazed (but lightly burnished) on a body of $\frac{2}{3}$ red earthenware to $\frac{1}{3}$ T material. The basic recipe for the engobes, which Barbara has kindly allowed me to reproduce, is: borax frit 15%; nepheline syenite 30%; ball clay 30%; china clay 15%; tin oxide 5%; zircon 5%. Pigment oxides and underglaze colors are added. This is a fairly involved 'slip' but one which obviously repays the labor of making it up. It has the advantage that a single batch is suitable for all the colors.

The six groups of materials listed by Rhodes are:

1 The clays, including china clay for its whiteness and to control shrinkage.
2 *Fluxes*—the various base fluxes used in glazes.
3 Fillers—mainly flint.
4 Hardeners—borax and gums.
5 *Opacifiers*—zircon etc.
6 Colorants—the *pigment oxides*.

Rhodes also lists a number of recipes. It is possible to use a commercial white casting *body* on most conditions of clay or on biscuit (which should be dampened) (Behrens CM 20/4). Wally Keeler, in CR 112, quotes a very simple engobe for a slip on biscuit as 40 china clay: 60 feldspar.

Too great a shrinkage of the engobe will cause cracking or *crazing*; too little, scaling and flaking. Materials should not be too finely ground. A recipe is given at *brushed slip*. A *vitreous* engobe can replace a glaze (see also at *slip*). Parmelee discusses engobes at length in CG.

ENGRAVING

A design cut into clay, usually with a wooden or bamboo tool cut to an angle or to a rounded point. This is preferable to a sharp metal point, which will give a weak and furrowed line. Experiment on various conditions of clay, up to leather-hard: the drier the clay the tighter and sharper will be the cut line. The traditional glaze for use over engraving is a semi-transparent colored stoneware such as *celadon* on a fairly pale body. The increased depth of glaze in the cut line deepens the color and delineates the design.

EPSOM SALTS

Magnesium sulfate $MgSO_4.7H_2O.246.5$. It has been mentioned as a glaze *suspender* or *flocculant*: 3 parts of water to 1 part salts giving a concentrated solution of which 2 teaspoonsful to a pint is an average addition.

EQUILIBRIUM DIAGRAM

See *phase diagram*.

EQUIVALENT WEIGHT

A term used in connection with glaze formulas to indicate the amount, or unit, of an *oxide* which enters into a glaze. This is usually but not always the same as the molecular weight of the raw compound or mineral.

Red lead, for instance, is Pb_3O_4, while the unit entering into the glaze composition (that at the head of the column when translating *formula-into-recipe*) is PbO. If we include three parts of red lead this will give nine parts of lead oxide, PbO. To keep the arithmetic correct we divide the molecular weight of red lead by

three. $\frac{685}{3}$ = an 'equivalent' weight of 228.3. Such modifications are noted against the compounds concerned in the appropriate entry in this book. Colemanite is the most common example in glaze computation.

ESTUARINE CLAY

Clays which have settled in a river estuary 'one of the better clays' Cardew. Often deposited in thin layers with considerable variations. The *ball clays* of Wareham, Dorset, England, are valuable estuarine clays.

ETRURIA MARL

An ancient clay (carboniferous, three hundred million years ago) used for bricks, tiles and for *engineering bricks*. High iron content. Occurs on sites other than those at Stoke-on-Trent, from which it derives its name, though the term 'marl' is misleading since the clay is low in lime.

EUTECTIC POINT

That mixture of two or more substances which has the lowest melting point of the whole series. Some mixtures have more than one low or eutectic point.

A eutectic diagram looks like this:

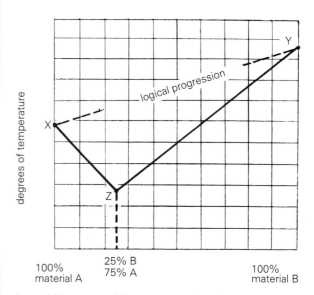

It would be reasonable to suppose that the mixtures of two materials with different melting points would melt as indicated by the line marked 'logical progression' in the diagram. This is not the case, however and there is a eutectic point (Z) which represents the most easily fusible mixture. (X) represents the melting point of material A (e.g. if each division on the scale represents 200°C. this would be around 1075°C.); (Y) is the melting point of material (B). For further explanation see text.

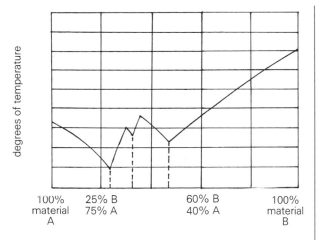

A more complicated graph which shows how two materials may have more than one eutectic. Although the most effective mixture is given as 75/25 there is a broken progression from there on, the least useful combination being 65/35 until 60/40 is reached. The diagram is purely illustrative and does not refer to any specific materials although in practice (B) would be silica (flint, quartz) and (A) an RO (flux). Multiple eutectics are more likely to occur when one of the materials in a recipe (and there are generally more than two) is itself a complicated compound such as feldspar. Eutectics are therefore very difficult to establish but the fact that this sort of reaction can occur can throw some light on otherwise inexplicable behavior in a glaze. It also suggests that a precise control of temperature can be as important as a precise recipe for economical firing. Another aspect is that two of the materials may develop their eutectic (become melted and glassy) before others present, giving a milky or speckled glaze or a variable surface. (See text at calcium.)

In this case the eutectic would be 75% A and 25% B.

It will be seen from this diagram that even though one material may have a much lower melting point than the other, the eutectic is lower still. It follows that an increase in the amount of either material—i.e. a movement to one side or the other of the low point—will raise the melting point of the mixture. This must be remembered when compounding glazes, an increase of the nominally *fluxing* material not necessarily continuing to 'soften' the glaze.

Glaze formulas for clear glazes aim at the eutectic. For expressing eutectics of three materials a *triaxial diagram* is needed; for more than three the problem becomes, mathematically speaking, very involved. Eutectic combinations form from materials within a pottery body, forming fluid glasses and lowering their *refractoriness* and *deformation point*. Glazes also go through liquid-in-solid phases.

The alumina-silica eutectic of 1595°C. occurs at 5.5 alumina: 94.5 silica.

Near equal mixtures of calcite, kaolinite and quartz have a low eutectic below 1200°C. This is equivalent to the formula 1.0 CaO. 0.35 Al_2O_3. 2.49 SiO_2. (Cardew). The eutectic of potash, at 770 C., is 1 K_2O. 0.5Al_2O_3. 5.5 SiO_2.

As mentioned above, the matter is further complicated by the fact that some mixtures have two or more eutectic points although one proportion usually predominates.

EXOTHERMIC

Releasing or creating heat by chemical reaction. Occurs in the firing of most clays at 900–1000°C. causing a more rapid rise in temperature for the the same heat input.

EXPANDING PULLEY

A pulley wheel in which the flanges are separate. They are held together by a spring, but can be forced apart by the strong pull of an A-shaped belt. As the belt approaches the center of the pulley, the speed ratio will be altered. The system has been utilized for varying the speed of a *power wheel*. See PQ 34 for building details (Bill Read).

The principle of the expanding pulley. Figure (A) shows the belt (black section) near the perimeter of the pulley when under minimum tension, the spring S holding the faces of the pulley together. (B) If the tension or pull on the belt is increased it forces the halves apart and the comparative speed of the pulley is increased.

EXPANSION

Expansion takes place when a material is heated. In pottery materials there are three types of thermal expansion:

1 The reversible expansion common to most materials, which occurs steadily and progressively upon heating, with contraction upon cooling. Oxides have different rates of expansion which have been worked out as

coefficients. An understanding of these is of great help in compounding glazes, especially with reference to crazing.

2 The expansion associated with quartz and cristobalite *inversion* which takes place very suddenly at 573°C. and 220°C. respectively. These are reversible.

3 The expansion which occurs in a clay body up to about 750°C. (when it will have been altered to ceramic) and is not reversed on cooling. A low-fired biscuit pot will be slightly larger than the dry clay pot. As soon as *vitrification* begins it involves a non-reversible shrinkage. At Crowan Pottery, Harry Davis fired very soft biscuit and then packed his glazed pots actually touching one another in the saggars, the shrinkage being sufficient to part them before the glaze melted.

A fourth, very slight, expansion can result from moisture *adsorption* by the fired pot. It will be enough to cause delayed *crazing* if the glaze is already in slight *tension.*

A de-airing pugmill extruding a strip of clay for cutting into tiles. (Courtesy Gladstone Engineering.)

A diagrammatic illustration of an expansion joint in the corner of a kiln which can be packed with ceramic fiber for insulation. A straight run of bricks may also need provision for expansion.

EXTRUSION

The forming of clay through a *die* on a pugmill or *wad box.* Coils and more elaborate shapes can be extruded and are used by potters for the coiling method of building, for making handles, and for decorative additions to pots. Sculptural constructions are also made using larger extruded shapes. A machine known as a clay 'bulley', made by Dragon Ceramex, will extrude square, circular and many other forms up to 12″ across. Mass-produced slab pots!

Bricks, pipes, and other articles are formed by extrusion in industry.

FACET

Thrown pots and bowls can be beaten or cut to produce facets or panels. Cut bowls are thrown thickly and cut with a wire while still soft, or may be roughly beaten prior to cutting; the resultant circle within a polygon is an attractive contrast. The facets are often used as a frame for further decoration; sgraffito, brushwork, alternate color slip or glaze dips, etc. Beating may be done up to the leather-hard stage and will give a softer effect than cutting which can have a crisp directness as exemplified in the work of John Reeve and others.

Boldly cut facets on a thrown bowl, by John Reeve.

FACTOR

See *conversion factor.*

FAHRENHEIT SCALE

A temperature recording scale in which the interval between the freezing and boiling points of water is divided into 180 degrees (degrees designated with a small "°"), with the freezing point put at 32°F and the boiling point at, 212°F. To convert a given temperature to the celsius or centigrade scale, subtract 32; multiply by 5; divide by nine.

Example: 2300°F. − 32 = 2268 × 5 = 11340 ÷ 9 = 1260°C.

FAIENCE

Applied to once-fired tin-glazed wares of eighteenth-century France, the name derived from Faenza where tin-glazed *majolica* was extensively made. Later used to denote any glazed earthenware. The French call the fine-bodied English earthenwares 'faience-fine'. In the USA it indicates a clear-glazed decorated pottery, a definition still further from its origins. Even more surprisingly it is applied to any large ceramics used on buildings.

FAIL-SAFE DEVICES

When mechanical or electronic (or human!) systems fail to shut off a kiln the results can obviously be disastrous. A clock-switch or a heat fuse can be fitted which will mitigate the worst effects and are advertised in suppliers' catalogs. However, by their nature, they must operate at a temperature above the optimum and are designed to protect the shelving and the kiln itself rather than the wares. A heat-fuse is used like a thermo-couple and is connected to the electrical supply through a contactor. See also *kiln-sitter*. A simple alarm clock or, better still, an alarm wrist watch, can save many a heart-ache.

FAT CLAY

Any highly plastic, workable, fine-grained clay.

FAT OIL

The thick, varnish-like residue resulting from the exposure of turpentine to the air for a period of time. It can be prepared by leaving pure turpentine (not turpentine substitute) in a cup for a few days until only a gummy residue remains. Take care that there is no turpentine on the inner sides of the cup or it will flow over and down the outside (Billington). Fresh turpentine can be added periodically. It is the traditional vehicle for underglaze and, especially, on-glaze colors. (See also *anise*.)

FEATHERING

A type of decoration in which *trailed* lines and dots of *slip* are drawn out by means of a thin and preferably pliable tool, such as the center rib of a feather. If the tool is drawn in alternate directions an overall pattern develops. The technique should be used with discretion —design values can be lost in an excess of random feathering. With skill, a number of variations can be developed—curved lines, or a quick flick at the end of a stroke, for instance. The technique is often combined with design trailing, e.g. for delineating a bird's beak or fish scales.

Both the base slip and the trailed line must be wet and fluid. One should avoid cutting into the clay beneath. Use the feather fairly upright; if its length is dragged through the slip, a dead and muddy line will result. Turn the dish to reverse the line direction. Feathering on upright or convex surfaces, as done on seventeenth century beakers, for instance, needs considerable skill.

A close-up of a nineteenth century trailed dish which has been feathered back and forth in parallel lines.

FELDSPAR, felspar, minerals

Feldspar is now the internationally agreed spelling. A large group of minerals which have decomposed from granite and *igneous* rocks and are thus allied to clay. Of world-wide occurrence.

The main group consists of the alumino-silicates of potassium, sodium, calcium, and, more rarely, barium. The ideal formulas, never quite achieved in nature, are:

Potash feldspar	Orthoclase Microline	$K_2O.Al_2O_3.6SiO_2$	556
Soda spar	Albite	$Na_2O.Al_2O_3.6SiO_2$	524
Lime spar	Anorthite	$CaO.Al_2O_3.2SiO_2$	278

Most feldspars are mixtures and are selected according to the predominance of one or other base.

A typical analyis of an orthoclase spar by weight:

K_2O	10.3				
Na_2O	2.5	Al_2O_3	17.5		
CaO	0.25	Fe_2O_3	0.2	SiO_2	68.2
MgO	0.12				

There is a series of mixtures between soda and lime spars known as the *plagioclase*. There is no potash-lime series.

Feldspars are the most useful minerals in ceramics, apart from clays. Used as a primary *flux* above 1200°C. and as a secondary flux in earthenware. Also in *bodies* and *engobes*. Many spars begin to melt at 1180°C. and continue to form complex fluids up to 1500°C. They are natural *frits*. Molten feldspar has a high *viscosity* which assists the standing-strength of porcelains and helps prevent glazes running during firing.

China stone is a slightly more refractory spar containing all three bases. *Nepheline syenite* is a fusible feldspathoid, high in alumina. (See also *feldspathic, spodumene, petalite etc.*)

FELDSPAR CONVENTION

The normal *analysis* of clays will list the *oxides* present. A rational analysis, listing the assumed *minerals* present, is more useful as a guide to its behavior and in calculating its *Seger formula*.

Under the feldspar convention, it was assumed that the minerals in clay were kaolinite, feldspar and quartz. Recent research suggests that *mica* rather than feldspar more accurately fulfils the theoretical grouping of oxides. Hence the *mica convention*. Both however are arbitrary, and the practical value of considering feldspar as a mineral in the rational formula is not greatly diminished.

Cardew points out that the mineral *illite* may have to be considered, and that some kaolinite may be replaceable by *montmorillonite*. Recent research on the subject stresses the importance of illite and the comparative dearth of kaolinite in many clays, even to the latter's virtual exclusion. None of this alters the observed behavior of clay but can illuminate certain aspects of it.

FELDSPATHIC, glazes, minerals

Containing feldspar. Generally used in connection with stoneware or porcelain glaze where the mineral is used to provide the primary flux. Characteristically a smooth clean glaze if sufficiently thickly applied, but without a strong character.

The feldspathic minerals constitute a large family: as well as those discussed under *feldspar*, there is also *leucite* which, with *nepheline*, is sometimes called a feldspathoid.

FELDSPATHOID

A term sometimes applied to the more distant members of the feldspar family: nepheline and leucite.

FELSPAR

Alternative spelling, see *feldspar*.

FERRIC CHROMATE

See *iron chromate*.

FERRIC OXIDE

The stable red oxide of iron, Fe_2O_3. The source mineral is hematite. Ferric oxide has a high melting point (1565°C.) and does not act as a flux. The *ferrous* oxide, however, behaves very differently.

All iron compounds revert to the ferric form in an oxidized fire. Many will be listed in merchants' catalogs, all with the formula Fe_2O_3. A 'synthetic' ferric is produced, very fine and pure, but I have not found that it noticeably improves color. Crocus martis is a natural ferric: ochre, sienna and umber are earthy oxides. Ferric is the coloring matter in red clay. Hematite produces the sparkle in *aventurine* glazes.

Ferric can be used as a pigment in all glazes, with a normal maximum addition of 12%. The red quality is lost in most glazes where ferric produces yellow-brown to black. Iron precipitated onto the surface in *kaki* glaze holds nearest to the original color. (See *red glazes*.) Results are more interesting and variable if red clay is used to supply ferric. (See also *iron*.)

In ash glazes, in an oxidising (or neutral electric kiln) fire, quite good reds can be achieved. See recipe at *oxidised stoneware*.

FERROSO-FERRIC OXIDE

Fe_3O_4, ($FeO.Fe_2O_3$) see *iron, magnetite*.

FERROUS OXIDE

The 'lower', black oxide of iron FeO. 72. m.p. 1370°C. 'Soluble in [fired] glazes up to saturation point (about 8%)' (Hamer). Will revert to ferric in an oxidized fire. Ferrous (reduced) iron in a body will act as a flux, causing it to melt, slump, or slag if present in quantity. In high-temperature glazes it is considered to be ferrous iron which produces the typical reduced greens and blues. (See also *ilmenite*.)

FERRUGINOUS

Impregnated with iron. An iron oxide-bearing mineral. *Ochre* for instance is a ferruginous earth.

FETTLING

Term used more often in the industry than by craft potters. It signifies the trimming and smoothing of a leather-hard pot, especially the sharp edges left by molds. Cardew uses the term to cover the removal of glaze from foot rings, lids etc, but this is unusual. Fettling is best done with a fine-bladed knife.

FIBERGLASS

See *glass fiber*.

FICTILE

Capable of being molded (as applied to potter's clays), or simply 'having to do with pottery' (SOED).

FILLER

A silica or other refractory addition to a clay body: to open or texture with sand, grog, etc; to control shrinkage; or to control or alter its behavior in the kiln. Hamer warns that silica of too fine a grain size (200 mesh or finer) may not behave as a refractory. 'Fillers' also often feature in engobe recipes. Rhodes mentions *pyrophyllite*.

FILTER PRESS

Equipment for dewatering clay, consisting of a concertina-like set of canvas bags which are filled with body slip. These are squeezed from either end, forcing out the water. Filter presses involve major engineering work and occupy a lot of space. They are of limited effectiveness with very plastic clays, which quickly coat the canvas and render it almost waterproof. For a more promising approach for studios see *vacuum filter*.

Filter presses are available in smaller sizes but are expensive and not often used by studio potters. They are more suitable for porcelain and other 'pastes' than for plastic clays.

FINGER-COMBING, finger sgraffito

Decoration in wet slip on the surface of a dish or pot.

A direct and clean 'finger wipe' on beaten pots by Phil Rogers.

A finger wipe softened by thick running hawthorn ash glaze, by Mike Dodd.

A swift and sure movement is essential in finger-combing. The technique can also be used with glaze.

Two or three fingers are drawn steadily across the slip, either straight or in a wavy line. The work is done a few minutes after slipping. The slip coat should not be too thick. A similar effect can be achieved with glaze and *glaze-over-glaze*.

FIREBRICK

A *refractory* brick, generally made from *fireclay* and *grog*. Industrial firebricks are given *P.C.E.* ratings. In America these are:

1 Superduty—P.C.E. 33.
2 High-duty—31.5
3 Medium heat duty—29.
4 Low heat duty—15.

Grade 2 is recommended for kilns. The P.C.E. refers to the deformation point. In England the grading is according to alumina content: those with more than 38% alumina are called aluminous fireclay refractories (1650–1750°C.).

The refractoriness of firebricks increases with their alumina content. They are strong and resist *spalling*, but their high density reduces *insulation* value. *Conduction* loss is five or six times that of the same thickness of a No. 23 grade insulating brick, with four times the *heat storage*. Against this, firebrick has greater strength and abrasion resistance than insulating brick. Firebricks are never used in electric kilns, but are more common in oil or solid-fuel fired kilns. See *bricks* for some available shapes of firebricks.

Super-quality firebricks are made from 'soaked' refractory minerals producing *mullite* and silliminite in the body. (See also *silliminite*.)

FIRECLAY

A general name for *sedimentary clays* usually associated with coal measures—they are very ancient deposits. Many are black and shaly, compressed to a coal-like consistency, and must be pulverized before use. The 'underclays' immediately beneath the coal seams break down more readily in water. In the best fireclays impurities, i.e. minerals or oxides other than kaolinite, alumina and silica, should not exceed 5%. Not all fireclays are especially *refractory*, however, and may contain carbonates of iron and calcium. Particle size averages 0.1–5.0 *microns*. Reasonable plasticity and dry strength. Fired color is buff to light-brown. Used by potters in refractory mixtures and as a body component. If used in large proportions, however, its carbon content can cause trouble such as *black core* and *bloating*.

Grading of the refractory clays is by alumina content. Those with 38% Al_2O_3 or more are called aluminous fireclays. The common fireclays have 35–37% alumina—the high-duty clays 45% or more.

Rich glaze quality and color in *celadons* and other reduced iron glazes is reputed to derive from the use of fireclay in bodies. Mr Noakes of Potclays called it 'sweated color'. The *pyrites* in fireclays can also add interest.

A Portugese flame-proof dish in soft earthenware, showing the curved base and interior glaze.

FIRECORD

A Japanese pot decoration. Straw rope is soaked in salt water and wound round a pot; the whole is then fired, giving semi-glazed lines.

FIRECRACK

May be due to the opening up of an incipient crack caused by mishandling in the leather-hard state, bad joins, uneven thicknesses in the pot wall (particularly the base), over-wetting, or joining soft clay to hard. In all these cases the crack will be rather ragged. If due to *dunting* the crack is likely to be curved and sharp. Dodd mentions too rapid a fire, but this is not confirmed in practice, although the termination of a biscuit fire at 500–600°C. (dull red heat) is likely to result in extensive cracking. (See also *shattering*.)

Bad packing in the kiln; too great a weight in a *bung* of pots or bowls; the sitting of one pot in the neck of another, etc, can lead to cracking during firing.

FIRE-EXTINGUISHER

Few cases have been reported of fires started by kilns (a bag of weed-killer may prove a greater danger as Mick Casson discovered), but precautions should be taken. If you employ assistants a fire-extinguisher is a statutory necessity. The solid (powder) extinguishers are recommended for electrical fires.

FIRING

The heat treatment of ceramic materials at least to the *sintering* stage, in practice to a minimum of red heat (600°C.). It is the indispensable factor in pottery. A kiln should therefore be the first consideration when setting up a pottery or school department. Neither sun heat nor a cooking-oven will 'fire' pottery. *Sawdust* kilns frequently fail to develop the minimum temperature.

Firing involves two cycles: heating and cooling. The following chart shows the principal changes and alterations.

Involved chemical and physical changes take place during firing: firstly sintering, then a series of melts in the fabric as *eutectics* are reached. Clay expands slightly up to about 800°C., then begins to shrink as particles come closer together, either taking part in the glass-making activity or packing in a glassy matrix. When a certain proportion of glass is formed, the ceramic will begin to flow. This is the deformation point of a body. The normal reversible expansions and *inversions* also cause molecular changes in volume. (See *crazing, thermal shock, etc.*) The speed as well as the temperature reached will affect the result of a firing.

It will be seen that the most significant changes take place early in a biscuit fire and late in a glaze fire. Firing schedules should take this into consideration. While science and logic both suggest slow firing and cooling the tolerances are, in fact, very wide. The Japanese kilns at Tamba were raised from 700°C. to 1300°C. in two and a half hours, and cooled nearly as quickly. Biscuit, in a bonfire, develops almost instantaneously, while *raku* shows what stresses an open body will stand without serious damage. *Bone china* has been fired to 1250°C. in seven minutes!

In test kilns glazes are fired very quickly. All one can say for certain is that the quality of a glaze will vary

°C.	BISCUIT	GLAZE	GLAZE and BODY	°C.
1400	Hardpaste porcelain vitrifies		WHITE HEAT	1400
1300	Vitrification of secondary clays	Most stoneware glazes molten		1300
1200	Vitrification of most red clays			1200
1100	Formation of mullite and cristobalite	Most soft glazes molten.	YELLOW HEAT	1100
1000	Most carbonates dissociate			1000
900	Contraction from here on		ORANGE RED HEAT	900
800	Sintering	Sintering		800
700	Some expansion		RED HEAT — Glazes begin to become rigid	700
600	Clay turning into ceramic	— Quartz inversions 573°C. —		600
500			DULL RED HEAT	500
400			BLACK HEAT	400
300	Most organic materials carbonising	— Cristobalite inversions 220°C. —		300
200	Adsorbed water driven off			200
100	All 'free' water evaporates. Clay drying.			100
0	HEATING	firing	chart COOLING	0

Carbons burning out — Increasing viscosity of glazes — Crystallization of glazes — Dunting range of bodies — Crazing range of glazes

considerably with the firing schedule, but only experience can show whether fast or slow firing gives the more desirable results.

See also *nitrogen* for an essential aspect of firing efficiency.

FIRING GRAPH

A *kiln graph* is the most economical and most easily interpreted method of recording a firing, but it must be based on a minimum of three readings, either from *cones* or *a pyrometer*. The graphs show how a single end-point can be misleading.

The progressive heat loss which occurs as the gap between the *ambient* temperature and the temperature inside the kiln increases always produces a slowly flattening curve, and explains why the last few degrees are sometimes so difficult to attain. Graph lines can start at intervals along the base line for successive firings, to facilitate direct comparison. (See *graphs, kiln log*.)

A firing graph with projections (dotted lines) of a kiln's possible further performance had the firing continued at a steady rate. It will be seen that, if only two readings are taken; (A) and (B) (the commencement and finish of the firing) the speed of the further temperature rise will be falsified. The line A–A1–A4–B shows intermediate readings on a pyrometer and these help in plotting a very different path which indicates that, in this case, the temperature rise will probably level out for the same input of energy, (the kiln failing to get any hotter) at below 1000°C.

FIRING SPEED

The rate of rise (and fall) of temperature during a firing will always affect the result. Rapid firing in a test kiln can therefore often be misleading. Obviously, in a biscuit firing, the thickness of the clay walls is crucial in avoiding bursts. A 1 in. thick wall would need a very

slow 50°C. an hour, at least for the first 700 degrees centigrade, whereas a $\frac{1}{4}$ in. could be taken at 150 degrees, always with the proviso of a slower first 200. (See *adsorbed water*.)

It is possible to fire most glazes very rapidly without harm though, as mentioned above, this will alter their fired character. The industry has, experimentally, successfully fired bone china in well under half an hour!

FLAKING

Usually applied to a fault in the *raw* rather than in the fired glaze. It is due to the surface coat shrinking less or much more than the body. *Flocculated* glazes (ash, colemanite) are prone to flaking, as are glazes too thickly or unevenly applied. Flaking of fired ware is called *shivering*.

FLAMBÉ

A glaze, generally on porcelain, streaked with reduced copper reds and purples, i.e. flame-like. Some crude modern copies are produced by an *on-glaze* method.

FLAMEPROOF WARE

Flameproof pottery, as distinct from *ovenware*, is difficult to achieve. The very considerable thermal shock due to expansion and the inversion of *cristobalite* in a high-fired body, combined with the comparatively low conductivity of ceramics (relative to metal, for instance) present almost insoluble problems.

The solution among primitive and less sophisticated communities is to use a body so soft and open that the shock can be accommodated within the structure. This involves a comparatively coarse body and presents glazing difficulties. A soft lead glaze is traditional, but this is frowned on today. The body needs to have a range of particle sizes and a minimum of 'free' silica. Porous red dishes up to 20 in. (500 mm.) diam. from Portugal and elsewhere are miraculously flameproof (and can be put onto a gas-ring) if soaked in water for twenty-four hours before being used for the first time. There is no obvious explanation, although the low firing to *sintering* without the formation of any glassy phases has been suggested. The effect of the water is even less obvious: perhaps *adsorbed water* helps to balance thermal shock?

Shape is a factor: For instance a shallow but continuously curved base which can expand without putting excessive strain on the wall. This may also be a reason for the predominance of rounded bases found in primitive pottery throughout the ages. There is no intermediate ceramic material between this type and a high-fired body of very low *thermal expansion*, e.g. true porcelain (1400°C.).

Cardew discusses the use of petalite and spodumene i.e. lithium bodies (PP 75–77). Zircon, also, has a *low coefficient of expansion*.

A raku pot with a body mainly of fireclay, reduced with gum leaves, by Joan Campbell (Australia).

FLANGE

A flat narrow projection, usually at right-angles, in the form of a collar or rim. Most commonly used by potters in connection with the seating of lids. (See under *lids* for several diagrams.)

FLASHING

Accidental and partial reduction or over-firing, usually on biscuit. Also applied to the effect, on a part of a glaze surface, of a tongue of flame or hot gas which smoke-stains or alters the degree of *reduction*. Wood ash settling on the surface can be a cause, also volatiles from a number of minerals and pigment oxides. See *chrome-tin-pink*, *copper*, etc. Deliberate flashing can be achieved by confining a piece of pottery in a saggar together with salt and/or other volatiles in open bowls. (See *fuming*, *volatilization*.)

FLASH WALL

See *bag wall*.

FLAT LINER

A long, slender square-cut flat brush. (See *brush*.)

FLATWARE

An industrial term for plates, saucers, etc. Flatware presents problems in throwing, drying and firing, especially when using highly plastic clay. This is evidenced by the dearth of hand-made plates. (See *plates*.)

FLETTON

An English building-brick. Named after the original centre of manufacture near Peterborough, but now made in vast quantities from a deeper and harder clay seam which stretches from Yorkshire to Dorset, known as Oxford (Jurassic) clay. It is shaly and contains organic matter which assists firing. Flettons are made by a semi-dry method. Suitable for *raku* and similar firings and for the outer skins of higher temperature kilns. Flettons are more porous and better insulators than firebricks, but are not for hot-face use except for very low heat (less than 950°C.) situations such as *sawdust firing*.

FLINT

A dark blue-gray boulder pebble found in chalk seams. It is a form of micro- (or crypto-) crystalline silica, SiO_2, of considerable purity.

A typical analysis by weight:

CaO	0.68				
Na_2O	0.05	Al_2O_3	0.29	SiO_2	97.9
MgO	0.01	Fe_2O_3	0.07	TiO_2	0.01

It is used to provide silica in glazes and bodies, and to whiten the latter. It is less pure but finer-grained than quartz, and thus more readily converted into *cristobalite*. The finer the grain of the flint the more effectively it will be involved in the glassy state. Hamer warns, however, that a very fine-grained silica cannot, therefore, be considered as a refractory.

Flint, like any form of silica, is a health hazard if inhaled and partly for this reason its use as a *setting* material is giving way to alumina. In America 'flint' refers to any form of ground silica including quartz.

FLOATATIVES

An American term for additions to slips and glazes which prevent them settling in water. The English equivalent is *suspender*.

FLOCCULATION, flocculant

The aggregation or coming together of particles in suspension. A flocculant is a material (an *electrolyte*) which causes this flocking. The effect of salt from the sea on river-borne clays is responsible for *estuarine* deposits. While a flocculant will hasten the settling of fine clay particles its immediate effect is to thicken (useful when glazing a low-porosity biscuit), and to keep larger particles of glaze, etc in suspension.

Gelatine and polymer adhesives will act temporarily, but this is a physical suspension rather than flocculation. Vinegar is also used but is unpleasant. The commonest inorganic material is *bentonite*. Calcium chloride, magnesium chloride (epsom salts) in very small proportions (a few drops of concentrated solutions) together with bentonite have been recommended in glazes. I have found ochre in a glaze to have a similar effect, as can also wood ash and colemanite. An unwanted result can be the increased shrinkage if the mixture gets too thick and water is added, causing glaze or slip to craze or peel as it dries.

FLUID, fluidity

A substance that takes the shape of the containing vessel. A liquid (or a gas).

The degree to which a material (glaze, slip etc) approaches a liquid is its fluidity. The reciprocal of *viscosity*. Glazes are less fluid than glass, which does not contain alumina. Alkalis increase the fluidity of glazes. (See *poise*, *viscosity*.)

FLUORINE

A gaseous element. F. 19. The fumes are a health hazard. Known as a halogen or salt-producer; it reacts with alkalis to form a lattice similar to that of common salt. It also reacts with other pottery oxides. Can cause blisters on release from a glaze—(see *fluorspar*). China stone is sometimes defluorinated. Cryolite, sodium fluoride and lepidolite will also provide fluorine. In CM 19/7 Behrens discusses fluorine and gives some simple recipes, e.g.

Lepidolite	52.0	
Sodium fluoride	2.8	
Fluorspar	12.4	Cone 4
Flint	32.8	

He mentions that the glazes may be smooth or 'cratered' (bubbled), but does not give further advice. 'Considerable color variation from the norm' may be expected from the pigment oxides.

FLUORSPAR

'Derbyshire spar'. CaF_2, 78. Decomposes in the presence of silica, forming a gas SiF_4, leaving CaO in the glaze. 'It perhaps has a catalytic effect on the calcium and other elements in the batch' (Cardew). Not widely used in pottery glazes, where over 5% may cause blistering. Can help to give a more transparent green stoneware glaze from chrome. Acts as a powerful flux in a multi-base glaze but the release of harmful gases must be catered for with good ventilation. (See *fluorine*.)

FLUTE

See *ocarina*, *whistle*.

A charming double flute or pipe by Neil Ions.

FLUTING

The cutting of grooves into the surface of a pot. Leach PB illustrates a fluting tool: a thin strip of metal with a short cross-cut about $\frac{1}{2}$ in. (12.5 mm.) from one end, beaten down to form a tooth which gives a controlled, curved cut (very like one of the individual cutting edges on a Surform tool). A fine wire-ended tool, perhaps with a 'stop' on it to prevent too deep a cut, is more easily available. Less 'accurate' but livelier cutting is done with a bamboo tool sharpened to a chisel edge towards the outer, harder skin of a large-diameter bamboo. When fluting round a large bowl or pot, the corners of the bamboo tool may wear away, altering the appearance and crispness of the cut and for this reason a steel tool is sometimes used.

The state of dryness of the clay will affect the character of the cuts. Fluting on softer clay is more fluid—or 'fluky', to quote Cardew. David Leach works on leather-hard clay and cuts with a sweep of the arm from a supported elbow, 'locking' the wrist to a fixed position.

The flutes can be fine and regular or wide and free, and are sometimes combined with combing.

Lively, swirling fluting on a temmoku glazed bottle by Leo F. Mathews.

FLUX, fluxing, fusible

In ceramics the term indicates an oxide, generally a *base*, which lowers the melting point of an *acidic* oxide, especially silica. Boric oxide has an ambiguous position. The fluxes are *network modifiers*.

Individual oxides may have a high or low melting point (e.g. Sb_2O_3 656°C., CaO 2570°C.) but it is the reaction between the oxide and silica which is of interest to potters. Lime can be a very fluid flux at stoneware temperatures. From the *eutectic* it will be seen that a 'fluxing' oxide will be increasingly effective up to a certain proportion; beyond that it will begin to reverse the effect and lead to *crystallization* of the cooling glaze. *Basic matt* glazes can be achieved in this way, but care must be taken not to develop an unstable formula with resultant *metal release*.

Oxides vary in their effectiveness as fluxes—i.e. the temperature at which they become active. With certain exceptions, a variety of bases will be more efficient than a single one. The following list is general guide, starting with the most active fluxes; the later ones are used in stonewares.

Lead oxide PbO
 Soft glazes only. Can be used as sole flux.
Boric oxide B_2O_3
 Essential in soft *leadless glazes*. The only *acidic* oxide in the list.
Potassium oxide K_2O
 Features in all types of glazes. A primary flux in stoneware and porcelain, secondary in earthenware. Efficient at lower temperatures.
Sodium oxide Na_2O
 All glazes. Can be a primary flux in soft glazes.
Lithium oxide Li_2O
 Efficient at low temperatures.
Strontium oxide SrO
 Some similarities to calcium but more effective at low temperatures though in this case it should be introduced as a frit (the carbonate will not start to be effective below about 1100°C.).
Zinc oxide ZnO
 Up to 3% effective in earthenware. The major flux in *Bristol* glazes (1180°C.).
Calcium oxide CaO
 Secondary flux in small amounts in earthenware. Can develop very fluid glazes above 1250°C.
Magnesium oxide MgO
 Used in small amounts. Most effective from 1150°C. upwards.
Barium oxide BaO
 Fairly refractory. Stonewares.

Of the pigment oxides, manganese is very fusible, copper and cobalt are weak fluxes. Iron is fusible only in reduction. Fluxes in a body will also, of course, form glassy melts leading to *vitrification*.

FLY ASH

Ash carried by draft through a kiln. Can be responsible for '*kiln-gloss*' or *flashing*. May also spoil the appearance of a lid or any horizontal pot surface in a kiln, especially when salt glazing.

FOAMED CLAY

Insulating-bricks made by generating bubbles, physically or chemically, in thick *slip*. These are trapped as it dries.

FOOT RING

Sometimes referred to as a 'foot rim'. Most bowls need a foot ring. It is, in effect, a low pedestal which can be thrown onto the turned, inverted bowl, or cut from the surplus clay left at the base when it was thrown. The bowl section should not vary to any great extent throughout its whole curve. The proportions of a foot ring—its height, width and splay—can make or mar a bowl form. It must be in tune with, and emphasize, the character of the bowl: its sturdiness, lightness, roundness etc. Physically it must support the curve: a small foot on a flat bowl can result in *slumping* or *warping*. The foot should be visible from an oblique viewpoint.

The ring width will appear to be smaller (narrower) when you are turning it than it will when the bowl is set right way up. Cut a somewhat smaller ring, therefore, than you think the bowl will need or, better still, use an inside *chuck* so that it can be removed and checked during the turning. Cut your initial ring quite wide so that it can be corrected later. Most foot rings are vertical but variations are possible, even the slightest of which can alter the general character of the bowl. (See *turning*.)

A footring being turned on a bowl. (For more detail see under turning.)

FORCED DRAFT

A mechanical augmentation of the normal chimney draft through a kiln. Air is either blown into the firing chamber, or movement in the chimney is speeded up with a fan. A fan can be used to blow air into the combustion chamber of a wood kiln which needs a great deal of ventilation. A forced draft kiln may need only a minimal chimney (see also *oil burners*).

FORMALDEHYDE, formalin

Chemical formula HCHO. Suggested as an additive to prevent the decomposition of gums used in glazes. Formalin is the liquid form. (See *suspender*.)

FORMER

A rather wider term than 'mold', which suggests a predetermined shape, and used to cover any constructed or 'natural' form which can be utilised in the process of shaping.

In addition to a biscuit bowl or other pottery shape into which clay can be pressed, many common objects—a pebble, a balloon, a bag of sand, a roll of paper or card—have been used as formers. Clay release is easier if the material of the former is slightly absorbent. In Japan, small pots and bowls have been formed over the elbow, the knee, or the hand. Carlton Ball MPWW deals with many variations as do many primers.

1

2

3

4

5

6

7

8

9

10

(1) and (2) Making a small dish over one's elbow!
(3) A joined-up group of small dishes made over stones.
(4) to (7) Stages in pressing a large dish or a unit of construction in a biscuit former or mold. First a block of fairly soft, usually grogged clay is pressed in with the palm of the hand and then eased into the shape, thinning the wall, with a darning head. Finally the surface is scraped and smoothed with a steel palette. Extensions of the form can be coiled onto the rim.
(8) to (10) Here a simple former has been made from four strips of leather-hard clay, with a rolled slab eased into the central space to make a shallow wide-rimmed dish.

(11) A raku dish made in this way by Sheila Fournier. (See also handbuilding.)

FORMULA

A chemical or *molecular* description of a material. A glaze may be written as a formula or as a *recipe*. A formula is written as a list of the elements or *oxides* which enter into the fired glaze; a recipe is a proportional list of the *minerals* and other materials which will most nearly approximates to the formula.

The *element symbols* are used in the formula. A small figure following and slightly below the symbol (e.g. Pb_2) indicates the number of *atoms* in the *molecule*. A figure preceding an oxide formula indicates the number of molecules of the whole oxide. Thus $3Al_2O_3$ represents three molecules of alumina, which is itself made up of two atoms of aluminium to every three of oxygen.

The ultimate or empirical formula merely lists the relationship between the atoms of the material, e.g. $Al_2Si_2H_4O_9$, or it might read $Al_2Si_2O_5(OH)_4$. These tell a potter little about the material, except that the second formula suggests that it is a *hydrated* mineral. If the same elements are grouped into oxides as Al_2O_3. $2SiO_2.2H_2O$, we can recognise kaolinite. This is the *rational formula*.

The symbols are, of course, relative ones, and do not refer to any practical amounts or weights. They can, however, be translated into weighable minerals and oxides. (See *formula-into-recipe, analysis*.)

FORMULA FROM PERCENTAGE WEIGHTS

To turn a weight percentage list of *oxides (analysis)* into a molecular *formula*, divide each number by its *molecular weight*.

Example:

46.5 SiO_2, 39.5 Al_2O_3, 14 H_2O

$$\frac{46.5}{60} = 0.775$$

$$\frac{39.5}{102} = 0.387$$

$$\frac{14.0}{18} = 0.777$$

If each is divided by the smallest number a molecular ratio is arrived at—$2SiO_2.Al_2O_3.2H_2O$ or the formula for kaolinite.

The figures derived from an analysis can also be used in *Seger formula* terms by adding the bases together and dividing all the figures by the total.

FORMULA-INTO-RECIPE

The fundamental equation is:

Molecular parts × molecular weight = parts by weight. 'Parts by weight' refers to physical comparative weights: gm., oz., or what you will. It is rarely possible, however, to use simple oxides in a recipe. They will more often be one constituent of more elaborate minerals. To simplify the arithmetic, various charts have been suggested. The molecular make-up or formula of a glaze or mineral is tabulated according to the *Seger formula*, i.e. in the proportions of the *bases*, *amphoterics* and *acids*, the sum of the bases being kept at unity. This can be transcribed into a list of physical materials with their proportional weights, as follows.

A simple lead glaze.
Formula: 1.0 PbO. 0.3 Al_2O_3.3.0 SiO_2

A chart is made up of as many columns as there are oxides in the formula, plus five more, and as many horizontal spaces as there will be raw materials in the recipe, plus two.

It will be seen that the 'molecular parts' figure is that represented by unity in the formula for the mineral. For instance, the clay is $Al_2O_3.2SiO_2.2H_2O$. The H_2O is lost in the firing and is ignored (although allowed for in the total molecular weight of clay); of the rest, the alumina is at unity so the figure of 0.3 is used. The *molecular weight* for oxides and minerals is given under each entry. The bottom line gives the totals for the oxides, which must correspond with the formula.

The recipe is always approximate, as the minerals are considered to be in exact accordance with the *ideal formula*, which is rarely the case. It is possible to have each mineral analyzed into its actual oxide proportions, but for the average craft potter this is impractical. Results of these computations can be taken as a reference-point and guide. The proof is always in the firing.

Decisions as to which materials to use to translate the formula are a matter of trial and error. Start with materials which will satisfy the *RO (base)* requirements. These may be oxides or carbonates such as litharge or whiting, in which case the decision is a simple one. In many cases this will not be so. Lead oxide is forbidden in schools, and a frit must be used. This will automatically introduce silica into the glaze batch. In the example

shown in chart B below, sesquisilicate is listed; this has the formula PbO. $1.5SiO_2$. For every one molecule of lead, one and a half molecules of silica are introduced. We could use the monosilicate, proportions 1:1, or the bisilicate, 1:2, entering the appropriate proportions of silica in its column. Working from left to right, alumina is the next oxide to be considered. It would be possible to use calcined alumina, but it is too coarse and, as a general rule, natural minerals are preferable to synthetic ones. We need a mineral which does not include unwanted oxides. China clay fulfils the requirements, introducing one alumina molecule to two silica. The 0.3

FORMULA-INTO-RECIPE—Chart A

PbO	Al_2O_3	SiO_2	Material	Molecular parts × weight		Parts by weight		%
1.0			Litharge	1.0 × 223	=	223	=	60.2
	0.3	0.6	China clay	0.3 × 258	=	77.4	=	17.4
		2.4	Flint	2.4 × 60	=	144	=	32.4
1.0	0.3	3.0	TOTALS			444.4	=	100.0

FORMULA-INTO-RECIPE—Chart B

PbO	Al_2O_3	SiO_2	Material	Molecular parts × weight		Parts by weight		%
1.0		1.5	Lead sesquisilicate	1.0 × 313	=	313	=	70.5
	0.3	0.6	China clay	0.3 × 258	=	77.4	=	17.4
		0.9	Flint	0.9 × 60	=	54	=	12.1
1.0	0.3	3.0	TOTALS			444.4	=	100.0

FORMULA-INTO-RECIPE—Chart C

K_2O	CaO	MgO	Al_2O_3	SiO_2	TiO_2	Material	Molecular parts × weight		Parts by weight		%
0.3			0.3	1.8		Feldspar	0.3 × 556	=	166.8	=	48.47
	0.5					Whiting	0.5 × 100	=	50.0	=	14.53
	0.1	0.1				Dolomite	0.1 × 184	=	18.4	=	5.34
			0.02	0.04		China clay	0.02 × 258	=	5.2	=	1.50
				1.46		Quartz	1.46 × 60	=	87.6	=	25.52
					0.2	Titania	0.2 × 80	=	16.0	=	4.64
0.3	0.6	0.1	0.32	3.3	0.2	TOTALS			344.0	=	100.0

alumina is therefore entered in the appropriate column and the accompanying 0.6 of silica in its column.

In satisfying the lead and alumina requirements we have, willy-nilly, put 1.5 + 0.6 silica into the batch, a total of 2.1. This falls 0.9 short of the required 3.0 parts and, luckily, there are two minerals which are nearly pure SiO_2: flint and quartz. This completes the formula. If we had used bisilicate of lead, only 0.4 parts of flint would have been required.

One more example with a longer formula: a hypothetical stoneware glaze.

Example:

K_2O	0.3	Al_2O_3	0.32	SiO_2	3.3
CaO	0.6			TiO_2	0.2
MgO	0.1				

Working from left to right as before: 1. K_2O. The most convenient material is potash feldspar which will also bring in, for one part of potash, one part of alumina, and six silica, e.g. for 0.3 K_2O, 0.3 alumina and $0.3 \times 6 = 1.8$ silica. See that these proportions are not more than are required. 2. CaO. This can be used as the carbonate, whiting, 0.6 parts. Nothing else is added in the process. 3. MgO. The most readily available source of magnesia is dolomite where it occurs in equal parts with calcium. If we use 0.1 parts of dolomite to provide magnesia we also add 0.1 parts of CaO. We must therefore reconsider the whiting and alter the 0.6 parts to 0.5, so that the total introduced by whiting plus dolomite does not exceed the formula requirements. 4. Al_2O_3. The feldspar has already provided 0.3 parts, leaving only 0.02 to be accounted for. Using clay we can add this amount, with the appropriate 0.04 entry under silica. 5. SiO_2. Feldspar has given 1.8 and clay 0.04. We require 3.3, or 1.46 more and can use flint or quartz. 6. TiO_2. Titanium oxide can be used, 0.2 parts. (See Chart C. on page 119)

In all three cases dealt with above it has been possible to satisfy the formula with common minerals. If, however, formula C had required 0.45 parts of potash, this would have given similar parts of alumina—more than required—and so feldspar could not have been used. In fact there is no common mineral which would have been suitable, and you would have had to resort to a *frit*. Where this situation arises it may be better to reconsider your formula, especially where a stoneware glaze is being formulated.

FORMULA WEIGHT

Also known as the *molecular weight*. The total of the atomic weights of all the elements which make up the formula. Example: clay, $Al_2O_3.2SiO_2.2H_2O = 2 \times 27$

(Al) + 2 × 28 (Si) + 4 × 1 (H) + 9 × 16 (O) = 258. The figure following the formula for each of the minerals in this book is the molecular or formula weight. (See also *equivalent weight*.)

FREE SILICA

That proportion of silica in a raw or fired body which is not combined with other oxides, i.e. remains as crystals. Quartz or flint added to the body may remain 'free'. During heating and cooling the free silica undergoes *inversions*, with consequent strain on the body. At temperatures above 1070°C. it is slowly converted into another SiO_2 form—cristobalite. Siliceous *ball clay* contains quartz grains. (See also *crazing*.)

FREMINGTON CLAY

A fine-grain, very clean, fusible red clay from Devon, U.K. comparatively low in lime and high in alkalis. Probably glacial. It is famous for its throwing qualities; has been used as a burnishing slip; and as a slip glaze with some extra fluxes and silica, at temperatures above 1250°C.

FRENCH CHALK

A preparation from *steatite (talc)*.

FRIT

A ground glass or glaze. The potter utilizes naturally occurring minerals as far as possible, but sometimes it is difficult to find an insoluble and non-toxic source for a required oxide. Borax, for instance, the main source of boric oxide, is soluble even after *calcining*. Litharge, white and red lead are all poisonous and are usually used as soft silicate glasses or frits.

Frits are always used on industrial pottery in order to ensure uniformity of color and other qualities, and to avoid uneven settling in the glaze batch. Frits have lost any combined water, carbon dioxide, etc. which may have been present in the raw materials. They are therefore concentrated and must be applied more thinly. The transparency of the glaze immediately after dipping can be misleading—one feels the coating is too thin. Frits settle rapidly in water. They are best used as a basis for further additions of raw minerals, i.e. treated as one item in a *recipe*. Common salt is reputed to assist *floatation*. To use frits scientifically one must know their *formula*, which should be treated like any other multioxide material. The lead silicates and the softer borax and alkaline frits are useful to the earthenware potter. With few exceptions (one being David Leach's stoneware) all prepared glazes are frits. Fritting can alter and control colors.

The potter can prepare his own frits in small quantities, but they are normally made by the industry and sold in a finely powdered state. Glaze materials, soluble and otherwise, are mixed and melted together in a special oven, often in the form of a revolving cylinder. When quite fluid the molten glaze is let out in a stream into a tank of cold water. It will break into fragments under the thermal shock, resembling granulated sugar. The grain-size is further reduced in a *ball mill* or *vibratory mill*.

The craft potter has to melt his materials in a bowl in the kiln, break the bowl away and pulverize the frit, or else heat them in a crucible and continue as above. If ground in a mortar and pestle, a teaspoonful must be dealt with at a time. A ball or jar mill is a virtual necessity. David Eeles makes large quantities of an alkaline frit for use in his fine celadon glazes, melting china clay, quartz, and soda ash in biscuited pots which have been washed over with quartz, then crushing and milling the frit. (Sutherland GNS.)

FUEL

Material used to produce heat by rapid *oxidation*. (See *gas, oil, wood, coke, paraffin*.) *Electricity* is not, in this sense, a fuel: it is energy supplied at one remove. Fuels vary in their flame temperatures. The maximum attainable heat has been given as around 1370°C. for wood, 1500°C. for coal, 1650°C. for oil. *Drainoil* is reputed to have a higher *Btu* rating per gallon than any other fuel.

FULLER'S EARTH

A calcium *montmorillonite* type mineral with impurities sometimes including iron oxide. Originally used for the 'fulling' or cleaning of wool. There are contrary opinions as to its plasticity. Cardew dismisses it as 'non-plastic; James Walford (CR 60) 'highly plastic'. It is possible that different sources for the 'earth' give different results, Walford's coming from North Africa, though the mineral is widely distributed in England and elsewhere. Walford suggests that it can be used in clay bodies in small quantities and also, after calcinating at around 850°C. in celadon glazes (10–15%), the fullers earth itself supplying the necessary iron oxide. He sprays the glaze onto the pot to avoid crawling. Suppliers: Ellis and Everard, and Frdk. Allen.

FUMES

The fumes from burning materials can be dangerous to health as can the products of *reduction*, especially *carbon monoxide*. The problem is most acute in electric kilns which are generally unvented. Well-ventilated kiln areas should be ensured. Some attempts to discharge the sulphurous and other fumes for electric kilns which often occur in the firing of clays and glazes have resulted in unacceptably low rates of temperature rise, but the Orton Ceramic Foundation advertise a Kiln-o-vent which must have been tested in this regard.

FUMING

Surface effects on bodies and glazes, generally at stoneware temperatures, obtained by firing pots in enclosed saggars with volatiles; the chlorides, sulphates, or nitrates of metals. Keep a good standard of ventilation in the kiln room. The fuming materials can be put into a small biscuit bowl in the bottom of the saggar; some potters layer them with sawdust or charcoal, some with sand to slow down the decomposition. See *volatilization*.

Salt glaze is itself a form of fuming, and Parks PGRG introduces copper fuming into his kiln by the use of old plumbing items of copper or brass in the hearth at the end of the firing, giving somewhat unpredictably placed red blushes on the ware. He also suggests two teaspoonsful of stannous chloride at red to black heat for mother-of-pearl effects.

FUSE, electric

A 'weak link' of easily melted wire put into a *circuit* to avoid the over-heating which would develop from the flow of more *current* than the *conducting* wires will take, i.e. from a *short-circuit*. Fuses are graded according to the current in amperes which they will conduct without failing, e.g. a 15 amp fuse will begin to overheat at 16 amps, and will melt at approximately 20–25 amps. Fuses may be of wire or a wire enclosed in a capsule. An *ELCB* fulfills a similar function. (See also *heat-fuse, fail-safe*.)

FUSE, fusion, fusible

To melt together. Fusible materials are those which melt easily or lower the melting point of a mixture such as a glaze. Some oxides are *refractory* in themselves but act as fusible agents (see *flux*) in a glaze.

FUSED ALUMINA

Used for abrasives.

FUSED SILICA

A translucent or transparent vitreous silica made by fusing quartz sand in an open furnace.

GABBRO

A basic granite, usually high in iron oxides (average 10%). Widely distributed (Cornwall, England).

Average analysis: MgCaO, 20%; Na_2K_2O, 2%; FeO/Fe_2O_3, 5% (but variable; no iron in Saxony gabbro, for instance); Al_2O_3, 20%; SiO_2, 48%. See also at *glazes from natural sources*.

GALENA

A lead ore, lead sulphide PbS, 239, s.g. 7.5. Conversion factor 0.93.

Widely distributed. Used on medieval pottery and seventeenth century slipware. Toxic but less so than litharge or white lead. Contains copper and other impurities (some silver is extracted) which enhance its value for slipware but not for more sophisticated glazes. Needs plenty of ventilation during firing to disperse the sulfur and to form PbO. Not, therefore, very suitable for electric kilns. Galena-glazed pots are often once-fired (as in the film *Isaac Button, country potter*). Other types of glaze in the same kiln may be spoiled. 'Up-draft kilns are best for galena glazes' (Leach).

Example of raw-clay galena glaze recipe:

Galena	66
Plastic clay	16
Flint	18

Weights can be transposed from *litharge* recipes.

A lead glaze will use part of the body surface to assist its maturity during firing; it will thus eat away thin *slip*.

GANISTER

A fine-grain silica rock found in lower coal measures (e.g. in Yorkshire, England). It is ground, mixed with clay, and used in silica refractories.

GARNET

A group of crystalline minerals used as abrasives and gemstones. The *RO* constituents vary, the general formula being $RO.R_2O_3.3SiO_2$.

GAS

Any substance in the gaseous state, scientifically defined as 'occupying the whole of the space in which it is contained' Uvarov DS. Its molecules are in a free state and not connected to one another in any pattern. Air is the most common gas. In everyday use 'gas' is usually taken to mean gas fuel.

GAS BURNER

Gas fuel must be mixed with air for *combustion*. This is normally done at the point where the gas escapes from the pipe. The burners may be divided into three groups:

1 Atmospheric or inspiratory burners where the forward movement of gas under pressure draws in the air needed for combustion.

2 Burners in which a current of air draws in gas, itself under small or nil pressure.

3 Where gas and air are mixed in a chamber behind the burner.

The first of these is the simplest and the most commonly used. Gas is easily ignited and the burners are more simple in construction and principle than those used for oil. See also Rhodes K for other useful information.

GAS EXPANSION

The expansion for a given temperature rise of any gas will be the ratio in *Kelvin* degrees. Example: air at 10°C. is at 283°K; at 1100°C. its equivalent in K is 1373°. The expansion will be $\frac{1373}{283} = 4.68$. Thus at atmospheric pressure a cubic meter of air at 10°C. will have increased in volume to 4.68 cubic meters at 1100°C. Kilns must be designed to accommodate such volume differences between cold air inlets and hot air outlets.

GAS FUEL

'Town' or coal gas has a high proportion of free hydrogen; 'natural' or well-gas is largely methane.

The Office of Gas Supply arrives at therms for costing purposes by multiplying the volume of gas (or the weight) by its calorific value and dividing the result by 100,000.

e.g. 7.500 cu. ft. of natural gas =

$$\frac{7500 \times 1,000}{100,000} = 75 \text{ therms}$$

or 350 lb. of propane =

$$\frac{350 \times 21,500}{100,000} = 75 \text{ therms}$$

(The therm is likely to be replaced by a European Community system.) The proportions of ingredients will vary a little but it will be seen that N.G. has none of the very poisonous CO while its high methane content gives it greater efficiency and, reputedly, a 'cleaner' and better firing in the kiln.

Cylinder or *bottled* gas (L.P.C.) produces nearly three times as many Btu per cu. ft. as natural gas. Supply gas is lighter than air and will rise, whereas L.P.G. is

% volume of	Coal gas	Reformed gas	Natural gas	Propane	Butane
Methane CH$_4$	15	25	94.5		
Higher hydrocarbons	5	2	4	C$_3$H$_8$	C$_2$H$_{10}$
Carbon monoxide CO	14	2	nil	Known as L.P.G. Liquid petroleum gases	
Carbon dioxide CO$_2$	4	14	nil		
Hydrogen H$_2$	55	57	nil		
Nitrogen N$_2$	7	nil	1.5		
Calorific value (gross)					
Btu/cu.ft.	500	500	1000	2500	3000
Btu/lb.				21500	21200
Specific gravity	0.49	0.49	0.59	1.5	2.0
Air required for combustion given as cu. ft. per cu. ft. of gas	4.5	4.5	9.5	24.0	31.0

by kind permission of South-Western Gas Corporation (UK) (Now part of British Gas)

heavier than air and will collect at a low level making it dangerous in enclosed spaces or basements.

GAS KILN

If gas supply is available in sufficient quantity (a 2 in. (50 mm.) mains is the minimum requirement), a gas kiln can provide clean, versatile, and comparatively trouble-free firing. Design can be of the open-chamber or *semi-muffle* type, and there are several ways of burning the gas. Most kilns mix the fuel and air at the primary air or burner point.

For smaller kilns, a pressure of around 8 oz. is required [somewhat higher than those of 15 cu. ft. (0.5 cu. m.)] or more. Your local gas supplier should be consulted.

The design of gas kilns, both for supply and *bottled gas*, allows of wide variations and can be very simple. 'Strict rules for [proportions of parts] should be viewed with some reserve' (Casson). There are normally several burners or jets.

Mick Casson has found that natural gas has a lazier flame than had town gas and that the burners are easily extinguished when burning low. Ideally the burners should be within the kiln wall. Good *secondary air* control is essential. Natural gas takes more air for combustion than did town gas and larger flues are needed. Great heat and strong reduction are possible. There is

some tendency for *spalling* and disintegration to occur in *refractories*.

As with other types, gas kiln design has been revolutionised by ceramic fibre and other new materials. Andrew Holden, in CR 87, describes the building, in a few hours, of a gas kiln using Sayvit bricks and ceramic fibre. Fordham Thermal Systems supply a kit for building your own 5 cu. ft. L.P.G. model. (See also *gas burner*, *inspirating burner*.)

GAULT CLAY

A brick clay with a high calcium content and consequent short *vitrification* range (maximum around 1100°C.). The iron content is bleached by the calcia to yellow or buff in a clay body, but when used as a *slip glaze* at high temperatures some samples will behave more like Albany clay.

GEOLOGY

Geology is the study of the whole physical earth; the study of the rocks which form the earth's crust and which is more important to the potter is known as petrology.

GERMANIUM, oxide

A metallic element Ge, 72.5. Oxide GeO$_2$ 104.5. Sometimes listed as a *glass-former*, i.e. with silica.

GERSTLEY BORATE

An impure colemanite or borate of sodium and calcium with some magnesium, from the Gerstley Mine, Death Valley, California. It has proved to be a particularly 'well-behaved' form of colemanite, only very slowly soluble in water.

Gerstley Borate appears in a number of American glaze recipes in proportions averaging 10–12%, especially for the lower stoneware range 1210–1230°C. Typical analysis (U.S.A. Borax Corp): 28% B_2O_3; 20.6% CaO; 5.3% Na_2O; the rest water and shale. Imported in the U.K. by Potclays Ltd.

GIBBSITE

A *hydrated* alumina mineral, $Al(OH)_2$, or, Al_2O_3, $3H_2O$. The alumina in kaolin is in the form of a 'modified gibbsite sheet' (Worrall). *Calcined* at a high temperature to eliminate high shrinkage. Can be used, with a little china clay, as a *batwash*.

GILDING

Dodd defines gilding as 'the painting of pottery with liquid gold to be fired on at 700°C. but as a general term 'gilding' usually indicates the application of gold leaf with an adhesive or as a paint. (See *gold*.)

GLACIAL CLAYS

Clays which have been transported by glaciers are deposited more or less as they are picked up; they are not separated into particles sizes as are river-borne clays. They are therefore often mixed with non-clay matter and with boulders—hence boulder-clay. Cardew cites the Fremington clay of North Devon in England as a possible glacial clay.

GLASS

A 'melt' of *inorganic* materials cooled sufficiently quickly to prevent crystallization, and retaining its *amorphous* structure. A super-cooled liquid. It has a three-dimensional *network* structure, but without the symmetry of crystals. *Glaze* is a special form of glass, containing alumina, and with a comparatively low thermal expansion.

Foremost of the materials which can form glass is silica. It will 'fuse' alone at 1713°C. but in combination with larger atoms of lower valencies it will melt at lower temperatures. These elements, generally the *bases*, weaken the network bond. Glass can be so soft as actually to dissolve in water (sodium silicate), or hard enough to withstand great abrasion or chemical reaction (salt-glaze, which is also a soda-silicate but of different

formation.) Window glass will lie somewhere between these extremes and is produced with little or no alumina. (See also *glaze, glass-formers, network modifiers, Seger formula* etc.)

GLASS CULLET

Pieces of transparent or colored glass. (See *cullet*.)

GLASS DECORATION

Pieces of glass or, especially, mirror glass have been used decoratively, set into pottery after firing. (See also *melted glass decoration*.)

GLASS FIBER

Fine threads of glass woven into a matted form for use in comparatively low-temperature insulation situations. Not recommended for kilns. A good electrical insulator.

GLASS FORMER

Or network-former. Only a few materials, all *acidic* oxides, can form glass. The most useful to potters are silica and boric oxide, the former being the prime essential in all glazes and in the great majority of ceramic bodies. Antimony oxide and phosphorus pentoxide are of some interest (the latter retaining much of its crystalline structure and giving the particular effects seen in *Jun glaze*), though it has no place in the glass network (Hamer).

The silica tetrahedrons form a random network of linked molecules in the liquid state which can be 'opened' or modified by *bases* to become fluid at a lower temperature. Quick cooling 'freezes' the random network, which cannot then arrange itself into crystals.

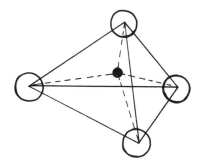

A representation of the silica molecule. A configuration of a small silcon atom (black) and four larger oxygen atoms set in a pyramid formation which is the basis of the silica glass-forming network. It does not exist as a separate entity but is extended in every direction, another Si atom sharing each face with a further O atom. In the whole complex there are therefore twice as many oxygen as silicon atoms and it is written as SiO2 in glaze formulas.

Germanium oxide and arsenous oxide are also listed. Under some conditions alumina can also assist in glass-forming.

GLASS MODIFIER

See *network modifier*.

GLASS MULLER

A sort of flat-ended *pestle* for grinding and mixing color, especially *enamels*, with medium. Used on a glass slab or glazed tiles.

GLASS PHASE

A stage in the heating of ceramics when glass begins to form in the fabric. If excessive the piece may collapse or *deform*. (See *vitrification*, *phase diagrams*, *clay*, *porcelain* etc.)

GLAZE

A ceramic glaze is a special sort of glass, differing from window-glass and glassware in its lower thermal expansion and higher alumina content, which increase its *viscosity* and help it to adhere to the clay body. The general principles are discussed under *glass*, *glass formers*, *network modifier*, *Seger formula* etc.

All glazes start as mixtures of a number of oxides and minerals with water. The craft potter may use these as *raw materials* even *once-firing* them on a clay pot, but an industrial pottery will use them as ground glass or frit. Prepared glazes are usually in the form of *frits*.

One can arrive at a glaze *recipe* either by the empirical trial-and-error method, or by the application of the principles of simple chemistry. Neither, alone, is sufficient. Science is one valuable aid among others, which include careful observation and intuition. Glazes are discussed in this book under *earthenware*, *stoneware*, *porcelain* etc., but the differences are not fundamental. They lie mainly in the choice of *bases*, some of which are not active at the lower temperatures (see *flux*).

The most useful guide to glaze computation, and the easiest to handle, is the *Seger formula*. This discusses glazes in terms of *molecular* equivalents rather than physical weights, but the translation from one to the other is not difficult to make (see *formula-into-recipe*).

The main factors governing the overall behavior of a glaze are:

1 *The base: silica ratio*. The normal practical limits of this ratio are 1:2 and 1:4.5. An average *soft glaze* will in the region of 1:2.8, a stoneware 1:3.8. Above 1300°C. the proportion of silica rises sharply and in hard-paste porcelains may be as high as 1:10.

2 *Choice of bases*. These vary in their effectiveness as fluxes (see list under *flux*). Multi-base formulas are generally preferred to single-base ones.

3 *The use of boric oxide*. Although a *glass-former*, boron operates at a very low temperature and its visible effect is that of a flux. It must be used where lead is not present in a soft glaze. It is usually listed as part of the acidic oxide RO_2, and this can lead to some untypical formulas e.g. 1 RO: 4.8 RO_2—the acid made up of 4.0 of silica and 0.8 B_2O_3—for a soft frit.

4 *The alumina ratio*. Alumina is essential for a stable, well-adhered glaze. The ratio for a clear, bright glaze is alumina:silica from 1:8 to 1:10. An excess is liable to produce a matt surface.

5 *Pigment oxides*. These will behave like other glaze ingredients, the acids rendering the glaze more refractory, the bases tending to soften the glaze.

A simple glaze recipe of equal parts feldspar, china clay, and dolomite on a porcelain body, giving a textured surface resembling salt-glaze. Handbuilt by Sheila Fournier.

A striking pattern on a hand-formed burnished terracotta dish with 'carved glaze'. By Louise Gilbert Scott.

Some materials such as iron oxide are influenced by the kiln atmosphere, and many stoneware glazes appear to achieve greater maturity in *reduction*.

For advice on the formation of glazes see *chemistry of pottery*, *Seger formula*, and under special glaze headings such as *earthenware glazes*, *aventurine*, *Bristol*, *celadon*, etc. The influence of the various *minerals* is discussed under their entries.

GLAZE-BODY FIT

Glazes and bodies undergo a number of expansions, contractions and shrinkages which affect the final state of the cooled ceramic. If the glaze has contracted more than the body after it has become rigid (700°C. and below) it will be in a state of *tension*, which can be relieved only by the glaze crazing. If the reverse is true and the glaze is in slight *compression*, then it will be stable and can also accommodate some thermal shock or expansion though *absorption*. Excessive compression of the glaze will have a similar effect on the body as that of tension in the glaze, *shattering* being the result in extreme cases, or the glaze may *shiver* away on rims etc. Large dishes which are glazed on one side are vulnerable.

Glaze-body fit is arrived at by sensible application of the principles of thermal expansion and inversions, and by the careful observation and evaluation of results from the kiln. (See especially *crazing*, *shattering*, *coefficients of expansion*.)

GLAZE FROM NATURAL SOURCES

All glaze materials, apart from frits and prepared colors, are, of course, 'natural' materials but some hardy souls wish to bypass the commercial suppliers and look for their own locally or sometimes much farther afield. Searching for and dealing with rocks and deposits suitable for glaze making involves some prior geological knowledge and subsequent hard and noisy work rendering them fine enough to use. Harry Davis was so keen he went to New Zealand to work on the basaltic (volcanic) rocks which abound there after he had exhausted his interest in igneous Cornwall! Cardew PP and, especially, Brian Sutherland's book of the same title as this short article, together with various issues of CR,—for instance the color plate of rock fragments in No. 118 and a series of diagrams by David Green in No. 84—will give a good start to a potter interested in this activity. Green analyses such common materials as fuller's earth, slate, and various ashes including coal ash. (See also *clay winning*, *crushing rocks*, *granite*, *grinding of rocks*, etc. and under the various mineral headings.)

GLAZE MELT INDICATOR

If a sufficiently large aperture is available, pieces can be extracted from the kiln during firing as indications of its progress. These can be pieces of the actual body and ware in the setting, or lead-glazed pieces which will become darker and colder as the firing proceeds (these should be of red clay). If the pieces are in the form of a ring or hoop they will be easier to withdraw with a simple iron rod. (See *Bullers ring*, *cone*, *draw trial*, *Seger formula*, etc.)

GLAZE MIXING

See advice at *weighing glaze ingredients*, and when you are sure that you have them all accurately weighed up they can then be sprinkled by hand into a large bowl or bin of water, taking care that you do not raise dust from the materials in doing so (or wear a mask). They will then soak more quickly without aggravating lumps. The exceptions to this method are talc and bentonite. The first needs mixing with other ingredients and should then be worked into a paste with a little water before soaking—otherwise it will float on the surface and refuse to mix. Bentonite should be similarly treated, adding water very gradually to form first a thick paste and preferably put through a 200 sieve before being added to the batch.

The soaked ingredients can usefully be first brushed through a coarse nylon sieve (such as a cook's sieve), preferably not a wire one as the metal may stain the glaze, before the appropriate lawn is used—usually 60 or 100 mesh for stoneware, 100–120 for earthenware—though special materials may have their own demands. Sieve twice if the glaze is to be used immediately and stir very thoroughly; the efficient melting of the glaze depends on the close association of each ingredient with the others.

GLAZE OVER GLAZE

A technique of decoration where one glaze is poured over another in part, as a complete re-coating, or in conjunction with *wax resist or sgraffito*.

In earthenware attractive results can be obtained by covering a *saturated glaze*, on which a bold, simple wax design has been painted, with a clear glaze. This is most successful on tiles, bowls and dishes, i.e. on semi-horizontal surfaces. The second coating should be poured or dipped while the first is still damp but not shiny. Practice is required, as with all glaze over glaze techniques, to assess correctly the comparative consistencies of the glaze batches used, and to avoid too thick a final layer. There will always be a degree of flow from one glaze to another, softening and altering the shape of the resist line. Fire experiments on a bat with plenty of alumina in case of running. A thinner top coat will give a crisper design but less contrast. It is advisable to wax the rim after the first coat. Stoneware glazes, being more viscous, run and merge less than *soft glazes*. Experiments can be carried out using a more *refractory* underglaze.

Panels can be dipped, or the pouring action itself can

An earthenware bowl with a saturated manganese glaze which has been painted with a wax design and then covered with a second (tin) glaze. The original waxed line has become finer and narrower with the running of the glaze.

Stoneware (reduced, 1280°C,) with a black glaze poured over a clear glaze. Underglaze cobalt blue brushwork plus, in a second firing at 780°C., further decoration with onglaze enamels By Kevin White (Australia).

be used to provide a pattern. A number of modern potters pour glaze, sweeps of contrasting color from the center line outwards give a variety of patterns. Glazes may also be treated like slip and trailed one onto another. A *flocculant* can give some *viscosity* in the trailer, but a sure and rapid motion is called for.

Glazes can be *sprayed*, either in the open air or with an efficient extractor.

The comparative thicknesses of the glazes, the types of glaze (*refractory*, *matt*, *opaque*, etc.), the colors, the soaking time in the kiln and other factors will all influence and vary the results.

A second glaze can be poured over a fired glaze. This will give a less contrasting effect. *Crazing* will sometimes absorb glaze when dipped, or a *crawled* glaze can be filled with another color by sponging a thick glaze into the cracks.

GLAZE STAIN

The term 'stain' is generally applied to the *fritted* colors in suppliers' catalogs, as distinct from the *pigment oxides* used raw. Variations in hue, apart from the combining of various oxides, are obtained by *sintering* with such non-coloring additions as alumina, soda, flint, etc. which alter the hue. When redissolved in a glaze, the stain may revert to the typical oxide color, and care must be taken to use only the glaze recommended for the color. Stains are more dilute than oxides and are added in proportions of around 10%, or as directed by the makers.

GLAZE THICKNESS

The thickness of a glaze coating is a critical factor in its behavior and fired appearance. Too thick, and it is liable to *peel*, *crawl* or *craze*; too thin, and it will fail to develop its true character. There is no one ideal consistency; each recipe has its optimum thickness which can be decided only by trial and experience. A reading with a *hydrometer* is useful, while tight-fitting bin lids will help to control the inevitable evaporation between firings.

Factors controlling glaze coating are:
1 *Biscuit porosity*. The glaze take-up depends on water being absorbed, leaving a solid coat of glaze material on the surface. Keep biscuit firings as standard as possible. The thickness of the pot wall is allied to porosity. A thin wall will saturate quickly and cease to develop further coatings—in fact the glaze already solidified can be re-saturated from the water in the batch and may wash off again. If this happens the pot must be cleaned, dried over a strong heat, and another attempt made. A thick wall will absorb more

moisture and thus retain a thicker coating. Good glazing therefore depends on even-walled throwing and making. An open, *grogged* body will obviously be more porous than a close one. The more porous the pot, the more water is required in the glaze batch in relation to solid matter. (See *tongue test.*)

2   *The batch consistency.* It follows from the previous remarks that a thicker mixture will result in a thicker coating. Test with a hydrometer, or more roughly by dipping in a dry finger or test-strip; note the reading for future occasions. A glaze may appear to thicken as it stands; this is a result of *flocculation* caused by soluble alkalis or colemanite. This glaze will have a jelly-like consistency. If further water is added, it may lead to excessive contraction of the glaze-coating followed by peeling. *Ash glazes* are liable to flocculation; more careful washing of the ash will help to minimize the trouble.

3   *Speed of work.* Quick dipping will give less time for absorption than a slow one, and thus cause a thinner coat to develop. Very slow dipping may saturate a pot wall so that the glaze will fail to dry. A steady but unhesitating action is called for. Do not shake violently after dipping; a short circular or twisting movement will cast off the drips.

4   *Type of glazes.* Glazes vary in their optimum thickness; and you may actually want to vary it for differ-

ent effects. Raw material glazes need a thicker coat than do frits which have already lost their volatile components. Also, frits, being powdered glass, will look very thin when the pot is lifted from the glaze but the coating will become opaque as it dries. In general a transparent glaze will need a slightly thinner coating than an opaque or colored one.

5   *Double-dipping* needs careful preparation, the first coat acting as a very porous body if allowed to get too dry. (See *glaze over glaze.*)

To summarize, as a general guide:

A thinner glaze mixture for:
Frits
Porous biscuit
Thick-walled pots
Slow glazing (difficult pots)
Clear glazes (earthenware)
A thicker glaze mixture for:
Higher-fired, low-porosity biscuit
Thin-walled pots
'Skimming' of tiles
Opaque glazes (generally)

GLAZE-TRAILING

Decoration derived from varying the glaze thickness of an oxidised dolomite/copper glaze which goes black where it is thicker. The bowl was dipped first one side and then the other, the center swathe being the overlapped portion. Pouring the glaze from the dish resulted in the lower darker area. By Robert Fournier. The technique can give subtle and integral designs.

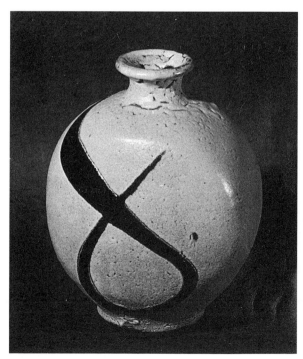

Typically rapid and emphatic black trailing onto a flattened bottle by Shoji Hamada. (See also photo at tube lining).

Glazes as well as slips can be *trailed*. The decoration is necessarily fairly broad in style. Trailing can be done on the biscuit, or on a glaze coating. A certain spread and softening of the line are inevitable when two glazes are used, but trailing can be quite crisp on biscuit or on a refractory glaze.

GLAZE TRIAL

One is always faced with the necessity to compromise in the making up of test glaze batches. Large quantities will be wasteful, but small samples are liable to error during weighing, in the relative dampness of the ingredients, and in preparation losses. 300 gm. ($10\frac{1}{2}$ oz.) must be considered a minimum batch. *Line blends* or *triaxial blending* allow larger initial batch weights.

The object of a series of glaze trials is to arrive at a useful *recipe*. Haphazard, unrepeatable mixtures are merely tantalizing. It is necessary to record at least the weights, subsequent alterations and the firing temperature. Never rely on memory. (See also *records, glaze trial log*.) The recipe is, of course, only one factor: others include the size of the kiln, speed of firing and cooling, kiln atmosphere and glaze thickness.

Glaze trials merely brushed onto tiles or shards are insufficient. Small bowls can be thrown very rapidly from cones of clay, cylinders can be cut into sections, or curved tiles about $2\frac{1}{2} \times 1\frac{1}{2} \times \frac{1}{4}$ in. ($60 \times 30 \times 5$ mm.) can be stood on end, or formed over a rolling-pin. Circular discs with a hole may be glazed and filed, or hung on a board or on the actual glaze-bin. For the ultimate trials, full-sized production pieces are used.

The golden rule for glaze trials or any other trial is: alter only one ingredient at a time. If two variables are operating together, it is difficult to decide which of them is primarily responsible for the result. This is admittedly a counsel of perfection and is not followed in all the permutations of the second series discussed below.

It is useful to test materials on their own (see *button test*), but, unless they are natural or artificial frits (e.g. feldspar or lead silicate) the essential reaction between the material or oxide and silica will not be shown. (See *calcium* for an extreme example.)

Trials with three simple materials such as a lead frit, clay, and flint can be of great education value with students. A simple series may run as follows:

Trial No	1	2	3	4	5	6	7
Frit	100			33	70	15	15
Clay		100		33	15	70	15
Flint			100	33	15	15	70

Nos 1, 2 and 3 are for testing the materials alone, No. 4 tests them in equal quantities; and 5, 6 and 7 are

tests involving an excess of one ingredient over the other two. The use of red clay would further differentiate the results. For stonewares, almost any three minerals can be tried in similar proportions.

An interesting series of glaze trials were achieved by a mixture of line blending and more intuitive experiment. The series may be taken as one model (among many) for a trial sequence. It by no means covered the field but it did give a useful general picture. The variables were: five similar batches of glaze, each with the accepted maximum proportion of a coloring oxide (i.e. 'saturated glazes'); a similar opaque glaze with 10% tin oxide which was added in various quantities to dilute the colors; and a softer frit which tested the effect of both dilution and a more fluid melt.

The series, which was repeated for each color and for eight permutations of two colors, was as follows:

Group A—single color

		Colored glaze	Tin glaze	Soft frit	
No	1	2	1		parts
No	2	2	1	1	parts
No	3	1	4		parts
No	4	1	4	2	parts

Group B—two colors

		Color (1)	Color (2)	Tin	Frit	
No	5	1	1			parts
No	6	1	1	1		parts
No	7	1	1	3	1	parts
No	8	1	4			parts
No	9	1	4	3		parts
No	10	1	4	5	2	parts
No	11	4	1			parts
No	12	4	1	3		parts
No	13	4	1	5	2	parts

The standard 'part' was a dessertspoonful. All tests were fired at the same temperature and on buff and red trial pieces.

To work back from any mixture to a recipe, multiply each of the ingredients of the constituent glazes in the mixture by the 'parts'; list them in a chart, find the totals and divide each figure by the total number of 'parts' as shown in the chart on page 130.

Example. In the chart Test No. 10 in the above series has been worked back to a recipe assuming that:

C (1) was
Lead sesquisilicate	60
China clay	15
Whiting	5
Flint	20
Copper oxide	2.5

Glaze	Parts	Lead ses.	Clay	Whiting	Flint	MnO$_2$	Tin	Frit	CuO
C1	1	60	15	5	20				2.5
C2	4	240	60	20	80	40			
T	5	300	75	25	100		50		
S	2							200	
Totals	12	600	150	50	200	40	50	200	2.5
Recipe	1	50	12.5	4.1	16.5	3.3	4.1	16.7	0.2

The same type of chart can be used for any mixtures or blends

and C (2) was a similar glaze with 10% manganese dioxide, and T was a similar glaze with 10% tin oxide, S being a soft frit.

GLAZE TRIAL LOG

The records which a potter needs to keep will vary with particular kinds of work. The closer one gets to a final

TEST no	1	2
RECIPE	Lead sesquisilicate 70 China clay 20 Flint 10 Tin oxide 12 (500 gms)	
TEST PIECE	Curved tile	
BODY	Red	
TEST SURFACE	Impressed	
GLAZE THICKNESS	Thin and medium	
KILN AND FIRING	1080°C Soaked Small kiln 10 mins.	
POSITION IN KILN	Middle	
NOTES	Biscuit low fired	
TYPE	Opaque	
COLOUR	White	
SURFACE	Shiny	
NOTES	Breaking well to red-brown at sharp edges Poor where thin	
ASSESSMENT	Good	
ALTERATIONS	None needed	
NAME	Soft tin glaze	

recipe, the more information one needs to keep. A possible log book is shown in the chart. The information on the actual glaze trial can be tied in with *kiln logs* or records; this is especially important in reduction firings.

GLAZING

It is probable that more pots are spoiled during glazing than at any other stage. That 'it will all smooth out in the firing' is a common delusion. Certainly some glazes are more accommodating than others. Opaque and colored glazes will show differences in thickness more clearly than transparent ones.

Bubbling, *crazing* and other ills can often be traced to faulty glaze-application. In all cases, the tidier a pot looks when it goes into the kiln the better it is likely to look when it comes out. Consistency of the batch is discussed under *glaze thickness*. Pots can be dipped, rolled, poured or sprayed. Speed and smoothness of movement are the keys to good glazing. Think carefully before starting each piece, and work out the best procedure for it.

Where there is plenty of glaze, the quickest and easiest method is immersing. Hold a pot by the rim and base, or a dish each side of the rim, using as few fingers as possible or, better still, a wire gripper (see *glazing gripper*). After a quick sweep through the glaze—with dishes the edge farthest from the potter enters the glaze first—hold the piece vertically to drain it for a few moments and then stand it down on a *stilt*. Pots, beakers, etc. in a shallow glaze should be held with two fingers on the base and two on the rim 'walked' round the pot so that the piece revolves in the glaze. Tip it the right way up for an instant to ensure that the base is covered inside, and then invert to drain.

Tiles can be held across the back with fingers and thumb and skimmed across the glaze surface, the leading edge entering first. With practice, a neat glaze line along the edges can be achieved.

For stoneware and other pieces which are not to be glazed over the base there are three possibilities. They can be filled, emptied and dipped in quick succession. Large pots may need to have glaze poured over them. If it is possible to grip the base, turn the pot as far round in one direction as possible, so that a smooth and complete revolution can be made as the glaze is poured. Use a big enough jug and a large bowl to catch the surplus. If the pot is too heavy or awkward it can be supported on a central stick, across two supports on the bowl, or on a turntable.

The 'water spout' dip takes some practice (try it when washing-up!), but it is ideal for the rapid glazing of beakers, wide-mouthed pots, bowls, etc. particularly

for stonewares. The piece is gripped by the foot or base, dipped to the desired level outside, then sharply lifted straight up until it barely leaves the glaze, the suction causing a 'water spout' to rise. Very quickly the pot is pushed downwards onto the rising column of glaze which will coat the interior even of tall jugs. After trying it, you will probably add 'sometimes', but with practice it is a very reliable method.

Spraying. Blowing glaze through a spray is dangerous. A bulb or mechanical pump should be used, together with an extractor-fan. It takes a good deal of spraying to achieve a thick enough glaze coating, but for slip glazes, thin layers and special effects it can be useful, though it always results in a somewhat mechanical finish.

Some general notes:

1 Pour some of the clear water from the top of a glaze before stirring. Keep this water handy in a jug and add again if necessary.

Stir your glaze very thoroughly and keep it stirred during use.

2 Label permanent containers clearly. Beware changing containers when re-sieving a glaze, which will be necessary from time to time.

Use a container of a suitable size and shape for the piece to be glazed.

3 Touch up holding marks with finger or brush immediately after glazing. Smooth the repair over as it dries, and carefully scrape down blotches or runs with a sharp knife (e.g. a photographic re-touching knife).

Although for tableware and much other pottery a smooth, even coating of glaze is desirable, it is obviously possible to use different thicknesses of glaze in a free and exciting way on more decorative or sculptural pieces. Even on tableware, the marks left by the gripping fingers of a skilful potter can add to the attractions of a pot. Other glaze faults such as *crawling* or even *peeling* can be used positively.

4 It is easier to protect a surface from glaze than to scrape it off afterwards. This can be done by brushing with wax. See *wax*.

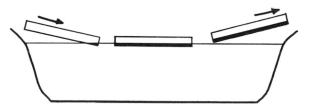

Glazing tiles by skimming them across the surface of a well-stirred glaze. The tile can be held with the thumb and finger or with a glazing gripper.

Glazing

Teapots present special problems, especially the clogging of strainer holes. One can fill the teapot with glaze and pour it all out of the spout. This saturates the strainer and a sharp jerk will free the holes, or you can blow sharply down the spout (don't eat the glaze!). Alternatively a pad of clay can be pressed over the holes prior to glazing, or they can be thickly *waxed*. (See also *poured glaze*.)

1

2

3

4

5

6

7

8

9

10

11

12

13

(1) to (4) Glazing by filling and dipping. The pot is filled to the brim with glaze, or partly filled and revolved as it is emptied, reversed, dipped immediately to the required depth, lifted out and given a slight sideways twist to shake off drips. The whole process is a continuous movement. For pouring glaze over a tall pot which can be gripped at the foot, it is first held (upsidedown) with the wrist turned as far round towards the body as possible. As the glaze is poured steadily from a large jug into a large bowl, the pot is given a complete revolution. (5) to (13) A teapot poses special problems in glazing. The series shown here embodies some of Geoffrey Whiting's methods. The flange and base are waxed in order to resist the glaze at these points, and the pot filled with glaze and emptied by pouring steadily from the spout (see text). The shoulder and end of the spout are glazed by inverting and dipping. The teapot is then turned right way up, gripped by the inside of the lid flange, and again dipped until the glaze levels overlap but being careful that none runs into the spout. The lid is dipped upsidedown just to the top edge of the rim.

GLAZING GRIPPER

Metal grippers are especially useful when glazing flat-ware or bowls. They can be cut from sheet alumina or curve. If the slowly increasing curve is continued beyond to work with a single strand on each arm, but two claws on one arm give a firmer hold. Two or three sizes will be necessary to cover the likely range of pots and bowls with 3–6 in. (70–150 mm.), 6–10 in. (150–250 mm.), and 10–14 in. (250–350 mm.) spans.

Interior grippers which exert pressure outwards have a limited but occasionally essential use. See at *raku*.

(A) A glazing gripper of galvanized or kiln element wire, and
(B) of sheet metal – aluminium or brass.

GLOBAR

A trade name for *silicon carbide* kiln elements.

GLOST FIRE

Term used for the glaze-firing of ceramics, especially in the industry and in America. More rarely applied as 'glost ware'.

GLOVES

Fire-proof, heat-insulating gloves or mittens are essential for *raku* and are sometimes useful for normal firings. If a pot is liable to burn your hand, however, it means that it is still too hot to take it from the kiln. There are special heat-proof gloves available though these may be expensive and leather gardening gloves or kitchen oven gloves are alternatives, though less efficient.

GOLD

Gold *enamel* is fired onto glazed pottery at about 700°C. It is used as a prepared liquid and painted on with a brush. Before firing it is brown and sticky. It is prepared as either a gold chloride (Billington), or as a gold sulphoresinate and a flux, perhaps bismuth (for 'bright' gold), or as gold powder in essential oils for 'burnish' or 'best' gold (Dodd).

Bright gold comes from the kiln shiny; burnish gold is dull from the firing and must be rubbed with a stone (traditionally a 'blood-stone' or agate) or with a glass burnisher to bring up the surface glint.

Leach mentions the admixture of gold dust with red enamel in Japan, which softens the crudity of the color. Experiment on these lines might be rewarding. Curious

colors result from the use of gold in raku firing. Painting with prepared gold will reveal any hidden crazing. Gold and tin oxide give *purple of cassius*. Pinks and reds in enamels are also obtained from gold.

The firing must be very precise, especially if the painting is done in thin strokes. A few degrees over and a purple may develop. On some glazes, however, the gold cannot be subdued even at 1000°C.

Gold enamel felt-tip pens are available for fine drawing.

GRAIN SIZE

Apart from the obvious textural effects of differences in grain size of grog, sand, etc. in a clay body, too fine a material will have ill effects on plasticity and can cause over-vitrification and deformation in the firing, especially in reduction. Hamer quotes a minimum of 200 mesh for flint in earthenware bodies and 80 for sand in stonewares.

GRANITE

Most *intrusive* rocks are in the form of granite, which is classified as an *acidic* rock, i.e. with a high silica content. An analysis of a typical granite shows some 70% of silica; 14.5% alumina; various bases in percentages from 4.5 potash to 0.05 baria; 3% or less of iron compounds with some phosphorus and titanium.

In decomposition, therefore, granite contains the ingredients of the pottery minerals—feldspar, stone, quartz etc.—and, at one remove, clay. The range of rocks of which granite is one is known as igneous (from fire). Ivan Englund discusses the 'average' granite, which he calls 'avgran', for use in glazes, (CR various issues, especially No. 87). Because it is such a hard rock, he recommends using dust from granite workings, or else heating it in a fire or kiln to weaken the molecular bonds. His final recipe suggestion as a 'starter' is: granite, 73; whiting 18; silica 9; bentonite 2. It will inevitably contain some iron oxide. (See also *crushing rocks*.)

GRAPH

A graph is a pictorial or diagrammatic representation of the relationship between two variables. The information it contains would take many sentences to describe; it can estimate intermediates between known points and can sometimes be extended to indicate probabilities.

A graph consists of a vertical measured line and a horizontal one, joined at their lower left-hand terminations. Each line is divided into regular units appropriate to the data. A familiar example will explain how to set out a graph.

GRAPH FOR VARIABLE TIME AND TEMPERATURE DURING A FIRING

(A) A typical firing graph with readings taken every two hours (horizontal figures). The broken lines connect the vertical (°C. figures) scale with the time divisions. The points of intersection are marked. The slowly flattening curve is typical of firing graphs (the increasing heat loss slowly balancing output). A possible 'projection' is shown as a dotted line.

The vertical numbers represent intervals of 100°C., the horizontal ones hours. At any point in your firing you can consult the pyrometer and draw a horizontal line from the temperature and a vertical one from the time which has elapsed since commencement. Readings every two hours are shown. The points of conjunction

(B) Another typical graph. The numbers could represent monthly pot production and the sequence of months. This graph suggests a somewhat erratic output but does show an overall improvement over the period. The number of pots could be related to their value and a second graph superimposed which will give a more accurate idea of the financial health of the workshop.

can be joined by straight lines or drawn as an estimated curve. If the slowly increasing curve is continued beyond the last reading it will give a rough indication of the maximum temperature the kiln may reach, or at what time it would reach a given higher figure.

Graphs can be drawn for any two sets of variables. A particularly ingenious one is described in Cardew PP, Appendix 8, to produce approximations to square roots below unity. Graphs do not have to show a steady progression, but can show broken lines and sharp angles, frequently caricatured as profit and loss graphs. The principle remains the same.

A graph may be misleading if based on insufficient or inaccurate information.

The use of squared paper facilitates graph-making.

GRAPHITE

A natural form of carbon. Also called 'blacklead' and 'plumbago'. (See also *reduction*.)

GRATE

The bars which support burning fuel and allow the passage of air through it. The development of the fire-grate (grating) marked a significant step forward from the flat surface with its heaped-up fuel and ash mixture. The earliest grates were composed of ceramic cylinders laid horizontally across stones. The grate made a hotter and more controllable flame possible, with the ash falling away and more easily disposed of. The modern type of grate was used by Bottger to achieve his remarkable 1300°C. plus for porcelain. The heat can either travel direct into the kiln from the fuel surface, or be drawn through the bars.

The development of refractory steels and casting has produced grates with a long life, but care must be taken that the ash never comes into contact with the underside of the metal or the bars will twist and fail. Oil or gas burners, of course, do not require grates. Parks recommends that the hearth or grate size should be one-third of the loading area.

GREEN GLAZES

There are two families of green colors in glazes: those derived directly from pigment oxides, usually copper or chrome; and those from reduced iron.

We will deal here mainly with the first group. Chrome is a hard, dense opaque coloring agent, and it is advisable to keep the proportions in a glaze to 1% or less. It will give green in a zinc-free multibase *lead glaze* at 1050–1150°C., and in stoneware glazes. At lower temperatures it may give very different colors. Combined with cobalt the color is brighter and somewhat less dense, though still liable to give a rather lifeless surface. Although *refractory* it will *volatilize* and can be a danger in the presence of tin oxide. (See *chrome-tin pink*.)

Copper, in proportions of 1–3% in an oxidizing atmosphere, will give a variety of greens in soft glazes: apple green in a lead glaze, a brighter color in a lead-lime-potash or leadless glaze, progressing towards turquoise as the alkalis are increased and the alumina content diminished.

Greens from copper or chrome can be modified or assisted by additions of other oxides. Cobalt has been mentioned (use only about 0.2% in the batch): iron, nickel, rutile, vanadium and antimony can be experimented with. Prepared stains have been derived from cobalt/uranium, zirconium/vanadium, and praseodymium phosphate. Iron and cobalt mixtures tend to give gray rather than green, but antimoniate/cobalt mixtures will give better results when used as a pigment, see below. Nickel oxide can give gray-green in a lead borax glaze. Some magnesium in the formula can improve the color. Most of these mixtures and stains are more suitable for soft glazes, but Fulham Pottery lists a zircon/vanadium/praseodymium green stain which will hold for temperatures up to 1280°C.

True turquoise in a soft glaze demands a soda-silica glass, which is somewhat unstable as a glaze. See also *Egyptian paste*. For stoneware, a *turquoise* to blue-green recipe is given at that entry. In fluid glazes copper will volatilize and is apt to be uncertain in its effect above 1200°C.

Kathleen Pleydell-Bouverie gives a sea-green or olive-green mixture for addition to *oxidized stonewares*:

Iron	1%
Manganese	0.3–0.5%
Copper	0.3–0.5%
Cobalt	0.5%

Copper is dangerous in lead glazes, see *metal release*, *soluble lead*.

For a discussion of reduced greens see *reduction*, and *celadon*.

GREEN GLAZING

A term sometimes applied to once-fired ware, i.e. glazed on the raw or 'green' clay. (See *once-fired ware*.)

GREEN PIGMENT

Copper, either as the oxide or carbonate (slightly toxic), is commonly used on earthenware glazes to produce various hues of a rather watery kind. It is normally used as a wash or filler for a design, and needs applying with care, since any excess will fire black and cindery.

Chrome is also difficult to use alone, being refractory and having a heavy opacity. Beware pink reactions from chrome. Prepared colors are generally mixtures of these oxides fritted with zinc, whiting, borax etc. to induce variety of hue. The coloring agent for Victoria green is stated to be $3CaO.Cr_2O_3.3SiO_2$. Cobalt can be added to chrome with advantage. Simple mixtures of cobalt and iron, or cobalt and antimoniate of lead (or yellow stain), can give subtle greenish colors in a tin glaze, sometimes partly separating out in a pleasant way. Green pigment is less often used on stoneware. Cobalt in a zinc glaze can produce a rather strident green. See also at *green glazes* for some less familiar compounds which are also utilized in green pottery pigments.

There are dangers in using copper in lead glazes, see *metal release*, *soluble lead*.

GREEN SLIPS

Chrome and copper in equal parts will provide a reasonably pleasant and stable green in slip. The first is too hard and opaque alone, the second too watery. 1.25% of each, in a pale buff slip, is adequate. Iron or a darker slip will gray the tone. Blue slip under a *honey* glaze will tend towards green.

GREENWARE

Unfired pottery. Leach uses the term for leather-hard clay suitable for turning and cutting, but it is also used for dry clay. Green strength is an important virtue in a body (see *dry strength*.)

GRINDING OF ROCKS

Most commercially supplied materials are in a finely-ground form—sometimes too fine. For breaking down experimental quantities of rock etc. a *mortar and pestle* can be used, or a *ball* or *jar mill*. A primitive but effective grinding pan used until recently at Soil Hill Pottery, Yorkshire was simply a circular metal container with a revolving central shaft which dragged flat stones round on chains. (See also *crushing rock*, *pan mill*, *vibratory mill*.)

GRINDING WHEEL

An abrasive disc which revolves on a central axis. The old, large wheels were turned quite slowly with a treadle; the modern wheel is spun at high speed by an electric motor. It needs to be true on the centre or considerable and dangerous vibration will be set up. The disc can be of bonded *silicon carbide* or *alumina* (marked 'C' and 'A' on British standard wheels); (see *abrasive*). There are many grades and grain-sizes. A hard grade of medium grain with a vitrified bond (marked 'V') would be of general use, but finer wheels may be necessary for glaze grinding.

GROG

Ground, fired biscuit (sometimes even ground up glazed ware, in porcelain factories). Incorporated into clay bodies to give texture, to impart 'bite' when throwing, to assist drying, or to increase firing strength. It will reduce the rate of clay shrinkage during drying and, in the firing, up to the temperature at which the grog itself was fired.

Standard grog is made from a refractory *fireclay* and is relatively inert at potters' temperatures. It is graded according to the size of grain, e.g. a '30 to dust' grog would be composed of all the grades which would pass a 30 mesh sieve. '30–60' will pass a 30 mesh but be retained by a 60. Some suppliers grade still more carefully, e.g. all through 40, 25% retained in 60, 25% by 100, 50% through 100 mesh. This would be a very fine grog, almost too small even for throwing clay. A grog which is too fine may be a hazard, causing the clay to absorb water rapidly. For a normal body up to 10% of grog may be added, but much more for large pieces and special work.

As a rough guide to grog size: that which passes a 50 sieve is no more than a calcined clay dust, through 30 would be a fine grog; through 14 a medium one; and through 8 mesh a coarse sample.

Grog can be made in small quantities by crushing dry clay to a suitable size and firing it in an unglazed bowl. Colored grog can be tried for particular effects, e.g. red-clay grog beaten into the surface of stonewares. Grog for raku can be crushed soft brick. (See also *ilmentite*.) An interesting grog recipe for coloring with chrome and other pigments is given in CR 102 by Mark Stanczyk; china clay, 80; frit, 16; bone ash, 4.

GROUND-HOG KILN

A semi-updraft kiln partially buried in a bank of earth. The earth acts as a heat insulator and building the kiln in a sloping barnk helps to create draft. The idea has parallels in the Eastern sloping kilns and could be utilised for 'primitive' firings such as raku. Rhodes quotes their use by country potters of the Southern Highlands of the U.S.A. (illustration in Rhodes, K). As a type, however it was widespread. Sometimes adapted today for temporary outdoor kilns at ceramic festivals and tutorials.

GROUND-LAY

A method of applying an even layer of pottery color by first coating the biscuit or glaze with a tacky oil, onto which the pigment is then dusted. Mainly used in the industry on bone china, but the principle, in a more flexible for, could be adapted to craft ceramics and modeling.

GROUT

To fill the joins between tiles or tessarae after they have been set in cement, glued, or otherwise fastened down. The grouting material should be of the same kind as the backing if set as described under *mosaic*. For tiles there are a number of proprietary grouting materials, but most are white and could well be stained to make the grouting less conspicuous. Portland cement can be used if dried very slowly under polythene (2–3 days).

GROWAN STONE

A Cornish china stone.

GUM ARABIC, tragacanth

Vegetable gum can be purchased as liquid or as powder. Powders are dissolved in water or denatured alcohol by soaking overnight, boiling for a few minutes and straining through a 40's mesh. A dessertspoonful of tragacanth dissolved in a pint of water is sufficient for around six gallons of glaze. Gummed glaze forms a 'surface (which) takes painted decoration better', (Sutherland GNS).

Sometimes added to glazes (e.g. raku), or colors, to give a harder coating when dry, avoiding rubbing and smudging. All gums will decay in time and spoil the glaze. A little *formalin* has been suggested to counteract decomposition.

Gum arabic has some *deflocculant* effect. Tragacanth promotes *suspension* or *floatation*. Dextrin is an alternative. Cardew mentions a gum and quartz mixture for painting lid flanges etc. to prevent sticking during firing. Fine alumina might be preferable in place of the quartz.

GUMBO

A very sticky surface clay (Rhodes).

GYPSUM

A widely distributed evaporate rock (from evaporation of salt water). A hydrated calcium sulphate $CaSO_4$ $2H_2O$. Shells embedded in clay and attacked by sulfuric acids from metallic sulfides form transparent gypsum crystals. Most gypsum is derived from *anhydrite*. The pure micro-crystalline form is alabaster.

When crushed and heated in a revolving cylinder to 120°C., gypsum loses more than half of its water of crystallization and becomes an unstable demi-hydrate powder. Upon the addition of water it re-assumes something of its original hard state. This is *plaster of paris*. If the powder or plaster is heated above 120°C. it becomes 'dead-burnt' and will not reset. So do not dry molds on a hot kiln. Hamer suggests using small quantities of gypsum in or under the first glaze of a double layer to promote oilspot in a fluid glaze.

HAEMATITE

The accepted English dictionary spelling but see under the simplified *hematite*.

HAKE

A soft, flat hand-made Japanese brush. 1½–3½ in. (35–90 mm.) wide. From 'hakame'?

HAKEME

A form of decoration using a white slip and a coarse brush often as a ground for iron brushwork. Early examples can be found on the rough pots and bowls of the Korean Yi period. Leach PB has a drawing of a hakeme brush described as 'a miniature garden broom made of the grain ends of the rice straw'. The technique has been used by Bill Marshall of St Ives and, of course, by Hamada, amongst others. The slip, which must be fairly thick or it may vanish under the glaze, (though this is not such a danger in stoneware), is normally spun onto the surface of the pot or bowl on a slow-turning wheel or banding-wheel. The effect is a subtle contrast

A type of hakeme achieved by a rapid dabbing of a slip-loaded brush onto the slip-coated surface of a bowl as it slowly revolves on the wheel.

between body and slip, the slip being a little lighter in color than the body. Leach recommends Pike's siliceous ball clay G.F.C. but other light colored clays will do, perhaps with the addition of some china clay and feldspar, though to go too far with additions to the natural clay will destroy the quality of the result which, to quote Honey 'implies a principle fundamental in all the arts— it speaks clearly of a process'. In the Far East some potters use a technique of dabbing a very wide brush rapidly up and down on a flattish bowl as it turns giving a regular broken pattern of slip—it needs a lot of practice!

HALLOYSITE

A kaolinite (clay) mineral in which the plate-like structure is rolled into tubes, causing high and uneven shrinkage due to their sudden collapse on drying. The mineral may be present in various clays. Found in New Zealand, Japan, North Africa, and Mississippi, U.S.A.

The possible structure of halloysite showing curled 'plates' which collapse during firing, leading to excessive and uneven shrinkage.

HANDBUILDING

A convenient term for the forming of ceramics without a wheel. Can include *coiling*, *pinching*, *slab building*, *molding*, or combinations of these. Bowls and other rounded forms can be stroked and beaten out of a ball of clay as in many primitive and traditional techniques. The illustrations show a bowl made by a combination of pinching, stroking and coiling, using rubber and *steel palettes*. (See also *formers*, *cut-corner dishes*, etc.)

Stages in the handbuilding of a bowl.
(1) to (3) A sufficiently large ball of fine-grogged clay is pinched into a hollow form, using both hands. This is further thinned and shaped by holding the curve in the palm and stroking the surface with the fingers of the other hand, finally smoothing with a kidney rubber.
(4) It is dropped into a biscuited bowl to stiffen.
(5) At the soft-leather stage the inside and the outside are further smoothed and shaped with a steel palette.
(6) to (8) The bowl is reversed onto a whirler, an area brushed with slip, and a foot coiled on.

9

10

11

(9) and (10) The base is carefully levelled with a needle awl and finally worked into the curve of the form with a palette.
(11) The finished bowl.

HANDLE

The forerunner of the handle was the pierced lug, one on either side of the pot. These can be found in the Shang Yin pots from Central China and in ceramics from the near tropical countries from Africa to Peru. They are still used by potters, sometimes decoratively, sometimes when the pot is designed to be suspended, which was

their original use. From the lug to the true side handle intended for grasping with the hand was a considerable step but intermediate stages appear to be few.

There are many contrasting forms of handles: those applied to commercial pottery differ in some fundamental ways from those found on craftsman-potter's work. In industry the handles may be carefully considered in relation to the pot, but it is always made, in a press or slip-mold, as a separate entity. A distinct point of junction is thus apparent. A 'stop' or thumb-hold at the top may be worked into the design to prevent the hand from slipping. These handles need not have a smooth, arched flow of the pulled handle but may be angled or built up from broken curves. It is the clean articulation of parts which is distinctive of the best industrial ceramics.

At the other end of the scale, an English Medieval jug handles springs like a branch from the main form, to which it is firmly secured by strokes of the thumb. This apparently natural growth gives satisfaction from all angles, not merely from a profile view. The strong 'pulling lines' and bold wipe of the clay each side of the juncture are delights in themselves. The thumb movement at once fastens the handle and decorates the pot. Since this is a practical dictionary we will ignore quirky 'handles' which are designed as decorative or symbolic aspects of non-functional ceramics, an entertaining enough game which has been practised since the earliest examples, and mention only a few aspects of those handles designed for use.

The placing, shape, and size of a handle is dictated by its use. 'Size' also includes thickness or degree of sturdiness compatible with the material; earthenware, porcelain, etc. and the general character of the vessel. A handle which looks as if it might break when grasped will never give comfort or pleasure to the user.

Placing—the placing of a handle is governed by three main considerations : the curves of the main form: the number of fingers required to lift the vessel when full of liquid (the thickness and width of the handle must also be in direct relation to this weight); physical and formal balance.

Between the curve of the pot and that of the handle there is a space. Not only must this be sufficient to accommodate the finger or fingers comfortably, but the shape of the space is of great aesthetic importance. On a more or less cylindrical jug or beaker it may be no more than the simple letter D—the one-finger handle is an example—but on the inward curve between the belly and neck of a well-designed jug it will be very subtle. These related curves should merge into a whole.

It is usually advisable to spring the handle across a concave section of the pot form. If it straddles a bulge a rather ugly crescent is formed and the handle may become awkwardly long, or difficult to hold, or both.

When dealing with the question of placing, one can say generally that a handle which springs higher than the rim of the pot will make it awkward to invert for draining, while one that is too near the base will not allow a firm grip when picking up or setting down.

Within these limits, however, a case can be made for both high and low positions. For instance, the centre of gravity of a beaker may be said to be below the halfway mark as it is rarely quite full of liquid. A low handle should, therefore, give a better balance. On the other hand, the leverage resulting from a low placing gives less control when drinking from the beaker. This is a matter for individual discretion.

The recessed type of handle illustrated is really an alternative to a *knob* which, though it can be an asthetic crowning glory to a lid, in the case of the casserole can be a nuisance in practical use. The strap handle will allow for a larger vessel in a small oven and will also ensure that the lid won't get damaged when withdrawing the casserole.

The placing of a handle is crucial to the overall effect. Each of these positions alters the character of an identical basic form.

1

2

A classic jug form by John Lomas, illustrating how the inward curve of the body and the spring of the handle can result in a satisfying leaf-shaped space which may be as important as the actual form of the pot.

3

4

5

6

7

8

142

Michael Casson forming a handle on a large jug.
(1) After being well-wedged it is slapped into a tongue shape.
(2) and (3) The end is broken away with a flick of the thumb to leave a curved face which is then applied to a slip-coated area of the jug just beneath the rim.
(4) to (6) The handle is well pressed on and fastened all round the joint, the jug then being tipped over onto its back and supported on one palm while the other hand begins to 'pull' the handle with a steady stroking and squeezing motion.
(7) When the handle has reached the required length and thickness the jug is stood down and the handle curved over, the upper section supported by the hand.
(8) With one hand supporting the wall inside, the lower junction is pressed home and 'wiped' off with firm strokes of the thumb.

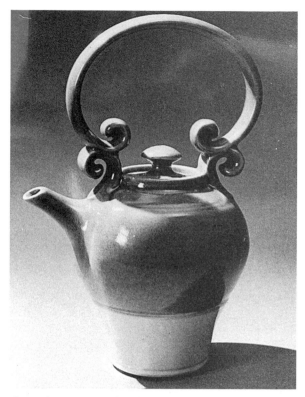

An exuberant teapot handle by Bill Brown.

Two stages in making a strap handle for a casserole.
(1) The lid, which can be flat as shown, or in the form of a shallow inverted bowl, has two semicircles cut from the centre leaving a 'bridge' between them.

(2) A separately thrown small bowl is then luted on beneath it.

Handles put to an original use by Jitka Palmer.

143

HANDLE CUTTER

A shaped wire ring attached to a wire or wooden handle and used for cutting strips of clay for forming pot handles. An alternative to pulling or extruding but, like the latter, the cut handle results in an even thickness from top to bottom which is not always desirable. Widely available.

HARDENING-ON-FIRE

A separate firing, usually up to about 800°C., which fixes *underglaze* pottery pigments onto the *biscuit* in order to prevent smudging or washing off during glazing. The process is common in the industry, but for craft potters it can be avoided by painting onto the raw clay, or by adding a little clay to the pigment if it is to be used on biscuit, as practised by Geoffrey Whiting. If neat oxides are used, some will still be loose on the surface at 1020°C, and must be rinsed off before glazing. A little flux may be added—china stone will help with cobalt. *Gum* can be used when painting on biscuit or when glazing directly over the unfired colour but this will affect the glaze take-up.

HARD-LEATHER

Used in this book to indicate clay on the dry side of *leather-hard*.

HARDNESS SCALE

Also known as Moh's scale. Based on a series of minerals in order of hardness: each mineral can be scratched by the one below it.

1 Talc	6 Feldspar (orthoclase rock)
2 Gypsum	7 Quartz
3 Calcite	8 Topaz
4 Fluorspar (fluorite)	9 Corundum
5 Apatite	10 Diamond

The scale is used as a convenient reference, e.g. a mineral or rock might be rated 5–6, between apatite and feldspar. *Hard paste* porcelain rates 6–7.

For practical purposes the following has been suggested: No. 2 can be scratched with the fingernail; No. 3 with a copper wire; Nos 4–5 equates with window glass; Nos. 5–6 with a pocket knife; Nos. 6–7 can be abraded with a file; Nos. 7–8 will themselves scratch a steel knife blade. The main use of Moh's scale is as a preliminary clue to the identification of rocks.

HARD PASTE

The name given to 'true' porcelain of European type firing at 1350–1450°C. and composed of china clay (kaolin) with china stone or feldspar. Craft potters rarely fire to this range and it is difficult to find a pure clay which can also be thrown on the wheel. The theoretical ideal composition of hard paste is 25% quartz, 25% feldspar, 50% kaolin. CR3 gives a recipe (Richard Parkinson) for a throwable 1320°C. porcelain. (See under *porcelain*.)

HARE'S FUR GLAZE

A name given to a range of mottled or streaked dark brown Chinese glazes. Rhodes asserts that these are slip glazes. Fairly fluid, and subject to blistering—the healed over blisters causing the darker marks. I have found that manganese as well as iron, if heavily loaded into a glaze, will give something of the same effect. The temperature is critical and varies with the glaze. (See also *temmoku*.)

HARKORT TEST

A method of testing glaze for its liability to *craze*. The piece is heated repeatedly and at successively higher temperatures from 120°C. to 190°C., and plunged into cold water between each stage. A note is made of the temperature at which crazing becomes apparent. The higher the temperature stage, the longer its probable craze-free life (from 3 months to $2\frac{1}{2}$ years). There are other factors in crazing besides *thermal shock*, but a simple form of this test gives an indication of the strength of your glaze and of glaze-body fit. In professional equipment the pieces are heated under steam pressure.

HARP, bow

A clay-cutter in the form of a semi-circular hoop of metal or bamboo with a wire or wires stretched across it. The harp can be used for trimming clay—e.g. rims on the wheel or the edges of *molded dishes*—or it can be dragged through a block of clay to cut slabs. In the latter case it needs to be sturdily constructed with the wire fixed at a given distance from the ends, so that, when the cut is made and the ends pressed tightly to the bench surface, an even thickness slab results. A number of

A 'harp' with two wires on a metal frame for cutting multiple slabs.

notches can be provided to control the cut, or several wires used at once. For slab cutting, very strong steel piano wire is used (some ingenious ideas are suggested by potters in Fournier PT). There is always a slight tendency for the wire to rise in the middle. Considerable strength is needed to cut a large block into several slabs.

HARRISON PYROMETRIC CONES

See *Seger cones*

HEALTH HAZARD

The inhaling of the dust from clay, glazes, and other powdery materials is the main hazard in the general run of studios. Those who use abrasives to smooth dry clay or biscuit are especially vulnerable and more than one potter has suffered. Some materials are more dangerous than others but inhaling or ingesting any of them is a **bad thing**. Use all materials wet where possible and be especially careful when sweeping or brushing. There are a number of sweeping compounds on the market; in England Dusmo Farinol and Sweeping Component Daventry are two suppliers. The outlay may seem unnecessary until you begin to get short of breath! The really dangerous materials are marked 'toxic' under their headings but see also *poisonous materials* for further discussion and my set of rules for a long life.

HEAT

Heat is the result of the translation, rotation or vibration of molecules. It is energy which can be put to work

Three ways in which heat can be distributed.
(A) Convection. Air (or any gas), when heated, will rise and cooler air flow in to take its place. Convection occurs only to a small extent inside an electric kiln (unless top and bottom spyholes are open together, a dangerous proceeding), but it is the basic mechanism in a fueled kiln, creating the draft in the chimney. In all kilns it is a factor in heat loss from the outside.
(B) Radiation. Heat given off from a hot body (kiln elements, burning fuel, etc) to pots, kiln furniture and walls in a kiln and, as the temperature rises, from hot wall to pack and from pot to pot. Air is not involved in radiation which spreads out in straight lines like light rays.
(C) Conduction. Heat is transferred through all materials in a kiln, though at different rates according to their composition.

by potters to rearrange the *molecular* structure of matter, e.g. forming ceramic from clay. In a fuel-burning kiln it is the result of the chemical combination of carbon with hydrogen and oxygen; in an electric kiln it is the result of *electronic* and molecular movement. It can be transmitted by *conduction, convection* and *radiation*. Heat is not gauged merely in terms of temperature. In the firing of pottery, time is also a factor. (See *heat work*.)

HEAT CONTROL

Solenoid connectors to gas burners can be used with a

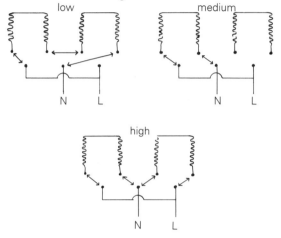

(A) Connections for a multi-position electric switch heat control.
Low heat. *The current passes through two circuits in series. For drying.*
Medium. *One circuit only. Burning off wax etc.*
High. *Two circuits in parallel. Full power.*

(B) Results from two 120v circuits with neutral (U.S.A.)
Low. *120v through two circuits.*
Medium. *One circuit at 120v.*
High. *Two circuits in series (no neutral) at 240v. Full power. (Courtesy Wikey CCEK).*

controlling pyrometer to vary the heat input and thus the firing speed automatically. A somewhat expensive luxury. For general kiln control see *controlling pyrometer, heat fuse, kiln sitter, pyrometer*.

The diagrams on page 145 show how simple heat control in an electric kiln can be achieved by switching between circuits.

HEAT-FUSE

Electric current can be conducted through a short length of metal inside the kiln which will melt at a given temperature, break the *circuit*, and cut off the supply to the kiln elements. Similar in appearance to a *pyrometer*. The fuse must be rated somewhat above the optimum firing temperature and its object is to prevent a total burn-out of the kiln. It is not an automatic cut-off for ' normal firing.

As well as the melting heat fuse which has only one 'life', resettable fuses are available with 50° Centigrade increments of control up to 1350°C.

HEARTH

See *grate*.

HEAT INSULATION

See *insulation of heat*.

HEAT LOSS

Heat can escape from a kiln in various ways. With combustible fuels the chimney takes away probably a third or more of the heat produced at the hearth. Hence the attempts by down-draft, multi-chamber kilns, and other designs, to utilize as much heat energy as possible before the chimney is reached. Simple updraft kilns are the most spendthrift, the ancient Eastern climbing kiln or the modern electric kiln probably the most economical. In the industry, the tunnel kiln wastes very little heat.

Heat loss through walls can be controlled by the use of special *insulating bricks, ceramic fiber, mineral wool block,* etc. though only the first two are suitable for hot-face use and all are easily abraded or broken. Heat loss increases as the difference between the *ambient* and chamber temperature increases. It is also proportional to wall area (rather than to the volume of the firing-chamber). A perfect cube is ideal in this respect, a long narrow rectangle the least efficient. The total area can easily be worked out and compared with volume. A 2 × 2 × 2 ft. (0.6 × 0.6 × 0.6 m.) chamber will have a volume of 8 cu. ft. (0.216 cu. m.); a 4 × 2 × 1 ft (1.2 × 0.6 × 0.3 m.) chamber will also contain 8 cu. ft. (0.216 cu. m.). The first, however, has 24 sq. ft. (2.23 sq. m.) of wall area (four sides, floor and roof) while the latter has 28 sq. ft. (2.6 sq. m.) or 16% more. Wall loss will obviously vary with the type of bricks or other insulation used but it has been estimated at up to 20% at higher temperatures.

Bricks will also store heat, i.e. use up energy in getting hot themselves. This will vary dramatically between a close, heavy *firebrick* and an open, *insulating-brick* (See *heat-storage*.) If, for reasons of strength and heat resistance, the *hot-face* must be of firebrick, this should be as thin as possible and backed by more insulating material. (See *insulation*.) When other heat expenders such as the production of steam and poor combustion are taken into account, not much more than 20% of the actual hearth heat is available to fire the pots. (See also *thermal conductivity*.)

Too little attempt is made to utilize chimney and other heat losses in a kiln for space-heating, clay drying etc. While there are problems with fumes from electric kilns, they certainly warm the studio and a gas kiln could also be utilised for space heating as well as firing. I have even cut ducts, fitted with fans, through walls to distribute kiln heat through the house.

HEATPROOF WARE

See *ovenware*, and *flameproof* ware.

HEAT RESISTANCE

The power of resisting change (to the molten state) when heated. (See *refractories, eutectic* etc.)

HEAT SHOCK

Taking pots from too hot a kiln can cause *crazing* or *dunting* which may not occur during slower final cooling. (See *thermal shock*.)

HEAT STORAGE

The amount of heat that kiln bricks, kiln furniture, saggars etc. will 'hold', i.e. that amount required to heat them to the point where they radiate as much energy as they take in. This storage represents wasted fuel; bricks should be chosen with as low a heat storage as is compatible with abrasion resistance etc. (See also *heat loss*.) The denser the brick, the more heat it will absorb. The average firebrick will store some 30,000 BTu (30.6 MJ) per square foot 9 in. (230 mm.) thick; a high quality insulating brick 6–8000 BTu (6–8 MJ). The familiar household storage heater utilizes the heat storing properties of heavy brick.

HEAT-TREATMENT

The control of temperature during cooling to create

special effects, especially crystal formation. The temperature may be held at various stages, or a degree of reheating may be practised. Changes can also be made in the glaze by means of subsequent refiring at submaturing temperatures. Many of the interesting glazes from Scandinavia and Germany are heat-treated.

HEAT-WORK

In the firing of pottery there are two factors, temperature and time, which taken in conjunction will represent the energy input or heat-work. Thus *soaking* will alter glaze qualities although the temperature remains constant. *Pyrometric cones* respond to heat-work in a similar way to glazes, and this is their principal advantage over *pyrometers*.

HEMATITE, haematite

The mineral of ferric iron Fe_2O_3. Described by Billington as 'an iron-earth . . . found in a stonelike form'. Has been recommended for coating pots prior to burnishing to give a good color, but the type of hematite generally offered by merchants is too pure and the burnish tends to fade. The inclusion of some fine-grain red clay could help. (See *burnish*.)

HOLDCROFT BAR

Holdcroft *Thermoscope*. Special ceramic bars $2\frac{1}{4}$ in (57 mm.) long, supported at each end and used like *pyrometric cones*. A bar will sag at the temperature indicated by its number. Numbers are from 10–360. Temperatures are in °C.

No 40–700°	No 230–1100°	No 270–1250°
No 120–905°	No 250–1140°	No 280–1280°
No 190–1000°	No 260–1200°	No 290–1300°
No 210–1060°	No 265–1230°	No 360–1490°

Similar bars, now more widely available are Pyro mini-bars (used in *kiln sitter*).

HOLE CUTTER

Double-edged, semi-cylindrical knives for cutting holes for teapot strainers and other purposes are available from many suppliers and perform a quick, neat job if the clay condition is just right. There are several sizes from around $\frac{1}{8}$ in. to $\frac{1}{2}$ in. wide. Some are tapered, allowing for variable sized holes from one tool.

HOLLOW DISH-MOLD

A concave mold of plaster or biscuit in which a dish is formed. It is the easiest type of mold to make. Hump molds can be made from it.

   Method. The illustration shows a block of clay

which has been cut with a tool and finally shaped with a template to an inverted version of the required dish shape. Make sure that there is a sharp and clean angle between the clay and the board and ensure that this is not undercut at any point. A watertight wall of clay, corrugated card, metal or leather is built round the clay shape and about an inch from it. This is then filled with plaster of paris poured steadily onto the middle of the clay form until it rises to a level $\frac{1}{2}$ in. (12 mm.) above the highest point. This is left to set, the wall removed, the whole reversed, and the clay-former peeled out. The surfaces of the mold can be scraped smooth and clean and the top inner edge cut to a sharp corner. The outside corners are bevelled with a plane. (For use see *dishes*.)

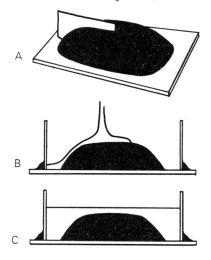

Making a hollow dish mold.
(A) shows a block of clay which has been cut to the desired shape. Start with a flat-topped block, cut the plan shape with the aid of a card template, then steadily pare the curve away with a wooden spatula tool. Finish with a template of metal, stiff card or wood as in diagram. The template is scraped round the form until it touches at all points. Build up any area which has been cut too low. Ensure a sharp, clean angle between the clay and the base board. The slope of the sides should not be too steep or, in use, it will be difficult to ease a slab clay into the finished mold. There should be a flat or even slightly dipped area on the top of the former so that the dishes made from it will sit firmly.
(B) A wall of lino, corrugated card, or similar material is built round the completed former and made water-tight as shown in the section. A smooth mixture of plaster (see plaster of paris *for mixing) is poured steadily over the former, giving it time to flow into the surrounding wall without cavities, and continue until the level is about $\frac{1}{2}$in. (12mm.) above the clay, as in diagram (C). When the plaster is set the wall is removed and the clay former peeled out and the outer corners of the mold beveled. Keep the inner corners sharp. (See also* pressed dishes.*)*

A hollow dish mold in use, of the type shown in the diagrams. The clay is first beaten flat with the palm, rolled to the required thickness, lifted by the cloth or, if it is firm enough, directly by the hands as in the photograph and lowered into the mold. (See also pressed dish, rolling clay.)

HONEY GLAZE

A general name for a high-lead glaze with some iron oxide, generally introduced by the use of *red clay* in the recipe. The natural impurities in the old slipware glazes gave a slightly yellowish or 'honey' tinge which had a unifying effect on the design. A typical modern 'honey' glaze recipe is:

Lead sesquisilicate	70
Feldspar	10
Red clay	12
China clay	6
Whiting	2

fired at around 1070°C. (See also *lead frits*.)

HORNEBLENDE

An intermediate *igneous* rock. Complex silicates of calcium, magnesium, iron and sodium.

HOT FACE

The inner surface of a kiln wall.

HOT-FACE BRICKS

Bricks capable of standing great heat and, in a solid fuel kiln, abrasion and *spalling*. The various qualities of high-alumina *firebrick* are generally used, except in electric kilns where the more efficient but softer insulating-brick composes the hot-face and often the entire wall. (See *insulation*, *heat loss*, etc.)

Used with care, the more efficient *ceramic fiber* blanket or block can replace hot-face bricks in many situations.

HUMP-MOLD, mushroom-mold, drape-mold

Dish molds with a convex surface. Useful for *trailed* and *feathered* dishes. The disadvantage of the type is that the dish may crack across it when drying. A hump-mold without a foot can be used as a 'master' from which to reproduce hollow molds. If a hump-mold is cast from a hollow one, the expansion of the plaster can cause trouble and it is advisable to line the hollow mold with a thin sheet of clay to accommodate this expansion. Hump-molds can also be made from metal pie-dishes (thinly greased before casting). If other concave shapes are used, always bear the expansion factor in mind—it is powerful enough to split glass or pottery.

The diagrams below show the methods of making a mold from a pie-dish.

A hump mold made in a metal piedish.
(A) The dish is lightly greased with warm Vaseline or similar and filled with an even mix of plaster of paris until the level is just below the point where the dish wall begins to turn outwards towards the rim.
(B) The central area of the set plaster is scored or roughened, and a wall of card, lino, or similar sheet material is set on it, made water-tight with clay, and filled to a depth of about 2in. (50mm.) with plaster.
(C) The completed (reversed) mold.

HYDRATE, hydration

A compound containing *chemically combined water*. Clay is a hydrated aluminium-silicate. Firing drives off the water leaving alumina silicate. In this case the operation is irreversible, but this is not always so. With *gypsum* it is partially reversible under certain conditions. Hamer recommends that any glaze containing a hydrate, e.g. colmanite, be fired slowly to 800–900°C. to avoid damage to the glaze layer during dehydration.

HYDROCARBON GASES

Gases of carbon and hydrogen compounds, e.g. methane CH_4. The paraffin series are hydrocarbons, also *natural gas*. Mentioned in connection with *reducing atmospheres*.

HYDROGEN

A gaseous element H, 1. Lightest substance known. Inflammable (see *gas fuel*); combines with oxygen to form water, H_2O. True *acids* will contain hydrogen in their formula but the acidic oxides used in pottery do not. Originally used (as unity) to calculate *atomic weights*, but now superseded by oxygen for this purpose. Hydrogen is the unit of *valency*.

HYDROMETER

Or 'slip-gauge' (Leach). An instrument for determining the specific gravity of a liquid/solid mixture, i.e. the consistency or thickness of a slip or glaze. A hollow glass cylinder (a test-tube, for instance) or a wooden road about 1 in. (25 mm.) × 6 in. (150 mm.) is weighted at one end so that it floats upright. The more solid matter present in the mixture, the greater the length of

A simple hydrometer, crosshatching indicating the weighted end which holds it upright in the liquid. The dotted line (A) indicates its level in pure water. In a glaze it would float higher, as at line (B), giving a reading of 4 to 5 on the scale marked on the hydrometer. The divisions on the scale are arbitrary and used for comparative reference. If wood or a permeable material is used it must be protected with paint; it will sink lower if it absorbs water and will falsify the reading.

hydrometer which will show above the surface. A scale can be marked on it, using its position in clear water as a base line. Its value lies in its ability to compare one glaze with another or to maintain a standard for any one glaze. Approximate readings for true weight and volume can be noted by testing the hydrometer in a batch of known dry weight and water content.

Pottery supply merchants now list hydrometers, but they are not difficult to make. Wooden ones must be protected by paint or varnish from absorbing water.

HYDROXYL, hydroxide

An *ionic* combination of one oxygen atom and one hydrogen atom forming part of a *compound*. Known as the OH- group and shown as (OH) in formulas. The alkalis, boron and phosphorus can form hydroxides.

HYGROSCOPIC WATER, substance

Term occasionally used to indicate the *chemically combined water* in clay.

A hygroscopic material, however, is one capable of absorbing water from the surrounding air. Exceptionally hygroscopic substances are *deliquescent*, e.g. potassium carbonate.

IDEAL FORMULA

The theoretical formula for a mineral, to which natural materials approximate: the simple ones, such as flint or whiting, very closely; more complex formulas such as the feldspars less so. The ideal formulas are used to represent natural minerals in simple glaze computations. For greater accuracy, in the industry for instance, a true formula derived from analysis would be used. Because of possible divergencies, it is advisable for potters to buy their raw materials in as large quantities as they can house (they are cheaper pro rata, too) so that they can become familiar with their actual properties as distinct from those expected from an 'ideal formula'.

IDENTIFYING STAIN

See *distinguishing stain*.

IGNEOUS ROCK

From 'fire' (Greek). Rock which has been molten and has formed during the cooling of the earth, or by intrusions from a molten core into the earth's crust in more recent times. In some cases the cooling has been slow and the rocks have had time to crystallize into individual minerals. *Granite* is the prime example. These old rocks are generally acid, i.e. they have a high silica content of 70% or more.

The molten material which has been forced through the crust—volcanic or extrusive rock—has solidified rapidly as lava and has a very fine *crystalline* grain. This materials tends to be basic with 50% or less of silica, *Basalt* is the commonest. One might say that the granite systems represent the body and the volcanic rocks the glaze of a ceramic.

Feldspars and *kaolinite* clays have decomposed from granitic rocks: *montmorillonite* more probably from extrusive ones. In England many igneous rocks are often used as roadstones, and could be used as a foundation for a stoneware glaze. It is worth trying any hard rock dust that you can get. *Chemical Analyses of Igneous Rocks* was published in 1931 (South West England) and 1956 (Northern England) by Her Majesty's Stationery Office, and there are similar sources of information elsewhere. A useful table of the mean compositions of igneous rocks is given in Sutherland GNS.

ILLITE

Described variously as a hydrous *mica* or a clay mineral. 'In London clay the mineral is thought to be 90% illite' (Cardew). Worrall doubts its separate existence: 'It seems likely that (illite, etc.) are mixtures rather than pure minerals.'

Illite has less potash and more *OH* groupings than mica and may have been converted by seawater from kaolinite. Secondary clays often contain a proportion of illite, even, some believe, to the exclusion of kaolinite.

The name originates from Illinois, where it was first isolated.

ILMENITE

An ore, ferrous titanate, $Fe_2O_3TiO_2$, 152, m.p. 1365°C. s.g. 4.7. A similar combination to rutile, but with more iron. Found as beach-sand in Australia, South-West India, America and Scandinavia. Grinds to grog-like granules and can be used in bodies or glazes to provide speckle—'a peppery appearance' (Rhodes). The iron will dissolve at the perimeter of the granule to give an amber 'halo'. 1–3% is the normal addition. Can be bought in various grades.

IMPERVIOUS, impermeable

Will not *absorb* water or allow water to pass through. In pottery the degree of vitrification controls permeability. There are strict industrial tests. (See also *porosity*.)

IMPRESSING

Impressed decoration has been one of the most popular techniques of the mid and late twentieth century. The ideal of a close integration between pot and decoration is combined with direct and spontaneous 'instant' action and an enhanced glaze interest.

The *roulette* or *stamp* are less favored than the chance patterns developed by 'found' objects: a broken edge of wood, a cog-wheel, rolled string etc. This can result in freedom and freshness, or incoherence and muddle, according to the degree of skill and sensitivity employed.

Order and design are more easily obtained by restricting one's impressing tools to two, or even to a single one, building up a pattern by repetition and variation of placing. If several sheets of clay are rolled out, experiments can be made before working on a pot. Impressing is very suitable for *slab pots* and can be done before the piece is assembled. *Beaten decoration* is a related technique.

Any relief materials, woven or uneven surfaces, can be utilised to obtain an impressed pattern on clay: anaglypta paper, wood, leaves, trellis, plastic mats of all sorts, the list is endless. The design needs to be reasonably 'abstract' and used with sensibility if it is to become integrated with the form of the ceramic and not merely used for its own sake.

A wide variety of impressed marks made into a slab of soft clay by common, everyday objects.

IMPURITIES

In a mineral, any oxide or material not included in the *formula*. 'Purity' is the prime object of the industrial potter, since it ensures uniformity. The careful extraction of iron traces from clay by electromagnets is an instance.

Commercial suppliers are industrially orientated and the craft potter has to accept a greater degree of purity than he sometimes wants. The alternative is to go and find materials for himself (see *glazes from natural materials*). The subtlety and quality of the older ceramics — early Chinese blues, slipware glazes etc. — arose partly from impurities which it was beyond the technology of the time to remove. There is no genuine way of returning to unrefined materials except by pioneering in the way that Cardew and Harry Davis have done, and more recently Brian Sutherland and others.

We can still use some composite natural materials, e.g. red clay to introduce iron; colemanite instead of borax frit, etc. David Green EP suggests trials with everyday materials such as scouring powder, fertilizers etc. Copper metal can be *oxidized* in a kiln or in salt water, iron oxide can be scraped and ground as rust and so on. See *button test.*

Leach tells of Hamada's 'building stone' used neat as a glaze. Potclays once listed an interesting 'black feldspar' and suppliers should be encouraged to include the less common minerals. Some are, in fact, widening the range with basalt and similar materials. In the West, generally, we put a premium on time and take the quickest way out.

INCISING

See *engraving.*

INCONGRUENT MELTING

Pottery materials may dissociate during firing into compounds with varying melting points, i.e. into liquids within a solid. The whole structure melts incongruently. This is especially true of bodies, although it also occurs in glazes, during the firing. (See *eutectic, melting point.*)

In bodies it helps vitrification without deformation and, in glazes, renders them sufficiently viscous not to run from the pot.

INLAY

A technique of decoration used in medieval floor tiles, Korean Koryu wares etc. The clay is inlaid with another of a contrasting color to a depth of up to about 1/16 in. (2 mm.). The typical pattern is fairly bold and broad, although the Korean wares mentioned were often very fine in line.

Early potters used wooden stamps with which to impress the pattern, but the usual method today is to cut with a wooden or bent-wire tool into leather-hard clay. The cavities are then filled either with slip or with soft clay. When the slip has stiffened, scrape the surface with a straight-edge to remove excess inlay clay and to leave the design sharply defined. A finer line can be filled with thin slip or pigment. (See also *mishima.*)

Potters also inlay more involved 'sculptural' clay forms in contrasting colours, not to mention non-ceramics such as silver, plastics, and other materials. See also *neriage, rolled inlay.*

Tile inlay. The design has been cut into a leather-hard tile and slip brushed or trailed into it. When stiff, the surface can be cleaned level with a knife or scraper. (See also mishima.)

A finer type of inlay on a handbuilt bowl.
(1) and (2) A manganese/cobalt/clay mixture is brushed into engraved lines and the surface gently scraped clean.

Sharp, precise line inlay on porcelain by Nicholas Homoky.

Jukta Fischer constructs her pots from patchwork sheets of various colored clays and then inlays with further colored bodies to a depth of about half the thickness of the wall. Underglaze additions of small details (such as polka dots on a handle) complete the scheme. When quite dry the pot is sanded with a fine-grade wire wool. Sprayed alumina matt glaze, earthenware.

INSOLUBLE

Will not dissolve in water. Clay, for instance, will mix intimately with water but will not dissolve and disappear as sugar does. Glaze materials must be insoluble for the following reasons: solutions are likely to crystallize out: if surplus water is poured from a settled glaze, then the dissolved material will go too; the solution will be carried into the pores of the *biscuit*; the solution is likely to separate out onto the surface of the biscuit; it may cause *flocculation*; if the solution is caustic it will affect your skin.

Ash contains soluble alkalis, hence the need for washing. Borax can be rendered insoluble only by fritting with silica. *Lead* is used as a *silicate*: although insoluble in the water of the glaze it can enter the human system as a solution. Colemanite is slightly soluble. Luckily 90% of the potter's minerals are insoluble.

INSPIRATING BURNER

A gas-burner in which the gas pressure draws the air of combustion into the mixture. The converse is the aspirating principle where air pressure draws gas in. (See *gas burner*, *Venturi burner*.)

INSULATION OF ELECTRICITY

Electricity is a good servant when under complete control. All electric kilns (and other equipment) must be protected against current-carrying wires making contact with each other or with any other *conductor*—including the potter!

It is not practicable to insulate the actual connections between the ends of the elements and the wires connecting them, though the wires themselves can be covered with woven asbestos, and the whole system must be shielded from the possibility of being touched. This type of heatproof wire is not always available and the alternatives are butyl-rubber and silicone-rubber insulating-material. The latter has a rating of 140°C maximum. They are both expensive. Porcelain beads strung on wire were once widely used, and a potter could make his own in the form of short tubes. All connections to the kiln should be housed in flexible metal tube, or in metal or plastic conduit.

The main insulating materials are, air, rubber, most dry ceramics, dry wood, dry thick cloth, insulating tape and plastic.

INSULATION OF HEAT

The prevention of *heat loss* or thermal *conductivity*, especially, for potters, through the fabric of a kiln. A major consideration in design, and the choice of materials. *Air* is an excellent insulator, and is utilized by trapping it in small pockets in a brick or other rigid heatproof material. Thus the insulating properties of a brick will decrease as its density increases.

A *hot-face* may need strength at the expense of insulation, but all backing material should conserve heat. These can be of low temperature insulating ceramic, such as Moler's red slabs, *diatomite* brick, or at least an open textured house brick (Flettons). Clay and ash or even coke mixtures are possible in situations protected from the air. Aluminium foil will reflect heat back from its surface.

Newer insulators, suitable particularly for electric kilns where strength is not a necessity, include *ceramic fibers*, *micropore* (expensive but several times more efficient than the best brick), alumina bubbles, Kipsulate and proprietary brands of non-asbestos heat-proof sheeting, see *asbestolux*. 3–6 in. (75–100 mm.) of ceramic fiber can replace some 18 in. of firebrick as an insulator but the more rapid rise and, especially, the fall in temperature will alter the character of a glaze. Super-efficient insulators are therefore subject to the law of diminishing returns. (See also *heat storage*.)

For making your own insulating bricks Pete Brown (CR 58) suggests: 4 parts (by volume) fireclay or a mixture with china clay; 1 part coarsely crushed firebrick; 5 parts fine sawdust. Fire slowly at first then fast as soon as the sawdust carbon has burnt away.

The rate of heat flow through various materials is shown diagrammatically in the accompanying figure.

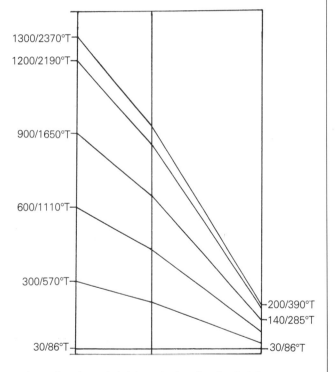

A section through brickwork showing the hot face temperatures, probable values at the junction with an insulating brick, and at the outside surface. The heat does not, of course penetrate instantly and this sort of diagram is based on a given period of time that the hot-face is subjected to a particular temperature. As the whole wall becomes hotter its heat storage capacity decreases and the outer temperature, and consequent radiation and convection, will rise. A very slow firing is therefore less fuel efficient in this respect and the top temperature becomes more difficult to attain.

INTERFACE

The area, in a section through a pot, where glaze and body merge into one another. When a glaze melts on the surface of clay it 'uses' or reacts with it in fulfilling its glass-making function. The interface is at its most diffuse in stoneware, porcelain and in once-fired earthenware. A well-developed reaction is responsible for the tight grip a glaze has on a body. Its development aids craze resistance. Alumina is an important factor in its formation. Calcium in body and glaze is reputed to increase the development of interface, and may have been added to Delft bodies for this purpose.

INTERMITTENT KILN

Kilns which are filled, heated, cooled and emptied. All studio kilns are of the intermittent type, while most industrial ones are now continuous. The nearest we get to a *continuous kiln* is in raku-firing. Intermittent firings are inevitably more wasteful of fuel, but they involve a certain rhythm which gives satisfaction and which the industry, feeding an unending production line, has lost.

INVERSION-POINT

The temperature at which an alteration in *crystalline* form takes place, involving a change in volume. (See *quartz inversion, cristobalite*.)

ION, ionic exchange, bonding

An electrically charged *element* or bonded group of elements. *Atoms* with 'incomplete' *electron shells* (other than two or eight) may gain or lose electrons to other atoms. They become electrically bonded and build up into a lattice or crystalline structure. Single molecules are seldom formed by this type of bond, which is known as *electrovalent*. Most *silicates* are formed by ionic bonding.

If an atom loses an electron it is left with a positive charge, and vice-versa if it gains one. Electro-positive ions are written R^+; if they lose more than one they may be R^{++} or R^{2+}. Silicon shares four electrons with oxygen atoms and becomes Si^{4+} in what is known as the SiO_4 grouping. Electro-negative ions—the gainers of electrons—are shown as R^-. The *alkali* metals form electrovalent compounds.

These theories provide explanations of the observable habits of inorganic compounds, and do not destroy the usefulness of the hypothesis of a single *molecule* or unit. Although mentioned as an SiO_4 grouping above, the quartz lattice in fact is a three-dimensional structure in which, overall, there are twice as many oxygen as silicon atoms, each O_4 group being linked above and below with two atoms of silicon. In a formula we therefore refer to the proportion of atoms in a complex or lattice as SiO_2.

Ionic exchange can take place on the surface or edges of crystals in order to stabilize the electrical charge. In clays the *bentonites* have a greater capacity for exchange than *kaolinites* and are therefore more variable in their composition.

IONIC RADIUS

The comparative size of an atom which controls its powers of combination with others. See *atomic radius*.

IRIDIUM

A metallic element Ir. 192. Mentioned by Billington as a source of fine stable blacks and grays, but its rarity and expense preclude its use at present.

IRON

A metallic element. Fe. 56.

Oxides: Ferric, Fe_2O_3, (hematite)	160	m.p.	1550
Ferrous (reduced) FeO	72	m.p.	1360
Ferroso-ferric Fe_3O_4 (*magnetite*)	232	m.p.	1538

(For other iron compounds see under *crocus martis*, *ilmenite*, *rutile*, *ochre*, *sienna*, *red clay*, *copperas*, *iron chromate*, *synthetic iron oxide*. Also *Albany clay*.)

The average percentage of iron in magnetite is 72; hematite, 70; limonite, 60; pyrites, 46.6; ilmenite 36.8. (Peter Smith CR. 96) He also finds pronounced differences in the analyses of similarly described iron oxides; empirical trials are therefore essential when following a given recipe.

In earthenware, iron gives buffs and browns (1–8%) or more reddish colors in a high alkali, lime-free glaze. It can be combined with other oxides for black, or to modify cobalt, etc. Red clay is the most subtle source of iron for many colors and glazes; in *honey* glazes and in many stonewares where it also has a fluxing action in reduction. It can be used in high proportions in a glaze (15–20% and more). As a pigment, mixed with manganese and cobalt, e.g. 30% cobalt carbonate; 35% manganese dioxide; 25% ferric oxide; and 10% red clay, it approximates to *asbolite* for brush painting on stoneware though it may separate to some degree giving golden flecks in oxidation. Crystalline glazes are produced from hematite. Avoid zinc with iron. In coarse particles, such as ilmenite, iron produces specking.

Chemically an amphoteric, it will have little effect in an oxidizing fire but will behave as a flux in reduction. The most stable iron form is the *spinel* $FeO.Fe_2O_3$, or Fe_3O_4.

Iron leads the field as a coloring agent in reduced glazes with a range from brick-red to blue. (See *celadons*, *reduction*, *temmoku*, etc.)

IRON CHROMATE

Chromate of iron, ferric chromate, $FeCrO_4$. By analysis Fe_2O_3 34.6. Cr_2O_3 49.8. In a glaze of 0.5–2.0% will produce grays. Also used in bodies as a stain. Brown with zinc. Used in crystalline glazes. May be used to modify other pigment oxides. If used for brushwork 'the edges can variously bleed with different colors' (Hamer).

IRON EARTHS

A series of impure, clayey, high-iron compounds, sometimes with manganese. They are generally more stable to 1400°C. than iron oxides, and are preferred by some potters for introducing iron into glazes, slips and pigments. (See *ochre*, *umber*, *sienna*.)

IRONING OF COBALT

Reddish to black patches on cobalt caused by too high a concentration. Due to crystallization of cobalt silicate (Dodd). Generally considered a fault, but can sometimes be pleasant on a brushstroke. To avoid ironing, cobalt can be diluted with china stone or a frit; or modified with other oxides, e.g. red clay or manganese.

IRON SPANGLES

See at *spangles*.

IRONSTONE, ironstone ware

A hard iron ore. Ironstone ware has a dark colored vitrified body.

ISOTOPE

It has been found that, though *the proton* number of an element is constant, the number of *neutrons* varies. Since the *atomic weight* is the sum of these fundamental particles, an element can have more than one 'weight'. The deviations from the formerly accepted weight are called isotopes. Luckily the ratio of the number of isotopes is constant in a mass of material, so that an atomic weight can be worked out which is an average or mean number. Thus if two-thirds of an element has a weight of 14, and one-third a weight of 15, the atomic weight of a mass of that element would be 14.33 recurring (a hypothetical case). As a result, the convenient whole numbers have given way to several places of decimals. (See also *atomic theory*, *atomic weights*, *atomic numbers*.)

JAR MILL

A small *ball mill*, usually turned by friction on revolving horizontal rods about 2 in. (50 mm.) in diameter. The jars range from 2 pints (1 liter) to a gallon (5 liters). The advantage of the jar mill mechanism is that various sizes of jars can be used, and more than one jar at a time. The critical factors are those given under *ball mill*.

The jar can be of a hard ceramic. The lid must be quite watertight, and capable of firm closure. Size from 4 in. (100 mm.) internal diameter upwards. The mechanism is shown in the diagram. Only one roller is driven, the other(s) run free. One might compromise by constructing the drive and purchasing the jars from a merchant.

Diagram of a jar mill showing the drive from the motor to one of the rollers, the second running free. In practice some gearing or speed reduction system, would be needed between motor and roller, and a computation made for the roller and jar revolution speeds by a comparison of their relative cirumferences.

JASPER WARE

The name given by Wedgewood to a fine-grain, unglazed, *vitreous* stoneware, often stained with oxides. A quoted recipe:

Ball clay	26
China clay	18
Barytes	45
Flint	11

JERSEY STONE

An American equivalent to china stone.

JIGGER

The pivotted arm of a *jigger and jolley*.

JIGGER AND JOLLEY

A machine for molding hollow ware and flatware. The clay is squeezed between a profiled metal tool (the template or 'die') and a revolving plaster mold. The face of a plate or saucer is formed by throwing a slab of clay onto a revolving mold, while the shape of the back and the thickness are controlled by the die, which is brought down by means of a pivoted arm onto the spinning clay, squeezing and cutting away the surplus. For hollow shapes the outside is formed by the mold, and the inside by the die.

It is essentially an industrial operation for large-scale production of identical pieces. It needs some skill (although automated systems are now taking over) but is obviously a mechanical technique. To say that the method destroys the 'plastic feeling' is to ignore the fact that the bodies used have little plasticity anyhow. Plastic clays such as the craft potter uses are rather sticky to operate. 'Jiggering' usually refers to hollow ware, and 'jolleying' to flatware.

Hollow forms are limited to those which will lift directly from the mold—fundamentally cylinders or forms approaching inverted cones, and without 'return' angles (see diagram at *mold*). Footrings are minimal on most shapes.

Several hundred molds may be used for one service, each piece being left to stiffen before it can be removed from its mold.

Amateur jolleys can be rigged up for special

Robin Welch using a jigger and jolley machine for forming a plate. (Photo Eileen Lewenstein.)

purposes—cutting the clay former and the plaster foot of a circular dish mold, for example. Jolley arms can be purchased. The template or die can be sheet brass or wood.

A simple cylinder jolley mold and some of the variations derived from the basic shape. Robin Welch workshop.

JOLLEY

See *jigger and jolley*.

JORDON CLAY

A light-burning stoneware clay from New Jersey, USA.

JOULE

The standard international unit of heat quantity (work or energy). Symbol J.

1 Btu	=	1050 J
	=	1.05 kJ
1 Therm	=	100,000 Btu
	=	105,000,000 joules
	=	105,000 kJ
	=	105 MJ
kJ	=	one thousand Joules (10^3)
MJ	=	one million Joules (10^6)

JUG SHAPE

A satisfactory jug shape combines a generous and well-defined form with utility. Cardew suggests a combination of beaker and sphere and gives advice on throwing this basic pottery form. The 'inverted beaker' shape has, however, been much favored. Medieval English pottery provides a patternbook of splendid jugs in a wide variety of shape and finish. The *jug handle* is crucial to its form and should be balanced by the *lip*.

Points of utility to be remembered are that a jug must be easily cleanable, though with modern kitchen tools it is not essential to be able to get one's hand inside. It should withstand moderate thermal shock.

'Jug with Birds' in earthenware by Alison Britton.

Three fine, strongly formed salt-glaze jugs by Sarah Walton. Note thumb stops on the larger pieces.

When full, its weight will be more than doubled and the handle should be *seen* to have sufficient strength to lift it without danger. The handle should not rise above the rim of the jug.

Today, in common with the cup, teapot, and other humble ceramics, the jug has been subjected to many variations, deformations, and indignities. These are aesthetic matters and outside the scope of this book.

A sophisticated and finely proportioned version of the Medieval style by Bernard Leach. Subtly scored, and with a strong rim and apt handle.

JUN GLAZE

The new spelling of 'Chun'. A type of *opalescent* Chinese glaze which has fascinated many craft potters. It has a milky bluish tinge but does not contain pigment oxides, the color arising from suspended globules of 'glass in glass' (Cardew) known as 'optical color' (see *color*), or 'scattered light from suspended particles of colloidal size' (Hamer) which are difficult to control. If overfired the result will be transparent; if underfired dull and semi-matt. Chinese Jun was often associated with colloidal copper reds.

Phosphorus, usually derived from wood ashes, is probably a necessary ingredient. The glaze is unaffected by kiln atmosphere except that the body color will show through to a degree and will influence that of the glaze. Cardew PP (pp 142–3) deals at some length with 'Jun' glazes. He recommends a thick application over a darkish body or even a temmoku. Talc is a useful addition. The 'Jun' effect can also result from suspended particles (dicalcium silicate which may precipitate in the molten glaze has been suggested to aid suspension), or from minute bubbles of gas.

Rich, overlapping, fluid Jun glazes on a pot by Peter Rushforth (Australia).

KAKI

Japanese for 'persimmon', applied to a series of red-brown, broken-color, *reduced*-iron glazes. In Mashiko the use of a local building-stone, crushed, gave kaki glaze without additions. Leach mentions glazes with a high *feldspathic* content, some limestone and about 5% iron oxide. Several recipes are given in Leach PB 170–1. They have a higher iron content—up to 20–30% of ochre—and also suggest that the color can be obtained in *oxidation* which is, anyhow, necessary during cooling to allow the formation of red iron crystals on the surface. Rhodes includes kaki under *slip glazes*, and there is some parallel here with the ochre recipes. Certainly the iron needs to be in sufficient quantity for some to be precipitated onto the surface where it will react with oxygen and crystallize on cooling. (See also *red glazes*.)

A translation from Japanese to American materials of a kaki recipe gives:

Nepheline syenite	38.7
Colemanite	20.0
Zinc	8.1
Barium	9.85
China clay	25.8
Flint	33.3
Iron	2.0–6.0% addition

KALIUM

See *potassium*.

KANTHAL

Suppliers of a wide range of electrical resistance materials for use in kilns and furnaces. Originating in Sweden, they are now made under licence in other countries: in England by Hall and Pickles of Sheffield; in the USA by Kanthal of Bethel, Connecticut. Alloys are made into wires, strips, rods, tubes, ribbons etc.

For potters' kilns the A1 quality wire is the most widely used element material. It will run at a maximum of 1350°C. but, since there is always lag between element temperature and that of the kiln, the working maximum firing temperature is nearer 1300°C. The wire will last longer at 1275°C. The diagram illustrates the average life/temperature relationship according to the 1963 Kanthal Handbook. In my experience well-designed and carefully wound elements should last up to

200 stoneware firings in *oxidation*. They become thinner and slower with use, and the coils tend to collapse sideways but they are economical, if not abused.

Kanthal 'Super' is a special molybdenum/silica alloy rated at 1700°C. Kanthal A is suitable for earthenwares.

Wires are supplied in 37 different diameters in two series or gauges called s.w.g. (standard wire gauge), and

This graph illustrates the average life/temperature relationship according to the 1963 Kanthal Handbook. The 1970 edition gives a more optimistic assessment of probable life and it is possible that the quality has been somewhat improved but, if the left-hand figures are taken as the number of firings, the above graph corresponds fairly closely to my experience of coiled elements. Kanthal have not responded to my request for recent information. Note that the figures on the graph denote wire temperature: the chamber temperature would be around 40/72°T. lower in each case.

SOME DATA ON KANTHAL A1 RESISTANCE WIRE   *Maximum wire temperature 1350°C.*

Wire gauge		Diameter		Resistance in ohms per foot	ft/lb.
		in.	*mm.*		
s.w.g.	18	0.048	1.219	0.3786	179.4
B. and S.	16	0.0508	1.290	0.3376	160.3
s.w.g.	17	0.056	1.422	0.2781	131.9
B. and S.	15	0.0571	1.450	0.2677	127.1
s.w.g.	16	0.064	1.626	0.2129	101.0
s.w.g.	15	0.072	1.829	0.168	79.85
B. and S.	13				
s.w.g.	14	0.08	2.032	0.136	64.6
B. and S.	11	0.0907	2.304	0.1059	50.3
s.w.g.	13	0.092	2.337	0.1031	48.87

B. & S. (Brown & Sharpe). Diameters between 1.6 mm. (approx. 1/16 in.) and 2.35 mm. (approx. 3/16 in.) are the most useful to potters. These are in the ranges 16–13 s.w.g. and 14–11 B. and S. The higher the gauge number, the thinner the wire. The thicker wires are recommended for stoneware firing. (See also *electricity, electric kilns, elements, electrical, winding elements,* etc.)

KAOLIN

The name derives from the Chinese *Kao*—high, and *Ling*—hill, a ridge or mountain where it was discovered. It is synonymous with china clay, the latter name being preferable to avoid confusion with *kaolinite*, the pure, theoretical clay substance or mineral.

KAOLINITE

The 'ideal' clay mineral $Al_2O_3.2SiO_2.2H_2O$, 258, to which china clay approaches most closely. The true kaolinite crystal consists of alternate layers of SiO_4 groups and $Al(OH_6)$ groups see *gibbsite*), arranged in the lamellar structure which gives clay its quality of plasticity. In most natural clays this 'stacking' has been disorganised to some degree, allowing the intrusion of alkalis, iron etc. For a molecular stacking diagram see Worrall C. and Hamer PDMT, and diagram at *clay*.

The mineral is the result of the decomposition of alumina-silicate rocks, e.g. feldspar. Non-kaolinite clays include the *montmorillonites* and it is now widely believed that most secondary clays may contain only small percentages of kaolinite, if any. See *clay, illite*, etc.

KAOLINIZATION

The action of hot gases, mainly CO_2 and H_2O, have in geological time acted on *feldspathic* minerals to leach out the alkalis and to form kaolinite. A very simplified notation for the process is:

Feldspar + steam + carbon dioxide, rearranged as Potassium carbonate + quartz + clay. In chemical terms:

$$K_2O.Al_2O_4.6SiO_2 + (2)H_2O + CO_2 = K_2CO_3 + (4)Si_2 + Al_2O_3.2SiO_2.2H_2O.$$

There are doubts as to whether kaolinization, by weathering, is still proceeding.

KELVIN

Symbol K. A temperature scale allied to Celsius but beginning at 'absolute zero'—minus 273°C. (See also *absolute temperature scale, centigrade, conversion factors, gas expansion, sintering.*)

KEUPER MARL

Also known as Mercia mudstone. A source is given in Sutherland GNS: Keuper Marl (Brickworks) Hartlebury, Hereford, G.B. but it is widely distributed and Potclays sell a 'Keuper Red' clay. Mentioned in connection with *oil spot* and *slip glazes*.

KICKWHEEL

A foot-operated potter's wheel. There are two main types:

1 The genuine 'kicked' wheel. The potter sits over a large stone flywheel which he rotates by direct friction with the sole of his foot. This is the traditional wheel of the Mediterranean and other countries, and is occasionally used by the modern craft potter. There is often no tray, so throwing must be fairly dry.

2 The crankshaft wheel, where the 'kick' is transmitted to the shaft via a bar or connector. The potter may stand on one leg and swing a frontally suspended bar with the other. This type is not recommended for serious potters; one's stance is unstable and the strain on the standing leg is considerable. It is however found in many schools and colleges. The seated type is better-designed, affording greater control with the minimum exertion. The direct drive to the shaft imposes a limited speed but recent refinements include a geared wheel giving a ratio of about 1:1.5 between kick-bar and wheel head speeds.

The kickwheel is especially useful for turning. Many potters prefer its direct and instinctive control to the one-remove of the power wheel. A well-made seated kickwheel with a good flywheel, about 60 lb or 25 kg., can be worked for hours without unduly tiring the potter.

There are many wheels on the market. Sturdy construction, good bearings, quietness and comfort are points to check. Wheels are not difficult to build if one has minimal carpentry and/or metalwork skill. Use a hard wood for the frame—beech is excellent. The frame is triangular in plan, each side about 36 in. (1m.) long. Height depends on the stance you like to adopt when throwing but the average is 30 in. (800 mm.). Joints should be short mortice and tenon, not glued but pulled in tight with studding (threaded $\frac{1}{2}$ in. or 12 mm. rods with a nut at either end. The bar is supported in some designs by a vertical chain and, as a result, swings in an arc. This is comfortable for the leg, but is a difficult movement to transmit to the crankshaft. A flexible leather connector may be used, but a better system mechanically is shown in the photographs, where the support is taken back diagonally to the same pivot line

Two views of one type of kickwheel (with tray removed). It was constructed, in oak, in 1947 and has been in continuous use ever since. The timbers are $3\frac{1}{2} \times 2\frac{1}{4}$ in. (90 × 55 mm.). The connecting rod is from an old car, the flywheel from a lathe. A thrust bearing (again, the clutch bearing from a car) is set at the base of the crankshaft with a ball-bearing at the top, protected from the water by a disc of ply and plastic. The kickbar support is taken back to the axis of the bar, giving a smoother motion than does a chain-supported action.

as the kick-bar itself, ensuring a true horizontal drive. David Ballantyne developed a geared wheel in which the arc and horizontal drive are ingeniously combined. The actual wheel shaft is normally made of 1 in. (25 mm.) steel, but an increase to $1\frac{1}{8}$ in. (28 mm.) will reduce 'whip' very considerably. Any wheel which has an uncomfortable action or involves too bent a back must be avoided.

The jointing system used in the kickwheel illustrated. A short mortise and tenon is made between the horizontal and upright timbers which should fit adequately but not be glued. A hole is drilled straight through the upright, the mortise (B), and horizontal bar as shown, and a slot cut large enough to take a washer and a nut at (A). A length of $\frac{1}{2}$ in. (12 mm.) studding (threaded metal rod) is inserted, screwed into a nut in the slot, and the whole joint drawn up tight with a second washer and nut at (C). As the wood contracts or compresses the nut can be tightened while, conversely, the whole structure can easily be dismantled. A touch of grease will prevent the nuts rusting on.

KIDNEY TOOL

The kidney-shaped tool, embodying several curves, is a favorite one with potters. It may be of hard or soft rubber, or of thin, pliable sheet-steel. Sheet-steel kidney tools are called 'steel palettes'. They are also made in aluminium (from Cromartie) and rubber, the latter useful for smoothing surfaces and even for burnishing. Other uses for the tools are scraping, smoothing, turning and pressing. The hand-builder will find them invaluable.

KIESELGUHR

A German name for *diatomite*.

KILN

Called an 'oven' in the industry. Essentially a box of refractory bricks, into or around which heat is introduced either by combustion or by radiant heat. A kiln must be capable of reaching at least 600°C. (1112°F.). A cooking-oven, therefore, cannot be used as a kiln. In small kilns the ware is packed straight into the box, in large ones it may be protected and supported by *saggars*.

The very primitive, but nevertheless often effective, brushwood bonfires cannot be said to have used a kiln at all. In some cases the pots were covered with a layer of shards as protection and to retain heat, and this represented the first step towards a kiln. Cultures which aimed at a finer type of pottery soon began to enclose their wares in brick or stone boxes which allowed a greater control and higher temperatures. In the simplest kilns, a fire is lit under the floor, the heat rises through the pots and out at the top. The whole kiln acts as a chimney. Though more economical and reliable than a bonfire, its heat utilization is low. The final step was to direct the heat against its inclination across the kiln setting and, eventually, downwards through it. A strong draft or pull is essential; this is provided by a tall chimney (a straight-up kiln needs no separate chimney) as in most Western kilns, or by a stepped series of firing-chambers as in the East. All intermittent kilns are variations or improvements on these types. An electric kiln has no combustion or draught and is thus a simple fire-proof box.

Rhodes gives an excellent account of the history, types, and designs of kilns. Kilns come in countless sizes, shapes, and degrees of complexity and it is impossible to deal with them in a dictionary. Just one piece of advice if you are considering building your own is to start from a module of the size of available kiln shelves plus an inch or so to get your fingers round the edges when deciding on the plan of the chamber. David Miller (CB 85) has designed an original cross-draft for salting with the front wall lifted by pulleys for packing and removing pots, but perhaps the most startling of all appeared in CR 115. (Sebastian Blackie). A paper kiln! The pots,

A trolley kiln (see also illustration at truck kiln*) for wood-fired salt-glaze at the workshop of Janet Mansfield (Australia). Note* catenary *form (see text).*

surrounded by wood blocks, are piled onto a cone shape on a steel grid and the whole covered with layers of glossy paper brushed with slip. The structure is lifted by the grid and dried out over smouldering embers. Eventually the wood blocks turn to charcoal in the absence of air which burns in its turn to produce temperatures of anything between 950 and 1250°C. before the paper finally collapses.

(See also *insulation of heat, up-draft, down-draft, chambered kiln, brazier kiln, clamp kiln, sawdust firing, gas kilns, oil kiln, electric kiln, climbing kilns, ground-hog kiln*.)

KILN FURNITURE

Term applied to pieces of *refractory* material used to support pots during firing, including *shelves* and *props*. More particularly, the term refers to the small equipment designed to prevent glazed ware sticking to kiln shelves.

The commonest piece of kiln furniture is the *stilt* which has three radial arms ending in upright conical points. *Spurs* have one point up and three down; three or more can replace a stilt when supporting larger dishes or irregular shaped pieces. Triangular sectioned *saddles* will hold tiles or flat-based models. There are ingenious constructions called cranks, which hold similar sized plates or tiles apart from one another in a pile or bung. Tile bats may also be called cranks and can be built up on their own 'cranked' or turned-over edges, or with spacing cubes (bits).

It is important to bear in mind that all clays become *pyroplastic* during firing. When placing 'furniture', try to imagine that the piece of pottery (especially flat plates and dishes) is still plastic and can sag under its own weight. A plate will warp on a small out-of-center stilt or on spurs placed too far apart. See *warping*.

Kiln furniture, in the sense of stilts and similar articles, is intended for oxidized earthenware only, it will fail at temperatures over 1200°C. Even shelf props, if cast, may collapse in stoneware reduction firings unless specifically made for this purpose. Stoneware pots, therefore, are normally left with unglazed bases.

See also *batt, kiln shelves, prop*, and under the individual items mentioned.

KILN GLOSS

A, usually accidental, partial shine on a pot caused by local vitrification or to the deposit of ash or other fluxing material onto the surface.

KILN LOG

A record of firings is always useful, especially with a

Firing no 22. Feb 3rd '73. Sunday.
Tight pack. Middle hot, floor cooler
12 hours 50 mins 1270°C   173 units
Probable voltage drop 1–3 p.m.

No	1sts	Value	
15	Plates	20	Cobalt too strong
12	Saucers	3	
16	Cups	6	
	Tall pot	5	
	"	3	Ash 1 glaze
	"	7	Ash 2 glaze
30	Egg cups	7	
7	Various Small pots	10	Blue slightly oversized on middle shelves
	2nds		
2	Plates	1	Underfired
2	Saucers		30 Spinners (floor left)
1	Tall pot	2	50 Crawled (floor left)
		64	80

new kiln or during the first year of work in a new pottery. A kiln log will materially assist *pricing and costing.*

The record can be a very full one, or merely a list of pieces with length of firing and top temperature noted. It is advisable to keep the same sort of record each time so that the data is comparable. Priorities will vary with type of kiln and work fired. If your kiln has a chimney it will be sensitive to the weather. Leach always recorded not only weather but also oil pressure, temperature of kiln at various stages, atmosphere, and damper positions, for all of which he developed a private code. Cardew suggests recording the weight of clay used in the kiln setting which will also give density of packing, an important factor affecting firing. A broader indication of density such as 'loosely packed', 'large pots', 'very full', or the number of shelves used, is more practicable. In electric firing the weather is not of direct consequence unless the kiln is in a very cold and drafty place, but *voltage drop* may occur in winter.

A firing-graph will replace many words and may be used as a basis of the kiln log. A possible layout is shown above.

A reduction graph will show 'steps' in the line. A deliberate stepped firing known as 'fire-change' is used in Japan. Geoffrey Whiting used a '*stepped graph*' in an electric kiln to obtain special colors (see also *heat treatment.*)

KILN SHELVES

Kiln shelves are made of compacted high-alumina clay, *sillimanite* or *silicon carbide*. It is difficult to make one's own bats. The underlying science which controls the behavior of shelves under load is a complicated one. Some of the problems are discussed in Cardew PP. Silicon shelves are more conductive than clay, but are expensive.

One of the major manufacturers in England, Acme Marls, has provided the following data on shelf performance in the kiln:

SPECIMEN DEFORMATION DATA ON KILN BATS

Temperature in °C	900–1050			1050–1200			1200–1250			1250–1280		
Thickness in mm.	12.5	17.5	25	12.5	17.5	25	12.5	17.5	25	12.5	17.5	25
Size of bat												
47.5 × 41.5	14	40	77	6.5	22	45	0	7	19	0	0	6
44.5 × 42	16	42.5	81	7.7	23.5	47	0.6	6.5	21	0	0	8
40.0 × 28	14	35	60	7.4	21	36	2.2	9	17	0.25	3.5	7.5
35.5 × 21	12	32	59	6.5	19.5	37	2.5	9.5	20	0.5	4.5	10

These figures represent the loads in lb. which the shelf will take without deformation. The load to be spread reasonably evenly over the surface. Calculations made for alumina shelves and reproduced by kind permission of Mr. H. Gautby of Acme Marls, Hanley, Stoke-on-Trent.

1 Cracks may be due to fast heating or cooling—the hot load cooling slowly while the shelf cools more rapidly. Also to gross overloading, usually because of a badly placed prop.

2 An overloaded bat will normally bend and will ultimately tear.

3 The life of a shelf is dependent on how much it bends in the firing; this is governed by the load, the unsupported span, the temperature and the thickness.

4 The bending rate will also depend on the time that any given temperature is maintained.

5 It is quite in order to turn shelves over to correct bending.

6 A bat bends more rapidly at the beginning of its life than at the end.

7 Concentrated loads will have the effect of reducing the life afterwards.

8 A good test for a cracked bat is to support it on a pad in the center, cover it with fine, dry *alumina*, and hit it sharply to make it resonate. The alumina parts where there is a crack.

The table gives a rough idea of the normal distributed loads which bats will stand at different temperatures. There is no smooth graduation in the series for different thicknesses. A bat must carry its own weight as well as the load and this must be subtracted from the gross loading.

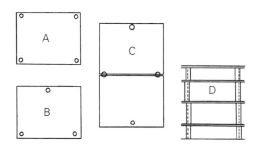

The propping system for kiln bats. (A) shows a logical but unsatisfactory position for supports: it is difficult to get a firm seating on four columns and the stresses are along edges or across long diagonals. System (B), using three props, gives an automatically firm seating and shortens the diagonal spans. Two closely adjacent shelves can be supported as in plan (C). In the elevation (D) the props are not immediately under one another, as is the ideal state, but the dotted lines show that the shelves are nowhere cantilevered, i.e. the weight is all taken by the columns and not by the shelves, so this degree of variation of position is acceptable. (See cantilever.)

KILN-SITTER

The action of a mechanical electric kiln switch. Other systems may be more sophisticated but the principle remains similar.

A gadget for shutting off your kiln while you are out enjoying yourself! It does not measure temperature direct but uses a metal arm which rests on a *Pyro mini-bar* or similar, and which drops as the mini-bar bends and switches off the kiln. Fairly widely available from suppliers and kiln factors.

KILN WASH

A thin layer of *refractory* material spread over the *hot-face* of the kiln. *Air-setting cements* have been suggested for this, washed over with a brush or sprayed on (see *Sairset*). 'Pebesil' is another commercial surface-cement which can be applied to soft *insulating*-brick to make it more abrasion resistant. It has high heat-retention. (See also *bat wash*.)

KILOWATT

Symbol kW. 1000 watts.

KIMMERIDGE CLAY

A Dorset brick clay, often contaminated with lime or bituminous substances.

KNEADING CLAY

See *wedging*.

KNIFE

A really sensitive knife which will also be strong enough for use on clay is very difficult to find. The ideal is a blade ½ in. (12 mm.) wide and tapering, about 1½ in. (38 mm.) long with a fairly fine back edge, and with a comfortable handle. 'Stanley' knives are too short and clumsy; scalpels with renewable blades are too delicate and too sharp for safety: penknives do not always have a good grip. Photographic touching-up knives are useful. A local cutler will generally grind a knife to your specification. Some merchants now offer more attractive knives than the usual *fettler*.

Reward Supplies sell a good range of potters's knives. Cromartie's is long and slim (and looks a little dangerous) and is made with a soft or hard blade.

KNOB

The knob of a *lid* is no trivial object. A quick survey of ceramics will reveal not only rich variety but also show that the lid and its knob or handle can be the crowning glory of a pot. Modeled knobs of considerable size and intricacy, such as the splendid teams of stylized horses, are found on early Greek pots. Those from the Far East may be more subdued, but are carefully considered in relation to the overall form of the pot and sometimes have a touch of fantasy. Michael Casson's early knobs

and Ian Godfrey's often crowded and dominant lids are modern examples.

The principle underlying good design is to provide a stem of length adequate to accommodate finger and thumb, spreading out to a wider top. No matter how elegant or aesthetically suited to the main form, a knob which cannot be easily gripped and held must be accounted to a failure. But within these limitations there is a multitude of possible forms. The knob should not be too high on ovenware.

The illustrations show various ways of making the knob. It can be modeled and luted on; turned from the thick base of a thrown lid; thrown onto the leather-hard turned lid; inset into a cut lid; or made in the form of a pulled handle or a simple thumbed-down coil.

Three ways of forming a knob.
(1) Turning the shape from the stem of a thrown lid (see lids).

(2) Throwing a knob on a flat casserole-type lid.

(3) Throwing a hollow knob on a recessed lid.

kW

The symbol for a kilowatt or 1000 watts. A kilowatt hour (kWh) is the electricity consumed by one kW piece of apparatus in one hour. (See also *electricity*, *units of electricity*.)

KYANITE

A mineral $Al_2O_3.2SiO_2$, similar to *sillimanite* but with different physical properties. Considerable volume increase at 1300°C., when it breaks down into *mullite* and *cristobalite* (Dodd). Has been mentioned as a *bat wash*. Obtainable from Kyanite Mining Corporation, Dillwyn, Virginia, U.S.A.

LACE decoration

Open-weave cloth or lace can be soaked in slip and laid on a clay surface or used in modeling. The fibers burn away in the kiln to leave a clay skeleton of the fabric. Early porcelain figures often used the technique, sometimes even as 'free' items of modeling, i.e. not laid on a surface.

LACUSTRINE CLAY

Clays which have been deposited, in geological time, on the bed of a lake. Similar to *estuarine clays*.

LAMELLAR

In the form of sheets or scales. Clay is considered to be lamellar in structure and this is the general explanation of its plastic qualities. (See *clay*, *plasticity*.)

LAMINATED CLAYS

See agate, marbling, neriage.

A powerfully designed laminated clay dish by Michael Bayley.

A laminated-clay pot by Mal Magson.

165

LATEX RESIST

A preparation used in the manner of *wax resist*. Its main advantages over wax is that it can be used cold, but more especially, that it can be peeled off, leaving a clear, sharp image similar to that gained from *paper resist* but with the possibility of a much freer and more spontaneous use of line and mass. The resisted areas can be repainted or treated in any other way. It is suitable for work with pigment, slip and glaze, especially glaze-overglaze techniques. The treatment is necessarily fairly broad. John Maltby uses latex to produce remarkable designs which could not be achieved by any other technique. Another attractive feature is that brushes can be cleaned in water (before the latex sets). See illustrations in Fournier DPD.

A film of rubber laid on as a resist can be lifted off and further detail then added to the resisted areas.

A detail of a dish by John Maltby showing the resisted area from which the latex has been peeled away, glaze trailing being subsequently applied in the spaces.

LATTICE

A regular three-dimensional pattern or network of linked atoms building up into a *crystalline* substance. Quartz, for instance, has a lattice unit of one silicon atom and four oxygen atoms in a pyramid or tetrahedron. Further Si atoms share half the electron charge with each of the O atoms, the pattern being repeated in every direction. This is known as the SiO_4 lattice. This crystalline lattice has a tight structure but it can be altered and weakened by the intrusion of other atoms (see *network modifiers*, and diagram of SiO_4 under *glass former*.)

LAVA

Volcanic rocks of variable composition equivalent to around 50% feldspar and 50% ferro-magnesium minerals (Frazer, CR 17). The iron content is high and the rock yields dark-colored temmoku-type glazes. See *basalt*.

LAWN, lawn mesh

A fine-meshed *sieve* originally of woven silk or fine linen (hence the name) but now usually of phosphor-bronze wire. The mesh (the tiny holes where the wires cross each other) is graded according to the wires per linear inch (25.5 mm.): 80 wires per inch for a number 80 lawn, etc. Some quoted apertures for comparison are:

No 30 (U.S.A. 35)	0.50 mm.
60	0.25 mm.
80	0.18 mm.
120	0.125 mm.
200	0.075 mm.

It will be seen that the aperture halves as the number doubles. Lawns are seldom made below 40 mesh, the coarser wire or nylon sieves taking over for wide apertures. Hamer quotes a 2:1 relationship, e.g. a 100 mesh with a hole 1/200 of an inch wide. Luckily the numbers for lawns are reasonably comparable in Britain and the U.S.A. In Europe, however, the system is quite different. This is all fairly academic for the potter who soon comes to know which sieve number best suits his purpose.

Lawns are mounted on ash-wood, plastic or metal rims. (See also *sieve*). A phosphor-bronze lawn carefully used will last a lifetime. Useful rim sizes are 6 in. (150 mm.) for glaze trials, 10 in. (250 mm.) for slips, 8–12 in. (200–300 mm.) for glaze batches. Color sieves or 'cup' sieves about 3 in. (75 mm.) across are made for pigments. Lawn mesh sizes in general use are: 60–80 for slips and many stoneware glazes; 100–120 for earthenware glazes; 200 for pigments and stains.

If you have unmounted lawns or a piece of lawn

from a broken frame, a fairly easy do-it-yourself sieve can be made by cutting the base from a circular plastic box or bucket or cutting a section from a plastic drain-pipe (limitations on the diameter of the latter), laying a piece of lawn on the top and fastening it by carefully melting the plastic rim beneath it with a soldering iron or, as Lynn Carter suggests for smaller sieves, heating the lawn on a hotplate and pressing the plastic onto it. Other useful ideas may be found in Fournier PT, and see also *sieve*.

LAWN PROVER

A small glass magnifier, set above a one inch square aperture through which one can count the wires in a lawn to determine its gauge or number. Could be of use to check the mesh of unmounted lawns.

LAYERING CLAY

See *agate, marbling, neriage, wedging*.

LEAD, oxides, compounds

A metallic element Pb, 207.
Oxides:
Litharge PbO, 223.
Peroxide, red lead Pb_2O_3, 686 (useful equivalent weight 228.5)
White lead (basic) $2PbOCO_3:Pb(OH)_2$, 775 (equivalent wt. 258)
Galena (sulfide) PbS.239.

A *base*, and a powerful *flux* in the 750–1150°C. range. It is the principal or only base in most soft glazes which do not contain boric oxide. The rich quality of many early glazes owes much to the use of lead. Its *coefficient of expansion* is in the middle range and lead glazes are reputed to adapt to tension better than others.

Litharge is the traditional oxide for slipware glazes. Galena has been widely used in the past but needs a very well-ventilated kiln. Lead is now normally used as a frit, see *lead frits, lead glazes*.

Lead oxide is toxic both as a raw material and in an unbalanced or ill-fired glaze from which it may be dissolved by food acids. The addition of copper oxide will greatly increase this danger. (See *soluble lead*.)

LEAD ANTIMONIATE

A compound of lead and antimony, quoted as $Pb_2(SbO)_4$. Composition variable. Toxic. Used as a yellow pigment—'Naples' yellow. Dilute with a lead frit for painting. Up to 8% can be added to a soft lead glaze. Not suitable for use in stoneware. (See also *antimony, yellow*.)

LEAD BOROSILICATE

A low-solubility frit containing oxides of lead, boron and silicon, with other trace compounds as stabilisers. Available W. G. Ball. Ltd.

LEAD FRIT

The use of lead in the form of *silicates*, now compulsory in schools and factories though studios and some colleges may still use the oxides.

The commonest frits in use are:
Lead monosilicate $PbO.SiO_2$, 283. m.p. 670–750°C.
Lead sesquisilicate $2PbO.3SiO_2$, 627. ($PbO. 1.5SiO_2$ 313) 690–850°C.
Lead bisilicate $PbO.2SiO_2$, 343, 710–800°C.

The actual frit batch can include small amounts of alumina (up to 3%), or titania. Podmores also quote a 'coated' frit, reputed to be less liable to *metal release*.

Sesquisilicate is perhaps the most useful for potters. Monosilicate does not comply with British regulations governing lead in glazes. The melting points given above are derived from those quoted by various suppliers. Apart from simple silicates, many lead frits are available for temperatures up to 1150°C. The simplest basis for bisilicate/clay proportions is 3:1. Use iron oxide or red clay for a 'honey' glaze. (See also *low solubility glaze*.)

LEAD GLAZE

Lead can be used as the only *flux* in an earthenware glaze. The formula limits are:

1 PbO. 0.23–0.35Al_2O_3. 2.0–3.5SiO_2 with an average 1:0.3:3.0 firing at 1100°C with a recipe:

Lead sesquisilicate	70.5
China clay	17.4
Flint	12.1

See also 'honey glaze' for the use of red clay in the recipe. This is useful for *slipware*, especially slip-trailing.

Lead can be combined with other bases but must represent at least 0.5 of the *RO group*, e.g.

0.6	PbO
0.2	K_2O
0.2	CaO

If the lead equivalent is less than 0.5, boric acid must appear in the RO_2 column, unless it is a high soda glaze. A glaze recipe, embodying frit, by Anthony Phillips (CR 123) is given as:

Lead bisilicate,	57
Boric frit,	25.6
China clay	10.3
Flint	7.1
Bentonite	2.
Firing at 1105°C.	

If there is any significant lead content in a glaze it is generally labelled as a 'lead glaze'. The mixed base glazes are more purely transparent and viscous than simple ones, and are therefore chosen for underglaze painting and for tin glazes (see *majolica*).

Once-fired earthenware generally utilizes lead oxide as the main or only base. Higher proportions of the oxide are used—although not the 100% litharge mentioned by Billington. Some typical recipes: 70% litharge, 12% plastic clay, 18% flint, or 75% lead bisilicate, 10% china stone, 15% plastic clay.

Most pigment oxides readily dissolve in lead glazes giving yellow-brown from iron, apple-green from copper (but beware, see *soluble lead*); blue from cobalt; purple-brown from manganese. Lead and soda glazes produce brighter colors and have been suggested for soft-glaze *black*. Lead oxide is toxic and if the formula is not a balanced one can constitute a health hazard even when fired in a glaze. (See discussion under *soluble lead*.)

Glazes recommended by Kenneth Clark in CR 9:

Lead bisilicate	72.8	Lead sesquisilicate	52.8
China clay	12.1	Feldspar	31.1
China stone	13.5	Whiting	5.6
Flint	1.6	China clay	7.2
1060–1080°C		Flint	3.3

Strontium is used in some countries as a substitute for lead oxide in glazes.

The laws on lead glazes have been tightened in recent times and it is now used much less as a flux. Any new lead glaze, if it is to be used on tableware or pottery which may come into contact with edibles must be laboratory tested for metal release. Some pottery merchants (e.g. Potclays) offer this service.

LEADLESS GLAZE

A glaze with not more than 1% its dry weight of PbO (British regulations). Most leadless glazes (rather confusingly marked 'L' in suppliers' lists) have no lead content at all. It is replaced, in effect, by boric oxide, although this is listed with the RO_2 in the *Seger formula*. The bases can include, soda, potash, strontium, lime, magnesia, and zinc oxide.

There is no form of insoluble boric oxide which can be used in a soft leadless glaze. Calcined borax is the nearest approach, but it will crystallize in a comparatively short time (as will very soft leadless frits). Colemanite can help, but introduces lime. A leadless frit which melts at 1000°C. or lower can be mixed with raw materials such as clay to aid suspension and strengthen the dry coating. Many suppliers quote the formulas for

their frits; these can be entered in the glaze formula computation (see *formula-into-recipe*).

High soda frits, e.g. Na_2O. $\quad$ 3.5 SiO_2
$\qquad\qquad\qquad\qquad\quad$ 2.0 B_2O_3

will produce a turquoise from copper, but the lack of alumina renders it unstable. A more regular L frit might read:

$$\begin{array}{ll} 0.27\ Na_2O & \\ 0.13\ K_2O & 4.7\ SiO_2 \\ 0.59\ CaO \quad 0.42\ Al_2O_3 & 0.96\ B_2O_3 \\ 0.01\ MgO & \end{array}$$

firing at 1040°C.

It will be seen that the silica and alumina ratio is much higher than one would expect from the normal Seger ratios. This is caused by the anomalous position of boron which, in practice, acts as a flux and could quite logically be listed with the bases. In the above formula this would bring the silica equivalent down to 2.5. Leadless earthenware glazes have been compounded from strontium and zinc additions. (See *Bristol glaze*.)

Leadless fritted glazes need to be applied more thinly than lead or raw glazes. Colors from manganese, copper and cobalt are apt to be unsubtle and strident. They should not be fired with high lead glazes which can coat them with a thin skin of lead oxide and make them dangerous in use.

The term has little meaning in connection with stoneware and porcelain glazes, which are outside the lead range.

LEAD SOLUBILITY

See *soluble lead*.

LEAN CLAY

A clay or body of low *plasticity*. *Aging* will help some lean clays.

LEATHER-HARD

A stage in the drying of clay when it has become almost rigid but is still damp. One might elaborate by using the terms 'soft-leather' and 'hard-leather' to indicate stages either side of leather-hard, and these are occasionally used in discussions in this book. Work done at leather-hard includes *turning*, *engraving*, *sgraffito*, *planing*, and techniques involving the use of metal tools.

At this stage most of the drying shrinkage will already have occurred—the particles are just touching one another. The size difference between leather-hard clay and soft biscuit is small. There is just enough plasticity in leather-hard clay to allow gentle beating to change its form. Clay can still be joined, but it is advisable to score and slip, or to work up a slip with a little moisture by rubbing the two parts together. For absorbent clays (which include most of those made up by merchants) raw clay glazing (*once-fired ware*) is best done at *hard-leather* dryness.

LEPIDOLITE

A mineral with the ideal formula $(LiNaK)_2,(F.O-H)_2,Al_2O_3, 3SiO_2, 472$, m.p. 1170°C. A typical analysis by weight:

K_2O	8.3
CaO	0.4
MgO	0.08
Li_2O	3.6
Al_2O_3	25.5
FeO	0.16
MnO	0.06
F	5.33
SiO_2	54.0

A *lithium* mica, with a lower melting point than feldspar, beginning its fluxing action at around 1150°C. Difficult to grind. A source of lithium for bodies and glazes, but its use is complicated by the release of fluorine as a gas during firing which can cause bloating in a body and bubbles in a glaze.

LEUCITE

A mineral $K_2O.Al_2O_3.4SiO_2$. Potash feldspar melts incongruently into a liquid plus leucite, which is an explanation of its high viscosity. Leucite can be formed when alkalis attack fireclay. Known as a feldspathoid. It is found in *lavas* (Australia, U.S.A. etc).

LEVIGATION

Defined in the Oxford Dictionary as to 'reduce to a fine powder', but in pottery it is taken to mean the separation of particles in a flowing stream (of slip), the finer ones remaining in *suspension*, the coarser sinking to the floor of the vessel or channel. China clay is levigated to remove the relatively coarse micas etc., the dumping of which produces the 'white mountains' of St. Austell.

A long, shallow trough with a sloping floor. The liquid mixture flows in at A and out at B at a slightly lower level. During the slow passage through the trough coarser particles will sink and the finer ones remain in suspension to flow out at B.

Cardew PP illustrates a levigating trough 12 ft. (3.5 m.) long, with 1 in 14 slope and a 2 in. (50 mm.) high check-gate at one end. Slip is fed in at the higher end, heavy particles sinking below the 'gate' level while the fine ones flow over it. Hamer illustrates a stepped type of trough. The natural levigating action of rivers has led to the accumulation of fine clay particles in their estuaries.

LIAS CLAY

Λ calcium-contaminated brick clay.

LID, lid seating

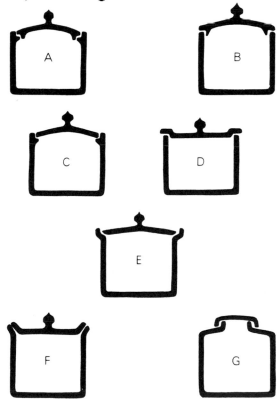

Seven types of lid seating
(A) with a flange on both lid and vessel, typical of teapots and jars.
(B) has a flange on the lid only, and is useful where the maximum aperture is needed at the mouth of the container, but it must be a good fit. The edge of the lid normally overhangs the sides of the pot so that it can be lifted without a knob so long as it is not larger that a handspan.
(C) A flange on the pot only. Typical of casseroles.
(D) An inset lid (see photograph of throwing method).
(E) The flange formed from an outward slope of the rim.
(F) A tapered lid and flange, self-adjusting to a degree but necessitating true circles for a snug fit.
(G) A lid for a small-mouthed jar or bottle.

The covered pot is a comparatively sophisticated object, and we do not find ceramic lids in general use until after the craft had graduated from *coiling* to *throwing*. Those who have tried to make a well-fitting lid on a coiled pot will appreciate the difficulties.

The design of a lid depends as much on the method

Two types thrown lid.
(1) The required diameter of the outside of the flange is measured.

(3) and (4) Forming an inset lid. The required diameter is similarly measured with calipers, a short upright wall thrown with a mound of clay left in the center of the lid. The top half of the wall is then eased over and outwards and the knob thrown from the central mound. (See at knob for an intermediate action.)

(2) The clay is brought up into a cone from the top of which an inverted lid is thrown.

A powerful stoneware lidded jar by Janet Leach.

used to stop it falling off as on its formal relationship with the pot. The diagrams below show several ways of securing a lid. Apart from F, each involves a horizontal surface for the lid to sit on, and an upright wall or flange to prevent sideways movement. The tapered lid will automatically accommodate a tighter or looser fit but its success depends on the maintenance of two perfect circles—not always achieved in pottery!

The simplest way of throwing a lid is flat on the wheel head as in photos 3 and 4. A domed lid is thrown upside-down either as a simple curve or with a flange as in photo 2. The knob may be turned from the stem of clay left at the base. An excellent example of lid type G in the diagram is shown in the porcelain jar. (See also *box, calipers, knob*.)

Isaac Button throwing the seating for a casserole lid.

LIFT-OFF KILN

See *top-hat kiln*.

LIME

Lime, strictly speaking, is a burnt limestone CaO, an unstable *anhydrous* material (quicklime) which may be slaked with water to produce $Ca(OH)_2$. In ceramics the word is used, imprecisely, to indicate whiting, $CaCO_3$, or a calcium material which will be converted into CaO in the glaze or body melt, as in 'lead-lime-potash glaze'. Used to produce lime matt glazes, which need careful firing, avoiding over-firing, and giving time for the crystals to form during cooling. These glazes are not usually suitable for tableware, but will give good colors with pigment oxides. See also *calcium*.

LIMIT FORMULA

A term used by Rhodes CGP to indicate the minimum and maximum amounts of any oxide which can be used in a particular formula. The silica limits are given as 1–5 (compared with the RO of 1, see *Seger formula*); alumina 0.05–0.5; KNaO maximum 0.4; CaO up to 0.7 (at 1250–1300°C.); B_2O_3 0.15–0.6. The limits, of course, varying with the temperature at which the glaze is to be fired. See also *glaze, saturated glaze*, and under the individual minerals and oxides.

LIME-BLOWING

Pellets of lime in clay will be turned into quicklime in the firing. Moisture will subsequently slake the lime which expands and breaks pieces of pot away. If lime is suspected in a pot, dip it into water and put aside for checking in a day or two.

Philip Stanbridge, in British Ceramic Review, Summer 91, discusses and enlarges on some interesting research by Harry Fraser and Derek Basnett. They have concluded that it is possible for dispersed lime in a clay or glaze to coagulate into nodules under the influence of damp and warmth, even though the original slip may have been passed through a fine lawn. Blunged bodies are said to be less prone but are not immune. If, therefore, you find spit-outs in fired bodies due to lime fragments soon after receiving the clay then it is probably a supplier problem, but clay which has been kept moist and warm for a longer period may possibly develop its own nodules spontaneously.

Stanbridge suggests that acid rain may be leaching more lime into our water supply, aggravating the problem. The only treatment at present available is to add barium carbonate (toxic, but not a great danger in the small quantities of 2–3% required, see at *efflorescence*), or a biocide chemical which might have its own hazards and prevents the natural and useful 'souring' of clay. Clay suppliers continue to work on the problem.

LIMESTONE

The sedimentary rock of calcium carbonate or *calcite*. Formed from lime in solution or from organic deposits (fossil shells), and sometimes as pure as 98% calcite. There are mixtures of calcite and clay (marls), and sandy (quartz) limestones. Chalk is an earthy variety. Marble is an 'altered' limestone.

LIMONITE

An hydrated iron oxide; a 'bog ore'. Crumbly and often fairly pure. The mineral of *ochres*. Recommended for mixing with cobalt; 'very nice for brush decoration' (Harry Davis).

LINE BLEND

A method of working out intervals in a series of mixtures of two different colors, glazes, etc.

The simplest blend is:

A— 100 75 50 25 0 —A
B— 0 25 50 75 100 —B

each vertical pair being tested.

The principle can be extended to any number of intervals. For a slightly different approach discussed in practical detail see *color trials*, also *glaze trials* for working blends back to a recipe.

LINE TAP

A form of connector for thick electric wires, especially

(1) A line tap, showing the parts separate and assembled. These are, of course, not insulated and are used only in fully guarded situations. (See Fournier EKP.)

(2) The great advantage of the line tap is that two spanners can be used as shown here. This not only ensures a tight connection but it also makes it easy to undo, even if corroded, without breaking a brittle element tail.

useful to potters for joining kiln *elements* to their connecting wires, and for joining the neutrals in a *three-phase star system*. The Sherardized finish does not corrode. If difficult to buy, ask your Electricity Company.

LIP

There is some overlapping and confusion over the use of this term to describe a part of a pot. It is sometimes applied to the upper termination of a pot or bowl, also variously called the 'edge' or the 'rim'. For the purposes of this entry 'lip' is taken to mean the pouring lip of a jug, mixing bowl, etc.

The lip can be formed immediately after throwing by a steady out-and-over pull or a side-to-side stroking motion with one finger, while the finger and thumb of the other hand support the rim at each side. Alternatively a somewhat crisper type of lip can be beaten out with the side of a rigid finger, after the pot has been turned or at soft-leather stage. Moisten the clay and give full support with a crooked finger under the lip as it is formed. Finish with smooth sweeps round the curve.

An applied lip. (A) a small flaring cup shape is thrown and a segment cut from it with a wire. An equivalent area of the neck of the jug is either cut right away, left with a bridge across the top (as (B)), or pierced with holes. The segment of the thrown shape is then luted onto the jug. (C) A section cut away from a jug lip to form a raised lip.

172

(1) Tapping or beating a lip from soft-leather clay. The underside of the lip must be supported so that the clay is pressed between the two surfaces and not stretched or it will split. A wipe of water on the rim before starting will help. Finish with a side to side movement.

(2) The supporting and forming positions of the fingers when pulling a lip from a newly-thrown jug. Other potters may vary these positions but the principle of two supports and side to side stroking followed by an out and downwards finish to form the edge of the lip is common to most methods.

A lip which curves slightly downwards at the very edge is more likely to pour well than one which finishes with an upward slope. The last drop of liquid will fall from the end of the lip rather than round it (to dribble down the side of the jug). Similarly a sharper edge will cut the flow more efficiently than a rounded one, though there are obvious limits.

Two other forms are:
1 The ewer type in which a flared rim is cut down for the greater part of its circumference, the section of the original rim acting as a raised lip.

2 Lips made separately, either thrown as a small inverted cone which is cut in two, or molded, and luted onto the rim. The rim behind the lip can be cut away entirely: a bridge can be left across the top; or it can be perforated.

Whichever method is used, make the lip generous and well-defined. It will then be aesthetically attractive as well as efficient in directing the flow of liquid. A somewhat involved type of reportedly 'non-drip' lip is described in Fournier PT p.60.

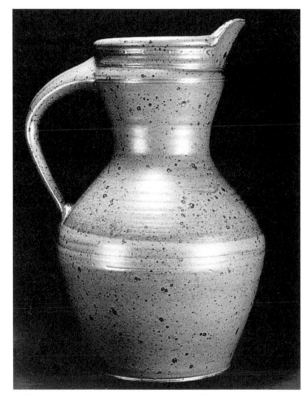

A fine large pitcher by Doyle Long (U.S.A.) with an upstanding spout/lip luted onto the form.

LIQUID PETROLEUM GAS

L.P.G. (See *bottled gas*.)

LIQUIDUS

The line on an equilibrium or *phase diagram* above which the components become a liquid or, conversely, below which a liquid begins to precipitate solids.

LITHARGE

Lead monoxide PbO.223. A yellow or orange powder

which like all lead compounds is toxic if taken into the body. Potters working on their own may use litharge but in factories and schools a *frit* must be used. Litharge glaze must not be used on table-ware unless it has been passed as safe (see *soluble lead*).

Litharge produces a rich, transparent glaze very suitable for slip-trailed ware. A typical recipe:

Litharge 50, china clay 17.5, flint 32.5, firing at 1080–1100°C.

Litharge-tin glazes, with high lead content and 12–15% of tin oxide, used over a red clay, will break on the edges to a brick-red. Lead/soda glazes will also work well for this technique, e.g.:

Litharge 46
China stone 52
Bentonite 2

For a black or dark brown glaze use 9% manganese and 1% tin. Avoid litharge glazes if contact is likely to be made with acids, vinegar, or ferments. (See *raku*, *lead*, *green glazing*, *once-fired*.)

LITHIFY

To turn to a stone-like state, generally by natural pressure and heat, e.g. shale is lithified clay.

LITHIUM

An alkaline metallic element. Li, 7.
Oxide Li_2O, 30. Lithia,
Carbonate Li_2O_3, 74. An insoluble ('slightly soluble' Hamer) form. See also *petalite*, sometimes referred to as lithium feldspar.

Acts in a glaze like soda or potash, i.e. with a strong fluxing action, and has the added advantage of a low *thermal expansion*. Will brighten colors.

Lithium compounds have been expensive and are still around six times the price of feldspar. Lithia, however, is light in weight (the lightest of the metals) and the addition of only 0.5–2.0% markedly affects glaze *fusion*. Its use is frequently suggested by Behrens in all types of glaze and in amounts up to 20% of the batch. Even *raku* recipes may contain 10% lithia (with very soft frit, clay, and flint). 3% lithia in a stoneware glaze can bring its melting point down two or three cones. Around 2% of other fluxes, e.g. calcium borate, can be replaced with lithium.

Lithium has been tried in porcelain bodies. The common lithium minerals have certain disadvantages, e.g. the fluorine content of *lepidolite*. (See also *petalite*, *spodumene*, *amblygonite*.)

LITHOGRAPHY

In ceramics, a method of making transfers printed in lithographic oil, the color being dusted onto the oil. They are applied to ware coated with a tacky varnish. Now generally replaced by slide-off transfers, called 'decals' in the USA.

LOAM

A clayey earth with sand and gravel.

LOCAL CLAY

It is fun, and always instructive, to dig clay from the ground but you are not very likely to find good, workable deposits in regions where they are not already known. The study of local industries of the past may reveal clay workings, also the names of fields, etc. Few geological books deal specifically with clays. In America the State Geological Departments may be able to help; in England the British Geological Survey. Also organizations such as CoSIRA (Council of Small Industries in Rural Areas).

If you have access to any local rock-formation studies take note of Cardew's dictum that 'it is broadly true that the younger geological systems and strata are more likely to yield workable clays than the older ones'. Brick clays will seldom take a glaze satisfactorily. Details on the testing of clays may be found under *clay testing*; (see also *clay*, *body*, *clay-winning*).

L.O.I.

See *loss on ignition*.

LONDON CLAY

A brick clay (Oligocene period, ca. 25 million years ago) from the Home Counties (those counties around London). *Vitreous* at about 1000°C. 'Possibly 90% *illite*' (Cardew).

LOSS ON IGNITION

The loss in weight when strongly heated (of a clay or mineral) through the dispersal of carbonates, etc. For clays the figure quoted in catalogs is the percentage of its dry weight lost at 1000–1100°C. With frits the temperature will be below the fusion point.

To ascertain the L.O.I of a mineral or rock, weigh it very carefully; fire it and weigh it again. The percentage figure will be: dry weight minus fired weight; divided by dry weight; multiplied by 100. The loss can be very considerable, up to 50% for dolomite which means that a fired glaze will have only half the amount listed in the *recipe*. Ash, on the other hand loses hardly anything at all since it has already been 'fired', and frits, of course, nothing. The loss from feldspars is negligible; from colemanite and talc around 20% and 40% respectively.

LOW SOLUBILITY GLAZE

Frits which comply with the Pottery Health Regulations not to 'release more than 5% of its dry weight of soluble lead when subjected to specific tests in hydrochloric acid'. Often marked L.S. in catalogs.

LUG

A small handle or pierced piece of clay on the side of a pot. Originally for suspending a pot on a rope, lugs are now often used purely decoratively. (See also *cane handles*.). Fournier DPF illustrates a variety of modern variations on the lug handle.

Shell-shaped lug handles on a painted earthenware dish by Bennett Cooper.

A sturdy lug on a porcelain teapot by David Leach.

Lug handles formed from flattened coils on a dish by Joanna and Andrew Young.

Lugs used decoratively on a stoneware bottle by Janet Leach.

LUMP WARE

In the industry 'defective ware of the lowest saleable quality'. The grades are: best, seconds, lump.

Rather too much 'lump' appears as 'seconds' in some studio potteries!

LUSTER, lustre

Thin metallic coatings on glaze, producing *iridescence*. The metal is obtained by reduction either in a reducing atmosphere or by the addition of a reducing agent to the metal *salts*. The luster is applied to an already fired glaze, preferably an *alkaline* one, and refired just hot enough to adhere the metal to the glaze surface – 650–800°C. They can be bought ready to fire, or reduced in the kiln from a paste of red ochre with silver sulfide or copper carbonate and a little gum. The Fe_2O_3 in the red *ochre* is reduced to FeO and, together with the clay constituent, inhibits the re-oxidation of the underlying luster metal during cooling. Care must be taken, when using an ochre paste not to take the temperature above the softening point of the glaze. Bismuth can be used for a 'mother of pearl' effect.

An overall luster glaze can be obtained by silver nitrate, bismuth sub-nitrate, or copper sulfate in concentrations of 1–3%. The pots must be reduced during cooling until the color has gone from the kiln. Soft 900–1000°C. glazes are used. Parmelee also mentions iron chloride dissolved in sodium resinate, or manganese and copper sulfates treated in the same way. Silver color is derived from platinum. Luster is a tricky technique and the result may not always be as expected; repeated experiment will be necessary.

The Arabian lusters were made from silver sulfide, cinnabar (HgS), iron oxide, and alum in vinegar; fired in a smoky kiln. The lusters from sixteenth century Spain must have been fired in a comparatively simple way and without sophisticated chemicals. Rhodes K shows a simple updraft 'Spanish luster kiln'. Lusters can be pro-

Luster brushwork from the Alan Caiger-Smith workshop. The color has 'bled' a little at the edges of the strokes, a common occurrence with certain types of luster.

The seductively varied surface (which needs the subtle color to show its real quality) of a luster-glazed vase by Greg Daly (Australia). An 'alkaline glaze with copper, bismuth and silver' fired in an electric kiln to 1000°C. followed by a third firing to 800°C. with heavy reduction down to 620°C.

Luster used unconventionally on a low-fired bowl by Robin Welch.

176

duced in reduction in an electric kiln with wood, mothballs, gas, etc. Raku frequently exhibits luster from alkali/copper glazes. Ochre reduced luster will need cleaning with a mild abrasive when taken from the kiln. See Fournier DPD and Hamer for more detailed discussion and Caiger-Smith LP for a lifetime of experience and an answer to most queries. He also features in John Anderson's film/video 'Lustre firing' (Films for Potters).

LUTING

The joining of plastic or leather-hard clay with *slip* or water. Called 'sticking-up' in the industry. Clay models, especially children's work, often disappointingly fall to pieces as they dry due to poorly joined or insufficiently moist junctions. Clay surfaces at any stage will adhere more firmly with a thin layer of water or slip between them. Only the soft clay used on coil pots built by the fingering down method seems not to require slipping. Scoring the joint is an extra precaution but a little liquid will usually suffice at the plastic or soft-leather stages. One can rub up a slip with one's finger between the surfaces to be joined.

LYNN SAND

Or Llyn sand. Given by Billington as a ground quartz, and by Leach as a pure form of quartoze sand. Does not now appear in suppliers' lists.

MACALOID

A superior form of bentonite. 'An excellent suspender'. Listed by Reward Products.

MAGNESITE

The natural mineral of magnesium carbonate $MgCO_3$ with some $FeCO_3$. Widely distributed. Is the chief ore of magnesium. It can be substituted for talc in *ovenproof* bodies. Used also for basic *refractories*.

A listed calcined magnesite has an analysis MgO 88.2, Al_2O_3 1.0, SiO_2 4.3. Potclays list a pure form with 94% MgO.

MAGNESIUM, oxide, compounds

An unstable metallic element Mg, 24.
Oxide MgO, 40, magnesia, m.p. 2800°C.
Carbonate $MgCO_3$, 84. Decomposes to oxide at 350°C.
Sulfate $MgSO_4$ $7H_2O$, 246.5. Epsom salts.
The ore of the mineral is magnesite. It is also derived from seawater. *Steatite* (soapstone) is an hydrated silicate of magnesia.

Although a refractory oxide it is *basic* and will, like calcium, act as flux in higher temperature glazes. It is classed as one of the *alkaline earths*. The normal formula equivalent is around 0.3 parts of the *RO*. *Talc* and *dolomite* are most generally used by potters as a source of magnesia. They also, of course, introduce silica and lime respectively. 5% is an average weight in a recipe but it can be exceeded. Magnesia can give a pleasant 'buttery' surface to a glaze. The carbonate, either precipitated or as ground magnesite, is slightly soluble. Its effect on cobalt can vary: giving purple or even red (Rhodes), or, used as talc can 'quench' the blue to a blue-gray (Cardew). It is considered by many to be an essential ingredient in Jun-type glazes, but it may turn celadons brownish. Used in *fireproof bodies (cordierite)* and as magnesia *refractories*.

A calcined magnesia is listed by Reward Products.

MAGNETITE

The *spinel* oxide of iron Fe_3O_4 ($FeO.F_2O_3$). Also known as magnetic iron ore (loadstone), or black iron oxide. It may be prepared by roasting scrap iron in the kiln at about 1100°C.—'Blacksmith's scale'.

MAJOLICA, maiolica

In the pottery industry and in merchants' catalogs, a 'majolica' glaze indicates a soft, *opaque*, colored glaze firing 980–1080°C. However the majolica technique as understood by craft potters, is the painting with metal oxides on a white, generally tin-opacified *earthenware glaze*.

The art of majolica painting has suffered an eclipse but it still has unexplored potential and great satisfaction can be derived from its practice. It is very flexible and can be treated as broadly or as finely as you wish. The basic technique is simple enough. A pot or plate is evenly coated with an opaque glaze such as a lead-lime potash glaze with 10% tin oxide. The use of a light *terracotta* body will give warmth to the glaze. The design is painted straight onto the raw glaze. One may start work as soon as the wetness has gone from the surface, which then accepts the color like a dampened water-color paper. Alan Caiger-Smith, however, works on the dry glaze. The timing depends partly on the physical strength of the dried coating (which will usually be rather powdery if frits are used). *Gums* or other binders can be added to the glaze.

The oxides are ground with water, either in a mortar or with a palette knife on a glazed tile. See also *pigment oxides*. The depth of color will depend on the amount of water used. Most oxides will become transparent and each stroke will be revealed after firing even though they appear as a solid block of color when raw. Many of the unfired oxides are black and this can lead to confusion. It will help to use those carbonates which have distinctive hues, though these will change in the firing. The carbonates are slightly toxic. Cobalt and manganese are the most stable colors: copper is rather watery with blurred edges; lead antimoniate is refractory and needs softening with lead oxide or frit and careful application; iron is rather fugitive, varying from a pale amber to dark brown within a single stroke. Chrome is rarely used because of possible pink reactions.

With practice one can work with these particular properties and turn them to advantage. Oxides can be mixed. Rather firmer greens can be obtained with antimony/cobalt mixtures. Much of the older majolica painting uses a thin outline of cobalt or manganese to give definition to the washes of copper and antimony.

A long-haired *brush* is traditional but all kinds may be used, care being taken not to abrade the glaze coating or to saturate it. Painting should be rapid and direct—it has more affinity with Eastern *calligraphic* styles than is often realized. The Italian majolica glazes were compounded of *tin-ash* with a lead-clay-sand frit and after painting a thin coat of clear glaze was applied. The clear glaze would also have been mixed with the oxides to help them to *flux*. Colors will vary with the type of glaze and *opacifier*. Tin oxide is kinder to the pigments than zirconium: leadless glazes will develop more brash hues than lead ones. The glaze must be applied with care, runs or thick areas pared down with a sharp knife, and the firing carefully controlled. The high degree of opacity may cause some *crawling*. As mentioned the body may be a mixture of red and buff clays.

Painted majolica pots are difficult to handle when packing the kiln. One may use siccatives to fix the glaze or color, but if the painting is designed with this problem in mind, and if the piece is held firmly, the difficulty can be minimized. With top-loading kilns the pot can be held by the inside.

The term, spelt 'majolica', is confusingly applied to overall color opaque glazes by historians and the industry. Some writers therefore prefer 'maiolica' to indicate the raw glaze painting described above. 'Majolica' is also used for large industrial sculptural ceramics, probably after the Della Robbia plaques and figures.

MALM

A natural high-calcia brick clay. Will melt to a glass at 1200–1250°C.

MANGANESE, oxides, compounds

A metallic element Mn, 55.
Oxide MnO, 71.
Dioxide MnO_2, 87 (pyrolusite) loses oxygen at 535°C.
Tetraoxide Mn_3O_4, 229.
Carbonate $MnCO_3$, 115.

A coloring oxide, typically brown or purple-brown in a glaze but capable of variation. Used in concentrations of 2–10% in soft glazes and even higher in stonewares.

In a lower oxide state it is *basic* in effect, i.e. softens or fluxes a glaze. On heating, however, it alters to Mn_2O_3 and to Mn_3O_4. As the *valency* rises it acts as an *amphoteric* and then as an *acidic* oxide. In earthenware glazes, therefore, and especially in lead recipes it can be considered as quite a powerful flux: in oxidised stoneware it will behave more like alumina. The alteration or decomposition results in the release of gas which can lead to *bubbles* or craters in the glaze at around 1070°C. This bubbling in soft glazes can be avoided by using prepared glaze stains but this is expensive. Fraser recommends replacing whiting with *wollastonite*. A soak near top temperature may allow the bubbles to settle down, or firing a little lower plus soak. In high temperature reduction it should, theoretically, revert to its basic state. 2% has given a gray in reduction. Fully reduced MnO gives a green similar to chrome.

As well as a variety of purple-browns (often lurid in a leadless glaze), manganese can produce pink. I have

A stoneware casserole on a candle heater. The glaze is heavily loaded with manganese dioxide (20%), giving a lustrous surface effect. By Robert Fournier. (See also saturated glaze, super-saturated glaze.)

seen a salmon blush on tin glaze over black (manganese) slip. A pink *stain* is prepared from manganese, alumina, and borax. It is used with other oxides for *blacks*. 10% and over will cause metallic surface deposits giving *iridescence* and other effects. Manganese and zinc have a low *eutectic* and the mixture is best avoided. Manganese and copper can give a muted gold surface on biscuit, but the mixture has a tendency to run. Manganese is sensitive to the presence of sulfur gases, which may explain why it bubbles in a glaze on some bodies and not on others. Painted onto raw clay or biscuit it will fire to a dull gloss at 1090°C. and can also be used on stoneware. (See also *copper/manganese gold*.)

MARBLING

Marbled or variegated slip patterns can be achieved in two ways:

1   Tiles, small pots, pottery figures, etc. can be dipped into a bowl of *slip* onto the surface of which contrasting colored slips have been dribbled or *trailed*. The traditional Sussex 'pig-bank' is decorated in this way.

2   Slip may be trailed directly onto a dish or pot which is then either shaken sideways or given a sharp twist. Use a minimum of movement—if the effect is not immediately attractive, continued shaking will only make it more muddy. The colors tend to become less defined after glaze firing, due to overlapping slip becoming slightly transparent and showing the color beneath. This effect can also be turned to advantage.

Marbled *bodies* result from layered clays of different colors. The clays should be of similar shrinkage—it is advisable to use a single clay variously stained. The layers are sharply smacked together, pressed into a convenient shape, sliced through, and then used for making

A well-controlled slip-marbled dish by Jane Smith.

pottery in the normal way but with a maximum economy of movement. The surface of thrown pots will be smudged but the design can be sharpened by turning or by scraping, when leather-hard, with a steel palette. (See also *agate ware*).

Dipping a pinch-pot pig money-box into a bowl of black slip into which white and red slips have been trailed, giving a very fluid marbling effect.

MARL

An imprecise term given to some iron-bearing secondary clays, generally with calcium impurities. Examples: Keuper marl, of variegated color and containing magnesium carbonate and gypsum, Etruria marl, however, is almost lime-free. Cambridge marl contains some 40% CaO. The term is applied to a low grade fireclay (e.g. saggar marl). Leach mentions the use of a marl with a finely dispersed lime content for slipware. Much traditional slipware must have been made with this type of clay, which is common all over England.

MASK

The danger of breathing unhealthy dusty materials by potters varies with their working habits (see *dust, poisonous materials, etc*). The simplest mask, obtainable from pharmacies, is a light metal shape into which filter pads are fitted, and which is held in place with elastic round the back of the head. More elaborate and more effective models (resembling gas-masks) are now often provided with two filters to make breathing easier.

Wearing this clumsy equipment is anathema to many people but some effective filter should always be used when spraying, sanding dry clay for any length of time, and any work which results in a prolonged dusty atmosphere (or air holding fine droplets in suspension, as with spraying).

The double filter mask in use. Easier for breathing but large and clumsy. Essential, however, for assistants to potters or suppliers (this picture was taken at Bath Pottery Supplies, U.K.), where dry potter materials are handled or spraying done. Simpler, cheaper pad masks are available for occasional use but this more efficient type is recommended if regular spraying, sanding, or other dust-producing processes are practised.

MASKING TAPE

Masking tape resist decoration on a raku bowl by David Roberts.

Ordinary adhesive masking tape has been used by potters as a resist material on clay or biscuit. The simplest but often striking effect is of broad stripes, though the tape can be cut and manipulated to produce other designs.

MASSIVE FORM OF ROCK

The rocky, solid, or block form of a mineral, e.g. steatite.

MASTER MOLD

Or block-mold. A high quality copy taken from a hollow mold and from which 'case molds' can be made. In the case of simple dish molds, the 'block' would be in the form of a solid inverted dish (which can be used as a drape or *hump mold*).

MATRIX

The 'ground mass' of a mineral or ceramic material in which larger crystals are embedded.

MATT, mat

A non-shiny surface. Term sometimes confused with *opaque*. Opacity is, in fact, involved, since a fully transparent glass does not have *crystalline* structure and does have a bright surface. The matt effect is due to the break-up of reflected light by minute variations in the surface level. A matt glaze will, therefore, tend to stain or mark more easily than a shiny one.

Matt glazes can result from under-firing but these are less satisfactory than those due to the development of very small surface crystals. Slow cooling in the upper temperature range (maturity down to 800°C.) will assist crystallization. Alumina in slight excess of the optimum balance with silica; high base glazes; titanium; barium in low boron glazes; zinc oxides; hematite; lime (below 1200°C.); will all tend to make a glaze matt. 3% of copper oxide may produce a rather ashy matt black. Lime matts are a result of the formation of wollastonite (Shaw SCP).

MATURING OF GLAZE

The optimum condition of a glaze when it has fully melted or otherwise achieved its potential. Most potters believe that the involved physical and chemical changes need time fully to 'mature'. This is not always proved in practice. In the older kilns it was not possible to fire quickly and the idea of a long, *soaking* fire may be linked with this fact.

The same glaze will give quite different results in different kilns and firing schedules, and I have found that some of the most attractive and apparently 'mature' glazes have come from fast firings. The question is an open one, but the subtleties of a well-developed interface and other considerations will for many potters swing the balance in favor of longer firings. A twenty-minute soaking certainly helps *earthenware glazes* to settle down.

MEASURING SPOON

These can be bought in various sizes from a $\frac{1}{4}$ teaspoon to a tablespoon. Scrape the surface of the material flat for accurate measurement. Useful for small tests and especially for line blends of glazes etc. Attempts have been made to translate weight recipes into spoonsful (see CM 15/10) by taking density into account, but it is much easier to weigh larger amounts of glaze and slip materials. The measuring spoon could find a use in schools where scales are not always available.

MELTED GLASS DECORATION

Ordinary commercial window glass will melt at around 1060°C.—above or below this figure according to its type. It will also stand heating up to 1270°C. or more without trouble. On cooling it has the very high contraction natural to soda glass. This may be powerful enough to tear stonewares apart.

Molten glass is very fluid and, if not contained in a well or cavity, will flow like water. This quality can be turned to advantage in certain freely modelled dishes or other pieces, giving a 'frozen fall'. Too thin a coating will *devitrify* to a dull powdery surface: this can also occur on any melted glass surface—forming a white powder (with the glass beneath it dull and faulted), which may even appear weeks after the glass has been fired. Refiring is more likely to scum the surface with

1

bubbles than to cure the fault, unless further glass is laid on top. Colored glass is more liable to this fault than clear glass. (See illustration under *devitrification*.)

The glass will always be very 'shattered' in appearance through excessive *crazing* but, as the surface usually heals over the effect is decorative and mysterious. Glass can be colored by laying it over glaze or pigment and firing them together. It is best used in a well-broken but not powdered form—the latter may involve too much trapped air. Wrap the glass to be broken in thick newspaper, thick plastic (for flat sheets), or a cardboard box, and hammer it from the outside. You can usually get a supply of broken pieces from a local builder's glass cutter. Window glass is easier to handle and more reliable in melting than bottle-glass. (See also under *box*.)

2

(1) and (2) Broken pieces of window glass are placed on the unfired glazed surface of a slab dish. After firing the glass has melted together and the pigment in the glaze has stained it. Not all types of glass or glaze are suitable – only trials will show which will work. (See devitrification.) Note the fierce crazing just below the surface which, however, appears miraculously smooth.

MELTING POINT

The point of change from a solid to a liquid *phase*. In some cases this takes place completely at a given temperature (and pressure) and without change in composition. This is known as congruent melting. Many pottery materials, however, go through mixed solid and liquid *phases* i.e. they melt incongruently.

This behavior is of great service to the potter, allowing the development of *vitreous* stonewares and porcelains without collapse and assisting the *viscosity* of glazes. Reference books will often quote the melting points of the metals and oxides we use, but the knowledge is of limited use. To take magnesium, for instance: the m.p. of the metal is 651°C., that of the oxide 2800°C. Apart from the startling difference between these two figures, neither of them tells us much about their behavior in a glaze or body. It is more important to know where it stands in relation to the *Seger formula*, and its habits and effects in conjunction with silica.

Melting points in reaction with other materials will always differ from those of the oxide or mineral on its own—this is the limitation of the *button* test for individual materials, instructive though that can be. The study of ceramics is the study of *eutectics* rather than of individual melting points.

MENDING CLAY AND BISCUIT

'Mending' is used in the industry to mean the luting or joining of clay, as in the assembly of porcelain figures. Leach mentions the mending, in the more usual sense, of kiln props, etc. with powdered fireclay and *water-glass*. Repairs to unfired clay, can be made with slip up to the hard-leather stage but joins in dry clay or biscuit are unreliable. One may sometimes get away with the use of vinegar to repair dry clay, but one cannot be certain that it will hold: it should not be used for broken handles, for instance. Stress cracks will mend only temporarily.

Certain high temperature cements are advertised for dry or biscuit pots, which, the makers claim, can be glazed over without showing. One type is called 'Alumide': the name is a clue to its content. However if a pot is badly broken or cracked it will never fire very satisfactorily. (See also *stopping*, and *repairing pottery*.) Potclays sell a 'Magic Mender' for 'broken greenware or cracks in biscuit'.

METAL

A metallic *element* will generally unite with oxygen to form a *base*. Tin, titanium, zirconium, germanium, and aluminium are exceptions, forming acidic and amphoteric oxides.

METALOID

An element with some metallic and some non-metallic characteristics. The oxides are *amphoteric* (Uvarov DS) though two metaloids which occur in glaze formulas, arsenic and antimony, are glass-formers and listed with the *acidic* oxides. The metaloids belong to the fifth group of the *periodic table*.

METAL RELEASE

The tendency of some heavy metals (high atomic numbers) to dissolve out of a glaze and into vinegar, fruit juices, or any strong alkali or acid. The most dangerous are lead (see *soluble lead*) and cadmium. Copper is also involved, especially in the presence of lead oxide. Cadmium is used mainly in orange and red enamels. Neither these nor cadmium glazes should be used on the inside of tableware, storage jars, or kitchenware. Some merchants are now rating their colored glazes and frits on a metal release scale, those with high potential danger to be used on decorative ware only. Associated more with earthenwares than stonewares. Barium carbonate is mentioned as suspect. One need not panic over possible metal release. If glazes have well-balanced formulas and are accurately fired, the great majority of pots would be less liable to be dangerous than, say, household bleaches. Tests for metal release are offered by some potters' merchants.

One test has been given as: a 4% solution of acetic acid must not dissolve sufficient metals in 24 hours to color it. In some countries the tests are more stringent.

METAMORPHIC ROCK, mineral

A rock which has undergone transformation by natural agencies. *Igneous* or *sedimentary* rocks subjected to great heat and pressure are 'altered' and change their texture and appearance and sometimes their mineral composition. Limestone, for instance, re-crystallizes to form marble. Sillimanite is a metamorphic mineral.

METHANE

A *hydrocarbon*, CH_4. The principal constituent of natural gas. (See *gas fuel*.)

MICA

A general term for a group of minerals composed of hydrated *silicates* of alumina, with other silicates e.g. of the *alkalis*. The characteristic mineral of schists, and the glittering crystals or scales in granite. Some deposits will readily cleave into sheets. Feldspars are altered to *kaolinite* and mica in the formation of china clay. The shallow troughs which *levigate* the china clay are known as 'mica drags'.

Biotite mica contains iron and magnesium and is sometimes present in feldspars and other ceramic minerals. Muscovite is white mica, ideal formula $H_2KAl_2(SiO_4)_3$ or $K_2O.3Al_2O_3.6SiO_2.2H_2O$ with fluorine sometimes given as an element. There may be wide variations from this formula. It can be used as a 'natural frit' in bodies, especially for ovenware, where it will strengthen the fabric against thermal shock. Mica will begin to decompose into *mullite* and liquid at 1050°C.

The lamellar structure of mica has affinities with

clay, though it is not plastic. This structure also makes mica difficult to grind. In the past the alkali fraction in clay has been attributed to feldspar in a *rational analysis* but it is now generally given to a mica percentage (*mica convention*) which leads to a re-assessment of the kaoline content. Sheet mica is sometimes used as a heat-proof window for furnaces.

MICA CONVENTION

In a *rational analysis* of clay the assumption, for many years, was that the bulk of the mineral could be described as kaolinite, feldspar and quartz. It is now considered that the alkali content can more accurately be discussed in terms of mica. The new computation alters the proportions of the other compounds. See Cardew PP for details.

MICHIGAN SLIP-CLAY

A red fusible clay similar to *Albany slip*.

MICRON, micrometer

One-millionth of a meter. Symbol μ(m). A millionth may be written 10^{-6}. Used in the discussion of light wavelengths, and very fine clay particle sizes. 1 micron = 10,000 ångström units.

MICROPORE

A very efficient heat insulating material for the outer skins of kilns. One half inch (12.5 mm.) is reputed to replace 3 in. (75 mm.) of brick. (See also *insulation of heat*.)

MILL

To grind finely, or, a machine for grinding materials to a powder. (See *ball mill, jar mill*.)

In CM 19/5 it was suggested that one could shake marbles and glaze in a glass jar to mill glaze materials. This sounds energetic and a little dangerous!

MINERAL

In the process of the earth's cooling, and of its subsequent weathering, breaking down and re-combining, combinations of *elements* have formed with distinctive physical and chemical properties and, in the present environment, a degree of stability. In some crystal structures, *ionic* substitutions can occur causing variations in the detailed make-up of the mineral. Since the *electron* charges and the *atomic radii* must be similar to the displaced ions, the overall characteristics of the mineral remain within a certain range. *Rocks* consist of various minerals. Most minerals are of *inorganic* origin. The mineral is deemed to have an 'ideal' formula: the actual

material used will be the nearest approach in nature to this formula. Thus china clay or kaolin is often 98% kaolinite mineral. The principal rocks, ores and minerals of interest to potters are:

Alabaster. A pure form of micro-crystalline gypsum.

Albite feldspar. $Na_2Al_2O_3.6SiO_2$, 524. Igneous.

Amblygonite. Variable. Lithium, alumina, phosphorus, with a little silica.

Anorthite feldspar. $CaO.Al_2O_3.2SiO_2$, 278. Igneous.

Andalusite. $Al_2O_3.SiO_2$, 162.

Asbestos. Variable silicates of calcium, iron, and magnesia. Serpentine, amphibole.

Asbolite. Impure cobalt ore.

Barytes. Rock of barium sulfate, $BaSO_4$.

Basalt. Basic rock, high in iron. Volcanic.

Bauxite. Ore of aluminium. Residual.

Beidellite. Alumina-rich montmorillonite clay mineral.

Bentonite. Clay mineral of montmorillonite group.

Biotite. Mica mineral with iron and magnesium.

Borax. $Na_2O.2B_2O_3.10H_2O$, 381.5. Evaporate.

Boro-calcite $CaO.2B_2O_3.6H_2O$, 304.

Brucite. Ore of magnesia. $MgO.H_2O$.

Calcspar. Calcite. Crystalline $CaCO_3$, 100. Deposit.

Carolina Stone. See *china stone*.

Cassiterite. Ore of tin, SnO_2.

Chalcopyrite. Ore of copper. $CuFeS_2$.

Chalk. Soft limestone. $CaCO_3$, 100. Deposit.

China Stone. $Na_2O.Al_2O_3.8SiO_2$, 644. Igneous.

Chromite. Ore of chrome. $FeO.Cr_2O_3$. Ultrabasic, metamorphic.

Colemanite, $2CaO.3BO_2O_3.5H_2O$.

Cobaltite. Ore of cobalt. $CoAsS$.

Copperas. Ferrous sulfate, $FeSO_4$.

Corundum. Crystalline Al_2O_3. Igneous. Ultrabasic, or limestone rock.

Cuprite. Ore of copper, Cu_2O.

Crocus Martis. Fe_2O_3, 160.

Cryolite. Na_3AlF_6, 210.

Diaspore. Clay high in alumina.

Diatomite. Mainly SiO_2. Organic deposit.

Diopside. $CaO.MgO.2SiO_2$. Solid solution. Pyroxene, metamorphic.

Dolomite. $CaCO_3.MgCO_3$, 184.

Feldspar. See *albite, anorthite, orthoclase*.

Flint. Micro-crystalline SiO_2, 60. Boulder pebble in chalk.

Fluorspar. CaF_2, 78.

Galena. PbS, 239. Ore of lead.

Ganister. Fine-grain silica rock. Coal seams.

Garnet. Various, $RO.R_2O_3.3SiO_2$.

Gerstley Borate. See *colemanite*.

Gibbsite. $Al_2O_3.3H_2O$.

Granite. Variable; bases, alumina, silica, phosphorus, iron, titania, etc. Igneous, intrusive.

Gypsum. $CaSO_4.2H_2O$.

Halloysite. Clay mineral with a rolled plate structure.

Heavyspar. See *barytes*.

Hematite. Mineral of Fe_2O_3.

Hornblende. Silicates of calcium, magnesium, iron, and sodium. Amphibole, intermediate.

Illite. Micaceous clay mineral.

Ilmenite. $Fe_2O_3.TiO_2$, 152.

Ironstone. A hard iron ore.

Kaolinite. The ideal clay mineral, see *clays* as main dictionary entry. Igneous.

Kieselguhr. See *diatomite*.

Kyanite. $Al_2O_3.SiO_2$.

Lava. Basic rocks of variable composition.

Lepidolite. $(LiNaK)_2.(FOH)_2.Al_2O_3.2SiO_2$, 472.

Leucite, $K_2O.Al_2O_3.4SiO_2$. Feldspathoid, lavas.

Limonite. Ore of iron, $2Fe_2O_3.3H_2O$.

Limestone. Rock of calcite, $CaCO_3$. Sedimentary.

Magnesite. Mineral of $MgCO_3$, with some iron.

Magnetite. Magnetic iron ore, Fe_3O_4. A spinel.

Marble. Altered limestone.

Mica. Variable; hydrated silicates of alumina, with alkali silicates.

Monothermite. $0.2R_2O.Al_2O_3.SiO_2.1.5SiO_2$. Weathered Mica.

Mullite. $3Al_2O_3.2SiO_2$. Dissociation of kaolinite.

Muscovite Mica. $(NaK)_2O.3Al_2O_3.6SiO_2.2H_2O$. Alkaline, igneous.

Nepheline Syenite. $Na_2O.Al_2O_3.2SiO_2$, but variable with some potassium, Feldspathoid.

Ochre. Earthy iron oxide.

Orthoclase Feldspar. $K_2O.Al_2O_3.6SiO_2$, 556. Igneous.

Perlite. Fine-grain acidic laval rock. Rhyolite.

Pegmatite. General granitic or feldspathic rocks. Sometimes a synonym for china stone.

Petalite. $Li_2O.Al_2O_3.8SiO_2$, 612.

Petunze. Chinese equivalent of china stone.

Plagioclase. Feldspar series between albite and anorthite.

Pitchblende. Ore of uranium.

Pyrites. Metal sulfide minerals, e.g. FeS, CuS, CoS.

Pyrolusite. Ore of manganese, MnO_2.

Pyrophyllite. Clay family substance, $Al_2O_3.4SiO_2.H_2O$.

Quartzite. Rock of crystalline silica. SiO_2, 60.

Rutile. Crystalline titania, TiO_2. Polymorphic.

Salt. NaCl. Deposit.

Sand. Various coarse rock particles.

Sandstone. Rock of silica minerals, cemented with clay, lime and iron.

Shale. Lithified clay.

Sienna. An hydrated iron-manganese earth.

Sillimanite. $Al_2O_3.SiO_2$. A clay mineral. Metamorphic.

Smaltite. Ore of cobalt. $CoAs_2$.

Soapstone. 'Massive' impure talc.

Spangles, Magnetic iron. Fe_3O_4.

Spodumene. $Li_2O.Al_2O_3.4SiO_2$, 372. Pyroxene, granitic.

Steatite. See *soapstone*.

Stibnite. Sb_2O_3. Ore of antimony. Replacement deposit.

Talc. $3MgO.4SiO_2.H_2O$, 379. Metamorphic magnesium-rich rocks.

Umber. A ferruginous earth. Hydrated.

Vermiculite. Biotite mica altered by hydrothermal solutions.

Volcanic Ash. Variable basic rocks, with iron.

Witherite. Rock of barium carbonate.

Wollastonite. $CaO.SiO_2$, 166.

Zincblende. Ore of zinc. ZnS.

Zircon. $ZnSiO_4$. Occurs as sands, etc.

MINERALOGICAL CONSTITUTION

The type and proportions of minerals present in a material, as distinct from its chemical constitution.

MINERAL WOOL BLOCK

An insulating material of compressed mineral wool (typically calcium silicate). Made in various sizes up to 3 ft. × 1 ft. (1 m. × 0.3 m.). A number of proprietary makes include: Caposil, Supertemp, Kipsulate, etc. The material is rather weak and friable, easily compressed locally, and very dusty in use (wear a mask), but is a very efficient insulator. $1\frac{1}{2}$ in. (38 mm.) of mineral wool block will replace 3 in. (76 mm.) or more of standard insulating brick. Its low mass—a piece 1 ft^2 (930 $cm.^2$) by 1 in. (25 mm.) thick has an average weight of about $1\frac{3}{4}$ lb. (790 g.)—enables kiln weight to be cut considerably. Maximum operating temperature of 900–1000°C. (around 1750°F.) confines its use to the outer skins of kilns. *Ceramic fiber* block is similar in appearance but has a higher operating temperature range.

MINI-BARS

Non-tapering pyrometric indicators which are smaller than standard cones but work in similar way except that they are laid horizontally across two supports, one at each end. The cone sags in the middle as it softens. Used especially for operating *kiln-sitters*. Pyro mini-bars are widely available. (See *Holdcroft Bar*.)

MINIUM

Red lead Pb_3O_4. (See *lead*.)

MISHIMA

A delicate, often starry, form of inlay originating in Korea and widely practised in Japan. The design, usually in fine lines, is stamped or impressed into clay at the *soft-leather* stage, and then filled with brushed-on slip which may or may not be scraped flat. (See also *inlay*.)

'Mishima' or slip inlay on a pot by Lex Dickson (Australia). The pattern is carved into the leather-hard clay and then brushed over with repeated layers of porcelain slip. When the inlay is just proud of the pot

surface it is scraped back flat with a sharp tool. (Photo by Chris McLaren). See also illustrations at inlay.

MIXING CLAYS

Most commercial bodies are combinations of clays, each chosen for a particular quality. These are rendered into *slip*, combined in *recipe* proportions, *filter-pressed*, and *pugged*. A similar routine but with the filter press replaced by weathering and drying in troughs can be practised by the studio potter who has sufficient space and energy.

In the last few years many potters have bought dough mixers from old bakeries to mix clay powder and water to a plastic state. For most potters, however, it is a case of pugging already plastic bodies, or hand-*layering* and *wedging*. Cardew warns against wedging *short* clays into plastic ones, the whole mix tending to assume the lowest level of plasticity. He recommends a slop mix, at least for china clay.

It is possible to spread layers of dry clay onto a sheet of thick plastic in a wooden frame, slaking with water at each layer. The corners of the sheet are then folded in and the whole left to soak for a few days before kneading.

MODELING

The sculptor models from the outside, generally applying clay to a solid core. The figure cannot be fired without the intermediary of a *mold and cast* (see *press mold*). In this book discussion is limited to techniques which allow for direct firing, e.g. modeling by *pinching*, *coiling*, *slab-building*, *throwing*, etc.

With some skill, practice, and ingenuity most forms can be constructed by these methods, although, in general, the pottery figure will be stylized, compact, and self-supporting. Clay is an amiable and versatile material but imposes its own limitations. Some of the most fundamental of these are:

1 It shrinks during drying and firing—if soft clay is applied to stiff clay, tensions and cracks will result.
2 Clay will not adhere to itself simply by being pressed together; moisture or slip must be used.
3 Air and water will expand on heating and can destroy the fabric if trapped in it.
4 Clay will become *pyroplastic* during firing.

An open, grogged clay, and a maximum wall thickness of $\frac{1}{2}$ in. (12 mm.) will help in all cases.

Simple models may be made from thumb pots and slabs. For a more involved slab figure, but one still within a student's capabilities, see Fournier CC. The superb coiling technique of Rosemary Wren can be studied with advantage by all interested in building larger pieces. (See film 'Creatures in clay'.) All her figures are totally self-supporting both during building and firing. Inverted T-shaped coils are used.

1

2

(1) A realistic sculptural approach to animal modeling: a bear by Robert Fournier, and (2) the more stylized anteater of Rosemary Wren.

If a large piece has more than one support, e.g. the legs of an animal, it is advisable to biscuit and glaze fire on a flat slab made of the same body; the slab will therefore contract at the same rate as the figure. The slab should be bedded on alumina, as should any wide-based construction. Any horizontally extended parts of the model may need separate support in the kiln. Coil a hollow supporting cylinder from the same body. See at *armature* for crushed paper support.

An impressive 'Bridge' by Brian Newman.

A 'standing window' by Sheila Fournier.

MODELING CLAY

The so-called 'modeling clay' listed by many pottery merchants is, too often, a characterless white body with low plasticity and poor dry strength. A red or buff clay with good plasticity, opened with a fine grog, makes the best body for modeling.

Many attempts have been made to prepare a clay body which will have high dry strength without firing. (See *Newclay*.) These are not, of course, ceramic materials in the true sense.

MODELING COMPOUND, unfired

There are several mixtures of clay with hardeners on the market, all fairly expensive, for semi-permanent models and the like. Newclay was one of the first; Darwi (Cromartie) is another.

MODELING TOOL

The most useful clay modeling tool is a spatula-ended hardwood tool, see *spatula*. A large range of other shapes are available but many of them are too lumpy and insensitive for good work. Flexible steel palettes are invaluable for working on large surfaces and built-up forms. 'Surform' tools and clay planes do a similar job. An ordinary penknife or a small fettling knife can be used as the clay hardens. Good metal tools are made in a variety of spatula and saw-tooth shapes. One can cut one's own tools from hardwood or even wooden meat skewers if nothing better is available, or from bamboo. Several splendid bamboo tools are now on the market. For hollowing-out a strong wire-ended tool is essential.

A few familiar tools are more valuable than a wide range of expensive purchases.

MODULUS, elasticity, rupture

A constant factor for converting units or indicating relationships between one system and another.

There are equations for arriving at the breaking point (the modulus of rupture) of a kiln shelf; these are essential to a manufacturer. See Dodd DC for details.

The modulus of elasticity is the extent to which a material may be distorted under stress without failing. The industry calculates glaze-body relationships in these terms. For the average craft potter however, insufficient data is available to put these equations to practical use. (See also *conversion factor*.)

MOH'S SCALE

See *hardness scale*.

MOISTURE CONTENT

There is always some moisture in powdered minerals, though few of them suffer deterioration from damp. An appreciable or uneven moisture content can, however, cause error when weighing up a *recipe*, and one should keep all materials as dry as possible. If one of your materials is noticeably damp, dry off a weighed amount and note the loss in weight. The equivalent percentage can then be added to the *batch weight*.

MOISTURE CRAZING

Crazing due to the adsorption of water into the body after firing, causing it to swell very slightly. More likely in earthenware. Can take place days or weeks after firing. (See *crazing, adsorption*.)

MOISTURE EXPANSION

See *adsorption, moisture crazing*.

MOLD, mould

In its widest sense a mold is any former over or in which clay can be shaped. Molds such as one's own elbow, a sand-filled bag, or a stone, are dealt with under *formers*. More specifically a mold is a biscuit or *plaster of paris* 'negative' of the shape required and is normally used for repetition work. Virtually all industrial pottery is made by means of *press molds* or *slip molds*. (See also *jigger* and *jolley*.)

Molded work will, inevitably, be more mechanical in appearance than hand-built or thrown pottery. The *cast*, however, can be treated merely as a starting point, to be worked on or beaten into a more original and creative shape. Of the types of mold used by craft potters the commonest is the dish mold, especially when decoration is the main interest. A square of cloth or canvas can be suspended from the corners to make an 'instant' mold. A *rolling pin* is a handy tool which can be utilized for molding or forming cylinders.

Of the true molds, the press-mold is fairly widely used (some of Leach's large square bottles, for instance) and is often combined with coiling or throwing e.g. the neck of an oblong bottle. *Slip-molds* are not very relevant to the craftsman, although again simple basic forms can be utilized as a base for further work, or in building larger constructions. They come into their own for casting bone china and other very friable and delicate bodies.

The limitation of the mold is that it cannot deal with 'returning' forms unless it is split into sections.

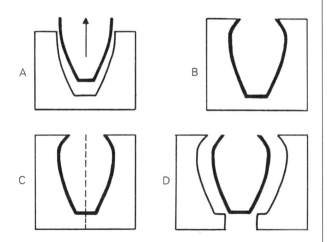

The principle of molded forms. In (A) the beaker shape can be lifted directly from a one-piece mold (as in jigger and jolley work), but if the form has any shoulder or 'returning' shape, as in (B), this will prevent its removal. Such a shape can be accomodated in a two-piece mold separated vertically as shown in (C) and (D).

There is a limit to the number of pieces a mold can be divided into. Involved shapes are cast in sections in separate molds, the pieces being luted together.

(See *hump molds, hollow molds, dish molds, slip molds, press molds, formers, plaster of paris*, etc.)

A very simple dish mold or former, using a square of cloth suspended from each leg of an inverted stool.

A lively and well-observed 'choir' of singers which look as if they might have been made from slab or pinchpots but, in fact, were pressed from cone-shaped molds and then varied by modeling, adding, and cutting away. By George Martin.

MOLECULAR FORMULA

See *formula*.

MOLECULAR WEIGHT

The sum of the *weights* of all the atoms which make up a *molecule*, or in the case of minerals, the whole *ideal formula*.

Examples:

Ferric oxide $Fe_2O_3 = (56 \times 2) + (16 \times 3) = 112 + 48 =$ molecular weight 160.

Dolomite $CaCO_3.MgCO_3 = 40 + 12 + (16 \times 3) + 24 + 12 + (16 \times 3) = 184$.

As mentioned under *molecule*, the term is used for convenience, and is not strictly accurate in cases where the first oxide or molecule mentioned in the formula is more or less than unity, an equivalent correction must be made before it can be used in glaze calculations. (See *equivalent weight*.)

MOLECULAR WEIGHTS OF COMMONLY USED GLAZE MATERIALS

For molecular weights of *oxides* see under that heading.

ALBITE FELDSPAR	524	
ANORTHITE FELDSPAR	278	
BARIUM CARBONATE	197.3	
BONE ASH	310	(103)
BORAX	381.5	
BORO-CALCITE	304	
CHINA CLAY	258	
CHINA STONE	644	
COLEMANITE	412	(206)
CRISTOBALITE	60	
CRYOLITE	210	(420)
DOLOMITE	184	
FLINT	60	
FLUORSPAR	78	
GALENA	239	
ILMENITE	152	
LEAD MONOSILICATE	283	
LEAD BISILICATE	343.5	
LEAD SESQUISILICATE	313	
LEPIDOLITE	472	
LITHARGE	223	
LITHIUM CARBONATE	74	
MUSCOVITE MICA	–	
NEPHELINE SYENITE	292	
ORTHOCLASE	556	
PETALITE	612	
POTASSIUM CARBONATE	138	
QUARTZ	60	
RED LEAD	685	(228)
SILLIMANITE	162	
SODIUM CARBONATE	106	
SPODUMENE	372	
STRONTIUM CARBONATE	147.5	
TALC	379	(126)
WHITE LEAD	775	(258)
WHITING	100	
WOLLASTONITE	116	
ZIRCON	183	

Numbers in brackets indicate equivalent weights for glaze calculation.

MOLECULE

The smallest particle into which a substance can be divided while retaining the properties of the original substance. Molecules are built up of *atoms* united by electrical bonds. (See *atomic theory*.) Strictly speaking, only those atoms united in a covalent bond are true molecules; most *salts* and metallic *oxides* are *electrovalent* compounds and thus aggregates of *ions*. The true molecule is considered to exist in the *gaseous* state only. However, for convenience and simplicity, it is applied (as in *molecular weight*, for instance) to any well-defined combination of more than one atom.

MOLOCHITE

A pre-fired china clay made by English China Clays, St. Austell, U.K. P.C.E. 1770°C. Used as a refractory grog. Has some valuable qualities in bodies. The whiteness of molochite makes it suitable for use in porcelain bodies which it also renders more refractory and slump-resistant. Because it has been vitrified at great heat, the 'free' silica is combined with alumina to produce mullite and silica glass. See CR 125 for article by Hamer. He warns that not all calcined china clays mentioned in catalogues are Molochite which is a registered product made only by English China Clays.

An 80's mesh Molochite is listed by Cromartie, although the PQ article mentions only Whitfield and Sons Ltd. who presumably also supply other grades.

MOLYBDENUM

MoO_3, 144. Very high melting point. Toxic. Sometimes used in the industrial preparation of yellow stains.

MONOTHERMITE

A mineral, $0.2R_2O$, Al_2O_3, $3SiO_2$, $1.5 H_2O$, produced by the weathering of hydrated mica, and present in fireclays.

MONTMORILLONITE

A group of minerals allied to *kaolinite* and included in the clay 'family'. They differ from kaolinite in being of a much finer grain and having a slightly different cell structure (details in Cardew PP and Worrell C).

'Small flat hexagonal crystals', Hamer. The bonds between the layers are weaker, allowing more water to penetrate. The outer layers of *electrons* exhibit a negative charge which together with a less stable structure allows the substitution of *bases* (Ca, Mg, Na, Fe, especially) for some of the alumina.

The composition is therefore very variable. The weaker 'bonds' also mean that they sheer easily and this gives the material an exceptional kind of plasticity. However its very high shrinkage and the release of silica during firing preclude its use alone or in any great quantity in a pottery body. The usual form of the mineral used by potters is *bentonite*, and the proportion in a body or glaze 2–3%. There are montmorillonites with little or no plasticity, e.g. fuller's earth.

It is thought possible that most secondary clays contain some montmorillonite in their make-up. The mineral is usually the result of the decomposition of basic rocks such as *basalt*, rather than acidic granite.

MOP

A large round *brush* without a point. Does not leave brushmarks to the same degree as do flat *dusters*.

MORTAR

Bricklaying mortar for kiln-building is usually a mixture of 10–30% fine grog with fireclay or china clay. A little soda silicate, about $\frac{1}{8}$ of a pint to 10 lb. of dry clay (or 0.07 liters to 4.5 kg. may be added to give a degree of dry setting. The mortar is used in an almost liquid state and is spread thinly—'buttered'—on. It is less a jointing material than a levelling bed.

Normal bricklayer's mortar is composed of lime and sharp sand. This may be used for exterior work exposed to the weather. Sand/cement is not generally recommended. Cardew warns against the use of mortar in the foundations of a kiln.

Commercial mortars or 'cements' are available, e.g. Sairset, which can also be used as a *kiln wash*.

MORTAR AND PESTLE

Mortars, thick-walled semi-circular bowls generally made of biscuit porcelain, and pestles of the same ma-

Grinding a teaspoonful of color in a mortar.

terial on a wooden handle, are used together for grinding materials; however they are used much less frequently, now that most minerals are supplied in a finely ground form. For experimental quantities they are still useful, for grinding a rock sample, for instance. Do not overfill the mortar—a teaspoonful at a time will grind more efficiently than a larger quantity. All materials must first have been broken to at least sand-size with a hammer. For general workshop requirements a *ball* or *jar mill* can replace the mortar and pestle.

MOSAIC

Small pieces of stone or ceramic fitted together to form an overall pattern or design. The traditional mosaic is flat, or with the pieces very slightly tilted to catch the light. Modern mosaic or wall-decoration includes the use of impressed, textured and three-dimensional effects.

Small tiles or 'tesserae' can be cut from slabs of clay and finished either separately or in blocks. In the latter case a fairly coarse (wide) cut is taken not quite through the clay, the tesserae being broken apart at a later stage. With care they can be glazed as a block. Mosaics can be built up from random pieces; from more formal units such as a square or triangle; or from pieces shaped to fit the design. The last involves drawing the design full scale on a sheet of thin paper and dividing it into conveniently shaped pieces which are numbered on the reverse side. The design is then laid on a slab of clay, the shapes and numbers traced through with a suitable tool. If too large to be conveniently handled as whole it can be cut into sections, each laid on a slab of clay. The clay pieces are cut apart when at soft-leather stage, and trimmed. They must be glazed individually and reference can again be made to the original design as regards color. Glazed tesserae should be set on alumina for firing. The tedious work of glazing can be avoided by the use of vitrified *colored bodies*. *Egyptian paste* and *enamels* are other possibilities. The breaking of glazed slabs or tiles into pieces is not very satisfactory. A tile cutter could be used but this is also a long job.

It is difficult to dry large or long pieces of tesserae so that they remain flat. One system is to lay them on an absorbent material (e.g. kiln shelves or Asbestolux) and dry quickly on a hot surface such as the top of a firing kiln or a stove.

The pieces can be assembled in several ways:

1 As the Byzantine mosaics were set; piece by piece into a cement background e.g. a *lime mortar* (or a retarded *plaster of paris* could be used).
2 If the tesserae are of even thickness or an uneven

surface is acceptable they can simply be glued onto a wooden base.

Transfering a design from a drawing to clay tesserae for building into a mosaic.
(1) The design is made on tracing paper and each piece numbered.
(2) The sheet of paper is reversed and laid onto a slab of clay, the shapes and the numbers traced through with a pointed (but not sharp) tool.
(3) The numbers will now be on the back of the tesserae which, with the paper removed, can be cut apart with a knife.

3 If the face needs to be quite flat, e.g. for a table top, the pieces must either be assembled face down, or a sheet of 'Contact' or other adhesive plastic laid over the glazed face and smoothed on. Sandwich the whole mosaic between two boards and turn it over. Level the back with a fairly liquid cement (no sand) or with a proprietary tile cement. Battens fastened alongside the mosaic can help in achieving a level. The whole can be adhered to a wooden base either with a bonding glue or even with a layer of Polyfilla or similar cement. The mosaic must be turned face-up before the cement has quite set (usually three or four hours later) so that the design can be cleaned off and grouted with a similar material. To grout, wipe over with a liquid mixture, working it into all the cracks, then wipe the tesserae clean with a rag. An edging, preferably of metal, is needed to finish off a table. This can either be made to size and dropped over the finished mosaic, screwed to the wooden base, or it can be made in angle iron and fitted over the back while the mosaic is reversed, and previous to the final grouting. Mosaics can also be built up on plastic clay by pressing pellets of colored body on to the dampened surface. This is very suitable for mosaic tiles in schools.

A mosaic table of earthenware triangles in blue and turquoise glazes, by Robert Fournier and Albert Shelly.

MUFFLE

In a kiln, an internal shell or box which protects pottery from the effect of flame or hot gases, these being directed between muffle and kiln wall. A saggar is a kind of muffle. Some gas kilns are semi-muffle, protected at the base and about half way up the walls.

MUG

See *beaker*.

MULLER

See *glass muller*.

MULLITE

A compound of alumina and silica, $3Al_2O_3.2SiO_2$, m.p. 1880°C., which results from the *dissociation of kaolonite* at high temperatures. This leaves a proportion of *free silica* which is steadily converted into *cristobalite* up to 1660°C. Some mullite begins to form at 1000°C., and most of the alumina is in this form at 1340°C. The crystals are needle-shaped and are believed to have a 'felting' effect, strengthening stoneware and porcelain bodies. Mica at stoneware temperatures produces mullite (Cardew PP).

MULTI-WIRE CLAY CUTTER

See *harp, bow.*

MUSCOVITE

A mica with the theoretical composition (Na_2K_2O). $3Al_2O_3.6SiO_2.2H_2O$. The form of mica considered to be a constituent of most clays. (See *mica.*)

MUSHROOM MOLD

A convex dish mold on a stem or stand, over which plates and dishes can be formed. (See *hump mold.*)

NAPLES YELLOW

A color derived from antimoniate of lead with a little ferric iron for use at temperatures up to about 1090°C. Use as a pigment, or add 5–10% to glazes.

NATRUM

An element, symbol Na, see *sodium.* 'Washing soda' is a crystalline sodium carbonate; 'natron', a sesquicarbonate.

NATURAL GAS

Gas derived from wells or bore-holes in the earth's crust. (See *gas fuel.*)

NECK

The narrow terminating section, often more or less elongated, of a bottle-shaped pot. A long neck may be thrown separately, or thrown onto the shoulder of a pot from a thick coil. See film 'David Leach' (Films for Potters).

A triple-necked hand-built stoneware bottle with poured glaze. The necks were formed round a brush handle. By Robert Fournier.

NEEDLE AWL, pricker

'Pricker' is the American term. A fine awl for cutting clay. A simple type can be made by pushing a coarse needle through a cork, but this will snap off rather easily. Commercial awls are stronger and are set in a wooden handle. Use 'Fine' grades for clay cutting, especially for the rims of thrown pots; thicker awls with a blunt point for less delicate work.

Using a needle awl (pricker) to level the top rim of a thrown pot. Note the oblique angle which avoids rucking the clay (not to mention spearing the finger!), and the positions of the other fingers ready to whip away the ring of clay as soon as the cut is complete.

NEGATIVE EXPANSION

Only one oxide, that of boron, expands on cooling, i.e. has a negative value for its coefficient of expansion. (See *coefficients of expansion.*)

NEPHELINE SYENITE

Nepheline is theoretically $Na_2O.Al_2O_3.2SiO_2$ but as it almost invariably contains some potash it may be written $K_2O.3Na_2O.4Al_2O_3.8SiO_2$, 1168, equivalent weight 292, m.p. 1200°C. Syenite is a crystalline rock of feldspar and hornblende.

The natural material is variable in constitution but always high in alumina and soda when compared with feldspar. It usually contains some iron which can be extracted magnetically. Deposits in Canada and Norway.

It is an interesting material to use in glazes, making possible formulas which are difficult to convert with feldspar. It is also used in small quantities in porcelain bodies.

A typical analysis by weight (Podmores):

Na_2O	8.1				
K_2O	9.0	Al_2O_3	24.9	SiO_2	56.3
CaO/MgO	1.7	Fe_2O_3	0.1		

Compare with a feldspar percentage analysis. It differs from spar in tending to have a more defined *melting point* and at a lower temperature. In stoneware glazes it can be used empirically to replace some of the feldspar. Rarely used in earthenware but a recipe was given in CM 19/6 (Behrens):

Nepheline syenite	69
Frit (3134)	20
Whiting	10
Bentonite	1

NERIAGE

A form of decoration used in Japan. Slabs of contrasting clays are laid one on another, cut into strips, and rolled or folded into a block. These are sliced end-on so that a whorl or other design of marbled color is obtained. The pieces are pressed into a mold side by side to form a continuous skin.

Neriage has become very popular in the West where involved and highly decorative effects are achieved. See Fournier DPD for more details and illustrations.

A startling and involved 'Lunar Bowl' in neriage technique by Dorothy Feibleman.

Spirals derived from the neriage technique used as inlays. By Felicity Aylieffe.

NETWORK, former, modifier

A molecular three-dimensional pattern of linked atoms, a lattice. In glass this pattern has a certain underlying regularity of formation but is random in detail (*amorphous* or non-crystalline).

Only a few acidic oxides can initiate a glass network (see *glass-formers*); the chief of these is silica. On its own, silica needs a very high temperature to vitrify or develop a glassy nature, but the atomic pattern can be loosened, or modified by other oxides so that a fluid

The technique of neriage is not a new one as this bowl from Song China proves.

material is formed at a lower temperature—as low as 650°C. The larger atoms intrude into the network and, themselves having weaker electrical *bonds*, lower the cohesion of the whole structure. Sodium and potassium have the ideal *ionic valency* and radii for this purpose. Calcium is interesting in that small quantities will modify a glass above about 1080°C. and yet the glaze (or the body, in the case of bone china) will tend to be stable and viscous. At higher temperatures and concentrations, however, this behavior may be reversed and 20% or more at 1290°C. can make a glaze very fluid.

NEUTRAL ATMOSPHERE

A kiln atmosphere which is neither strongly oxidizing nor reducing. The flame uses all the available oxygen without forming carbon monoxide—a state of perfect combustion. An electric kiln is usually neutral although the combustion of impurities in body or glaze can cause a slightly reducing atmosphere in a tightly closed kiln.

NEUTRON

The electrically neutral particle in an atomic core. (See *atomic theory*.)

NEWCLAY

A proprietary name for a clay containing nylon fibers which give it a degree of dry strength. For use in junior schools where it is not intended to fire the work into ceramic. Its principal use is in modeling. Hardeners can also be added to form cements as the clay dries. Supplied by Newclay Products Ltd. There are also other types of clay mixes which develop some physical strength without firing, sold by some of the larger suppliers.

NICKEL

A metallic element Ni, 59.
Black or green nickelous oxide NiO, 75, s.g. 6.7.
Black nickelic oxide Ni_2O_3, 166.
Also quoted as NiO_2. Black nickel.
Decomposes into the monoxide at 600°C.

A fairly refractory oxide, producing in oxidation muted browns, grays, and greens, of a not usually very exciting nature. Tends to be unstable at over about 1200°C, 'causing a scum'. (Hamer).

1–3% is soluble or partially soluble in a soft glaze, the lower percentage tending to gray, the higher to brown, but with varying effect in different types of glaze; at its least attractive in *borax glazes*. It often contaminates cobalt to which it is a near neighbor in the *periodic table*. Will tend to increase glaze mattness. Gives uncertain and sometimes unexpected colors in *reduction*: Rhodes mentions yellow and purple; blue has

also been mentioned. The tendency towards blue in any type of glaze will be increased by the addition of zinc oxide. A formula quoted in Webb CNS is:

ZnO	0.33			
Pbo	0.32	Al_2O_3 0.2	SiO_2	2.5
N_2O	0.35		B_2O_3	0.2

Nickel with titanium in a feldspathic glaze has been known to produce yellow. Lithium has been recommended for inclusion in nickel glazes.

Nickel is most often used to 'quench' or modify other coloring oxides. 'Nichrome' resistance wire is nickel/chrome.

NITROGEN

The second constituent (with oxygen) of pure air. It is inert and, in a firing, takes a great deal of energy (fuel) to heat up. It is important, therefore, only to admit sufficient air into a kiln to combine the oxygen and fuel into carbon dioxide; any excess is wasteful of energy. The Glendale Control leaflet (see list of Suppliers) states that one third of the input (natural gas is quoted) is 'wasted' in heating the nitrogen in the air intake. The weight of this nitrogen is quoted in tonnes! The use of an *oxygen/carbon sensor* could therefore save both fuel and firing time.

NON-VITREOUS, non-vitrified

A pottery body in which the *glass phase* is absent or has barely begun, e.g. soft earthenware or any porous biscuit. In the USA the official definition is a water absorption above 10% for pottery or 7% for tiles.

OCARINA

From the Italian for 'little goose'. An ovoid pottery wind-instrument, traditionally of porcelain but can be made from any pottery material. (For details of the mouthpiece, see *whistle*.) There should be eight finger-holes. To quote Scholes: 'the pitch is affected by the number of holes left open, i.e. if one hole is left open it does not much matter which, and so with more than one'. The range of the notes will rise as the clay shrinks in drying and firing and it is difficult to get a particular pitch. The notes are controlled by the size of holes not by their position which can be purely for comfort in use (Neil Ions CR 90). CM 19/2 also gives advice on making the instrument. The ocarina has a charming sound when properly used.

The whistle or ocarina in bird form has a long history (the original meaning of ocarina is 'little goose') and this is a charming modern variation by Neil Ions.

OCHRE

A natural hydrated earthy *ferric* oxide. $Fe_2O_3.H_2O$, 178, together with impurities and often some clay and sulfur. Yellow ochre contains *hydrated* iron oxide: red ochre *anhydrous* ferric oxide. Yellow ochre can be *calcined* at 550–600°C. to form red ochre, which is more stable and inert, or the red (terracotta) ochre can be purchased already prepared. Both forms can be used in slips, pigments, and glazes, though the yellow ochre sometimes has a *flocculating* effect which makes it difficult to use in any quantity in a glaze or slip batch. The raw ochre usually produces a yellower color than iron oxide, because of the bleaching action of calcium 'impurities', which effect, however, can be reversed at high temperatures and in reduction. Leach suggests using calcined ochre for celadon glazes (Leach PB 166). He also quotes Old Seto Yellow as containing 25–40% ochre, the glaze used thinly and oxidised. Emmanuel Cooper puts as much as 20% in his 'oil spot' glaze at 1260°C. with nepheline 70% and alkaline frit 10%.

Ochre is commonly used as a reduction vehicle in *lusters*.

OHM

Symbol Ω. A unit of electrical resistance, named after G. S. Ohm, a German physicist, (1787–1854).

Example: To obtain 30 amps at 240 volts in an electric kiln we need a wire resistance of 240 (E) ÷ 30 (I)=8 (R) ohms. Element wire is rated at ohms per foot.

Thus if the wire you are using has a figure of 0.07 ohms per foot length then you will need 8 ÷ 0.07 = 114 feet.

Useful equations:

$$R = \frac{E}{I} \text{ or } \frac{E^2}{P} \text{ or } \frac{P}{I^2}$$

(E in volts, I in amperes, P in watts). (For further clarification see *electrical symbols*.)

OIL, fuel, burner

Various grades of petroleum can be used in the firing of pottery, the more unrefined oils producing more smoke. A medium grade has been quoted at 135,000 Btu per gallon (3.3 MJ per liter).

Oil must be transformed from a liquid into a mist or vapor before it will burn efficiently. This can most simply be done by *drip-feed* onto a hot metal plate; more controllably by atomizing the oil by means of a jet of air at the burner. This involves the provision of air-pressurizing equipment. Rhodes (K 69–75) describes several types of burner. The domestic heating burner would be adequate for a 2 cu. ft. (0.06 cu. m.) chamber but lacks control and would probably give too rapid a heat rise. The 'Swirlamiser' burner is reasonably priced and has had good reports. All oil kilns will burn more effectively when hot.

The advantage of oil over other fuels are its relative cheapness and the ease with which its temperature and atmosphere can be controlled. On the other hand it tends to be noisy and smoky, while the flame is not kind to kiln *refractories*. It is more suitable for high-fired pottery than for earthenware. (See also *forced draft* and *drainoil*.)

OIL-FIRED KILN

Oil is most efficient in medium and large kilns—10 cu. ft. (0.3 cu. m.) and upwards. Built on the site, they are often constructed by the potter. Some detailed instructions were given in CR 16. Rhodes K deals quite extensively with oil kilns, as do several other books including Cardew, Leach, Olsen, etc.

Oil-fired kilns tend to be variable in performance and need a reasonably isolated site because of the noise and smoke – not to mention a 600 gallon tank some 12–16 feet (3.5 – 5 meters) above the ground (although pumped oil from a surface tank is also a possibility.) A low, stable flame is difficult to maintain at the beginning of the firing and some potters practise pre-heating with bottled gas.

OIL SPOT GLAZE

An effect derived from crystalline formations on the

surface of a high iron glaze. Both Sutherland GNS and Hamer PDM suggest the use of what he call *mafic* clays (containing iron, magnesia, and lime) and 'mudstones' such as Keuper Marl (an Albany clay slip is also mentioned) in a viscous glaze, taking care not to overfire.

ONCE-FIRED POTTERY, glazing

Also known as 'green-glazed pottery'. A technique which bypasses the *biscuit* stage by glazing the raw clay and firing both together. There are hazards, especially when using the average commercially supplied body: collapse or blistering due to rapid absorption of liquid from the glaze; the scaling away of the glaze due to shrinkage differences; and the bubbling of the fired glaze. However, a majority of the world's ceramics have been once-fired and a number of modern potters have successfully overcome these difficulties, including Colin Pearson on stoneware, Lucie Rie on porcelain, and Alan Frewin on slipware.

The traditional once-fired earthenware glaze has a high lead content together with some plastic clay. A simple example (firing at 1100°C.) based on suggestions by Alan Frewin is given below (suitable for decorative pottery, especially slipware, but see at *soluble lead* if tableware is envisaged):

Lead sesquisilicate	58
Body clay	38
Whiting	4

Used on body of 45% red clay, 45% buff clay, and 10% grog.

It is also possible to adapt leadless and, of course, stoneware and porcelain glazes for once-fired ware. Some plastic clay (varying between 10% and 40%) is normally added to the glaze batch to allow for the necessary shrinkage. The glaze can be applied at the leather-hard stage, though some clays with a high dry strength and low absorption will take the glaze when quite dry. In some cases, however, glazing a bone-dry body can lead to the development of bubbles in the fabric (*bloating*) both before and during firing; thin-walled pots being no less liable to trouble than thick ones. In spite of this, in his book Parks PGRG, a valuable and enthusiastic guide to the technique, the author recommends bone-dry clay and appears to have little trouble with it. If a bubble does develop his instructions are to press the blister flat from both sides.

Alan Graham (CR 75) suggests a deflocculated glaze so that less water is taken up for a given thickness of glaze. Obviating the water absorption problems entirely, Dennis Parks (CR 46) dusts dry glaze or wood ash straight onto damp flattish surfaces or onto the shoulders of pots, etc. This can be most effective on a damp slip or siccative, but it must be remembered that dusting is always a health hazard and an effective mask would be advisable.

Christopher Buras, in CR 84, also ignores the possible blisters from water adsorption and glazes 'white bone-dry pots' quickly and thinly with the following glaze recipe. There is no magic about the body he uses – the well-tried Potclays St. Thomas's Body (oxidising).

Ball clay	10
Petalite	20
Potash feldspar	40
Quartz	10
Dolomite	10
Bentonite	5

He fires at 1250°C in an electric kiln.

Almost any recipe can be adapted for glazing on unfired clay but experimentation will always be necessary to achieve a glaze which will match the shrinkage and other characteristics of the body you are using. To adapt a stoneware glaze one can start with a normal biscuit-glazing recipe and replace the china clay with ball clay. e.g. 50 feldspar, 20 whiting, 20 ball clay, 10 flint. A little bentonite will increase shrinkage if the glaze peels. Zinc oxide has a high drying shrinkage if it can be accommodated in the formula. (See *Bristol glaze*.)

According to Parks the clay can be adjusted for minimum absorption by a *pH* value as near neutral as possible. A binder or added bentonite in glazes can help to avoid lifting off, especially when one is poured over another. Up to 12% of bentonite has been suggested, replacing either the ball clay or the feldspar in the recipe.

Isaac Button glazed inside and out at one go but his was a remarkable clay and, for the average potter, it is safer to glaze the inside and leave for an hour or so before tackling the outside. To accommodate the expansion Dennis Parks lightly sponges or sprays the unglazed area with water, especially the outsides or bases of bowls and large plates. Handles will dry before the body of the pot and should be protected or moistened. Spray equipment is useful for large structures. Glaze can also be brushed on though this tends to drag on dry clay and is easier on leather-hard surfaces.

The ware needs careful and thorough drying and a steady firing with plenty of ventilation to allow the easy escape of *hydrocarbons* from the body which the covering glaze will tend to inhibit. A burst pot can obviously cause widespread damage with the whole load needing to be unpacked and cleaned.

The firing cycle must combine the typical *graphs* of a

biscuit and a *glost* firing and it may therefore take a longer firing than either alone. Interaction between body and glaze is greater than when the glazing is done on the biscuit. Some of the body surface will combine with the glaze to assist its maturity, especially in earthenware. *Slips* and *engobes* must be of adequate thickness or they will become transparent or disappear completely.

ON-GLAZE

Color applied to a pre-fired ceramic, generally at a low temperature. (See *enamels*.) A very wide range of color is available at 700–900°C. It is a more explicit term than 'over-glaze' which may also include majolica painting. True on-glaze color adheres to the surface of a glaze but barely penetrates it.

OPACITY, opacifiers

When light cannot pass through a glaze but is reflected back from its surface, the glaze is termed opaque. Opacity is caused either by reflective matter suspended in the glaze, or by an uneven (matt) surface. (See also *translucent*.) All glazes will become transparent or nearly so if fired to a high enough temperature.

The principal opacifying agents operate by remaining as suspended, white, undissolved particles distributed through a glaze, as minute bubbles, or in the case of zirconium and titanium as recrystallization during cooling (it follows that slow cooling when using these materials is useful, see also below). The main opacifying agents are the oxides of tin, zirconium, titanium, and zinc; the average addition to a *soft glaze* being 8–12%; rather less for stoneware. A degree of opacity can be caused by the formation of crystals on the surface, which can be stimulated by calcia and baria in quantities in excess of their requirement in the fluxing process. Chrome is an opacifying colouring oxide. Refractory oxides such as alumina can be increased in a glaze giving an opacity which is linked with a matt surface. Bubbles which have been unable to escape from an earthenware glaze (often inhibited by too thick a coating) may appear as uneven milky white patches. The formation of crystals to induce opacity is assisted by low alumina levels in the formula.

OPALESCENT

Applied to a semi-translucent, cloudy glaze showing *iridescence*. Like an opal. A high boron content can induce opalescence (Rhodes) and it is a quality sometimes found in reduced *raku* glazes. The so-called 'Jun' glazes (relatively high in MgO and low in Al_2O_3) show opalescence. (See *optical color*, *color*.)

OPEN BODY

A body with large pores. Usually contains *grog*. Normally applied to unfired clay mixtures. At stoneware temperatures an open body may *vitrify* but the surface texture will remain characteristically rough or coarse.

Very fine-grain clays need 'opening' with *fireclays*, calcined china clay, or grog. Grog is more efficient in assisting drying than the addition of *sand*. An open body will usually have a lower wet/dry shrinkage and greater standing strength, but also faster water absorption. A low-fired open body will have high resistance to *thermal shock*. Modeling clays are usually open to allow for possibly excessive wall thicknesses.

OPTICAL COLOR

Certain glazes without coloring oxides will nevertheless give an appearance of color e.g. *Jun*. The effect arises from very fine particles which approximate to the wavelengths of light e.g. around *0.5 microns*. A very thin coating on a glaze can also produce color, like oil on water; bismuth mother-of-pearl luster is an example. The colors are frequently bluish. Cardew mentions the hypothesis of the suspension of one glass or glaze within another to explain Jun blues.

OPTICAL PYROMETER

Commonly the 'disappearing filament' type, where the temperature is measured by the comparison of two light sources: firstly the light from a lamp filament, which is adjustable and secondly the light radiated through the kiln spyhole. Both are viewed through a red filter which renders them monochromatic. The system takes advantage of the fact that the intensity of light at any one wavelength depends on the temperature of the 'hot body'. The brightness of the filament is adjusted until it matches that of the kiln when it will apparently disappear. The setting on a connected *ammeter* reads on a scale as a temperature. The device needs recalibrating at intervals. If your kiln has a small spyhole some sort of stand or tripod is essential. It has been found to produce somewhat subjective results.

ORANGE-PEEL GLAZE

A finely crinkled surface usually associated with *salt glazes* and which will vary in texture according to the grain-size of the underlying body. A sprayed-on glaze will also sometimes develop this texture.

ORGANIC CHEMISTRY

The chemistry of substances produced by living organisms. More recently confined to the study of *carbon* compounds, excluding the metallic *carbonates* and the oxides and sulphides of carbon (Uvarov DS). The term is useful in a general sense but can be imprecise in particular instances.

ORTHOCLASE

Potash feldspar $K_2O.Al_2O_3.6SiO_2$, 556. (See *feldspar*.)

ORTON CONES

American *pyrometric cones*. They are numbered in a similar way to Staffordshire and Seger cones but their temperature equivalents differ and there are complicated tables for speed of heat rise and size (length) of cone. As with all heat measuring devices, experience is a better guide than lists of temperature equivalents. (See also *cones*.)

The range for standard 63 mm. cones at a temperature rise of 150°C. per hour is given as:

Orton Cones
Temperature at which the point of the cone has curved over level with its base.

Cone No	Temp. °C.	Nearest staffs	Temp. given in RCGP
020	635	021	
018	717	018	
016	792	015	
015	804	014	
013	852	012	
011	894	010	875
010	894	010	
09	923	09	930
08	955	08a	
07	984	06	974
06	999	05	
05	1046	03a	1030
04	1060	02	
03	1101	1	1080
02	1120	2	1095
01	1137	3	1110
1	1154	3a	
2	1162	4	1135
3	1168	4a	1145
4	1186	5a	1165
5	1196	6	
6	1222	6a	1190
7	1240	7a	1210
8	1263	8a	1225
9	1280	9	1250
10	1305	10	1260
11	1315	11	1285
12	1326	11	1310
13	1346	12	1350

It will be seen that the equivalents given in R.CGP are variations on the temperatures quoted by suppliers of the cones, especially in the 7–11 range. His glaze recipes presumably refer to his cone chart, e.g. cone 9, the glaze melting at around 1250°C. Evan Rutherford offers his experience of Orton cones in CR 86 and has found that Seger cone 8 more nearly equals Orton 9 which doesn't coincide with the above tables though it is nearest to column four. As they are all based on similar principles the rate of firing should not be a factor, but see first paragraph above. It is the results that you obtain from your particular kiln and methods of firing which are important – empiricism is all!

OVAL SHAPE

Oval dishes may, of course, be pressed in oval molds (see note below), or they may be derived from circular thrown bowls either by beating or by the following method. Cut a leaf-shaped sliver from the center of the base (which must be thrown with a reasonable and even thickness). Only about $\frac{3}{16}$ in. (5 mm.) at the widest point need be removed. Make the cuts at an angle, both sides sloping the same way, damp the faces with slip and ease them together by pressure from each side of the dish. The work should be done at the soft-leather stage. Another method is to cut out two sections near opposite walls of the dish and to press the faces together again. These joins tend to be stronger than the centre cut illustrated. Oval pots are usually pressed into shape; beating may destroy the surface quality. A third system employs a previously thrown sturdy wall and rim which is luted onto a thrown slab cut to the required shape.

To draw an oval; lay a sheet of paper on a drawing board or wooden surface. Fix two drawing pins at a distance from one another $1\frac{1}{8}$–$3\frac{7}{8}$ in. (30–100 mm.) less than the breadth of size of oval that you require. Make a loop of string which, when held taut, from one pin, extends $\frac{5}{8}$–2 in. (15–50 mm.) beyond the second pin. With the loop over both pins, hold the string taut with

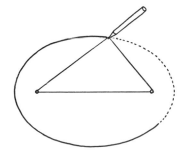

System of drawing an oval as described in text.

1

2

3

Forming an oval dish from a circular thrown one.
(1) and (2) A narrow leaf shape is marked in and cut away at an oblique angle.
(3) The faces of the slot are slipped and brought together by pressure on the walls of the pot, allowing the angled cuts to ride a little over one another so that a firm join can be smoothed over.

the point of a pencil and the oval can be drawn by moving the pencil round the loop of string. The larger the loop compared with the distance between the pins, the nearer the shape will approach a circle. See diagram.

A glaze-trailed oval oven dish by Ray Finch.

OVEN WARE

There are a number of factors governing the efficiency of ceramic cooking vessels. Our chief concern is with the expansion and contraction which occurs at oven temperatures. A low-fired open body like that of African cooking pots, and some Mediterranean and European wares, can accommodate these strains within the fabric of the pot (see also *flameproof ware*). At harder earthenware temperatures some *cristobalite* will form in the body. This helps to prevent crazing, an important factor in hygiene (though Cardew maintains that a case of food poisoning due to a crazed cooking vessel has still to be proved), but cristobalite also has an *inversion* within the oven range. A reasonably open-bodied earthenware dish fired below 1050°C. and with a low-expansion glaze (see *coefficients of expansion*) is, theoretically, the most likely to be successful. Against this is the fact that porous ware has low conductivity and heat applied to one point will not rapidly be dispersed through the fabric. Oven heat, however, is reasonably even; it is when taking the dish from the oven and putting it down on a metal or conductive surface that trouble may occur. This depends as much on the cook as on the potter.

A well-fired stoneware casserole has a good chance of resisting the thermal shocks of cooking, with the proviso above. Advice from various sources for increasing this resistance includes: a minimum of free silica in the body; the use of high alumina clays, such as high-grade fireclays, which will help the development of *mul-*

lite without a release of excessive silica; an *open* stoneware body, not quite vitrified, which may be less brittle than a glassy one; *mica* minerals and zircon sand have been mentioned as suitable additions to the body; the increase of thermal conductivity can be increased with *silicon carbide* (but this poses glazing problems); and the addition of sillimanite.

Finally, the form of the piece can help, a well-rounded casserole approximating to the sphere being under less strain. A wide, flat base is not recommended for ovenware. See the curved form illustrated under *flameproof ware*.

The glaze should, of course, be in slight *compression*. If lead is used, the glaze must be well-balanced in its formula and adequately fired. A low solubility or a leadless glaze is advisable.

High magnesia bodies and glazes are mentioned by Behrens, and he gives recipes which include quite high proportions of talc and Penco frit in both bodies and glazes. The use of lithia has also been suggested.

OVER-FIRING

Over-firing means firing above the temperature at which the desired result would obtain. Thus an overfired opaque glaze will go *translucent*; a matt glaze, shiny. The fluidity of the glaze is increased and with it the possibility of the glaze running onto the kiln shelves. *Volatilization* will lead to blistering and a thin 'starved' glaze. An over-fired glaze will always show a different color and appearance. Earthenware tin glazes will often stand considerable over-firing without disastrous results. *Oxidized* stonewares are more liable to violent change in a short temperature range than are reduced ones. Very occasionally desirable characteristics may emerge but an overfired body will vitrify, probably bloat, distort and eventually melt and collapse. Prolonged soaking may have the same effect as higher temperature. Excessive over-firing will severely damage the kiln and kiln furniture. Elements should be used with a maximum temperature rating at least 50°C above the firing temperature. (See also *flashing, pyroplastic deformation*.)

OVERGLAZE

Colors applied on top of the glaze. In its widest sense it includes *enamels*, though these are better described as *on-glaze*. It is possible to paint onto a fired glaze with the pigment oxides or stain thickened with gum or fat oil, but overglaze color is more easily applied by the *majolica* technique on the *raw glaze*.

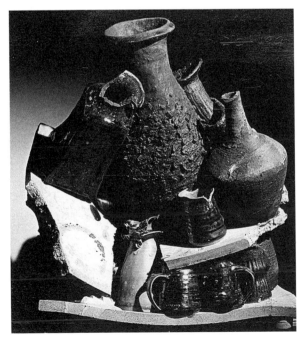

An impressive heap of melted and vitrified pots and kiln furniture (see also pyroplastic *deformation) from a grossly over-fired kiln which continued burning over a week-end, the 'automatic' controls failing to switch it off. (See* fail-safe *for a means of avoiding such a calamity.)*

A large dish by Robert Barron (Australia). Shino glaze with overglaze decoration.

OXFORD CLAY

The raw material of many English bricks, e.g. the Peterborough Flettons. Carbonaceous material burns in the brick during firing, which therefore requires a minimum of fuel.

OXFORD FELDSPAR

A feldspar from Maine, U.S.A. More siliceous than English spar and approximating nearer to *china stone*. Mixed feldspars (potash and soda spars) could form an

English equivalent.

Analysis by weight

K_2O	7.9	Al_2O_3	17.0	SiO_2	69.0
Na_2O	3.2	Fe_2O_3	0.1		
CaO	0.4				

OXIDATION, oxidize, oxydize

The combination of a metal or other element with oxygen to form an oxide. All pottery materials are used in the oxide form. Although one may refer to the metal as, for instance, in 'an iron glaze', it is the oxide that is always implied. The abbreviation occurs quite frequently in this book.

Heat is generated during the process of oxidation. The burning of fuel is the rapid oxidation of *carbon* into *carbon dioxide*, CO_2. Most elements oxidized during the cooling of the earth. Metals etc. can be oxidized in a workshop or factory.

Oxygen is present in the atmosphere in *molecules* of two oxygen atoms which can receive transfer of *electrons* from another *element* according to its valency. Thus $2Mg + 2O$, $4K + 2O$, etc. are generally written MgO and K_2O respectively. Elements may have more than one oxide form, one of which will be more stable than the others.

OXIDE

A compound of an *element* with oxygen. The combination may be in various ratios, e.g. 2:1 as in potash, 1:1 in lime, two ratios representing the first group of the *Seger formula* where the middle group of oxides is in 2:3 proportions; and the last group in 1:2 ratio. There are other, less common, ratios such as 3:4, e.g. magnetic iron Fe_3O_4.

Elements may combine in more than one ratio although one of these will be more stable and normally only one enters into combination in a glaze.

Oxide entering fusion	Molecular wt.	Name	Materials commonly used to supply oxide
Al_2O_3	102	Alumina	Clay Minerals, Feldspars, Alumina Hydrate
B_2O_3	69.5	Boric Oxide (Boric Acid)	Borax, Colemanite, Frits
BaO	153.3	Baria	Carbonate, Barytes
CaO	57	Calcia, Lime	Whiting, Dolomite, Anorthite, Feldspar, Wollastonite, Wood and Bone Ash, Fluorspar, Colemanite
CoO	75	Cobalt Oxide	Black and Gray Oxides, Carbonate
Cr_2O_3	152	Chrome, Chromic Oxide	Green Oxide, Iron Chromate
CuO	79.5	Copper Oxide	Black Oxide, Carbonate, Red Oxide, Oxalate
Fe_2O_3	160	Iron Oxide, Ferric	Hematite, Red Ferric, Black Magnetite, Spangles, Ilmenite, Ochre, Sienna, Copperas, Red Clay, Synthetic Red Iron
K_2O	94	Potash	Orthoclase Feldspar, Pearlash (Carbonate), Nepheline, Stone, Wood Ash
Li_2O	30	Lithia	Oxide, Carbonate, Petalite, Spodumene, Amblygonite
MgO	40	Magnesia	Carbonate, Talc, Dolomite
MnO	71	Manganese Oxide	Dioxide, Carbonate
Na_2O	62	Soda	Albite Feldspar, Nepheline, Borax, Alkaline Frits, Salt, Carbonates, Silicates, China stone
NiO	75	Nickel Oxide	Black or Green Nickel Oxide
(P_2O_5)	173	Phosphoric Oxide	Bone and Wood Ash
PbO	223	Lead Oxide	Litharge, Galena, Red and White Lead, Silicate Frits
SiO_2	60	Silica	Flint, Quartz, most Clay and Feldspathic Minerals, Talc, Silicate, Frits, Lithium Minerals
SnO_2	151	Tin Oxide	Oxide
SrO	103.5	Strontia	Carbonate
TiO_2	80	Titania	Precipitated Oxide, Rutile
U_3O_8	842	Uranium Oxide	'Depleted' Oxide, Sodium Uranate
V_2O_5	182	Vanadium Oxide	Oxide, Ammonium Metavanadate
ZnO	81	Zinc Oxide	Oxide, Calcined Oxide
ZrO_2	123	Zirconia (Zircon)	Zirconium Oxide, Zircon (Silicate), various prepared forms to assist dispersion.

The suffix -a is often applied to the root name of the element to indicate the oxide. Thus, aluminum—alumina; titanium—titania; silicon—silica. The suffix -ic indicates the higher (most oxygen) ratio (the stable form) and -ous, the lower more unstable proportion. For instance: ferric—ferrous (iron); cupric—cuprous (copper); cobaltic—cobaltous.

Water is hydrogen in 2:1 combination with oxygen. It will be seen that oxides bear no obvious physical relationship to the elements which make them up. (See *compound*.) Carbonates are oxides in combination with CO_2. They are written not as $RO.CO_2$, but RCO_3 (R being the element in combination). Oxides in combination with one another form more elaborate compounds such as *minerals*.

Each oxide used in pottery is discussed under the entry for each particular element. To save continual reference, however, the principal oxides are listed on p. 200 with their molecular weights or *equivalents*.

OXIDIZED STONEWARE

Stoneware fired in a clear atmosphere with plenty of air. Electric kilns will normally have an oxidized or at least a neutral atmosphere. Many potters regard reduction as the apex of achievement in stonewares, but there is still a wide field to be explored in oxidation. In the latter the 'interest' must be integral to the glaze itself, and the potter's handling of it. Janet Leach, describing Hamada's Mashiko pottery, says that all 5000 pots in his eight-chamber climbing kiln were oxidized, except those in the first chamber.

In my experience, manganese and copper are more useful than iron as coloring oxides, but potters are deriving *kaki* and other iron stonewares from oxidized firings. (See also at *saturated glaze* and under oxide headings). A recipe which gives pleasant black, deep red, and yellowish colors and which I have used on tableware for many years is:

Feldspar	51
Hardwood ash	32
Flint	8
China clay	6
Bentonite	3
Red iron oxide	7.5
Synthetic iron oxide	7.5

If the glaze turns out to be dark or dead-looking, dilute with the plain glaze mixture (without the iron) until satisfactory. The type of ash will alter its behavior. Fired at 1230–1250°C. in an electric kiln.

Ochre is another useful material in oxidation and

20% or more has been used in a glaze but it sometimes has an unwanted flocculating effect.

The maturing range of glazes seems to be shorter than in reduction, making careful and precise firing essential. The firing can be rapid—7 to 8 hours. Up to 20% red clay can be included in the body. A stepped *firing graph* i.e. soaking or even dropping the temperature at certain points in the firing (Japanese 'fire-change') may be essential for certain effects.

OXIDIZING FIRE

A clear fire with plenty of air intake, in which *oxides* remain unaltered and any *elements*, such as carbon, will find sufficient oxygen in which to oxidize freely. In a closed electric kiln organic matter may consume the oxygen early in the firing and give rise to a slightly *reducing* atmosphere. In a fuel-burning kiln plentiful *secondary air* must be admitted.

Earthenware, with the exceptions of *copper reds*, *lusters*, and some *raku*, is fired in a fully oxidizing atmosphere. (See also *stoneware glazes*.)

OXYGEN

A gaseous element O, 16. An odourless invisible gas essential to life, and to combustion. The most abundant element in the earth's crust. Comprises about 21% of dry air. Present in the atmosphere as *molecules* of two oxygen *atoms*. Combines with elements to form *oxides*.

OXYGEN/CARBON SENSOR

An electronic instrument for the fast and accurate monitoring of kiln atmospheres in relation to the oxygen/carbon balance, i.e. the proportions of oxygen, carbon dioxide and carbon monoxide. Fuel efficiency levels and degree of reduction can thus be ascertained. A reasonably priced sensor can be obtained from Glendale Controls. Effective for temperatures above 700°C. (See also *nitrogen*.)

OXYGEN FORMULA

A system of calculating glaze formulas and recipes by means of comparing cation to oxygen ratios. It is explained in CR 27 by Michael Gill. I asked John Anderson for his views on the system and he replied that 'the article does not appear to make out any case for the use of The Oxygen Formula in a practical situation', and he goes on to advise that 'the Seger . . . formula being directly expressed in terms of oxides—as, frequently, are compositions of minerals—would seem to make for easy conversion to a recipe.'

PACKING KILNS

An evenly and reasonably closely-packed kiln is not only economical but is also likely to fire better than a half empty one. Kilns and pots vary too widely to give more than a general guidance. In fuel burning kilns space must be allowed for the proper circulation of hot gases, and the pack or setting will control the behavior and efficiency of the firing. Keep the density as balanced as possible, especially in an electric kiln. Do not crowd closely packed shelves into one side of the kiln but try to disperse them.

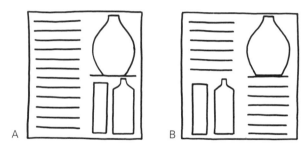

Packing of a combination of large pots and close shelves in a kiln. In arrangement (A) the density is unbalanced and although (B) would still entail tall props it will better maintain an even temperature throughout the pack, especially in an electric kiln.

When packing a top-loading kiln it is easy to see whether the pots are laterally separated but the height must be checked to avoid rims sticking to the underside of kiln shelves. This most easily done by laying a strip of wood across the supports and ensuring that all rims lie below it.

Large kilns may be packed with a combination of *saggars* and *shelves* (See L.PB.)

In the biscuit fire, pots may be piled in *bungs* (see *boxing*) but it must be remembered that clay has a degree of *pyroplasticity* at all firing temperatures and will warp under any uneven strain. An oval shape set in a round one may deform both. The rim of a jug is seldom flat and a thin tile bat should be inserted if pots are to be set on top. (See also under *biscuit firing*.)

In the gloss pack, glazed surfaces must not touch each other, although they can be set very close for high-fired stoneware, since the shrinkage during firing will further separate them. (See also *bat, bung, kiln furniture, prop*.)

In an electric kiln tall pots, especially slap pots, will incline towards the elements if packed too close to them, due to the greater shrinkage on that side.

PADDLE, paddling, paddle and anvil

A beater or bat-shaped wooden tool (see *beater*) which can be used either for shaping or decorating pots, or for stirring glazes and slips. In America the term 'paddling' may be used for beating. Many primitive peoples used a paddle to thin a pot wall by beating it against a rounded surface (like a *darning head* and known as an anvil) held inside the pot.

A beating or stirring bat cut from a piece of 4 in. × 1 in. (20 × 100 mm.) timber and about 14 in. (360 mm.) long.

PAINTED SLIP

See *brushed slip*.

PAINTING ON POTTERY

Pots can be decorated with brushed color at any stage from wet clay to fired porcelain as follows:

1 On the raw clay with pigment oxides or *underglaze* colors.

2 On biscuit with oxides or underglaze *stains* (but see *hardening on*).

3 On the unfired glaze with oxides or suitable glaze stains.

4 On the fired glaze with *enamels*.

All can be used on earthenware, stoneware, or porcelain, although the range of possible pigments decreases as the temperature rises. (For further discussion see *brushes, brushwork, calligraphic, majolica, paper resist, wax resist* as well as the individual pigment oxides, etc.)

PALETTE, knife

The Oxford Dictionary defines 'pallet' as 'a flat wood blade with handle used by potters'. A palette knife, however, is of flexible steel with a round-ended blade on a wooden handle, and is used for grinding and mixing colors in water or enamels in oil, working the knife from side to side on a glazed tile.

A *steel palette* is a thin, very flexible piece of sheet steel, usually kidney-shaped, a valuable tool. (See *kidney tool*.

Using a palette knife for grinding and mixing colors on a tile. A sideways motion is used, raising the forward edge of the knife at each stroke to compress the color. Use a minimum of color at a time.

PAN MILL

A primitive grinding mill in which hard stones (chert) are dragged over a paved area by rotating paddles. Used until recently in English potteries. More sophisticated mills use heavy metal rollers on a perforated metal floor, but the principle is the same. Smaller versions are available, or can be constructed by a potter.

PAPER FOR PLACING

See note at *placing sand*.

PAPER RESIST

A technique of decoration with characteristic bold, open patterns. As with all resist methods it is the background which is colored with slip or pigment, the design being reserved in the original surface color. Of especial value to the beginner or student who is usually more fluent with scissors than with a brush. The design can be altered and developed at will before its actual application to the dish or pot.

Method: paper resist can be practised in association with *glaze on glaze* but is most useful on leather-hard clay. Cut or tear the design in a thin, fairly absorbent paper such as typing copy paper and apply it to the surface of the pot or dish with a little moisture. Designs can be built up of a number of pieces of paper which may overlap. Sponge over the surface of the paper when finally in position, and work the edges gently but very firmly onto the clay. The coloring material should have been prepared previously and be ready to apply. As soon as any excess moisture has dried from the surface, brush your *pigment* on with broad, even strokes, or flood the surface with *slip*, pouring gently to avoid floating the paper. Put aside until the surface has dried to leather-hard and then remove paper with a needle or fine knife, making sure that you have found all the pattern!

When designing for paper avoid large areas: they will look very blank on the finished piece. A large shape

(1) A thin-paper design is adhered to the pot with a little water and a sponge.

(2) The color is brushed with firm, broad strokes over clay and paper.
(3) The paper peeled away to show the resisted design.
(See another example at counterchange.)

can be given interest by cutting smaller design elements within it. A simple but effective idea is to cut a single shape, a fish for instance, and then to slice it into several sections placing these a little apart. The result will be an 'exploded' shape broken up with lines of color. One can also mask off larger areas and use a second color. For resist on biscuit (color, vitreous slip, or glaze), self adhesive labels might be useful.

To soften the hard edge, paper can be torn instead of cut. This will introduce a greater element of freedom and lessen the danger of over-representational design.

PARALLEL WIRING

Many pieces of electrical equipment can be taken from a *single phase* (2 wire) mains input. The number is limited only by the ability of the input wires to carry the load. To maintain full voltage, however, each must be wired directly to a line and neutral connection (See diagrams under *series*.)

PARIAN BODY

A favourite Victorian material for unglazed models, etc. A white, vitreous though not usually translucent semi-porcelain. for the modern potter a white clay originated by Dorothy Fiebleman and obtainable from Pottery-crafts approximates to it. It can be thrown and fires at 1120–1180°C. when it will have a degree of trans-lucency.

PARTS OF A POT

Just as we use the word 'body' for the clay fabric of a pot so the pot itself is described in human terms: foot, belly, shoulder, neck. Leach also calls the termination of a pot the 'head' but this term is less commonly used. The top edge is the 'rim'. A pot may also have a 'waist' e.g. a diabolo shape. 'A Potter's Portfolio' (Leach) includes an analysis of pottery form in these terms. The relationship between them is the art of pottery form. In general, these analyses are more easily applicable to the traditional full-bodied pot forms.

PASTE

A term often used by archaeologists and historians to indicate any *body* mixture. To a potter it suggests a body with low plasticity and smooth, e.g. porcelain or bone-china, and especially the artificial, prepared mixtures used for the old *soft-paste* wares.

PASTRY CUTTER

Circular metal cutters sold at large kitchen equipment shops. Invaluable for cutting circles and rings of clay from slabs. (See *coiling, slab pots.*) At one time the cutters were sold in sets of up to 16 sizes but these are difficult to find. Other shapes are available but these are usually too definitive to be of much use.

P.C.E.

Abbreviation for *pyrometric cone equivalent*.

PEARL ASH

Potassium carbonate, K_2CO_3. Billington gives potassium oxide also as 'pearlash'. Present in wood ash. *Deliquescent* and soluble. Unsuitable for raw glaze but used in *frits*.

PEBBLE MILL

A *ball mill* using flint pebbles.

PEELING OF GLAZE

The lifting of glaze from a pot can be due to very low thermal expansion with consequent excessive compression strain, although this could better be described as *shivering*.

Glaze can also peel or flake away from the pot surface during drying, or early in the firing, and this is often caused by excessive shrinkage of the glaze (e.g. from a *flocculated* ash batch) or from too thick a coating. An over-plastic slip can peel and crack. Zinc and colemanite, as well as ash, can cause shrinkage. The use of calcined materials or the substitution of china clay for

A pinched pot form by Sheila Fournier glazed with an ash glaze which flocculated in the bin, causing excess shrinkage as it dried. The peeling has been used as a deliberate decorative effect in the well of the piece. Stoneware.

plastic clay will help. Glaze which has begun to peel in drying will *crawl* in the firing.

PEGMATITE

Geologically the term is given a very wide connotation, from granitic minerals to nearly pure quartz, and branching into lithia-micas and the syenite group. Pottery books will, however, often use 'pegmatite' as a synonym for Cornish granite or *china stone* with a formula of RO (made up of soda, potash, and some lime and magnesia). Al_2O_3. 7.0–7.5 SiO_2.

PEN

Gold and silver enamel felt pens are available (Potclays).

PENCIL

A pointed sable brush, also listed as majolica pencils. Underglaze colours are also obtainable, made up into pencils or *crayons*.

PERCENTAGE COMPOSITION

The percentage by weight of the elements or oxides in a compound. (See also *analysis*.)

To derive percentage composition from a formula:

1 **The percentage of elements in an oxide**

$$\frac{\text{Total atomic weight of the element}}{\text{molecular weight of compound}} \times 100$$

Example: the amount of oxygen in MnO_2

$$\frac{2 \times 16 \text{ (atomic wt. oxygen)}}{87} \times 100 = 36.8\%$$

leaving 63.2 of manganese metal.

2 **The percentage of an oxide in a compound.**
Example: the amount of calcia in whiting, $CaCO_3$

$$\frac{\text{Molecular wt. calcia, 56}}{\text{Mol. wt. calcium carbonate 100}} \times 100 = 56\%$$

Some 44% of the recipe weight will therefore be lost when the *carbon dioxide* is driven off during firing.

The equation can be extended to work out the percentages of *oxides* in *minerals*.

PERCENTAGE RECIPES

A recipe can be listed as *batch weights* with a random total, or as parts of a hundred. It is much easier to compare recipes in the latter form.
Example: two batch weight recipes.

	A	B
China stone	74.0	128.4
China clay	116.1	185.7
Whiting	90.0	144.0
Quartz	105.0	168.0

If we bring each of these recipes to percentages, we find that they have the same proportions (to the nearest whole number: stone 20, clay 30, whiting 23, quartz 27).

It is therefore worth bringing all batch weights to percentages both for easy comparison and also to get an immediate impression of the proportions, and thus the sort of glaze or body likely to result.

Method: Total the batch weights and divide each of the items in the recipe by this total, then multiply by 100.

i.e. $\dfrac{\text{Item}}{\text{Total}} \times 100$

Example:
From the above batch A. the total is 385. To work out the whiting percentage.

$90 \div 385 = 0.2337$
$0.2337 \times 100 = 23.37\%$

PERIODIC TABLE

A table or chart in which the elements are arranged in order of their *atomic numbers*, and grouped according to their electron configuration and *valencies*. As far as their behavior in ceramics is concerned the groupings are often appropriate. In Group 1 (one electron in the outer shell) we find lithium, potassium and sodium vertically adjacent, as are the slightly less 'efficient' fluxes calcium, strontium and barium. However another important base—lead—is found in Group IVA with the glass-formers, silica, and germanium. Many of the colors are contained in the Group 23–29 and are called the *transitional* elements.

The table's practical value is limited but the information it contains can give some explanation and forecast of behavior. Hamer deals very fully with the table and its relevance to potters.

PERLITE

A fine-grained acidic laval rock (rhyolite type), composed of 70–75% silica; 12–14% alumina; and 6–8% alkalis. Swells when rapidly heated—'expanded perlite'. Used in the making of insulating bricks. Expanded perlite can be found in garden stores for use in potting soil. It burns out or melts (loses its expanded form) at about 1260°C. Can be used as a 'grog' at lower temperatures as in raku, helping to resist *thermal shock*, or to develop apertures and small craters at stoneware temperatures. Useful in 'sculptural' experiments. See William Hunt's article in CR 70.

IA	IIA	IIB	IVB	VB	VIB	VIIB	VIII			IB	IIB	IIIA	IVA	VA	VIA	VIIA	0
1 H				THE PERIODIC TABLE OF THE ELEMENTS													2 He
3 Li	4 Be											5 B	6 C	7 N	8 O	9 F	10 Ne
11 Na	12 Mg											13 Al	14 Si	15 P	16 S	17 Cl	18 Ar
19 K	20 Ca	21 Sc	22 Ti	23 V	24 Cr	25 Mn	26 Fe	27 Co	28 Ni	29 Cu	30 Zn	31 Ga	32 Ge	33 As	34 Se	35 Br	36 Kr
37 Rb	38 Sr	39 Y	40 Zr	41 Nb	42 Mo	43 Tc	44 Ru	45 Rh	46 Pd	47 Ag	48 Cd	49 In	50 Sn	51 Sb	52 Te	53 I	54 Xe
55 Cs	56 Ba	57 La	72 Hf	73 Ta	74 W	75 Re	76 Os	77 Ir	78 Pt	79 Au	80 Hg	81 Tl	82 Pb	83 Bi	84 Po	85 At	86 Rn
87 Fr	88 Ra	89 Ac															
RARE EARTHS Lanthanides			58 Ce	59 Pr	60 Nd	61 Pm	62 Sm	63 Eu	64 Gd	65 Tb	66 Dy	67 Ho	68 Er	69 Tm	70 Yb	71 Lu	
ACTINIDE Series			90 Th	91 Pa	92 U	93 Np	94 Pu	95 Am	96 Cm	97 Bk	98 Cf	99 Es	100 Fm	101 Md	102 No	103 Lw	

A salt-glazed platter by William Hunt (U.S.A.) with "substantial additions of expanded perlite, which leaves many small voids like soft brick, but with far more durability".

PERMEABILITY

The rate at which one substance (a liquid or a gas) can pass through another. In pottery, the rate at which water will pass through a ceramic body. It gives some idea of the size of the pores as distinct from total pore volume, which is demonstrated by *porosity* tests. Scientific tests for permeability are beyond the potter's range but simple comparative trials can be made. For example one can test several similar-sized but differently fired containers by filling them with water, and sitting them in glazed saucers. The rate at which the saucers fill will be a rough comparative test of permeability.

PETALITE

A mineral LiO_2, Al_2O_3, $8SiO_2$, 612. A *fluxing* mineral with a rather high melting point. Sometimes referred to as a lithium feldspar. Can be used as a source of lithia in glazes and porcelain bodies. Should be pebble-ground. A sample analysis by weight:

Na_2O	1.1			
MgO	0.3	Al_2O_3	16.0	SiO_2 77.2
CaO	0.2			
Li_2O	4.3			

Related to spodumene, which has half the amount of silica in its formula. Lithium minerals are recommended by Cardew for flameproof bodies, using as much as 60% petalite to 40% plastic clay for very low *thermal expansion*.

A 1280°C. recipe from the late Katherine Pleydell Bouverie is:

Petalite	15.0
Feldspar	22.5
China clay	7.5
Quartz	11.5
Ash	22.5
Whiting	22.0

See also *once-fired pottery* for a 1250°C. recipe by Christopher Buras (CR 84).

PETROLOGY

The study of the rocks of the earth's crust as distinct from the earth as a whole (geology).

PETUNZE

The Chinese equivalent of *china stone* or *feldspar*.

PHASE DIAGRAMS

A diagram or graph showing changes in the physical state or composition of various mixtures of two materials at increasing temperatures. Shows *eutectics* and the degree of *vitrification* or glassy liquid likely to be present at a given temperature. The diagram for alumina and silica is important to potters, especially in the manufacture of refractories.

There follow two simplified diagrams based on McMurdie and Hall's Phase Diagrams for Ceramists (American Ceramic Soc. Inc. 1956).

1 Mixtures of potash and silica in the range between 60/40 and 10/90 K_2O/SiO_2, and between 700 and 1300°C. There are two eutectic mixtures at 55/45 and 33/67.

2 Mixtures of calcium feldspar (anorthite) and silica.

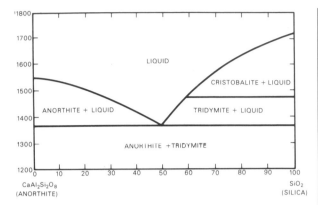

Here there is a eutectic at almost equal parts with solid solutions either side. It can be seen that additions of quartz or flint to anorthite feldspar will lower its melting point.

PHASE, electrical

A line of electricity supply. (See *single phase, three phase*.)

PHASES OF MATTER

Distinct physical states which include *states of matter* and also changes within solids and liquids. Thus alumina, and silica compounds at high temperatures have phases where liquids are present within solids. Most phase changes occur at a definite temperature, but ceramic materials are very involved and the process is 'dynamic' or continuous with overlapping phases. One can discuss, for instance, 'glass phases' in a pottery body. (See also *phase diagrams*.)

pH FACTOR

Refers to the hydrogen ion concentration in a solution, denoting relative acidity or alkalinity. pH7 is neutral, i.e. pure water: lower numbers are increasingly acidic: the higher numbers alkaline. Used in testing casting slips.

PHOSPHORUS

Element P.31. Pentoxide P_2O_5. 173.

One of the glass-forming elements (i.e. high valency, 5, and low ionic radius, O.35 A). Wood ash for example usually contains 2–5%, and *amblygonite* larger concentrations. The element occurs only in the combined state in ceramics, the main source being bone-ash, $Ca_3(PO_4)_2$, calcium phosphate. Small amounts of calcium phosphate are considered a help in Jun glazes. It probably has a subtle effect on glazes (and on bone china body) which is not fully understood. Although acting as a glass-former it 'does not enter the silica chain', Hamer.

PHOTO-ELECTRIC PYROMETER

A heat measuring device in which the light given off by a 'hot body' in a kiln is measured and transformed into an electric current which will operate a pointer on a dial, similar to a photographic light-meter. Normally used only for high temperatures.

PHOTOTROPHY

A slight and short-lived deepening of color as seen in rutile/titanium glazes (totalling 15%, Hamer) when a cover, e.g. a cup in a saucer, is removed.

PIGMENT OXIDES

The various metals whose *oxides* provide *color* or *opacity* to glazes are dealt with in detail under their individual headings. Ordinary oil paints and other painting pigments will provide color in fired pottery only to the degree to which they contain these metals—all organic materials burning away.

Their number is few but there are many variations and combinations. It is somewhat misleading to give a tidy list of colors resulting from the use of the oxides. Cobalt, for instance, can confidently be quoted as providing a strong, stable blue, but it can also give viridian green with zinc, or even purple and red with magnesia under certain conditions.

It is well-known that a range of colors from red to blue can result from the use of iron, while copper can give apple-green, turquoise, purple, red, or copper lustre. The final hue, the result of the absorption of certain wavelengths from white light, is dependent on the material in which it is dissolved or suspended and on the particular oxide or compound which has been formed in the glass.

The fired color will bear little resemblance to the raw oxide unless it is undissolved in a glaze e.g. painted onto the biscuit when it will be largely unaltered from the unfired oxide. In this case copper and manganese, though of different qualities, will remain black, iron will lose its brightness but remain red-brown to black, and cobalt may develop a gray-blue.

The principal oxides are those of the metals:

1 *The common coloring materials:* copper, cobalt, chromium, manganese, iron, nickel antimony, and their variants such as ilmenite, ochre, rutile, etc.
2 *The rare or precious metals:* vanadium, cadmium, selenium, uranium, gold, silver, platinum.
3 *The opacifiers:* tin, zirconium, titanium, zinc.

To minimize the confusion when using oxides for painting, slightly different chemical forms can be used e.g. the *carbonates* of copper or cobalt which, at least, are distinguishable from manganese!

Most carbonates are poisonous. The prepared colors listed in suppliers' catalogs are *fritted* mixtures of oxides with other ceramic materials. Chrome is often included to give stability to the darker colors and in reaction with tin to give pink. Oxides are stained to give an approximation to their fired color. The hues listed may not be true for all glazes, they are not immune to the variations mentioned above.

Temperature is another factor in the quality of color. In general, the lowest temperatures produce the brightest colors, e.g. a bright red can be obtained from iron or chrome at below 900°C. It is also true, however, that cobalt in stoneware can be pretty lurid, as can high temperature reduced copper. Finally, the kiln atmosphere is crucial, whether *oxidizing* or *reducing*.

Reference books list theoretical maximum percentage proportions of pigments in glazes and slips. These are good guides to the relative coloring power of oxides but it is instructive to exceed the limits in test batches. In some cases, copper for instance, an excess will destroy the glaze surface, producing an ashy black, but very considerable proportions of iron or manganese can be used.

Some generally recommended maxima are: copper 3%, iron 12%, chromium 5%, nickel 3%, rutile 10%, ilmenite 5%, manganese 10%, iron chromate 3%, antimoniate of lead 5%, cobalt 2%, the opacifiers 10%. The impure and 'diluted' ochres, etc. can be as high as 25%.

There is no harm in trying combinations of any pigments. (See *color trials*, *line blends*. etc. Rhodes CGP 138 and 206–7 gives useful lists of mixtures). The colors mentioned, however, are those which are likely to develop in a 'neutral' glaze: the actual results may be different under your particular conditions. A few mixtures can generate *volatile* particles which will affect other glazes. Copper has this tendency and can stain right through a pot wall to show on the other side. (See also *chrome-tin pink*.) Dolomite and zinc glazes may produce a similar mushroom pink reaction in stoneware. (See also *color*, under the individual *element* headings, *painting on pottery*, *majolica*, *enamels*, *colored glazes*, etc.)

PINCH POT

Also known as thumb pots. Pressing one's thumb into a ball of clay and squeezing it up into a hollow shape is the most instinctive and intimate way of handling clay. It is often presented to the beginner as the first and not very important step towards making 'real' pots, but this is to seriously underestimate the technique. Not only

can one's fancy run free but, with practice, quite large thin-walled shapes with subtle organic qualities can be achieved. The technique is soothing and satisfying.

Simple pinched pots are especially suitable for sawdust, raku, and other primitive firings.

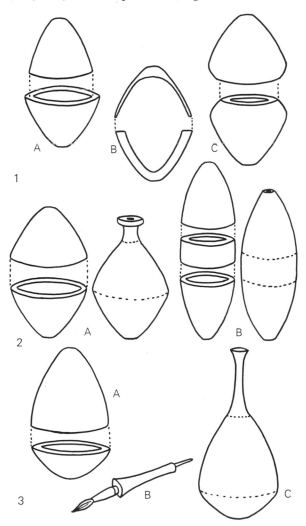

Assemblies and additions to the basic pinch pot shape. (1) Three common faults which can occur when forming the sections of multiple pots. (A) The openings are of different sizes. (B) The walls are uneven and the top half too thin to secure an adequate join. (C) It is almost impossible to join walls which are inturned.
(2) The second diagram offers some suggestions for double pinch pots. (A) an aperture can be cut after joining and shaping, and a neck modeled or coiled on. (B) A short cylinder or collar can be inserted to give a taller form.
(3) By varying the proportions of the parts high or low-bellied shapes can be obtained. A tall neck may be modeled round a paintbrush or suitable rod and luted on for a bottle form.

1

2

Method: As the clay will dry fairly rapidly during the process, moist plastic material should be used— normally a red clay. Grog may be added but if used in excess the necessary plasticity is lost. If cracks appear on the surface smooth them over immediately. To make a single pot roll the clay into a ball, the rounder the better for a symmetrical shape. Hold in one palm and start to press the thumb of the hand centrally into the lump, turning with short movements as the thumb penetrates. When down to within ½ in. (12 mm.) of the base grip the pot between the thumb inside and the fingers outside and begin to squeeze the walls to an even thickness, revolving the pot about ½ in. (12 mm.) between each pinch. Do not try to thin the wall haphazardly; keep up a steady and rhythmic series of movements. Work round and round in an ascending spiral towards the neck of the pot. If a shoulder is required on the finished shape, keep the mouth as small as possible.

Do not stand the pot on its base while soft; rest it on its rim or in a suitable hollow support. To control the spread of the shape hold it sideways in the palm and squeeze slightly round the circumference after each 'pinch'.

The pinch pot can be used as a unit or basis for future work. Examples are illustrated. Multiple pinch pots luted mouth to mouth, or with a 'collar' between, can be built up to quite respectable sizes. Oval balls of clay can be pinched into asymmetric forms. The finished pots can be *burnished*, or colored, slipped or glazed in the usual way.

For large bowls the initial pinching can be done with all the fingers inside the bowl, while a combination of pinching and stroking is used for the walls. See illustration under *handbuilt pots*.

PINHOLING IN GLAZE

A particularly aggravating glaze fault, found most often in *viscous* stoneware glazes. According to most authorities, pinholes result from blisters or bubbling in a glaze which has not quite settled down. Recommended as precautions: a thinner glaze coating; a more fluid glaze; the avoidance of *over-firing*; a heat *soak* at melting temperature. Rhodes also mentions over-zealous *reduction* early in a firing as a contributory cause. Even 'perfectly' fired pieces, especially plates, can show pinholes. I have noticed that the holes are often quite deep, suggesting pits in the body over which the glaze refuses to flow, rather like paint over cracks in woodwork. In these cases they show no signs of a burst bubble. Clean clay and the careful smoothing of 'flatware' will help; you may well find the same glaze to be perfectly smooth on a vertical surface. Sulfur released from the clay (made

(1) A pinch pot is formed by squeezing a ball of clay between the thumb inside and the fingers outside, steadily turning the piece after each 'pinch'. Outward spread is controlled by gripping the whole pot with the palm and fingers of the other hand. Larger shapes are possible using both hands (see handbuilding*).*

(2) When two pinch pots have been joined together, rim to rim, the shapes can be perfected by rolling the 'egg' as shown. This is done before cutting any aperture. The pressure must be steady and gentle or the wall may split.

An unusual form arrived at by the pinching technique by Sheila Fournier.

very evident to the nose by some bodies) may also be a cause. Air trapped between particles of glaze powder is suggested by Dodd. Glaze which regularly pinholes is difficult to cure without adding more *flux* which will change its character. Try altering the body clay.

PINT WEIGHT

The weight of solid matter in a pint of slop glaze or slip. Usually quoted in oz.: 26–28 being the average for casting slips; 28–30 for glazes. (See *Brongiart's formula*.)

PIPECLAY

A white clay of the type used in the manufacture of tobacco pipes and, in general, applied to any discovered pocket of white-firing, possibly *calcareous* clay. According to some authorities it was un-plastic and siliceous but Worrall describes it as plastic and fusible. It is sometimes associated with fireclays, which may be why Leach uses the term in connection with a wide range of marls and fireclay, but another explanation may be that 'pipe clay' is also applied to any clay made into drainage pipes.

PITCHER, pitchers

In the singular the word is applied to a large water *jug*. (In USA any jug e.g. cream pitcher.) In the plural it applies to broken pots, generally biscuit, which may be crushed and used for *grog*. Electrical porcelain factories grind glazed pitchers to add to the body. (See also *jug*.)

PIT FIRING

A pit dug into the ground, 24–30 in. deep, and used as a 'kiln' in a similar way to *sawdust firing*.

PLACING

A method of 'placing' a piece of pottery with more than one base or leg. It can be set on a slab of the same clay as the body of the piece which, in turn, is placed on a generous layer of sand or calcined alumina to allow it to shrink without splitting. The arrangement can be carried through drying, biscuiting, and glaze fire with the same slab.

The setting of pots in a kiln (see *kiln packing*, etc). *Wads* of clay are 'placed' between *saggars* for ventilation and stability. Hamer uses the word to mean the packing of pots in saggars, bedded in sand; an industrial technique for high-fired biscuit.

PLACING SAND

Fine white or 'silver' sand used for *setting* earthenware and high-fired biscuit, or it may be used under large pots or multi-based ceramics providing tiny 'rollers' over which the piece can move as it shrinks. For most setting purposes, however, *alumina* is replacing sand. Some potters even use several thicknesses of glossy paper in electric kilns. These may be cut to the shape of the base. Quite a lot of smoke will be generated.

PLAGIOCLASE

A series of feldspars between albite and anorthite, i.e. with variable amounts of soda and lime as the base oxides. The mixtures occur because of the similarity in *ionic radius* of the atoms of soda and calcium. Although the series is continuous it is divided, for convenience, into half a dozen mineral types. These are listed in Cardew PP 47.

The two types of feldspar are considered to be 'melted' into one another (see *solid solutions*).

PLANE

A clay plane is similar to a woodworking plane but has a somewhat larger aperture in front of the cutter. Alternatively the Surform type of plane can be used, with the advantage that blades of various sizes and curved shapes can be bought. Clay particularly with grog, is highly abrasive and no metal edge will last long. If used with discretion the clay plane can be a valuable item of equipment, especially for the hand-builder.

Using a Surform plane on a grogged surface.

PLASTER OF PARIS

Mixing plaster of paris. (1) and (2) It is sprinkled into a bowl of water until small islands stand above the surface, or the measured proportion of plaster is used up. Do not stir at all until all the plaster is in the water and allow it to soak for a minute or so. (3) Mix thoroughly by swinging the hand to and fro beneath the surface of the liquid.

A partially dehydrated gypsum known as a demi-hydrate ($CaSO_4.\frac{1}{2}H_2O$) which, when mixed with water,

recombines to form a soft porous stone. It has the quality, partly by reason of a slight expansion during setting, of reproducing in great detail the shape and surface texture of any material or object onto which it is poured and allowed to set. It was known to the ancient Egyptians and to the Greeks but its name derives from the fact that the original modern material was prepared from deposits in the Montmartre district of Paris.

Plaster of paris is made in various qualities, from a coarse, yellow-pink builders' plaster to a very fine-grain white 'dental' plaster. There is a special type supplied for pottery molds. The so-called 'dental' plaster is quick-setting and rather too close and hard for our purposes. Plaster of paris is prepared by roasting crushed gypsum in a revolving retort to 120°C. Commercial pottery of all kinds is formed in or on plaster molds, the shape being as much conditioned by the plaster as by the clay. Its main use in a school or pottery will be for non-circular dish molds, or in the form of slabs or bowls which will absorb moisture from very wet clays. Pieces of plaster in clay will cause it to split or bloat in the kiln. If it is heated to 150°C. or above it will become 'dead-burnt—weak and powdery—so do not put molds to dry directly onto a hot kiln.

Method for mixing plaster. Once plaster has been stirred into water it is difficult to add more without forming lumps or even nodules of dry powder. Start, therefore, with up to half a bowl of water, as required, and sprinkle handfuls of plaster into it, without stirring, until the powder is heaped into 'islands' just above the surface. Leave these to soak for a few minutes and then stir vigorously, keeping the hand beneath the surface to avoid aeration. A proportion of $2\frac{1}{2}$–3 lb. to 2 pints (1.25 kg to 1 liter) of water will give about 80 cu. in. (1000 cu. cm.) of a reasonably hard mix.

Materials can be added to alter the performance during setting: lime added to the plaster will lessen expansion; dextrin, milk, vinegar, sodium carbonate, and size have been mentioned as setting retardants and/or hardeners; warm water, salt and alum can accelerate setting but may also aerate. Molds should not contain additional materials.

PLASTIC
Capable of being easily molded. (See *plasticity*.)

PLASTICITY
With reference to ceramic materials, especially clay, it is the property which permits the shape to be altered by pressure and yet retain the given shape when the pressure is removed. The 'yield point' of a clay will vary with the type and with the amount of water present.

The sheet structure of clay is a possible explanation of this behavior. Between each leaf or sheet of clay material (which is molecular thin) a layer of water will lubricate movement relative to one another, while the electrical attraction is sufficient to hold the leaves in place when not under pressure. This simplified view has not been definitely proved and the movement may be between larger particles. *Colloidal* gels from bacterial action have also been suggested as a contributory factor. Clay is unique in possessing true plasticity allied to dry strength. Shaw SCP illustrates the distinction between the flat plates of *kaolinite* and the curled or tube structure of *halloysite* which has otherwise similar constituents.

In common use the term is widened to include general workability, but excess plasticity can render a clay unworkable. The *bentonites* (montmorillonites) cannot be used alone and, like the *ball clays*, are valued for their very plastic nature but are used as additions to a body rather than as a working clay. Plasticity involves a high water content with fine grain and consequently high shrinkage and, frequently, *fusibility*.

Clays may be arranged, as a general rule, in the following order of increasing plasticity: *china clay, fireclay, stoneware clay, buff secondary clays, ball clay, red clay, montmorillonite clay.* (See also *aging, thixotropy, weathering,* etc.)

PLASTICS

A series of synthetic resinous or other 'organic' polymerized substances shaped in a liquid state and allowed to set. Low melting point. (See *polythene*.)

There are 'thermosetting' and 'thermoplastic' plastics, the second softening under mild heat, the first staying more rigid. The first type includes the polyeurethenes, silicones, and epoxy resins; the second, polythene, polystyrene, etc. The first type is obviously more useful to the potter for storage, etc. where they may come into contact with warm conditions. For homemade sieves as described under that heading, the second type would be necessary.

PLATE

Making hand-made plates creates problems of throwing, warping, 'humping', and uneconomical packing in the kiln. Therefore they are not widely produced. Some potters jigger and jolley their plates but this is tantamount to failure on the part of a craft potter. With practice, care and the use of large circular *throwing bats*, it is not difficult to make plates on the wheel. The illustrations show some of the stages.

After centering (by the *annular* method) the block of clay should be pressed down to a wide, shallow block before actual throwing starts. Leave plenty of clay for the rim which should be firm and well-defined. Alternatively, a thick even coil can be laid round a thrown or rolled slab and thrown up to a rim. Avoid a ridge or hump just before the wall of the rim begins to rise, and also any suggestion of a dip in the middle. A slight rise is preferable towards the center—the cutting wire will tend to rise as the plate is cut off. Use the wire with the wheel turning very slowly. Trimming with a pointed tool close to the wheel head will help to keep the wire flat and low. Leave the plate on the bat until it is *soft-leather*. If adequately thrown it will need no turning but if a foot ring is turned leave a second ring nearer the center to support it. At the hard-leather stage, plates can be inverted to dry on their rims.

Ray Finch *once-fires* large plates to minimize *dunting*. In the biscuit fire the heat-retention of the kiln shelf can cause trouble and some potters biscuit their plates and flat dishes on clay pellets to allow air under them. I have not found this necessary when using shelves up to $\frac{1}{2}$ in. (12.5 mm.) thick. Plates may also be glazed in the well only and fired *boxed*.

Stages in throwing a plate.
(1) The first spreading, down and outwards pressure using the palm or a sponge.

(2) The rim is formed, taking care not to make a depression just inside the rim.

(3) If felt necessary, the well and curve can be smoothed and adjusted with a metal kidney tool.

(4) The angle between the bat or wheelhead and base is cut to a bevel.

Plates are most easily thrown on a circular bat and removed when somewhat stiffer. When turning, a second footring nearer the center of the base, as shown in the photograph, will help to prevent slumping in the firing.

PLATINUM

Used as the salt, platinic chloride, to obtain silver *enamel* for overglaze painting. Bought as a liquid pigment. Platinum and its alloy with rhodium are used in the *thermocouples* of high temperature *pyrometers*.

PLUCKED WARE

Scars caused by glazed ware touching the kiln wall or supports, or each other during firing. Very evident on old salt-glazed pots.

The splendid German Bellarmines (Bartmannkrugers) were apparently piled against one another in the kiln. The resultant scars are very evident in this photograph.

PLUMBIC

Apertaining to *lead*. Note however that 'plumbago', the 'lead' in lead pencils, is, in fact, a graphite.

PLUNGE POTS

A name given to the technique of making pots by pressing a batten of wood into a block of clay. The walls can be thinned by stroking and easing the clay upwards against the wooden former, or by slicing away surplus clay with a wire. Very direct and lively pots can be formed.

(1) Thrusting a rolling pin into a block of clay.

(2) The clay is eased up along the roller to form a taller pot.

(3) The wall is reduced to a reasonable thickness by cutting facets with a wire, these facets being normally integral to the form of the piece.

A carved-side plunge pot form by Leslie Pearson.

POISE

A unit of *viscosity*. Occasionally quoted when discussing glazes at the melting stage. The viscosity of water at 20°C. is 0.010 poise, molten glass varies widely, of course, but its viscosity is at least 5000 times as great.

POISONOUS MATERIALS

Marked as 'toxic' where applicable at each main entry. Quite apart from those used by the potter, many materials in daily use would not be recommended for breathing in or ingesting! Similarly, in the pottery, care should be taken at all times. A few rules I have always carefully adhered to are:

1 Not to eat or drink in the workshop;
2 Not to raise dust when sweeping or cleaning up; as far as possible use all materials in a wet state;
3 When dealing with powdery materials, spraying, cutting any form of asbestos, or rubbing down large

areas of dry clay surface, wear at least a handkerchief round the nose and mouth or a mask (very cheap from a chemist);

4 Ventilate the kiln room well during firing, especially with electric kilns.

The prime villain among pottery materials is considered to be lead oxide, with others not far behind. Be wary of barium, antimony, dusty silica (flint), and most of the carbonates. As mentioned, fumes from firing can be very noxious, not to mention carbon monoxide and natural gas which are heavier than air and can collect at ground level. Silica is well-known for causing lung congestion and worse. Poisons in the fired piece are more complex, sometimes being released in use by the action of acids such as fruit acids. Copper can cause trouble, especially in association with lead, if in an unbalanced (often a matt) glaze. Selenium and cadmium are suspect. A well-fired (not overfired) balanced glaze will usually be blameless. It is possible (and if lead is used on tableware, legally necessary) to have glazes tested for toxicity. (See *soluble lead*.) The longevity of many potters, however, does not suggest exposure to great danger. A degree of knowledge and care are all that is necessary.

POLISHING CLAY

The actual application of furniture or other polish to pots after firing can have undesirable effects, especially if the pot is wetted. Use sparingly, if at all, on burnished pots.

The Elers brothers were reputed to have polished their red stonewares on a lapidary's wheel. Some faults in glazed ware can be polished using an electric drill and a very fine abrasive. (See *burnishing*.)

POLYTHENE, polyethylene

A synthetic material (the polymer of C_2H_4, if it interests you!), useful, cheap, and at once a bane and a blessing to potters. Because it is chemically inert it is suitable for glaze and slip containers, while in its sheet form it has eased the potter's problem of keeping pots moist, doing away with the rotting rags and the usually inefficient *damp-cupboard*, not to mention the rusting biscuit tins. On the other hand it has, more than any other material, been responsible for the rapid decline, almost to the point of extinction, of the traditional country potter throughout the world. (See also *plastics*.)

PORCELAIN BODY

In China the definition of porcelain (T'zu) is wider than is generally accepted in the West; it could be any fine, pale body of primary clay with a distinctive ring when struck, fired to *vitrification* but often too thick to show

the *translucency* which we expect today. Essentially porcelain is kaolin and silica with a little *flux*, fired to vitrification point. This is 'true' or hard-paste porcelain and requires a high temperature in the region of 1350°C. An increase or multiplication of the bases (or of the acids, boron or fluorine) can lower the melting point and it is possible that the Eastern kilns averaged no more than 1250°C–1300°C.

Richard Parkinson asserts that 1360°C. is needed fully to develop the 'felted mass of mullite needles bonded in a glassy cement' by which he defines true porcelain, and that the lower temperature mixtures such as David Leach's 1270°C. body, give a white stoneware. To a degree, this is a matter of words and preferences. Certainly the bentonite porcelains lack the white purity of the harder types and one must learn to counter what Harry Davis calls their 'evil properties'. The color is better in reduction. The best of modern porcelain bodies throw pleasantly and thinly up to about 9 in. (22 cm.), and can be used for pinching and slab pots, although the joins tend to show up after firing, the edge of the clay taking on a slightly different color to the face. Try mitered joints.

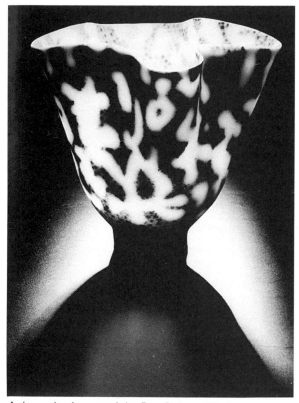

A dramatic photograph by Ron Sloman (St. James Gallery, Bath, U.K.) emphasising the transluscency of a porcelain bowl by Mary Rogers.

The basic recipe for porcelain is 50% kaolin (china clay), 25% feldspar, 25% flint or quartz. It is wise to leave the feldspar at 25% although this may be replaced in small part by nepheline: silica can be reduced to a 15% minimum. This leaves the clay. English kaolins lack plasticity, limiting the development of porcelains in England and frightening off studio potters. By swapping a proportion of kaolin for ball clay the throwing qualities are improved but the translucency diminished. Rhodes suggests up to 15% ball clay. 2–5% 'white' bentonite will make a body throwable but will increase shrinkage and impurities. Bentonite will also greatly increase *thixotropy*, apparently stiff or even leather-hard clay may soften suddenly and alarmingly under pressure or when turning. Practice can overcome the dangers here. More serious is the tendency to warp in drying and firing.

The amalgamation of the body ingredients needs to be thorough for complete fusion of the particles. Parkinson recommends a 300 screen lawn but this seems excessive—many particles would not pass through. For many potters the simple compounding of already finely ground materials, followed by efficient hand kneading and a week or so of 'resting', will suffice. (See *clay preparation*.)

Two recipes:
David Leach.

Grollegg china clay powder	53
Potash feldspar	25
Water-ground quartz	17
White bentonite	5

Firing to translucency 1250–1280°C. Substitute some quartz for china clay if *crazing* is persistently encountered.

Parkinson (published in CR.3)

EEC JM china clay	51
Potash feldspar	18
EEC BB ball clay	7
Fine (300 mesh) quartz	24

Firing 1320–70°C.

Richard Parkinson also suggests that these high temperatures can be obtained in an electric *silicon carbide element* kiln.

A traditional commercial earthenware body, fired to 1280°C. or more, can also be used. This yields a low translucency 'proto-porcelain'. (See also *electrical porcelain*). There are dolomite based procelains. The English industrial porcelain equivalent is *bone china*. Bernard Leach's recipe given in PQ 1 is near to the 'earthenware' body type: china clay 25, black ball clay 33, feldspar 30, quartz 12.

PORCELAIN GLAZE

Hard paste porcelain glazes have a very high silica equivalent. Parmelee quotes 7.0 SiO_2 with bases $0.3K_2O/0.7CaO$, for 1320°C. and even as much as 12.0 with $0.5K_2O/0.5CaO$ for a high-gloss glaze at the same temperature. These very nearly correspond to the Seger cone formulas. The alumina equivalents in the above examples are 0.8 and 1.3 respectively. At the other extreme, the low temperature bodies (1250–70°C.) may have glazes with as low as 2.0 parts silica. This proportion has been found in analyses of Chinese glazes, and also features in a formula given by Victor Margrie in CR 2 for a barium semi-matt glaze.

K_2O	0.32			SiO_2	2.0
BaO	0.34	Al_2O_3	0.4	SnO_2	0.1
CaO	0.34				

This has been translated into raw materials:

Potash feldspar	58.1
Barium carbonate	22.0
Whiting	11.1
Alumina hydrate	4.1
Tin oxide	4.7

(see CR4 which also contains other recipes).

Feldspar is the principal mineral in most porcelain glaze recipes. It will melt into a viscous glaze at cone 10 and over, and so needs only the modification of additional alumina, usually as china clay, with perhaps the diversification of the fluxes with lime or zinc. Magnesium can give a milky quality and a slightly subdued surface. Glazes for the lower-fired porcelains can be similar to those for stoneware.

A glaze suitable for use on the porcelain body developed by David Leach has been quoted as:

Feldspar	12
Dolomite	12
Quartz	22
China clay	14
Ball clay	9
Petalite	28
Bentonite	3

My standard white stoneware glaze works quite well, although it may craze.

Feldspar	40
Nepheline	20
Whiting	15
China clay	10
Talc	10
Flint	5

Firing at 1260°C.

POROSITY

Used by potters in a general way to indicate both water *absorption* and *permeability*. Defined as the proportion of pores, both open and sealed, compared with the total volume, and normally refers to the fired body of a ceramic. The open, connected pores allow water to seep into and through a pot, the closed pores simply increase heat insulation (and marginally decrease strength).

Earthenware biscuit is porous and must be covered with an unfractured (uncrazed) glaze in order to be rendered watertight. Porosity declines as molten materials fill the pores i.e. with an increase in *vitrification*. There is no sudden change from one state to the other; stonewares are porous to a small degree. An increase in *fluxes*, such as a little red clay, will aid vitrification.

A rough test for porosity is to weigh a dry pot, immerse it in water for twelve hours and re-weigh; the difference being the weight of water absorbed.

John Temple (CR 39) confidently asserts that porosity (and even small cracks) can be remedied by filling wth strong tea and leaving overnight! For waterproofing pieces not to be used for eating or drinking or holding food of any sort, one can flood them with a liquid polyeurethene (or there are special commercial equivalents in pottery suppliers' catalogs), pour out the surplus and leave to dry for several days, taking care not to allow a thick pool to form in the bottom of any curve. This of course, is something of a last resort and the customer must always be informed.

POT, potting

A vessel, generally rounded, for holding liquids or solids. The development of *'ceramic sculpture'* has led to a blurring of the definition but if a hollow fired clay shape has any sort of hole near the top it may be considered to be a 'pot'. The word is also used as an adjective in place of 'pottery' and as a verb 'to pot' i.e. to make pottery.

POTASH

The common term for potassium oxide, as in 'lead-lime-potash glaze' etc.

POTASSIUM, oxide, compounds

A metallic element K, 39.
Oxide K_2O, 94 Potash
Carbonate K_2CO_3, 138, Pearl ash

A base, strongly *alkaline*, and a powerful *flux* in glazes and bodies. Both the oxide and carbonate are *deliquescent* and *soluble* and can be used only in a *fritted* form. There are a number of 'natural' frits (minerals) containing potash, including: orthoclase feld-spar, wood ash, nepheline syenite, china stone, and to a smaller degree, many other vitrifiable materials, e.g. clay. Potassium is frequently associated with sodium, so much so that the *RO* for some minerals may be written KNaO indicating a variable mixture.

Potash occurs in all but the simplest glazes and at all temperatures. Equivalents vary between 0.1 and 0.5 of the RO group. Its effect on the coloring oxides is more neutral than soda or zinc. Potassium nitrate replaced some of the lead oxide to produce the 'coral red' of Chinese enamels (Nigel Wood).

POT GAUGE

A tool used to assist in the repetition throwing of pieces of a similar size and shape. It consists of one movable arm which is set with its point just clear of the rim of the pot, or with two arms the second of which indicates the widest point of the circumference.

In its simplest form the pot gauge can be merely a stick set in a wedge of clay; this is all that most of the old country potters would have used. Two modifications of the jointed arm type now in use by craft potters are recommended, a stiff rubber end to the pointer, and a means of swiveling the whole gauge to one side so that it does not inhibit *centering*. It is brought into position again when the pot is well under way. (See also *card measure*.)

(1) The simplest form of pot gauge: a rod stuck into a wedge of clay.

2

3

(2) and (3) Show a more sophisticated form of pot gauge. Each arm is adjustable in length and vertical movement, and is fitted with a soft rubber end. To obviate the disadvantage that the gauge can inhibit movement and may be knocked out of true, the whole assemblage can be pivoted so that it can remain set but be swung out of the way. The use of a single screw in the base allows this movement.

POTSHERD

A broken piece of pottery. (See *pitchers*.)

POTTERY

Fired clay objects. The term is narrower in its application than ceramics and is often used for the less sophisticated types of earthenware or, sometimes, for hand-made ceramics in general. As its root 'pot' suggests, it is applied mainly to containers, though these may be asymmetric and purely decorative. May be used as an adjective as in 'pottery modeling' i.e. modeling carried out by means of recognized pottery techniques such as coiling.

POURED GLAZE

Decoration by poured and splashed glazes.
(1) A large plate by Nigel Cox; the reduced copper on a white ground brilliantly controlled to produce a striking pattern.

(2) A more managed pour on a handbuilt bottle by Robert Fournier. The pot was abruptly twisted to develop the design as the glaze flowed down. Odd, unwanted dribbles were wiped away.

Pouring swathes of glaze across a plate or pot has long been a decorative technique. It was popular in the early days of studio pottery with Chaplet, Delaherche and others. The possibilities are many; from the simple pouring of glaze onto the shoulder of a pot, often over another glaze, to the more deliberate shaping of the run of glaze as in the work of Janet Leach, myself, and others. The shape of the surface will influence the result as will a quick sideways twist of the vessel as the liquid flows down. Very controlled designs can be achieved on dishes. Dry (matt) ash glazes are very suitable for pouring over the more rugged types of slab pots and constructions. Interesting if chancy effects can be obtained by pouring over a revolving pot. See Fournier DPD for illustrations of the great variety of poured glaze effects.

POWER WHEEL

A potter's wheel driven by a motor. The simplest system for transmitting the power of an electric motor to a wheel head is where a rubber or leather drive is brought into contact with the flywheel of a traditional kick wheel by foot pressure, springing back when the foot is removed. In a sophisticated version in general use in England, the drive wheel can be moved to any position from the center to the circumference of the flywheel, thereby controlling the speed of the wheel head.

In the typical industrial wheel the speed is modified by two slightly convex cones which can be swiveled on their axes relative to one another. Other systems are the expanding pulley, and the variable speed motor. The latter is now available without any great loss of torque at lower speeds and is thus likely to supersede other methods which are generally noisier and lose power through friction. The motor has a slight whine which some potters may find unacceptable. The average commercial wheel can handle 10–25 lb. (5–12 kilos) of clay according to the strength of its construction. It is important to try various wheels before purchasing: if the potter and his wheel are not in 'sympathy' it is difficult to do good work.

The simplest form of drive from a leather wheel attached to an electric motor onto the perimeter of a large flywheel. The motor unit is sprung so that it lifts from the flywheel when pressure on it is released, giving a degree of control.

PRASEODYMIUM, oxides

A metallic element Pr, 141.
Oxides Pr_2O_3, 330; PrO, 157.

One of the 'rare earths' or 'lanthanides' group. Fulham Pottery quote a zircon/praseodymium yellow for use up to 1280°C. Considered to be a more stable yellow than *vanadium*.

PRESSED DISH

Dishes formed by pressing sheets of clay into molds. (See *dishes*.)

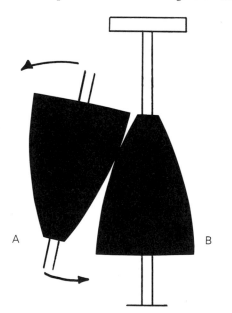

The double cone principle of transmitting power and varying the speed of the wheel head. The left-hand cone is driven from a shaft or motor and is so mounted that it will swing in the direction of the arrows while remaining in contact with the second cone, to the shaft of which the wheel head is attached. As the comparitive diameters in contact vary, an infinitely graduated speed is transmitted to (B) from the fixed speed of cone (A). In the diagram the speed of (B) would be near its maximum. (See also expanding pulley.)

Making a pressed dish. (See also hollow mold for illustrations of preliminary rolling.)

1

2

3

4

5

6

7

8

9

(1) and (2) The clay slab is cut to the approximate shape of the mold, carefully lifted, supported with the hand as shown and dropped into a hollow mold (or it can simply be reversed into the mold from the rolling cloth).

(3) and (4) The bulk of the surplus clay is cut away before sponging the slab snugly into the curve of the mold with gentle strokes from the center towards the perimeter.

(5) and (6) The edge is trimmed flat in two stages: the first by using a wooden spatula at a slight upward angle (use the outer edge of the mold as a guide) and cutting with sweeping movements towards the outer edge to avoid parting the clay from the mold. The final cut is made with the tool held level with the top face of the mold.

(7) After a final smoothing of sharp corners, the dish is left to stiffen a little.

(8) Cover with a board and invert with mold and board held tightly together. The mold can then be lifted away.

(9) The outer edge of the dish may be sponged or planed.

PRESS MOLD

A mold in which the clay cast is formed from plastic clay, as distinct from a slip mold. The term can indicate a mold into which clay is pressed, as in dish molds, or a hollow mold, the sections of which are pressed together. It may be designed with an aperture large enough to put one's hand in, so as to press slabs or pellets of clay into a continuous skin around the inner wall.

Other types may be taken apart, each section being dealt with separately, the edges scored and slipped, and the whole pressed together. A channel is cut to take the surplus clay as it is squeezed from the join, and which would otherwise prevent the parts making close contact. The handles for industrial tableware are often press-molded.

Its advantages over the slip-mold are: grogged and other mixed bodies can be used, the wall is generally firmer and thicker than a slip wall; pressed forms can be regarded simply as a basis for further work or as a unit

in a construction; the cast piece can be deformed by pinching, beating, etc.

Squared bottles are often made in two-piece press molds; the neck being thrown and luted on. *Jigger* and *jolley* work is a form of press-molding. (See also *dishes, molds.*)

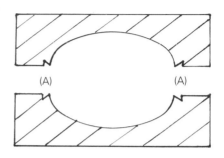

(A)   (A)

The clay mold is left a little proud of the surface and is scored and slipped in order to make a sound join when the two halves are pressed together. It is inevitable that some wet clay will be squeezed outwards and to accommodate this a channel is cut all round the inner edge as shown in the section diagram at (A). If this is omitted the two halves may not come completely together.

PRICING

See *costing.*

PRICKER

An American term for a *needle-awl.*

PRIMARY AIR

Air which is mixed with fuel to promote initial combustion; that drawn into the gas or oil behind or at the burner, or through the grate to burn solid fuel. Air introduced subsequently into the flame or hot gases is *secondary air.* The control of air input promotes *oxidizing* or *reducing* atmospheres. An electric kiln does not need primary air.

PRIMARY CLAY

A clay which has remained on the site where it was formed from the parent mineral—usually from granite via feldspar. The china clay of Cornwall is the classic example. Often called kaolin.

The term is also sometimes used as a synonym for *sedimentary clays.* Primary clays however are generally thought to have been formed by chemical action from below (by hot gases from the earth's core) whereas sedimentary clays are usually weathered minerals and may have been moved and re-deposited.

PRIMARY PHASE

The first *crystalline* phase to appear when a liquid (glaze) is cooled (Dodd). (See also *phase diagrams*.)

PROP

Refractory kiln furniture used for supporting shelves. Props may be in the form of blunt cones thrown from grogged fireclay, square columns, or units which will rest firmly one on another. There are a number of ingenious designs on the market, some of which are illustrated. Props may be cast, but slip-cast props will fail in high temperature and reduction and this is not always made clear in catalogs. H.T. insulating bricks can be cut with an old saw into suitable props for light loads. (See also *crank bits*.)

Interlocking props for kiln shelf supports.
(A) Domed and recessed
(B) castellated
(C) cast
The last is not suitable for reduction firings. Check with supplier.

PROPANE

The third hydrocarbon of the paraffin series $CH_3CH_2CH_3$. Rhodes quotes a heat value of 2558 Btu per cu. ft. or 93,000 per gallon (21.56 MJ per liter). An equivalent electrical consumption to a gallon of propane is therefore around 27 kWh (perhaps 20 kWh of useful heat). More efficient than *natural gas* but less so than butane. (See also *bottled gas*.)

PROTON

The positively charged particle in the core of an atom. (See *atomic theory*.)

PROTOPORCELAIN

An early or transitional porcelain, usually applied to pre-Song Chinese ceramics. Cardew discusses the analysis of a protoporcelain glaze in terms of the Seger formula and finds silica equivalents as low as 2.0 parts (Cardew PP 133–134). The barely translucent fabric obtained by firing a commercial earthenware body to vitrification has been termed protoporcelain.

PUG, pug mill

A machine composed of a metal barrel or cylinder tapered at one end, through which clay is forced by rotating blades in order to consolidate it into a firm column. Dodd makes a distinction between a pug and a pug mill, but this is not maintained in practice. The barrel can be vertical or horizontal, usually horizontal in smaller pugs. A vacuum chamber can be inserted half-way along the barrel to *de-air* the clay. The clay must be shredded as it enters the vacuum chamber. A pug mill can be constructed by a potter who is also something of an engineer. A de-airing pug has been developed by Harry Davis for studio potters to build. (Davis PA).

There are several machines on the market, usually with outlets of 2–3 in. (50–77 mm.) and handling about 3 cwt. (153 kg.) an hour. A pug will only work with clay which is in reasonable condition. Very wet or dry clays must be soaked together before they are put through, otherwise the block of clay in the pug may begin to turn as a whole. The action of the blades is to propel the mass forwards as it cuts it up but, in practice, some pressure is often needed at the hopper to keep it moving. A pug mill is a useful but not essential item in a small workshop. If several bodies are used it will need cleaning at each change of use, a tedious process. Clays should be 'rested' after plugging. (See Davis PA.)

PULLING A HANDLE

A method of forming a pot handle by stroking and squeezing a 'tail' of clay—see illustrations under *handle*. The term is misleading as you will soon find if you try to stretch a piece of clay by pulling. The handle may be formed separately or from a tab of clay attached to the jug.

PUMICE

A volcanic acidic laval rock (rhyolite group), composed of around 73% silica: 13% alumina; and various small amounts of iron and alkalis. Its texture is spongy, having many cavities caused by bubbles of gas trapped in rapid solidification. It is usually used as a mild abrasive in the form of powder or a block. As much as 40% has been used to give a clear glaze at stoneware temperatures. Has also been recommended as a *matting* agent.

PUNCH TEST

A rather rough and ready test for glaze-body fit. As described by Dodd: a $\frac{1}{16}$ in. (1.5 mm.) center punch is placed on the glaze surface and hit hard enough to break it. If cracks radiate from the point of impact, the glaze is in *tension*; if a circular crack has formed it is in *compression*. Score highest marks for the latter!

PURPLE OF CASSIUS

A pigment composed of chlorides of gold and tin. The over-firing of gold enamel on a *tin glaze* will produce a pale version.

PURPLE STONE

See *china stone*.

PUTNAM CLAY

A white, fairly plastic *primary clay* from Florida, U.S.A.

PYRITES

Metal sulfide minerals.
Iron pyrites FeS_2.
Copper pyrites $CuFeS_2$, 'Fool's gold'.

May occur as small nodules in clay, especially fireclay. Rigorously extracted by the industry, but the dark, slightly ashy spots which they develop on a reduced glaze are considered decorative by many craft potters. Larger nodules however can be unsightly in their effect. There are also tin pyrites and cobalt pyrites (smaltite).

PYROLUSITE

An ore of manganese dioxide.

PYROMETER

A device for measuring high temperatures, as distinct from low temperature mercury thermometers. The commonest type consists of two parts. A fused, silica or *sillimanite* tube containing wires of dissimilar metals, the thermocouple. For high temperatures the wires must be made of platinum alloys and are therefore expensive; for soft glazes they may be of base metals, chromium, nickel, etc. It follows that you must not use a pyrometer for firings above those specified by the manufacturers. When the tube is inserted into the kiln a minute current of electricity is set up, proportional to the temperature. This is measured on the second part of the instrument, a galvanometer or a potentiometer, and transmitted to a dial calibrated in degrees of temperature, which may be analogue (with a pointer) or digital (giving the actual temperature in figures). (See *controlling pyrometer*.)

The pyrometer will, of course, measure only temperature and not *heat-work*. Its main value is in indicating intermediate stages of firing; for the 'end point' *pyrometric* cones are very reliable. Pyrometers are very delicate instruments and are not infrequently damaged

The pyrometer system. The thermocouple (enclosed in a refractory sheath) which generates an increasing microvolt charge as the heat increases and is connected to an indicator where the tiny current operates either an arm on a dial or an electronic temperature figure.

in transit or by other means. The calibration can be inaccurate and it is wise to check against cones. However, once the difference between a reading and a cone indication has been established it can usually be applied over the whole scale. Instruments are made with automatic switch-off or 'soak' mechanisms; these can be very useful but do not trust them absolutely. The electronic devices are reputed to be more reliable than the motorized ones.

Other forms of heat-gauging devices are the photo-electric pyrometer and the *optical* or disappearing filament type. The latter has the advantage of portability. The pyrometer is a very useful but not absolutely essential aid to firing and if economy is necessary there may be more urgent needs on which to spend money. (See also *thermocouple*.)

PYROMETRIC CONE

Heat indicators in the form of sticks or elongated pyraminds of ceramic materials which deform at a given temperature. (See *cones, Orton cones, Holdcroft bars*.)

PYROMETRIC CONE EQUIVALENT, P.C.E.

The measurement of *refractoriness* of a clay or ceramic material obtained by firing a test of the material with cones. The cone number nearest the softening temperature of the test is the P.C.E. of that material.
Example: a high duty fireclay (U.S.A.) has a P.C.E. of 33; cone 33 melts at 1730°C.

PYRO MINI-BARS

See *mini-bars*.

PYROPHYLLITE

A clay-family substance with the formula $Al_2O_3. 4SiO_2. H_2O$. Used in some bodies and naturally present in many clays.

PYROPLASTIC DEFORMATION

Long words to describe the warping or bending of ceramics as they 'soften' at high temperatures. Applied especially to the bending of *kiln shelves* under load.

PYROSCOPE

A general term for heat-work recorders which operate by change of size or shape. (See *cones, Buller's rings, Holdcroft bars*.)

QUADRIVALENT

Having a *valency* of four, as silica, tin, etc. The oxides reading RO_2 the *acidic* oxides.

QUARTZ

A natural crystalline silica, SiO_2. Occurs as visible crystals (rock crystal) or as silica sand, quartzite or *ganister*, and in many clays.

Ground quartz is allegedly purer than flint and is preferred by many potters although the difference is difficult to detect in the fired body or glaze. Fused quartz is very resistant to chemical change and has a low *thermal expansion*; it is used for crucibles, etc. (See *silica* for further information.)

QUARTZ INVERSION

A volume change in the crystal of silica due to a 'straightening out' during heating into a state of greater symmetry of the SiO_4 lattice. It occurs instantaneously at 573°C—the increase in size being given variously at between 0.45 and 1% linear expansion. On cooling the crystals revert to their previous squeezed or deformed state at the same temperature with a corresponding contraction. These changes are in addition to the normal coefficient of expansion of silica.

If the silica is heated beyond 1050°C. it begins to change into cristobalite which has its own inversion at a lower temperature. The forms of crystal are known as alpha (sub 573°C.) and beta quartz (above 573°C.). Flint is, of course, also affected in the same way. The inversion occurs only in 'free' silica and not in silicates (glasses) or in altered silica; cristobalite, tridymite, mullite etc. which behave in different ways. More than about 25% of silica as crystals in a cooling body can shatter it, but smaller additions can give the contraction necessary to put a glaze into compression (see *crazing*). The inversion of flint is said to be less abrupt and taxing

than that of quartz, because of its microcrystalline structure. The failure of a kiln at around the inversion point can lead to severe shattering of pottery, as also can slow cooling, especially from the top temperature to around 1050°C. in stonewares and porcelains which allows the formation of crystals of silica out of the melt.

QUARTZITE

A *metamorphic* rock, formed from quartz sandstone cemented by silica. The name is also applied to a pure silica rock.

QUICKLIME

Anhydrous lime, CaO. Unstable and is slaked with water to produce $Ca(OH)_2$. The stable $CaCO_3$ form is used in ceramics.

R

There is no element with the symbol R and so the letter is useful to denote any appropriate element of an oxide, as in the *Seger formula* $RO.R_2O_3.RO_2$.

RADIATION, heat

The heat given off by a 'hot body'. *Electric elements* give radiant heat. In a fuel burning kiln, most of the work is done by hot gases, but radiation from the walls and from pot to pot plays an increasing role as the peak temperature is reached, levelling out the heat through the setting. This is one of the chief values of *soaking*.

RAKU

A technique involving a rapid firing cycle, the pots being placed in and removed from the kiln at or near the optimum firing temperature. In Japan it was merely left to cool but in the West it is now usually *carbonized* or *reduced*. Most raku is low-fired but this is not invariable —some Japanese raku was stoneware.

It was raku that brought Bernard Leach into ceramics. Its Japanese symbol means 'enjoyment'—a 'conscious return to the direct and primitive treatment of clay' (Leach). Eastern raku was usually oxidized, often painted, and air cooled. Modern western techniques have developed along the lines of sawdust reduction and quenching in water.

Raku may be made in any style but, because of the thermal shock to which it is subjected, the typical piece has been fairly small, sturdy, often asymmetric in form, and hand-built. All these criteria, however, have been superceded in the late twentieth century when the size and complexity of pieces was dramatically increased, partly due to the ceramic fiber revolution in kiln design. So wide in scope has the technique become that one of its progenitors in the West, Paul Soldner, has coined 'ukar' as an anti-raku joke title. Much modern raku is almost indistinguishable as such at first glance and many immensely skilful and sophisticated methods and finishes are employed.

Surfaces are often left smooth; the often remarkable richness of color and surface obtained from plain or painted glazes, and the contrast with the gray or black of the body in reduction, can be weakened rather than enhanced by excessive texturing or modeling of the clay. Neriage, inlay, and other decorative techniques are also employed.

The reduction (often, more correctly, *carbonization*) is achieved by covering the pot when it is still red-hot with sawdust, peat or leaves. Variation will result from partial immersion. The firing chamber or saggar should be kept free of coke or fuel. Wally Keeler (CR 1) states that, whatever the kiln atmosphere, pots will oxidize on removal. This has not been my experience: if coke falls into a saggar it is very difficult to get an oxidized glaze out of it. In Japan the system is sometimes reversed: the pots are carbonized in random patterns by biscuit firing in an open trough with charcoal dropped amongst them. The smoked pots are then covered with a clear glaze and cooled in air.

Method: the body must be open and *grogged* but need not be coarse-textured. Buff clay is usual but red clay and mixtures can be tried. The pots are normally biscuit fired to about 900–1000°C. in an ordinary kiln. Pots could be biscuited in the raku kiln, packing before firing starts, but this limits the pieces available for glazing; there should be sufficient available for a firing every twenty minutes or so for two or three hours. Once the kiln has reached cone 016 (Staffordshire) or 750–800°C., the lid or front is removed and completely dry, glazed pots which have previously stood on the kiln to get warm are quickly placed in the chamber with long tongs. They are loosely packed to allow for expansion but may be laid directly on one another. An inspection after about twenty minutes will show whether the glazes are shiny and fluid, and if this is the case, the pots are removed one by one with tongs and either laid in or covered over by sawdust, wood chips, straw, paper, or any organic substance to effect the 'reduction' of body and colors, then plunged into cold water (use a metal not a plastic bowl!) When cool the glazes will need scrubbing with a nail brush to reveal their surfaces. The

muffle is repacked as soon as one batch has been removed and the cycle recommences. See the films 'Raku English Style' for a complete session in detail, and 'Robin Welch' for raku firing with individual larger pieces.

The development of the light-weight *top-hat kiln* has widened the possibilities for raku firing but the excitement of removing pots with tongs from a red-hot kiln is less evident.

Glen Byers' book 'Raku' is an excellent and wide-ranging guide to the technique.

The act of removing a piece of glazed pottery from a simple raku coke kiln as described in the text and diagrams. (From the film/video 'Raku, English Style', see Suppliers at end of the book.)

A raku pot by Paul Soldner (U.S.A.).

Two fine, large, superbly controlled coiled pots in raku, by David Roberts.

RAKU GLAZE AND PIGMENT

Almost any glaze which will melt below 900°C. is suitable for the soft earthenware type of raku. Leach's white lead recipes are now somewhat tabu but low-temperature frits, e.g. lead silicates or alkaline frits, can be used with a little clay to provide some alumina

(5–15% clay). Frits may also be obtained which are complete in themselves, including borax and high-alkali melts. 2–5% of bentonite will assist suspension and glaze coating. These glazes will *crystallize* after a few weeks and it is advisable to dry them out after use. Alkaline (soda) frits develop exciting glaze colors especially from copper.

Any coloring oxides can be used. 2% each of CoO, MnO_2, Fe_2O_3 for black. 5% of tin will opacify and can produce a mother-of-pearl sheen in reduction. Always glaze reasonably thickly. Areas or strips of unglazed body will give an attractive contrast but should not be overdone. Enamels and gold can be used for painting, in addition to the ordinary oxide pigments, and can contrast with the rough clay in a stimulating way.

Some typical raku recipes:

1	Soft alkaline frit	93
	China clay	4
	Bentonite	3
	Copper oxide (for turquoise)	3
2	Lead sesquisilicate	50
	Soft borax frit	50
	China clay	2
	Bentonite	2
3	A simple and unusual recipe from CM 15/10	
	Gerstley Borate (colemanite)	80
	Feldspar	20

Harold MacWhinnie in CR 104 lists seven raku glazes, all crackled and also using up to 80% *gerstley borate* with nepheline syenite and clay.

Most of the pigment oxides can be used on raku, as paints, in slips, or in the glazes. Copper is the most lively, giving green, red, luster, and any variation in between. In-glaze lusters can be used. Enamels are possible and Byers K discusses *fuming* in the kiln itself for special and remarkable, if sometimes rather lurid, effects. Some special raku pigments have been suggested, e.g. for:

iron-red: frit, iron oxide and yellow ochre.
green: frit and copper oxide.
blue: cobalt, a lead frit, and flint.
white: alkaline frit with china clay and zircon or tin oxide.
yellow: lead frit with a 3:1 mixture of ferric oxide and antimony.

(See also note on raku *crackle*.)

RAKU KILN

A raku kiln must satisfy the following conditions: it must reach 800°C. and maintain that temperature for several hours, the chamber or muffle must be readily accessible and easily opened and closed with the kiln at full temperature; reasonably oxidizing conditions must prevail. There must be no danger (e.g. from shock in an electric kiln) when inserting metal tongs into the chamber.

One of the most popular and easily built is the *brazier kiln*. The Japanese type kiln, illustrated in Rhodes, Reigger and Leach resembles a Roman kiln, a long firemouth feeding into a circular chamber via a perforated hearth. Flame throwers, oil burners, acetylene burners, etc have all been utilized by modern western potters. Wood and coke fuels are commonly used. Electric raku poses problems. Firstly the kiln must be absolutely protected from damp or rain, but the pots must be reduced in the open if everybody is not to be choked and blackened; secondly the elements must be completely shrouded from any possible contact with the tongs; thirdly a complete *muffle* within the kiln is essential. CR 1 describes one type and the illustration below shows another. In PQ 36, John Chalke has advice and a series of drawings for raku kilns. Reigger and Byers give a good coverage of kiln types, the latter concentrating on the latest lightweight oil drum and top-hat kilns using ceramic fiber. These can quickly be built by the potter, and are also supplied commercially, e.g. by Fordham Thermal Systems. See also diagram at *brazier kiln*.

(1) David Roberts lifting one of his big pots from a top-hat kiln *and*
(2) plunging it into a bin for reduction. Note tongs adapted to hold pot inside the neck.

A special muffle or saggar, coil built in a well-grogged clay, for use with a top-loading kiln to enable it to be used safely for raku firing. The first photo shows the saggar itself, the second in place in the kiln. The wide flanged rim gives space which prevents the elements over-heating. When firing, of course, the lid is lifted by means of a metal hook or tongs – not the finger!

RARE EARTH

Actually these are neither very rare nor 'earths' (they are true metals); they are the elements numbers 57–71 in the *periodic table*. A few are coming into use in ceramics, though mainly as prepared pigments. Praseodymium yellow will fire to 1300°C. Others are used in optical glasses but may well become available to craft potters.

RASORITE

Listed as B_2O_3 66.3, Na_2O 30.0 i.e. a form of borax.

RATIONAL FORMULA, analysis

The description of a material in terms of its *oxides* in a *formula*, or its *minerals* in an analysis. Thus *feldspar* can be written as $K_2.Al_2.SiO_{16}$ or, as its rational formula $K_2O: Al_2O_3: 6SiO_2$. From the latter one can associate the mineral with the Seger *formula* to arrive at some idea of its reaction in the fire. A rational or 'calculated' analysis will list the probable minerals present, and is used for rocks and clays. Cardew PP Appendix 10 gives the method for arriving at a calculated analysis from an 'ultimate' or oxide one. Shaw considers rational formulas to be of little value to craft potters but the information helps to build up an overall picture of the material.

RAW CLAY

Green clay; unfired clay.

RAW GLAZE

A glaze in which none of the constituents are fritted. The term 'raw-glazing' is often confusingly applied to *once-fired* ware, where the term 'raw-clay glazing' would be more accurate.

(For further information see under *once-fired ware*.)

REACTIVE SLIP

A fusible slip which will start to melt before the covering glaze and thus will 'burn' through it. Potclays issue a series for firing at around 1200°C.

RECIPE

A list of materials, with proportional physical weights, which make up a specific slip, glaze, body, or color. Distinct from the *formula* which is expressed in theoretical atomic or *molecular parts*. *Percentage weights* are preferable to batches for comparing one weight with another.

Beginners in pottery are often hopeful that a good glaze recipe will solve their problems. However the recipe is only one (albeit a prime one) of the variables which affect the fired glaze. Others include the particular samples of raw materials used, the speed of firing, and the body on which it is put.

Trials and alterations may be necessary to arrive at a mixture which will suit your unique conditions. Some knowledge of the principles on which the recipe is based will prove invaluable: the first step towards preparing your own individual glazes. (See *chemistry of pottery*, etc).

RECIPE-INTO-FORMULA

A recipe will give some idea of the possible behavior of a glaze but the *Seger formula* will be more instructive and may be compared with those of known glazes.

The chart used for the computation is the reverse of that used in *formula-into-recipe* and, for simplicity, the formulas used are the 'ideal' ones. The results are therefore approximate. Greater accuracy would demand an analysis of your particular samples, and would involve much more arithmetic although the principle still holds good. There are several variations on the system. See also Cardew PP Appendix 10.

In the first column we list the recipe figures followed by the mineral or oxide they represent. This figure is then divided by the *molecular* (or unit) weight of the material; the resultant figure representing the unity figure in the formula, the alumina in clay for instance, or the potash in feldspar. This figure is entered in the appropriate column and multiplied in the others according to the formula ratio, e.g. clay, 1 alumina to 2 silica; feldspar, 1 alumina to 1 potash to 6 silica.

In the illustrative charts overleaf the examples dealt with under *formula-into-recipe* are reversed.

To bring the figures to the Seger formula:
1 Total the bases.
2 Divide each of the totals in the base line by this figure.
3 Arrange as $RO.R_2O_3.RO_2$.

RECORDS, workshop

Some records, such as the total sales of work produced, are required by law and you will also need proof of expenditure to set against income from sales (see *costing*.) The extent of your additional records depends on your temperament and style of work. Kiln logs are useful and can save worry and spoilt firings. Tests and trials of materials and glazes will be a waste of time without adequate records. One's memory is fallible and one doubts it most when the unexpected occurs.

It is not practicable to record all the factors which influence a result but the mere note of recipe and temperature is not quite enough. The following data will enable a fair appraisal to be made

1 A test number for identification; a running number with or without a prefix. Codes are apt to get muddled or forgotten.

2 Percentage recipe and the amount actually weighed.

The batch can be divided into fluid measures to facilitate future additions, line blends etc.

3 Type of test piece—cylinder, tile etc. and whether fired flat or upright.

4 Body color and texture.

5 Glaze thickness; vital in the appearance of the glaze.

RECIPE-INTO-FORMULA—Chart A (Reverse of formula-into-recipe, Chart A)

%	Material	Parts	÷	Mol. wt.	=	Mol. parts	PbO	Al₂O₃	SiO₂
50.2	Litharge	50.2	÷	223	=	0.225	0.225		
17.4	China clay	17.4	÷	258	=	0.0675		0.0675	0.1350
32.4	Flint	32.4	÷	60	=	0.540			0.540
100.0				TOTALS			0.225	0.0675	0.675
	Molecular equivalents						1.0	0.3	3.0

RECIPE-INTO-FORMULA—Chart B (Reverse of formula-into-recipe, Chart B)

%	Material	Parts	÷	Mol. wt.	=	Mol. parts	PbO	Al₂O₃	SiO₂
70.5	Lead sesquisilicate	70.5	÷	313	=	0.225	0.225		0.337
17.4	China clay	17.4	÷	258	=	0.0675		0.0675	0.135
12.1	Flint	12.1	÷	60	=	0.202			0.202
100.0		100.0		TOTALS			0.225	0.0675	0.674
	Molecular equivalents						1.0	0.3	3.0

RECIPE-INTO-FORMULA—Chart C (Reverse of formula-into-recipe, Chart C)

%	Material	Parts	÷	Mol. wt.	=	Mol. parts	K₂O	CaO	MgO	Al₂O₃	SiO₂	TiO₂
48.47	Feldspar	48.47	÷	556	=	0.087	0.087			0.087	0.522	
14.53	Whiting	14.53	÷	100	=	0.145		0.145				
5.34	Dolomite	5.34	÷	184	=	0.029		0.029	0.029			
1.5	China clay	1.5	÷	258	=	0.006				0.006	0.012	
25.52	Quartz	25.52	÷	60	=	0.425					0.425	
4.64	Titania	4.64	÷	80	=	0.058						0.058
100.0		100.0		TOTALS			0.087	0.174	0.029	0.093	0.959	0.058
	Molecular equivalents						0.3	0.6	0.1	0.32	3.3	0.2

6 Position in kiln.

7 Kiln and firing as *kiln log*.

For the recording of clay tests see under *clay testing*. Briefly the record should be of plasticity and workability; soluble materials; shrinkage; raw and fired colors; absorption; deformation and faults and the behavior of glaze on sample. Other useful records can be kept of weights of clay for reproduction items, with their size and shape. (See *card measure*.)

RED CLAY

An iron-bearing *secondary clay*. Includes brick clays. Although called 'red' clay its fired color is brown or terracotta. It is present in vast quantities and a great variety of qualities all over the earth's surface.

A potter needs a plastic but not sticky clay, fairly smooth and with a shrinkage within 12% plastic-to-fired. It should contain negligible 'free' impurities such as lime fragments and soluble alkalis.

The fine particle size adds to the plasticity but also lowers the *fluxing* temperature, and red clays are normally used only for earthenwares, notably slip-wares. In England the Etruria marls are well-known high-iron clays some of which, from the Staffordshire region, will stand up to 1260°C. in an oxidizing fire without serious trouble. They are vitrified and 'self-glazed' at this temperature. In *reduction* red clays will generally fail or melt as the iron is turned to its fusible *ferrous* state.

Red clay may be added to other clays, and also to glazes to provide iron in an ultra-fine form. In stoneware glaze it also provides valuable fluxes, and up to 50% can be used. 5–10% of a suitable red clay in a stoneware body can lessen the possibility of *shattering* during cooling in the kiln or afterwards. A body of 7 parts Potclays Buff Body to 1 part of their Staffs red clay in oxidation at 1230–1260°C. gives the hardest, most unchippable body I have known for tableware and other purposes. *Slip glazes* are high-clay glazes or are composed mainly of very fusible clays such as *Albany clay*. Local red clays may be useful as pigments.

RED COLOR AND GLAZE

Reduced copper reds are the only true reds available to the studio potter at 1100°C. or over, although red colors (often nearer purple or terracotta) are becoming available in this range and also up to 1300°C. Various red glazes appear in merchants' catalogs for lower temperature firing under careful conditions up to about 1050°C. Most are opaque. The standard, slightly purplish red up to around 1140°C. is *chrome-tin pink*.

Selenium is a comparatively new oxide and with cadmium will give orange and red but the compound is difficult to stabilize and is subject to *volatilization*. Research is improving the performance of these frits. Chromium oxide at around 900°C. in a high-lead low-alumina glaze will produce red. A possible recipe: white lead 66%, china clay 10%, flint 21%, soda ash 3%, with 3% chrome or 5% potassium bichromate. Until recently uranium has been unobtainable but is now appearing again as 'spent' uranium. It is a source of orange-reds up to 1020°C. A *chrome-tin* reaction will give pinks, as will zircon-iron compounds at higher stoneware temperatures (Dodd).

Iron reds rely on undissolved crystals of Fe_2O_3 which are difficult to maintain in the fired glaze. Cardew recommends a pure nepheline in the batch (C.PP 145) with a high-alumina, low-calcium formula. Rhodes reverses this advice. In Cardew's type however the color is from an undissolved suspension within the glaze, while the latter is derived from precipitated surface crystals. The glazes need applying fairly thickly. Formulas quoted in Cardew PP include

$$K_2O \quad 0.8 \qquad Al_2O_3 \quad 1.17$$
$$Na_2O \quad 0.2 \qquad Fe_2O_3 \quad 0.05 \qquad SiO_2 \quad 5.35$$

Difficult to transform into a recipe. The use of an alkaline frit may help.

A recipe suggested by Peter Smith, and which approaches the formula is:

Nepheline Syenite	42%
Potash feldspar	35%
Fremington red clay	20%
China clay	3%

Another recipe for iron red appeared in CM 37/20 (John Reeve). The calcium content controls the ability of the glaze to dissolve the iron oxide. Potterycrafts make a high-temperature iron/zirconium red; Ivo Mosley suggests adding as much as 60% to an underglaze slip.

Soaking and slow cooling to 1000°C. are reputed to help. The aesthetic attraction of a bright red on craft ceramics is open to doubt even if it becomes easily available. Of course it is always possible to use *enamels* which exhibit a very fine range of reds. Geoffrey Whiting has produced a persimmon red at 1200°C. in an electric kiln by varying the temperature rise, a method known to the Japanese as 'fire change'. Details have not been published. Titanium is reputed to enhance the redness of iron in very fluid glazes.

(See also *ash glaze, kaki glaze, oxidised stoneware glaze,* the last for a broken-red 1250°C. recipe.)

RED LEAD

Lead peroxide Pb_3O_4, 685 (equivalent weight 228). Also known as 'minium'. Poisonous. A strong flux in a glaze. Although forbidden in schools or potteries where assistants are employed, it can still be used with great care by the studio potter. Traditional slipware glazes used red lead and it figures in several of the older raku glaze recipes by Leach and others.

RED PIGMENT

Similar considerations apply to red pigments as to red glazes: they are plentiful in the enamel range and below 1000°C. Underglaze reds include the ubiquitous *chrome-tin* sometimes with vanadium. Above 1050°C. most compounds revert to brown, but there are prepared fritted colors from iron/vanadium and other compounds for use at stoneware temperatures. (See *red color and glaze*.)

RED SLIP, body

Like red clay this is brown rather than red and is normally a simple liquid red clay. Lighter colored slips and bodies can be stained with iron oxides or with prepared body *stains*, often iron-based, to give red-browns, pinks, and 'coral' up to as high as 1280°C. These need a white body to develop their color.

REDUCTION

The extraction of *oxygen atoms* from *oxides*. The most startling color changes in reduction are those of the iron and copper oxides. More subtle alterations take place in other oxides, in the glaze quality and in bodies. The reduced oxides are usually unstable and will revert to their 'higher' oxide unless protected from the air by dispersal in a glaze. Precipitated iron will re-oxidize (see *kaki*, and *red color and glaze*).

Reduction is generally considered to be the result of starving the fuel of oxygen during the firing, creating *carbon monoxide* and *hydrocarbon gases*. CO is a very poisonous gas and kiln rooms should be well ventilated. David Ketteridge (CR 12) mentions reduction by hydrogen as it forms water with oxygen 'stolen' from the glaze oxides, e.g. $Fe_2O_3 + H_2 = 2FeO + H_2O$, or elemental carbon by a simple equation yielding the metal and CO. This contradicts several accepted theories including that of the negative role of smoke. Searle in PQ 8 lists CO, H, coal gas, incompletely burned oil and finely divided carbon in luminous flames as the chief reducing agents. The wide variety of results from 'reduction' suggests that more consideration should be given to the fundamental chemistry. The CO/CO_2 and the H_2/H_2O ratios control the degree of reduction (together with elemental carbon) and it is possible to measure the atmosphere with instruments placed in the kiln or the chimney flues, now available to the studio potter, e.g. from Glendale. (See *oxygen/carbon sensor*.) The reduction in a kiln is normally sufficient to produce only the ferrous iron oxide FeO, but copper oxide is easily reduced to the metal under certain conditions, (see *luster*). The moisture given off by burning fuel helps to develop celadons. It has been noticed that a humid day is better for reduction than a dry one.

Reducing atmospheres are built up by the adjustment of *primary* and *secondary* air controls, judicious use of the *damper*, and sometimes the extraction of chimney bricks to cut down the draft. Reduction started before 800°C. may stain the glaze gray or black which subsequent firing will fail to burn away. During reduction the fuel is inadequately burned and the temperature may fall; reducing periods are therefore interspersed with clear-fire conditions. With wood or coal firing, each stoking tends to set up reducing conditions willy-nilly. Alternatively a semi-reducing atmosphere can be maintained from about 1000°C. so long as the temperature can be steadily increased.

Other cycles have been recommended: Ray Finch reduces for 55 minutes of every hour from 1000–1240°C. but not sufficiently fiercely to prevent a steady rise in heat, then continuously until the peak temperature is reached, soaking for half an hour in *oxidation*. Some potters maintain a neutral atmosphere from 1050°C. with a reduction at the end; or give half-an-hour of reduction at 1000, 1100 and 1200°C. Shaw mentions reduction starting at top temperature and continuing during cooling to 800°C.

The weather has its effect. I have found that a still, bright fine day is more conducive to success than a dull or windy one. It does not seem to matter whether or not one 'cleans' the kiln at the close with an oxidizing fire. When a kiln is reducing, flame may appear at cracks and spy holes wherever the gases come into contact with free oxygen. Any sign of 'escape' should be ignited to reduce the danger from carbon monoxide. Beware gas burners 'blowing back' into the pipes: turn off and re-light if this happens.

Glazes can be reduced in a neutral atmosphere, e.g. in an electric kiln, by means of local reducing agents incorporated into the glaze batch itself. Soot, charcoal, animal charcoal, and silicon carbide can be used, the last mentioned being the least effective. A fairly viscous glaze is needed to prevent re-oxidation. The more fluid the glaze the more reducing agent is needed. The amount will vary with the kiln as well as the glaze and experiments should be made with additions of between

10% and 20% to the batch. Copper and iron will respond to this type of reduction (Peter Smith). In electric kiln reduction, two outlets, one lower front and the other top back are advisable in order to direct the reducing agent right through the pack, with the top outlet controllable.

Stephen Coulsting reduces with gas in an electric kiln, heavily at 1050°C. and at intervals with decreasing strength to 1210°C. then continuing the firing to 1310°C. He suggests a number of inlets, including the floor. Care must be taken not to introduce the gas at temperatures below 1000°C. in order to avoid minor explosions. He recommends butane as a rapid reduction agent, though propane and natural gas are possible. Details in CR 88.

Nitrogen piped into an electric kiln or, preferably, a closed saggar, can maintain an 'inert' atmosphere and, if iron is introduced into the glaze as black iron oxide, FeO, it will not reoxidise and a 'reduced' effect can be obtained. The system, however, would prove expensive. For checking the CO levels in any type of kiln there are meters which register the gas, normally used by garages to test exhaust gases; also Gendale sell an oxygen sensor.

Kiln furniture will be affected by reduction and it is advisable to check with the manufacturers that it is suitable. Cast props are very vulnerable. Shelves need to be thicker: $\frac{3}{4}$ in. (18 mm.) for alumina or silliminite bats, slightly less for silicon carbide. Obviously a *refractory* body must be used for pots, often a ball clay strengthened with fireclay, china clay, and flint. Few red clays will stand up and all are more liable to fail during reduction than in oxidation. A proportion of red clay—usually about 5% through this varies widely—can aid vitrification and warm the body color, a darker body often giving improved glaze color. In glazes the red ferric iron is most commonly used. 2% or less for celadons; up to 12% for other effects (see *temmoku, kaki*), black iron oxide, crocus martis, ochres, and other forms of iron have also been used with good results. Reduced iron may be the spinel $FeO.Fe_2O_3$ (the formula for 'magnetic' iron).

Reduction is a skill which can be learned only with practice in your particular kiln. A kiln log is essential. In an electric kiln reduction is usually a trial activity only, although the development of *silicon carbide elements* widens the scope as has already been mentioned. Porcelain has responded to small sticks of wood about 5 in. (125 mm.) long and $\frac{1}{4}$ in. (6 mm.) square inserted into the lower spyhole during the last half hour of firing, giving a gentle greeny-buff color to a $1\frac{1}{2}$% iron glaze at 1270°C. *Kanthal* wire will stand occasional reduction without damage (or even regular reduction according to some potters). (See also *electric kiln, Kanthal.*)

Copper reduction will take place at lower temperatures than iron: 600–800°C. for producing copper-red *enamels* and *lusters*. It may be taken to the extreme of producing the metal by the same method as on-glaze painting and in *raku* firings. $\frac{1}{2}$% of copper, or less, is added to a glaze for high temperature reds. See *copper red*. Cobalt is not altered; manganese may produce a gray, or green.

Peter Smith has kindly made available the following recipes for reduction glazes in a neutral atmosphere:

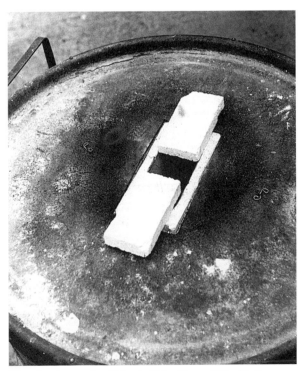

The simple gas-fired kiln, built by Steve Mills (Bath Pottery, U.K.) shown at top-hat kiln *is frequently used for raku firing but also for cone 9 reduction firings (1285°C); the atmosphere controlled by this equally uncomplicated vent in the lid, constructed of pieces of cut brick. Following a fast rise to top temperature, cooling is slower and accompanied by prolonged reduction.*

Feldspar	72	
Whiting	13	
China clay	7	A green matt
Flint	8	tableware glaze
Calcium phosphate	5	(bone ash)
Charcoal	8%	of total
Ferric oxide	3%	of total

233

Use animal charcoal if available as it contains calcium phosphate. This recipe gives a celadon type glaze without the calcium phosphate:

Fremington red		
clay	28.2	
Cornish		
stone	28.2	A viscous celadon
Whiting	21.1	type glaze.
Flint	7	
Ball clay	14.1	
Ochre	1.4	

plus 10% of charcoal, coal-dust, or graphite.

The above glaze is viscous but can be made shiny by the addition of 10% flint or quartz. The reducing agent should then be increased by 5–10%.

Add extra iron for temmoku.

RE-FIRING

A second glaze firing for faulty ware is seldom successful. The glaze may change its whole character on re-fire, only very occasionally for the good. In all cases it is advisable to re-coat the pot with glaze, or to rub it well into crawling etc. Use a thick glaze mixture, and warm the pot before re-dipping. Repeated re-firing will destroy the fabric of a pot.

REFRACTORIES

Heat-resisting materials used in those parts of the kiln which must stand high temperature and reduction without deforming or spoiling: bricks, tiles, shelves, supports, saggars, etc. The term is most often applied to the bricks.

High grade fireclays, high alumina bodies, and silicon carbide are some common materials. Special types are made from chrome ore, etc. The official rating of a refractory is a P.C.E. of 18 or above. Ciment Fondu is a refractory cement for use up to 1320°C. Some refractories are also designed to insulate—the lightweight bricks used in electric kilns for instance—others such as silicon carbide shelves to conduct heat.

Study of the alumina-silica *eutectic* will show why high alumina refractories are preferred. Even though a material whose make-up approaches the eutectic is way above our working temperatures, a certain degree of *pyroplastic* movement is always likely because of small amounts of impurities which lower the melting point. Refractories need a long soaking fire to develop a mat of *mullite* needles throughout the fabric. (See also *bricks, fireclay*, etc.)

REFRACTORY MATERIALS

Applied to oxides or minerals which are heat-resistant in their own right or which tend to raise the firing temperature of a glaze. The *acidic* oxides are considered refractory, especially silica, tin oxide, titania, chrome, zirconia and antimony. Zinc and boron have ambiguous positions. Alumina in molecular proportions greater than 1–8 compared with silica has a refractory effect. Lime has a very high melting point (2615°C.) but acts as a base in high temperature glazes above 1200°C. Barium has a similar role.

REGENERATIVE PRINCIPLE

In kiln design: the use of heat given off by cooling ware to pre-heat other chambers. The *climbing kiln* is very efficient in utilizing heat. A regenerative brick kiln is illustrated in Rhodes K 53.

RELIEF DECORATION

See *applied decoration, boss, sprigging.*

REPAIRING POTTERY

For broken pots the most commonly used glue is Araldite. Equal amounts from two tubes are mixed on a wooden surface with a wooden tool. As the glue takes several hours to harden, some method must be found to hold the join tight together meanwhile. Adhesive tape, string, clamps, and rough 'molds' are possible depending on the size and shape of the piece. If several breaks are involved it is better to do the job two or more stages. For earthenwares a less permanent and quicker drying glue is sufficient, but whichever is used wash, dry, and dust any loose pieces from the break before sticking. When the join comes together make absolutely certain that the faces are flush with one another; run your finger gently along the join to feel for any step. The glue must be used thinly and care should be taken not to let it set on the surface. Contact glues are less satisfactory as there is no second chance once the pieces are pressed together.

A good join will scarcely show but if the surface is broken then it will need filling with Polyfilla or something similar. The colors can be matched in water paint and touched in. For glazed ware the join can be carefully worked over with nail varnish using a fine brush. The riveting of pottery is now seldom practised.

For cracks or pre-firing damage see *stopping* and *mending*. A remarkable claim is made by Susan Bennett in Fournier PT that hairline cracks incurred after the glaze fire by careless handling may heal in a subsequent refire.

REPETITION THROWING

While many believe that the role of the craft potter lies in producing the one-off piece, the basis of much professional work is the repetition throwing of tableware, etc. It is a test of ability to control clay on the wheel, and each piece can still be given its due quota of care and attention.

A 'set' does not involve the absolute uniformity of the industrial product but rather a family resemblance and an identity of feeling and character. This is easier to achieve with a distinctive shape and color than with a simple, more anonymous form. There is more to matching pieces than mere design: the clay mix, the weight, the throwing method (movements and pressures) and the surface spirals are all fundamental to the result. Take care to control the base thickness and, of course, the finished size which can be checked with *calipers, a card measure*, or a *pot gauge*. Allow half a dozen trials before starting the actual group or run. Do not change your wheel or throwing position. Use clay balls of equal softness.

When turning, handling, etc, follow the same rules and do the whole group at one session, endeavoring to establish a rhythm of work and movement. Practice each stage on your trial pieces and use the same tools, etc, throughout. Variations in the details of decoration can add interest providing that a good match has been achieved in the early stages.

There is great satisfaction, in addition to technical development, to be obtained from repetition throwing, which is not so different from the creation of the 'one-off' piece as some imagine.

RESIDUAL CLAY

There is some disagreement on the use of this term. Many authorities use it as a synonym for primary clay. Cardew, however, links it with sedimentary clay; a clay that has been leached or weathered to remove impurities, e.g. fireclay.

RESISTANCE WIRE

All materials set up some resistance to the flow of electricity. This is measured in ohms. The wire for kiln elements (Kanthal, nichrome, etc.) is made in various grades and thicknesses which offer greater or lesser resistance, as measured in ohms per foot run. The greater the length of any given wire the less current will flow, while an increase in diameter will increase current flow. (See also *electricity, electric kiln wiring, Kanthal, silicon carbide*.)

RESIST METHOD

Resist techniques are essentially methods of obtaining a design with a colored background as opposed to a colored stroke on a plain background. The resist agent can be wax or paper or flat objects such as leaves. The

Repetition throwing on the grand scale in the workshop of Richard Batterham.

Delicately resisted glaze 'landscapes' on porcelain by Val Barry.

material to be 'resisted' can be slip, pigment, or glaze. Paper is more suitable for slip. (See *paper resist, wax resist.*) On a more mundane level wax can resist the glaze on foot rings, lid flanges, etc., when dipping pots. (See *wax.*)

RHEOLOGY

The science of flow and deformation. These are crucial factors in the behavior of pottery materials under heat. Also applied to flow characteristics of plastic clay and casting slips.

RHYOLITE

A medium or fine-grained glassy acidic rock in the granite bracket but containing less iron oxide.

RIB

A wooden or metal tool for smoothing or assisting in the throwing of a pot on the wheel. So called because the older potters used a bone for this purpose. Ribs often have one flat and one curved edge and are made of a flat sheet of a rigid material. Isaac Button cut himself ribs from an old spade, but they may also be of wood—sycamore, box, obeche, bamboo etc. They are normally used on the outside of a pot to minimize throwing ridges. Average size about 3 × 4 in. (75 × 100 mm.). A pliable *steel palette* can sometimes be useful.

(2) Using a bamboo rib during the latter stages of throwing for trimming the base of a pot on the wheel.

RICE HULLS

Rice husks burnt to an ash yield 96% and more of silica. Where they are plentiful (e.g. Italy) they may be used in the manufacture of *refractories.*

RIDDLE

A coarse-mesh sieve. A garden riddle can be used for separating the larger particles from the finer ones when dealing with crushed rocks, wood ash, etc. A cook's nylon sieve is useful for the initial breaking up of weighed-up glaze materials (in water, of course).

RIM

The top edge of a pot or bowl.

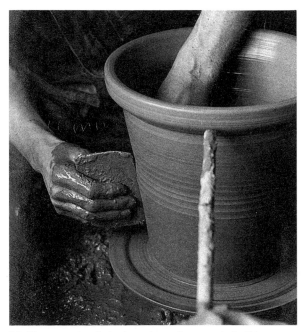

(1) The use of a rib in throwing a flowerpot; in this case it is merely an oblong piece of iron cut from an old spade.

The rim is more than a simple termination of the form and should have shape and character of its own. It should therefore be carefully considered in all cases; a weak rim can spoil a good piece. The rim can even become the focal point of interest as in this 'stepped' rim on a strongly formed bowl by Rachel Northam.

A manipulated rim which gives interest and character to a simple form. By Geoffrey Fuller.

ROCK

The earth's crust is made up of minerals and rocks. Rocks are usually conglomerates of minerals and have no *ideal formula*. They are not necessarily hard; clay, to a *petrologist*, is soft rock. The minerals in a rock may be detectable with the unaided eye, e.g. the mica in granite. Rocks are graded according to their base/silica content into basic, intermediate, and acid rocks. The first are dark in color, 'heavy' or dense, and fine grained; volcanic *basalt* is characteristic. Acid rocks tend to be lighter in color, coarser grained and with a lower specific gravity. *Granite*, the mother rock of feldspar and kaolinite, is the commonest. The syenites (nepheline) are intermediate. One may liken the acid rocks to the body of a pot and the basic rocks to the glaze. A rough color guide to the iron content of a rock has been given as: less than 1.5%, a very pale blue; 1–1%, light green; 2–2.5%, olive green; 5–10%, black.

RO GROUP

The symbol for the total of *bases* in a *glaze formula*, R indicating any suitable element and also covering the R_2 alkalis. The RO is kept at unity for easy comparison with the *amphoterics* and *acids*. (See *Seger formula*.)

ROLLED INLAY

A method of decoration in which a pattern or design is cut from thin slabs of colored clay, laid onto a clay sheet of a contrasting color, and pressed into the surface with a rolling pin. Coils can also be used in place of slabs though with rather less control. The technique was originated, as far as I have been able to verify, by Sheila Fournier in an article in PQ No 10 (1956). Sabina

Jack Doherty with his thrown variation on rolled inlay: in this case the colored clay motifs are adhered with slip to a thick-walled, partly formed pot and then thrown into the main body of the piece.
(1) and (2) In the first picture he is applying the inlays to a half-thrown pot; in the second photograph throwing is continued, and the wall made smooth and flat.
(3) Shows an early stage in the similar treatment of a bowl.

Teuteberg rolls colored clay designs into slabs with a mechanical roller, transfers the decorated slabs to molds and forms her tablewares by *jigger and jolley*, details in CR 100. (See also illustrations for a similar system of *thrown inlay*.)

ROLLING CLAY

Rolled slabs of clay are needed for a number of techniques: dishes, slab pots, etc and these are more likely to fire successfully if the slabs are made in a craftsmanlike way.

Use a dry cloth for rolling on: a fine hessian or some material which will stretch a little but not crease easily. It should have no knots or bad faults. Check that the cloth is laid on a surface which is smooth and free from grit or pieces of clay. Start with a well-wedged bubble-free block of clay beaten out to the general shape you require for the finished slab (e.g. a round block for a circular dish). Beat with the fist or palm to about $\frac{3}{4}$ in. (20 mm.) thick. At this stage, and at all future stages, give the clay and cloth an occasional quarter turn and also lift the slab from the cloth and let it down again to prevent it from working into the weave. If the clay really sticks to the cloth it cannot stretch any more. Using a good wooden rolling pin long enough for the work in hand, roll with a firm steady pressure and avoid thinning the edges. Turning the slab as mentioned above will help to maintain a level surface. Thickness can be gauged with the eye, or an edge cut through with a needle awl to show thickness.

Guide sticks can be used. These are strips of wood about 1 in. (25 mm.) wide, as thick as the slab you require, and a little longer than the widest part of the slab. The sticks are used only in the latter stages of rolling. If bubbles appear these must be sliced through

The use of laths of wood to control the thickness of a rolled slab means that one can adjust the thickness to suit the work in hand. It is also easier to roll with deeper laths to start the process and to replace them with thinner guides as the work proceeds.

with a needle and not merely pricked. Make sure that your rolling pin is not warped. Door knobs or other circular pieces of wood on the ends of rolling pins can be used in place of sticks as slab thickness controls.

Today more potters are using mechanical rollers such as those supplied by Cromartie and other potters' merchants. These are fast and accurate but, like all mechanical devices, may eventually have their effect on the finished product. (See also *hollow mold*.)

Door knobs or small wooden wheels can be attached to a rolling pin as shown to control clay slab thickness as an alternative to guide sticks.

ROLLING PIN

A straight, wooden rolling pin at least 14–16 in. (35–40 cm.) long is required for pottery. Do not leave the pin on a damp surface where it will warp—hang it up.

ROLLING PIN POT

A rolling pin (or a cardboard cylinder) can be used as a mold or former for cylindrical pots. Wrap a sheet of paper round the roller and tape the edges. Roll out your slab in fairly damp clay and ease it round the cylinder. The joint can be pinched together forming a ribbed pattern, overlapped, or bevelled and joined flat. The base may be luted on at the time of making or later when the pot is leather-hard (the base clay must be in a similar condition to the pot, of course). After an hour or so remove the rolling pin but leave the paper lining in the pot. The lining will have sufficient strength to hold the pot upright but will crease as the pot dries and shrinks; it can be removed as soon as the cylinder will stand unaided, or left in and fired away in the kiln.

2

3

6

4

7

5

In fact this pot is being made round a card cylinder but the principle is the same as when using a rolling pin.
(1) and (2) A sheet of paper is wrapped round the cylinder and fastened.
(3) and (4) An oblong slab of clay is cut to the height of the pot, and the width measured by folding it over the cylinder.
(5) and (6) The joint can be made in a variety of ways: overlapped; with slanting lapped cuts which can be worked into an invisible join; or, as shown here, the two ends slipped and fastened together in a pattern of pinches.
(7) A base is cut to size and luted on.
(8) Finally the card cylinder is removed, leaving the paper lining as a support until the pot is dry enough to stand on its own.

8

ROULETTE

A tool for producing a repeat decorative impressed pattern. The technique is of great antiquity. A roulette is an engraved wheel or cylinder which, when rolled over clay, produces the pattern. It was much used by Roman potters. 'The edges of old English ovenware dishes were notched by this means' (Leach). In the film 'Isaac Button, country potter', Isaac Button is seen impressing the name of his pottery as a continuous band round flower-pots. Ladi Kwali rolled a carved roulette round the shoulder of her pots, combining it with free pattern (see also the film 'Ladi Kwali').

The most readily available roulette 'blank' is a piece of blackboard chalk, which can easily be carved with a simple pattern. Biscuit rollers can be mounted onto a wire handle or onto a forked twig with a piece of thick wire. Roulette wheels can be shaped for concave and convex surfaces.

(1) An engraved stick of chalk used as a roulette, rolled over a soft clay surface to produce a repeat pattern.

(2) A large roulette wheel with full address both advertises the Pottery (Isaac Button at Soil Hill) and decorates the pot.

A simple roulette wheel, which could be of pottery, plaster, or wood, and mounted on a wire or other form of axle so that it can be rolled over plastic clay to impress a repeat pattern or motif.

RUBBER RESIST

Rubber can be used in a liquid form as a resist material, see *latex resist*.

RUN SLIP

One of the slipware techniques. The *slip* is trailed in blobs around one edge of a dish or on the shoulder of a pot, usually on a wet base-slip of a contrasting color. A shake will run the blots across the dish or down the sides of a pot, giving pleasant, liquid shapes. In a bowl, a sideways twist can give variety. Some practice is required and the shaking should be restrained. The comparative consistencies of the background and trailed slip will directly influence the resulting pattern.

(1) A leather-hard dish is flooded with slip and immediately trailed with blobs of contrasting color round one edge.

(2) Without delay the dish is held vertically and the blobs given two or three sharp downward shakes. Triangular dishes are especially suitable but all shapes can be used.

(3) A completed dish.

RUST

Hydrated iron oxide, $2Fe_2O_3, 3H_2O$.

Actual rust can be scaled from iron and used for decorative purposes; beating it into the surface of a piece, or adding to glazes and slips.

RUTILE

One of the crystalline forms of titania. To a chemist rutile is synonymous with titania, TiO_2, but to a potter it indicates the impure iron-bearing ore of titanium, an accessory mineral of *igneous rocks*. Also occurs as ilmenite beach sands, $FeTiO_3$.

The distinctive mottled appearance of rutile in borax glazes has led to its use ad nauseam on commercial tiles, etc. The titanium content will opacify a glaze. Small amounts (1–3%) of rutile are useful in modifying other pigments in earthenware and stoneware glazes. In reduction, rutile may give a bluish glaze.

SADDLE

An item of *kiln furniture*. A bar of *refractory* material used to support tiles, etc during firing. In section it is a concave triangle. Supplied in sizes 1–11 in. (25–280 mm.) long by $\frac{3}{8}$–$\frac{3}{4}$ in. (10–20 mm.) across.

A saddle, used during firing to support tiles or wide-based pots which are not glazed beneath the foot. Most kiln furniture of this type (spurs, etc) are suitable only up to the higher earthenware temperatures. Check with supplier.

SAGGAR

A clay box in which pottery is fired to protect the ware from flame and ash. Used in larger kilns as the unit of a bung. The box is made of well consolidated refractory clay with up to 50% graded grog. It can be coiled, slab built round a drum, formed on the wheel using soft clay and a rib, or by a combination of thumping and throwing. Industrial saggars may also be jolleyed or cast. Wall thicknesses average about $\frac{3}{4}$ in. (20 mm.). Saggars may be oval, circular, oblong, or square (but always with rounded corners). The industrial norm is a 17 × 23 in. (420 × 575 mm.) oval but they come in all sizes and thickness of wall. For some purposes they have holes in the sides. With the coming of cleaner fuels, smaller kilns, and 'continuous' firing the use of the saggar has declined sharply and it is becoming difficult to purchase them.

The striking result of 'saggar firing' on a pot by John Leach. He stands a pot on a bed of sawn-wood dust in a saggar, then packs further sawdust around it, sometimes adding straw or even rolled newspaper. The level of the packed material controls the misty white line to some extent. The saggar is made as airtight as possible with a lid and wads and the whole fired in a reduced stoneware kiln. The chamber temperature is around 1290°C but the actual pot is insulated by the carbonized sawdust and, surprisingly, remains slightly porous; having been subjected to no more the 1100°C. at the most. Carbon, in the absence of air, is very refractory and is also one of nature's insulators.

SAGGAR CLAY

A *refractory* mixture of clay and grog, the latter may be in proportions of 50% or more. The inclusion of grog from broken used saggars is useful. The 'dust' should be removed from the grog. The clay content is generally fireclay, but the inclusion of some vitrifiable clay will set up a liquid phase which will help the growth of *mullite* crystals. *Sillimanite* is a useful addition. Up to a point saggars will get stronger with firing. Cardew discusses the problems involved in making saggars in PP 158–60.

SAIRSET

A commercial name for an *air-setting* kiln *cement* or mortar for jointing bricks or facing walls.

SALT

Common salt is sodium chloride, NaCl, a colorless, *soluble crystalline* substance. It is believed to assist glaze *suspension* but its main use in ceramics is in the production of *salt glaze*. The re-crystallization of salt in cruets can cause trouble: a *crazed* earthenware glaze will allow dissolved salt to permeate the body and it may lift the glaze away.

A chemical salt is a compound: the reaction of an *acid* with a *base*, e.g. sodium sulfate, barium chloride, etc. A glaze may be considered as a salt, or as a salt into which additional material is dissolved. Salts are, in general, more stable than their separate constituents.

SALT GLAZE

Stoneware ceramics, generally once-fired, with a glaze achieved by throwing common salt or rock salt onto the hot fuel, normally at around 1200°C. and upwards (but see note below). The NaCl decomposes into chlorine gas and sodium, the latter reacting with the silica of the clay to form a thin, slightly orange-peel textured glaze which is very hard and resistant to corrosion. Developed in Germany, it went out of favor for tableware around 1760, its use since confined mainly to cheap jars, bottles, and drainage materials. Several craftsmen potters are now reviving the technique, which produces a very integrated and interestingly variable finish. The degree of glaze texture will depend on the grain size of the clay body. A fine, white stoneware body will show a correspondingly fine 'orange peel'; a porcelain will be even smoother.

A *siliceous* clay or a wash of silica slip has been recommended, although alumina is also needed. More complete glazes, or *ash*, can be applied, the salt being used as an additional flux. Borax additions will produce a thicker and more lustrous glaze but at the expense of the typical texture. Carbonates of copper, etc thrown onto the fire have been reported to produce psychedelic color. Anne Shattock uses stains (Mason Stain Co. U.S.A.) in slips to produce colored salt glaze in a neutral atmosphere (CR 95). Some Potterycraft stains are also suitable. Mary Rich uses lusters over her salt-glazed pieces.

A good deal of modern salt-glazed ware is decorated in subdued colors which, though attractive, can be somewhat at odds with the powerful surface/color textures of salt glaze on stoneware. A milder color break in the glaze itself, e.g. on a finer-grained body, would help.

Most fuelled kilns (i.e. other than electric) which have a reasonable chimney to carry away the chlorine fumes, can be utilised for salt glaze. The Wren family developed small coke and gas kilns to produce excellent salt glaze. Hamada used the technique for several years. Once a kiln has been used for salt glaze it cannot be used for *feldspathic* glaze firing, as the deposited salt will be released on to other glazes. All *lid* flanges etc. should be washed with pure alumina or silica to minimize sticking. Be generous with alumina on shelves, tops of props, etc. The technique is hard on refractories but high-alumina shelves, etc are reputed to stay reasonably free from glaze though Parks PGRG prefers silicon-carbide shelves with a thick coat of kiln wash. Firebricks are vulnerable, although the Wrens fired their gas kiln for salt glaze some 90 times without serious damage. Rosemary Wren recommends slightly damp salt (table salt, rock salt, or 'water-softener' salt) at 1 lb. to every 3 cu. ft. (5 kg. to 1 cu. m.) of kiln space, applied in three doses, starting at the highest temperature. The temperature will drop after salting. Beware blow-back of steam when using damp salt. Wear goggles. See also *fuming*—of which salt glaze is, of course, a variety.

Brushed and trailed slips with sponged oxides under salt-glaze. By Rosemary Cochrane.

Lively trailing on a rich brown salt-glaze, fired in the wood-fired kiln shown at kiln, by Janet Mansfield (Australia).

Guy Sydenham (CR 65) uses a seawater drip into the firemouth just behind the flames. Extra salt can be dissolved in the water where necessary and he finds this kinder than solid salt to both pots and kiln. David Miller, in CR 85, explains low temperature salting—950–1000°C. He uses a vitreous slip (*engobe*) with copper carbonate, etc.

Bowls will become glazed all over by the salt but enclosed spaces such as mugs and bottles may need a

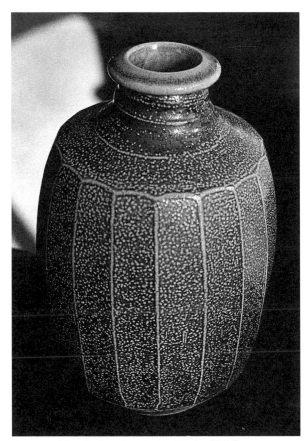

A powerful salt-glaze faceted bottle by Phil Rogers.

thin wash of a suitable glaze inside. Wally Keeler (CR 77) has the simplest possible glaze for salting: equal parts feldspar and china clay. Jane Hamlyn fires her lids in a perforated saggar to avoid the unsightly marks of *fly ash* settling on them during firing.

In 1991 the new Environmental Protection Act (Great Britain) was enacted to control the emission of harmful polluting substances. This is not intended to affect small scale craft businesses but salt glaze potters are advised to gain authorization, on the grounds that their level of production is 'trivial', from the H.M. Inspectorate of Pollution. Addresses and information from Frances Lord, Grants Officer, Crafts Council, 44a, Pentonville Road, London N1 9BY.

SALTPETRE

Potassium nitrate KNO_3. Soluble and normally used only in frits.

SAMPLING

Natural materials may vary slightly throughout a batch. A true sample must be made up from small amounts taken from various parts of a batch. A lengthier system is to divide the batch into four, discarding two parts and remixing the rest, continuing the process until only a sample amount remains.

SAND

Coarse particles of rock, generally impure silica. 'Sand-size' is given as 0.6–2.0 mm. Some sands contain heavy mineral impurities such as zircon, rutile, ilmenite. Seashore sand can contain large quantities of shell (calcia), basalt, and powdered shale.

The use of a pure silica sand as a *placing* material has largely given way to alumina. The grain shape varies and some sands are much more rounded than others. Some potters prefer smooth granules but sharper types are more likely to increase standing strength. Its addition to bodies will give 'bite' to throwing clays; will assist drying (though not as efficiently as grog); and decrease shrinkage. However it introduces '*free*' *silica* which may give trouble at the inversion point if used in large quantities. Builder's sand is supplied in 'sharp' and 'soft' qualities, the former being washed sand. The impurities in builder's sand can add interest to a body. Beach sands are variable and will need washing to remove salt, etc; river sands are preferable. Zircon sand has been recommended for *saggars*, *refractories*, and for *ovenware*. Sand additions can lead to pitted glazes especially in oxidized stoneware.

SAND SIZE

Given as 0.6–2.0 mm. Rocks or minerals must be broken at least to sand size before grinding in a mill or mortar.

SANDSTONE

A rock of silica (quartz or sand) particles cemented with clay, lime, and iron oxides. White clays may be found in association with sandstone.

SATIN GLAZE

A name given in suppliers' catalogues to semi-matt glazes 'usually of the zinc-titanium type', Dodd.

SATURATED GLAZE

A glaze with the maximum color content which it is capable of dissolving. Liquids can hold more material in *solution* at high temperatures than at lower ones; some metal or oxide may therefore be precipitated onto the surface of the glaze during cooling. Pigment/glaze ratio varies with the oxide and, to a lesser extent, with the glaze formula. 3% of copper in a lead glaze can produce a metallic black but a glaze will still be shiny with 10% or more of manganese dioxide; some stoneware glazes can dissolve as much as 25% in oxidation. In general, the more fluid the glaze the more color in solution it will accommodate.

A list of 'saturation points' is therefore misleading but as a comparative guide the following list may be useful. Average for *soft* clear *glazes*, color in solution:

2%	cobalt
2.5%	copper
4%	nickel
6%	chrome
8%	lead antimoniate
10%	iron
10%	manganese

Some types of *kaki* are examples of *supersaturated* reduced stoneware glazes where the surplus iron has been precipitated onto the surface, to re-oxidise during cooling.

SAUCER

Its design must always be considered in relation to the cup which is to be set on it. Saucers tend to flatten during firing and should be thrown with a slightly generous curve or lift. The foot ring is placed outside the line of the 'well' both for stability and strength. Saucers are thrown either as short cylinders, the walls of which are then thrown outwards to the desired shape, or as a plate is thrown, the edge being shaped from a ring of clay

Sections through two types of saucer. The second, with a wider well and shallower rim can double as a small plate.

after the well is formed. The well must be flat or slightly dipped or the cup may spin. One can finish the well at the turning stage. Saucers can be turned with a foot ring but this is time-consuming and they are often left as cut from the wheel, merely trimming the outer corner to a bevel.

SAWDUST FIRING

The firing of pots in slow-burning sawdust is fun but as an educational exercise may be misleading. The heat generated is not often sufficient to turn clay into ceramic and the pots will disintegrate in water. A low initial biscuit fire will rectify this and the sawdust treatment

Three types of sawdust kiln.
(A) A simple, dry-built brick box with a sheet metal cover raised slightly on shards or brickbats. It burns reasonably well but the pots are liable to dunt.
(B) A dustbin perforated to allow air for combustion.
(C) A saggar or brick box insulated with soil, the lid is propped as in (A).

will then be a mainly decorative one, subtle graduations of color resulting from *reduction* and *carbonization*. With practice and care, a measure of control can be exercised. In our so-called temperate climate the sun is rarely hot enough to avoid the all too common mishap of *dunting* as the piece is exposed during the firing. An *open* body helps but also increases the difficulties of *burnishing*. A rounded form with a sturdy rim is most likely to survive. The inclusion of sand or other silicas is not recommended, the firing always hovering round the *inversion* point.

Method: A brick box is dry-built, usually about an 18 in. (450 mm.) cube. Ventilation holes can be left between bricks but these increase the incidence of dunting. In some designs earth is banked round the kiln for insulation or a dustbin is pierced with holes and used instead of a brick box. Galvanized metal may give off poisonous fumes when heated and should be avoided. Whatever type of kiln is used, an outer baffle wall or windbreak is useful. An easily removable and fireproof cover must be provided, set on three or four pieces of brick to allow air to enter. The box is filled with alternate layers of dry sawdust and pots until full, finishing with 3–5 in. (80–130 mm.) of sawdust. It is ignited from the top and burns downwards; a sprinkling of paraffin (kerosene) on top will facilitate lighting. There is little point in 'topping up' with sawdust and if this is done there is the slight danger that the sawdust, given sufficient air, may ignite with a mildly explosive force. As the sawdust burns down pots will be exposed and settle down onto those beneath. Put the strongest ones at the bottom. As mentioned above, success is most likely on a hot, still day.

SCALES, weights

The most useful weighing balance for the small potter is a $\frac{1}{2}$ oz.–2 lb. (15–1000 gm.) 'sweetshop' scales. A 15 lb. (7 kg.) set is also useful for weighing clay and larger glaze batches. The cheaper spring balances are rarely accurate enough, but dial scales working on a counterweight principle can be adequate for throwing clay lumps. Good quality *beam scales* are the most reliable but are expensive. There is also a torsion balance which is reputed to be very sensitive from 0.1 gm. up to 2 kilograms. 'Electronic' scales are becoming more common with digital read-outs but they still rely on a mechanical system.

Gram weights are sold in sets from $\frac{1}{2}$ gm. to 1 kg., graded in such a way that all weights between can be measured. The set is 1×1 kg., 1×500 gm., 2×200 gm., 1×100 gm., 1×50 gm., 1×25 gm., 2×10 gm., 1×5 gm., 2×2 gm., 1×1 gm., $1 \times \frac{1}{2}$ gm.

SCEWBACK

A sloping-faced brick (see *springer*).

SCRAPER

The ordinary triangular paint scraper with the sharp corners filed away provides the best scraper for cleaning tables, etc. A cook's rectangular plastic scraper is also excellent and is less likely to damage polythene bins etc. The steel palette can also be brought into use and is the best tool for shaping and finishing hand-built pots. (See illustration under *hand-building, former*.)

SCREEN

A wire mesh or perforated plate for sieving materials. The term is often applied to the coarser meshes. (See also *lawn, sieve, silk screen, vibratory sieve*.)

SCUMMING OF CLAY

A white efflorescence which can mar the surface of fired terracotta. It is due to soluble basic salts, often calcium sulfate which has been brought to the surface by capillary attraction during drying, the crystals being crushed by the fingers while working on the clay. It is almost impossible to remove. If a salt-free clay cannot be found, the addition of 1–2% of barium carbonate will help. This however is a toxic material. Barium sulfide (barytes) can also be used. (See *efflorescence*.)

SEAL, stamp

All potters, whether amateur or professional, should have their own stamp with which to identify their pots. A seal is usually about $\frac{1}{2}$ in. (12 mm.) across and must be simple in design—initials, a monogram, or a cipher. More information (the name of the pottery for instance) can be shown on a *roulette* seal.

(2) A seal used as an item of decoration on the porcelain box by Sheila Fournier.

(3) A seal cut in relief to give an intaglio impression (which can be inlaid with color, glaze or slip).

(4) Geoffrey Whiting's pottery seal (A for Avoncroft Pottery) and his monogram on a coarser clay body.

(1) Cutting a seal directly into leather-hard clay (which will, of course, give raised initials in use).

The design may be either in relief or recessed (intaglio). The former is useful for pots that have become rather dry but the latter is more impressive. If you have a steady hand the seal can be cut directly into leatherhard clay; otherwise it is cut into a wood or *plaster* block from which casts can be taken. One can paint or scratch one's signature straight onto the pot—these are 'marks' rather than seals. A stamp pressed onto a little pellet of clay gives a raised seal which is attractive and can be a decorative item on a plain pot. It also minimizes the risk of pushing the stamp right through a thin pot wall.

SEAT EARTH

The material immediately beneath a coal seam—often *fireclay*. 'The seat earth for vegetation' (Worrall C.) i.e. the vegetation which produced the coal.

SECONDARY AIR

The air supply allowed into the kiln to assist the *combustion* of the fuel beyond the actual source of the flame, i.e. to *oxidize* any unburned carbon or gases given off by the fuel. Manipulation of secondary air can control kiln atmosphere. Secondary air will be more efficient if it is pre-heated. Kiln design should take this into account, directing it through a hot zone before it enters the chamber.

SECONDARY CLAY

A clay which has been transported from the site of its formation by water, wind, or glacial action. The clay is thus ground and *levigated* to a fine particle size which increases its plasticity but, inevitably, it picks up impurities in the process. Some may be very pure (e.g. English ball clays) but most are fusible and fire to a *terracotta* color. In some cases (*fireclays* for example) the impurities have been leached out again later, the clays becoming more refractory.

SECOND

Given by Dodd as 'pottery ware with small not readily noticeable blemishes', a definition which some potters would be advised to study. (See also *lump*.)

SEDIMENTARY CLAY

Sometimes confused with primary clay, these are very variable in character and origin. The common factor is that they have been deposited in depressions in the earth's crust (lake basins, etc) and most of them have been formed by the decomposition of feldspar. They are weathered clays often containing *micas*, hydrated iron oxide, lime, 'free' silica, etc. English *ball clays* probably have their origin in a *primary clay* which has been washed away and re-deposited as a fine-grain but reasonably iron-free material.

SEDIMENTATION

Although all solid particles will eventually settle in a liquid in which they have been suspended, the heavier and larger ones will settle first. Thus the finer particles carried by rivers tend to travel the furthest, finally coming to rest in estuaries or lake basins, forming reasonably pure clay beds. Sedimentation is used to separate heavier minerals from lighter, e.g. mica from china clay. (See also *levigation*.)

SEGER CONE

A *pyroscopic* device in the form of an elongated pyramid of ceramic material graded and numbered to 'squat' at a given temperature. The mixtures represent a logical series of steps originated by Hermann Seger, a nineteenth century German ceramic chemist. (See *Seger formula*.) Modifications have been made for the lower temperatures but the principle on which the series is based still holds.

The RO group is made up of 0.3 K_2O. 0.7 CaO, while the alumina is kept at one-tenth of the equivalent of the silica. A No. 6 cone is: RO. $0.6R_2O_3$. $6.ORO_2$; a No. 9 in the ratio 1:0.9: 9.0. The silica ratio will be seen to be higher than that used in stoneware glazes but some porcelain glazes have similar formulas. (See *cones* for a list of cone numbers and equivalent temperatures.)

SEGER FORMULA

Originated by the German chemist Hermann Seger more than a century ago, this is still one of the standard procedures for representing a glaze formula and is used in this dictionary because of its comparative simplicity. The system lists oxides as comparative molecular equivalents in three groups: *basic, amphoteric,* and *acidic,* written $RO.R_2O_3.RO_2$, R denoting any appropriate element. The RO group also includes R_2O oxides, e.g. potash, and the sum of all the basic oxides is taken as unity—1.0 equivalent. In this way the other constituents can be directly and immediately compared. The R_2O_3 is represented by alumina; ferric oxide may also be included. When we come to the acid group certain ambiguities creep in. The principal acid and the foundation of all ceramics, SiO_2 fulfils the role, as do TiO_2, SnO_2, etc but boric acid, antimony, and others have amphoteric type formulas (B_2O_3 etc) and are still listed with silica. The symbol RO_2 is therefore not to be taken literally but as including all the *glass-formers*

The placing of B_2O_3 continues to be questioned since it acts more like a *base* or flux and falsifies the silica proportion (see *leadless glazes, glaze formula,* and under the oxides of individual elements.)

SEGER RULES

Hermann Seger's rules for dealing with *crazing* and *peeling* of glaze.

For crazing adjust body thus:

1 Decrease clay content
2 Increase flint
3 Replace some clay with kaolin (china clay)
4 Raise biscuit fire
5 Decrease feldspar

(Nos. 1 and 5 refer more specifically to industrial bodies.)

For crazing adjust glaze thus:

1 Increase silica base ratio
2 Replace some SiO_2 with B_2O_3
3 Replace high molecular weight bases with low weight ones

For peeling, reverse these adjustments.

SELENIUM

A non-metallic element Se, 79. 'Resembling sulfur in its chemical properties . . .; occurs as selenides of metals', Uvarov DS. A *metalloid*.

Used in combination with cadmium, as sulfides, to produce low temperature orange and red glazes and enamels. Quick cooling helps to retain color. Normally only available as a complete fritted glaze. A quoted frit is:

soda ash 15.0, nitre 2.0, cryolite 6.0, fluorspar 14, borax 29.0, sand 34.0, with 3% selenium.

At the present time the maximum firing temperature of selenium reds is around 1040°C. (See *red, glazes*.)

SEMI-MUFFLE

A muffle in a kiln which does not completely protect the ware. In effect a bag wall on each side.

A semi-muffle kiln. The example shown is an up-draft type but can be adapted to down-draft. Many gas kilns are of this type.

SEMI-PORCELAIN

According to the Brussels Nomenclature it has: 'The commercial appearance of porcelain without being really opaque like earthenware or truly translucent like porcelain. These products may be slightly translucent in the thinner parts such as the bottoms of cups (and) . . . can be distinguished . . . because the fracture is rough grained, dull, and non-vitrified . . . a fracture clings to the tongue'. Some studio porcelains come into this category.

SERIES WIRING

A number of resistances wired one to another. This reduces the voltage to each one and the total resistance will be the sum of all the resistances in the circuit. Thus two similar lamps in series will reduce the power by a factor of the square of half the voltage—in other words you will get a very dim light! The various kiln elements in a circuit are wired in series and so must be calculated as if they were one unbroken length, but the various circuits are wound in *parallel*. Series/parallel switching is used for slow/medium/fast kiln controls. (See *heat control*.)

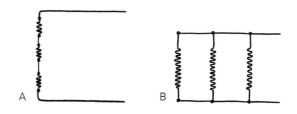

(A) Three resistances connected in series, e.g. may represent three kiln elements but all wired one to another so that they 'share' the voltage, the resistance being the sum of all three. (B) The same equipment wired in parallel, i.e. each at full voltage.

SESQUISILICATE

'Sesqui' is strictly $1\frac{1}{2}$, but in molecular formulas this is expressed as the whole number relationship 3:2. Thus, in the commonest of these compounds, lead sesquisilicate, the relationship is 3 molecules of silica to 2 of lead oxide, $2PbO.3SiO_2$.

SETTER

Supporting refractories for pots during firing which closely follow the contours of the ware, or separate it from the shelf (see *placing*). Dishes can be set on sand or alumina in the biscuit firing (as is *bone china* biscuit). Tile setters are thin, flat shelves sometimes called 'cranks'.

SETTING, density

A *kiln* pack, including *shelves* and *furniture*.

Setting density will influence kiln behavior, a full kiln generally firing better than a half empty one (see *radiation*). However, problems of heat transfer can arise from too solid a pack—of very close tiles for instance. The professional potter will arrange his work with the kiln setting in mind so that the space can be fully utilized, yet allowing for variety. (See *packing kilns*.) Setting density can be recorded in terms of weight; the number of pieces; the market value; or, at least described in general terms as 'very full', 'loose pack', etc which will be of some help in assessing firing graphs and the practical results.

SETTLING OF GLAZE

The settling of solid material in slips and glazes, often to form a hard cake on the bottom of the container, is a perennial headache for the potter. Frits are especially prone to settling. Attempts to stir up a hard, settled glaze are often a hopeless task and the only way to deal with it effectively is to pour off all the liquid. The cake of glaze will then usually come away quite cleanly and can be cut and broken up with the hands and reworked little by little into the liquid.

The suspension of glazes depends on several factors (see *flocculant, suspender, suspension*).

S.G.

Abbreviation for *specific gravity*.

SGRAFFITO, sgrafiato

Decoration in which slip or other coating is scratched or cut away to reveal the clay body beneath. A variety of tools can be used: the fingers for very wet slip (also called 'finger combing'), a stiff brush, a knife, or more traditionally, with a bamboo or cane tool cut to a flat end resembling a very broad pen nib. The condition and thickness of the slip at the time the design is cut will also affect the result. Glaze and pigment, as well as slips, will respond to sgraffito treatment. Sgraffito through glaze is necessarily treated in a broad and simple way; at the other extreme, through pigment, designs can be worked out in very fine lines.

Designs are too varied to discuss in a short article. Compare, for instance, a Leach bottle with a decorated Greek amphora for extremes of sgraffito styles. The line should be fluid and yet taut, rapidly executed and, once cut, left alone. Backgrounds can be cut away leaving textured areas which will throw more solid shapes into relief. Do not become carried away by the fascination of

The typical sgraffito cut through soft, though not liquid slip with a chisel-ended cane tool.

Eric Mellon at work on one of his decorated bowls, using a sharp metal tool. He often combines sgraffito with brushwork. (See a fired example of his work at underglaze.)

the work and do not forget the vital correlation between the decoration and the form of the piece, which is as important for dishes and bowls as for pots. The alternative term 'sgrafiato' is sometimes used for designs in which the background is cut away, as opposed to linear pattern. James Tower's combination of resist and sgraffito between a light and a dark glaze proves how the simplest of techniques can result in successful and subtle work. (See also *combing, finger combing, wax resist*.)

Another excellent example of fine-line sgraffito on a bowl by Greg Daly (Australia). It was glazed with cobalt/copper glazes, fired in oxidation to 1280°C. and then decorated with resin luster.

SHALE

As the water was squeezed out of clay in geological time by strata movements, pressure and heat, it hardened or 'lithified' into mudstone and shale. Slate is a further, metamorphosed stage. *Fireclays* are often shaley and need grinding for use.

SHATTERING

The break-up of the pot fabric after glaze firing, happily a rare phenomenon. It is almost always due to an excess of fine, 'free' silica in crystalline form and to the shock of its *inversion*. This not only strains the body itself but can also put a glaze into a state of such extreme *compression* that it splits the body. Associated with *peeling* (see also *Seger rules, crazing, quartz inversion*). A large dish glazed on one side only is at especial risk, a thick glaze coating more dangerous than a thin one. Glass, melted in a ceramic piece as a decorative effect, can break the piece through excessive contraction and tension.

To cure compression-shattering use less flint or quartz in the body and/or higher contraction bases in the glaze. Cool rapidly to about 950°C. in order to

minimize crystal formation, and increase body fluxes to form silicates, which do not 'invert'. Geoffrey Whiting found that 5% of a red clay cured bad shattering. A clay with a high incidence of the trouble may be best discarded. (See also *shivering*.)

A glaze in high compression on the top face of a dish can exert sufficient outward thrust to break or shatter the body.

SHELF, kiln

See *bat, kiln shelves*.

SHIVERING

The action of glaze breaking away from the body, especially on rims and edges. It is usually suffering from *over-compression* associated with a poorly developed interface. The treatment generally recommended is as for *shattering* or *peeling*. The replacement of some of the feldspar with nepheline syenite or china clay with ball clay may help, especially with ash glazes. Rim crawling is a similar complaint, the glaze lifting away from the body at a sintering stage. It is difficult to cure (see *crawling*).

Slip can also 'shiver', especially a white slip on a red body, and this is most often caused by unequal slip/body shrinkage. Add more plastic clay to the slip, a fusible ball clay for instance. If shivering happens during drying, apply the slip to rather stiffer clay, or apply it more thinly. Slip shivering during the cooling of the kiln may be associated with quartz or cristobalite inversions and can be helped by the addition of about 5% of flint.

SHORT CIRCUIT

See *circuit, fuse*.

SHORT CLAY

Clay with poor plasticity or workability, also known as 'lean' clay. Large-grain, pure clays are short; ball clays are *fat* or plastic. Most bodies contain both types. 2–3% of bentonite in a short body will impart some of the qualities of plasticity. Shortness can result from *over-wedging* or *pugging*, or from too small a water content.

A few days' rest in a damp atmosphere will restore a normally plastic clay, and a week or two will help a short one.

SHOULDER

The upper part of a pot where it turns in towards the neck or rim. It is the most eye-catching area of a pot and generally takes the most important part of the decoration.

SHRINKAGE OF CLAY

Clay progressively decreases in length and volume during both drying and firing though the rate of decrease is not constant over the whole cycle (see below). Firing shrinkage is non-reversible, and is not to be confused with heat expansion and contraction (*coefficient of expansion*) which all materials undergo during heating and cooling, or with silica *inversions*.

There are two phases. First, wet to dry shrinkage caused by the evaporation of films of water of plasticity from between the particles of clay. This varies with the fineness of grain; a red surface clay or a bentonite may shrink too much to be any use to the potter at all. English *ball clays* have a high wet/dry shrinkage. The maximum for a useful body should not exceed 10%. The shrinkage is reduced by the addition of flint, sand, or grog. (See *clay tests* for shrinkage test.)

Second, firing. There is little or no shrinkage from leather-hard clay to a low biscuit, in fact there may even be a slight expansion. However, as soon as glasses begin to form in the body through heat reaction between basic impurities and silica, the unmelted particles pack closer together and an overall lessening in volume occurs, continuing at an increasing rate to complete vitrification.

(A) In plastic clay the plates or particles are held apart by layers of water. As the water evaporates the particles come closer together.
(B) The interstices can still hold some water and the diagram can represent either leather-hard or dry clay. Hence the comparatively low shrinkage between leather-hard and dry clay.

Some approximate shrinkage rates:
Etruria and brick clays
wet/fired to 1000°C. .... average 12%
Fireclays
dry/fired .... average 3%
China clay
low wet/dry shrinkage;
if fired up to 1300°C. 12%
Ball clays
wet/dry .... up to 12%

(For the effects of 'shrinkage' in glazes see *crazing, glaze/body fit*.)

Showing the shrinkage of slab pots, all made to a similar size, at various stages from clay to fired pot. From left to right: wet plastic clay; leather-hard clay; dry clay; biscuit; stoneware. It is obvious that the greatest shrinkage occurs between the first two and between the last two. From dry to biscuit is minimal. (See text.)

SIENNA

A hydrated iron-manganese ochrous earth. Similar to umber but with less MnO. (See also *ochre*.)

SIEVE

Regular mesh or perforations which will control the grain size of a material which is passed through the sieve. Made of metal, metal wire or nylon.

Useful sieves (screens or lawns) for potters are $\frac{1}{2}$ in. (12 mm.) garden sieves for removing the worst roughage from ash, stony clays etc; 8 or 16 mesh cooking sieves usually of nylon, which can be used for the first breaking down of a slip or glaze batch and for grog; 60 to 100 phosphor bronze lawns for slips and stoneware glazes; 100 or 120 for earthenware glazes; and 200 mesh for colors. The number indicates the wires per linear inch (see *lawns*). In practice some slightly larger particles will pass through because of unevennesses in the weave (which may be forced apart by clumsy usage) and oblong particles which slip through endways. Grog is graded by sieve range.

Use only a brush for working material through a sieve, not tools or fingers! The most accurate grading is probably given by a vibratory sieve, but this sort of precision is rarely required in craft work.

Using a sieve, deeper rim uppermost (the number of students who instinctively used a sieve with the shallow section uppermost always surprised me), and supported on two sticks over a bowl, the glaze worked gently but firmly through with a nylon washing-up brush.

SIEVE FRAME

Lawns must be mounted on frames. These are usually circular and vary in size from 3 in. (75 mm.) to 12 or 14 in. (300 or 350 mm.) wooden or polypropylene frames. The standard frame is about 4 in. (100 mm.) high and is designed to be used with the deeper wall upwards so that it will hold the maximum quantity of liquid (many students use sieves upside down). 8 in. (200 mm.) is a good average diameter for a frame. Wooden (ashwood) frames inevitably overlap at the joins and are difficult to clean completely and it is advisable to keep one sieve for each major class of work: for transparent glaze, white opaque, and colored for example. The more recently developed plastic frames in which the lawn can easily be replaced should be an improvement.

As mentioned at *lawn*, it is possible to fuse lawns onto plastic frames (of the right type, see *plastics*) from round plastic boxes with the bottom cut out, or from pipes, with a soldering iron or by heating the lawn on a stove top. This, when successful, forms a neat and waterproof junction.

SIEVE, use of

It is easier, and quicker in the long run, to use more than one sieve size when preparing a slip or glaze, working from coarse mesh to fine. For slips and glazes made up from commercially supplied materials sieving is more a question of breaking down loose aggregates rather than separating particle sizes. Use a 'cooking' sieve of nylon for the first break-down and then the appropriate lawn for the resultant slurry (see *lawn, sieve*). Sieve a glaze at least twice through the finest sieve if it is to be used immediately, to assist the intimate mingling of particles.

A newly made-up slip will improve if left to rest for a day or so.

Slips should ideally be sieved every time they are used but this can be confined to the amount required. Glaze will need resieving every so often anyhow, bits of pot, grit, and other rubbish will fall into it. It is advisable to pour the glaze from its container to ensure that a 'cake' does not form on the bottom which will alter the constituents of the remaining mixture.

In persuading the mixture to pass through the lawn use an appropriate brush—never a rigid tool or your fingers—and do not work it too hard. Use plenty of water—it can always be poured from the settled mixture later. A thick sludge will form a coating on the lawn and never pass through. The ideal is to use little or no direct force and in this respect the *vibratory sieve* may not be a complete luxury. If slips or high-clay glazes are forced thickly through a sieve they will only re-unite on the other side and the result will be nearly as lumpy as the original. More water, as mentioned above, will make easier work, more effective screening and prolong the life of the sieve which, with care, should last many years.

SILICA

Silicon dioxide SiO_2, 60, m.p. 1610–1713°C. Normally oxides are discussed under the element but silica is such a fundamental material in ceramics that an exception is made for it. All ceramics are based on silica both in the body and glaze, except for a few specialized industrial products. It is the principal *glass-forming* oxide.

Used as a white powder, it is derived from *calcined* and ground flints or ground quartz. Its place in the Seger formula is with the acidic oxides (though its refractory character may be modified if it is introduced in too finely ground a form). Many sands are mainly silica. It is more often used to produce *silicates* than on its own (see *fused silica*). Crystalline silica has an *inversion* point at 573°C., changing from alpha to beta forms with a linear expansion of about 1% (given variously at 0.45–1.0), with an equivalent contraction on cooling. It ceases to be stable at around 870°C. and will begin to convert to *cristobalite* from 1050°C.

However most of the silica in a glaze, and to a lesser extent in the body, will unite with bases to form silicates, in which case the reverse beta to alpha inversion does not occur. Silica also combines with alumina and these have a *eutectic* at 1595°C. (see also *phase diagrams*) and form *mullite* and *corundum* at different temperatures according to their respective proportions. For a full and exhaustive discussion of the nature and uses of silica in bodies and glazes the reader is referred to the article in Hamer PDM.

SILICA REFRACTORY

A silica brick or other material containing 90% or more silica and a P.C.E. (i.e. deforms like a pyrometric cone) of not less than 1500°C.

They are resistant to deformation under load but, as might be expected, are subject to *thermal shock* in the *inversion* ranges. Potters' *refractories* are therefore more usually *aluminous*.

SILICATE

A compound of a *base* or bases with silica, that is, a salt. Many pottery minerals and all clay and glazes are silicates, many of them complex. In its simplest form a silicate may be written $RSiO_3$ or $RO.SiO_2$, the 'R' indicating the other element involved, but there are also other combinations. Clay includes combined water in its formula and is thus a 'hydrated aluminium silicate'. The frit, lead monosilicate, is one part lead oxide to one part silica, $PbSiO_3$ or $PbO.SiO_2$.

SILICEOUS

Rich in silica: often in a 'free' or separate crystalline form. Applied to refractories and sometimes to ball clay.

SILICON

A non-metallic element Si, 28, Oxide SiO_2, 60. (See under *silica* for general information.)

SILICON CARBIDE

SiC, 40, s.g. 3.2. Low thermal expansion, 5.0 (see *coefficient of expansion*). Made by fusing coke and sand.

Silicon carbide's excellent thermal shock resistance, refractoriness, and thermal *conductivity* make it a useful material for *kiln shelves*. It is also a conductor of electricity, a property which has been utilised as silicon carbide heating elements. Silicon carbide shelves, however, because of the way they are manufactured are not a great hazard in electric kilns.

It has been used in a powdered form as a glaze ingredient to produce 'crater' glazes (it bubbles with the release of the carbon), and in speckled red copper glazes as a local reducing agent. For the latter to be effective the kiln must be sealed during the last part of the firing and during cooling. Hamer recommends the addition of around 1% of tin oxide as a 'stabiliser' in silicon carbide glazes.

SILICON CARBIDE ELEMENTS

Kiln *elements* in the form of straight hollow rods. Middle range diameter just over ½ in. (14–18 mm.). The performance of these elements has been greatly

(A) A single silicon carbide element. The ends which pierce the kiln wall are rated at only 0.5 ohms (compared with 4.5 ohms in the working portion) in order to save current and prevent overheating in the enclosed space.
(B) shows the end of a bar through the kiln wall. The hole diameter must be at least 1.25 that of the rod. The braid and clip connector is shown diagramatically.
(C) The bar is self-supporting from the points where it enters the wall. The kiln face is grooved so that the bars need not stand out too far into the kiln chamber. Care must be taken to protect bars when packing the kiln. See Fournier EKP for more advice on the use of SiC rods.

A hairpin type SiC element.

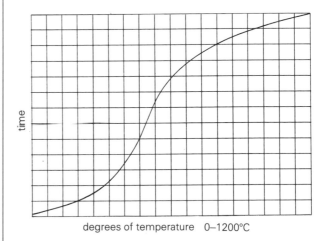

degrees of temperature 0–1200°C

Approximate heating curve for silicon carbide elements from cold to 1200°C/2190°F.

improved since their introduction in the nineteen-thirties. They no longer need an expensive transformer, which once cost more than the kiln. Crystal growth within the rod increases its resistance to the passage of electric current by about 10% every thousand hours, the kiln consequently taking longer to fire. An ingenious system has been invented by Peter Taylor by which the wiring, on three phases and neutral, can be modified to compensate almost indefinitely for this loss by increasing the voltage through each element from 60 through to 120 volts.

The rods are self-supporting, the working area producing the bulk of the heat. The ends, which must be $\frac{1}{2}$ in. (12 mm.) longer than the kiln wall thickness, are designed to offer less electrical resistance. Connections are made with braid and clips. The use of modern refractory insulators can reduce the wall thickness to six inches or less. The cost of these elements is greater than that of equivalent wire ones, but they should have a very long life and are less affected by reduction. They are fairly brittle and need the protection of a board against the possibility of damage when packing the kiln. Details of a silicon carbide kiln were given in CR 17, and in Fournier EKP. (See also at *truck kiln*.) In CR 3, Richard Parkinson suggests that temperatures as high as 1380°C. should be possible using silicon carbide elements!

Notes on silicon carbide elements
Wiring systems for resistance alteration compensation (by kind permission of Peter Taylor).

Using 12 elements or multiples of 12; three phase supply:

A. 3 series of 4 in star connection. 60 volts per element.

B. 4 series of 3 in star connection. 80 volts per element.

C. 3 series of 4 in delta connection. 100 volts each across phases.

D. 6 series of 2 in star connection. 120 volts per element.

Change when firing time has increased by 25%, e.g. from eight to ten hours. Average resistance increase 10% per thousand hours. See diagram at *Star and delta*.

No support is needed if the correct size is used for the length of span.

Up to 32 in.–14 mm. diameter

Up to 39 in.–16 mm. diameter

Up to 50 in.–18 mm. diameter

SILICONE

A series of organic compounds of *hydrocarbons* with silica $(R_2SiO)_n$ some of which will stand temperatures up to 300°C. Used as sealers and water-repellents, they have been mentioned as a last-ditch method of waterproofing the bases of leaking or scratchy pots.

SILICOSIS

A disease caused by fine *silica* dust inhaled over a long period. The dust cannot be eliminated from the lungs and so builds up to a solid substance. The studio potter is not at special risk unless he is in the habit of sandpapering dry clay. Reasonable hygiene and *cleanliness* are essential, working as far as possible with liquid or damp materials especially in handling glazes, ash, etc. *Alumina* can replace silica for *setting*, for spreading on kiln shelves, etc.

SILK SCREEN

A decoration technique, especially useful for tiles. A stretched piece of silk or other fine mesh material is marked with a design and those areas not required to be colored are varnished or otherwise made *impermeable*. The 'screen' is then laid flat on a tile and color (generally an *enamel*, but possibly other pigments) is brushed through or pressed through with a squeegee or roller. (See more information in Fournier DPD.)

SILLIMANITE

A brown or gray metamorphic mineral Al_2SiO_5 $(Al_2O_3.SiO_2)$. A highly refractory material (melting point around 1900°C.) found as a type of fireclay. Its heat resistance and high thermal *conductivity* makes it valuable for *kiln furniture*. Chief sources S. Africa and India. There is a sillimanite zone in N. Scotland. Kyanite and andalusite are similar in composition but have different properties. It is also made into bricks suitable for bag walls.

SILVER

A metallic element Ag. 108. A clear yellow is derived from silver salts for temperatures up to 1000°C. Silver-colored *enamel* is made from platinum. Silver sulfide with *ochre* can be used for lustre, with *reduction* near top temperature of 700–800°C. and during cooling. Silver enamel felt pens are available (Potclays).

SINDANYO

A type of very hard and durable asbestos sheet. It has a special use for *throwing-bats*. Expensive but almost everlasting and unmarked even by steel turning tools. Obtainable from Bell's Asbestos.

SINGLE FIRED WARE

See *once-fired ware.*

SINGLE PHASE SUPPLY

The normal household electricity supply, conducted through a live and a neutral wire. Usually 60 amps, with 30 amps the maximum for any one piece of equipment, e.g. a 7 kW kiln of about 3 cu. ft. However, some electricity authorities are now allowing 40 amps or more on a reasonably new line and it is worth contacting your local electricity authority for advice. Single phase motors are dearer and marginally less efficient than *three phase*—the alternative form of supply.

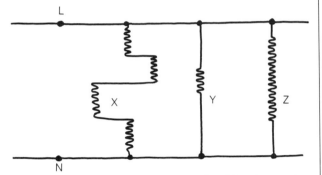

A single phase supply. Between the line (L) and neutral (N) various items of equipment can be connected so long as the total load does not exceed the strength of the mains input wires to conduct without overheating. In the diagram X might represent a 5kW. kiln; Y a 200 watt lamp; and Z a 2kW. electric fire. If all were on together the total load would be 7.2 kW. on the input wires.

SINTERING

An intermediate stage in the firing of a ceramic, either glaze or body, where the *liquid phase* has not yet begun but 'solid state reactions or intercrystallization' (Dodd)

Sintered particles of clay or other material. The points of contact have fused together giving a stronger fabric but with very little shrinkage between dry clay and low-fired biscuit. In practice the particles would have begun to assume a more spherical shape.

or the beginning of a reaction between two solids has fused the material causing a decrease in porosity and an increase in strength. The sintering temperature of a material is called the *Tamman* temperature, being between 0.55 and 0.6 of the K. temperature of fusion (Cardew). If the melting point is 1500°C., then the material will sinter at about 0.6 of the K. temperature, in this case 1773 (1500+273; see *absolute temperature*).

Thus, $1773 \times 0.6 = 1064K$ or 790°C.

A certain expansion takes place in clays up to sintering temperature.

SKIPPING

Sometimes used to indicate the *peeling* or *shivering* of glaze or slip on the rims of pots or bowls.

SLAB POT

Pots built up from slabs of clay can be very diverse in form and character. They may have the sharp clean lines which result from cutting the pieces from leather-hard clay, or the squashy, rounded forms of plastic clay building.

Leather-hard slabs are cut with a fine bladed knife held quite vertically, scored at the edges and luted together with slip made from the body clay. Press well home with a wooden spatula. The surfaces can be decorated before or after assembly by *impressing, beating, applied* clay etc. or by *wax resist, brushwork* or poured glaze. Several pourings of thin ash glazes will give an attractive and appropriate finish.

As mentioned in the text, straight lengths of wall in a slab pot tend to warp during drying and firing and may be strengthened by the addition of a strip attached at right-angles to the wall as shown.

Slab Pot

The proportions of a slab pot are all-important. Rules cannot be laid down but a rectangular plan tends to be of more interest than a square one. The clay is usually fairly well grogged for stoneware, but there is a wide field in earthenware. If the technique is used for open containers, the rim needs to be strengthened with an additional strip forming an inward or outward angle in order to counteract the almost inevitable warping. Cylindrical slab pots are described under *rolling pin pots*. The inside corners of larger slab pots will need reinforcement with thin clay coils worked well into the angle.

Slab pots make good lamp bases. Large composite pots can be built up from smaller ones. Curved surfaces can be partially dried over a former before assembly.

Building a slab bottle.
(1) The sizes of the various pieces having been worked out (remember to allow for extra wall thicknesses at top and base, for instance), cut the sections from a soft-leather slab of clay, keeping the cutting tool; awl, spatula, or knife, quite upright.
(2) The neck aperture can be made with a pastry cutter.
(3) All joints are moistened, using slip or slurry (made from the body clay or it will show as a different color).
(4) and (6) The first pieces are put together and the inside joins are sealed and cleaned off with a square-ended tool. Some potters work a thin coil into the angle.
(7) When the open box stage is complete the joins are further pressed together with a firm stroking action.
(8) The top and base are applied to the walls. The base can be set inside the pot, if desired, when only three walls have been joined together. The top and base can be treated in various ways: the top can be left open if the walls are sturdy, or fitted with a narrow flange; a true slab neck can be made; or a thrown neck can be added. Other finishes will occur to you. Similarly, a slightly recessed foot, either circular or oblong will give a certain lightness to the pot if this is desired.
(9) and (10) show a thrown neck luted on when half-dry.
(11) Corners may be left sharp, beveled, or rounded.
(12) For curved slab shapes a biscuit former is useful.

6

7

8

9

10

11

12

Two possible finishes for the necks of slab pots, using circular cutters. Both have the effect of keeping the walls rigid.

An unusual slab-built dish by John Maltby.

A slab-built sculptural stoneware boat by Sheila Fournier.

Made in the early 1970's this is still one of the most powerful slab pots ever constructed. By Ian Auld.

Slab-built porcelain (a risky technique), which is also a pot, the back being a steady curve. By Sheila Fournier.

SLAB ROLLER

Mechanical slab rollers are available but are something of a luxury and take up space unless large scale or large production work is envisaged. Several suppliers list them, and a number of potters are very enthusiastic about them.

SLAKE

Apart from the pint after a long day's potting, to 'slake' also indicates the disintegration of clay and other materials in water. This will occur most readily with clay when it is bone dry and broken up into at least pebble-sized pieces.

SLAG

The product of the reaction between *fluxing* materials e.g. ash, and a *refractory* kiln lining. Also applied to a non-metallic fusion which floats on metal during its extraction, or to any encrusting, semi-molten material—'our slipware body . . . would turn to slag at 1300°C.' Leach (see also *basic slag*).

SLICK

The movement of a metal blade over clay tends to bring water and fine particles—a 'slick'—to the surface. It sometimes causes lamination in pugged clay.

SLIP

Any clay or body mixed with water to a smooth creamy consistency. Originally used to provide a thin coating of the then rare light-firing clays over a red body, but has also been used world-wide for decoration, (see *feathering, hakeme, run slip, sgraffito, trailing,* etc).

A quick way of making the occasional slip, when joining slab pots, for instance. A piece of almost dry clay is rubbed over a Surform, as in illustration, into a saucer or bowl of water when it will quickly become saturated.

The term 'slip' is generally reserved for liquid 'natural' clays or bodies used for decorative pottery. Those which contain significant proportions of non-clay materials are known as 'engobes'. 'Slip-casting' is an exception. (See various colors of slip, e.g. *black slip, blue slip, green slip* and for technical notes *engobes, slip making, slip recipe,* etc.)

A method of flooding a plate, dish, or bowl. An adequate amount of slip is poured into a dish which is immediately tipped slightly and revolved, spreading the slip just up to the rim. The movement is almost complete in the picture. Surplus slip is poured out as neatly as possible with only the gentlest shake of the dish. Do not use too thick a slip.

SLIP CASTING

The making of pottery in *plaster* molds using liquid body or slip. The *mold* is filled with slip; the absorption of the plaster causes a thin wall of clay to be deposited on the inner surface. Surplus slip is then poured off and the cast is left to dry and shrink away from the mold, when it can be removed (see *molds*). Casting-slip is made up of a clay with up to 75% china clay, stone and flint. Nevertheless it is still too *viscous* to be used for casting and must be *deflocculated*.

A perfect cast is not easily obtainable. In addition the seam line left by the mold join is almost impossible to eradicate; even if trimmed quite flat it is liable to rise again during firing. A possible cure is to biscuit the piece to a low temperature and then to refettle seam lines at this stage. Some of the faults which may occur are dealt with in the table issued by the British Ceramic Research Association (under *casting-slip*). Detailed instructions for slip casting for the craft potter were given in CR 9 by William Hall. Cromartie advertise a slip-casting machine which will maintain the slip in condition *and* fill and drain molds, large and small!

SLIP DECORATION

Slip may be used as a complete or partial covering on a pot or dish. A 'bib' can be dipped, or contrasting colors poured over. Other techniques include *brushed slip, sgraffito, trailing, feathering, marbling, run-slip* and *hakeme*, and they are dealt with under those headings.

Slip decoration at its best is very direct and free. Essentially an earthenware technique, it is also sometimes used on stoneware using special *engobes*.

SLIP GAUGE

An instrument for measuring the consistency of slip or glaze. (For details see *hydrometer*.)

SLIP GLAZE

A slip derived from a very fusible clay which will melt to a hard glossy surface at stoneware temperatures. *Albany clay* is commonly quoted, also *Fremington clay*.

One can make up a slip glaze using 50% or more of a suitable red clay with other glaze ingredients. The difficulties lie not in the actual melting of the glaze, but in countering the effects of high shrinkage during drying and *sintering* stages. Dolomite, feldspar, colemanite or a frit will lessen shrinkage and increase *fusibility*. Additions of iron, rutile, or spodumene (Rhodes) will alter its behavior. Two simple slip recipes by Andrew Holden are mentioned in CR 45.

> Ball clay, 50;
> Whiting, 50

for a 'bright yellow', and,

> CY ball clay 50;
> Potash feldspar, 50

a 'rich orange red'. Stoneware firing.

Any red or surface clay may have the necessary qualities to make a glaze, and experiments with local materials are always worthwhile. Slip glazes are useful for *oxidizing* conditions, though not so variable as in *reduction*. They will always be dark brown, red-brown if you are lucky, or black. It is possible that *temmoku* and other dark-colored Oriental glazes were slip. If a slip-glaze shows bubbles or blisters, a slightly higher or longer firing may help.

SLIP MAKING

For plain colors, the clay is broken into small pieces and soaked in water. when well saturated, the *slurry* is brushed through a coarse *sieve* and then through a 60 mesh. Brush lightly with plenty of water.

If pigments are to be added, the ingredients must be weighed dry. The clay must therefore be used as a powdered body, or thoroughly dried and broken into small pieces. The appropriate proportion of pigment oxide is ground separately and passed through a 200 *lawn*. The liquid color can be added to the clay at the slurry stage before all is passed through a 60 or 80 mesh two or more times. Newly made slips should be 'rested' for a few days before use.

SLIP PAINTING

See *brushed slip, engobe.*

A press-molded plate with painted slips and sgraffito, by Kim Walker. (See also brushed slip, slip, *and illustration with technical details at* engobe.*)*

SLIP RECIPE

The following are the simplest recipes for slips for trailing, etc. (all dry weights) but there are countless more intricate ones.

White or buff slip	100% buff clay (throwing clay)
Red slip	100% red clay
Black slip	100% red clay + 9% manganese dioxide. Cobalt oxide 0.5% can be added for a blacker slip
Blue slip	100% buff clay + 0.5–1.5% cobalt oxide
Green slip	100% buff clay + 1.25% chrome and 1.25% copper oxide

(See also under slip headings, i.e. *black slip* etc.)

If slip crazes or *shivers* (*peels* or *flakes*) see under these headings for possible remedies. Stoneware slips are generally iron slips, variation being obtained by reduction. (See also under *casting slip, engobes*.)

SLIP TRAILER, tracer

These vary considerably in shape, but are all designed to direct a controlled stream of slip onto a surface.

1 The commonest type is a soft rubber bag with a glass or plastic nozzle. The bag is filled with a funnel.

2 Stiff rubber bulb containers have the advantage that slip can be drawn in by suction, but the control is not so delicate as with the first type.

3 A rigid container with a direct outlet—sometimes a quill. A pottery tracer can be made which fits snugly into the palm. It will have two holes: one is for the quill or nozzle, and the thumb fits over the other to control the entry of air and thus the outflow of slip. Two or more streams of slip have been used.

4 A rigid container with a rubber tube. Slip can be forced out of the nozzle by blowing down the tube. A baby's bottle is a possible container.

5 Cloth icing bags. These tend to drip after some use.

6 Paper containers, wrapped over like a sweet bag. Used by Odney Pottery, who published details in PQ 2. These are made of waxed paper or soft plastic. A segment of a circle is held point downwards and wrapped over the hand. Fastened with a pin or dab of clay.

7 A cup or container with one or more holes in the base. This method needs free, sure and rapid movement. Hamada used a ladle with a hole for trailing slip and glaze.

2

1

(1) Filling a soft rubber bag type slip trailer. A funnel in the mouth of the bag is filled with slip which will

3

probably need 'milking' in by gripping the top of the neck and sliding the fingers downwards. This is repeated until the bag is almost full. It is not always easy to introduce the funnel into the bag: damping the inside will help but the outside must be dry in order to maintain a grip.
(2) A more involved slip trailer designed by Peter Smith, the flow controlled at the mouthpiece. (3) Overleaf.

A triple-spouted trailer was used on this eighteenth century dish. Such a trailer could be constructed from a flattened pottery form (two joined pinch-pots would be suitable) with a hole in the top over which the thumb or a finger could be conveniently placed to control the flow of slip, and three smaller holes cut in the end to take the trailing spouts, either built-in or inserted. Quills would probably have been used originally. Similar multi-trailers, slab-built, were made with sections to separate different colored slips.

SLIP TRAILING

A decorative technique. (See *trailing*.)

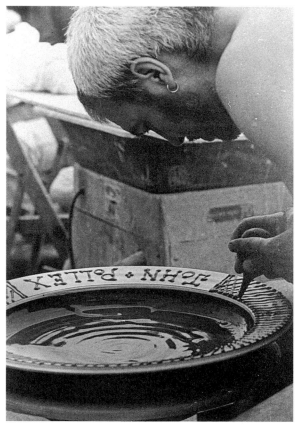

Lettering responds well to slip trailing and here we see John Pollex at work, completing the border with traditional cross-hatching.

SLOP GLAZE

A *suspension* of glaze materials in water; a glaze ready for use, in fact.

SLOP WEIGHT

The weight of solid material in a slip or glaze. Industrial pottery materials are measured and combined as slop weights. (See *pint weight* and *Brongiart's formula*.)

SLUMPING

The collapse of a pot in the kiln due to *pyroplastic* deformation, i.e. in a semi-molten state. Impure clays and porcelains will slump if over-fired, as a result of the high degree of glass formation in the fabric. (See *over-firing*.)

SLURRY

A thick, half-mixed slip, or a rough, wet, sandy mixture used for *clamming* etc.

SMALT

A fused mixture of cobalt, silica and a flux. A sort of cobalt frit, or glass, sometimes used as a pigment or for staining.

SMOKE

Unburnt particles of fuel, mainly carbon, caused by insufficient air in the combustion-chamber of a kiln. Smoke coming from the chimney is a sign of wasted fuel (as well as being antisocial and perhaps illegal), but in the firing chamber elemental carbon assists *reduction*.

SMOKED WARE

A body or glaze discolored by a smoky *reduction*-fire. Early reduction, below about 900°C., can stain pots with carbon which will not burn out. The black body of *raku* and *sawdust* firings is a mixture of reduction and smoking or carbonization. *Celadons* are rather liable to smoking.

SOAKING, heat

Maintaining a glaze or body in a kiln at a certain temperature, generally at the maturing-point. Many potters believe that a soaking period is essential to the maturity of a glaze. A slower firing from about 1000°C. will have similar results. A kiln graph, with its steadily flattening rocket-like curve, will show that many kilns slow down considerably after 1200°C. and give a soaking effect with little deliberate control.

Time must be allowed for the glaze in its fluid state to release gases, and for the resultant bubbles to smooth out, but an excessively long firing can set up secondary reactions which aggravate the trouble. The act of reduction will slow down or reverse the temperature rise, and this 'stepped' firing may be crucial to the development of some iron colors (see *kaki*).

Most *earthenware glazes* benefit from a soak of about 20 minutes, but it must be remembered that the glaze is fluid and may be slowly running down the pot. A *controlling pyrometer* is needed to soak an electric kiln efficiently. A degree of soaking can be achieved by switching on and off at intervals of one or two minutes. Use a second cone one number above the optimum temperature to ensure that the kiln does not get too hot. Alternatively one can set the 'medium' control if the kiln is wired in this way; this will retard the cooling rate.

Stoneware is more subtle in its reactions, and it is difficult to lay down rules. *Oxidized* glazes are often very susceptible to even ten degrees of over- or under-firing and I have found a soak to be a mixed blessing. Very fast firings in a test kiln have produced more exciting and silky-surfaced glazes than have the same recipes in larger, slower kilns. Triple *cones* are useful for soaking without a pyrometer, the higher number warning if the optimum temperature is being exceeded.

SOAPSTONE

Or steatite. An impure, 'massive' form of *talc*. Frequently used in 'soft paste' recipes. Now used in electroceramics and in *cordierite* bodies.

SODA

Refers, in pottery, to sodium oxide Na_2O. Used to describe glazes which contain sodium oxide, e.g. lead and soda glaze. Pure forms soluble but contained in many minerals. (For fuller discussion see under *sodium*.)

SODA ASH

Anhydrous sodium carbonate Na_2CO_3, 106. *Hygroscopic* and soluble. Used in alkaline frits, also as a *deflocculant* for casting slips. Ann Hirondelle (Washington, U.S.A.) quotes a soda ash glaze for cone 7–8 in reduction:

Silica	55
Soda ash	30
Plastic kaolin	15
Nepheline syenite	10

which, with a variety of pigments gives attractive broken glazes. She does not say how she copes with the solubility of the soda ash but stresses the use of 'cold water only'.

SODA GLAZE

Soda alone can produce a glass with silica, and this may be so 'soft' that it will dissolve in water (water-glass). The turquoise soda and copper glaze was used by the ancient Egyptians and though considered to be unstable has lasted for three thousand and more years! (See also *copper, turquoise, Egyptian paste*.)

A majority of glazes contain some soda which must be introduced as a *frit*, the raw compounds being soluble, or as a *mineral* (see *sodium*). The molecular equivalent of soda is usually kept at a maximum of 0.3, on account of its high thermal expansion. High-soda glazes will nearly always *craze*. Soda is inextricably mixed with potash in many minerals, so that the symbol NaKO may occur denoting random proportions. Piccolpasso mentions the calcining of wine lees with sand to produce a soda silicate for *majolica* glazes (marzacotto). Pigments will give brighter colors in soda glazes.

SODA, washing

Hydrated, or hydroxide of, sodium carbonate $Na_2CO_3.10H_2O$. Crystalline.

SODIUM, oxide, compounds

A metallic element Na. 23. (Natrum).
Oxide Na_2O, 62. 'Soda'.
Other compounds are listed below.

An *alkali*. A large *atomic radius* similar to potassium, with which it is often found in combination giving rise to the compound symbol KNaO. A very powerful *flux* (network modifier) with silica. All soda glasses need some lime or alumina to prevent their becoming soluble in water. Very high *coefficient of expansion* (37.0).

All simple compounds of soda are soluble and must be used as *frits*, or as 'natural' frits, e.g. the *feldspathic* minerals. Small amounts of soda figure in the analyses of most clays and of many other pottery materials. The high thermal expansion leads to the crazing of glazes, and the molecular equivalent is normally kept to within 0.3 parts. Brightens most colors, turning copper turquoise if in a high concentration.

Soda compounds and minerals used in ceramics:
Sodium carbonate Na_2CO_3, 106. Soda ash.
Sodium bicarbonate $NaHCO_3$, 107.
Sodium chloride NaCl, 58. Common table salt.
Sodium silicate, $Na_2O.SiO_2$, but in practice variable. $Na_2O.2-3.5SiO_2$. Water-glass, i.e. a glass which will dissolve in water. A deflocculant. Used also in *airsetting cements*.
Washing soda $Na_2CO_3.10H_2O$, 286.
Caustic soda, the hydroxide NaOH, 40. Unstable.
Sodium tannate. An efficient deflocculant. Prepared from NaOH and tannic acid.
Sodium uranate (see *uranium*).
Sodium borate (bi-borate) $Na_2O.2B_2O_3.10H_2O$, 382. (See *borax*.)

Chief soda minerals:
Albite feldspar $Na_2O.Al_2O_3.6SiO_2$, 524. Also some soda in nominally orthoclase feldspar.
China stone Na_2O (or NaKO).$Al_2O_3.8SiO_2$, 644.
Nepheline syenite Na_2O ($0.75Na_2O$. $0.25K_2O$). Al_2O_3 $2SiO_2$, 182.

All are variable within certain limits.

SOFT GLAZE

A glaze which matures at around 1150°C. or below, and includes in its formula lead or boron. *Earthenware* (and *bone china*) are covered with a 'soft' glaze. The term is comparative in the sense that the glaze can be scratched with a steel knife. The converse term 'hard glaze' is not, however, in general use.

SOFT LEATHER STAGE

Used in this book to indicate clay slightly damper than leather-hard—that is, at the point where it has stiffened but can still be deformed manually without breakage.

SOFT PASTE

A general term for all the experimental and glassy bodies which were developed in Europe from the time of the Medicis to the end of the eighteenth century, in an attempt to imitate oriental porcelain. The factories of St. Cloud, Bow, Chelsea etc. used soft paste. The material was immensely difficult to handle and fire, having little plasticity and a rapid and very fluid glass phase at maturity. Soapstone, bone ash, alkalis, tin, oxides, white clays, are among the ingredients mentioned. Firing temperatures around 1100°C., but variable. The very soft glaze with which they were covered took *enamels* very well. The bone ash/china clay mixture finally triumphed in England around 1800 (Spode), and continues to hold its own against hard paste porcelain. (See *bone china*.) Some porcelain bodies in current use among craft potters hover between soft paste and true *hard paste*. A soft paste for low-fired (1020°C. or less) beads and jewelry can be made up from roughly equal parts of ball clay and frit. Fire on a bed of alumina.

SOFT SOAP

A potash soap which remains in a liquid or jellified state. Used to lubricate the surfaces of plaster molds, to prevent plaster casts sticking, e.g. when reproducing dish molds. (See also *molds*.)

SOLAR FIRING

A long way from the sun-dried bricks of early times is the elaborate 'solar kiln' described in CR 59 by Zelijko Kujundzic—elaborate, that is, except for the 'kiln chamber' itself which was a 3 lb. coffee can! A large, circular parabolic reflector concentrated the sun's rays onto the can which contained a small pot surrounded by ceramic wool, the narrow beam being directed through a hole in the top directly into the pot itself. The main problem was keeping the reflector aligned exactly to the sun. Temperatures of 1060–1260°C. were attained.

Fun, but a lot of time and energy for a small result and it is obvious that much more technical work needs to be done before it becomes a viable technique.

SOLID SOLUTION

Materials dissolved one into another at high temperatures, reverting to a homogeneous solid mixture on cooling.

SOLUBLE, solubility, solution

A soluble material is one which will dissolve in a liquid to form a solution, an intimate combination but without chemical change, e.g. sugar in water. Materials which are soluble will crystallize out of solution and are not suitable for raw glaze batches. Pouring the water from the top of such a glaze will also pour away dissolved materials, altering the constitution of the glaze. There may be slightly soluble elements in any mineral or material, and it is always a wise precaution to retain the poured-off water for re-use if necessary. Dusting of soluble glaze materials onto wet clay (even immediately after throwing) with a garden 'puffer' has been suggested (CM 18/2)—it would be advisable to wear a mask during this process—but the usual method of using them is in the form of frits. The alkalis and boron are soluble in all their simple compounds, even colemanite is slightly soluble.

Glaze is a super-cooled liquid and we can therefore refer to certain materials and oxides as being soluble in a glaze, e.g. most of the *pigment* oxides will, up to a certain concentration, yield transparent color. The *acidic* oxides are mainly insoluble. Tin, for instance, will remain little changed in suspension rendering the glaze opaque. Glaze will also form compounds, one of which will dissolve in the other (see *solid solutions*). Liquids, including glazes, will hold only certain proportions in solution, the excess remaining in its original form or being rejected (precipitated). Hot liquids will hold more than cold ones; certain oxides may therefore come out of solution as the glaze cools, especially if this takes place slowly. Iron may do this in stoneware (see *red color in glaze*). 3% or more of copper and 12% or more of manganese will have the same effect, the degree of precipitation varying with the *fluidity* of the glaze. In an 'under-fired matt' or a high-base stoneware glaze the oxide may not dissolve at all: copper, for instance, giving gray instead of green.

Soluble materials (soluble in water) used in pottery:

Boric oxide   Most boron minerals including borax, calcined borax to a lesser degree. Colemanite is slightly soluble.

Soda   Most silicates and carbonates of soda, salt (sodium chloride), borax.

Potash   Oxide and carbonate, pearlash. Soluble form in many ashes.

Frits   Very soft frits may dissolve in part to re-crystallize after a few days.

SOLUBLE ALKALI

Plant ashes contain *soluble* and *caustic alkalis*. These may *crystallize*; invade the fabric of the biscuit; cause flocculation of the batch with attendant cracking of the glaze coating; and make it impossible to pour liquid from the batch without altering its behavior. Ash is therefore usually 'washed'. (For method see *ash preparation*.)

SOLUBLE LEAD

Lead and lead oxides are soluble in the bloodstream, where they act as cumulative poisons. The lead in a fired glaze, unless it is very stable, may also be 'dissolved' by the action of strong acids, such as those in certain fruits and vinegar, and by fermentation.

Raw lead compounds are forbidden by law in all but a few situations, and their use in manufactured materials is controlled. The potter working on his own may use them but not his employee. In Britain all lead (or cadmium) glazes on any table ware must conform to British Standard BS 4860, and all potters using them should have their work tested regularly and obtain certificates to that effect. Fritted *lead silicates* are powdered glass, which (in spite of detective fiction) is much safer in use. The *frits* must be made to certain standards of solubility (not more than 5% must dissolve in a standard hydrochloric acid test). Those that pass this test are labelled low sol. or LS frits. Monosilicate is too 'soft' to satisfy the regulations; sesquisilicate and bisilicate are usually satisfactory but the latter is recommended. Suggested starting recipe:

Bisilicate	65
China clay	25
Whiting	10

The dangers to the potter can be minimized by common sense and hygiene; the fired product presents a more involved problem. Shaw SCP states that 'lead glazes are brilliant, highly craze resistant and, if properly fritted, are absolutely safe in use'. He gives the rule that the *bases* plus *alumina* must equal at least 2.0 parts of silica in the molecular formula (see *Thorpe's ratio*).

Copper will increase lead solubility; indeed, Harry Fraser goes so far as to warn against the use of copper even with leadless glazes if there are also plumbic glazes in the same kiln.

Of other commonly used oxides:

Boric acid ⎫ increase solubility
Alkalis   ⎭

Alumina ⎫
Silica   ⎪
Lime   ⎬ decrease solubility
Zinc   ⎪
Barium   ⎪
Zircon   ⎭

There is, however, some doubt about the role of zinc oxide.

At high temperatures, lead is *volatile* and may be inhaled from a kiln. Do not open the kiln door when ware is very hot. It can also be deposited as a thin skin on leadless glazes, rendering them dangerous in use.

A test for the presence of lead not completely involved in the melt has been described in various magazines (Tactile, New Zealand Potter, CR): Two ounces of vinegar are left in the test pot for 12 hours. The vinegar is then poured into a glass and 2 oz. of fresh vinegar poured into a second glass. One-eighth of a teaspoon of liver of sulfur is mixed with 2 oz. of hot water, and two teaspoonsful are added to each glass. If the test vinegar is tinged tan or brown compared with the fresh batch, then heavy metal is present.

(See also some further notes at *lead, metal release*.) Some potters' suppliers (e.g. Potclays) offer a testing service.

SOLUBLE SALTS

Sulfates and carbonates of calcium, magnesium, and sodium are present in some clays and may 'migrate' to the surface, especially when they are much handled in modeling. They are most apparent on red clays (see *scumming*). *Egyptian paste* relies on this phenomenon to develop its glaze. *Filter pressing* tends to eliminate salts. Soluble alkalis are also a feature of ash (see *ash preparation*).

SOLUTION

See *soluble*.

SOLUTION COLOR

Colors derived from metal oxides dissolved in a molten glaze. (See *color*.)

SORTING TOOL

'Sorting' is the removal of the sharp points of glaze left by *stilts* etc after glaze-firing. A sorting-tool is a type of cold chisel with a tungsten carbide or other very hard edge. To use it, hold the pot firmly in one hand and bring the tool down sharply and square onto the pot just behind the snag to be removed, so that the tool catches the snag as near to its base as possible. Repeat with short, sharp movements, working into and under the blemish. With skill the blemish will sheer off after very few jabs.

SOURING

The aging of clay to improve plasticity and other qualities.

SPALLING

The breaking away of flakes or larger pieces from the faces and corners of *refractory hot-face* bricks in the kiln. *Thermal shock, crystalline inversion*, inadequate expansion allowances and *slag* formation are among the causes. *Free silica* should be minimal in the refractory fabric. Sudden heating or cooling will alter the expansion of the face of the brick compared with its back, and can cause deep spalling.

SPANGLES

Iron spangles, magnetic ferroso-ferric iron Fe_3O_4, 233. Magnetite. A coarse black iron oxide used to produce speckling in bodies and glazes.

SPAR

Feldspar and allied minerals are often referred to simply as 'spars'.

SPATULA TOOL

A tool with a flattened, curved and rounded end. It can be of wood or metal and is a most useful tool for potters.

A wooden spatula tool, one of the most useful in the potter's collection.

SPECIFIC GRAVITY

The ratio of the mass of a material to that of an equal mass of water at 40°C. A specific gravity (s.g.) figure of less than one will therefore indicate that the material is 'lighter' than water (i.e. will float). The s.g. of clays and most common ceramic minerals averages 2.6; feldspars slightly less, and quartz a little more at 2.65. This is useful when using *Brongiart's formula*. The mass or weight of a material divided by its volume will give its density. The equation must be either in lb./pts. or kg./liters. The figure obtained is divided by the s.g. of pure water, but since this is 1.0 the density and s.g. are the same.

The s.g. value will also control the settling speed of pottery materials in water. Lead compounds (s.g. around 11), will drop quickly and such glazes must be stirred repeatedly. The high s.g. of zircon sand limits its use in refractories, saggars etc., for which it would be otherwise very suitable; high concentrations make these too heavy.

SPECIFIC HEAT

The heat required to raise a unit of a substance through one degree. (See *British thermal units, calorie, joule*.)

SPINEL

A mineral built up into regular *crystals* from a *bivalent* and a *trivalent* (tervalent) metal. The general composition is $MO.R_2O_3$, where M equals magnesium, ferrous oxide, manganese, zinc, cobalt or nickel; and R equals ferric oxide, chromium or aluminum. The typical mineral is magnesium aluminate, $MgO.Al_2O_3$. Magnetic iron oxide $FeO.Fe_2O_3$ is a spinel, and cobalt also forms spinels. They are considered to be the most stable form of oxides.

SPINNER

A plate or saucer which has sagged or warped in the center of its base so that it will not sit firmly, i.e. it can be spun round. This may be caused by careless *turning* or may develop during drying. Test before packing in the kiln and, if necessary, flatten with a pad of glass paper which can also be used on soft biscuit.

SPIRAL WEDGING

See *wedging*.

SPODUMENE

A *lithium* mineral $Li_2O.Al_2O_3.4SiO_2$, 372. Similar to *petalite* which has eight molecules of SiO_2, and is likewise sometimes referred to as a lithium feldspar.

Undergoes an irreversible expansion from alpha to beta forms at 900°C. Used in bodies where a low *thermal expansion* is required. Cardew PP 76 discusses the compounding of an artificial spodumene body or the use of spodumene rock (60%, 60–200 mesh) with plastic clay for flameproof bodies. A very simple glaze recipe using 54.5% spodumene to 45.5% talc is given by Behrens in CM 20/3. (See also *lithium*.) Brian Dewsbury uses up to 20% of spodumene in stoneware electric kiln firings. Obtainable in G.B. from Cromartie and others.

SPONGE

Various synthetic sponges are now made, but none can equal a fine-grain natural sponge for sensitivity and working qualities. The ideal type is the 'elephant's ear' Turkey sponge, about $2\frac{1}{2}$ in. (65 mm.) across. Natural sponges are becoming rarer and more expensive. If you can visit a supplier to choose your own, so much the better. The 'grain' should lie all in one direction with no holes or tears. Once found, a good sponge is worth treasuring; wash it after use and avoid highly abrasive surfaces.

Synthetic bath-sponges with large holes are best for swabbing and cleaning. The type which dries stiff can more easily be cut to shape and used for throwing, but most of them become loaded with clay, which is difficult to wash out.

SPONGED DECORATION

Apart from the sponging on of color to represent foliage, etc. which has been practiced for a long time, Anthony Phillips (CR 123) uses cut sponge shapes with slips, laying one color over or beside another to build up 'a more mysterious decoration'. The earthware glaze eats away some of the finer layers and creates a feeling of translucency. Artificial sponges can be cut or burned with a hot rod into quite large motifs for sponging color, slip, or glaze onto pottery.

SPONGE STICK

A natural or polyester fiber sponge fastened to the end of a dowel or stick, and used for absorbing surplus water from pots during throwing. A small natural sponge stretched tightly over the end of a $\frac{1}{2}$ or $\frac{3}{4} \times \frac{1}{4}$ in. (say 15×7 mm.) stick can be used as a *throwing stick*.

SPOUT

A tapering tube which conducts and controls the flow of liquid from a tea or coffee pot etc. It is useful to bear the definition in mind, especially with regard to 'control', when designing a spout. The object of the taper is to build up a pressure or weight of liquid so that it issues in a steady, arching stream. A large and clumsy spout will not do this efficiently. Nor will it pour well if the grid behind the spout will not allow more water to pass through it than can issue from the narrowest part of the spout.

Spouts are usually thrown, leaving sufficient extra clay top and bottom for trimming. The form can be straight-sided, concave, or slightly bottle-shaped. Trim the large end to fit the pot at the correct angle, about 45° to the vertical, and ensure that the other end is at least level with the lid flange, if not higher. If the lower part of the spout is too thick it can be trimmed inside with a knife. Mark the outline on the pot and drill grid holes before scoring, slipping, and luting it on.

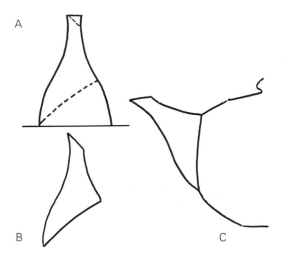

(A) The shape of a thrown teapot spout which, when cut along the dotted line (B) and attached to the body of the pot as (C) forms a spout with a single curve above and a double curve below.

11

12

13

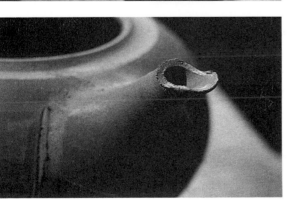

14

Michael Casson applying a spout immediately after throwing.

(1) to (4) Showing stages in the throwing with the last picture especially important, all trace of slip on the surface being removed with a rib so that it is dry enough to handle.

(5) and (6) The spout is removed from the block of clay on which it was thrown and cut through to the appropriate angle with a wire.

(7) and (8) The top of the base aperture is eased upwards with the finger, and the spout pressed onto the pot just firmly enough to make a mark.

(9) to (12) Within this line the grid is cut through, the spout placed in position, and fastened on with a few careful but free-moving strokes.

(13) The end of the spout is now cut. To allow for the twist ('unwinding') which often occurs during firing, the wire is held sloping slightly downwards to the left when facing the pot, as in the picture. (14) The last picture shows the spout, completed only a few minutes after throwing.

A modern Japanese teapot by Futoh of Tokoname with an unusual slab spout.

Trimming the small end presents problems. Clay has what Cardew calls 'memory', that is, it will continue to twist during firing in the direction of the throwing strain. This means that the spout may be pointing sideways after firing if it has been trimmed horizontally. Slower, 'easy' throwing will help. Allowance can be made when trimming by facing the spout away from you and cutting it to slope slightly to the right and point a little to the left. Some potters avoid the difficulty by leaving the end of the spout as a right-angle, but the form must be very carefully worked out if this is not to look blunt and unfinished.

Spouts have been *press molded* and applied to thrown pots, but not with conspicuous success. Thrown spouts are usually applied at soft leather stage, but Michael Casson and others lute them on almost immediately after throwing. This demands great skill but at its best can be very fresh and integrated in its effect. A spout may be 'pulled' (see *handles*) into a curve when half-dry. The very tip of the spout should be reasonably sharp, and its pouring qualities will be enhanced by a slight downwards curve (see *lip*).

A salt-glaze coffee pot with a bold 'bridge' spout. By Ruthane Tudball.

SPRAYING

The application of glaze or color by rendering it to a fine mist under pressure. Usually done with a spray-gun similar to those used for paint etc. The granular nature of ceramic suspensions will clog some types, especially the cheaper electric drill-sprayers. A more sophisticated and efficient set-up involves an air-pressure pump and pressure tank. Spraying is practiced in the industry, but has limited value in the small workshop. It is noisy, and an additional spray-booth with an exhaust fan is strongly advised. A mask should always be worn. Sprayed glaze is liable to uneven thickness and to *pin-holing*. Although small amounts of glaze can be used, there is considerable waste. The cost of equipment, with a booth, is also considerable.

Spraying is useful for *once-fired* wares, especially large plates and other bulky pieces. Color can be sprayed onto *resist* or, from a finely controlled jet, 'drawn' on the dish or pot. It is difficult to avoid a mechanical, commercial appearance. A number of professional potters are, however, experimenting with sprayed decoration.

For more than purely experimental work a booth is essential both to restrict the spread of colors and glazes which can quickly invade every corner, and more importantly, the lungs of the potter. An extractor booth is one luxury which will repay the effort of acquiring or building.

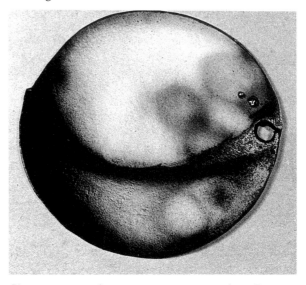

Pigments sprayed onto a matt stoneware glaze. By Robert Fournier.

SPRIG

A bas-relief or medallion made in a small press-mold and stuck with slip onto a pottery surface. Typified by eighteenth century bi-colored sprigging, salt-glazed bellarmine masks, and in the industry by Wedgwood's cameos. The craft potter can still devise new and entertaining uses for the sprig.

A simple sprig mold with casts.

The sprig-mold can be cut directly into clay and then biscuit fired, the design can be cut into a slab of plaster, or the sprig can be modeled separately and cast in plaster. To make a cast, work plastic clay firmly into the mold with a flat tool and flatten the back. It can be removed by pressing a damp metal spatula or *palette knife* onto the back and lifting sharply. Position the sprig on the damped surface of a pot and press gently with a wooden tool in the hollows of the design. Do not attempt too large a sprig; it is better to build up from smaller units.

SPRINGER

Or scewback. A brick with one sloping face from which an arch can be 'sprung' when building a kiln. (See *brick, bricklaying*.)

SPUR

A small piece of kiln furniture with one point up and three down. For use at earthenware temperatures only.

SQUARE LINER

Long slender brushes with the end cut square. For lining with the whole length of the brush.

STABLE, stability

A stable glaze has a well-balanced formula, is adequately fired and will not react easily to acid or other corrosion. An excess of bases or coloring oxides may render a glaze unstable. Stability is always desirable, but especially so in lead glazes (see *lead solubility* and *metal release*). Adherence to the generally recommended ratios of the Seger formula will assist in computing stable glazes. (See *Thorpe's ratio*.) Materials can be added to a recipe to render lead, for instance, less likely to be dissolved from the glaze. Titanium and calcium are used in small quantities in lead frits.

The physical stability of a pot is also a virtue. Tall shapes with very small bases are seldom good pot forms. The strengthening of a narrow-waised pot with a metal rod is an acceptance of failure. An uneven base is aggravating, and all pots and bowls should be tested before firing. A slightly hollow or concave base may be achieved during making or turning by tapping with the finger when soft-leather. A wobbly base can be flattened by holding the pot hard down on to a wetted wheel head or whirler, which is then revolved. Dry pots can be sandpapered in the same way.

STACK-THROWING

Term sometimes used to describe several small pieces of pottery thrown from one large block of clay. The top surface clay should be well compressed after cutting off each piece so as to minimize the chance of cracking because of excessive wetness remaining from the previous throwing.

(1) Throwing from a cone of clay – stack throwing – in this case a small glaze test bowl.

(2) A method of cutting off with a needle awl held slightly sloping upwards towards the center of the base giving a slight recess (if you are clever!).

STAFFORDSHIRE CONE

A range of pyrometric cones. Most numbers correspond within 10°C. to Seger cones. Graded in 10°C. steps above 08 (940°C.) up to 11 (1320°C.), except 1200–1215° and 1215–1230°. The numbers are prefixed by H. A nought in front of any number indicates a temperature below 1100°C. (See under *cones* for list.)

STAIN

A term widely used in pottery, but without a specific meaning. It can indicate an organic *identifying stain* (used industrially for different bodies, especially porcelain) or any oxide or prepared pigment used for coloring bodies, slips or glazes. The term might with advantage be restricted to fritted, prepared colors, in which sense it is generally used in merchant's catalogs. Stains for clay bodies or decoration as well as glazes are sold by most suppliers, some formulated for stoneware or porcelain firings.

High temperature bright colors for slips are available and Ivo Mosley (CR 86) reduces his colors from 850°C. to within 100°C. of his top temperature to maintain their brilliance but he warns that some 'high temperature stains' will be less successful than others. He quotes Deancraft for good browns and yellows, Potterycrafts for greens and reds, Fulham for yellow.

STAMP

An embossed or intaglio stamp can be used to build up a pattern on clay. *Impressing* is a type of stamping but the term can also indicate the printing of color onto the surface without involving impression. Sponge 'root', cut into patterns, has been used for stamping designs onto pottery. Some potters' 'marks' are rubber-stamped with pottery pigment. (See also *seal*.)

STANDARD BLACK

A color derived from 4% each of cobalt, manganese, and iron oxides. (See *black glazes*.)

STANNIC

Applied to a tin compound or a glaze containing tin. From 'stannum', the international name for tin, hence its symbol Sn. More exactly 'stannic' indicates quadrivalent tin oxide, SnO_2 as distinct from the 'stannous' bivalent SnO.

STAR AND DELTA WIRING

Systems for wiring *three-phase* equipment.

(A) Star wiring for a three phase kiln, each line connected back to a common neutral. This will give full mains voltage on each phase or circuit. (See also three phase.)

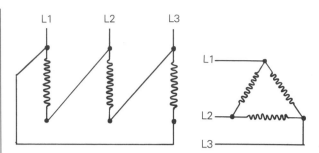

(B) Delta wiring for three phases. Element circuits are connected across phases to give 415 volts from a 240 volt supply. The neutral is not employed in this system.

STATES OF MATTER

The three most distinct states of matter are the gaseous, the liquid and the solid. No chemical change takes place between these states, but only the physical 'loosening' of the bonds between the *molecules*. Energy, usually heat, is involved in the changes.

STEATITE

The massive form or rock of talc. Soapstone. One of the softest rocks. Can be carved into pot and other forms and is still known as 'pot-stone'. Also used as 'French chalk'.

STEEL PALETTE

A very thin, flexible, sheet-steel tool, rectangular or kidney-shaped. Made in two thicknesses and several sizes, averaging 5 in. (127 mm.) across. Invaluable for scraping and smoothing plastic clay, especially for *hand-building*. Can be used as a throwing *rib* or, occasionally, for *turning*.

STENCIL

Allied to *resist* a stencil is a piece of shaped card, paper

Brushing color across a paper stencil on a dish.

or other fairly stiff material laid onto a surface so as to control a design. It can have apertures cut in it, through which color can be applied; it can be used as a resist shape, producing a blank shape on a background of color; or to divide a surface into two areas. The comparative rigidity of stencils confines their effect to simple shapes and masses, often as a foundation for other decoration. Sponging or dabbing the color will give sharper outlines than will brushing, alternatively pigment can be sprayed on. Shallow dishes and tiles present no problems, but stencilling is more difficult on a pot. *Paper resist* is a form of one-off stencilling. Leach used a stencil to divide his 'mountain' dish designs.

Stiff-paper shapes, one cut from the other, have been held against this dish and sprayed over. The occasional 'leaks' of color under the edge of the stencil help to soften the otherwise hard lines. By Sheila Fournier.

STEPPED GRAPH

A variation on the steady rise in temperature of a kiln graph which shows periods of heat maintenance or even a fall, associated usually with reduction or *soaking*.

STICKING-UP

The assembly of parts of a model, teapot, or similar construction, either at the leather-hard or a softer stage. An industrial term.

STILT

An item of *kiln furniture*. It has three arms radiating from the center, with vertical points, generally at the end of each arm. Glazed pieces are supported on appropri-

ately sized stilts, the points about $\frac{1}{4}$ in. (6 mm.) in from the edge of the base. The point adheres to the glaze and breaks away when the stilt is removed. Stilts are therefore expendable, though they may last three or four uses. Designed for the industry with its thin, *fritted* glazes, a stilt can become firmly welded into thick or carelessly applied *raw glaze*. Glaze the base sparingly, therefore, or wipe some of the glaze away. Do not jam the points into a *foot ring* or extend them beyond the ring. *Spurs* may be used in place of stilts for large dishes. Remember also that the pot will shrink, but the stilt will not. Remove stilts with a sorting tool.

Sizes are available from 25–100 mm. (1–4 in.) point to point. 'Egg stilts' are triangular in plan, with a hole in the center. Stilts are for use in *earthenware* firings only, and will fail in stoneware.

A stilt support for pots. For earthenware only.

STONEWARE

According to the Brussels Nomenclature—'dense, impermeable, and hard enough to resist scratching with a steel point . . . more opaque [than porcelain] and normally only partly vitrified'. Stoneware is distinguished from earthenware by:

1 Its higher firing-temperature. The generally accepted minimum is 1200°C., and the range is 1200–1350°C. Bodies with artificially lowered *vitrification*-points have been marketed.

2 Its degree of vitrification. A *porosity* of not more than 5%. The higher fired stonewares will also be *impermeable*. The surface has a close and glassy appearance but may be rough to the touch.

3 A well developed reaction zone across the interface, giving greater integration and subtlety of glaze.

4 Low iron-content in the body. Red clay will not form a true stoneware, though it may be added to a *refractory* body.

5 Does not need either lead or boron in its glaze, although the latter is sometimes used in small quantities.

6 Jun glazes and celadons in reduction.

In spite of stoneware's apparent advantages over earthenware, the qualities of the two types of ceramics are so different that neither has an inherent superiority.

STONEWARE BODY

A naturally *fusible* but reasonably iron-free plastic clay is the basis for a stoneware body. Many *fireclays* and other *sedimentary clays* may be suitable as the major constituent. Sources of 'stoneware' clay are reported in the USA in Colorado, Wyoming and New Jersey (Jordon clay).

Most stoneware bodies are mixtures of a number of materials each chosen for their particular qualities.

1 For plasticity: ball clays and red clays, up to 40% of the first and 20% of the second.

2 For fusibility: natural fusibility from the ball and red clays. Additional non-plastic fluxes such as feldspar, stone, (5–15%), or 5% of talc have been mentioned.

3 Refractoriness and low shrinkage: china clay, quartz or flint (15–20%), sand, grog (ideally the body biscuit), or aluminous fireclay.

4 For color: red clay, or 5–10% of *ochre* (Leach).

5 Texture *grog*, sand, coarse fireclay up to 25%.

Ilmenite will cause glaze speckle. The materials should be blunged to a slip for maximum efficiency.

Many potters buy a prepared plastic body which when bought is often too smooth and characterless, but which can be modified as above. (Cardew warns against wedging china clay into a plastic body.) Others buy dry powdered materials and work them together in a *dough mixer*.

STONEWARE CLAY

A general name for plastic, refractory, *secondary clays* which are not as fine-grained as *ball clays* or as deep-seated as *fireclays*. In Germany and the U.S.A., and in other parts of the world, grades of clay can be found which will fire to 1300°C. with few if any modifications. They have no massive commercial use and are therefore more difficult to obtain than kaolins and fireclays.

STONEWARE GLAZE

A range of glazes firing between 1200°C. and 1350°C., with the great majority in the midway range, 1260–1310°C. The two oxides which feature so prominently in soft glazes (lead and boron) have little or no place in stonewares, which are generally based on feldspars or wood ash.

The average formula for a stoneware glaze is $RO.0.35Al_2O_3. 3.5SiO_2$, but there are numerous combinations outside this ratio, e.g. above 1300°C. the silica ratio can rise sharply, while formulas with only 2.0 parts of silica have been reported in analyses of Chinese glazes. At temperatures of 1250°C. plus it is difficult *not* to produce a glaze of some kind by mixing two or three ceramic minerals. The classic starting point is 40 parts feldspar, 30 flint, 20 whiting, 10 clay; but in other recipes the feldspar is much more dominant, e.g. 70 feldspar, 13 flint, 10 whiting, 7 china clay.

Try line blends or triaxial mixtures of nepheline syenite, talc, barium, china stone, with other more exotic minerals such as petalite, basalt, etc., also with red clay and, of course, ash. It is useful to be able to translate any interesting result back to a glaze formula (see *recipe-into-formula*). The effects of the various oxides and minerals are discussed under their headings. (See also *oxidation* and *reduction*.)

Iron is the principal coloring oxide in reduced stoneware glazes, which seem to have a wider firing-range without violent character changes than do oxidized glazes. In the latter the range is wider but the effects, in general, are not so subtle. Manganese and copper have a place, the latter in matt glazes to prevent *volatilization*. Cobalt needs to be well 'quenched' with iron, red clay etc if it is not to be strident.

STOPPER

A decorative, tree-like stopper on a bottle by Mary Rich. Note slightly conical neck form.

Ceramic stoppers are rarely air-tight. The old bungs were often wound with straw. A tapered stopper in a similarly formed bottle neck helps, but corks or flanged plastic stoppers are usually used. One should start with available cork sizes and throw the pots to fit them rather than the other way round. Cardew, in 'Pioneer Pottery', describes an ingenious tool he made for cutting screw threads on bottle necks and stoppers.

STOPPING

Mixtures for filling cracks in biscuit ware. Merchants list 'red', 'white' and 'stoneware' stopping—generally composed of china clay, flint and a little flux. If a biscuit pot has cracked, this suggests strain which may cause further damage in the glaze fire, and the piece is better discarded. With modeling there is more justification for attempted repair. The stopping called Alumide, its makers claim, can be glazed over.

STORAGE OF CLAY

Clay improves with *aging*, and facilities for storing clay in a damp atmosphere are very desirable. For large quantities, some sort of clay 'cellar' with non-absorbent walls, a tile foor, no ventilation and a close-fitting door is ideal, but for most craft potters something more modest is called for. The *polythene* bags in which plastic clay is often delivered provide storage, if unpunctured, for many months. Similarly, plastic sacks, bin-liners and the like can be utilized for mixed and *wedged* batches, which should be rested for at least a day or two before use. Damp the interior of the bags with a sponge to avoid dry flakes of clay.

Clay bins present problems: drying layers of clay on the sides; the decomposition of zinc on galvanised surfaces; and the difficulty of extracting clay from a pressed-down mass. If clay has been pugged, try to keep the rolls separate so that they can be more easily lifted out; sheets of stiffish polythene between layers help. Pug your clay fairly soft. A full bin is more efficient than a half empty one. Asbestos-substitute tanks need filling with water first to saturate them. Plastic bins keep clay damp, but are easily damaged by scrapers. They will also melt easily, and can crack in frost.

STRAW ASH

A highly refractory ash, usually containing up to 75–80% silica. An exception is 'bean straw ash' (L.PB).

STRONTIUM, oxide

A metallic element Sr, 87.5.
Oxide SrO, 103.5. Strontia.
Carbonate $SrCO_3$, 147.5.

An *alkaline earth*. The slightly *soluble*, non-poisonous but expensive carbonate is used as a glaze flux. Similar to calcium, which it can replace. Strontium glazes should be low in lime, however, if crystallization is not required. Parmalee states that good earthenware glazes can be had by replacing some other bases with strontia, and that colors also benefit. The oxide provides a long firing-range and is very craze-resistant. There are no common strontia-bearing minerals. Strontium earthenware glazes are reported to be widely used in Russia, the oxide replacing lead.

STUDIO POTTER

An artist craftsman working alone, or with very few assistants, who takes part in all the ceramic processes so that the final piece has his or her individual stamp or character. It is not a very satisfactory term, and others have been suggested: craftsman potter; artist potter; workshop potter; hand potter; non-industrial potter; ceramist, etc. As the industry becomes more and more remote from its craft origins, perhaps simply 'potter' will soon be sufficient.

STUPID

An old term for a *wad-mill*!

SULFIDE, sulfate

Many elements will form a salt or binary compound with sulfur. Its release during firing, however, can have ill-effects on glazes, and the form is rarely used. Galena is a sulfide of lead, barytes a sulfate of barium which liberates sulfur dioxide during firing. Plaster of paris is $CaSO_4$ ($\frac{1}{2}H_2O$). (See also *sulfuring*.)

SULFUR

An element S, 32. Combines with metals to form binary compounds, sulfides. Sulfur may be present in clays, especially fireclays, and in some concentrations in yellow ochre. Its presence is made obvious when firing an electric kiln! Mentioned in the 'Dictionary of Science' as 'essential to life', but it is not good for the lungs for all that!

SULFURING

The dulling of a glaze surface through attack by sulfur. Parmalee discusses the effects at length CG 308–11. Sulfur as sulfites—salts of sulfurous oxide SO_2—will burn away, but those of SO_3, sulfuric oxide, are resistant to change by heat. Early ventilation is therefore necessary to clear fumes from the kiln, especially in *soft-glaze* firings. At higher temperatures a *reducing* atmosphere is more likely to drive out the sulfur in sulfates.

Leadless glazes and those with a high calcium or barium content appear to be at greatest risk from sulfur gas. The sulfur gases liberated by some clays in an electric kiln are a nuisance, or worse, and the pottery room should be well ventilated.

SUMP OIL

See *drainoil.*

SUPERSATURATED GLAZE

A glaze with more coloring oxide than it can dissolve, the surplus being precipitated on cooling. (See *saturated glaze.*)

SURFACE COMBUSTION

Fuel gases burn more readily on contact with hot surfaces. This will be obvious to anyone who has tried to start a *drip-feed* kiln from cold. Kiln design should take this into account; the heating of *secondary air* is important.

SURFACE TENSION

An effect, resembling that of a stretched elastic skin, seen at the boundary or surface of any liquid. For instance, when gently pouring liquid from the surface of a glaze it will pile up on the rim before bursting through and running off. Glaze, in its liquid state, has a high surface tension value—some 200–300 as compared with 74 for water. This will be seen from the globules of glaze which hang at the foot of an over-fired or over-glazed pot. *Crawling* in its final stages is influenced by surface tension, the glaze failing to 'wet' the surface. The surface tension of the glaze is greater than the gravity effect which would otherwise spread it over the surface. Cracks in the glaze coating, the primary cause of crawling, increase the surface area and thus the tension. Dust under the surface will have a similar effect. Zinc and magnesium are reputed to lower the surface tension.

SUSPENDER, floatative

A glaze or slip additive which will help to retard *settling* and aid *suspension.* This can be by physical means, using gums (tragacanth, dextrin, arabic), size, bentonite or ball clay, or by the electrical or molecular effect of salt, deflocculants or ammonia. All have intrinsic disadvantages. Organic materials (Parmelee also includes quince pips and blood!) decompose if glaze is kept for long periods and need the further addition of *formalin.* *Deflocculants* thin the mixture; salt introduces unwanted *soluble* ingredients. Dodd mentions calcium chloride to prevent settling—about 0.02%. Epsom salts have been mentioned, as has *Macaloid.*

All in all, perhaps the best suspender is a good wide paddle and a strong arm.

SUSPENSION

All insoluble materials stirred up in a liquid will eventually sink to the bottom again. Fine particles will remain suspended in the liquid longer than coarse ones; those with a low *specific gravity* will remain longer than those with a high one. A lead frit will thus have the worst of both worlds. *Colloidal* particles will remain longest in suspension, hence the use of bentonite. Suspension does not of course refer to *soluble* materials. Some glazes will stay in suspension for a longer period if the container is tightly sealed.

Glaze becomes liquid during firing. Certain oxides, generally *acidic* oxides, will fail to dissolve but will remain in suspension in a fundamentally unaltered state. These are the opacifiers, notably tin and zircon.

T°

Symbol for degrees of temperature.

TABLEWARE

A general term for pottery directly concerned with the serving of food and drink. (See *plate, cup, saucer.*)

TAILINGS

The portion of a material which will not pass through a particular *screen*, for instance, coloring oxide in a 200 sieve. The tailings go back into the *mortar* for further grinding, (or more often in practice, down the sink!).

TALC

A mineral, a hydrated magnesium silicate $3MgO.4SiO_2.H_2O,379$ (convenient equivalent weight 126). Low *coefficient of expansion* (2.0).

The chief mineral of soapstone and steatite. Used as an insoluble form of magnesia in glazes. Dolomite is now more commonly used for this purpose. Typical analysis by weight:

MgO	32.0	Al_2O_3	7.0	SiO_2	56.5
CaO	3.0	Fe_2O_3	1.5		

Small amounts, 2% in the batch or up to 0.3 of the RO, will act as a *flux;* more than this will tend to make the glaze *viscous,* but can impart a pleasant sheen to the surface. Lowers the *thermal expansion* (see *cordierite*). It affects some colors—iron goes brown, cobalt a less intense blue. Can be mixed with cobalt when this oxide is used as a pigment.

Talc has a fine, powdery nature and is difficult to mix with water in a glaze batch, floating on the top and blowing away in the slightest breeze. It is advisable to mix it well with the other dry ingredients, and to slowly add the water to the batch.

TAMMAN TEMPERATURE

The *sintering* point or temperature range.

TEAPOT

Like the jug in the hands of Alison Britton, the humble teapot has become a jumping off place for riotous imagination and has suffered many transmogrifications and indignities over the last ten years: multi-spouted, deformed, pornographic, Victorian kitsch, (the variations are endless); forms which are beyond the scope of a practical dictionary.

A good teapot is difficult to make but, when successful, few things can give a potter more satisfaction. One of our most distinguished potters, Geoffrey Whiting, gave this advice in PQ 7:

'A teapot needs to be fairly broad and certainly stable. Throw as thinly as possible, and keep the opening as small as is compatible with easy filling and cleaning. Throw the spout on a fairly thick base, which should be wide enough to allow a grid, the holes of which have a slightly greater cross-sectional area than that of the narrow end of the spout. Make the knob on the lid something worth getting hold of, and vent the lid with a generous $\frac{1}{10}$ in. (2 mm.) hole.'

It is vital to trim the spout so that it is at least level with the top of the teapot (see also *spouts*). Punch plenty of grid or strainer holes, each about $\frac{1}{8}$ in. (3 mm.) across, and leave the ragged edges inside the pot severely alone until quite dry, when they can be chipped away without blocking the holes. Mark and score the spout position and attach with slip. Geoffrey Whiting prefers a spout which grows 'smoothly out of the body of the pot and makes a continuous unbroken line with it', but other teapots show more articulation between spout and pot.

The *handle* is very important. It must be efficient and comfortable, with room for three fingers on a medium pot and four on a large one. Its form and the area of void its loop encloses must balance the spout and the lid. Always attach the handle after the spout, and with the completed lid in place. 'You [may] find that, to form a comfortable efficient hold, the handle looks wrong on the pot . . . in which case you may have to redesign the whole thing. This sort of difficulty is implicit in the nature of design and craftsmanship and it is no good

Still among the best teapots ever made is the classic form by the late Geoffrey Whiting. If there is any criticism, the knob could have been a little bolder to match the strength of the rest of the form.

A compact, multifaceted teapot with paneled glaze and brushwork decoration. By John Maltby.

An attractive example of the modern 'fun' teapot which had almost overtaken the practical type in the 1980's, harking back, in a sense, to Victorian styles.

being afraid of it. Pencil sketches will help but do not allow yourself to become a slave to paper designs. They militate against the freedom and spontaneity the thrown shape should always have.'

Arched-over handles can be of *cane* or clay. They must be high enough for comfortable removal of the lid. The *lugs* of a cane handle should be sturdy; a good deal of weight depends from them. (See also *spouts, handles, cane handles, glazing, lids, knobs*.)

TEMMOKU, tenmoku

The Japanese name for very dark colored *reduced* iron stonewares of early Chinese types, including 'hare's fur', 'oil spot' and other effects on a near-black glaze, which can also break to an iron-red. Quoted percentages of iron in the batch vary widely: 4.5–5% with slow cooling (Cardew); 10% burnt sienna, or a slip glaze of the Albany variety (Rhodes); up to 12% (Leach); a precise 7.6% from Dodd, who also gives this recipe: feldspar 50, whiting 10.9, magnesite 2.3, kaolin 5.9, quartz 23.0.

Margaret Gebhard (CR 88) suggests the following recipe for a once-fired (raw-clay glazed) 1240°C, (soaked for 25 minutes) electric kiln oxidised firing:

Potassium feldspar	40
Nepeheline	15
Whiting	10
Red clay	35

with an additional 2.5% red iron oxide and 1% *spangles*.

It obviously depends upon the type of glaze, usually a fairly fluid one, and on how much iron it will dissolve. A supersaturated glaze will tend to break with lighter browns. (See also *black glazes, red glazes, iron* etc.) Shaw WJC mentions managenese, chromium, and cobalt in connection with temmoku glazes.

TEMPERATURE COLOR

The optical effect of rising heat (in the absence of light) is a change from black to blue-white, through reds, oranges and yellows. It is difficult to give names to these 'colors' which will make them recognizable when peering through a kiln spyhole. Green EP gives a color chart, but the light reflected from an illustration is different in kind from the radiant heat color. With these reservations in mind, the following table may have some use.

Seger cone	T°C°	T°F°	Color
022	600	1110	dull red
015	800	1470	red
010	1000	1830	cherry red, between red and orange
1	1100	2010	orange
5	1180	2160	light orange
7	1230	2250	pale yellow
10	1300	2370	yellow-white
12	1350	2460	white tending to blue

Intensity of light, in fact, produces color effect.

TEMPERATURE CONTROL

See *heat control*.

TEMPERATURE DEGREE

Temperature conversion tables—Centigrade (Celsius) Fahrenheit, and Kelvin

C.	F.	K.	C.	F.	K.
−273	−477	0	1000	832	1273
−18	0	255	1050	1922	1323
0	32	273	1080	1976	1353
10	50	283	1100	2012	1373
50	122	323	1120	2048	1393
100	212	373	1140	2084	1413
120	248	393	1150	2102	1423
200	392	473	1180	2156	1453
225	437	498	1200	2192	1473
250	482	523	1220	2238	1493
300	572	573	1230	2246	1503
350	662	623	1240	2264	1513
400	752	673	1250	2282	1523
450	842	723	1260	2300	1533
500	932	773	1275	2318	1548
550	1022	823	1280	2336	1553
573	1063	846	1285	2345	1558
600	1112	873	1300	2373	1573
660	1220	933	1310	2390	1583
700	1292	973	1325	2417	1598
750	1382	1023	1335	2435	1608
800	1472	1073	1350	2462	1623
870	1598	1143	1380	2516	1653
900	1652	1173	1400	2552	1673
950	1742	1223	1450	2642	1723

Heat produces internal activity in matter: 'hotness' or temperature is a measure of the kinetic energy of the *molecules* of which the matter is composed. Heat leads to fundamental alteration and rearrangement in the basic atomic structure. Certain reactions (e.g. *oxidation*) in themselves produce heat. Temperature is one factor in *heat-work*.

The degree of heat is indicated by a constant scale. Those in common use are based on the interval between the freezing- and boiling-points of water. The

Centigrade or Celsius scale divides this interval into 100 degrees and commences at freezing point, 0°. The freezing point in the Fahrenheit scale is 32°, and the interval is divided into 180 degrees, giving 212°F, as the boiling-point. Conversion cannot therefore be made directly except by memory. The arithmetic is:
Centigrade into Fahrenheit—divide by 5, multiply by 9, add 32 to total.
Fahrenheit into Centigrade—subtract 32, divide remainder by 9, multiply by 5.

TEMPERING CLAY

Adding water to clay powder, or distributing it more intimately. This can be done with a *paddle* and bin, with a *dough mixer*, or, really professionally, by *blunging and filter pressing*. See also *mixing clays*. In the historical sense, the word 'tempering' is often used to indicate the addition of non-clay materials to a body; for instance, shell, grit, grog, sand, etc.

TEMPLATE

In general, a template is any guide or mold shaped to the outline of a piece of work. In pottery it is generally confined to describing a sheet of card, metal, or other stiff material cut to the profile of a pot, plate, bowl, or mold and used as a guide to scrape or model the clay surface to the desired curve, see *jigger and jolley, hollow mold*. It can also be applied to card or paper resists used in decoration where these are held against the piece rather than adhered to it, as with *stencil*.

TEMPORARY KILN

The spate, in recent years, of large 'sculptural' ceramics has given rise to firing problems. When pieces are too heavy or too awkward to be packed into a standing kiln, simple dry-built kiln structures have been erected round them and the whole fired *in situ*. Firing is generally by oil, carried out through strategically placed burner apertures. More than one burner is needed. A simple *up-draft kiln* might be easier to fire. (See also diagrams in Rhodes K,). Raku and sawdust kilns are also generally temporary structures, erected and taken down in a few minutes. A more traditional structure erected as a temporary kiln can be very instructive with regard to kiln design and performance. See also *raku kiln, top-hat kiln*.

Like all kilns of this type their weight and complexity for the same degree of insulation, has been considerably reduced by the development of *ceramic fiber*.

TENSILE STRENGTH

The resistance a material exhibits to being torn apart by tension or pulling. The tensile strength of glazes and bodies is important, one or the other usually being in a state of tension. *Soft glazes* are reputed to be more 'elastic' or resistant than stonewares, but it is easier to get a stoneware glaze into *compression*. (See *crazing, shattering*).

TENSION

A state of tensile or 'pulling' strain. Glazes under tension will *craze*.

TERRACOTTA

Literally 'cooked earth', the term most commonly indicates unglazed red clay modeling or architectural ceramic. It is also applied to the color of fired *red clay*. Rhodes equates terracotta with a low-grade open *fire-clay*, but this would not be a widely understood meaning. Cardew describes a 'terracotta' wood-firing kiln for temperatures up to 950°C.

TERRA SIGILLATA

A reddish-brown, slightly glossy surface found especially on Roman pottery. Probably a very fine (*colloidal*) *red slip*. Potash additions (wine lees) have also been mentioned. Behrens suggests: clay 40, water 100, soda ash 4. Allow the slip to settle, pour water from the surface and use only the top one-third or so—the finest grain (see *suspension*). Colors in the form of carbonates and also zinc or titanium can be added before sedimentation. Parks PGRG, mentions the proprietary water softener Calgon or sodium hydroxide: around 1 to 200 parts. The fine particles can be further improved by milling.

Fiona Salazar sprays her basic slip onto pots, burnishes them, then adds decoration, using several coats of stained ball clay slips brushed on, followed by a final reburnishing (CR 107). Her slip recipe is: 3500 centiliters water; 1500 grams ball clay; 7.5 grams sodium hexamater phosphate (SHP). The last item is ground before adding to the slip. After 48 hours water is syphoned off and the top layer of fine clay particles used. Duncan Ross (CR129) uses some red clay in his bodies, fires in saggars with sawdust after a preliminary biscuit fire to 1000°C; uses masking tape as a resist between slips; and controls carbon penetration by varying the thickness of the slips. He finishes with a light coating of paraffin-based wax.

TERTIARY AIR

An infrequently used term for a supply of pre-heated air to the chimney of a kiln to assist combustion of smoke and to minimize pollution. The chimney can be large enough to accommodate pots for biscuit-firing, it will then act like an up-draft kiln.

TESSHA

A Japanese glaze of the temmoku family but more metallic and breaking to iron reds. The standard 4.3.2.1 glaze (see *stoneware glaze*) with the addition of 26% quartz and 13% Fe_2O_3, in reduction, is given for tessha. The firing schedule will radically affect the glaze. Quick cooling to 900°C is recommended.

TEST-KILN

The value of very small trial kilns is limited. By their nature they fire and cool more quickly than a production kiln and this, together with other factors, will give misleading results. They are more useful in earthenware, the results approximating more closely to those from larger kilns than in *stoneware*. On the credit side, they can give a general impression at various temperatures and can reveal gross errors in glaze mixes before a full pack is spoiled. Tests are always more valid, however, when worked in with the general run of production in normal kilns.

Electric test-kilns can be built quite cheaply and quickly, although the limited *element* lengths will necessitate a thinner gauge wire than is normal for high temperatures. 90 ft. (27 m.) of 17 s.w.g., producing 2.5 kW, can generally be housed in a test-kiln.

TEST-PIECE

See *glaze trial, temperature indicator, draw-trial*.

Test pieces for glaze, etc.
(A) A thrown cylinder can be cut in two as shown or, if wider, into four or six segments. Each will give an upright inside and outside surface, simulating a pot.
(B) A small bowl, thrown on a stack.
(C) A ring with a hole in it is useful for hanging on a board or for stringing together.

(D) Strips of clay can be dried over a rolling pin so that each piece will stand on a curved edge.
(E) A shallow dish from the center of which several glaze tests may be poured, keeping a series together for reference and comparison. It is somewhat instructive if the tests overlap.

TEXTURE

The same root as 'textile'. The 'Oxford English Dictionary' gives 'an arrangement of threads'. In general usage the term indicates fine markings or irregularities of the surface, or the degree of smoothness of the surface, as apparent to sight and touch.

With the increase in *hand-building* and the decline in

Texture can be developed by the instrument or tool used for cutting through the clay (see cutting off). Here is an extreme example:
(1) Slicing through a block of clay with a defunct kiln element.

(2) The striking three-dimensional pattern achieved by this means.

Strong texture achieved by rolling soft clay onto a ridged surface, the slabs further manipulated into this striking standing form by Peter Wright.

Subtle, varied fluted textures on a 'Windswept bottle' by Gordon Baldwin.

brushwork and pattern-making, texture is often the main interest provided by the surface. Sand or grog is either beaten into the surface or exposed by working it over; coarse metal oxides (e.g. ilmenite) or even fragments of metal (e.g. copper filings) produce varied texture on a surface. More consciously controlled markings are made with hacksaws, fine combs etc, or by beating with engraved or string-bound bats etc. (See also *impressing*.)

Christopher Selwood (Chisholm Institute of Technology, Vic. Australia) suggests adding organic materials—sawdust, crushed coke, etc either singly or together—or inorganic materials including silicon carbide, pumice, basalt, or scoria (the slag from metal workings), or laval deposits, to give physical texture to clays, or colour breaks and speckle to the overlaying glaze.

THERM, thermal unit

A unit of quantity of heat equivalent to 100,000 British thermal units or 29.3 units of electricity. Around 100 cu. ft. of *natural gas* are needed to produce a therm; one gallon (4.55 litres) of *propane*; or $\frac{3}{4}$ gallon (3.4 liters) of fuel oil.

A 'therm' unit is used by gas companies to price their product based on the calorific value of a cu. ft. of gas; 200 ft.^{3} of town gas or 100 ft.^{3} of natural gas produce one therm. (See *gas fuel*.)

Even the best-designed kiln will not utilize all the heat produced, and the 'useful therm' is reckoned at about two-thirds of the 'true therm'. *Electricity* is direct conversion and there is almost no loss. One gas therm is therefore equated with about 20 kWh. In *joule* units one therm equals 105 Mj.

THERMAL CONDUCTIVITY

The rate at which heat passes through a material. High conductivity is required in kiln furniture, a low rate in kiln walls. Materials with low conductivity are 'insulators'. The variation between common ceramic materials can be startling, e.g. silicon carbide is given a factor of 120, while a white porous insulating brick may be as low as 0.8. The factor is arrived at by computing the Btu's per square foot of face area per hour per degree Fahrenheit per inch of thickness, written Btu/ft.^{2}/h/°F./in. Other measurements can replace certain items, such as square meters for ft.^{2}, or °C. for °F., but it is the comparative figures derived from any one factor which are of practical interest. The diagram for conductivity through a brick shows a section through the thickness (through the kiln wall); the *hot-face* temperature is marked on one side by dividing the upright into degrees

281

(like a *graph*). The outer face is also similarly divided and the temperature indicated is that which is maintained when the brick has reached full *heat storage*. The flatter or more horizontal the line, the more complete is the thermal conductivity and the poorer are the *insulating* qualities.

Two bricks of different constitution are often used in a kiln, the inner one chosen for strength and physical heat resistance, the outer one for low thermal conductivity.

It will be seen that, as the hot face temperature rises, the initial heat input into the kiln will go to warm the brick itself (heat storage); when this is complete the outer temperature will rise in direct relationship with the inner one. At a certain temperature the radiation (which increases with the difference between the outer face and the *ambient* temperatures) will equal input into the kiln, and the chamber temperature will become static. (See also *heat loss*.)

Air, except when in free movement (*convection*), is a poor conductor of heat. The inclusion of pores in a material will therefore lower its rating, and it follows that dense, heavy materials have a much higher conductivity factor than lightweight 'open' ones.

heat storage   51.500 Btu/ft²   heat storage   78,050 Btu/ft²
conduction loss 1450 Btu/ft²   conduction loss   540 Btu/ft²

The conductivity and heat storage of firebricks. (See also heat.)

THERMAL EXPANSION

The expansion which all materials undergo when heated, and which is normally reversed on cooling. (See *coefficients of expansion*.) Not to be confused with *inversions*, or with the structural changes which occur in a clay body and are not reversible (see *shrinkage*).

THERMAL SHOCK

Bodies and glazes as a whole, or some oxides within them, undergo changes in volume during firing, some of which are reversible on cooling. If expansions and contractions cannot be accommodated within the structure,

then damage will occur. The *inversions* of quartz and cristobalite will cause thermal shock. The latter, which spans cooking temperatures, is the more important in ovenwares. Quartz inversion is instantaneous and can damage a high-silica ceramic in the kiln. Alumina rather than silica refractories are therefore preferred. Limit *'free' quartz* or flint additions to bodies to 20%, and cool reasonably slowly over the 600–150°C. range. Rapid cooling of a glaze can cause shock and *crazing*, especially if it is high in alkalis.

As well as firing stress, pottery is liable to thermal shock in use, as when taken from an oven and placed on a cold surface. For discussion of this hazard see *flame-proof ovenware*.

THERMOCOUPLE

The activating part of a pyrometer. Two wires of dissimilar alloys are fused together at one end. For temperatures below 1100°C. the alloys are usually Chromel and Alumel, but above 1100°C. pure platinum is used with an alloy of platinum and rhodium. The fused junction is protected by an aluminous porcelain, mullite, or a similar refractory sheath and inserted into the kiln, protruding about an inch (25 mm.) beyond the hot-face. The ends of the wires outside the kiln are connected by special compensating cable to the pyrometer indicator, so completing the circuit. As the wire junction gets hot a small voltage (only a few millivolts) is generated which is measured by the indicator and moves a pointer across a dial calibrated in °T. The length of the connecting cable will affect the reading so do not shorten or lengthen these wires once the pyrometer is installed. Ensure as far as possible that the terminals do not get too hot, or the indicator either too warm or cold. See *pyrometer* and in Fournier EKP for more detailed information.

THERMOTROPHY

Most potters will have noticed that the colors of glazes when opening a kiln while the contents are still just too hot to touch show some rather startling variations; white glazes appear creamy-grey and the quality of reds and browns is altered. Some glazes, especially those containing titania will again alter color if subsequently heated, a phenomenon which can surprise a cook when withdrawing a casserole, for instance, from a hot oven. This change of color at comparatively low temperatures is known as thermotrophy. An associated effect is that of *phototrophy* which is activated by light (or the lack of it) rather than heat.

THIMBLE

An item of *kiln furniture*, now more rarely listed by

merchants. One thimble fits into another, and each has a short horizontal arm. Three piles, set into bases, provide support for similar sized plates or tiles. Used for *earthenware* only. The term '*cranks*' is applied to similar constructions listed in suppliers' catalogs.

THIXOTROPY

A factor of *plasticity*. A clay body 'softens' momentarily under pressure (e.g. of the fingers when throwing) and solidifies again when released. It controls standing strength. The *lamellar* structure of clay with strong electrical bonds between the layers seems to hold the key to this behavior but other explanations have been suggested, e.g. 'house of cards' or 'scaffold' structures. In general scientific terms, thixotropy indicates an increase in *viscosity* with the passage of time, as in thixotropic paints.

Excess *electrolyte* can produce thixotropy in slips, causing them to 'set', becoming fluid only when stirred. See also the converse of thixotropy at *dilatancy*.

THORPE'S RATIO

An equation controlling the *base* (especially lead/silica ratio) in a glaze. A simplified version given by Kenneth Shaw in CR11 (after Mellor) to help computation of safe lead glazes (*low solubility*) reads:

$$\frac{RO + R_2O + Al_2O_3}{RO_2 \text{ (mainly SiO}_2)} = \text{a maximum of } 0.5$$

Examples:

Formula 1. PbO 0.8
K_2O 0.2 $Al_2O_3.25.SiO_2 2.0$

gives $\dfrac{0.8 + 0.2 + 0.25}{2.0} = \dfrac{1.25}{2} = 0.625$

Formula 2. PbO 0.8
K_2O 0.2 $Al_2O_3\ 0.3.SiO_2\ 3.0$

giving $\dfrac{1.3}{3.0} = 0.43$

Formula 1 is in excess of the maximum and is therefore likely to be outside the allowed solubility limits; Formula 2 is a better figure.

This is to be taken as one guide only in working out glazes: the alumina/silica ratio and other factors must also be considered. (See *glaze, Seger formula, etc.*)

THREE PHASE SUPPLY

An electrical mains input through three lines or 'live' wires and one neutral. A high load can be equally distributed over the lines, each supplying a third of the required wattage, or they can be connected in such a way (line to line) to increase the voltage. This enables the electricity company to balance its supply and also reduces the cable size necessary for each phase. The normal domestic supply is on one live and neutral only —*single phase*—and this may be limited to a total load of about 60 amps. For wiring diagrams on three phase supply see *star and delta*.

Kilns of over 4 cu. ft. (0.11 cu. m.) capacity will need more than one phase. Sometimes a two phase supply may be installed. The cost depends on the distance from the mains cables to the meter position and to your kiln. In England it appears to be fairly arbitrary and negotiable. (See *electric kiln, element* etc.)

Electric motors are marginally cheaper and more efficient on three phases. Some authorities will allow up to 70 kW on one phase, especially where three phase is not available.

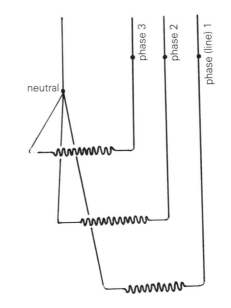

Diagram of a three phase supply. Each circuit in a kiln or other piece of equipment is taken from one phase and back to a common neutral. (See also single phase, star and delta.*) More than one piece of equipment (resistance) can, of course, be taken from each phase but these must be in* parallel *i.e. each taken from a mains line to obtain full voltage.*

THROWING

The hand forming of hollow shapes on a revolving wheel head. Various techniques of coiling, pinching, and molding preceded throwing, probably assisted by a 'slow wheel' or turntable and the precise date of its inception is unknown but there is evidence of throwing some thirty centuries B.C. The changeover from built to wheel pots seems to correspond with a change from women to men potters.

Throwing, when treated in a direct and spontaneous way, gives a distinctive quality to pottery, offers a wide range of shapes, and allows of infinite subtle variations. It is the hall-mark of the individual potter and the general public is coming to appreciate its qualities. It can never recover a prime position in pottery which, industrially, is the place of the mold and the *jigger and jolley*, but it is likely to maintain an honourable and distinctive place. A thrown pot is often distinguished by the spiral groove, especially on the inside, and which can be strongly marked or only just perceptible.

It is an extremely personal technique and one cannot dogmatize on method. The following is an outline of the principles. The clay is well kneaded and formed into a ball or blunt cone with a rounded base, which is brought sharply down onto a damp but not wet wheel head with sufficient force to drive any air from under the base and to attach it firmly to the wheel. It is then 'centered'—for details see *centering* and *coning*. At all stages the surface of the clay is moistened (lubricated), but not saturated, with water or slip. Some potters throw almost dry. For the actual throwing, the thumb (or fingers for a very large pot) is pressed steadily into the clay precisely on its vertical axis until it is $\frac{1}{4}$ in. (6 mm.) or so (more for bowls which are to be turned) from the surface of the wheel head. The rest of the hand is cupped round the clay during this process, and the whole gently supported by the left hand. The thumb is then thrust at right-angles to the first movement, parallel to the wheel head, supporting the clay with the fingers outside until thumb and fingers are within about $\frac{1}{2}$ in. (12 mm.) of one another. The right hand is now raised slowly while gripping the revolving wedge of clay which is squeezed and allowed to flow between thumb and fingers resulting in a thick-walled cylinder. The thinning and raising of the wall is continued using both hands, the middle finger of the left hand (supported by the others) replacing the thumb inside, and the crooked forefinger of the right hand exerting the outside pressure. Shape can be introduced by increasing the pressure inside or out, by raising the inner finger slightly above the outer (for concave profile) or vice versa for convex shapes. It must always be remembered that clay can be worked only by squeezing it between two surfaces—it will not stretch. This holds good for any pottery technique. Widening a pot on the wheel by means of pressure on the inside only will cause it to split or slump.

More concrete instructions are to be found in Colbeck TT but personal tuition and continual practice are essential. (See also *bowl, jug, turning, lids.*)

Isaac Button throwing a large flowerpot.
(1) to (3) Opening out, using both thumbs inside and squeezing the clay up to the fingers outside and into a thick collar which is gripped and lifted with a slight change in position, the little finger crooked over to exercise control over the rim. Note that the extra thickness required for the finished rim is already apparent. In illustration (4) the hands are in the usual position for thinning the wall, the knuckle outside and the straight fingers inside. (5) The still slightly narrow pot is brought up higher than the guide stick so that, when brought out to full width, it is the correct height as at (6). The outside has been smoothed with a rib.

1

2

3

4

5

6

THROWING GAUGE
See *pot gauge*.

THROWING STICK
Called 'egote' in Japan where they are much used. Shaped wooden sticks used as interior *ribs* when throwing, especially narrow-mouthed vessels. (See illustration

285

under *egote*.) The more usual Western method is to pull up a wider pot and throw the shoulder inwards. (See the film 'Isaac Button, Country Potter'.) Sometimes a stick with a sponge on the end is used.

THROWING BAT

See *wheel bat*.

THROWN INLAY

See *rolled inlay*.

THUMB POT

See *pinch pot*.

TILE

The industrial tile, usually 4 × 4 in. (100 × 100 mm.) or 6 × 6 in. (150 × 150 mm.) is power-pressed from a barely damp powdered body in a die or metal mold. This minimizes shrinkage and warping (the latter being the main obstacle to making tiles from plastic clay) but it also destroys any quality in the finished ceramic. Thicker tiles may also be extruded from between rollers. A number of potters use industrial tiles as surfaces to be decorated with brushwork, trailed glaze, etc.

There is an account of pre-industrial tile-making in Berendsen TGH. Roughly cut rolled tiles were piled up to 'yearn' (even out their moisture content) before a final rolling and cutting using an iron-edged template. They were fired in pairs, upright, bedded in 'wads'. Throughout the history of the tile there has been a steady diminution in thickness from around $\frac{3}{4}$ in. (20 mm.) to $\frac{1}{4}$ in. (6 mm.). The average thickness of a hand-made tile is $\frac{3}{8}$ in. (10 mm.).

Methods of making tiles:

1 Slabs can be rolled out freehand or with the use of guide sticks: the tiles cut at leather-hard with a fine knife using a square template.

(A) The halved joints of a tile frame.
(B) The frame assembled. See at (3) in text. It helps if two people cooperate with this type of tile frame, one holding, one pulling. Alternatively the frame can be held steady by two nails in a board, spaced to hold the outer arms.

2 A block of clay cut into appropriately sized slabs with a multi-wire 'harp' and then treated as above.

3 Wooden frames or plaster molds: a two-piece mold with a separate base needed for the latter. Clay is beaten into the frame with the palm of the hand and the surplus is scraped off with a ruler, wetting the clay for the final smoothing movement. Turn the frame 45° between each pull. Lay the frame on a square of paper before commencement to avoid the clay sticking to the table.

1

2

3

(1) Cutting a tile with the aid of a card template.
(2) and (3) Two stages in the use of a tile cutter.

Part of a large tile panel 'The back of the Moon' by Maggie Angus Berkowitz. White glazes were trailed and brushed on, fired, and then a dark blue transparent glaze poured over the figure. A silicon carbide glaze was used on the 'Moon'.

Tile-mosaic tables by Albert Shelly and Robert Fournier. (See note in article on mosaic for the system of keeping these long triangles of clay flat while drying.)

4 Metal tile cutters, with ejection plates, can be purchased. Usually made for 4 in. (100 mm.) squares or circular tiles. The tile is cut from a rolled-out slab.

Methods of drying tiles:

1 Tiles can be dried in the open, turning them over frequently to correct warping.

2 Between absorbent bats, such as asbestos sheets or several thicknesses of newspaper.

3 Leach suggests that tiles cut from a large sheet of clay should be not quite separated so that they hold each other flat.

4 Smaller or thinner tiles can be dried very rapidly on a hot surface such as a kitchen range, or the top of a hot kiln. Lay them on a kiln shelf.

Tiles can be biscuited in piles of five with a *setter* on top. They are glazed by skimming the surface over a well-stirred glaze; or they can be sprayed.

Tilework has always included other shapes than square, and has often had relief treatment. There is a greater variety today than ever before, in shape, size, and finish. On the walls of our rather dim modern buildings they can add a touch of gaiety and interest, but their use is seldom really understood or fully exploited, and there is a wide open field for the potter to explore. (See also *mosaic*.)

Commercial tile setters.

TIMER

A one-hour or five-hour cooking timer is an invaluable aid when firing. In a classroom, or when engrossed in other work it is easy to forget the passage of time. The warning ring has saved many a pot from disaster!

TIN, oxide

A metallic element Sn (stannum), 118.5.
Stannic oxide SnO_2, 151.s.g.6.7.

A useful *opacifier* at all temperatures, with unique qualities which cannot be matched by zircon, etc. It is *acidic* and *refractory*, and does not *dissolve* to any great extent in a glaze up to about 1200°C. but remains suspended as a white powder. It has a tendency to cause *crawling*.

Its principal use is in *soft glazes* for *majolica* painting or colored glazes, the latter often rather misleadingly called tin enamels or majolica glazes in suppliers' catalogs and by historians. Tin gives a pleasant texture, and a soft clear color from oxides. Make additions of 9–10% in a lead glaze; up to 15% in a soft litharge glaze on red clay; 3–5% in stonewares. Beware *chrome-tin pink* reaction (see also *tin glaze*). A little tin oxide is reputed to assist *copper reds*.

TIN ASH

Tin *calcined* with lead, used as a more fusible white pigment than tin oxide alone. The early majolica potters used mixtures varying between 2:1 and 4:1 lead/tin, calcined and ground as one of the ingredients of their glazes.

TIN GLAZE

Any glaze which owes its opacity to tin oxide. An adequate glaze coating is needed to achieve *opacity* but not so thick as to crack and subsequently crawl. *Calcined* clay, or the use of *tin ash* is reputed to help prevent crawling in a soft glaze. (See *tin* etc for percentage additions.)

Ideally a tin glaze will include around 0.5 RO equivalents of lead oxide. The tin will increase the *viscosity* of a glaze, which is an asset in *majolica*, helping to prevent the running of colors. High-lead glazes with 15% or more of tin will break red on the edges of red clay pots. Michael Casson's early and immensely attractive work used this technique. Alan Caiger-Smith in PQ 35 states 'a glaze deriving . . . alumina and silica from stone or feldspar is likely to have richer color-carrying properties than one dependant on china clay'. Much other useful information is to be found in this article and in his book Caiger-Smith TGP. Tin can also be used in a stoneware glaze although its opacifying effect diminishes at high temperatures.

TIN OVER SLIP

A flask by Robert Fournier, built from two shallow thrown bowls and decorated with sgraffito through black slip covered with a tin glaze (10% in an earthenware glaze). Note the dark line on the edges of the form and the cuts where the manganese has broken through, giving emphasis to both. The manganese in the slip can also, sometimes, give an attractive rosy tint.

A useful and versatile technique for earthenware. A lead glaze with 10% of tin oxide is used over slips which have rather more than the normal pigment content, e.g. black slip with 15% MnO_2, or blue slip with 2% CoO. The slip is used as a vehicle for dispersing the oxide evenly over the surface of a dish or pot—a difficult feat by brushing or any other method. The iron in red clay will produce only a faint gray if any color at all; the chrome in green slip will have little effect but the copper will give a watery green. We are, therefore, largely limited to blue and black slips but a great variety of shades will result from varying thicknesses of glaze and with practice this can be used to great advantage. The technique is used in combination with *sgrafitto, paper resist,* and *wax resist.*

Strangely, a lower tin concentration in the glaze does not necessarily lead to stronger color from the slip, the effect being watery and much less striking than with the full *majolica* type glaze. The color will also be directly affected by the firing temperature and degree of *soaking.* A slightly higher fire, or a softer glaze, than normally used for over-glaze painting will give improved results. Do not glaze too thickly.

TITANIA

Oxide of titanium TiO_2.

TITANIUM, oxide, compounds

A metallic element Ti, 48.
Titanic oxide TiO_2, 80, titania, m.p. 1850°C.
Sesquioxode Ti_2O_3, 144, c.o.e. around 16.

Precipitated titania is white but the rutile and anatase forms are brown. It will tend to produce a cream color when used as an opacifier when 'it dissolves almost completely in the glaze and recrystallizes on cooling' (Royle). Very small proportions can be used to stabilise lead and coloring oxides (up to 1%) especially in frits. The iron-bearing form produces rutile mottle (ad nauseum on commercial tiles, etc) and is used with pigments. It is an agent in *crystalline glazes.* Tends to give yellows with chromium. In some *Bristol* glazes titania can turn iron green according to Parmalee who quotes 0.1 of titania to 0.9 of iron. In *reduction,* various colors from blue to red have been reported. 'Rutile', though strictly a form of titania, is used to describe the iron-bearing mineral.

T MATERIAL

A plastic, refractory grogged clay containing *molochite.* Obtainable from Potterycrafts, Potclays and Fulham Pottery. It was a favorite clay of Hans Coper, and is ideal for modeling and pottery which requires some 'tooth' or a light surface texture. It is expensive—five times the price of stoneware clay but many think its virtues outweigh its cost. Potclays also issue a similar and somewhat cheaper 'Y' material.

TOKI

According to Dodd, a Japanese name for a high-fired earthenware of the composition: 70% clay; 10% pegmatite; 20% grog.

TONGS

Tongs are required for *raku*. Now usually listed by merchants, or can be made from flat or round iron rod. Rod will be more efficient if beaten flat at the hinge. About 3 ft. (1 m.) long, they should open 5 or 6 in. (125–150 mm.) at the working end. They must be light and easy to use; wooden handles will help grip and insulation. A distinction is made between the shape of the gripping ends for red and black raku in Japan, see Sanders WJC. A more elaborate type are 'accordion' tongs. Kemper Manufacturing Co. California, among others, supply raku tongs.

Typical raku tongs made from two 4 × ¾ in. (5 × 20 mm.) metal strips. The jaws are twisted at right-angles to the handles. The whole can be about 3 feet (1 meter) long. Wooden handles at the 'cold' ends will insulate and give a better grip.

TONGUE TEST

If the tip of the tongue is touched against a biscuit pot one can get an idea of its porosity by the extent to which the tongue sticks to the pot momentarily. The more porous the biscuit the more it will adhere. If the surface feels slippery and the patch stays wet or absorbs only slowly, the biscuit is partly vitrified and will take up very little glaze when dipped.

TOOL

There are as many tools as there are potters but one can list half a dozen or so essential ones. Some of these are shown in the photograph; these and others are discussed under *steel palette, beater, turning tool, chamois, spatula.*

Some of the essential tools of the potter, all quite cheap and simple: a nylon or metal wire on wooden handles; a natural sponge; a scraper; a hoop turning or scooping

tool; a wooden spatula; a fine needle awl; a small knife; and a plane.

TOP HAT KILN

A type of kiln in which the muffle is lowered over the piece to be fired instead of the ceramic being inserted into it. Modern light-weight ceramic fibers have made the top-hat kiln more practical for the studio potter and it is often used for raku and other rapid firings. The muffle is either lifted off manually (using gloves) by means of handles, or it is suspended from a counterweighted pivoted arm which makes control easier and safer, but involves more construction and a more permanent site.

In the industry the top-hat type of kiln has long been employed in firing large electrical ceramics such as power-station insulators.

Gas is the usual fuel for potters' top-hat kilns but it is possible to use other methods of heating.

kiln to be lowered over pot

counterbalance weight

The system for a 'top hat' kiln which is too heavy to be lifted directly from the pot by hand. The kiln and its base are drawn in section to show a flange on the base and an overlap in the kiln wall which will hold it in place when lowered over the pack.

David Roberts' top-hat kiln showing lifting gear and counter-weight for raising the upper section.

Steve Mills (of Bath Pottery Supplies) with his safety-first variation on the top-hat design (more of a flat-hat kiln in this case!) constructed from a paint drum lined with ceramic fiber blanket. (See text and also ceramic fiber.)

Steve Mills, of Bath Pottery Supplies (U.K.) has doubts about the safety of the top-hat kiln and cites scorched trousers and, even more dangerous, the red-hot pack toppling over when the 'lid' is lifted off. He prefers a horizontally split kiln, with the lift-off section being rather less than half the total height. This leaves the pack intact though still easily removed, and the pots suffer less thermal shock. Like David Roberts he utilises a simple paint or oil drum lined with ceramic wool. See also *ceramic fiber* for details of the cheap and simple fastening he uses.

TOP LOADING KILN

While most pottery kilns open in the front, some are packed from above. Both types have advantages. Top loaders, usually *electric kilns* (though *raku* is often top loaded), are easier for the potter to build, and they can be heated all round. Pots can be tightly packed laterally. When firing, the top is at a convenient level for the supervision of drying pots and it can also provide an extra working surface in a small workshop. The height is limited by the potter's ability easily to reach to the floor of the chamber; the width by the available roofing bats which support the top bricks or slabs. The maximum capacity is therefore in the region of 12 cu. ft. (0.34 cu. m.) e.g. 2 ft. (60 cm.) high × 2 ft. (60 cm.) deep × 3 ft. (90 cm.) wide, although the width is not so crucial.

Full details of top-loader construction is given in Fournier EKP. Many commercial models are available, most of them hexagonal or round.

TORN PAPER RESIST

See *paper resist*.

TOWING

The industrial term for the act of smoothing the outer edges of plates, etc on the wheel, traditionally with 'tow' but also with glasspaper or scrapers.

TOWN GAS

Gas fuel produced from coal at a gas-works as distinct from *natural gas*. It is now almost obsolete in Great Britain. (See *gas*.)

TRAGACANTH

See *gum*.

TRAIL AND FEATHER

Slip trailed lines and dots which are feathered through, generally at right-angles. The decoration is done on a flat slab of clay, the plate or dish being formed over a hump-mold when the surface is partly dry. (See also *feathering, trailing*.)

TRAILER, tracer

See *slip trailer*.

TRAILING

Decorating by means of slip or glaze extruded through a nozzle onto the surface of a piece of pottery. A similar technique to cake-icing but with a more fluid material.

The trailing may be done straight onto the body clay, as was practised in the seventeenth century notably on the fine 'Toft' and other large platters. 'Dry' trailing is linear in character—masses may be filled in with washes of brushed slip.

Trailing onto a wet-slip surface allows a more flowing style. The design can be trailed onto a flat slab of clay, the dish being formed when the surface has dried somewhat. The clay can be eased into a *hollow mold* from the edges of the slab, or made over a *hump-mold*. The back must be kept damp with sheets of damp newspaper or the clay will crack. Alternatively the dish can be made first, covered with slip when stiff enough to handle, and the design applied immediately. This is easier as far as making the dish goes but more difficult in the actual trailing. Drop the dish back into the mold as a support when trailing.

Contrasting slips can be spooned into roughly sponged-off areas on the surface of the dish to give some solidity to the background. *Finger combing* can be com-

bined with trailing. The consistency of the slip will affect the style of the design—the thinner the slip the faster and freer will be the trailing movement. A very thick slip will give lumpy results, physically and aesthetically! A sure and unhesitating movement is called for, the design growing as much from the immediate behavior of the slip as from premeditated ideas. A sharp blow on the work-table, or lifting the corner of the mold a fraction and letting it drop again, will spread and unify the trailed line with the background. Trailing on pots is possible but difficult, the face to be worked is generally held nearly horizontal. (See also *slip, slip trailers, glaze trailing, feathering,* etc.)

TRANSFER, decal

Designs, printed onto special paper backgrounds, which can be applied to biscuit or glazed ware, the paper peeling or soaking away. (See *lithographic transfer*.) They have little place in craft pottery although *silk screen* printed transfers have been used effectively on tiles. There are firms which will make transfers to your design for repeated pieces, e.g. Pamela Norton Ceramics.

TRANSFER PEN

Supplied by Potclays to be used on special paper to trace a design and to transfer it onto a pot surface.

TRANSITIONAL ELEMENT

The elements nos. 23–29 in the *periodic table* together with some of the *rare earths*. These elements form coloring oxides.

TRANSLUCENT

Temmoku glaze over red clay trailing. Fired at 1280°C. By Wayne Hathaway.

The transluscency of a porcelain bowl by Lucie Rie. Oxidized fired in an electric kiln. (See also porcelain.)

Transmitting light, but not *transparent*. Objects between the translucent object and the light source will be seen through it as shadows. It is one of the properties of porcelains and occasionally of thin stoneware. The term is also applied to semi-transparent soft glazes with 3–6% tin or titanium oxide, and other glazes, cooled slowly to promote crystallization.

TRANSPARENT

Transmitting light without diffusion so that objects behind the transparent material can be plainly seen. A majority of glazes, if taken up to full fusion, will be transparent or nearly so. Transparency is a characteristic of glass. Lessened or destroyed by *opacifiers*, and by *underfiring*, by the development of *crystals* during slow cooling, by trapped bubbles, and by the opalescent effect of mixed glasses within the melt. Also, of course, by coloring oxides, especially the *acidic* or refractory ones. The ratio of 0.1 Al_2O_3:1.0SiO_2 should be maintained for transparency in glazes.

TRI-AXIAL BLENDING

Or ternary system. A diagrammatic method of studying the effects of the various mixtures possible with three materials or colors. (See *line blends* for two materials.) Four variables would require the construction of a pyramid.

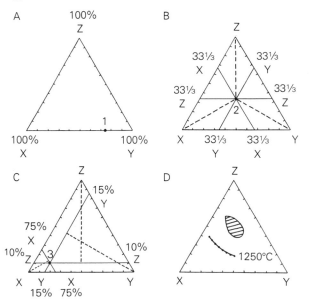

The triangle used has 100% of each material at the corners. Halfway down each side indicates, therefore, 50% of each of the materials denoted at the extremities of that line, and pro rata at any point along the line. In fig. B point 2 is at the center of the triangle. The lines which intersect at this point cut the sides at $33\frac{1}{3}$%. An off-center point 3 in fig. C makes this clearer and 3 would indicate a mixture of 75% of X, 15% of Y, and 10% of Z.

A line drawn within the triangle represents any mixture at any point on the line. It might be labelled 1250°, meaning that all the mixtures within that range would melt at that temperature. An area marked within the triangle would similarly indicate all the possible combinations within the area. For instance, it might show all the mixtures of three materials which would be craze-free, those outside the area being liable to crazing. See fig. D. Tri-axial diagrams are also used for phase diagrams. In CR nos. 97 and 99, tri-axial blending is dealt with in detail.

TRIDYMITE

A primary phase of silica, probably with a disordered crystal lattice and with several *inversions* between 170°C. and 870°C. Stable up to 1470°C. It seems likely, however, that the involved make-up of plastic bodies may often prevent the formation of tridymite although it has been used with *crisobalite* to mitigate the later's sudden contraction (or expansion) at 226°C.

TRIP SWITCH, ELCB
(Earth Leakage Circuit Breaker)

A type of electrical mains switch, usually installed by the supply company, which will cut the current as soon as it detects any earth leakage. If, when one tries to switch the current on again, it persists in 'tripping' this indicates a continuing fault or short circuit which must be detected before supply can be resumed. A thunderstorm, a surge of current, or a fault on a neighbor's installation can all trip the switch off, in which case it can merely be reset. There is usually a switch for each main group of circuits, and a special one would be installed for a kiln. Many electrical gadgets now have circuit-breakers incorporated.

TRIVALENT, tervalent

Elements which combine with three atoms of hydrogen. The oxides (since oxygen is bivalent) are written R_2O_3, e.g. alumina, ferric iron, boric oxide.

TRUCK KILN, trolley kiln

A kiln from which the loading area (usually the floor and front wall or 'door') can be inserted and withdrawn before and after firing. The packing can then be done in the open but must be fairly sturdily packed so that it will not be disturbed as it is wheeled back into the kiln shell.

An electric truck kiln heated by silicon carbide rods. (1) The very clean and simple interior. The brick wall facing the camera is attached to the trolley and not to the chamber.

(2) One of the trolley packs being wheeled out after firing. The trolley is a double one with a brick wall between the packs so that the other half, in this picture, would be following into the chamber, loaded with unfired ware. Photographs courtesy of Labheat. (See also illustration at kiln.)

TRUE POROSITY

The sum of open and closed or sealed pores in a fired body.

TUBE LINING

A Victorian term and technique developed from the Spanish 'cuenca', and having parallels in early Staffordshire and other slipwares. Thickish lines of slip are trailed onto a plate or pot, building up enclosed areas which can later be filled with slip, color, or colored glazes. CR 119 shows some brightly colored examples by Clive Davies. A variation is to glaze the whole piece white and then paint within the spaces. (See also *cuenca*.)

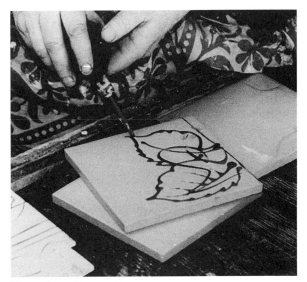

The main outline on this complicated tile panel by Maggie Berkowitz was tube-lined to keep it visible when glaze and oxides were added.

TUNGSTEN

A metallic element W (Wolfram), 184.
Trioxide WO_3, a yellow, insoluble powder, m.p. 1473°C.
Could be used for high temperature yellow pigment, possibly with molybdenum (Billington). Also used in very hard steel alloys.

TUNNEL KILN

A kiln in which ware is transported through a hot zone in the middle of a long tunnel. The firing is a continuous process. The nearest a studio potter can approach the tunnel kiln is with a kiln with doors back and front, the ware being packed on trolleys and wheeled in. This is still, however, an intermittent firing. (See *continuous kiln*.)

TURNING

The trimming of a thrown pot on the wheel. This can be done immediately after *throwing* but more generally when *leather-hard*. Excessive turning will destroy the lively effect of throwing. However very short bodies such as *porcelains* are sometimes thrown thickly and turned to a thin wall. It is obvious that the Chinese practiced a good deal of turning. The little industrial ware still thrown is turned on a horizontal lathe like a piece of wood, the *short* body making very high turning speeds possible.

Jugs, bottles, and most pots can be trimmed as the final action of throwing; alternatively they can be turned at a drier stage but still right way up, re-adhering them to the wheel head with a little water. If a flat base is given a sharp tap with the fingers to make it slightly concave, the pot will have more stability.

If a *foot ring* is required the piece must be inverted. For tall pots a hollow *chuck*, or a *cup head* and a wad of

Turning the foot ring on a bowl.
(1) The rough flange left from cutting-off is removed by a vertical cut followed by an upward-sloping cut from the outside, both with a pointed triangular tool, giving true surfaces for further work.
(2) The outer wall of the ring is trimmed with a square tool.
(3) and (4) The inner face of the ring is incised, and the interior cut away with a square tool, working from the center outwards. Leave the foot ring a little wider than finally required to allow for accidents.
(5) The curve of the bowl is perfected, the ring cut down to its final size, and the outer edge beveled. The bevel gives a pleasant line of shadow beneath the bowl and also prevents chipping.

clay can be used. A solid chuck is generally used for bowls or squatter shapes. Bowls and many pots can be adhered to the wheel head simply by moistening the rim. The clay should be leather-hard, the parings coming away crisply like wood shavings. If it is too soft it will stick to the tool. If too hard the work will be slow and tedious. See also *chatter* for the method of dealing with the corrugations which sometimes develop when turning; also *plates, knob*.

Turning in the industry. On the rare occasions when the wheel is still used bodies are thrown relatively thickly and turned on a fast horizontal lathe.

Supporting small-necked pots for turning.
(A) (In section) a thrown, diabolo-shaped supporting chuck in leather-hard clay, adhered to the wheel-head with a little slip.
(B) A cup head used in turning a smaller pot centered and held in place with a coil of clay. Note in (A) that the pot drops in as far as it will go but does not touch the bottom of the chuck, while in (B) the pot is set firmly down before the coil is applied.

TURNING TOOL

The only essential feature of a turning tool is a short, firm cutting edge which can be held at a right-angle to the rotating pot. The actual design varies widely. The standard tool is made from a $7 \times \frac{1}{2}$ or $\frac{3}{4}$ in. (180 × 12 or 20 mm.) iron strip. A 1 in. (25 mm.) length at one end is bent to 90° and cut either to the shape of a rectangle, a triangle, a rounded end or a 'leaf' shape. A V-shaped nick cut away at the angle makes for cleaner working. The cutting end of the tool is then bevelled to a sharp edge all round. Loop tools are also made, using a thinner steel strip and a wooden handle, and there are other designs. Each potter will recommend the type to which he has become accustomed.

Clay is abrasive and tools need regular sharpening. They should not, however, be honed to a knife edge, which is as liable to *chatter* as is a very blunt one. A slight burr seems to help. A *steel palette* can be used for turning a large plain area. A bamboo tool is a pleasant tool to use for trimming the foot of a pot immediately after throwing.

The four shapes most useful for turning tools. (See also hoop tool under *tools*, and another useful type at *electric kiln*.)

TURQUOISE GLAZE, color

Generally derived from copper oxide. For the purest color, soft glaze must be virtually free from alumina while soda must predominate in the RO. Such a glaze lacks stability (pure soda-silicates are soluble in water) and is very liable to *crazing*. A recipe of one part sodium silicate to one part quartz with 0.5% copper carbonate would make a turquoise frit, but in practice small additions of alumina or lime would have to be made. Published formulas include equal parts of CaO and Na_2O with no alumina and 2.6 SiO_2, 0.6 B_2O_3 and more involved glazes which include small proportions of alumina, lime and zinc. A *frit* is always needed for this type of glaze. (See also *Egyptian paste*.) Any type of turquoise frit will work better on a *siliceous* body or slip. The Egyptian bodies are reported to consist of up to 90% silica by analysis.

Turquoise stoneware glazes are rare but can be developed from formulas high in calcium and barium, using dolomite to introduce some magnesium. None of the rules governing soft glaze turquoise seem to apply. Use about 2% copper carbonate. A quoted glaze is nepheline syenite 56, barium carbonate 25, ball clay 6, flint 7, copper carbonate 3. It is my experience that the color in stoneware is very dependent on a precise firing temperature and on the thickness of the glaze. It is always variable.

Small amounts of vanadium and zircon are reputed to produce turquoise in an alkaline glaze.

A turquoise-to-blue stoneware glaze I have used for many years is:

Feldspar	52
China clay	10
Dolomite	19
Barium carbonate	19

with 0.8% copper oxide; 0.95% copper carbonate.

Some variation is possible in these percentages, and with the firing temperature which can be between 1220°C. and 1250°C. Not really suitable for tableware as it is likely to be attacked by strong fruit acids, etc. Will give a variety of colors if one layer of glaze is poured over another.

TWADDLE DEGREES

Symbol °Tw. A system for denoting the *specific gravity* of a liquid.

°Tw=(s.g.−1) × 200.

Used for solutions of sodium silicate in casting slips.

TWO PIECE THROWING

Large pots may be thrown in two or more sections (the method is also useful when working with porcelain or other short bodies). A neck can be thrown from a coil or squat cylinder stuck to a half dry base. It is possible to build up very large forms section by section, throwing from a fresh coil as each previous one stiffens. Shrinkage of the last thrown section must be taken into account. Leach shows a considerable outward bulge immediately above the join in his diagram in Leach PB.

Alternatively the two sections of a pot may each be shaped on the wheel, luted together when stiff enough, and the join worked together on the wheel, perhaps with a throwing stick inside. The rims to be joined must be broad and fairly flat and, of course, of similar diameters. (See also *amphora*.)

TYPES OF POTTERY

Firing temperatures and categories of pottery:

Temp. (°C)	Type
700–800	*enamel* colors
	raku
800–1000	soft *earthenware*
	Building *bricks* (Flettons, etc)
950–1150	*soft paste* porcelains
1000–1140	range of most craft earthenwares
1150–1200	hard earthenware (industrial)
1160–1180	*Bristol* glazed ware
1200–1250	*bone china* (biscuit firing temperature)
1220–1320	*stonewares*
	salt glaze
1255–1275	low-temperature *porcelain*
1320–1350	porcelain
1350–1430	*hard paste* porcelain

μ(m)

Pronounced mu. The symbol for a *micron* or 0.001 of a millimeter (one-millionth of a meter). Many clay particles are less than 0.5 microns in size.

ULTIMATE ANALYSIS

The chemical breakdown of a material into its constituent oxides (see *analysis*). Also called an 'element analysis'.

ULTIMATE FORMULA

The arrangement of atomic symbols as the total numbers present in the formula e.g. $Al_2Si_2H_4O_8$, as distinct from the *rational* or oxide formula Al_2O_3, $2SiO_2$, $2H_2O$.

UMBER

A natural *ferruginous* earth or *hydrated* iron oxide with some manganese oxide. Allied to ochre and sienna. *Calcined* as burnt umber.

UNDER-FIRING

Under-fired biscuit will be very porous and breakable. The word will have a different meaning in terms of temperature for different materials. In general the more fluxes and impurities there are in the clay, the lower will be its optimum firing temperature. For stoneware, *biscuiting* is simply a method of making it possible to dip the pots into glaze without disintegration, but for earthenware other factors are involved and a very low-fired biscuit is not recommended. (See *crazing, cristobalite*.)

Badly under-fired glazes will be *opaque*, with rough *matt* surfaces and probably with a quite different color to the mature glaze. Slightly under-fired tin glazes are liable to *crawl*.

UNDERGLAZE COLOR

Pigments applied to the raw clay or biscuit and covered with a glaze. When used on biscuit they must either be fixed in a *hardening-on* firing, or a gum or other binding material must be mixed with the color. The latter will tend to influence glaze take-up. The binder generally used for stoneware underglaze painting is simply a little clay. Underglaze colors are limited to those oxides, mixtures, or prepared *fritted* pigments which will withstand the temperature of the glaze which is to be put over them.

If simple oxides are used on raw clay it may be found that some color is still loose after the biscuit firing. This must be washed off under a tap and the pot thoroughly dried before glazing. A little *flux*—a frit, china stone, etc.—mixed with the oxides will help them to adhere, especially cobalt which often fails to *sinter*. An addition

Underglaze painting on stoneware, covered with a transparent ash glaze. By Eric Mellon.

of a plastic clay, as mentioned above, will at least prevent the color from blurring when dipped in glaze.

Christine Rainbird (CR 120) suggests protecting underglaze painting on biscuit with two coats of hairspray to avoid smudging when handling or packing in the kiln.

Most pigment oxides yield *transparent* color (chrome is an exception). Opacity can be increased by the addition of tin, zinc, etc. or china clay and flint. (See also *pigments*, and under the individual *elements*.) Commercially prepared underglaze colors are fritted compounds with various 'fillers', flint, clay, etc. and opacifiers which may include chrome for the darker colors. Leadless or low lead glazes are usually recommended. In the workshop, a *jar mill* is useful for preparing underglaze colors.

There is an optimum thickness of application for all colors. The oxides, especially copper, need careful handling. Practice and experience are needed to get the best from them.

Reward issue 'one strike' concentrated underglaze colors; useful for fine line work.

UNDERFIRED CLAY, bricks

Clay will not become a ceramic until it has been subjected to a temperature of at least 550°C. A cooking oven (max. circa 275°C.) is obviously insufficient, as is sun heat. Some clays, however, dry very hard, perhaps because of a particular grain structure or the presence of cementing materials. A great number of the houses in the Mediterranean countries and elsewhere are built of unfired bricks or slabs reinforced with straw and chaff, sometimes called *adobe*. Several attempts have been made to produce a material with the plastic advantages of clay but which will not easily break on drying, using fibres of nylon, etc to form a sort of felting throughout the body, or the addition of resins as setting cements. (See *Newclay*.) Materials described as 'air-hardening clays' and given names such as Airset, Marblex, Mexican Pottery Clay, etc. are widely available.

UNITS OF ELECTRICITY

The units of immediate interest to potters are discussed under *volt, ampere, watt, ohm*.

The 'unit' on which the pricing of electricity supply is based is one *kilowatt-hour*, symbol kWh, the amount consumed by a 1000 watt appliance (e.g. a single bar electric fire) in an hour. The same fire would consume 5 kWh in 5 hours; if rated at 1.5 kWh then it would consume $7\frac{1}{2}$ kWh in 5 hours, and so on. To estimate the cost of firing an electric kiln:

Kilowatt rating × hours of firing × cost per unit, thus a 6 kWh kiln × 10 hours firing × 8p per unit = £4.80p.

The sum is slightly complicated by the fact that the kiln may not be running at full all the time, or there may be a standing charge in addition to the unit cost, but a little common sense can allow for these. Reckon one-third the rating if you have a 'slow' setting and two-thirds for a 'medium'.

UNITY FORMULA

Applied to the *Seger* arrangement for glaze formulas, where the first group of bases (broadly, the fluxes) add up to one: e.g. soda 0.2; calcia 0.5; potash 0.3; total 1.0. This allows instant comparison with the 'amphoteric' and 'acid' figures (groups two and three), and an appraisal of the probable fusibility or refractoriness of the glaze. (See *formula, formula into recipe, Seger, etc.*)

UP-DRAFT KILN

The simplest form of true kiln: a fire beneath the floor, the hot gases and flame rising through the ware to a chimney or vent at the top. The heating tends to be uneven—hot at the base—and a great deal of heat is wasted.

Nevertheless it was the type in use for thousands of years and is still fired. Interesting variations are found; in Cyprus a perforated hollow dome is built inside the kiln, and the pots stacked in the space between it and the outer wall. A wood fire is burnt inside the dome which is reached by a low tunnel. There is no chimney—merely vents in the top. Sometimes bottomless pots are stuck over holes in the upper part of the kiln, often pointing downwards. The form of the kiln itself acts as a chimney.

In up-draft gas kilns a *semi-muffle* may be used, or the jets injected horizontally through separate flues, greatly extending the life of the floor refractories. See many illustrations of up-draft kilns in Rhodes K.

In an up-draft kiln the flame and hot gases travel through a perforated floor and up among the pots to a short chimney or simple vent.

URANIUM, oxides, compounds

A metallic element U, 238.
Oxide UO_2, 270.
Sodium uranate $Na_2.2UO_3.nH_2O$.
'Depleted' oxide U_3O_8,s.g.7.3.

The radioactive potentialities of uranium are well known and it has not been available since 1944. However, the depleted oxide is now appearing in the catalogs, albeit still expensive.

The use of uranium as a pigment oxide is generally limited to *soft glazes*, giving reds and oranges up to about 940°C. and turning to a cool yellow at higher temperatures. A high-lead glaze is recommended, with a little tin oxide. Boric oxide and whiting are to be avoided. At stoneware temperatures Leach gives a recipe for Kawai's yellow which used 2% uranium oxide in the traditional 4:3:2:1 recipe (see *stoneware glaze*) with an additional 15% of feldspar. Uranium is liable to turn gray or black above 1260°C.

V

VACUUM FILTER

An idea developed by Harry Davis. The usual method of squeezing the water from slip is reversed, a semi-vacuum being used to draw it out. No heavy machinery is required and the equipment is neither bulky nor costly. See his book PA. A similar system has been developed in the U.S.A.

VACUUM PUG

See *de-airing pug*.

VALENCY

The way in which *atoms* combine. The inert gases contain 8 *electrons* in their outer shell (helium has 2) and other atoms with different configurations aspire to this stable state, borrowing or sharing electrons with neighboring atoms. Shared electrons take part in 'covalent' bonds.

The transfer of electrons results in an unbalanced electrical charge on the nucleus (electrons being negatively charged) and the formation of 'ions' (see also *electrovalent*). Chemical action, the formation of *compounds* and new materials, is the result of one or other of these bonds or a combination of them.

The ratio in which atoms combine is thus in terms of

simple whole numbers, and the valency is the number of hydrogen atoms with which an atom or an *element* will combine (or which it will replace). A *compound* or *molecule* must balance these numbers if it is to be stable. Thus tin has a valency of 4; oxygen 2 (as in H_2O) and they combine in the ratio which will balance them— bring them both up to 4—i.e. two oxygen atoms with valency 2=4, one tin atom with valency 4=4 or one tin (Sn) to two oxygen (O) written SnO_2. Many elements can be made to combine in different ratios i.e. have more than one valency, but there is often a single stable combination, or oxide, e.g. TiO_2, Al_2O_3. The transitional elements in particular occur in nature in more than one combination, e.g. iron as Fe_2O_3 and Fe_3O_4.

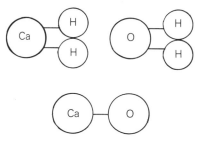

Valency, the combination values of atoms in a molecule. (See atomic theory, electron, bivalent, molecule, etc). Calcium, Ca, will combine with two hydrogen, H, atoms and is thus bivalent. Oxygen, O, is also bivalent and the two can therefore combine in the ration of one to one, giving the oxide CaO.

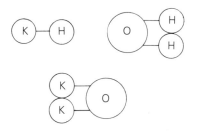

(B) Potassium, K (Kalium), is monovalent (will combine with one hydrogen atom) and thus two of its atoms must be present to balance the bivalency of oxygen, giving the oxide K_2O.

VANADIUM

A metallic element V, 51.
Pentoxide V_2O_5, 182 m.p. 685°C.
Ammonium metavanadate $NH_4 VO_3$, 117.

A fairly rare mineral found in *bauxitic* clays and also recovered from fuel oil soot. Both forms listed above can be purchased. The pentoxide, however, is water soluble and can penetrate the skin—wear gloves. John Chalke has mentioned that his glaze stirring sticks assume a yellowish green color when using vanadium! Vanadium

is used in proportions of 5–10% to produce a yellow color; rather weak in a clear glaze but stronger in combination with titania and tin oxide.

Zirconium–vanadium blues have been quoted and are available in prepared form (as is also the yellow stain), the blues being suggested as a substitute for copper in lead glazes in order to avoid the latter's tendency to increase *lead solubility*. Similar high temperature stains are also available. Gray colors with tin have been mentioned. The metavanadate is reported to be refractory to 1300°C, and to be unaffected by reduction, though Behrens mentions blue from reduced vanadium. The pentoxide can be used in oxidised firings.

VAPOR GLAZING

This form of usually partial glazing or coloring uses volatiles (materials which become gaseous on heating) which will attack or become attached to a pot surface altering its color, texture, or degree of shine. Salt-glaze is a form of vapor glazing, but the term is normally restricted to the use of *volatiles* (usually contained in a small

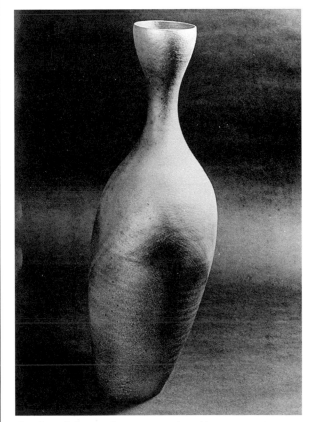

An altered thrown form, vapor-glazed in a saggar by Joanna Constantinidis. A monochrome print does not do justice to the subtlety of the silvery and other nuances of the surface color.

bowl) and enclosed with the ceramic in a sealed saggar. During the firing the vapor causes flashing or color changes to the surfaces. The technique is slightly hit-or-miss but can produce fascinating and striking results. Joanna Constantinidis has been very successful in this field. See also *flashing, volatilization* for materials which can be used.

VELLUM GLAZE

A merchants' term for an opaque glaze with a dulled or satiny sheen. Often achieved by means of various combinations of oxides of tin, zinc, and titanium in the glaze recipe. Magnesia may also help to promote a silkier surface.

VENTURI BURNER

An inspirating gas burner with a constricted flow just beyond the point where the gas exits. This increases the speed of the gas flow and draws air in from behind. The principle was formulated by the Italian scientist Venturi. See Rhodes K, for illustrations.

VERMICULITE

An expanded (exfoliated) mica. Fairly refractory. Main use as a heat insulator for temperatures up to 1000°C. Has also been mentioned as a type of grog for lightweight brick and, finely ground, for other bodies. From S. Carolina and Montana.

VIBRATORY MILL

Upright mills for grinding frits and other materials are now standard in the industry. They do not revolve but are vibrated at very high speed and the time taken to reduce sand size or even $\frac{3}{4}$ in. material to powder is dramatically reduced. They have not yet appeared widely on the studio potters' market although Fraser GCP illustrates an Op-po mill which grinds $\frac{3}{4}$ in. to 'the desired fineness' in a few minutes!

VIBRATORY SIEVE

A sieve or lawn which is shaken rapidly in a lateral direction by an eccentric drive on an electric motor. Marketed by various suppliers. Something of a luxury for most potters but the action gives a more even particle separation and is kinder to the lawn than is brushing through. (See *sieve, use of.*) Chris Aston, in CR 96, describes the building of a vibratory mechanism employing weights bolted to a revolving spindle.

VINEGAR

Contains 3–6% acetic acid. It has a deflocculating effect on clay and can be used to repair dry pots or modeling

(so long as the damage is not a result of strain). Work the vinegar with a brush onto both surfaces and press them together. It has been successful with large coiled pots but must not be used for handles. Odors reminiscent of fried fish shops during firing!

Rada CT suggests grinding luster colors in a mixture of vinegar with gum arabic; they can then be thinned with water. Vinegar will also slow down the setting of plaster of paris.

VISCOSITY

Resistance to flow offered by a liquid, due to internal frictions. A very fluid glaze would run from a pot at peak temperature (and sometimes does!) but the presence of alumina increases viscosity, distinguishing *glaze* from *glass*. Viscosity also prevents glaze from soaking too readily into the body of a pot, and inhibits crystal growth. The unit of viscosity is the *poise*.

Magnesia increases viscosity, as will zircon and tin oxide. The alkalis have the opposite effect and are vigorous in promoting *fluidity*. Lime has an ambiguous role. It will increase viscosity at low temperatures and, in certain proportions, in stoneware. The point of maximum fluidity will vary from 15–35% at 1250°C. and over. *Celadon* needs high viscosity (Cardew).

Water decreases in viscosity as it is heated to a factor of 3 between 0°C. and 40°C., hence the greater efficiency of hot water in various processes. It is known that the temperature of the water affects clay during throwing.

VITREOUS

Glassy, or containing glassy materials. Vitreous bodies will have low *porosity*. 'Vitreous' slip or *engobe* is one with a high *base* content and is fired to fusion point. Vitreous silica, or *fused silica*, has been heated to translucency (see also *thermocouple*). Any pottery body or associated mineral will become vitreous if heated sufficiently.

VITREOUS SLIP, engobe

Slips compounded with fluxing oxides can be used on stoneware and porcelain to produce slightly glossy colors on biscuit or to affect the color of overlaying glazes. Geoffrey Eastop (CR 121) mixes clay and whiting, modifying the result with borax frits. In place of the calcium he has also tried wood ash. His experiments with colors make interesting reading.

VITRIFY, vitrification

To assume the nature of a *glass* (glaze) or to form glassy melts within a fabric which flow into the pores and allow the particles to become more closely packed. It involves the breaking down of *crystalline* structures. A vitrified body will be non-porous and *impermeable*, although in pottery this is rarely completely achieved (see *porosity*).

Vitrification—the progressive fusion or glassification of a clay—is accompanied by shrinkage and leads eventually to deformation and collapse. The temperatures at which it occurs will vary with the *fusibility* of the clay (the number and type of fluxes) and the alumina content. The 'vitrification range' is the temperature interval between the initial glass formation (beginning of shrinkage) and eventual deformation. The first figure is around 850°C. for plastic clay, and deformation varies between 1030°C. for a very impure red clay to 1450°C. for the most refractory kaolin porcelains. Aluminous fireclays will have an even greater range.

Porcelain is a mixture which will vitrify to *translucency* without collapse.

VOLATILE, volatilization

The remarkable deposits of volatilized lead on the wall of a country potter's kiln.

In ceramics the terms refer to those materials which pass into vapor with increasing temperature; water, of course, will turn to steam at 100°C. but above red heat chlorine and carbon compounds release gases at around 700°C.; sulfur and fluorine at 1000°C. Copper will begin to volatilize at 1000°C. and increasingly at 1200°C. and can stain neighbouring pieces, especially in reduction, or can be seen to stain right through a body. The fluorine from fluorspar can cause glaze pitting. Lead will volatilize increasingly with temperature, slowly coating kiln walls and furniture if used with regularity, as will other bases, zinc and soda. Volatilized lead in a high-fired closed electric kiln can be a health hazard when unpacked. Volatilized sodium from salt is the basis of salt-glazing, but potters can also produce many remarkable and attractive effects on bodies and glazes by enclosing volatiles (the sulfates, nitrates and chlorides of metals) in a saggar with pots, known as *vapor glazing*.

The term is also used to denote the removal by heat of CO_2 and other components of a glaze batch but this is better described as *decomposition* or *dissociation*.

VOLCANIC ASH

Volcanic lava frequently produces *basic* rocks which can eventually decompose into clay of the *montmorillonite* type. The typical volcanic rock is *basalt*, which can be used for dark colored stoneware glazes.

'Volcanic ash' is available cheaply in the U.S.A. and has been quoted as roughly equivalent to 70% feldspar, 30% flint. It is probably more fusible than this sounds for it is also said that 25% volcanic ash with 75% red clay will *vitrify* at earthenware temperatures. It can be combined with Gerstley borate as a glaze.

A sample of volcanic ash has been analysed (parts by weight):

MgO	0.35
CaO	1.0
Na_2O	3.6
K_2O	4.5
Al_2O_3	13.0
Fe_2O_3	3.0
SiO_2	73.0
Cl_2	0.03
H_2O	1.5

Around 10% is suggested as a secondary flux, while as much as 50% has been used for a clear, fluid glaze.

VOLTAGE

Symbol E (electromotive force, or e.m.f.). The force which carries one ampere of current against one ohm of resistance. The unit is the volt, symbol V.

Useful equations:

$$E = I \times R, \text{ or } \frac{P}{I} \text{ or } \sqrt{P \times R}$$

(I, current in amperes; R, resistance in ohms; P, power in watts.)

VOLTAGE DROP

If more than a certain amount of current is taken from an electrical supply, the 'pressure' or voltage will drop and all appliances will become less efficient, e.g. lights will dim, kilns take longer to fire. Power is proportional to the square of the voltage, and for a voltage drop of up to about 20% the loss of power will be approximately double the percentage, e.g. from 240 V to 220 V is an 8.3% voltage drop but 16% less power is produced if the resistance remains constant. See discussion in Fournier EKP.

WAD, wadmill, dod box

The 'wad' is a coil or extruded column of clay used for coiling or other modeling, and, using fireclay, for *placing*, and separating saggars, etc.

A wad box or wad mill is a simple hand-operated screw plunger enclosed in a cylinder with a die at the aperture and is used to extrude plastic clay in coils or wads. Can be utilized for *coiling*. Some catalogs suggest that it is a sort of *pug*, which it is not.

See *extrusion* for larger scale work. Various small extruders are sold, e.g. the Kemper Klay Gun, which forces clay by means of a plunger through shaped *dies* in the manner of cake icers.

WARPING

Deformation which can take place at any stage in the making of a pot. Few fired pieces escape totally—try spinning a commercial saucer on the wheel. Warping will be aggravated by:

During making and drying	High wet/dry shrinkage
	Uneven clay walls
	Very thin rims
	Poor *wedging*
	Unsupported weight, including open slab boxes
	The joining of clay of different consistencies
	Unlevel bases or *foot rings*
	Uneven *drying*
	Plastic 'memory' (see *clay memory*)
During the biscuit fire	Close proximity to kiln wall
	Unsupported weight
	The *boxing* of pots on jugs
	'Bungs' too high
	Bent kiln shelves
During the glaze fire	Unsupported weight
	Bent kiln shelves
	Overfiring
	Inefficient *stilt* support (earthenware)
	Molded dishes which are too flat or thin.

Pots which are deformed during drying may revert even if the fault has been corrected in time. Wooden cones are useful for rounding out cups etc. An extreme case of unsupported weight is the handle of a porcelain cup pulling it out of true during firing. The industry beds bone china in alumina (its high fire is its biscuit fire) but the craft potter must design self-supporting ceramics. (See *kiln furniture*.)

(1) Badly placed stilts and spurs causing warping due to unsupported weight.

(2) Some other common causes of warping during firing. (A) Bent kiln shelves. (B) Uneven foot rings or bases. (C) Very thin rims. (D) Long unsupported sides (see slab pots *for possible remedy). (E) The boxing of uneven or dissimilar pieces.*

WASHING ASH

To remove *soluble alkalis*. Steep the ash in plenty of water and stir well. When the solid matter has settled, pour off the clear liquid. Refill with clean water and repeat the process. Three washings are usually sufficient. At the first wash the liquid may be sufficiently *caustic* to harm the hands, so wear gloves. (See also *ash*.)

WASTER

A spoiled pot which is discarded, often on the site of the kiln. Archeologists owe a great debt to wasters.

WASTE HEAT DRYING

Optimum use is made of very little of the heat generated by kilns. It is worth planning your pottery so that heat liberated during cooling has some work to do, either as space heating or to dry pots. *Top loading* kilns are very useful in this respect. Fans and ducts can distribute heat: more simply it can be directed through a gap to an upper floor. Kiln exhaust gases can first be directed beneath a drying cabinet before reaching the chimney. See film 'Isaac Button, Country Potter'.

WATER

The 'oxide' of hydrogen, H_2O, 18.

The normal water supply contains impurities and these can, to some extent, affect the behavior of clay and glazes. Water impurities have been mentioned as a contributary cause of *crawling* after a pot has been sponged with very 'hard' (high calcium) water, and the pH of the water can affect glazes and slips; alkalis deflocculate, acids have the opposite effect. Though the amounts in tap water are not usually strongly operative, they may explain some variations in the behavior of slops.

Water in pottery can exist in a number of forms:

1 In its familiar liquid state, mixed with clay to promote plasticity or in excess of this to produce slip. This water is drawn or driven off at temperatures up to 100°C. (see *drying*).

2 As *adsorbed* water, not obvious as a liquid and more tenacious in its hold and can only be completely dispersed by heating to 120–200°C.

3 The H_2O which is built into the molecular structure of clay, sometimes known as 'combined water'. This needs considerable heat—500°C. plus—before it will separate as vapor, with fundamental and irreversible changes in the fabric.

Other *hydrated* minerals may lose their H_2O at different temperatures, *plaster of paris* for instance at a much lower heat. Water decreases in *viscosity* as it is heated and hot water will have a different effect from cold on many materials including clay. (See also *adsorption, absorption, hydration*.)

WATER GLASS

Sodium silicate $Na_2O.SiO_2$, with grade from 1.2 to 1:3.5 soda/silica ratio. Used as a *deflocculant* and in *air-setting cement*. *Soluble* in water. (See also *mending*.)

WATER OF PLASTICITY

The water content of clay in the range between soft plastic and leather-hard. Clays vary in the percentage of water needed to attain plasticity, the average being about 40% of the dry weight.

WATER SMOKING

The evolving of vapor at temperatures beyond 100°C. 'Bone dry' clay will still contain *adsorbed* and mechanically held water which will continue to vaporize up to 250°C. in bentonite type clays especially. Care must be exercised throughout this range. The term probably arose because the combination of steam and smouldering organic matter combine in a steamy smoke.

WATT

Electrical unit of power (P): the rate of working in a *circuit* where electromotive force is one *volt* and the intensity of current is one *ampere*. Symbol W. Named after James Watt.

Useful equations:

$$P = \frac{E^2}{R}, \text{ or } E \times I, \text{ or } I^2 \times R$$

(E in volts, I in amperes, R in ohms.)

The load or power of a kiln or other electric appliance is stated in watts, as in a 60 watt electric lamp. Multiples of 1000 watts are called kilowatts or kW, e.g. a 4.5 kW kiln—4500 watts.

WAX

Used in a fluid form for *wax resist* decoration or resisting glaze when glazing. Candle melted on its own is not satisfactory since it sets hard before it can be properly applied. Mixtures of paraffin wax, or candle with paraffin are very inflammable. Equal parts of candle and a thin oil makes a very usable mixture, kept warm over an electric or gas ring in a double saucepan or old fashioned glue-pot.

There are several proprietary cold wax emulsions and resist materials on the market. They are generally less workable and some must be left to dry and have poorer 'resist' qualities. A liquid latex resist is now sold, it can be removed from the surface at any time and one can envisage interesting decorative possibilities. Very low temperature paraffin waxes are also available.

Wax can be applied by using sticks of candle like crayon (see *wax resist*).

Do not leave your brush in the wax: it may burn during heating or may develop a permanent bend. On the other hand do not attempt to clean it with water—this will destroy the hairs. Stroke the hairs flat and leave to set either hanging or lying flat. Take care not to drip the wax where it is not required—it is difficult to remove. Turpentine removes a certain amount, but absorption is still affected. Badly waxed pots may need refiring to remove the wax.

WAX RESIST

For decoration. Wax designs are applied to a pottery surface in order to repel liquid pigments, thin slips, or glazes. The wax is usually applied as *free* brushwork, but a design can also be drawn with a wax crayon or piece of candle. The work can be done at various stages:

1 On the raw clay, generally when leather-hard. The wax design is applied and color or slip is spun on or laid over the whole surface with a brush, or poured or dipped. The waxed parts will be left in reserve against a painted background. The wax rarely repels the overlaid color completely and the small blobs and dots of color within the resisted areas give the technique its attractive and distinctive character.

2 A reserved biscuit design will result from waxing on the raw clay for once-fired pottery, or on the biscuit before glazing.

3 The unfired glaze surface can be waxed and painted as on the raw clay or covered with a second glaze coat of contrasting type for *glaze over glaze* techniques.

3

(1) Wax has been painted onto a plate and the first band of pigment applied.
(2) and (3) The color is laid on at different strengths to give added variety to the pattern.

Wax resist combined with glaze trailing and other techniques on a dish by David Frith.

1

2

Calligraphic wax brush strokes on a spun luster dish by Alan Caiger-Smith.

A more mundane but extremely useful and time-saving application of wax resist is to coat bases, foot rings, lid flanges, and all those parts of a pot which are to be free of glaze. The whole piece can then be dipped or poured. A heavy *whirler* or banding wheel is essential for the efficient waxing of thrown pieces. (See illustration under *glazing*.)

WEALD CLAY

A variable brick clay from S.E. England.

WEATHERING OF CLAY

Exposure to rain, sun, and frost will improve the working qualities of most clays, breaking them down and oxidizing pyrites and other metals, leaching out soluble alkalis, and by the development of an intimate and uniform water content. Long weathering, over geological time, has probably been a major factor in the plasticity of clay. The minimum useful period for weathering, usually done in outside troughs with some protection from excessive rainfall and dirt, is a year.

Weathering is a different process to *aging* or *resting* but they all assist workability.

WEDGING, MIXING, & KNEADING CLAY

Originally 'wedging' referred to the cutting of two wedge-shapes from a block of clay and banging one down on the other. It is now loosely applied to the whole process of the hand mixing of clays and working them into a consistent, bubble-free mass.

There are two stages in mixing clays of different types or consistencies:

1 Layering. The clays are cut into thin slabs which are slapped down alternately on one another. If grog is being added it can be spread between the layers. Harder and soft conditions of the same clay can be alternated. The whole pile is then cut vertically; one half lifted and brought smartly down on the other, taking care that the layering remains horizontal. Repeat until the layers have merged.

2 The mass of clay is cut into balls of 3–6 lb. (1.5–3 kg.). These are kneaded either by the forward and inwards thrust of the 'bull's head' method or by the spiral method which allows for somewhat larger blocks of clay.

Mixing and wedging clay.
(1) and (2) Blocks of clay (light and dark, hard and soft, etc) are sliced into layers about ½ in. (10 mm.) thick and slapped down alternately one upon another.
(3) to (5) The mass is cut through vertically and the blocks are again combined, bringing one smartly down

on the other while taking care to keep the layers horizontal – this is crucial.
(6) and (7) (overleaf) The block is compressed, recut, and the process continued until the layers merge together.

1

2

3

4

5

6

7

8

9

10

11

12

13

14

15

In (8) this is almost complete.
(9) The final mixing is generally done by kneading, using one of two allied methods. For up to 7lb. (3kg.) of clay the 'bull's-head' method is suitable, so-called because the typical overlapping layers resemble an animal's head as shown in illustration.
(10) and (11) show the main block lifted towards the potter and then forced down and back with the pressure of the palms, the hands enclosing the sides and exerting a certain inwards pressure which prevents undue sideways spread. The base of the block must grip the bench surface so that the whole mass is spread over itself as it is forced away from the potter's body. Keep the arms fairly straight and use your body weight to

exert pressure, which will be less tiring than working from the elbows (do not use too high a bench).
A pellet of colored clay placed on the forehead of the 'bull' should travel downwards and finally disappear under the base as the work continues.
(12) to (15) attempt to show stages in spiral wedging. The basic movement is not very different from the above but the pressure is applied to one corner of a large mass forming a spiral shell shape as the work proceeds. The clay is lifted, rolled a little forwards, gripped and thrust down and away. In the last picture the spiral is finally being worked into a suitably compact shape by slapping and rolling it on the bench.

WEIGHING OF MATERIALS

When weighing out large amounts of glaze materials it is usually necessary to split the weight into thousand gram lots. In order not to lose track of the amount weighed it is useful to tip them into separate heaps (in a large bowl) which may overlay at the base but remain recognizably separate and can be counted. This is in addition to noting each batch in a notebook.

Very small batches of 300 grams and under for the total glaze batch are notoriously liable to inaccuracy and misleading results, and are of limited value as trials.

WET FIRING

A rather controversial system of drying clay during the actual firing. CR 1 gives particulars. The method resembles that of raku in some respects. The newly thrown, wet pot is inserted into the red-hot kiln. Cooling by rapid evaporation, the principle of refrigeration, may be the factor at work. Even as described by an enthusiast the technique seems hedged about by provisions, exceptions, and uncertainties, such as the danger of a minor explosion. It sounds fun as an exercise in the unlikely but does not seem to have been generally accepted as a technique.

Little has been heard of the system since this article was written for the first edition of this book.

WHEEL, throwing

A potter's wheel is, essentially, a flat circular slab of wood, metal or stone so mounted as to revolve on a vertical axis. There is generally a heavy flywheel which stores energy and ensures a steady and even movement. It probably evolved from a slow wheel used for coiling etc. In the Far East a stick is inserted into a hole in the rim of the wheel head which is spun round by this means and then withdrawn, the throwing being done before the impetus is lost. The European wheel has a wide stone flywheel which is spun by the sole of the foot on its surface. Manually powered wheels using pulleys and ropes featured in the eighteenth century factories. The traditional English wheel is the cranked wheel described under *kick wheels*.

Wheels are now usually powered by a self-contained electric motor. (See *power-wheel*.)

WHEEL BAT

A circular bat which can be removed from the wheel head complete with the thrown pot. Useful when making plates, large pots, shallow bowls, and for repetition throwing.

They can be made of wood, plaster, or mineral wool sheet (see *ejector head* for plaster type). Wood is 'sympathetic' to the touch and has good clay-release properties but can warp or soften in use. Waterproof plys are available. Potter's Mates' supply $11\frac{3}{4}$ in. (300 mm.) bats and special wheel heads. Of the asbestos type materials *Asbestolux* is easily shaped but is too absorbent and needs partial sealing, for example with a polyurethene varnish, to make it usable. *Sindanyo* bats are expensive but very hard and durable. Bats can be fastened to the wheel by means of two short lengths of metal rod set into the wheel head, one in the center and one about $2\frac{1}{2}$ in. (70 mm.) from it. The bats are drilled to fit over these 'pins'. Alternatively they can be adhered to the wheel head by a ring or thin slab of clay. (See illustration under *bat*.)

WHIRLER

A hand operated turntable also called a *banding wheel* although this term has a narrower application. Used for decoration, waxing, or glazing and for modeling and hand-building. There are many types and designs: in some the base will fall away if the whirler is lifted by the head. These are dangerous and should be avoided especially in schools. The head may be of aluminium or cast iron—the latter gives greater stability and momentum. You should choose as heavy a model as you can handle. Weights vary from 4–36 lb. (2–15 kg.) 15lb (6.5 kg.) is a useful average.

WHISTLE

Richard Dunning in PQ 13 gave full instructions for making clay whistles. A pinched or thrown pear shape is formed as shown (A) with an initial hole cut through it. The mouthpiece and the aperture through which the note is formed are shown in the second drawing. The 'whistle stick' (C) is thrust through the mouthpiece and out at the top of the bulb. A small pad of clay has been luted over the initial hole (D), which was made large enough to trim the inside shape of the bulb. A small wedge of this pad is now cut away (E) back from the

The basic form of the whistle. 'Whistle stick' is $\frac{1}{2} \times \frac{3}{4}$ in. (12 × 16 mm.) at the widest end of the wedge, about 8 in. (200 mm.) long. (See text for further explanation.)

point where the stick emerges, as in the second drawing. The stick is very carefully withdrawn. The sixth drawing shows how the points 1,2,3 and 4 should lie in a straight line while 3 should present a sharp edge. Point 1 to point 2 should be about $\frac{1}{2}$ in. (12 mm.).

The whistle can now be tried—it is often helpful to 'tongue' the breath, as when playing a recorder. If it does not produce a clear note the aperture is probably at fault and careful trimming may put it right. The one error which cannot be put right easily is too wide an aperture, due to miscalculating in the first place the angle of the stem to the body; too much air escapes. It is better to start again. Tuning holes are made, when the whistle has stiffened, with the handle of a paintbrush (5 and 6). Each successive hole gives a note of higher pitch; see *ocarina*.

The whistles can be decorated, or bird and animal forms constructed. Make sure that the tuning holes are where your fingers can easily reach them. Straight pipes (*flutes*) are possible, even double pipes as made by Neil Ions, see CR 90 where he describes an alternative system of forming the mouthpiece.

WHITE, glaze, body, pigment

Tin oxide will give the purest and best quality white *opaque* earthenware glaze. Zircon is also efficient but harder and shinier. Use 8–12% of either in a *soft glaze*. Titania will opacify but tend to produce a cream. Zinc and *Bristol* type glazes can be very white. Stoneware glazes are often naturally white and opaque: barium, zinc, and lime can assist, the last, perhaps, in the form of bone-ash.

A white body will always be a 'short' one. China clay and flint are used to whiten bodies in the industry. Small quantities of cobalt are sometimes added to impart a certain spurious whiteness. Porcelain is normally very pale in color and will have a whiter appearance if fired in reduction, the iron traces being bluish instead of cream. White *engobes* are mixtures with very little ball clay and various fillers—see recipes in Rhodes CGP.

Tin-ash may be used as a white pigment or tin oxide mixed with a little frit.

WHITE LEAD

'Basic' lead carbonate $2PbCO_3.Pb(OH)_2$, 775. Convenient equivalent weight 258 (see also under *lead*).

Poisonous, use with great care. A very active *flux* in soft glazes and gives clear transparent glaze for use with tin oxide for *majolica*. Now forbidden in schools or where labor is employed. White lead was formerly the standard material for lead–lime–potash glazes. Specimen recipe:

White lead 43, feldspar 30, whiting 5, china clay 8, flint 14.

WHITING

Finely ground cretaceous chalk, practically pure—97% —$CaCO_3$. (See *calcium carbonate*.) Decomposes to oxide at 825°C. The most commonly used glaze material for the introduction of *lime* into bodies and glazes.

WICKET

The door of a kiln. Usually bricked up for firing.

WIRE

See *resistance wire, element, electric kiln wiring, cutting wire, harp, bow*.

WITHERITE

A comparatively rare rock of almost pure barium carbonate.

WOLLASTONITE

Calcium metasilicate $CaO.SiO_2$, 116. m.p. 1540°C.

There are natural and synthetic forms with thermal expansions of 11 and 6 respectively. Sometimes used as a part substitute for feldspar in low temperature vitreous bodies. Can be used as a source of calcium in glazes. Wollastonite with barium and about 20% of clay is used for the very strong bodies of electrical porcelain. Whiting and flint mixtures give a cheaper equivalent. David Eeles has rendered his stoneware glazes free from opacifying bubbles by replacing whiting (with its release of carbon dioxide) by wollastonite which has no such loss on ignition.

WOOD ASH

See *ash*.

WOOD FIRING

Wood firing, at its best, gives a quality to both earthenware and stoneware which is unmatched by other fuels. It entails long and continuous work both in the preparation and firing. It is a fuel of comparatively low specific gravity and a great volume of material is required to fire a kiln: $4\frac{1}{2}$ cords of wood (about 580 cu. ft.) were used by Michael Cardew to fire his large (100 cu. ft.) kiln to stoneware. The calorific value is less than half that of oil. The Chinese potters are said to have been largely responsible for vast tracts of desert through their rapid destruction of the forests. This role is now taken over by newsprint, although a more conscious effort is made to replace the trees. Nevertheless, wood of the right type, condition, and size is not easy to obtain and comparatively few potters rely on it as their only or principal fuel. It is more often used as a boost towards the end of a firing, fed through subsidiary fireholes. Its long clear flame makes it an ideal fuel in many ways, especially for stoneware.

Leach specifies dry pine 3–8 in. (75–200 mm.) in diameter and 2 ft.–2 ft. 6 in. (600–750 mm.) long. At the height of the firing up to twelve such logs are burned every four minutes. Common deal cut-offs from timber-yards can be used but are likely to come in small and odd-shaped pieces which makes the use of the semi-automatic grate impossible and thus increases the time taken up in stoking and surveillance. Advice on wood firing can be found in Leach PB, Cardew, and Rhodes K.

WORKABILITY

'An evasive synonym for plasticity' (Dodd). Nevertheless the word sums up the various qualities which a potter requires in his clay: plasticity, standing strength, low water absorption, together with the less tangible qualities of 'feel' and texture.

WORKING SURFACE

The working surface for potting should be slightly porous, so that clay comes away cleanly, but not so porous as to dry it too rapidly. Nothing fulfils these requirements as well as a sound wooden bench, preferably, though not necessarily, a hardwood. Education Authorities are 'hooked' on plastic surfaces on which it is impossible to *wedge* or work with damp clay with any comfort. They are not even particularly easy to clean and they damage easily with metal scrapers.

YELLOW, glaze, pigment

The sources of yellow color in ceramics are antimony, uranium, vanadium, iron and cadmium, and the compounds zircon/praseodymium and chrome/titania have been mentioned. An ochre yellow stoneware glaze quoted is: a red-firing clay 55; limestone 26.25; quartz 18.75.

Uranium will give a cool yellow at medium temperatures and is mentioned in a stoneware recipe- in Leach PB. Antimony must be fritted with lead and used in a high-lead soft glaze for its best color, see lead antimoniate. A yellow pigment frit recipe is: red lead 15, antimony 10, tin oxide 4. Vanadium is used as the pentoxide or as ammonium metavanadate for high temperatures (to 1280°C.). Cadmium is used only at low temperatures and is even then difficult to stabilize. Iron yellows are cream or brown-yellows. See under the various materials mentioned for percentages in a glaze, etc. and *antimoniate of lead* for use on *majolica*.

Nigel Wood tells us that the fine Imperial Yellow of Qing China was derived from 3.5% ferric oxide in a lead/silicate base.

YELLOW OCHRE

See *ochre*.

YING CH'ING

Translated as 'shadow blue' or 'sky blue', the term is used to cover a large family of pale blue-green reduced iron glazes from the East, usually on engraved porcelain. The term is now in some disfavor among ceramic historians but remains a convenient description for similar glazes used by craft potters today.
David Leach's recipe gives a close approximation using 1% of iron oxide in reduction to about 1255°C.

25	Feldspar
25	Whiting
25	China clay
25	Quartz

ZAFFRE

An impure cobalt arsenate, or a roasted mixture of cobalt ore and sand. Now largely obsolete as a pigment, but it sounds as if it might yield a more attractive color than the present vivid cobalt blues.

ZETTLITZ KAOLIN

A Czechoslovakian kaolin, high in alumina.

ZINC, oxide

A metallic element Zn, 65.
Oxide ZnO, 81, c.o.e. 6.5, s.g. 5.6.

In small quantities, up to 2%, it acts as a flux in many glazes and increases *craze* resistance. Larger additions tend to opacify and promote a *matt* surface. Used in both earthenware and stonewares. The *Bristol* glaze was an attempt to replace lead with zinc. The $ZnO.Al_2O_3.SiO_2$ eutectic is high at 1360°C. but the inclusion of other bases will lower this figure. Zinc has a balancing effect in glazes.

The raw material has a high shrinkage which gives trouble in a glaze on biscuit, though it is advantageous on once-fired ware. Shrinkage is reduced if the ZnO is calcined. An example stoneware formula:
0.4 KNaO
0.3 CaO. 0.6 Al_2O_3. 3.5 SiO_2
0.3 ZnO

Zinc has a strong effect on pigments: poor color with iron, brighter with copper (sometimes a pink!), brown with chrome, with cobalt mauve or even an intense green have been obtained—these reactions all in oxidation. A versatile oxide but somewhat unpredictable and must be handled with care.

ZIRCON

See *zirconium*.

ZIRCONIUM, oxide, silicate

A metallic element Zr, 91.
Oxide ZrO_2, 123, *zirconia*, m.p. 2700°C.
Silicate $ZrO_2.SiO_2$, 183. 'Zircon'.

The oxide has an *inversion* of about 2.5% at 1200°C.

Zircon sands occur abundantly in Australia. They are very refractory. Zircon is used as a glaze opacifier, it operates mainly by recrystallization during cooling. The first 3% of zircon will dissolve in a glaze and not recrystallize (Derek Royle CR 32). For opacity, use glazes low in alkalis, higher in lime and alumina. Zircon can replace some or all of the tin oxide, giving a harder, shinier, more scratch-resistant surface. Less favorable reactions with pigments which are, however, very stable in a zircon glaze over a wide range of temperatures. The zircon needs to be well mixed with the batch either by grinding or very thorough stirring if it is not to show white specks. Special coated zircon is made to assist dispersion. Up to 12% is required in a soft glaze for opacity, but up to 30% can be added to promote crystalline and broken color effects in a soft glaze. Zircon has a low *thermal expansion* and will increase craze resistance, at the same time making a glaze more *viscous*. A trade name for a prepared zircon is Zircopax.

Used in the manufacture of *refractories*, e.g. platinum melting crucibles, sparking plugs, etc. Can be used as a bat wash and kiln wash: 10 zircon to one clay.

Suppliers mentioned in the dictionary

Acme Marls Ltd.
Clough Street,
Hanley,
Stoke-on-Trent,
Staffs,
England
(Kiln shelves and refractories)

Allen, Fdk, & Sons (Chemicals) Ltd.
Hatherley Wharf,
Bow Common Lane,
London E3 4AX,
England
(Fullers earth)

Ball, W.G. Ltd.
Anchor Road,
Longton,
Stoke-on-Trent,
Staffs,
England
(Pottery materials)

Bath Pottery Supplies
2 Dorset Close,
Bath,
BA2 3RF,
England
(General supplies (and new ideas!))

Bryant, Victor
Terracotta Software,
18 Latchmere Rd,
Kingston,
KT2 5TW,
England
(Computer programs for potters)

Ceramatech Ltd.
Unit 16,
Frontier Works,
33 Queen Street,
London,
N17 8JA,
England
(General supplies)

Cinva-Ram Press
c/o Bellows-Valvair,
200 West Exchange Street,
Akron,
Ohio
44309,
U.S.A.
(General supplies)

Craftsmen Potters Shop
William Blake House,
7 Marshall Street,
London,
W1V 1FD,
England
(Tools and books)

Cromartie Kilns Ltd.
Parkhall Road,
Longton,
Stoke-on-Trent,
Staffs,
England
(Kilns and equipment,
pottery materials)

Dragon Ceramex
5 Nomix Park,
Congresbury,
Avon,
BS19 5HB,
England
(Extruders)

Dusmo Farinol
Miller Road,
Bedford,
England
(Sweeping compounds)

Ellis & Everard (Chemicals) Ltd.
Star Road,
Partridge Green,
Horsham,
W. Sussex,
England
(Fullers earth)

Fordham Thermal Systems Ltd.
Studlands Park Industrial Estate,
Newmarket,
Cambs,
England
(Ceramic fiber modules, gas kiln kits)

Fulham Pottery Ltd.
Burlington House,
184 New Kings Road,
London,
SW6 4PB,
England
(General supplies)

Gladstone Engineering Co. Ltd.
Foxley Lane, Milton,
Stoke-on-Trent,
ST1 7EH,
England
(Pugmills, clay rollers, etc)

Glendale Controls
10 Derwent Crescent,
Whitehall,
Kidsgrove,
Stoke-on-Trent,
Staffs,
England
(Oxygen/carbon Sensor)

Hall & Pickles Ltd (Kanthal)
Wire Division,
Ecclesfield,
Sheffield,
England
(Kiln wire)

Hewitt, David
7 Fairfield Road,
Caerlon,
Newport,
Gwent,
NP6 1DQ
Wales
(Computer programs for potters)

Hogg, Dr. C.S.
17 St Sulien,
Luxulyan,
Bodmin,
Cornwall,
PL30 5EB,
England
(Computer glaze and body
calculations for the studio potter)

Insight
IMC,
134 Upland Drive,
Medicine Hat,
Alberta,
TI1 3N7
Canada
(Computer programs for potters)

Kanthal Corporation
Bethel,
Connecticut,
U.S.A.
(Kiln wire)

Kemper Manufacturing Co.
California,
(Tools available from Potclays)

Kyanite Mining Corp.
Dillwyn,
Virginia,
U.S.A.
(Kyanite, etc)

Labheat
(present address unknown)

Laser Kilns
1 Cooperdale Road,
London,
E9 6AU,
England
(Slab rollers and equipment)

Mason Stain Co.
PO Box 76,
East Liverpool,
Ohio, 43920
U.S.A.
(Ceramic colors)

May, J.B.
19 Church Road,
Boldmere,
Sutton Coldfield,
West Midlands,
B73 5RX,
England
(Computer advice)

Newclay Products Ltd.
Overston House,
Sunnyfield Road,
Chislehurst,
Kent, England
(Fiber-strengthened and
self setting clays)

Orton Ceramic Foundation
6991, Old 3c Highway,
Westerville,
Ohio,
U.S.A.
(Kilnovent)

Pamela Moreton Ceramics
226 Holt Road,
Cromer,
NR27 9JW,
England
(Decals, Transfers)

Potclays Ltd.
Albion Works,
Etruria,
Stoke-on-Trent,
Staffs,
England
(General suppliers)

Potter's Mates
Malcolm Headley-Saw,
Cust Hall,
Toppesfield,
Halstead,
Essex,
CO9 4EB,
England
(Lotus wheel head system, and
other equipment)

Potterycrafts Ltd.
Campbell Road,
Stoke-on-Trent,
Staffs,
England
(General supplies, materials and
equipment including the
Fiebleman Parian body)

Rath Fibertech UK Ltd.
10 Omega Court,
352 Cemetery Road,
Sheffield,
S11 8FT,
England

Reward Products Ltd.
Units A & B,
Brookhouse Industrial Estate,
Cheadle,
Stoke-on-Trent,
ST10 1PW,
England
(Materials, tools, and equipment)

Steetley Minerals Ltd.
Worksop, England
(White bentonite)

Sweeping Component
Unit 4,
Prospect Way,
Royal Oak Industrial Estate,
Daventry,
England
(Sweeping compounds)

Watts, Blake, Bearne and Co.
Courtney Park,
Newton Abbot,
Devon,
England
(Ball clays)

West Shore Machine Works
Box 512,
Trona,
California
93562,
U.S.A.
(Hand operated rock crusher)

Whitfield & Son Ltd.
23 Albert Street,
Newcastle,
Staffs,
England
(Molochite)

Films mentioned in the dictionary

Isaac Button
Creatures in clay
Raku, English style
Geoffrey Whiting
David Leach
Lustre Firing

and others, obtainable from:
FILMS FOR POTTERS
John Anderson,
East View,
The Green,
Long Melford,
Suffolk,
CO10 9DU,
England
(Also available as video cassettes).

Bibliography
Books mentioned in dictionary

AUTHOR and CODE LETTERS

Aldred, F.	RE	*Refractories in the electrical industries.* Electricity Council
Berendsen, A.	THG	*Tiles, a general history.* Faber & Faber, London, 1967.
Billington, D.	TP	*The technique of pottery.* London, Batsford, 1962.
Byers, I.	R	*Raku.* Batsford, London, 1990.
Caiger-Smith, A.	LP	*Lustre Pottery.* Faber & Faber, London and Boston, 1985.
Caiger-Smith, A.	TGP	*Tin-glaze pottery.* Faber & Faber, London, 1973.
Carlton Ball.	MPWW	*Making pottery without a wheel.* Van Nostrand Reinhold, New York and London, 1965.
Cardew, M.	PP	*Pioneer pottery.* Longmans, Harlow, 1969.
Ceramic Review.	CG	*Clay and glazes.* Eds. Cooper and Lewenstein. Craftsmen Potters Association of Great Britain, 1988.
Chandler, M.	CMW	*Ceramics in the modern world.* Aldus, London, 1968.
Clark, K.	PC	*Practical pottery and ceramics.* Studio Vista, London, 1964.
Clark, K.	PM	*The potter's manual.* Macdonald, London, 1983.
CM	CM	(Periodical) *Ceramics Monthly.* Columbus U.S.A.
Colbeck, J.	TT	*Pottery, the technique of throwing.* Batsford, London, 1969.
Colson, F.	KBSM	*Kiln building with space age materials.* Von Nostrand Reinhold, 1975.
CR	CR	(Periodical) *Ceramic Review.* Craftsmen Potters Association of Great Britain, London.
Davis, H.	PA	*The potter's alternative.* Methuen. (Australia). 1987; Chilton (U.S.A.), 1990.
Dodd, A.E.	DC	*Dictionary of ceramics.* Newnes-Butterworth, 1967.
Flight, G.	CM	*Ceramics manual.* Collins, London, 1990.
Fournier, R.	CC	*Ceramic creations.* Sterling, New York, 1972.
Fournier, R.	DPD	*Illustrated dictionary of pottery decoration.* Prentice Hall Press, New York, 1986.
Fournier, R.	DPF	*Illustrated dictionary of pottery form.* Van Nostrand Reinhold, New York, 1981.
Fournier, R.	EKP	*Electric kiln construction for potters.* Van Nostrand Reinhold, New York, 1976.
Fournier, R.	PT	(Ed), *Potters tips.* Ceramic Review, Craftsmen Potters Association of Great Britain, 1990.
Fraser, H.	GCP	*Glazes for the craft potter.* Pitman/Watson-Guptill, London/New York, 1973.
Green, D.	EP	*Experimenting with pottery.* Faber & Faber, London, 1971.
Hamer, F.	PDM	*Potter's dictionary of materials and techniques.* A & C, Black/Watson-Guptill, London and New York, 1st and 2nd Editions.
Hamer, F & J.	C	*Clays.* Pitman/Watson-Guptill, London/New York.
Holderness, A.	IPC	*Inorganic and physical chemistry.* Heinemann Educational, London, 1963.
Leach, B.	PB	*A potter's book.* Faber & Faber, London, 1945.
NZP	NZP	(Periodical) *New Zealand Potter.*
Parks, D.	PGRG	*A potter's guide to raw glazing and oil firing.* Pitman, London, 1980.
Parmalee, C.	CG	*Ceramic glazes,* 2nd (revised) edition, Industrial Publications Inc., Chicago, 1951.
PQ	PQ	(Periodical) *Pottery Quarterly.*
Rhodes, D.	CGP	*Clay and glazes for the potter.* Pitman, London, 1967; second edition, Chilton (U.S.A.), 1973.
Rhodes, D.	K	*Kilns: construction and operation.* Pitman, London, 1969; second edition, Chilton (U.S.A.), 1981.
Rhodes, D.	SP	*Stoneware and porcelain.* Pitman, London, 1960.
Riegger, H.	RAT	*Raku art and technique.* Studio Vista, London, 1970.
Sanders, H.	WJC	*World of Japanese ceramics.* Kodansha International Ltd, Tokyo/Palo Alto, California, 1969.
Shaw, K.	SCP	*Science for craft potters and enamellers.* David & Charles, Newton Abbot, 1972.
SOED	SOED	*Shorter Oxford English Dictionary.*
Sutherland, R.	GNS	*Glazes from natural sources.* Batsford, 1987.
T	T	(Periodical), *Tactile.* Canada.
Uvarov, E.	DS	(Ed), *Dictionary of science.* Penguin, 1969.
Webb.	CNS	*Cobalt, nickel and selenium.* Mond Nickel Company.
Wikey, M.	CCEK	*Calibrating and calculating the electric kiln.* Marshall Craft, 1001 Martin Avenue, Santa Clara, California, 1974.
Worrall, W.	C	*Clays: their nature, origin and natural growth.* Applied Science Publishers, London, 1986.